Tailoring

Tailoring

Third Edition

ALLYNE BANE
*Formerly Associate Professor
of Home Economics
Ohio University*

McGRAW-HILL BOOK COMPANY
*New York   St. Louis   San Francisco
Düsseldorf   Johannesburg   Kuala Lumpur
London   Mexico   Montreal   New Delhi
Panama   Paris   São Paulo   Singapore
Sydney   Tokyo   Toronto*

This book was set in Claro Light by University Graphics, Inc.
The editors were Richard R. Wright and Susan Gamer;
the designer was Barbara Ellwood;
the production supervisor was Bill Greenwood.
New drawings were done by John Cordes, J & R Technical Services, Inc.
The Maple Press Company was printer and binder.

Tailoring

1234567890MAMM7987654

Library of Congress Cataloging in Publication Data

Bane, Allyne.
  Tailoring.

  1. Tailoring (Women's)   I. Title.
TT519.5.B36   1974   646.4'5   74–5755
ISBN 0–07–003608–X

CONTENTS

1803024

PREFACE

In the five years since the preface to the second edition was written, fashion has been fun and mischievous; in a way, it has been fashionable to scoff at demanding fashions. This attitude nourished a love of casual, quick, temporary costumes planned for the mood of the moment and intended for an exciting but short life-span. During these years, traditional tailored costumes were too proper, too permanent, and too expensive in both time and money to enjoy their usual popularity with fashion sewing enthusiasts. But the tailored suit and coat survived, not as the uniforms they had been but rather as pants suits or disguised as capes or dashing ponchos.

As this third edition goes to press in 1974, fashions are pretty and ladylike again; and those who sew are rediscovering the delights of the little "wear-everywhere" suit and the elegant coat. However, tailored fashions will never be the same again. The pants suit will surely continue to rival the traditional suit. We will surely never again accept anything less than the freedom of expression we have enjoyed in the early 1970s. And easy-care fabrics, with their excellent performance and their washability, will surely continue to influence and even dominate the fabric market. The art of tailoring is as relevant as it has always been; it simply must be modified and adapted to the demands of each new fashion season.

The fashion arts continue to satisfy loyal devotees and to attract new ones, for the following reasons: (1) The variety, aesthetic appeal, and performance of new fabrics are responsible for some—perhaps much—of the increased interest in fashion sewing. Because their intrinsic excitement minimizes the need for complicated construction details, they have attracted many new enthusiasts who lack the patience to work with more difficult fabrics. Imaginative fabrics in interesting textures and designs have replaced the need for intricate design features to such an extent that teen-agers and those who either are inexperienced or possess limited natural talent can make effective costumes with professional results. (2) Current men's fashions in softer, more casual lines are not unlike women's fashions; they can be constructed with similar techniques and have consequently attracted new sewing fans, including men. (3) The high cost of ready-to-wear clothing, an ever-increasing percentage of which reflects labor costs, adds to the profitability of fashion sewing; many sewers who formerly made only utilitarian costumes are now buying designer patterns and exclusive fabrics for special-occasion costumes. At the same time, ready-to-wear costs have forced others who might never sew otherwise to turn to sewing as an economic necessity. (4) The increase in leisure time has changed the pattern of our lives; we now demand leisure activities that are not only time-consuming but also creative and mentally stimulating. The joys and demands of leisure, once known only to the rich, are a part of the life-style of an entire society. Many people of all ages in all walks of life now enjoy the precious luxury of time to pursue the fashion arts. Tailoring, being more time-consuming than sewing, is an ideal leisure-time activity. (5) The young people of today have a reverence for self-fulfillment and basic values; they have embraced the home arts and crafts and in ever-increasing numbers and are swelling the ranks of fashion-sewing enthusiasts.

Because the incentives which motivate fashion sewing are so diverse, it becomes clear that there is a great need for two methods of sewing. First, there must be a quick and easy method adequate for the simply cut designs favored by the young or inexperienced and practical for those who sew out of economic necessity. This method is appropriate for utilitarian garments and for obviously temporary clothing such as children's clothes, maternity wear, and "strictly for fun" fashions. With quick sewing methods comparable to those used in manufacturing, it is possible to compete with budget-priced and moderately priced ready-to-wear; this is an entirely adequate standard for some units of the wardrobe, and if necessary for all. However, the very speed and ease of construction made possible by shortcuts and compromises are not acceptable to many sewers, who demand an alternative at the other extreme. The second method is the couturier method. By contrast, this method is time-consuming, painstaking, and challenging because it aims at the highest standards of exclusive ready-to-wear and custom-made costumes. This method is favored by those who love good design and beautiful fabrics and so

always work at the high level demanded by international couturier patterns and costly fabrics. It is also favored by those who use it for special-occasion costumes or for any costume singled out for an extra measure of loving attention.

Both methods have merit. Rather than using one or the other exclusively, each sewer should combine features of both methods and should devise a personalized method by using different methods for different costumes or different parts of one costume, choosing quick methods for some of the simpler elements and couturier methods for more difficult or more significant details.

By its very nature, tailoring requires the painstaking techniques that characterize couturier methods. Tailoring differs from sewing in many ways; but the major and basic difference is that a tailored costume is molded to the shape it will assume on the figure by means of hand stitches to hold the various layers together so that they act as one, tapes to control certain edges and areas, and additional pressing techniques to create the desired shape and ensure that it will be retained. One does not have the usual choice between quick methods and couturier methods when one undertakes a tailoring project; although it is possible to do certain insignificant details by quick methods, in general the quality of the costume is greatly and adversely affected by compromises.

The scope of this text is limited to construction techniques of tailoring. However, the reader must understand that a successful costume, whether it is made at home or purchased on the ready-to-wear market, is a result of careful study in broad areas of textiles and clothing. Artistic principles must be applied in the choice of color and color combinations, in the use of texture and texture contrasts, in the selection of pleasing lines for the individual figure, and in the effective use of proportion and balance. The fabric (its fiber content, weave, finish, etc.) determines the character, the performance, and the care of the garment. The influence of fashion is an important consideration. Thoughtful study of current fashion magazines and a careful survey of newsworthy fashion in large department stores and specialty shops will strengthen fashion know-how; reference books on clothing selection and wardrobe planning and a basic book on the fundamentals of textiles will be required.

A text cannot replace the instruction sheet included with the commercial pattern; it can only supplement the excellent directions given on the pattern. In general, the tailoring techniques recommended here are very similar to those suggested by all the pattern companies and are almost identical to those included with Vogue patterns. The explanations of fundamental techniques are more detailed, however, and are fortified with more illustrations than is possible on an instruction sheet. The most typical constructions are explained in depth, and the principles involved are discussed in great detail. In many cases, the basic principle is applied to other similar but less typical construction details. But because it is quite impossible to cover every possible subtlety of construction, the instruction sheet of each pattern must supply the unique directions for that particular pattern. The reader must *thoroughly* understand the principle involved so that it can be applied to ever-changing circumstances and designs. Space for elaboration on fundamental problems was gained by omitting construction details that are used infrequently; for example, pocket construction is not included because pockets are unique features that must be made according to the directions with each individual pattern. I have a well-founded respect for patterns and pattern directions, a fact that will be

obvious on almost every page. When directions given here differ from those usually suggested on the pattern, the difference will be stated and explained. In almost every case, the reader will see that the changes and improvements are possible because of the space for elaboration that a text allows; rarely, if ever, will the difference cast a bad light on the quality of pattern directions.

This edition has been prepared for the following uses: (1) Primarily, it is planned as a text at the college level or for adult-education classes taught in a similar academic manner. (2) It will serve as a self-teacher for those who sew without formal instruction; this group includes members of county extension clubs, experienced and talented girls in 4-H clubs, and hobbyists of all ages. (3) It will serve as a reference for professional home economists (especially high school teachers) on the job, and as a self-teacher for any home economist who needs (or wants) to explore this area of learning more deeply than was possible in the limited time allotted to it in the college curriculum. I have assumed that the reader has had limited experience, that her experience is largely confined to basic sewing skills, and that she has had little more than an introduction to the theory of technical clothing construction; in short, I have assumed that she has had the equivalent of one or two basic clothing courses. Some instructors who teach in schools requiring only one elementary course as a prerequisite for tailoring have recommended that this edition start at a somewhat more basic level. I have followed their suggestion and included more basic information; but in so doing, I have not compromised on the final level of accomplishment.

Because I have started low and aimed high, this edition is considerably larger than the second edition.

Now that I am writing full time, it has been possible for me to make many improvements in this edition. It is more comprehensive in many aspects (such as content, examples for application, and alternative methods). I am confident that readers of the previous edition will welcome the improvements in organization. There are additional headings that break up long passages of text, help simplify processes, and allow for convenient reference by the instructor. For example, a lengthy passage may be very simply divided into three segments: "Initial Steps," "Construction in Progress," and "Finishing Steps." In most cases, similar or identical headings appear as legends for the accompanying illustrations. The illustrations (more numerous in this edition than in the previous one) will have greater value because they are combined in meaningful groups and have additional explanatory notes and descriptive legends. The introductory information in many sections is presented under the heading "Evaluation of Methods" and includes a detailed explanation of the advantages and disadvantages of two or more means of solving problems, along with suggestions for making a wise decision for each costume. This approach makes it possible to emphasize more effectively the continuing need for experimentation, which is essential when working with any new fabric, especially a newly developed man-made fiber or a blend of several fibers.

Many sections, like the examples listed below, have been greatly enlarged and improved. The information on pattern sizing and measurement standards of the Pattern Fashion Industry has been updated and is in better perspective now that the major sizing change of January 1968 is more firmly established; other factors having to do with sizing are clarified by greater emphasis on livability amounts in various types of garments and on the implications of style fullness in certain designs.

The chapter on pattern alteration has been greatly increased to include additional alterations and, when possible and advisable, to offer alternative methods. The numerous additional examples of basic alterations applied to a greater variety of designs are a marked improvement.

The chapter on fitting is also more comprehensive. I have stressed the wisdom of making a muslin test copy of all units of the costume, but have also included alternative solutions for those who will not make a muslin copy. These alternative suggestions (new in this edition) are necessarily less effective because certain radical corrections cannot be done after the costume has been cut in expensive fabric; they will, however, be adequate for those persons who do not require major fitting adjustments.

The information on the selection and handling of supporting fabrics has been entirely rewritten to clarify more effectively the differences between underlining and interfacing fabrics and to distinguish between the appropriate uses and construction techniques suitable for each.

Chapter 7, Fundamentals of Construction and Pressing, has been retained essentially as it was in the second edition, although the material has been updated and alternative methods have been evaluated in greater depth. It is an advantage for the reader to have these details appear in a tailoring text, so that she need not refer to another text. By confining them to one chapter, I was able to simplify and clarify other chapters which deal with new information and more complicated tailoring techniques. A new section titled "Aids to Accuracy" appears in this chapter. This unique feature should prove to be a favorite with all readers. It includes little simple-to-execute tricks for ensuring perfection when doing the small details (color points, band trims, pocket flaps) which are so very easy to do poorly and yet so difficult to do accurately. The material is presented in a way that suggests application to an infinite number of little (but entirely visible) fashion details.

There is much that is new in this edition. Instructors will welcome a comprehensive new section called "The Tailored Costume as a Learning Experience." This section is, in a way, a plea to the reader to select a fabric and a pattern design that will allow her to gain the experience she needs for long-range goals—for a lifetime of tailoring. The reader is encouraged to select a fabric that requires the typical tailoring techniques and responds well to them. Construction details are evaluated for their carry-over value; the student is encouraged to select a pattern which includes several of the details that appear most frequently on tailored costumes.

When one is making a first project—especially if it will be the only opportunity to work under an instructor—it is important to evaluate the design and fabric as learning experiences. But once one has mastered the fundamentals, one should enlarge on those experiences by using a variety of fabrics, designs, and construction methods. Chapter 11 is devoted to these special problems (fabrics which require additional time or are more difficult to cut or handle, unique construction methods, etc.). This chapter includes a very comprehensive section on matching plaid, checked, or striped fabrics; it has been greatly enlarged and clarified, and much new information has been added. The problems of cutting twills are explained;

the reader will be pleased to learn that they are not as troublesome as one is often led to believe. A new section on washable construction should be a welcome addition at this time when polyesters and other easy-care fabrics make up such a high percentage of the market. These fabrics can be tailored by traditional methods (in which case they must be dry-cleaned) or handled with certain modifications to render them washable. In general, washable construction requires that many tailoring techniques be eliminated; this method of construction is, therefore, not a wise choice for first projects. The basic fundamentals of double-cloth construction, an entirely unique method of construction used only on double-cloth fabrics, are included. This method requires no traditional tailoring techniques and so is not recommended for first projects.

A section of men's tailoring appears in this edition for the first time. Men's fashions of the casual type that are popular with men themselves and with those who undertake men's tailoring are not radically different from women's costumes in construction. In this section, I have pointed out the similarities and the differences.

The popularity of pants suits is evident in every chapter. Many pattern alterations are shown first on skirts and then adapted to pants; and there are several new pattern alterations that are especially effective for pants. Waistline casings, popularized by pants suits, are new in this edition. Because elasticized casings are so comfortable, I was prompted to find a way to extend their use; a method of modifying the traditional casing construction (with dart fittings for a semi-fitted effect) is the result. With these modifications, pants and skirts with comfortable casings can be worn with shorter and more snugly fitted tops and jackets.

As always, I am indebted to the textiles and clothing staff in the School of Home Economics at Ohio University—to Martha Graham, Norma Karhoff, Mary Doxsee, and especially to Ellen Goldsberry. Their suggestions before I begin work and their criticisms as work progresses are invaluable to me. They give selflessly of their time and their talents, but it is their great measure of encouragement and affection for which I am most grateful. My greatest debt is to the hundreds of my beloved students at Ohio University who made teaching such great fun for me and who supplied me with the courage to do the first book and the inspiration to do the others.

Allyne Bane

Tailoring

Chapter 1

EQUIPMENT AND FINDINGS

The efficiency of the worker is greatly increased by high-quality equipment which is planned for the specific purposes of home sewing and which also meets the user's individual needs. The wide range of market offerings makes it possible for every woman who sews to have equipment which will allow her to sew more quickly and conveniently. It is important to keep in mind that equipment is an aid to progress, not a substitute for work or a solution to all problems. Relatively few well-chosen items will be adequate; for example, two pairs of scissors will serve most needs very well and six pairs may possibly slow rather than speed progress. Avoid the pressure of current advertising ("buy this and make magic"); clever gadgets are not the secret of successful home sewing. The wise consumer will place a higher value on quality than on quantity and will select only the essential items (see the list on page 12), adding other specialized equipment only if and when the need arises.

Caution The home-sewing market is loaded with a great variety of gadgets and gimmicks, many of which profess to "make magic." Some are very useful, others are not, and all too many require much practice on test samples before work can progress on the garment. Many require more manual dexterity than the average home sewer possesses. The consumer should read the directions before buying, and then she must always test out the device with the number of thicknesses of fabric she will be using. She must not proceed to use the device on a garment until results are consistently acceptable.

For example, covering buttons or buckles with supplies and tools from a kit requires great patience and manual dexterity. Furthermore, kits for making self-covered buttons and buckles are available in a limited number of designs and the results do not meet the high standards of appearance and durability of similar items which have been professionally made. The modest saving in total cost is a questionable economy. One may want to have a small supply of these on hand for use when one cannot take the time (several days) to have buttons covered professionally. Before deciding to buy one of these kits, read "Button Selection" on page 382.

Another sales gimmick is the package of patterns for bound buttonholes. This sounds like a good idea, but these patterns cannot possibly be properly spaced for every design nor can they be planned for the particular size of button that will be used. A pattern for bound buttonholes is an excellent idea, but it should be made to order by the worker (directions are included in the text).

These are but a few of the items that

seem so promising at first glance. The wise consumer will evaluate each one carefully before purchasing, giving thought to the time, effort, and ability required for professional results.

Scissors and shears

Scissors and shears differ in design because of their intended use. See Figure 1-1. Shears are used for the initial cutting, when it is important to cut with long slashes for more accurate lines; therefore shears are offered in longer lengths. A length of 7 or 8 inches is recommended; the variation in length allows for differences in hand size

or personal preference. Shears have one ring handle for the thumb and an oblong handle for several fingers. They are available in right- and left-handed models. Both handles are shaped to fit the hand comfortably because they will be used for relatively long periods of time. They are made with bent handles (bent in the direction of the ring or thumb handle) so that the blades can be used parallel to the table with the fabric and pattern lying flat for more accurate cutting. Shears have one sharp point and one blunt point (either rounded or angled); the blunt point adds strength for cutting heavier fabrics. Shears have the bent handle pictured in Figure 1-1 and are available with angled blunt points (for heavy work) or with rounded blunt points (for light dressmaking uses).

Scissors are offered in a great variety of lengths (shorter than shears); they are used

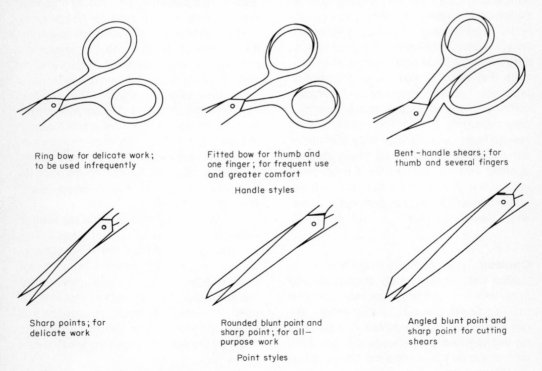

Ring bow for delicate work;
to be used infrequently

Fitted bow for thumb and
one finger; for frequent use
and greater comfort

Handle styles

Bent-handle shears; for
thumb and several fingers

Sharp points; for
delicate work

Rounded blunt point and
sharp point; for all-
purpose work

Point styles

Angled blunt point and
sharp point for cutting
shears

FIGURE 1-1 Scissors and shears.

for more intricate cutting on shorter edges. Because they will be used for shorter periods of time, most have ring-style handles for the thumb and one finger. Many have handles with fitted bows for greater comfort, and some that will not be used frequently have flat ring handles. Scissors may have two sharp points for very delicate, fine cutting; but most styles have one sharp point for close work and one rounded blunt point to give extra strength for fairly heavy cutting. The following are some of the most useful styles:

Embroidery scissors These have two sharp points and ring handles in lengths of 3½, 4, 4½, and 5 inches. They are used for the most delicate cutting and for applique work.

Sewing scissors These have one sharp and one rounded blunt point. They come in lengths of 4, 5, and 6 inches and are used at the machine and for general purposes as well as in-progress clipping and trimming.

Rip-stitch scissors These have one needle-sharp and one rounded blunt point. They are 5 inches in length and especially designed for ripping out stitches.

Light trimmer These scissors have one sharp and one rounded blunt point and shear handles (not bent). Available in 6- or 8-inch lengths, they are multipurpose scissors that combine many of the advantages of other shears and scissors.

Thread clip These special-purpose scissors, shown in Figure 1-2, are spring-operated and designed for clipping threads more quickly and easily at the machine. They are 4½ inches in length.

Knife-edge shears These special shears

have sharper blades that hold a keen edge longer. They are designed for cutting polyester knits and other fabrics (supple lining fabrics, fine silks, etc.) which are difficult to cut. Women who sew most of their wardrobes will consider this an essential piece of equipment.

Pinking shears These make zigzag slashes to give a neat seam finish that will resist or delay (but not prevent) raveling. They are available in a wide price range (from about $1 to about $10) depending on the type of metal used; the more expensive shears will cut heavier fabrics more easily and retain sharp edges longer. They are available in lengths of about 7 to 9 inches.

Few if any readers will need all the scissors described above. The average woman who sews will be able to do excellent work conveniently and efficiently with just two pairs: shears (or scissors of the light trimmer style if she will sew infrequently) for the initial cutting and sewing scissors for clipping threads at the machine and in-progress trimming and clipping.

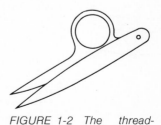

FIGURE 1-2 The thread-clip scissors.

CAUTION: When buying scissors or shears, take several scraps of various types of fabric along for testing; be sure to have some delicate fabrics in the collection. Before making the final purchase, test for defects and rough edges by making full, blade-length slashes in several fabrics. Make clips into several fabrics to test the cutting edge at the points.

Measuring aids

Accurate measurement is of paramount importance throughout the entire cutting, sewing, and finishing sequence. The essential aids, listed on page 12, should be of a very high quality; the worker can economize by acquiring special-purpose tools only if and when frequent need warrants their purchase.

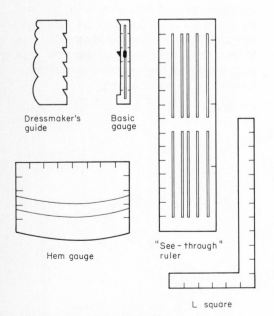

Dressmaker's guide

Basic gauge

Hem gauge

"See – through" ruler

L square

FIGURE 1-3 Measuring aids.

Tape measures These are available in fabric (limp and easy to handle, but they stretch with continued use) and plastic (firm and somewhat stiff, but these retain their original accuracy). The tape measure should be 60 inches long, marked in $\frac{1}{8}$-inch divisions. They are available with numbers beginning at opposite ends or at the same end on the two sides.

Yardsticks These are available in metal (more expensive) or wood. The metal ones, being thinner, provide a better edge for drawing lines and making accurate measurements. If a wood yardstick will be used, rub the edge with fine steel wool to make it satiny smooth so that it will not snag delicate fabrics. Wood yardsticks warp and must be replaced frequently.

An L square or T square This will be needed to establish right-angle corners. The L square is shown in Figure 1-3.

Short rulers These are essential tools that will be used frequently and must be of a convenient length. For greatest efficiency the worker needs both a foot-length and a 6-inch ruler.

Professional hem markers These are available in two basic types: the pin marker and the chalk marker. The garment hangs between the standard and the free arm, and when the free arm is pressed in place, it holds the garment in a position to be pinned or marked with chalk.

A gauge This is a measuring aid with a sliding marker than can be adjusted to indicate the measurement needed. Metal gauges are available in a variety of designs, some of which are shown in Figure 1-3.

Special-purpose measuring devices The

imaginative woman can economize (and often improve her work as well) by making measuring devices for special purposes. Thin, flat cardboard (comparable to a manila folder) and plastic calendars used for advertising are good materials for making gauges for special measurements, while the cardboard backing from seam tapes, elastic, etc.—or a tablet back—is adequate for general-purpose uses. A tablet back can replace the L or T square for short measurements, and a yardstick, held between wooden blocks for support and marked with tape at the proper level, can substitute for a professional hem marker. Cardboard gauges, notched for a special measurement, are more accurate and easier to use than professional gauges because there are no extra lines to distract the eye. Many of the special-purpose measuring aids shown in Figure 1-3 can be duplicated in cardboard at no cost. Some of the professional devices pictured do offer the advantage of transparency (which is convenient but not essential), but this advantage must be weighed against the advantages that only the made-to-purpose gauge can provide.

Findings for marking fabric

For fine couturier work, tailor's tacks are the most accurate method of transferring pattern markings to fabric. For work on simple designs, the following items will be helpful:

A tracing wheel used with carbon paper This can be used to trace important markings (seamlines and dartlines) on the muslin test copy. Tracing wheels are available with needle-pointed edges for fine lines or sawtooth edges for more distinct lines. Carbon paper is available in packages of several colors to contrast with most fabrics.

Several types of chalk These will serve marking purposes well. Ordinary blackboard chalk, sharpened to a fine point, gives a distinct line on most fabrics. Clay chalk in flat squares can be used on flat-surfaced fabrics, and waxed chalk, available in flat squares or pencil form, is more effective on wools and nubby fabrics. For greatest safety, these chalks should be used on the underside of the fabric only. If chalk will be used on the right side of the fabric, test it on a scrap of fabric to be sure it will not leave a permanent line.

Sewing thread

The size-use chart on page 6 will be useful for choosing thread in an appropriate size and type for a particular use or purpose; the higher the size number, the finer the thread. The new market offerings in the last part of the chart have gained wide acceptance in a relatively short time; some knowledgeable people in the industry feel they may well replace cotton and mercerized thread in the future. The reader may be sure that there will be other threads, similar and improved, that will reach the market soon; and she should be prepared to reevaluate the old favorites and discard the old for the new if the new item proves superior.

Many authorities recommend the use of silk thread for the structural seams of a wool costume because of the strength and elasticity of silk. The author does not consider that silk thread is necessary; the special thread planned for use with polyesters is more elastic than silk and it, as well as mercerized thread, works very well. If the reader would like to use silk

SEWING THREAD: SIZE–USE CHART

Name and characteristics	Sizes and uses
Cotton A thread made of 100% cotton, usually from 3 to 6 cords twisted together	Sizes 8 to 100 (very fine) Sizes 40, 50, and 60, appropriate for most dressmaking fabrics
Mercerized cotton A thread with a finish added for extra strength and luster	Size A (50), for general-purpose sewing Heavy-duty, for slipcovers, etc.
Silk A thread made of silk for more elasticity, higher luster, and greater strength	Size A (comparable to cotton thread of size 80 or 100 but more expensive, with fewer yards on the spool), for top-stitching and basting in preparation for pressing
Buttonhole twist A heavy, strong thread made of silk	One size, D, for tailored buttonholes, decorative and prominent top-stitching. Only 10 yards on a spool.
Nylon A strong thread that is elastic and resistant to wear and tear	Size A (comparable to silk A), for use with fabrics that will not be pressed at high temperatures. Available in a transparent thread of two shades (light and dark)
New special-purpose threads Poly Spun (Talon) Dual-Duty (J and P Coats) Poly Bond (Belding Corticelli) and others These are mercerized cotton threads wrapped in polyester threads to make them elastic and stronger and resistant to knotting	Available in one size for use with permanent-press fabrics and all knit fabrics in which elasticity is desirable Appropriate for almost any fabric

PINS: SIZE–USE CHART

Name and characteristics	Sizes and uses
Bank pin A heavy utility pin not suitable for dressmaking purposes	Size 14 (⅞-inch) through 32 (2-inch)
Dressmaker pin A pin of medium thickness—type most commonly used (but not the best choice) for dressmaking	Sizes 14 (⅞-inch) through 24 (1½-inch) Sizes 14 and 16 most appropriate for dressmaking uses
Ball-point pins of dressmaker type for use with single knits and other delicate fabrics	
Silk pin A slender pin with a tapered point somewhat like a needle	Sizes 14 (⅞-inch) through 17 (1¹⁄₁₆-inch); ideal for dressmaking and essential for sewing on delicate fabrics

thread, she must realize that the cost will be much higher because each spool of silk thread contains fewer yards than a spool of other types of thread. In the school laboratory situation, if silk thread is used in the tailoring class the tension adjustment of both the bobbin and the top thread of the machine will have to be changed constantly; under laboratory circumstances, it seems wiser to use mercerized thread. However, the luster of silk thread is highly desirable for top-stitched details and for stitching the lining if the fabric is silk or a very sheer fabric.

It is wise to purchase one spool of silk thread in a contrasting color to use for basting edges preparatory to pressing. If a basting thread must remain in the fabric during pressing, there is a danger that a heavier thread will press into the fabric, leaving little marks that are sometimes difficult to remove; basting with a fine silk thread will prevent this.

Buttonhole twist and buttonhole gimp In a mannish-tailored garment such as a blazer, the buttonholes may be hand-worked, in which case buttonhole twist is used for the hand stitches. Buttonhole gimp, which is a cordlike thread, is required as a padding under the stitches to provide the strength to withstand hard usage.

Very frequently the pattern will call for buttonhole twist for use in sewing on buttons. This heavier thread is most desirable if the tailored costume is made of very heavy fabric and is planned for hard service (such as a reefer in heavy tweed). However, if the fabric is light to medium in weight and if it is obviously a decorative rather than a serviceable costume, mercerized thread is preferable for this purpose.

Buttonhole twist is recommended frequently for topstitched details because the very thickness of the thread makes the stitching more prominent and the high luster of the thread adds a desirable accent.

Pins

Three types of pins are shown in the size-use chart on page 6 but only two are appropriate for dressmaking purposes. Of the two, *silk* pins are far superior. Silk pins slide into fabric more easily, do not snag yarns of the fabric, and do not leave large pinholes; since they are available in many stores at a reasonable cost, there is no reason to choose another type. Pin size is stated in sixteenths of an inch—thus size 16 is 1 inch long, etc. Some experimentation will indicate the pin length preferred by the individual; in general, longer pins will be more convenient.

Pins with colored heads (easier to see on fabrics) are available; they are an attractive novelty but they are of the *dressmaker* type and so are not ideal for use with delicate fabrics. Some come in very short lengths that are not convenient with the heavy fabrics suitable for tailoring.

There is a *silk* pin, finer and longer than those listed in the chart (slim as a fine needle) that is ideal for dressmaking purposes. The author recommends these pins, about 1¼ inches long, which are made by the Iris Company and labeled "superfine, number 7." These pins are truly marvelous to work with and, for anyone who will sew a great deal, well worth the effort to obtain them and worth double their cost. Unfortunately the author knows of only one outlet, a foreign store, where they can be

NEEDLES FOR HAND SEWING: SIZE–USE CHART

Type	Sizes	Characteristics	Uses
Sharps	Assorted: 1–5, 3–9, and 5–10 Solid: 1–10	Medium-long needles with small, round eyes	General sewing
Crewel (embroidery needles)	Assorted: 1–5, 3–9, and 5–10 Solid: 5–10	Same length as sharps, with larger, longer eyes	Embroidery and general sewing; easier to thread
Betweens (tailor's needles)	Assorted: 3–9, 5–10 Solid: 3–9	Shortest needles, with small, round eyes	Delicate hand work, short stitches, all intricate work

MACHINE NEEDLES: SIZE–USE CHART

General-purpose needles

Sizes 9 and 11	For sewing fine, delicate fabrics To be used with fine thread
Size 14	For sewing medium-weight fabrics of usual suit and coat weight To be used with general sewing threads (about size 50)
Sizes 16 and 18	For heavy fabrics (duck, slipcovers, and upholstery fabrics) and when sewing many thicknesses, as in slipcovers and draperies To be used with heavy-duty thread

Ball-point needles

Medium and fine sizes (one company offers four sizes)	For use with single knits and other supple, limp lining and blouse fabrics

obtained. By special request from many students and friends, the directions for purchase are as follows: Make out a check for $5.50, payable to Grands Magasins (the name of a reliable department store). This will pay for about 1½ cupfuls of pins. Ask for one packet Stechnadeln (Iris) superfine, number 7. Mail to Grands Magasins, Lelmoli, S. A., Zurich, Krasse 3, Zurich, Switzerland, and allow a month to six weeks for delivery.

Needles for hand sewing

The three types of needles listed in the size-use chart on page 8 are those generally used for dressmaking purposes; the higher the size number, the shorter and finer the needle. The worker will find that packages of assorted sizes are convenient, and she will probably also want some packages in the solid sizes she uses most often. Those most convenient for dressmaking are assorted sizes 5 through 10 and solid sizes 7 through 10. There is a great variety of other types of needles for special uses; ask the clerk for information on other types to serve specific purposes. Curved needles are available for working on firm, curved edges (for doing upholstery, slipcovers, millinery, lampshades, etc.) Needles with self-threading eyes are available in assorted and solid sizes. They have a slit at the top of the eye, which separates for threading.

Machine needles

The general-purpose needles shown in the size-use chart on page 8 can be used on all sewing machines, foreign and American-made. Singer or White needles in sizes 9, 11, and 14 will serve dressmaking purposes very adequately. Ball-point needles, which are relatively new to the home sewing market (but well known to lingerie manu-

facturers), are indispensable for sewing on polyester single knits and other supple fabrics, especially those as limp as the finest Banlons. These needles can be substituted for general-purpose needles in sizes 9 and 11 for use on other sheer fabrics as well.

Fasteners

Some of the pattern companies state the size of fastener needed for the design in the list of notions on the back of the envelope. This is so helpful for those who are inexperienced that probably all companies will offer the extra service in the near future.

Snap fasteners   These, in black or silver, are available in both assorted and solid sizes. Sizes are as follows: 4/0 (slightly more than ⅛ inch in diameter), 3/0, 2/0 (about ¼ inch), 1, 2, 3, and 4 (½ inch in diameter). The size 4 snap is usually covered in fabric (to match the garment or the lining) for fastening the inner edges of double-breasted suits and coats, wrap-arounds, etc.

Hooks and eyes   These, in black or silver, are available in both assorted and solid sizes. Sizes are 0 (very small), 1, 2, and 3. Coat hooks and eyes are still larger; these are available covered in thread to eliminate the glare of metal. This thread covering can, if desired, be replaced with thread to match a particular garment.

Skirt hooks and eyes especially designed for waistband fasteners are wide, flat metal hooks that slide into flat metal bands. These provide strong support with little extra bulk. One company makes these sets with adjustable eyes for fastening in three positions.

Pressing equipment

The combination steam and dry iron This is the most convenient for general-purpose as well as home-sewing needs, although the standard dry iron, used with a dampened press cloth, is certainly acceptable. Steam irons are available with a variety of features to satisfy individual needs and tastes (the "burst of steam" feature has proved very successful). These irons require distilled water because tap water clogs and rusts the inside of the iron. Distilled water is available in most large chain grocery and drug stores, and the nominal cost is worth its convenience. Water conditioning companies offer a filter jar with chemicals that make tap water safe for steam irons; these jars must be replaced when the color of the sandy particles changes, for this indicates that the chemicals are no longer effective. A special product for cleaning clogged and rusted irons is available.

The ironing board This should be adjustable to various heights or, if not, to a comfortable height for the worker. It should be padded smoothly (a ridge or wrinkle will mar fabric) with a commercial cover or with cotton padding or layers of a blanket. The cover should be fresh and clean at all times. Pads are available with a variety of features and all include elastic tapes to ensure a smooth, tight fit. If the cover is to be made at home, use a firm fabric which has been washed many times so that all sizing has been removed; starch and other sizing materials adhere to the surface of the iron and burn, preventing the iron from sliding quickly and easily over fabric. Take care to devise some method for attaching the cover smoothly and firmly to the board.

The sleeve board This is a small board mounted on a firm base; it is tapered at one end and rounded (rather like the cap of a sleeve) at the other end. Pads and covers are available at a reasonable cost; if the board is padded at home, it must be handled with the same care given to the standard board. A tubular pressing aid can substitute for the sleeve board for most uses. The professional types are very firmly packed and covered with a wool fabric pulled tight for a smooth fit. A similar item can be devised at home by covering a rolled-up magazine with a piece of wool.

The point presser This is a board (sharply pointed at one end) mounted vertically on a firm base. It is convenient for pressing hard-to-reach seams and pressing close to corners (such as the point of a collar).

The tailor's ham This does not appear on the list of essential equipment on page 12 only because it is somewhat costly for those who sew infrequently; it is essential for those who sew often and those who do most of the family's pressing at home. It is egg-shaped (to provide a variety of curved surfaces) and is packed very firmly and covered with wool. It is indispensable for doing quality pressing on curved areas such as the seamed and darted areas around the hipline of fitted garments.

Press cloths These must be made of a smooth, flat fabric that will not mar the fabrics with which they will come into contact. The fabric should be heavier (duck, heavy muslin) to retain more moisture for pressing heavier fabrics and lighter in weight (muslin, voile) for pressing thinner, finer fabrics. It is essential that all sizing be removed, because otherwise it will stick to the iron and burn, and it may then rub off on the fabric that is being pressed. Fabrics that have been laundered often (a linen towel, pillowcases, sheets, etc.) make ideal press cloths. A piece of wool is excellent to use when pressing wool from the right side because its rough surface will help prevent shiny edges and ridges. A transparent cloth (silk organza) is convenient because it allows seams and darts to show through. A variety of press cloths is available on the market at a nominal cost.

Miscellaneous items

The rolling pressure foot This special foot, available for some (but not all) machines, is an aid in stitching spongy, thick fabrics which tend to push out of line under the pressure of the standard pressure foot. Its usefulness is increased when several layers of fabric are involved.

The seam ripper This is an indispensable item for removing basting stitches and ripping seams. It is available in several sizes.

A thimble This is essential for some workers, but others, who learned to sew without a thimble, manage very well for all but the heaviest work. The thimble should be selected with great care, for it must fit perfectly if it is to be useful. Those who do not like to wear a thimble may find that an adjustable one, which does not encase the entire tip of the finger, is more comfortable.

Sewing boxes These are available in a wide price range. Many are elaborately and impressively designed with a place for every single thing. They do make appropriate gifts for women who sew but actually most of those who sew a great deal do not use them because of the additional time it takes to return everything to its proper niche and

because these boxes are too large to be kept close at hand. The large deluxe types are not appropriate in a classroom, where there is neither table space nor storage space to accommodate them. The small supplies which will be used most frequently can be better and more conveniently kept in a small flat box which can be carried from the table to the machine and stored in a drawer. Cardboard boxes and plastic trays especially made for this purpose are really more convenient than the elaborately made sewing boxes.

Certain office supplies These are essential throughout the entire construction process and especially useful for making pattern alterations. Scotch "Magic" transparent tape (packaged in a green plaid container to contrast with the red plaid of the standard Scotch tape) is ideal to use instead of pins for pattern alterations. Those who sew a great deal will want to invest in one of the desk-type dispensers (about $2) because the tape can be removed quickly with one hand, leaving the other free to hold the surfaces to be taped. A roll of adding machine tape is convenient to store in the supply box and is of a practical width for pattern alterations as well as for many other uses during construction. Onionskin paper is helpful for doing pattern alterations because it is comparable in weight to the pattern tissue. Graph paper, simply marked in ¼-inch squares, is convenient for many uses because it is accurately premeasured with fine, distinct lines.

EQUIPMENT AND SUPPLIES

Essential items
Machine
Zipper foot
Shears (7- or 8-inch length) or light trimmer
   scissors (6- or 8-inch length)
Sewing scissors (5- or 6-inch length)
Tape measure
¼ pound of *silk* pins
Hand-sewing needles in assorted sizes
Machine needles in several sizes and types
Iron
Ironing board
Press cloths
Yardstick
6- and 12-inch rulers
Tailor's chalk
Thimble
Seam ripper
Scotch "Magic" transparent tape
Snaps and hooks and eyes in assorted sizes

Helpful items for later purchase
Pinking shears
T square or L square
Professional gauges
Hem marker
Tracing wheel and carbon paper
Sleeve board
Tailor's ham
Point presser
Buttonholer (for older machines)
Professional tape dispenser
Knife-edge shears
Rolling pressure foot

Special findings for the tailored costume

Findings and supplies for the tailored garment will be listed briefly on the back of the pattern envelope. They should be purchased at the same time the pattern and fabric are purchased to avoid unnecessary delay when work has begun. The findings will be familiar to most readers, although they may be put to new uses. The following brief discussion will be helpful to those readers who are making a first tailoring project.

Cotton twill tape This tape is firmly woven, is available in black or white, and comes in a variety of widths to serve many functional purposes. In the tailored garment it is used to strengthen and reinforce seams and areas that will receive hard wear. The ideal width is ¼ to ⅜ inch. The choice of color is not an issue in most medium-weight, firmly woven fabrics and becomes important only in lightweight, loosely woven fabrics, where there is a danger of the color showing through; in extreme cases the white tape must be dyed to match the color of the interfacing or the garment. Cotton twill tape shrinks a considerable amount, and therefore it must be washed in soap and hot water, dried, and pressed. The tailored coat will require approximately two 3-yard packages of twill tape. One 3-yard package is usually sufficient for a suit.

Twill tape made of linen is available in some well-stocked notions departments. Many tailors prefer it for men's wear because it is very flat and gives a firmer, crisper appearance to the finished eges.

Shoulder pads Fashions in shoulder lines make up one part, and an important part, of the silhouette picture. And because fashions in silhouettes are the most demanding, the issue of shoulder lines and shoulder pads becomes an important one. During World War II, the wide and square shoulder fashions demanded shoulder pads that were all of 1 inch thick; the pads were essential to the success of the costume, and good ones were very expensive. In the years since 1950 a natural shoulder line has been fashionable, and the shoulder pad has all but disappeared. The manufacturers of shoulder pads are constantly concerned with fashion, and as a result, shoulder pads available on the market are of a size and thickness to meet the current fashion needs. The woman who sews must be concerned with fashion in every detail. When shoulder pads are fashionable, she must be similarly concerned with the selection of the correct pad. If the pad plays a leading role, she must recognize its importance and be willing to spend more money for the right pad.

Shoulder pads serve many purposes, so that a pad may well be needed in those years when pads are not required by fashion. One purpose of the pad is to assure a smooth foundation on which the garment will hang. Persons with bony shoulders may need a thin pad to smooth the shoulder line. The pad can serve as a camouflage for shoulders that are too sloping or too narrow. Many persons have one shoulder higher than the other, and if the difference is extreme, extra padding can be added to the underside of one pad to compensate for the lower shoulder.

There are two basic styles of shoulder pads—square and round. See Figure 1-4. The square pad has a sharply defined angle at its outer edge. It is used for all garments with the usual set-in sleeve and regulation armhole. The round pad is smoothly molded and rounded at its outer edge. It is used for any garment which does not have a regulation armhole; for example, it is the cor-

rect choice for raglan sleeves, sleeves cut all in one with the body of the garment, and sleeves with a dropped armhole seam.

There are four sizes of shoulder pads; each is available in the round or square style. The size is determined by the amount of space the pad covers on the body and the thickness of the pad. The sizes are blouse, dress, suit, and coat, and the

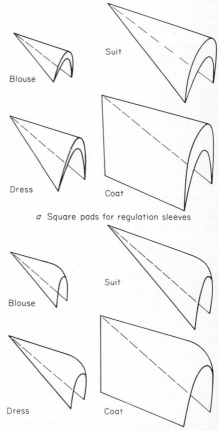

a Square pads for regulation sleeves

b Round pads for sleeves cut in one with garment

FIGURE 1-4 Shoulder pads.

amount of space the pad covers on the body and the height of the pad increase from blouse to coat. Blouse and dress pads are covered with fabric, usually white or black, and need not be covered with the fabric of the garment unless the addition of a nice touch to the inside of the garment or a better effect in a sheer garment is desired. Suit and coat pads are not covered with fabric because they are used in lined garments only.

Notice that all the pads except the coat model cover a triangular area on the body. Coat pads are made with a squared line in front and the usual diagonal line in back. This square shape in front allows the pad to cover a greater area, filling in the hollow between the shoulder and the bust for a smoother, better-tailored effect.

Shoulder pads vary greatly in price, from a nominal cost of less than a dollar to several dollars in seasons when a padded shoulder line has fashion significance. A great measure of the success of the garment depends on the shoulder line, and a good pad will provide a professional-looking shoulder line. It is well to select inexpensive pads for utilitarian garments and to buy better pads for the more significant wardrobe items. Certainly the time, effort, and money which go into the making of a suit or coat justify the added expenditure of a well-made, smooth pad.

NOTE: **If a pad is to be used, it must be purchased at the time the pattern and fabric are purchased. It will be used for the fitting of the muslin copy and for every subsequent fitting on the jacket or coat.**

Zipper The traditional length of the skirt and pants zipper is 7 inches, and in most cases this will be the length recommended on the pattern envelope. Some of the pattern companies suggest a 9-inch zipper for some utilitarian garments because the additional length will allow the woman with a small waist and larger-than-average hips to slip the skirt over her hips as she dresses; the 9-inch length, then, is recommended for practical purposes only. The woman with a small waist and large hips will require the 9-inch length in pants, shorts, and culottes. The woman with average waist and hip measurements can slip a skirt or pants over her hips if it has a 7-inch zipper, so there is no advantage in the 9-inch zipper for the average figure.

One is accustomed to seeing a 7-inch zipper, and the 9-inch length (on any figure but the very tall one) looks very long. The total costume will look more attractive with the shorter zipper, even if it means that the skirt will have to be slipped on over the shoulders. So the 7-inch length is the appropriate choice for those costumes which are more decorative than functional, while the longer length is acceptable for purely functional garments.

Findings for the waistband The waistband construction recommended in this book is different from that suggested by the pattern and will require some findings that will not be listed on the pattern envelope. Before purchasing the fabrics and findings for a suit, see "An Evaluation of Methods" on page 320. After deciding on the method, glance through the directions to see what findings will be needed.

Findings for finishing seams Depending on the fabrics used and the methods of construction chosen, there may be a need to finish seam and hem edges with seam binding or bias strips of lining or underlining fabric. The Hong Kong finish (page 287), which is highly recommended, is most attractive when done with bias strips to match the lining or underlining. By purchasing at least an extra ¾ yard for this purpose, the strips can be cut in ample lengths that will not require frequent seaming.

Muslin for the test copy The jacket or coat (and in most cases, the skirt or pants) will be tested in muslin in order to study the effectiveness of the design, to evalute pattern alterations, and to work out all fitting problems. See "Selection of Muslin for the Test Copy" on page 90.

Buttons It is not wise to purchase buttons on this first shopping trip. The choice of buttons for the jacket or coat is one of the most important decisions to be made, and careful testing should be done beforehand. Certain decisions can be made when the muslin copy is finished. More accurate decisions can be made when the garment has been basted together; testing out button ideas at that time will result in a far wiser choice than one could make on the first shopping trip. The issues involved with button selection appear on pages 382 to 384.

The Dior chain The metal chain is tucked under the edge of the lining of the finished skirt, jacket, or coat to add desirable weight to the garment. Although it is inserted in such a way that it is supposedly invisible, it does "peek out" as the jacket is slipped off, so that it adds a professional touch to the costume. Additional weight is the larger issue; weight may be required for the garment made of dress-weight woolen or for the jacket made for a person with rounded contours as an aid to creating smoother lines. These chains (in a choice of two weights) are available in notions departments for a nominal cost. Directions appear on page 473.

Chapter 2

PLANNING THE COSTUME

The woman who makes her own wardrobe runs an entire factory single-handed; she is the business manager, the fashion authority the designer, the layout technician, the machine operator, and the presser all combined in one. She must see that "profits" exceed expenditures; she must know current fashion and interpret it to her individual advantage; she must be an artist able to select appealing designs and appropriate fabrics, colors, and textures; she must be a scientist and a mathematician during the construction processes. Like clothing manufacturing, home sewing is a combination of art and science, and learning to master these conflicting talents is largely responsible for the challenges as well as the exciting rewards of home sewing. The "collection" made in the one-woman factory must meet the professional competition of ready-to-wear, and the woman who sews at home must be able to do a competent job of a great variety of work activities which are handled by specialists in the clothing industry.

The tension that builds up in the designer's office and filters through to every corner of the ready-to-wear factory is witness to the fact that clothing construction places heavy demands on a professional staff. The woman who sews at home can rival her competition successfully only if she understands that she is undertaking an ambitious project that is not quick and easy. Successful home sewing requires thought, effort, concentration, and practice.

The successful designer is a student of fashion as it is molded by worldwide cultural, social, psychological, and economic influences. She spends hours in observation, study, and thought before she sits at the sketching board; then she makes many sketches before making final decisions. She thinks of the role this costume must play in the ever-changing lives of her customers; she tests a variety of fabrics that will serve the needs of the design and the desires of her buyers; she experiments with colors, color combinations, texture, and texture combinations; she shops the vast market for just the right button or the perfect braid trim. She tests and compares a variety of possibilities before making each of the dozens of decisions she will make as the design progresses through various stages of manufacture. And she entertains second thoughts by discarding an idea that does not meet her exacting standards and beginning anew with a fresh and different approach. The woman who sews at home should strive to work in a comparably professional manner.

THE TAILORED COSTUME AS A LEARNING EXPERIENCE

Home sewing offers many advantages: possible savings in wardrobe costs, an opportunity to enjoy the luxury of quality fabric and good design within a modest income, the advantage of an accurate and flattering fit for every figure, the opportunity to preshrink fabrics and findings before cutting, the satisfaction of a personalized costume, and—for some the greatest advantage of all—the pleasures of creative expression. All these rewards are multiplied if the costume is tailored. There are several reasons: Tailored costumes are significant units of the wardrobe because typically they get frequent and hard wear, they are among the most costly purchases on the ready-to-wear market and therefore offer greater economic advantages, and they require more effort and ability, which adds to the pleasures of accomplishment.

There is some misunderstanding about the meaning of the term *tailoring.* The most common misconception is that tailoring and sewing are two identical activities and that the term *tailoring* is used to describe sewing if the costume is a lined jacket or a coat made of wool. This is not true. A lined jacket or coat can be sewn or tailored. Although both *sewing* and *tailoring* defy brief definition, the two are not interchangeable terms. In general, the basic difference between them is that tailoring techniques are an extension of sewing—they go beyond sewing in that they are additional techniques which are not usually used on dresses, blouses, and casual wear. Tailoring upgrades the appearance and the quality of the costume because these additional techniques are employed during construction (1) to combine all layers of fabric involved in such a way that they act as one and (2) to mold and shape the several layers to create the desired effect on the figure.

The all-important molding and shaping are done with padding stitches, tapes, and effective pressing techniques. In the tailored costume, certain seams are strengthened and stiffened with tapes for greater control. Supporting fabrics (underlinings and interfacings), which add body and enhance the fabric, are an integral part of the tailored jacket or coat. The tailored jacket or coat is always lined. Although skirts or pants do not require as much tailoring as jackets or coats, these accompanying pieces are usually lined to keep better pace with the costume. In all, the distinctive characteristics of tailoring are additional sewing techniques that require more hand work and greater attention to detail and so necessarily require more experience, more time, and more patience.

Another misconception is the belief that *tailoring* is a term used to describe sewing with wool fabrics. It is true that in the past the traditional tailored costume was made of wool. Wool, with its greater qualities of elasticity and resilience, responds more favorably than other fabrics to the shaping and molding which is a major concern in tailoring. This is not to say that other fabrics cannot be tailored; on the contrary, fabrics which are the most difficult to control and shape (denim, suiting-weight brocade, etc.) are greatly enhanced by the extra techniques employed in tailoring.

The tailored costume, especially if it is a first venture, as it will be with most readers, should be fun and exciting although it will represent many hours of work. Certainly it should be planned for a long, active life and be worthy of its special place in the wardrobe of the person who made it. But it is well to delay the excitement temporarily to consider a matter of greater importance. Because this book is planned primarily as a college text (or for persons taking a course under supervision), the tailored costume must be considered a project or an academic assignment — *a means of gaining the experience and knowledge necessary for a lifetime of professional and personal use.* Think of it this way: A costume, no matter how successful, is relatively insignificant, for it is nothing more than one costume which will eventually be discarded and forgotten. But with an academic approach centered on learning experience, the costume can be fashionable and exciting and, moreover, give birth to dozens of equally successful costumes in the future. The college student is well aware that the one tailored costume she will make under supervision is a requirement for her chosen career; certainly the student majoring in home economics education or extension has learned to plan her class projects around the experiences she will need to teach others. The reader who is working in an adult special-interest class, or working on her own at home, is wise to adopt a similar point of view; even if she sews only for purely personal reasons, her pleasures and rewards will increase as she learns to work at a professonal level. Therefore, *all readers should consider the first tailoring project for its educational merits, the more so if it will be the only opportunity to work under the supervision of a competent teacher.*

Fabric choices

Tailoring techniques can be applied to a great variety of fabrics with varying degrees of success. Basically, choices are limited to those fabrics with the character and body appropriate for jackets and coats — in other words, to fabrics of suiting or coating weight. They include woolens, polyesters and acrylics, velvets and corduroys, upholstery fabrics, fake furs, and others. But fabric choices are not limited to those obviously suitable for jackets and coats. The list can be extended to include many fabrics with less body if these are combined with underlinings of sufficient weight and hand to create the desired effect. Thus, suiting-weight cottons (denim, Tarpoon cloth, etc.), linens, and brocades can be adapted to tailoring purposes.

When choosing fabric, keep in mind that most of the major new learning experiences will be involved with molding and shaping layers of fabric to act as one — for example, handling the collar and lapel area to take natural, graceful lines on the figure. This is the reason most tailored garments are made of fabrics which are somewhat pliable. For the great advantage of learning the techniques of molding and shaping, the first tailored costume (even the first several costumes) should ideally be made of a fabric which responds to the technique. Of the fabrics listed above, the woolens and also the polyesters and acrylics are the best choices for first costumes. They will be responsive to tailoring techniques and in addition will afford the worker experience with the type of fabric she will encounter most frequently, both personally and professionally, in the future. Others mentioned above can be chosen after the worker has gained more experience; in every case, they present additional problems which will complicate learning processes on a first project. For example, the fake furs offer additional problems created by their bulk, their long fibers, and, in many cases, their design markings, which must be balanced in a way that is somewhat like matching plaids. The velvets and corduroys require special cutting and pressing techniques, and they are not as pliable as woolens, polyesters, and acrylics. Upholstery fabrics are interesting and effective, but they too are bulky and stiff. The cottons, linens, and brocades do not have inherent pliable qualities and so are not entirely responsive to the shaping techniques employed in tailoring. The above list does not include plastics, vinyls, suede, etc., which are popular fabrics on the ready-to-wear market; these are not recommended for class projects, because many tailoring techniques must be eliminated and because they create many unique problems of their own which require constant attention, distracting the worker from the fundamental tailoring experiences she set out to master.

NOTE: **Chapter 11, Special Problems, contains helpful suggestions for working with unique problems which are not part of the typical tailoring experience. Carefully review the contents of that chapter before purchasing fabric.**

Certain fabrics and textures, by their very nature, are easier to handle and will result in a more professional-looking finished product. The inexperienced person should have the advantage of this kind of fabric, and the experienced person will find her talents enhanced if she chooses a fabric responsive to tailoring requirements. In brief, the fabrics most adaptable to tailoring have the following characteristics:

They are firmly woven Loosely woven fabrics, particularly some of the novelty weaves with long floats of thread on the surface, present a problem of raveling and stretching.

They are somewhat pliable Although the hard-surfaced fabrics used in men's wear and similar rather stiff worsted fabrics make excellent tailored garments in the hands of the professional tailor, they do not ease well, they are more difficult to shape over curves, and they reveal every flaw of construction.

They have some surface texture interest The matter of surface interest is an important consideration for the novice. A very flat fabric, such as flannel, shows every little detail of construction. Design lines will be prominent (and this is an advantage), but at the same time every flaw, every stitch, and the slightest mistake in pressing will be magnified. By contrast, fabric with surface interest (nubby weaves, tweed, many of the novelty weaves) will hide flaws of construction.

The color is in the middle range To some extent, a fabric in a light color presents the same problems as a flat-surfaced fabric, so the choice of a flat-surfaced fabric in a light color is a serious mistake for the novice. The very light colors and white tend to reveal construction irregularities, and if the fabric is relatively lightweight, every seam and hem edge shows through to mar the beauty of the design. Black and other very dark colors are discouraging to some because they shine readily with improper pressing and tend to pick up lint during construction.

They are of a medium weight The very lightweight fabrics show every construction flaw, and unusually bulky fabrics are difficult to handle at the machine and present a problem of bulk in heavy seam areas. Medium-weight fabrics can be used for a greater variety of designs because most patterns are planned for "average" circumstances.

NOTE: **Fabric selection is discussed in detail in Chapter 4.**

Design choices

The choice of the design is a very personal decision which should center primarily on individual matters of taste, preference, wardrobe needs, figure flattery, and fashion. Even so, with the wide choice of excellent designs available on the market, it is possible to choose one that will serve these needs and will, at the same time, provide valuable learning experience. The reader should understand that there is much to learn on the first tailoring project, and if she will have only this one opportunity to study under supervision, it is very important that she choose a design which will give her a variety of experiences with the most typical and most difficult construction techniques she will encounter in the future. Ideally, these considerations should outweigh personal preferences on first projects. Anyone taking a course in tailoring must guard and cherish class hours; the assignment is demanding and time-consuming. One should not use these brief hours to master unique problems which are not a part of the tailoring experience. It is unwise to choose this time to solve the special problems of working with the vinyls or fake furs, for example, and likewise it is a mistake to jeopardize

this opportunity by choosing a pattern design so simple or so unusual that it does not require the very techniques which are the foundation of tailoring.

The following suggestions are offered as an aid to strengthening learning experiences. They are not intended to be so rigid and confining that they eliminate fashion excitement or personal satisfaction; actually most designs for tailored costumes featured in the pattern books satisfy the following educational requirements.

The pattern should be cut in relatively basic lines The excitement of a costume is a result of the combined influences of the character and texture of the fabric and its color and design, interesting little fashion details, and the design lines of the pattern itself. For a first tailoring project it is wise to gain interest with fabric, color, and details (these demand comparatively less time), and to simplify procedures by choosing a design cut in simple lines. Very intricately cut designs (such as some Vogue Paris Original and International Couturier patterns) require more time and ability than the average student can afford in the all too limited time available in a tailoring class; they require more difficult construction as well as more time and talent for pattern alteration and fitting. The reader will want to master these additional problems one day, but it is wise to undertake more demanding assignments after basic tailoring techniques have been mastered.

The pattern should require a lining Lining techniques are basic to the tailoring experience, and their importance is greater if the student has not had a previous opportunity to line skirts and dresses. But, more than that, the lining is essential to a well-tailored costume because it hides inner construction; if the jacket or coat is unlined, many tailoring techniques must be eliminated because they would be visible.

The great majority of patterns for tailored costumes include linings, but there are a few (usually designated "easy to make" in counter catalogues) which do not include linings. Most of these have front and neck facings with directions for finishing the edges in a way that will be adequate to prevent raveling and give a reasonably well-finished appearance. One of these designs can be chosen for a tailored costume, but the worker must make her own lining patterns from the major pattern pieces; directions appear on page 445. She will have to work without the benefit of specific lining directions written for a particular design, but she can follow general directions available in a text and will probably find them entirely adequate.

The student should understand the difference between a lined and a faced garment. A *lined garment* is one which has front and neck facings cut from the fabric of the garment and separate lining pieces which attach to the inner edge of the facings. A *faced garment* is one which has no front and neck facings; the lining (actually a facing cut exactly like the outside pieces) extends to the finished edges of the garment. If the jacket or coat will be reversible, it must be faced rather than lined; but for all other types of costumes, this construction is not recommended. The pattern companies offer a few of these designs (with understated lines and few fashion details) to satisfy their inexperienced customers and those who wish to use quick methods of construction. These are planned to be *sewn* rather than *tailored,* and they are not appropriate for tailoring projects. Faced patterns can be converted to use with lined garments if the worker makes her own facing patterns and lining patterns. However, this will not provide an ideal learning experience, because the special directions on the instruction sheet will have no value and the worker will be forced to rely entirely on generalized directions in a text.

The pattern should feature details which require fundamental tailoring techniques Much of the molding and shaping, which is the one technique above all others that distinguishes tailoring from sewing, occurs in the collar and lapel area. For this reason, the pattern should feature a collar of some type and preferably a separate collar and a lapel. The techniques of shaping can be learned equally well on a separate collar or on a collar cut in one with the jacket or coat front. However, the application of a separate collar is handled differently on tailored costumes (and other garments made of heavy fabrics). This construction, called the "notched-collar construction," is very difficult; and since it will be encountered on the great majority of tailored designs, it is well to undertake it at a time when a competent instructor is available. For this reason, a design with a separate collar (which must be attached) is recommended.

The pattern should feature some of the most difficult construction details that appear most frequently in typical tailored costumes A design with set-in or regulation sleeves will provide much more experience than one with sleeves cut in one with the major pattern pieces. The regulation sleeve is difficult to set into the armhole, and it requires more careful fitting as well. However, it is because of the far greater difficulty of inserting a lining in a regulation sleeve (and the difficulty is multiplied if there is a shoulder pad) that this is recommended for the most worthwhile classroom experience.

There are other construction details which appear frequently in tailored costumes, and the student should attempt to select a design which includes at least some of them. Some type of buttonhole (usually of the bound type) will be included in most tailored costumes; these are more difficult than their alternatives, which include zipper closings, snaps, and decorative frogs or hooks. An applied waistband for the skirt or pants will afford broader learning experiences than a simple elasticized casing; the casing provides little educational value, for it is simple to construct and eliminates the need for a zipper closing and careful fitting. Pleats, vent openings, decorative pocket laps, other applied trimming details, and pockets of every description are among the details that will give the worker valuable experience for her future personal and professional needs.

THE TAILORED COSTUME AS A PART OF THE PERSONAL WARDROBE

The fundamental function of the wardrobe is to serve the individual, and ideally it will be so well suited to the individual that she will be able to forget clothes and give her undivided attention to the work and pleasures of the day. If she must stop to think about what she is wearing before accepting a compliment, her wardrobe is a smashing success. The successful wardrobe should be balanced and coordinated in the following ways:

The style of living and the fashion consciousness of the community in which one lives is a major consideration, and the need to weigh this factor is influenced by the individual's need to conform. Those who wish to follow and blend in with the group must carefully study the prevalent tastes and accepted fashion of the community; while wardrobe choices can be quite different for those who are expected to set the fashion pace and those who wish to be distinctive.

The wardrobe should be balanced among the private, social, and professional activities of the individual; and although it is not possible to divide the effort and expense of a wardrobe mathematically, it is helpful to use percentages of time spent privately, socially, and professionally as a guide for making tentative decisions. The mother, confined by a young family to spending much of her time working and entertaining at home, can and should have an attractive wardrobe of casuals and hostess gowns and can easily manage with a minimum public-social wardrobe; if she is not working outside the home, her professional wardrobe will be composed of only those costumes necessary to enhance her husband's professional reputation. By contrast, the single woman devoted to a demanding career will need an extensive professional wardrobe, a few costumes that will serve her social needs, and some very comfortable at-home costumes to collapse in at night.

The cost of units in the wardrobe and the effort devoted to these units (for those who sew) should be influenced by their anticipated usefulness. Although the cost per wearing should obviously be greater for special-occasion garments (a wedding dress is the prime example) than for functional costumes, the cost per year or the cost per wearing is, in many cases, the most accurate way of allocating wardrobe expenses. The most expensive garment may well be the least expensive in terms of usefulness. For example, the most costly suit the author has made (about $60) has been worn rather like a uniform and is in its eighth year; judged on an annual or cost-per-wearing basis, it has turned into a bargain-basement item. The reader will be wise to give this method of planning wardrobe expense and effort careful consideration, while at the same time realizing that when the right costume for one very special occasion is required, a higher cost will be justified.

The degree or level of fashion will be a basic consideration. Some readers will be willing to pay the high price in time and money for a costume that will be avant-garde fashion this season, realizing that the high style of the design will limit its life-span. Others, more practical, will choose something more basic in design in hopes that it will give many years of service. The lasting quality of a design is largely a matter of silhouette. Those designs which follow the basic body lines often stay in fashion's favor for five to ten years, provided there is no drastic increase in skirt or coat length. Lines which do not conform to body lines, such as exaggeratedly wide shoulders, the pegged skirt, the very flared back in a coat or jacket peplum, the leg-of-mutton sleeve, etc., are design lines that are relatively short-lived. Consequently, the matter of silhouette, since it is so responsible for seasonal wardrobe expenses, will be one of the more important considerations in planning for the tailored costume.

The woman who sews usually feels a special kind of devotion for a costume she makes, especially if it is a tailored one and more so if it is a first venture in tailoring. She will spend a great deal of time making it and will put a great deal of love into it, and she will very probably want it to last forever. For this reason, it might be well to plan the first tailored garment in a design with simple lines which are not tiring and in a somewhat basic silhouette so that it can be enjoyed for many years. However, even if the suit or

coat is made in basic lines which ensure a certain fashion stability, the costume can be planned for an important role in the wardrobe.

Current fashion and individual style

Fashion has four components: design (silhouette or line), fabric (texture and texture combination), color and color combination, and details. Changes occur in each of these components, but fashion rarely if ever changes in every one in a given season. One season the newsworthy change may be in fabric; another season the excitement may be in silhouette. Changes occur in more than one of the fashion components in a given season, but the really big news is usually confined to one segment of fashion. Changes in silhouette have the greatest impact on the fashion world simply because they are so very obvious. The woman who hopes to wear a costume for many years will confine her choices to basic silhouette lines and will plan for excitement in other ways.

The first step in wardrobe planning is the careful study of the current fashion picture. The woman who sews is wise to realize that her greatest competition and most excellent source of inspiration is the ready-to-wear market. The remarkably high standards of design and construction of clothes available at a reasonable price make them formidable competition indeed. There is no reason, however, to draw inspiration only from merchandise one could afford on the retail market; it is far wiser and entirely possible to meet the demanding standards of the greater competition of exclusive, elegant costumes one cannot afford to buy ready-made. The quality of construction, even more than the quality of fabric, is obvious in exclusive ready-to-wear, and the little touches that make up quality construction are often quite simple to do. The woman who makes her own costumes is wise to visit exclusive departments for the purpose of establishing high standards and of "borrowing" tricks of the trade to add to her own collection. In other words, it is well to take advantage of the lessons to be learned from the most talented professional designers.

There are lessons to be learned from the buyer in the department store as well. She spends most of her budget on rather staple merchandise, while a much smaller percentage (approximately 10 percent) is allotted to current, exciting fashions. This smaller collection of high-fashion costumes is the prestige merchandise on which the fashion reputation of the store is based. The buyer, who must strive for fashion prestige, advertises these newsworthy fashions in window and departmental displays and features them in leading newspaper advertisements. By studying these ads and displays one can get a capsule view of newsworthy fashion, interpreted by a professional buyer and chosen especially to meet the needs of a particular community and region of the country.

While making a market survey, take cues from the kind of ready-to-wear clothing that is most appealing. All too often, the woman who buys imaginative merchandise loses her courage when she selects a pattern and fabric and chooses an uninspired design that she would never have purchased ready-made. This understand-

able lack of courage is a result of limited experience in pattern and fabric selection. The solution is to try to retain normal confidence and imagination; each venture in home sewing will increase the skill of costume planning, and each imaginative costume will build confidence for future costumes.

In addition to considering current fashion, the shopper must give careful thought to her own individual style. Fashion is not a dictator—rather, the individual is the dictator and should use fashion to her own advantage. Even in seasons when fashion is not as permissive as it was in the early 1970s, a woman need not be a slave to fashion as long as she stays within reasonable bounds; she cannot wear skirts 4 inches longer than those featured in current fashions, but she can wear them at a somewhat different length and still look fashionable. She can break one rule, and perhaps more, but she cannot break them all. A woman usually (and correctly) has a marked preference for a particular fashion trend because it is flattering to her (in terms of color, silhouette, etc.) or because she takes personal pleasure in it and finds it comfortable. If that preference is based on sound reasoning, the beloved fashion can be worn so often and so long that it becomes a "uniform." And if that fashion is artistically sound (the little Chanel suit is an excellent example), it can be varied and featured in every color and every fabric, and that very same fashion can make up an entire wardrobe for many years.

Components of an important costume

The costume can be planned for an important and distinctive role in the wardrobe by the effective use of all components of fashion (design, fabric, color, and details), by extra attention to little couturier touches which appear throughout the technical directions in this text, by the choice of interesting linings, and by the addition of companion pieces that meet professional standards.

Design (silhouette or line) Even if the silhouette will be basic enough to enjoy fashion stability, the design lines of the pattern can be the outstanding feature of the costume. For example, the design lines of a Vogue Paris Original or International Couturier pattern may well be so interesting that every other component of the costume should be subordinate to design. The design should be, in the opinion of the author, one that is of sufficient complication to ensure the appearance of an obvious expenditure of time and effort. It is foolish economy in both time and money to make a costume "in a jiffy." The oversimplified construction details and design lines of the kind of costume that can be made in a very short time (no collar, no pockets, faced rather than lined) fool no one. One has but to visit the budget shop in a department store to see costumes of that description, priced so inexpensively that there would be no advantage in spending the time to make them. By contrast, costumes in the exclusive departments of the store feature subtle design surprises and intricate touches that look as if someone cared. Costumes made at home should certainly show that someone cared, and the wise woman who sews will always keep in mind that every extra hour she spends in her workroom adds dollars to the apparent cost of the garment. The person who has become proficient in dressmaking and who is moving up to tailoring should not consider patterns planned for the novice. She is ready for more advanced work, and as soon as her experience warrants, she should consider Vogue Paris Original and International Couturier designs.

Many women commit the serious mistake of buying an attractive design and then subtracting all the excitement from it in an attempt to save time or effort. They rationalize that they do not need the pockets ("They aren't big enough to hold anything anyway") or the buttons and buttonholes ("I never button a jacket") or the cuffs ("They get in my way when I type"), and it takes just one or two "subtractions" to turn a beautiful design into a carbon copy of bargain-basement merchandise. If the suit is to be a bargain in time and effort, it is far wiser to buy that bargain ready-made. There are no shortcuts to a professional costume, and the smart woman who sews holds one thought uppermost in her mind: *Extra hours mean extra dollars in apparent cost, extra hours mean more elegance, and extra hours mean far greater creative satisfaction.*

NOTE: **Pattern selection is covered in detail in Chapter 3.**

Fabric (texture and texture combination) Because tailoring is a time-consuming process, the tailored costume deserves the very highest-quality fabric the consumer can afford to buy. Unfortunately there are very few bargains in fabric, and high quality demands a premium price. But there is no better way to add importance to the tailored costume than to make it of beautiful fabric; quality fabric gives pleasure to the beholder and wearer alike and, in addition, results in a garment which retains its beauty through hard wear and years of service.

The woman who has the ability and experience to ensure predictable, successful results can afford fabric of far better quality than she might be accustomed to buying. If home-sewn garments are to meet the competition of exclusive ready-to-wear, they must be constructed well and designed well, and they must be made of quality fabric. The first step toward ultimate success is to gain experience in construction and selection. A next logical move upward is to select a quality design. The last step upward (the final move because of the cost factor) is to buy quality fabric. The tremendous advantage of being able to afford an exclusive wardrobe on a modest income will have been achieved in these three logical steps forward.

The cost-comparison chart shown below may hold a pleasant surprise for some readers. It is based on prices of wool fabric, 54 inches wide, and on the amount of yardage required for a typical suit or coat. The three qualities of fabric listed might be con-

sidered minimum, average, and very good at present-day (1974) prices. The minimum-quality fabric would compare with that used in the $12.98 to $24.95 (possibly unlined) ready-made suit; the average-quality fabric could be compared with that used in the $49.95 to $79.95 ready-made suit; and the very good-quality fabric would compare favorably with that used in the ready-made suit priced at $79.95 and up to $125.

Obviously the differences in total cost are entirely dependent on the price of fabric, with all other costs remaining constant, but it is interesting to note that although the good-quality fabric costs four times as much per yard as the lowest quality, the total cost only doubles. Assuming that the reader is sufficiently proficient in construction to meet the high standards of the better and exclusive ready-to-wear, it is revealing to see that for an additional $11 above minimum costs, she can move up to the $49.95-and-up bracket. Quality fabric is an excellent means of achieving wardrobe excitement, and the cost is not as prohibi-

COST-COMPARISON CHART

	Minimum quality (estimated at $3 per yd)	Average quality (estimated at $7 per yd)	Very good quality (estimated at $12 per yd)
3 yd fabric	$10	$21	$36
	(see note below)		
Pattern	3	3	3
Findings (zipper, thread, buttons, miscellaneous)	3	3	3
Jacket lining (crepe at $2.50 per yd)	5	5	5
Skirt lining (crepe at $1.50 per yd)	3	3	3
Interfacing (muslin at 40¢ per yd)	1	1	1
Total cost	$25	$36	$51

NOTE: **Some extra yardage is allowed for straightening and preshrinking.**

tive on a cost-per-garment basis as it appears to be from a cost-per-yard comparison.

The weight, the very thickness of the fabric, has a great deal to do with the success of the tailored costume. It is a distinct advantage to see the design shown in a photograph (Vogue Paris Original and International Couturier designs are always shown in a photograph) because it will be pictured in an appropriate weight and texture, chosen by a professional designer. The suit pictured in a nubby tweed coating will often be a disappointment if it is made in a flat, hard-surfaced fabric, and the suit pictured in the sleek lines of worsted crepe may well lose its charm if it is made in a sturdy tweed. The experienced person is able to make a wise selection of fabric appropriate for the design, but the inexperienced person needs the help of the photograph and of the list of suggested fabrics on the pattern envelope.

NOTE: **Fabric selection is covered in detail in Chapter 4.**

Color and color combination   The choice of color is a very personal consideration, and rightly so. Color has tremendous powers of flattery (to the personal coloring of the individual, to the mood and personality of the individual), and the advantage of its flattery should be used in an individual way. In other words, unless one is working professionally in the fashion industry in a capacity that requires dressing in fashions of the current season, it is wise to favor flattering color over fashionable color; color is not a demanding component of fashion for most women. In fact, if the color is fashionable and not flattering, the choice is so obviously fashion-oriented that its advantage becomes a disadvantage.

The mood of a color or a combination of colors and the effect those colors have on the individual are of far greater impor-

tance than their fashion rightness. Women (and men) are sensitive to the moods of color, subconsciously if not consciously, in a way that has nothing to do with the personal flattery that color provides, and this sensitivity to color is more important than fashion to the success of a costume. The best color to choose, therefore, is one that is flattering and one that pleases the wearer, fashion be hanged! If the flattering and pleasing color happens to be fashionable, consider that a happy little bonus.

The inexperienced person who may not have confidence in her ability to choose color and color combinations wisely has many sources of inspiration and assistance. The survey of the current market and the study of current magazines and prestige advertisements, mentioned earlier in this chapter, will be of great help. Displays in the yard-goods department will be particularly helpful because many of these displays will be planned around a coordinated color and texture theme, selected by the professional buyer. Fabric manufacturers, ever sensitive to fashion and customer needs, are providing a great service by offering fabrics in a wide range of coordinated colors and textures.

Details   The details of fashion add great interest to the costume, but like color and to some extent like texture, fashions in details are not truly demanding. In other words, in most cases details add interest because they are interesting in and of themselves, not because they are fashionable. A relatively small percentage of women are aware of the seasonal fashions in "little touches." These details, then, offer fertile opportunity for individual preference and creative expression. Details are usually involved with little techniques of construction and the choice of accenting decoration, and although these details are a part of fashion, they need not be confined to a particular fashion season. The discussion of details is limited in this chapter because ideas for interesting accents will appear throughout the book. For example, button ideas appear on page 382, details to add interest to the skirt appear on page 302, and ideas for little details for the jacket or coat lining appear on page 440.

Every fashion magazine will picture interesting ideas that can be borrowed for future use. The woman who sews at home would be wise to collect pictures of unusual and appealing ideas to serve as an inspiration for future home sewing. An "idea scrapbook" should include suggestions for texture and texture combination, color and color combination, and details, for these three components of fashion will not be quickly outdated.

Interesting and exciting linings There is no easier way to add a touch of magic and a custom look to garments made at home than to choose exciting lining fabrics. The costume look, which adds so much in apparent cost with very little expenditure of money, is easily achieved by the clever choice and use of these fabrics. The suit with a matching blouse and jacket lining and the coat with a companion dress and lining are favorites of fashion largely because of the pleasant impact of the coordinated look. The success of these costumes is not automatic, however. The blouse and the dress must have substance of design and detail to keep pace with the tailored costume; an understated shift dress or a mere shell of a blouse can cheapen an otherwise attractive tailored garment. Lining fabrics that will match some other item of clothing must be chosen with extreme care. If the lining and blouse or dress are made of a gaudy print or in a design of poor taste, the fact that the two match will call obvious attention to the costume and thereby defeat the purpose. However, that is just a word of warning and is not intended to dwarf the imagination; the ability to dare a little and dream a little is an essential for successful wardrobe planning. The fashion surprise should not be disregarded, for adults like surprises as much as children. Because the lining is seen only momentarily, it provides excellent ammunition for the surprise attack.

The woman who is inclined to be extremely practical often resists any suggestion of a lining that will limit the use of every blouse in her wardrobe. It is true that the interesting costume cannot be entirely practical, but nonetheless it can be planned with many practical considerations. The cautious woman can choose a suit lining with design interest, and if the background is white, the costume can be practical because it can always be worn with white blouses.

The coat lining attracts more attention than the suit lining. In most cases the coat must be a more versatile wardrobe item, and the lining must be chosen accordingly. Many readers will want the advantage of a matching lining in the coat; it can be interesting as well as practical. The choice of satin, with its subtle sheen and highlights, will add interest and a look of luxury, and it need not increase the cost if it is made of one of the better rayon satins. The use of satin need not be confined to formal garments; a satin lining is in good taste in many tailored costumes with the obvious exceptions of those made in sturdy tweeds, typical man-tailored garments, and sportswear. There are several construction details, described on page 440, which will add interest and apparent cost to the coat lining.

Companion pieces These offer fertile opportunities for the imaginative woman. The blouse or dress coordinated with a coat or suit is such a companion piece. The "go-with" piece may be a hat, a purse, a stole, a belt to match the blouse or skirt, or any number of other "little" items. The companion accessory, if it is right, is a brilliant addition to the costume, but if it is wrong, it brings the entire costume down with it. The reader is urged to use the companion piece with imagination, while realizing that such pieces must be added with caution and with consideration to the several issues discussed in the following paragraphs.

There is a certain danger that the costume will look "homemade" if too many pieces are coordinated. This exaggeration will serve to illustrate: A suit with a blouse to match the printed lining, worn with a hat and purse in the suit fabric trimmed in the blouse fabric and with gloves dyed to match one of the colors of the printed blouse, would shout "homemade." This costume would be smart with a matching blouse or a hat of the suit fabric. But that *is all.* Hats should be trimmed with something that harmonizes in color and texture (ribbon, a cluster of fruit, a feather) rather than the blouse fabric. Accessories made in a harmonizing or coordinated fabric (velvet with a soft woolen suit or a coordinated plaid with a plain-colored suit) are often wiser choices.

Some fabrics, because of color or color combination or design, create so much interest that they must be used sparingly. One can imagine that a ruby-red coat with a lining and matching dress in a bold print of rich reds and greens would be stunning worn with stark black accessories, and it

is obvious that the same costume would be grossly overdone if, in addition, the print were used for a matching turban and pouch bag. Similarly, a tailored suit in a large, bold plaid (bright red and black) is a delightful addition to the wardrobe, but the same active plaid in a purse and matching beret, worn with the suit, would not be smart. However, the same plaid accessories would be attractive used with a suit in basic colors.

The quality of the companion piece must keep pace with and even surpass the suit or coat if the resulting costume is to look truly professional. No one is fooled by the fabric envelope, trying to be a purse, and yet the same envelope stiffened and padded professionally will enhance a costume. The hat based on a buckram frame (available at nominal cost in most large department stores) will add dollars in apparent cost to the total costume, and by contrast, a limp little pillbox will cheapen the costume. Decorations for the hat should have professional appeal. Trimming the hat is a problem because most of the trimmings available in the department store are basically dress decorations. If there is a very large city nearby, it is wise to shop in a millinery supply store to find appropriate accenting touches.

The companion piece will be a successful addition to the costume only if it is something that is currently fashionable, is being done by the leading designers, and is being worn by well-known fashionable women. This illustration will clarify the preceding statement: Ordinarily a little triangle of matching fabric, pretending to be a hat, would not keep pace with a lovely costume. And yet for a few seasons in the early 1960s, the little triangular head scarf was very fashionable, and one Paris designer, in presenting his 1963 fall collection, topped the entire collection (including the wedding gown) with little triangles tied in interesting ways. It is wise to study the market and copy only those accessory ideas which are currently fashionable.

FINAL DECISIONS—
BUYING PROCEDURES

A shopping trip makes far greater demands on the consumer who sews than on one who buys ready-to-wear, because the sewer must make dozens of decisions while relying largely on her imagination to visualize the finished costume. She needs every advantage. It is important that she be well informed, so that she need not depend on others for answers to pertinent questions. The sales staff is available, but not all clerks in the department will be competent to answer technical questions. There is usually one, obviously capable, who is interrupted with questions from the other clerks, and the wise consumer will wait in line for her counsel. Preparation for wise buying includes the mastery of fundamental knowledge that will lead to greater self-reliance and subsequently to a diminished need to question others.

Preparation for the shopping trip

Fabrics influence not only fashion but also the usefulness of the garment, and the wise consumer must be informed about new textile fibers and fabrics and the performance she can expect of them. The purchase of a current textile textbook is strongly recommended but an adequate capsule resume of new developments can be collected from articles in recent women's magazines and current publications of the pattern companies.

Fundamental theory As she shops, the consumer will need to use the information in several chapters of this text. The irreversible decisions she must make as she purchases fabrics and patterns call for thorough mastery of basic information. The novice recognizes her lack of background knowledge and remedies it with study; it is the person who has sewn for years (and naturally considers herself experienced) who often places herself in jeopardy. Her experience may or may not have been good, it may have been confined to one type of garment with limited and similar details, and, all too often, experience is weighted in the direction of sewing skills while completely failing to provide the underlying theory and science of construction. The experienced person will be wise to assume that she, too, has much to learn. There is no value in reading the entire text before beginning work; most technical directions should be studied while work progresses. The chapters listed below, however, must be studied before any purchase is made.

Chapter 1—Equipment and Findings The equipment that has been adequate for ordinary household uses and occasional clothing repair may not be of a quality that will serve specialized functions. A list of essential equipment and supplies for immediate purchase appears on page 12.

Chapter 3—Pattern Selection and Figuring Special Requirements The issue of pattern size and figure type (probably the most pertinent decision to be made) is included.

A warning to those who experienced but who have not used a pattern since January 1968: A sizing change, effective on that date and accepted by the entire Pattern Fashion Industry, will demand a different size from that used before that time; see more details on page 36.

The basic body measurements discussed on page 45 should be taken before the shopping trip; more comprehensive measurements will be taken just before doing pattern alterations. Pattern size is stated by bust measurement in most cases (skirts and slacks are two exceptions). The reader must avoid the pitfall of using her bra size as a bust measurement (she may measure two or more inches larger). Although the pattern size that will be required will very probably be the same as the size required in ready-to-wear, it is important to select the proper size and figure type from the charts on pages 50 and 51. Ready-to-wear sizes are not standardized as pattern sizes are, and so the consumer must not rely entirely on ready-to-wear sizing to determine pattern sizing.

Two convenient measurements to take and to keep updated are these: (1) The finished length the individual is currently wearing in full-length garments (taken from the base of the neck in the back to the hemline) and in other garments such as skirts and slacks (taken from the waist to the hemline). These finished lengths are stated on the envelope of each pattern and a comparison will reveal required pattern alterations and a possible adjustment in yardage requirements; directions on page 56 will allow the consumer to estimate accurately changes in the amount of yardage required. (2) The sweep of the garment (the circumference at the hemline) is stated on the envelope of each pattern. By measuring and recording the sweep of favorite costumes in her wardrobe (a flared skirt,

a boxy coat, legs of slacks, etc.), the consumer can better judge the effect of the various pattern designs under consideration.

Chapter 4—Fabric Selection and Preparation for Cutting Suggestions are given for fabrics that will serve their intended needs in the wardrobe, and, in addition, fabrics are evaluated for the handling skill. Tentering* problems (page 63) must be recognized before purchase; this information is especially important because poor tentering cannot be corrected on the polyesters, on bonded fabrics, and on washable woolens. This information is the more significant because bonded woolens and washable woolens tempt the consumer with their low price tags.

Selection of linings and supporting fabrics (underlinings and interfacings) is included. To better understand the use and functions of supporting fabrics before selecting them, see "Directions for Underlining Skirts and Pants" on page 303 and "Construction Methods for Supporting Fabrics" on page 353.

See page 382 for button selection and page 313 for zipper selection.

Chapter 6—Fitting the Muslin Test Copy It is well to glance through this chapter simply to see that the major fitting will be done in inexpensive muslin and perfected before

---

* *Tentering* is a process by which fabric is fastened to a frame which holds it in tension at a desired width while it is dried. If the process is done well, the crosswide threads are controlled to run at right angles to the lengthwise threads.

the costume is cut in good fabric. Those who have not worked with more expensive fabrics need the assurance of pretested results as they make this major purchase of fabric.

Chapter 11 — Special Problems   This chapter includes directions for solving the special problems which will not be encountered in a typical tailoring experience; much of this chapter has to do with fabrics which are not wise choices for first tailoring projects. If the reader will use a fabric or a construction method which is unique, it is especially important that she study the information in the appropriate section of this chapter before making a purchase.

Survey the pattern and fabric market

Some women prefer to select the fabric and then choose a pattern that will be suitable, while others plan the costume around the pattern. There is no one right way unless it is to do both at once, which is, perhaps, the way we all do it whether we realize it or not. The best method is to survey both fabrics and patterns without making a final decision, to come to the final decision with both patterns and fabrics in mind (a good time for a coffee break), and finally to purchase the pattern and then the fabric.

Approach the fabric department with an open mind. It is a mistake to go to a certain display (the wool counter, for example) while bypassing others (such as brocades and the cotton suitings and the polyester knits). Survey all displays; inspiration (an interesting color combination, the magic addition of a subtle texture accent) may come from an unlikely source.

The survey of patterns should be equally broad. Even if the reader has always chosen patterns from a certain company with complete satisfaction, the pattern that proves to be the favorite of a lifetime may appear, this very season, in a pattern catalogue she has never examined.

Fabric   The cardinal rule when buying fabric is *read the information on the bolt.* This information will include fiber content, width, and usually other helpful statements (shrinkage, washing or cleaning directions, expected performance, etc.). The customer can depend on this information; by contrast, statements from the clerk are less reliable. Bolts of fabric sold in department stores carry helpful information; some bolts sold in certain speciality shops carry nothing more than price, in which case the clerk must supply additional facts. Although clerks in these shops are usually honest, the novice who is not able to recognize questionable statements would be wise to confine her shopping to the department store which stands behind the printed information on the bolt. Questioning the clerk about shrinkage, fiber content, or fabric width is truly dangerous; she works with hundreds of fabrics and cannot be expected to remember technical data on each one.

Consider the important matter of fiber content   It is impossible to make a wise purchase of fabric without fundamental knowledge of the textile fibers and fabrics, their natural properties and characteristics, the performance one can expect from them, and the care they will require. For example, the consumer must understand that wool fibers blended with other fibers (rayon, nylon, etc.) will not perform the same as 100 percent wool fabric and that the acrylics or nylon, even when given the appearance and hand of wool, will retain their own inherent qualities. She must know what to expect of the bonded fabrics, washable wools, and low-quality wools, all of which carry temptingly low price tags. It is not possible to cover this material in depth in a tailoring book. The most basic and pertinent issues are discussed in Chapter 4 (Fabric Selection) but the reader must understand that she needs a more comprehensive background in textiles. College students will have had a course in textiles before enrolling in a tailoring course, and the reader who is working on her own will need to study a textile text before undertaking the major purchase of fabric for a tailored costume.

Measure the fabric to determine its exact width The width of the fabric is stated on the bolt; it may be stated in exact measurements (54 inches), or it may be stated in a way which will indicate that there may be some variation (52–54 inches). The latter is more helpful in that it serves to point out that all fabric widths may vary as much as 2 inches from the amount stated, a fact which many customers do not realize. It is well to carry a tape measure to check fabric widths; alternatively, the sales staff will perform this service on request. If fabric labeled "54 inches wide" is only 52 inches wide, the customer will be forewarned and can study the particular layout she will use to determine if she needs to buy additional yardage to compensate for the narrower width. In some cases she will need to purchase the pattern and make a special layout for the narrower width before purchasing the fabric. See "Figuring Special Yardage Requirements" on page 53.

Devise some means of visualizing the effect on the fabric under wearing conditions The bolt can be carried to a full-length mirror and held up to the figure to test the effect under near-normal circumstances of wear. A closeup mirror test is helpful for studying the effect of color only, but the

total effect of fabrics with a prominent design (plaids, fake furs, etc.) must be tested from a distance. The sales staff expect the customer to experiment and will, if time permits, assist her by draping the fabric on the figure to simulate the lines of the pattern design under consideration.

The customer may carry the bolt of fabric from one section of the department to another while searching for contrasting colors and textures and selecting appropriate linings and supporting fabrics.

Patterns Carefully study the section titled "Pattern Section—Figure Type, Size, Design" on pages 43 to 53 before making a final decision; technical and factual information is included in that section.

The appearance of the model in the fashion sketch may distract the customer, adding to the difficulty of visualizing herself in the design. This is especially true of the mature woman who must always work with a fashion sketch which pictures a much younger model (even in the women's and half-size collections). While the young models pictured in all fashion sketches of Simplicity, McCall's, and Butterick catalogues confuse the mature woman, the more sophisticated Vogue models may distract the very young. A simple aid to better visualization, recommended for all readers, is to cover up the faces of the models; this makes it easier to judge the design more accurately on its own merits.

Compare the finished length of favorites in the current wardrobe with the finished length stated in the yardage chart of the pattern. If the design is to be shortened several inches, cover a comparable portion of the sketch; if the pattern is to be lengthened, cover the fashion sketch with onionskin paper and extend the design lines accordingly. Proportions of the design are always influenced (and may be destroyed) by altering lengths several inches; for example, a jacket may have to be lengthened if the skirt will be lengthened several inches.

Compare the "sweep" (or circumference) of a comparable design in the wardrobe with the sweep of the pattern under consideration to better judge the effect of the design; this measurement is stated in the yardage chart.

Before making the final decision, make copies of several designs under consideration by quickly tracing the major design lines on onionskin paper; record the pattern name and number, the catalogue page number, and the yardage amounts required. In this way one can take time out to make the final decision at leisure or to present several tentative choices for the approval of an instructor.

General suggestions Before making the final decision, take time out for a coffee break. This is the time to find a quiet spot for more careful and detailed planning. Various ideas must be evaluated, color and texture combinations decided upon, etc. It is well to figure yardage costs, because it is possible that a more expensive fabric in a wider width will be less costly than a less expensive fabric in a narrower width. During this decisive period, keep this question in mind: "Is this the kind of costume I would purchase ready-made?"

Use the ready-to-wear departments to advantage Those with little confidence and imagination would do well to try on comparable designs in the ready-to-wear de-

partments. This is particularly helpful if the design lines are very different from those of costumes in the existing wardrobe or if the silhouette represents a radical departure from fashions of past seasons.

Test out ideas by making additional tracings of the fashion sketches. Using onionskin paper, trace the basic outline and design lines of the fashion sketch to test the effect of colors and color combinations by making additional tracings and coloring them as desired; a box of pencils in a variety of colors is a good investment. There is no need to work for perfection; quick shading will suffice, and the effect of plaid or stripes, etc., can be simulated very quickly with simple sketchy lines. Make additional tracings of each design to compare and evaluate all ideas under consideration.

Additional tracings will allow one to study the effect of certain details that might be added for a more personalized costume. Additional pockets and trimming details of all kinds can be sketched on a tracing for evaluation. This is an excellent way to determine the effect of cutting some sections on the bias in checked or plaid fabrics, for example.

Be imaginative with textures By studying the ready-to-wear market one can see that a shocking combination of textures can result in a stunning costume. The designers of high-fashion merchandise know the rules of appropriate texture combination, but occasionally they break the rules with exciting results. One of the most newsworthy costumes designed by the great American designer Claire McCardell was a cocktail or theater suit made of white duck (the same duck used for sturdy sportswear) lined in satin and accented with a collar and oversized lapels of black velvet. The rule book would not recommend duck combined with velvet, but happily Miss McCardell knew how and when to break the rules. Of course, the reader will want traditionally compatible combinations for most costumes she will make, but she should be courageous enough to break the rules once in a while.

The time to buy After experimenting with ideas and coming to a studied decision, it is time to return to the fabric and pattern departments to make the final purchase. The time spent on careful planning will give greater confidence as the purchase is made and greater satisfaction as the costume is worn.

Chapter 3

PATTERN SELECTION AND FIGURING SPECIAL REQUIREMENTS

The commercial pattern market is dominated by four well-established and reliable houses: Simplicity, McCall's, Butterick, and Vogue. Although Vogue, originally a separate company, is now owned by Butterick, fortunately the Butterick management has maintained the distinct identity of the two pattern houses so effectively that the consumer is unaware of their common ownership. The great popularity these companies enjoy has been earned by their fine reputation for reliability over many years. There are several minor companies (some quite good, some questionable) that have not enjoyed the time-tested popularity of these four. Every one of the major companies makes a reliable and accurate pattern and all deserve the confidence of the customer; every one is proud of its national and international reputation and will guard its good name with continued vigilance.

SIZING STANDARDS OF THE PATTERN FASHION INDUSTRY

Consistency and reliability of pattern size is the one single factor of greatest concern to the woman who sews. The pattern companies are devoted to serving customers well and have banded together to develop sizing standards for the entire industry. The major pattern houses (and most of the minor ones) follow body measurement charts established by the Measurement Standard Committee of the Pattern Fashion Industry. This means that patterns from all major companies are consistently sized (based on the same figure with the same measurements) within the company itself and among sister companies.

IMPORTANT NOTE FOR THOSE WHO HAVE HOME-SEWING EXPERIENCE BUT WHO HAVE NOT SEWN SINCE JANUARY 1968: Before January 1968, patterns were sized according to body measurements established by the Bureau of Standards; these standards were confusing because a person usually required a larger pattern size than she purchased in ready-to-wear. In an attempt to make pattern sizes correspond more closely with ready-to-wear, the Measurement Standard Committee of the Pattern Fashion Industry set up new standards which became effective in January 1968. In general, each pattern is simply labeled one size smaller (the old size 14 is now labeled size 12, for example), with the result that pattern sizes conform more closely to ready-to-wear sizes. In general, the customer will probably require a pattern one size smaller than the size she wore before 1968. Each customer must compare her measurements with the current body measurement chart.

Each pattern company has a dress form in one size of each figure grouping (size

10 or 12 is used for the misses' figure), and that dress form is made to specifications of the measurement standards of the Pattern Fashion Industry. Each company makes a basic pattern to fit the standard dummy, and because the companies that conform to the standard are working on dress forms of identical sizes, the resulting basic patterns are remarkably alike. Since the basic pattern is the foundation for all the designs in the collection, all patterns of all major companies are consistent in size. The woman who sews may be assured that when her pattern size and figure type are established, all designs from companies using the measurement standards of the Pattern Fashion Industry will give comparable results. Furthermore, she may be sure that the pattern alteration required on one pattern will be correct for patterns from other companies that conform to the established standards.

A common and dangerous misconception concerning sizing of commercial patterns   There are several reasons why many consumers mistrust pattern sizing — none of which can be rightly blamed on the pattern company.

1 The pattern is made for an average figure, and yet many people do not realize their figures are not average and some few do not wish to recognize their figure irregularities. These people will not alter the pattern to accommodate their individual problems. Actually, very few individuals are so perfectly proportioned that they need not make any pattern alterations.

2 Many who have lost or gained several pounds continue to buy patterns in the size they first used, perhaps 20 pounds ago; they do not realize that if weight is distributed fairly evenly on the figure, a change of 10 pounds will usually make a difference of one size. But these women insist, instead, that patterns are not sized the way they were

a year ago, and their criticisms are passed along to many others, several of whom will listen sympathetically and be convinced.

3 Many home sewers cut and sew inaccurately and then blame pattern sizing for the misfit.

4 Few figures are so perfect that they need no fitting adjustments, and yet many women who sew do no fitting at all. This is understandable, because fitting is one of the most difficult processes of clothing construction and, for this reason, it is often avoided entirely or mastered long after the home sewer has become expert in cutting and sewing. But fitting is related to sizing, and unfortunately pattern sizing is often blamed when fitting corrections have been neglected.

DIFFERENCES IN OUTLINE, SHAPE, AND CHARACTER OF PATTERN PIECES

For reasons stated above, all too many experienced readers are convinced that patterns are not reliably sized and that sizes differ within each company and even more among the various companies. These opinions, while incorrect, are founded on what appears to be fact, and for this reason *it is important that every reader understand that apparent contradictions do not alter the fact that patterns from all the major companies are consistently sized for the same body measurements.*

The outline of the pattern piece itself (if it is to be made at home or in a factory) is determined by three components which make up the total size or outline of each pattern piece and therefore the total overall size of the finished garment. These components are (1) body size or the measurement of the figure itself, (2) livability or fitting ease (room to move and "live" in), and (3) style fullness (fashion fullness or styling ease). The fact that body size is the only one of these three that is (and can be) controlled by measurement standards leads to the unfortunate misconception that patterns are not consistently and reliably sized.

Every company works on a dummy (representing the average figure) made to the standard body measurements of the Pattern Fashion Industry. Four different designers in the four major houses drape a basic garment on the dummy, allowing no style fullness but allowing extra size for livability or fitting ease. The amount of extra size the designer allows for livability varies at different levels on the figure because it is determined by the needs of that portion of the figure and the movement required of it. For example, there must be extra size in the bust and shoulder area to allow for arm movements, and there must be sufficient livability in the hip area to allow for figure expansion as the wearer sits; these two needs require different amounts of livability at the two levels. The designers of the four major pattern houses are trained professionals, sensitive to the need for livability and to its effect on the appearance of the costume and although they make four individual judgments, their decisions are remarkably consistent. For example, the amount of livability required for figure expansion in the hip area of a skirt is approximately 2 inches; one designer may allow 1¾ inches and another 2½ inches, while the remaining two designers allow the standard 2 inches. These

slight variations are responsible for the subtle differences between patterns from the four companies, but *it is important to understand that the size of the figure for which the pattern is made is based on the same standard body measurements; and so, in the final judgment, the patterns of the four companies are sized consistently with each other. And because that basic pattern is a foundation from which all patterns are made, all patterns made by any company which conforms to the standard body measurements of the Pattern Fashion Industry are sized consistently.*

The only accurate method of determining the slight differences in allowances for livability or fitting ease is to purchase basic regulation dress patterns in one size from all four companies and to superimpose them with center lines matching. There will be very slight differences in the slant of the shoulderline, the position of underarm seams, and in width or circumference, etc., but this test will prove that striking differences do not exist.

There are three reasons why amounts for livability or fitting ease must remain flexible and must not be standardized, and all have to do with the fact that designs will be more beautiful and functional if the designer has freedom to express and interpret each design and each type of garment as a separate entity. One reason has to do with the philosophy of the company. The companies which strive for mass sales must please the widely divergent tastes of the mass market and compromise those tastes somewhat by allowing the amount of livability the elusive "average" woman will prefer. Remembering that their average customers are, in general, more practical and less dominated by the need or desire to be fashion leaders, one could assume they might favor a bit more comfort (slightly more livability or fitting ease) than the typical Vogue customer, who may be willing to trade some comfort for a slimmer silhouette. This is not to say that it will be easy to detect the differences; they are slight and subtle.

A second reason for flexible, nonstandardized livability amounts has to do with the size and figure type of the wearer. Contrast the junior figure, with its characteristic slim, firm lines, with the half-size figure. Those with junior figures like to reveal them with more snug-fitting garments (less livability) and do not need as much extra size for movement and expansion of the figure. Those with half-size figures like to camouflage them with a looser fit (more livability), and their more generous proportions require more extra size for body movements and expansion. Those with half-size figures tend to favor comfort as well, and that calls for still more livability.

Finally, fashion explains why livability amounts cannot and must not be standardized. The amount of fitting ease influences the appearance of the garment in a delicate but substantial way. Therefore fashion is involved, and fashion, by its very nature, must be free and unrestricted. For example, in 1958 the typical boxy jacket was very boxy indeed, with as much as 8 inches of livability at the hipline and correspondingly large amounts in the bust and shoulder area; then, years later, the typical boxy jacket was slim and trim, with a hint of shaping at the waist and just enough livability at the hip level to allow it to hang smoothly over the skirt. In other words, fashion reaches all the way down to the fundamentals of basic fit, and the buying public would not want it any other way.

Average allowances for livability or fitting ease

The allowance for livability is based on the need for body movement and expansion at various levels of the body, and those needs differ with the type and cut of the garment. A few examples will further illustrate why

livability amounts cannot be standardized. A garment with a set-in sleeve constricts arm movements more than a sleeveless garment, and so livability amounts for the two must differ. A typical jacket or coat must have more fitting ease than a dress, because the thickness of a lining (and probably underlining) is involved and because it will be worn over a blouse or dress; however, if the jacket design is to be worn without a blouse (a suit-dress or a two-piece dress), less livability or fitting ease will be required. The thickness of fabric further complicates the issue of fitting ease for three reasons: (1) thicker fabrics are more constricting, (2) extra allowances must be made to accommodate the bulk of hems and facings, and (3) suits and coats of heavy fabrics are planned for wear over wool dresses and bulky sweaters. Consequently, suit and coat designs presented in the summer collections and pictured in obviously lightweight fabrics (printed linens, cotton suitings) are not cut as amply (less livability) as those shown in heavy fabrics in the winter collections.

The pattern companies which offer comprehensive collections of designs in all sizes and figure types for all ages and both sexes use dozens of basic patterns. Each one is based on the standard body measurements for that figure type, but each one includes the livability amounts adequate for a particular type of garment.

The chart (showing average livability amounts at the bust level) on page 41 illustrates that the overall all-around size of the pattern pieces for various types of garments varies greatly, therefore creating a demand for many basic patterns. The amounts of livability (body movement plus the effect desired) are stated for the bust level only because patterns are purchased by bust measurement and because these amounts vary more than those at any other level. The pattern pieces of several basic patterns, shown in Figure 3-1, further illustrate these differences in amounts of livability or fitting ease. *It is important to remember that the patterns are, in reality, all sized consistently in that they are planned for the same standard body measurements;* their differences simply allow for the special needs of each type of garment.

Careful examination of the chart will reveal why many experienced persons are convinced that patterns are not reliably sized. The total overall width or circumference of the finished garment at the bust level does indeed vary greatly—from 35 inches for the strapless dress to 43 inches for the coat. And yet all are consistently sized for the size 12 (bust 34) figure. *Important conclusion: If the customer always buys every pattern in her proper body size, she will benefit from the designer's experience and knowledge because every pattern will have the proper allowance for livability or fitting ease required for that type of garment and for the effect the designer intended to create.*

The person who refuses to believe that patterns are reliably sized will not buy a pattern in the proper size and will, therefore, encounter sizing difficulties. For example, consider the person who insists that patterns are too large and who therefore buys a size smaller than her bust measurement. This means that she must borrow 2 inches

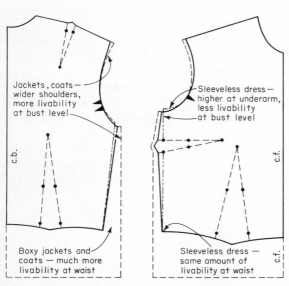

FIGURE 3-1 Livability amounts of two types of garments compared with the regulation dress with a sleeve.

AVERAGE ALLOWANCES AT THE BUST FOR LIVABILITY OR FITTING EASE

Type of basic pattern	Standard bust measurement, inches	Average livability allowance, inches	Total overall width of the pattern pieces, inches
Coat	34 (size 12)	8 to 10	34 + 9 = 43
Suit	34	5 to 8	34 + 6 = 40
Blouse	34	5 to 8	34 + 6 = 40
Dresses Regulation dress with set-in sleeves and waistline seam	34	3 to 5	34 + 4 = 38
Sleeveless dress	34	2 to 3	34 + 2 = 36
Strapless dress	34	1	34 + 1 = 35

from the allowance for livability and use it to make up 2 extra inches for her body size. She may get by with it on garments with large amounts of livability; for example, she may not detect a great difference in a coat. However, with 2 inches less livability in a suit (which should have about 6 inches) the suit will fit about like a regulation dress (4 inches) and the difference will be obvious.

Those who have been buying a size smaller than their figures require have been borrowing livability or fitting ease, in which case the garment has not fitted properly as judged by professional standards. By buying the proper size, the customer will profit from the designer's expert knowledge, talent, and experience.

Allowances for livability or fitting ease in the hip area These do not vary as greatly as those in the bust and upper torso. A fitted skirt must have enough livability to allow for leg movement and for body expansion as the wearer sits, and those demands are identical if the skirt is a separate unit or if it is a part of a dress, a suit, a suit dress, etc. The average amount of livability at the hipline is 2 inches, but the designer may add slightly more (2½ or 3 inches) if the skirt is planned for obviously functional wear, and she may add only 1½ inches if the skirt is a part of a highly styled cocktail suit that need not be as practical. The livability allowances in pants are somewhat greater (they average about 3 inches at the hipline) because these garments are more binding as the wearer sits.

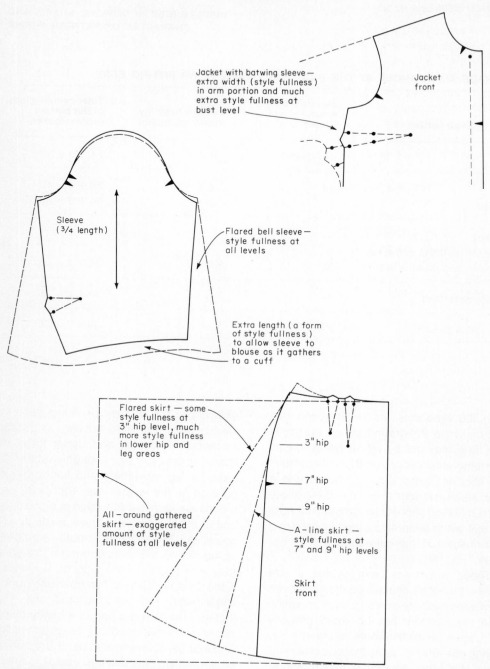

Jacket with batwing sleeve—
extra width (style fullness)
in arm portion and much
extra style fullness at
bust level

Jacket
front

Sleeve
(³/₄ length)

Flared bell sleeve—
style fullness at
all levels

Extra length (a form
of style fullness)
to allow sleeve to
blouse as it gathers
to a cuff

Flared skirt—some
style fullness at
3" hip level, much
more style fullness
in lower hip and
leg areas

3" hip

7" hip

9" hip

All—around gathered
skirt—exaggerated
amount of style
fullness at all levels

A—line skirt—
style fullness at
7" and 9" hip levels

Skirt
front

FIGURE 3-2 *Patterns with extra width, extra length, or both for style fullness (compared with basic fitted patterns).*

Allowances for style fullness
(fashion fullness or styling ease)

With the exception of garments made of stretch fabrics, the size of all garments includes the standard measurements for body size and a variable allowance for livability or fitting ease. In addition to these two basic components, some designs have an additional allowance for style fullness; gathered or circular skirts are examples of designs which require extreme amounts of style fullness to creat the effect desired.

Figure 3-2 shows several basic patterns (in solid lines) compared with patterns containing style fullness (in broken lines). It illustrates that the addition of style fullness greatly influences the outline, shape, and character of the pattern piece, resulting in a pattern that is larger (wider and sometimes longer) than the basic pattern. The extra allowance for style fullness may be great and can provide large amounts of extra width which the wearer can *(should not but can)* borrow to accommodate body measurements larger than those for which the pattern was made. Many persons who are convinced that patterns are not reliably sized have been purchasing patterns that are too small in designs with style fullness. They have thus been borrowing some of this fullness (perhaps several inches) for body size. Later, when they buy that same size in a fitted garment, they discover that it is too small. They conclude that patterns are not reliably sized, when in fact they have simply chosen a pattern without the style fullness they formerly counted on for extra body size.

Important conclusion: Buying a pattern ;n the proper size will ensure that all patterns of every type (from a strapless dress to a jacket or coat) will fit the figure properly, will provide an adequate amount of livability for body movements and for the effect that garment must produce, and, in

addition, will provide the proper amount of style fullness to create the desired fashion effect. The customer who has confidence in reliable sizing standards will buy a pattern of the proper size for her figure, thus gaining the extra advantage of having the important matters of livability and style fullness decided by a trained, talented, and experienced designer.

PATTERN SELECTION—FIGURE TYPE, SIZE, AND DESIGN

Standard body-measurement charts for all figure types of women (teen-age to maturity) appear on page 50 and 51. The charts for men and boys are on page 53. Children's sizes are included in the comprehensive collection in all counter catalogues.

Figure types

Patterns are made for several different figure types, and these types are comparable to those used for ready-to-wear. Therefore the woman who sews will probably wear the same size in the same figure type she has found most satisfactory in ready-to-wear. If she is not one of the lucky few who are perfectly proportioned for their size and figure type (a "straight size"), she will find the same general fitting imperfections in patterns that she is accustomed to correcting in ready-to-wear. While she can have ready-to-wear altered to take care of her particular figure irregularities (to a certain limited extent), she will be able to effect more comprehensive and more satisfactory solutions by altering patterns before cutting.

A brief description of each figure type is included with the measurement charts on pages 50 and 51. Read each description thoughtfully to determine which one (taken as a whole) best describes the figure; avoid being unduly swayed by any one portion of the description ("I'm short-waisted, so I must be a junior or a half-size"). The great majority of readers will have misses' and women's figures. A further aid in making a wise choice is to anticipate that the figure type required in a pattern is the same as the type that is most satisfactory on the ready-to-wear market.

Patterns in the proper figure type for the individual offer many advantages. The greatest advantage is that pattern alterations and fitting (both difficult steps in the construction sequence) can be minimized. Yardage amounts for the shorter figure types are more economical. The advantage of having a collection of designs planned especially for a particular type of figure means that the fashion details and the proportions of the design will be more flattering than those of an altered pattern; readers who have figures typical of any one of the figure types would be foolish to deprive themselves of these obvious advantages. However, if the figure can be as well (or almost as well) accommodated in an altered misses' size as in one of the other figure types, it may be wise to consider that solution to gain the advantage of the greater number and variety of designs offered in misses' and women's sizes.

The most accurate test to determine the proper size and figure type It is assumed the tailoring student is confident of her proper size and figure type from past experiences. If she is not, the following method

of testing is recommended. Study the body measurements charts, decide on the proper size and figure type and buy a basic pattern for a dart-fitted dress with set-in sleeves and a waistline seam. All the pattern companies offer dresses of this type. It is important to use the regulation dress described above because it involves size for body measurements and comparatively small amounts of livability or fitting ease; a small amount of livability keeps the wearer from "borrowing" to compensate for extra body size. After a careful judgment of size and figure type has been made, the pattern should be altered to correct the obvious figure irregularities indicated (bodice lengthened or shortened, extra size added at the hip level, etc.) and then cut from a firm-grade muslin. After the muslin is marked and basted, it should be tested on the figure for a careful analysis. There will be some fitting to do (unless the figure is perfectly proportioned), and many of these fitting corrections can be incorporated with pattern alterations for future sewing projects. Very subtle, refined fitting corrections are better left to fitting (rather than pattern alteration) in the future. If the muslin-test garment fits very poorly, reexamine the charts of figure types and sizes, and then make an amended judgment and another muslin test.

The fact that pattern size is standardized means that when the proper size and figure type are decided, tested, and reassessed (if necessary), all patterns in that size and figure type from all major pattern houses will fit the figure in essentially the same way.

Pattern size

Patterns should be purchased by bust size because pattern alterations are more difficult in this area than in the waist and hip areas. Four facts fortify this statement: (1) The pattern outlines are more complicated and intricate in the bust and shoulder area because it is composed of slanting lines (shoulder) and curving lines (neck edge, armhole edge of sleeve). (2) Many of the major design details are located in the upper torso area (closer to the face, visible when sitting, etc.). (3) The most prominent curves of the figure are located in this area, and creating proper shape for curves is one of the most difficult problems of pattern alteration and fitting. (4) Each alteration is further complicated by corresponding corrections which must be made on several other units of the pattern (if the size of the neck edge is changed, the collar must be altered accordingly, etc.). By contrast, alterations in the skirt are much simpler; the skirt pieces are usually more nearly rectangular in shape, design details are usually less numerous and intricate, the hipline curves of the average figure are not as pronounced as the bust curves, and in most cases, there are fewer corresponding pieces to be altered.

Careful consideration of these valid reasons for choosing the pattern by bust size will allow the reader to make exceptions to the rule under rare *(very rare)* circumstances. The woman with hips 6 inches larger (three sizes) than the size she should wear for her bust can never buy a suit pattern to fit her hips, for the upper torso portion of the pattern cannot be altered so extensively. On the other hand, the woman with large hips should buy a separate skirt or pants pattern to fit her hips and plan to do alterations at the waist.

Take basic body measurements

Bust, waist, and hip measurements are listed in the standard body measurement charts, and these three measurements should be taken before deciding on the size and figure type, remembering always that the bust measurement is most significant. Wear the undergarments that will be worn with the particular garment while tak-

ing measurements. If a padded bra will be worn, wear the bra while taking measurements; the extra padding must be considered a part of the body measurement.

Take measurements before a mirror, viewing the figure from the side to be sure that the tape is held in a horizontal position. Take bust and hip measurements at the level of the most prominent curves; it is well to take hip measurements at several levels to be sure that the largest measurement is recorded. Take measurements with the tape snug (but not pulled tight) around body curves; avoid the natural tendency to pull the tape too snugly around the waist; think of it as a belt or waistband that must be comfortable during several hours of wear. Record the measurements preparatory to studying the body measurement charts of the various figure types.

It is helpful to record "finished length" measurements before selecting a pattern. These measurements are listed in the yardage charts of each design. Comparisons will reveal the pattern alterations that will be needed and the resulting need for extra yardage or possible saving in yardage. Finished lengths for full-length garments are taken from the base of the neck in the back to the hemline; finished lengths for skirts, pants, etc., are taken from the waist to the hemline at the center back.

The sweep or circumference of the garment at the hemline is listed in the measurement chart on each particular pattern. If the reader measures and records the circumferences of several favorite costumes in her present wardrobe, they will provide a foundation for comparisons and will better enable her to judge the effect of the design under consideration.

A critical reevaluation of bust size

This must be made before deciding on the pattern size. The following explanation is of paramount importance and must be studied carefully and thoughtfully before proceeding. The general rule that the pattern should be purchased in the bust size is founded on four facts listed under "Pattern Size" on page 44, and all four are involved with complications of pattern alterations and fitting in the upper torso area. The general rule works well for those who have well-proportioned, average, or close to average figures. However, those with figures which vary greatly from the average need to reevaluate their bust measurements and, in view of their individual problems, consider revising the general rule.

The pertinent fact is that the bust and shoulder area (considered as one) is difficult to alter and fit; therefore the patterns should be purchased to best fit that area of the figure, leaving problems in other portions of the figure to be solved by pattern alterations or fitting. The average, well-proportioned figure has a bust measurement that "keeps pace" with bone structure—in other words, that "keeps pace" with the width of the shoulders and the width of the back. But there are many who have a very delicate bone structure (a small frame) with relatively narrow shoulders but who have a large bust measurement that is not a true indication of body size but is simply a result of a larger-than-average cup size or rib cage. *If the bust size and the bone structure are not compatible or do not "keep pace" with each other, the figure is not average and sizing problems must be anticipated.* The opposite problem may exist; an individual may have a large bone structure (wide shoulders and broad back) and a comparatively small bust measurement that is a result of a small cup size or rib cage. These irregular figures demand reevaluation before the pattern size is decided.

Contrary to popular opinion, the average cup size is relatively small. It is difficult to state the average cup size in definite terms because the issue is not one of cup size alone but rather involves the total curve in the chest area, and the total shape in that area is influenced to a very great extent by posture and the development of the rib cage and chest cavity. The somewhat ambiguous description below will provide an adequate basis for judging individual figures. The following figures have the type of average chest curve for which ready-to-wear and commercial patterns are made:

Figures with normal posture—B cup

Figures with very erect posture—A cup

Figures with erect posture and well-developed chest and rib cage—AA cup

Figures with sagging posture—C cup

Few persons with smaller-than-average bust curves need to reevaluate bust size in relation to bone structure because they usually wear padded bras to fabricate an average figure. Persons with large cup sizes (above C if they have average erect posture and certainly those with D and E cups) have bust curves that may not "keep pace" with their bone structure and they must reevaluate their bust measurements before determining the proper pattern size. These figures will be fitted better by a pattern that is the right size for their basic bone structure (width of shoulders and back); the pattern must then be altered to add extra width and shape in the front of the garment (only) for the larger-than-average bust curve. It is quite impossible to measure these figures to determine exactly which size will be best, and the only solution is to make a careful judgment of size and then purchase a basic pattern to make tests. The test pattern should be altered to accommodate the bust that is larger than average (directions on pages 175 to 186) and tested in muslin. Muslin testing will allow the person with an irregular figure to determine if the size is correct for the width of her shoulders and back and if the alteration for the bust curve is adequate. Possibly she will need to test another pattern size and other bust alterations, and if indicated, follow-up tests must be made. *These tests are very time-consuming, but they are absolutely essential because the larger-than-average bust, considered such an asset, is probably the most difficult figure problem any reader will encounter.*

In general, the person with a C or larger cup size should buy the test pattern in one size smaller than her bust measurement indicates. Muslin testing is absolutely essential when it is impossible to make precise, accurate judgments of size. The following guidelines are included to aid in selecting the size for a test pattern, but it must be understood that they are guidelines (for test patterns only) and are not foolproof scientific statements. In general buy the test pattern

One size smaller than the bust measurement for C-cup figures with erect postures and D-cup figures with sagging postures

Two sizes smaller than the bust measurement for D-cup figures with erect postures

Reevaluate all circumstances which may influence size It has been established that pattern sizing is standardized to fit the average figures established by the Pattern Fashion Industry and that differences in the overall shape and outline of pattern pieces reflect the varying allowances for livability and style fullness necessary to create a particular effect. It follows that once the proper size (and figure type)

has been established, a person will require the same size pattern in every type of costume; this, then, is her "true" size. However, it must be understood that a pattern is planned for certain "average" circumstances, and if the home sewer creates unusual circumstances, she may need to purchase the pattern *for that one particular design* in a different size than her tested and established "true" size.

NOTE: Knit fabrics are enhanced by a trim fit which forces them to stretch slightly over body curves. For this reason many patterns are planned especially for use with the popular knits; these patterns are made with somewhat less livability or fitting ease and with somewhat narrower darts that will create less shape. The consumer must be aware that these patterns cannot be used effectively with woven fabrics which will not stretch to accommodate body curves. Look for a note which will appear near the fashion sketch in the counter catalogue and on the pattern envelope. The note may read "suitable for knits," in which case the pattern can be used for either knits or wovens. Another note reading "For knits only" reveals that the pattern must not be used with woven fabrics.

Type of fabric to be used The fashion sketch pictures the pattern design in a fabric of appropriate weight; the go-with pieces and accessories pictured are a further indication of the "average" circumstances for which the pattern was planned. For example, coats and suits presented in the winter collections are pictured in winter-weight fabrics; sweaters, fur hats, and similar fashion accents pictured in the fashion sketch help to indicate that the costume is cut with enough livability to accommodate heavier facings and linings and the bulk of sweaters, blouses, and dresses which are worn in cold weather. By contrast, suits and coats of the summer collections are shown in lighter-weight suitings and pictured with brief, usually sleeveless blouses and dresses; these summer costumes are cut less amply (with less livability) than their winter counterparts. It is not wise to choose a winter design and plan to make it in a lightweight fabric suitable for summer (or vice versa), but if the home sewer decides to do so—to create unusual circumstances—she will probably need a different size pattern *for this one costume.* If she chooses a winter design to make in lighter-weight fabric, she should probably buy the pattern in a size smaller. On the other hand, if she chooses a summer design for winter-weight fabric, she may require a larger size.

If the home sewer creates sizing problems with unusual fabric choices, she must be alerted to additional sizing problems. For example, the difference in livability allowances for summer and winter designs is greatest in jackets and coats and not significantly different in skirts and pants; it is the jacket or coat which must accommodate the facings, linings, and go-with pieces which vary so much in bulk in the two extreme seasons. Therefore, if a suit pattern is purchased one size larger (in a summer design to be made of heavy fabric), the skirt will very probably be somewhat too large, and similarly, if a suit pattern is purchased one size smaller (in a winter design to be made of lightweight fabric), the skirt will very probably be somewhat too small.

Certainly, it is not wise to create unusual circumstances of this sort, especially for first tailoring projects. However, there are times when a more experienced worker will want to experiment and devise unique effects, and to do so she must carefully consider all factors before making a cautious judgment of pattern size. The following additional examples illustrate that the choice of fabric necessarily influences the size of the pattern required.

If a coat pictured in winter weight will be lined with a heavy quilted fabric or fake fur for greater warmth, and if the pattern does not recommend these heavy linings, the pattern should probably be purchased in a size larger than the "true" size required by the individual.

If a coat or jacket pattern, which includes facings and the traditional lining, will be used as a foundation for making a reversible garment, the heavier facing fabric (which will replace the facings and the lightweight lining) will create additional bulk and probably the pattern should be purchased in a larger size.

If a suit, pictured with a turtleneck sweater and obviously planned for street wear, will be worn without a blouse (rather like a two-piece dress), probably the pattern should be purchased in a smaller size than the "true" size the figure requires.

The author hopes the reader has noticed that the foregoing comments are somewhat ambiguous and that many statements are qualified with the word "probably." The evasive nature of the discussion should serve to alert the reader to the problems she may encounter. The experienced person who chooses a fabric markedly different from that for which the pattern was planned must expect sizing difficulties and proceed with caution. Furthermore, she must understand that she has created these difficulties *and that they cannot be blamed on the commercial pattern, which is properly sized for its intended use.*

The type of costume There are five different types of costumes in the counter catalogues which will, at first glance, appear to be suits and coats; and yet only two are true suits and coats, suitable for typical tailored garments to be worn over blouses, dresses, etc. The five are: two-piece dress, suit-dress, suit, coat-dress, and coat. The very great differences among these costumes have to do with the matter of sizing — specifically, with the livability allowances for body movement and the effect expected on the costume. Refer to the chart of average allowances at the bust level on page 41 to see that the livability allowances for a suit and dress are quite different and that the difference is still greater between a dress and a coat.

The term to describe the costume and a brief description of the costume appear close to the pattern number and the fashion sketch in the counter catalogue and also on the back of the envelope. The customer must take care to read these written descriptions because they reveal not only the type of costume but also other details that may not be visible in the fashion sketch.

Suit or coat patterns include the proper allowances for livability to accommodate the type of fabric for which they are best suited and an additional allowance to accommodate the go-with pieces with which they will be worn. Other types of costumes, which may look very much like suits and coats, do not have adequate livability allowances for blouses, sweaters, wool dresses, etc., and are not suitable for traditional suits and coats.

The two-piece dress is sized very much like a dress, with slightly more livability to give it something of the character of a suit; it is planned to look more like a dress than a suit. A pattern labeled "two-piece dress," purchased in the size the customer usually wears, will be much too small if cut of a heavy fabric and worn as a suit with

blouses. Similarly, the suit-dress is cut larger than a dress but smaller than a suit; it is planned to look more like a suit than a dress. However, it, too, is planned for dress-weight fabrics or relatively lightweight suitings and does not include an allowance for the bulk of blouses or sweaters. A pattern labeled "suit-dress," purchased in the size the customer usually wears, will be too small if cut of heavy fabric and worn as a suit over sweaters or blouses with sleeves.

The coat-dress, which is intended to be worn as a dress but to look like a coat, is cut considerably larger than a dress but much smaller than a conventional coat; it is planned to be cut of medium-weight fabrics similiar to typical suitings. This costume will not lead a double life as successfully as its name implies. It can possibly be worn over a sleeveless shift of a dress cut in limp, supple fabric, but if purchased in the size the customer usually wears, it will be much too small when cut of heavy fabric and worn as a winter coat.

Each of the five costumes mentioned is sized properly for its intended use. However, these costumes cannot be used interchangeably, and if the customer plans to use the costume as a suit or coat, she is wise to chose a design so labeled. If she does decide to adapt one of the other costumes to use as a suit or coat — thus creating unusual circumstances — she must understand that she will encounter sizing difficulties which *she had made for herself and which cannot be blamed on commercial pattern sizing.* It would be a grave mistake to attempt to adapt a two-piece dress pattern for use as a suit. If the home sewer choses a suit-dress for a suit or a coat-dress for a coat, she will need to buy the pattern

FIGURE TYPES—STANDARD BODY MEASUREMENT CHARTS

Junior sizes

Height—5'5"; bust higher than misses', well developed but not as curvaceous as the misses' figure; shorter-waisted than misses'; in general the figure is built on leaner, straighter lines than the misses' figure.

Standard body measurements

Size	5	7	9	11	13	15
Bust	30	31	32	33½	35	37
Waist	22½	23½	24½	25½	27	29
9" Hip	32	33	34	35½	37	39
Back waist length	15	15¼	15½	15¾	16	16¼

Junior petite sizes

Height—about 5'1"; full developed bust (like misses'); in general the figure is like the misses' figure but is smaller-boned, more diminutive, and shorter-waisted than junior and misses' figures.

Standard body measurements

Size	3JP	5JP	7JP	9JP	11JP	13JP
Bust	30½	31	32	33	34	35
Waist	22½	23	24	25	26	27
7" hip	31½	32	33	34	35	36
Back waist length	14	14¼	14½	14¾	15	15¼

Miss petite sizes

Height—5'2" to 4"; the figure is like the misses' in the bust and hips but is somewhat larger in the waist and about 1" shorter in back waist length than the misses' figure.

Standard body measurements

Size	6MP	8MP	10MP	12MP	14MP	16MP
Bust	30½	31½	32½	34	36	38
Waist	23½	24½	25½	27	28½	30½
Hip	32½	33½	34½	36	38	40
Back waist length	14½	14¾	15	15¼	15½	15¾

Misses' sizes

Height—about 5'6"; fully developed curves; the type of figure most mature girls and women have; longer-waisted than the junior figure.

Standard body measurements

Size	6	8	10	12	14	16	18	20
Bust	30½	31½	32½	34	36	38	40	42
Waist	23	24	25	26½	28	30	32	34
9" hip	32½	33½	34½	36	38	40	42	44
Back waist length	15½	15¾	16	16¼	16½	16¾	17	17¼

Women's sizes

Figure an extension of the misses' type cut in sizes for the larger, more mature figure; normal waist length.

Standard body measurements

Size	38	40	42	44	46	48	50
Bust	42	44	46	48	50	52	54
Waist	35	37	39	41½	44	46½	49
9" hip	44	46	48	50	52	54	56
Back waist length	17¼	17⅜	17½	17⅝	17¾	17⅞	18

Half-sizes

Height—about 5 feet 3 inches; fully developed figure with thicker waist, hips, and arms than misses'; narrower shoulders than misses'; shorter than misses' in every way—waist length, total length, arm length.

Standard body measurements

Size	10½	12½	14½	16½	18½	20½	22½	24½
Bust	33	35	37	39	41	43	45	47
Waist	27	29	31	33	35	37½	40	42½
7" hip	35	37	39	41	43	45½	48	50½
Back waist length	15	15¼	15½	15¾	15⅞	16	16⅛	16¼

at least one size larger than her tested and established "true" size. Obviously, the need for careful muslin testing is magnified under these circumstances.

The final decision Having decided which of the figure types best fits the figure, compare individual body measurements with those in the measurement chart. Do not expect measurements to correspond perfectly to the standard measurements. Keep in mind that patterns for most garments are purchased by the bust measurement, and do not be unduly concerned if other measurements do not correspond to those listed; measurements at other levels of the body will be corrected by pattern alterations. If the individual's bust measurement is 35 inches (halfway between size 12 and 14), she should make a careful judgment by considering two factors: general bone structure and the type of fit she prefers. If shoulders are somewhat wide or if she prefers an easier, looser fit, she should buy the larger size; if shoulders are narrow or if she prefers a snug fit, she should select the smaller size.

Use the special sections of the catalogue Because the large percentage of designs are in misses' and women's sizes, those who use patterns in other figure types can save time and avoid confusion and disappointment by turning to the special section of the catalogue where designs for special figure types are pictured. The section headings are very helpful for finding special types of costumes as well.

Study the fashion sketch Although the design is shown on a lengthened fashion figure, in every other way it is most carefully and accurately portrayed. Study the sketch carefully to become fully aware of details such as sections shown in contrast, whether the belt is made of self fabric or is purchased, length of sleeves, etc.

It is wise to select one view of the design as shown in the fashion sketch (in the catalogue and on the front of the envelope) and carry it through without variation. The experienced person often decides to use one feature of one view and another feature of another; but if she does so, she should understand the subsequent problems of yardage, cutting, and construction. If a pattern lends itself to use with plaid, it will be pictured in plaid in at least one view on the envelope front, and anyone who wishes to use plaid should buy only a pattern so pictured.

Examine the envelope and instruction sheet of every design under consideration The line drawing of the design on the back of the envelope reveals structural lines more clearly than the fashion sketch. The description in words, discussed in the preceding section, appears on the back of the envelope. A scale drawing of the pattern pieces will appear on the envelope or on the instruction sheet. The pattern pieces reveal difficulty of construction and estimated time requirements to the experienced person. The novice is helped somewhat simply by using the number and complexity of pattern pieces as a guide. The notions and findings required are listed on the back of the envelope.

Appropriate fabrics for the design are listed under "Suggested Fabrics" on the envelope. The person with developed taste will not need this help, but the person who is less competent in selecting compatible patterns and fabrics will find these suggestions invaluable. Special notes appear on the back of the envelope; such information as "napped fabrics not suitable" or "diagonal weaves not suitable" can make all the difference between success and failure.

One very important note appears on many patterns; it reads, "Extra fabric is required for matching plaids and balancing large designs." Each plaid or large design, by size or nature, requires a different amount of extra fabric for matching purposes. The pattern company cannot give a yardage amount that would be right for all purposes; therefore the chart states the amount of fabric required for cutting the pattern pieces, and the customer must figure the extra yardage required for her particular plaid or large design. Estimating yardage for matching plaid and for balancing large designs is covered on pages 474 to 478.

The words "with or without nap" appear in the yardage chart. As used here, the words "with nap" refer to all fabrics which have an up and down. These are fabrics with one-way designs and fabrics like corduroy, velvet, and napped woolens which show shading differences when worn unless all pattern pieces are cut in the same direction. In general, a layout involving a napped fabric requires more yardage. A more detailed discussion of napped and pile fabrics appears on page 495.

Carefully study the instruction sheet to see that the construction details involve some (and preferrably most) of the worth-while tailoring experiences outlined in "Design Choices" on page 20. In particular, study the construction of the collar and lapel area as detailed on the instruction sheet and compare it with the notched-collar construction on pages 407 to 413 of this text, this method of construction provides the most valuable learning experience.

FIGURING SPECIAL YARDAGE REQUIREMENTS

There are many circumstances under which a special cutting layout must be made and special yardage requirements figured for the individual costume: (1) when fabric will be chosen in a width not stated on the pattern, (2) when two patterns are combined to make one costume or when features of two different views of the same pattern are combined into one, (3) when sections of the pattern are to be made in contrast not planned for on the pattern, (4) when the pattern will be increased a substantial amount in width, (5) when pile or napped fabric is to be used with a pattern that does not include yardages for those fabrics, and (6) when estimating the extra amount of fabric required to match a specific plaid or prominent markings in fake furs.

It takes such a small amount of time and effort (before purchasing fabric) to make a special layout that will result in accurate and economical yardage requirements that it is a foolish economy to guess at yardage amounts for the special circumstances listed above. The economic advantage of the carefully executed special layout may result from a saving in the yardage (for the shortened pattern or for fabric in a width wider than the widths stated on the pattern) or from having enough (but not too much) extra fabric for the lengthened pattern, for pile or napped fabrics, or for matching plaid. It is always a careless and costly mistake to guess at yardage requirements for special problems, and the mistake becomes more serious as the price of fabric increases.

Those who believe that pieces can be shifted for more economical cutting should make a new layout before purchasing the fabric; savings are not possible under all circumstances and only a new layout will provide an accurate answer. The experienced person may be able to save ⅛ yard with intricate folding and cutting, but the saving must be worth the chance that she may make a mistake in her special layout (there is no mistake on the pattern), and must be worth her time and effort. A saving of ⅛ yard may be worth the time and effort to make a special layout if the fabric is $8 a yard and be a false economy if the fabric is $4 a yard.

To figure accurate yardage amounts by making a new layout

The layout can be made in the school laboratory or in the home by methods very similar to those used in the yardage department of the pattern company. There the layout artist works on very long tables, marked off with crosswise lines in ⅛ yard divisions and with lengthwise lines denoting all the various fabric widths. Pattern pieces are placed down in various positions to determine the most economical arrangement, after which the total measurement (yardage needed) is recorded. With a relatively short table in the home situation, one may have to do certain sections of the layout, record that amount of yardage, and then start another segment.

Steps of procedure See Figure 3-3.

1 Select a layout from the pattern in the proper size for a width of fabric comparable to the one that will be used (use a 54-inch layout for doing a special layout for 60-inch fabric). Changes will be made and pieces will be shifted to different positions, but there is value in checking work against a comparable layout done by a professional layout artist. Begin work with a similar type of layout and then experiment with more economical layout plans as work progresses.

2 Mark off the fabric width on a long table by taping a piece of string the proper distance from (and parallel to) a long edge of the table. Sketch *a* shows the string 30 inches from the edge (to indicate selvage edges) with the table edge indicating the fold of 60-inch fabric for a lengthwise-fold layout; and sketch *b* shows the string 36 inches from the edge (for one selvage), with the table edge indicating the other selvage edge of 36-inch fabric for a crosswise-fold or single-thickness layout.

3 Place pattern pieces in the marked-off area, beginning with an arrangement similar to the guide layout. Then experiment with other possible arrangements to find the most economical layout (professional layout artists spend hours experimenting on every layout shown on the instruction sheet). Take care to observe straight-of-material and place-on-fold lines. Be sure to allow space for cutting each piece the proper number of times; check work by studying the number of times each piece appears in a comparable layout. Move pieces as close together as possible.

4 Figure the amount of yardage required by measuring the required length on the table. Compare the two layouts in Figure 3-3 to see the difference in figuring amounts for lengthwise- and crosswise-fold layouts. The sketches show a four-piece skirt with seams at the centers and the sides. In

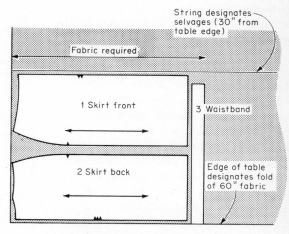

String designates selvages (30" from table edge)

Fabric required

1 Skirt front

3 Waistband

2 Skirt back

Edge of table designates fold of 60" fabric

a To figure yardage for fabric to be cut on a lengthwise fold

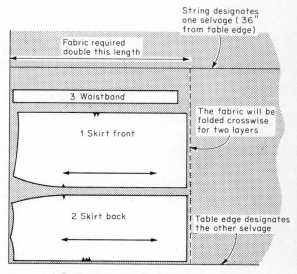

String designates one selvage (36" from table edge)

Fabric required double this length

3 Waistband

1 Skirt front

The fabric will be folded crosswise for two layers

2 Skirt back

Table edge designates the other selvage

b To figure yardage for fabric to be cut on a crosswise fold

FIGURE 3-3 *Figuring yardage amounts requires very careful attention to details.*

sketch *a* there are two layers of fabric be-cause the fabric is folded lengthwise; there-fore the yardage required is simply the length indicated by the arrows.

In sketch *b,* the space marked off is the full width of the fabric, indicating one thick-ness of fabric. If fabric will be folded on a crosswise fold (see the dashed line in sketch) to obtain the two layers necessary for a complete skirt, the layout will require twice the yardage indicated on the table. These sketches show the tremendous effect fabric width can sometimes (although not always) have on yardage amounts; this skirt requires almost twice as much 36-inch fabric as it requires in 60-inch fabric. There is some advantage (a matter of a few inches) in shifting the position of the waist-band in the 36-inch layout; waistbands can be cut on either the lengthwise or cross-wise direction if the design or nature of the fabric does not complicate the issue.

5 Measure the length on the table (dou-bling it if a crosswise fold is used), record the number of inches required, and make a rough sketch of the layout plan. Proceed making segments and recording the total number of inches each requires. When all pattern pieces have been accounted for, total the measurements of all segments and convert the inches to yards for the total amount of yardage required.

To figure yardage amounts by making estimates from a layout on the instruction sheet

Under some circumstances, yardage amounts can be accurately figured to meet individual needs of figure, fabric, or de-sign by studying the layout selected (prop-er size on proper fabric width) and revising the yardage requirements. This method of individualizing yardage amounts is ideal because it can be done very quickly in the department store. It is especially useful for figuring the amount of extra fabric for lengthening a pattern or the possible saving if the pattern will be shortened. The problem stated in Figure 3-4 shows the method of making estimates; in this particular layout, the estimates will be entirely accurate. How-ever, estimates made in this way are not al-ways as reliable. Some layouts are very complicated, with pieces dovetailed in such a way that reliable estimates are not pos-sible; with these intricate layouts, the only safe way to estimate yardage amounts is by making a new layout.

If the pattern will be altered considerably in length, select the layout to be used and then figure the amount of extra fabric re-quired or the amount that might be saved by working with that particular layout.

NOTE: If a pattern will be altered considerably in width (more than 2 inches in overall or all-around size), estimates cannot be accurately made from a layout. If a large width-wise al-teration will be made, the alteration must be made and a new special layout made before purchasing fabric. This is true even if there appears to be ample space for large alterations. The spaces between pattern pieces on the lay-outs have been somewhat exaggerated (more space pictured than actually exists), so pattern pieces can be more easily identified.

The sample problem in Figure 3-4 shows the method of determining the exact amount of additional yardage required for lengthened patterns. In the illustration, the pattern is lengthened as follows: skirt pieces, 2 inches; jacket pieces, 1 inch; and sleeve pieces, 3 inches. Study the sketch to see that because the upper sleeve and jacket back are laid in the same segment of the layout, it will be necessary to allow for the larger of the two alterations—the 3 inches for the sleeve. The same situation occurs in the area where the under sleeve and jacket side pieces are cut. Therefore, beginning at the left, this layout will require 2 inches, plus 3 inches, plus 1 inch, plus 3 inches for a total of 9 inches or ¼ yard. *When lengthening, allow for the larger of the alterations involved in each segment of the layout.*

Estimates from a selected layout must be done very carefully. For example, *when figuring savings for a shortened pattern, allow for the smaller rather than the larger*

of the alterations in each segment of the layout. If this pattern were to be shortened by the same amounts stated on the sketch, the answer would be quite different: there would be a saving of 2 inches in the segment where the skirt sections will be cut and a saving of 1 inch where the front facing and jacket front appear. However, because the jacket sections will be shortened only 1 inch, the savings in the two areas, where jacket and sleeve sections appear side by side, will be only 1 inch (each) despite the fact that sleeve sections will be shortened 3 inches. Therefore, if these pieces will be shortened rather than lengthened, the savings (beginning from the left) will be 2 inches, plus 1 inch, plus 1 inch, plus 1 inch for a total of 5 inches or ⅛ yard.

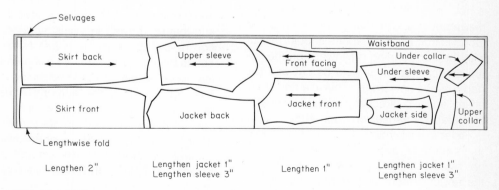

FIGURE 3-4 A sample layout showing how to revise yardage amounts by making estimates from the selected layout.

To figure yardage amounts for napped and pile fabrics

Napped fabrics are processed in such a way that fibers are picked up from the body of the fabric to produce a fuzzy surface; woolens are often napped to add interest and character. The extra fibers are brushed in one direction. *Pile fabrics are woven with extra short threads extending from the surface of the fabric and the extra threads bend slightly toward one direction.* Both of these fabrics give a different appearance depending on the direction the nap or pile runs; pile fabrics give a distinct color difference if one section of the garment is cut with the pile running down and others are cut with the pile running up. Both types of fabrics must be cut with all sections arranged so that the fibers or threads run in one direction in the finished garment; therefore pattern pieces must be laid on the fabric in one direction, with the upper edges consistently placed toward one end of the length of fabric.

The direction of the fibers or threads is not an issue as the yardage estimate is made but is of great importance when the fabric is cut. Napped fabrics should be cut with the nap running downward on the figure and pile fabrics should be cut with the nap running upward to achieve a rich color effect; specific directions for working with these fabrics appear on page 495.

Refer to the layout in Figure 3-4 and note that the upper edges of pattern pieces are not placed consistently toward one end of the length of fabric. In a without-nap layout, pieces can be turned end for end if they fit more economically in that position.

If napped or pile fabric will be used, the layout in Figure 3-4 is not acceptable, and if the pattern does not include a with-nap layout, the customer must (before purchasing fabric) estimate the amount of yardage required by making an estimate from an existing layout or by making a new layout; the latter is recommended. The following comparison of the two methods of approach will reveal the wisdom of making a new special layout.

Making an estimate from a without-nap layout This is by far the simpler method and, depending on the layout and the shape of the particular pattern pieces, it may be entirely reliable. Refer to the layout in Figure 3-4 and note that only the skirt sections and the upper sleeve are turned in a different direction from the majority of the pieces. Obviously, the skirt sections can be turned end for end without changing the yardage requirement; if the entire problem were that simple, there would be no need to make a new layout. However, the upper sleeve complicates the problem because there is not sufficient width in that segment of the layout to turn it end for end. In attempting to make a safe estimate, the author assumed (as most customers would) that the under sleeve would fit into the space where the upper sleeve is laid, and that by moving the waistband and the collars, the upper sleeve would fit into the space by the jacket side. An estimate must always be ample enough (better too much than too little); so the author's educated guess was that by moving the collars and cutting the waistband on the crosswise grain, it would probably require an extra ¼ yard (in addition to the amount stated for this layout) to cut the pattern of a napped or pile fabric.

Making a special with-nap layout See Figure 3-5, which shows the same pattern pieces in a with-nap layout and was made by rearranging the actual pattern pieces on a table. Note that the shape of pattern pieces is such that the under collar can be dovetailed into the space between the under sleeve and the jacket-front sections; this is simply good luck and nothing more —a result of the shape of these particular pattern pieces. By making the actual layout, the author discovered that no extra fabric was required to cut this pattern of napped or pile fabric; in this particular case, then, making a special layout saved the cost of the extra ¼ yard that would be indicated if the problem were solved by making an estimate. Depending on the cost of fabric, the customer may prefer to buy extra yardage to save the time for planning a new layout. However, all readers should understand that there are many times when an estimate will fail more seriously—when, for example, the estimate falls short of the amount required. If an estimate is low by only a few inches, it may (depending on the pattern pieces involved) require as much as an extra ½ or ¾ yard or enough to cut a whole pattern piece. Obviously a low estimate can be disastrous if the fabric is no longer available on the market.

A with-nap layout usually requires more yardage than a without-nap layout. If a pattern can be cut as economically from napped fabrics (and some can simply because of the shape of the pattern pieces), the pattern company will capitalize on this advantage by including yardage amounts for napped fabrics and showing the layouts with pieces laid in one direction with a heading that reads "with or without nap."

It should be understood that the sample layouts in Figures 3-4 and 3-5 were prepared for illustrative purposes by the author (they were not copied from an instruction sheet) and it is purely accidental that they require the same amount of fabric. *To repeat: With-nap layouts usually require additional fabric; and if the pattern can be cut as economically in napped or pile fabrics, the with-nap layout is the one pictured on the instruction sheet.*

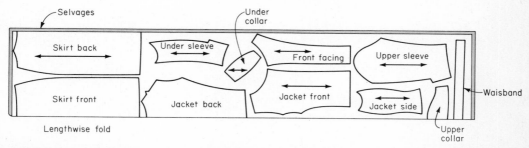

FIGURE 3-5   A sample layout with all pieces laid in one direction, for cutting napped and piled fabrics.

To figure yardage amounts for balancing one-way designs and matching plaids, checks, and stripes

The markings in fake furs and other woven or printed designs are usually one-way designs, planned for cutting in one direction. The same is true of the large majority of interesting plaids, which are uneven rather than even. If a fabric has a distinct up and down, it must be cut from a with-nap layout with the upper edges of all pattern pieces toward one end of the length of fabric. If there is no with-nap layout, one must be made by following directions in the preceding section. However, in addition to the yardage required for a with-nap layout, these fabrics require still more additional fabric for balancing or matching design units. Additional information on estimating yardages (and on other problems of working with large designs that must be balanced, or with plaids, checks, or stripes that must be matched) is covered in detail in Chapter 11.

Chapter 4

FABRIC SELECTION AND PREPARATION FOR CUTTING

It is not possible to cover the fundamentals of textiles adequately in a book devoted to tailoring. This chapter includes only the most basic information, and it is assumed the reader will study a recent, reliable text on textiles or, as minimum preparation for shopping, will study recent articles in popular women's magazines and in the informative brochures available from the pattern companies.

There are several fabrics to be selected for a tailored costume: the suiting or coating itself; supporting fabrics (underlinings, interfacings); lining fabric for the jacket or coat and possibly for the skirt or pants; fabric for go-with blouses, which may or may not be the same as the lining fabric; and muslin or some other inexpensive fabric from which to make a test copy.

WISE BUYING PRACTICES

Review "Fabric" on page 25 before proceeding. Some of the suggestions, mentioned briefly in that section, will be enlarged upon in the following discussions.

General Suggestions

The reputation of the store or merchant A reliable store or merchant is perhaps the first guarantee of a wise purchase. The store which stands behind its merchandise with a sound refund policy, building tomorrow's sales on today's fair transactions, is the only kind of store in which an inexperienced person should shop. Unfair practices exist in every business, and the fabric market is no exception. A practice which certain specialty shops (never reliable department stores) engage in is that of rewrapping fabric on empty bolts to gain the advantage of the information on the end of the bolt; for example, a wool-nylon blend can be wrapped on a reused bolt which reads "100 percent virgin wool." Since nylon is less expensive than wool, and certainly less costly than virgin wool, these practices result in what appear to be attractive low prices; unfortunately, it is the uninformed consumer who is most attracted by the too-low prices that are danger signals to more knowledgeable customers. Large department stores would not jeopardize their reputations with malpractices of this sort; their financial success depends on continuing business. But the unscrupulous merchant (especially in a city location) can make a reasonable profit on transient sales alone. The person who knows textiles well can shop anywhere with safety; the novice is wise to stay on the beaten path to a department store or a well-established fabric shop.

Informative labels and tags on the bolt Information given on the end of the bolt of fabric includes the fiber content by percentage, the finishes used, and the width of the fabric; often there are other helpful statements ("needs little or no ironing," "less than 1 percent shrinkage," etc.). In addition, there is often a hangtag with suggestions for care and other pertinent information.

The matter of fiber content is of the greatest importance to the woman who sews or buys ready-made, the more so in this age of man-made fibers. Synthetic or chemical fibers may be developed to have the look and general character of the natural fibers (wool, cotton, linen, silk) and results are so remarkable that even an experienced shopper may not be able to recognize differences without making scientific tests. On the other hand, some fabrics made of the man-made fibers may have a distinctive hand and appearance. The performance and care of the garment differ greatly with the fiber content. A wise consumer must know what to expect from each fabric and how to care for it, and this is largely dependent on the fiber content.

Check the width of fabric to uncover possible variations (width may vary as much as 2 inches from the stated width); ask the clerk to check the width with a yardstick or measure it with a tape measure. Al-though most wools are woven in the traditional 54-inch width, it is dangerous to assume that every wool will be 54 inches wide. Many imported wools are woven in different widths. For example, some homespuns from Scotland, which carry an attractively low price tag, are made in a 27-inch width, and twice the amount of yardage stated for 54-inch fabric will be required; imported challis, a dress-weight woolen, is woven in 36- and 42-inch widths; and many French imports are woven in 50- to 52-inch widths. Domestic woolens also may vary in width; many are woven in 58- to 60-inch widths. Similarly, the increasingly popular polyesters are woven in a great variety of widths, including 58, 60, 66, and 72 inches. If the width of fabric varies from the widths stated in the yardage chart (wider or narrower by even a few inches), a special layout should be made before purchasing fabric; see page 54.

Imperfections The customer has every right to examine fabric carefully; the wise buyer examines the entire length of fabric before it is cut from the bolt. Flaws in weaving or dyeing may be present and they may never come to the attention of the reliable merchant who purchased the fabric from a reliable fabric company. Loose threads on the underside are usually no disadvantage, but they should prompt an inspection of the area from the right side. If fabric has been on display in or near a window, evidences of sun fading may appear. Fabrics left on display shelves for long periods of time may show their age with dust or fading at the fold or selvage edges. The customer must be cautious, the more so during clearance sales, for it is just such damaged goods that carry the most attractive sale prices. Carefully inspect lengths of fabric which have been piled on counters for special sales for these may be snagged or otherwise damaged by excessive handling.

The quality of tentering and its implications

The process of tentering is one by which fabrics are stretched out to their full width, fastened to a rectangular frame, and dried under pressure. Ideally, they are fastened to the tenter framework in such a way that lengthwise and crosswise threads are in perfect right-angle position, as shown in fabric a in Figure 4-1. Less careful work reduces labor costs, and so the quality of tentering may vary; poorly tentered fabric,

with the crosswise threads slanting, is shown in fabric b in Figure 4-1. The 2-inch variation (from selvage to selvage) shown in fabric b is not at all unusual; a 1-inch variation is considered an acceptable standard by most fabric finishers. It is rare, indeed, to see the perfect positioning of threads

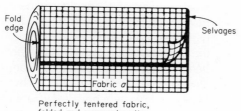

Perfectly tentered fabric, folded and wrapped on the bolt: quality of tentering is visible

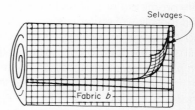

Poorly tentered fabric, folded and wrapped on the bolt: the slanting crosswise threads are visible

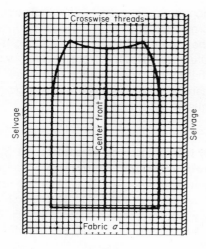

Perfectly tentered fabric with crosswise threads at right angles to lengthwise threads

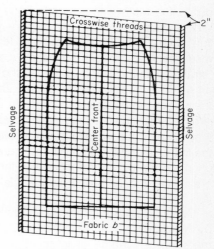

Poorly tentered fabric with crosswise threads slanting about 2 inches (a 2-inch variation) from selvage to selvage

FIGURE 4-1   *A comparison of perfectly tentered and poorly tentered fabrics.*

shown in fabric *a,* and it is not at all difficult to find fabrics on the market with a 2-inch (or, in some cases, a 4-inch) variation.

The quality of tentering is usually visible on the bolt of fabric; exceptions are those fabrics with a matted or fuzzy surface and certain fabrics in dark colors. Woven plaids or crosswise striped fabrics, fabrics woven with prominent crosswise threads or slubs, and loosely woven fabrics are very revealing. On closer inspection, almost all fabrics will reveal the direction of crosswise threads which can be compared with long edges of the bolt; see the threads close to the long edges of the two bolts in Figure 4-1. The wise consumer should examine the bolt of fabric to determine the quality of tentering and the effect it will have on the costume.

The implications of the problem are illustrated in the lower sketches in Figure 4-1, where the two fabrics are shown stretched out to full width with a simple basic skirt outline superimposed in proper position (with center-front lines on a lengthwise grainline); the skirt on fabric *a* looks "straight with the world" whereas the skirt on fabric *b* appears to be askew. Before the introduction of easy-care finishes, problems of tentering were not so grave because they could be corrected by straightening the fabric at home, as shown in Figure 4-5 on page 95; by this process the threads are shifted into the proper right-angle position.

Certain fabrics can still be straightened by this process, but the fabrics on today's market which can be straightened are very few—mainly woolens, and then only those which are not bonded and those which have not been treated to give them special qualities (such as wash-and-wear and permanent-press).

The easy-care finishes (drip-dry, easy-iron, permanent-press, etc.) are given special resin treatments during the tentering process. These finishes are applied at high temperature and pressure and, in essence, they lock the lengthwise and crosswise threads permanently into position. Therefore, poorly tentered fabrics which have undergone easy-care finishing cannot be straightened because the threads cannot be shifted.

Easy-care finishes are no longer confined to the fabrics which have been traditionally considered washable. Woolens labeled "washable" or "permanent-press" have been treated by a finish done with high heat and high pressure which locks the threads in position; if these wools have been poorly tentered, they cannot be straightened and corrected. The whole family of polyesters have easy-care characteristics and cannot be straightened. It follows that when the consumer evaluates a fabric with easy-care qualities, she must realize the implications of having to make the garment up with the fabric in the condition as purchased—with lengthwise and crosswise threads in the position in which they were held on the tentering frame. Study the following sections carefully to see that the choice of fabric (especially easy-care fabrics) must necessarily hinge on the quality of tentering.

If fabrics can be straightened to correct imperfect tentering In this case (for example, woolens with no special finishes), they must be straightened by following the directions on page 95. *If they can be straightened and are not corrected, they tend to straighten themselves in the finished garment, causing the garment to twist on the figure.*

Fabric *b* in Figure 4-1 was cut from the bolt by following along a crosswise thread, with the result that the full piece of fabric is a parallelogram that can be straightened (if the fabric is one of the few that can be corrected) by pulling it in such a way that the threads are shifted into proper position; this causes the whole piece of fabric to become rectangular in shape. Notice that the prominence of the cut edges on the bolt reveals that the fabric is poorly tentered.

Compare the sketches of fabric *b* in Figure 4-1 with comparable sketches of the same fabric in Figure 4-2. The clerk cannot always see a crosswise thread well enough to cut along it quickly, and so she may cut the fabric on a line parallel to the edges of the bolt as shown in Figure 4-2; furthermore, she may cut in this way to avoid revealing to the customer the full extent of off-grain variation, especially in fabrics with a variation of several inches. If fabric is cut parallel to the edges of the bolt, it will be rectangular in shape, as shown in the lower sketch in Figure 4-2; but if it is a fabric that can be straightened, the usable portion of the piece is in reality a parallelogram, as indicated by the dark lines in the sketch.

The first step in straightening the fabric (if it can be straightened) is to cut along a crosswise thread at both ends (see dark lines in the sketch); there will be a subsequent yardage loss on each selvage edge that will equal the total off-grain variation from selvage to selvage. This may vary from ½ inch to as much as 3 or 4 inches.

If the pattern will be shortened or if the variation is less than an inch, the amount of yardage stated on the envelope will be adequate; but if the pattern will not be shortened and if the total variation is several inches, the customer must purchase an extra ⅛ yard to compensate for yardage lost as the fabric is straightened.

NOTE: A similar loss will result when fabrics which cannot be straightened are cut from the bolt along a crosswise thread as shown in sketch *b* in Figure 4-6 on page 96.

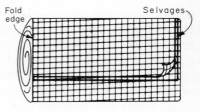

Poorly tentered fabric cut parallel to long edges of the bolt (not cut along a crosswise thread)

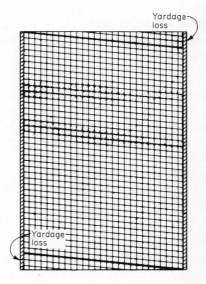

FIGURE 4-2 Yardage loss results when poorly tentered fabrics which can be straightened are cut parallel to the long edges of the bolt.

If fabrics cannot be straightened The reader would be wise to assume that 90 percent of the fabrics on the current market and an even greater percentage in the future may have easy-care qualities and therefore will be of the sort that cannot be straightened. The consumer must therefore decide at the time of purchase what effect the quality of tentering will have on the visual satisfaction of the garment. Visual satisfaction is the only problem; the customer need not be concerned about the finished garment twisting, because the threads are locked into position and they will not tend to straighten themselves on the figure. Visual satisfaction is largely dependent on the prominence of the crosswise threads and, to a lesser extent, on the pattern design to be cut from the fabric.

Refer to the two fabrics in Figure 4-1. Obviously fabric *a* will present no problems in any type of fabric cut in any type of pattern design. Fabric *b* calls for caution before purchase; it will be entirely satisfactory under the following circumstances:

If the crosswise threads are not visible, or if they are visible only at very close range. Examples are closely woven fabrics in a plain weave, fabrics with a crepey, matted appearance, pile and napped fabrics, and most fabrics in dark colors. These fabrics can be used with any pattern, regardless of style lines.

If the crosswise threads are visible (as in plaids, crosswise stripes, loosely woven fabrics) but the pattern design is one that is not based on close-to-rectangular pattern pieces. Examples are very flared skirts and circular skirts or capes.

If the crosswise threads are visible but the pattern is cut on the bias. When lengthwise and crosswise lines will appear diagonally on the figure, the quality of tentering is not obvious.

Poorly tentered fabrics, comparable to fabric *b* in Figure 4-1, cut of woven plaids, crosswise stripes, and checks, will not be visually satisfactory in most designs. The slanting lines in these will be obvious; crosswise lines cannot be matched at corresponding seams, and the effect will be exaggerated if the plaid or crosswise stripe is larger, wider, or in bold color contrasts.

Fabrics in one color which have a dominant crosswise thread or slub, and those woven in a jacquard weave which, even if subtle, reveals the direction of crosswise threads (many polyester knits have a visible design like a jacquard weave) will also be unsatisfactory.

Fabrics in which the lengthwise and crosswise threads are two different colors (denim, tweeds) are unsatisfactory. Even if they are closely woven, these are more revealing than fabrics in which both sets of threads are the same color.

Fabrics woven with heavy threads are unsatisfactory. Even if they are in a plain color and closely woven, these will reveal the direction of crosswise threads more readily than fabrics woven with fine threads.

Bonded fabrics (even if they are of wool which has not been resin treated) are unsatisfactory. These cannot be straightened without breaking the delicate bond between the two fabrics.

It becomes increasingly evident that poorly tentered fabrics have great limitations, and the important point to understand is that these problems must be recognized before purchase. Careful examination of the crosswise threads on the bolt of fabric is one way of judging the quality of tentering. A better test is to stretch the fabric out full width and place the selvage edges along the long edges of the sales counter and then compare the direction of crosswise threads with the end of the counter. Draping the fabric full length on the figure (with lengthwise threads hanging in a vertical direction) and studying the effect before a mirror will reveal the prominence of crosswise threads under wearing conditions.

High-quality tentering adds to the cost of the fabric, whether it is sold in yard goods departments or made into ready-to-wear. One cannot assume, however, that high cost ensures good tentering for it is only one of many processes in the manufacturing cycle which influence cost. In general (and only in general) the cost of well-tentered fabric is greater, and, judged on a basis of visual satisfaction, the extra cost is deserved. It is possible for fabric finishers to do perfect tentering if the customer is willing to pay the price. Customers can put pressure on the finishers to improve quality by refusing to buy poorly tentered fabrics and making the reason known to the salesclerk.

There is, however, another side to the story. The lower prices of poorly tentered fabrics are appealing to the many among the buying public who cannot afford to indulge in visual perfection and who, instead, are delighted simply to have a new costume. In other words, inexpensive fabrics must be available on the market, and those who demand higher standards must purchase more discriminatingly.

Anticipate the possible need for more yardage than is stated in the yardage chart

The amount of yardage stated in the yardage chart is the amount required to cut the pattern pieces as they are (with no alterations) on the proper grainline of plain fabric; in other words, the stated amount constitutes the total area (length by width) required to cut the pattern pieces. It is not

possible for the pattern company to include yardages in the chart to meet all the special needs of individual customers and fabrics. Some yardages are included for napped fabrics (or fabrics with one-way designs) with some patterns; these yardages are usually greater because all pattern pieces must be laid in one direction. There are many fabrics that will, because of their nature or design, require more fabric than the amount stated in the chart, but these special fabrics differ so greatly that no definite amount could possibly be stated that would be accurate for every conceivable fabric that will be used by the millions of customers who will buy each pattern. And so each customer must revise the yardage amounts to accommodate her individual needs and the demands of the fabric she will use.

There are several reasons why more yardage than the amount stated on the yardage chart may be required, and all of them must be considered before purchasing fabric. They are the following:

To compensate for the loss in straightening poorly tentered fabrics This will be necessary for (1) fabrics which can be straightened if cut parallel to the edges of the bolt (rather than along a crosswise thread) and (2) fabrics which cannot be straightened if cut from the bolt along a crosswise thread.

To make allowances for the special demands of certain fabrics This is done so that they can be cut in whatever way may be necessary to enhance their beauty. Most of these fabrics are discussed in Chapter 11, and in general they are fabrics which are not the wisest choices for first tailoring projects. Some fabrics which will require extra allowances are (1) fabrics with nap, pile, or one-way designs unless yardage amounts for these fabrics are stated in the chart; (2) plaids, large checks, crosswise stripes, and fabrics with a crosswise design motif which must be matched; and (3) any fabric with a prominent design unit (fake furs, etc.) which must be balanced on the figure. Before buying any of these fabrics, read the appropriate section in Chapter 11 and "Figuring Special Yardage Requirements" on page 53 and a section with a similar heading on page 474.

It is obvious that the pattern company cannot include yardage amounts to meet these divergent fabric needs. The customer must estimate the extra yardage her fabric will demand, but she must understand that while all the directions included in the page references stated above result in estimates that are reliable guidelines the unique demands of each of these special fabrics are such that it is impossible to figure the extra amounts with absolute accuracy. If one of these special fabrics is to be used, it is wise to select a fabric in good supply at the store, to buy the estimated yardage, and then to lay on the pattern pieces as soon as possible so that more fabric will be available should the estimate run short.

To compensate for a possible loss when the fabric is preshrunk One of the greatest advantages of home sewing is the opportunity to preshrink fabrics before they are made up, thereby ensuring adequate size and length for the lifetime of the garment. Fabrics should be preshrunk by cleaning them in exactly the same way the finished garment will be cleaned—with

soap or detergent, by hand or machine, by a professional dry cleaner, or in a coin-operated machine (the chemicals are sometimes stronger in these). Directions for preshrinking appear on pages 92, 97, and 294.

Preshrinking is absolutely essential for all fabrics in the lined garment because all fabrics (the suiting or coating, lining, underlining, interfacing, etc.) must act as one; preshrinking makes this possible. It is entirely possible that the lining may shrink in the crosswise direction while the fabric for the garment may shrink in a lengthwise direction, and the professional dry cleaners cannot prevent the disastrous results in the finished garment if both fabrics have not been preshrunk.

Wools which carry a label stating that they have been preshrunk may nevertheless shrink when pressed or cleaned; the amount of shrinkage is limited, but the demanding customer is wise to ensure her investment in time and money by having the fabric put through the cleaning process.

It is impossible to state the exact amount of extra fabric required for preshrinking because each fabric will, of course, respond in a different manner. An estimate of an additional ⅛ yard for a 3-yard length of fabric should be more than adequate for most fabrics of average to high quality. Less expensive fabrics, loosely woven fabrics, and crepes will probably shrink more than high-quality and firmly woven fabrics. Fabrics which have not been preshrunk during manufacture will shrink more.

To allow for pattern alterations to accommodate individual figure irregularities The person who will lengthen pattern pieces can make a very accurate estimate of the amount of extra fabric her pattern alteration requires, and likewise the person who will shorten pieces can estimate a possible saving of fabric; see "To Figure Yardage Amounts by Making

Estimates from a Layout on the Instruction Sheet" on page 56. Sizable additions in width of pieces (for example, more than a total of 2 extra inches in the hip area) create a greater problem than additions in length, because the pattern pieces may have to be shifted into quite different positions on the length of fabric. This may result in a need for considerably more yardage with some pattern layouts but not with others. Therefore the only safe solution is to do a new layout after the pattern is altered and before the fabric is purchased; see directions on page 54.

To allow for changes in or additions to the design Any change in the design as it is pictured in the catalogue and on the front of the envelope will affect yardage amounts. Experienced readers who may want to redesign patterns will need to make new layouts, individualized to their own demands, before purchasing fabric; see directions on page 54.

If the jacket or coat lining will be finished by the novelty Hong Kong method, extra lining fabric will be required; see page 287.

To allow for cutting the pattern with a less economical layout This section is included for experienced readers (only) who may value time more than money. If, after examining the particular layout that will be used, the worker finds that it has been planned for an open layout or for combination layouts which require more cutting time—and provided that she is experienced enough to see how, with additional fabric, the pattern could be cut on a lengthwise fold—she may decide to buy extra yardage for a lengthwise layout to save cutting time. The decision will hinge on the cost of the fabric. For some persons it may be advisable to buy an extra half yard of fabric at $4 a yard to save ½ hour of cutting time, but obviously this would be unwise if the fabric is $10 a yard.

SELECTION OF SUITING AND COATING FABRICS

Before proceeding, review the general information in several preceding sections of the text: "Fabric Choices" on page 18 (which includes recommendations based on the adaptability of the fabric to tailoring techniques and valuable learning experiences), "Fabric (Texture and Texture Combination)" on page 25, and "Fabric" on page 32.

NOTE: **Chapter 11 is devoted to the special problems of working with certain fabrics which are not recommended for first tailoring projects. Some fabrics appear in that chapter because they must be constructed by methods which are not standard to tailoring and therefore do not provide learning experiences with continuing value. Other fabrics are discussed there because they are difficult to work with and require more time than a tailoring course allows; these include plaids and fake furs. Before selecting fabric, glance through Chapter 11 to better understand the problems which will be encountered if these fabrics are chosen.**

Washable fabrics used for tailored costumes

Suits and coats can be made of any fabric of appropriate suiting or coating weight and hand. Wool was once the overwhelming favorite and is still a great favorite; but it has many rivals on the current market, and some of the most formidable are washable fabrics. In addition to washable woolens, these include polyester and acrylic suitings and coatings, suiting-weight cottons, and also blends of two or more of these. Of these, the polyesters, more than any other, rival and perhaps surpass the old favorite. The popularity of these fabrics does not hinge solely on their washability; for example, the crease-resistant and shape-retentive properties of the polyesters are partially responsible for their wide acceptance by consumers.

In choosing a washable fabric for a tailored garment, the wise consumer should base her decision on other qualities inherent in the fiber and the fabric, giving far less than the usual attention to the washability factor. *If a costume will be tailored with all the techniques that distinguish a "tailored" garment from a "sewn" one, the finished costume is not washable.* This is true even if all the fabrics involved are washable. After the many layers (including underlinings, interfacings, and linings) are combined and molded together in the tailoring processes, the finished costume cannot be laundered satisfactorily; there are just too many layers and too many stitches— in short, too much construction. If a washable fabric will be used for a traditionally tailored garment, the consumer must understand that its care and upkeep will be the same as for a wool garment—she must plan to have it professionally dry-cleaned.

The polyesters and acrylics are excellent choices for tailored costumes, because they are available in a great variety of appropriate weights and textures and readily adapt to tailoring techniques. In addition, they offer several economic advantages. The initial cost of a good-quality fabric made of one of these chemical fibers is less per yard than the cost of a comparable quality of wool. In addition, their wider widths (generally) require less yardage. Because

washing and machine drying at home will cause more shrinkage than the dry-cleaning process, these washable fabrics can be preshrunk at home even if the finished costume will be dry-cleaned; consequently, preshrinkage costs can be all but eliminated. The finished costume can be spot-cleaned with soap and water, and this adds up to great savings over the lifetime of the garment. *However, washability of the finished costume is dependent on the fabric and also on the construction;* if the costume will be tailored, the consumer must realize that she will not have this particular economic advantage and so must make a decision based on other merits of the fabric.

These washable fabrics can be made into suits and coats which can be laundered at home, but it must be understood that they will not be tailored; they will be sewn rather than tailored, and essentially this means that much of the very construction which makes the tailored costume what it is must be eliminated. Washable construction, then, does not include tailoring techniques and therefore it will not provide a good educational experience in tailoring. See "Washable Construction" on page 510. Washable construction (sewing rather than tailoring) is acceptable and appropriate for "little" suits and coats so long as the worker understands that the garment will not have the professional appearance of a tailored costume.

Washable woolens Many fabrics on the current market labeled "washable" are not really washable in the strictest sense of the word. Ideally, "washable" means that the fabric when washed retains its original beauty and character. The polyesters do; wool, rayon, and silk do not. *Fabric manufacturers, in an attempt to meet the formidable competition of the popular polyesters, are pushed to offer the washability feature on some fabrics which can be* washed but ideally should not be washed. The consumer should understand that wool fabrics will not be as beautiful when washed as when dry-cleaned and that the finishes which render wool washable destroy some of the elasticity expected of wool and so adversely influence its natural shaping and molding qualities. In addition, the wools offered as washable are not the highest-quality wools; wool is more costly than polyester, and if a wool is to compete with the polyester market, quality must be sacrificed.

An evaluation of bonded fabrics

Bonded fabrics are two layers of fabric held together by an adhesive; the underlayer, rather like a lining, is usually an acetate or nylon tricot, and the upper layer may be one of an almost unlimited variety of knitted or woven fabrics. Wools and knits are most frequently bonded, but other fabrics such as crepes and denims can also be bonded for extra body. These fabrics have been well received by the consuming public, although discriminating customers have discovered that their apparent advantages at the moment of purchase are often offset by their failure to withstand the long-term demands of wear and care. The following evaluation is based on long-term values; when viewed from this longer range, the advantages are not impressive. However, it must be understood that future developments may lead to fabrics which will withstand the tests of long hours of wear and the demands of washing or cleaning.

Two fabrics bonded together have more body than two separate layers of the same two fabrics; the adhesive which allows the two to act as one has a firming effect which adds apparent body. Because of this firming effect, two quite flimsy, shoddy fabrics can be bonded together to make a fabric which feels very firm and durable; most

unfortunately, the average consumer, attracted by the low price that is possible if shoddy fabrics are used, is too often fooled into thinking she is buying quality merchandise. On closer inspection she may find that there are as few as six or eight threads per inch in the wool fabric which feels so firm and durable to the hand. She must understand that the tricot lining layer will not prevent stretching and that loosely woven fabric will stretch with wear. If the reader can obtain samples of bonded fabrics, she can see the actual quality of most of these fabrics by peeling off the lining layer. The consumer must realize that she will not get the same service from a bonded wool as from an all-wool, unbonded fabric of comparable weight and hand.

Bonded fabrics do not need an additional lining for protection from the body (dresses, etc.), but jackets and coats will need the usual lining to hide construction details. The no-lining advantage is a legitimate selling point, but it must be balanced against the disadvantage of excess bulk and thickness in facings and hems where no lining is required.

The bonding process makes it possible to use knit fabrics which are too open and lacy to be cut and sewn without a backing fabric. Jerseys, which are difficult to work with otherwise because of edge-curl, can be, if bonded, cut and sewn with greater ease. These are legitimate advantages, although the lacy fabric will stretch even when bonded and the pliable quality characteristic of jersey will have been altered by the bonding process.

Bonded fabrics are frequently poorly tentered because they are usually loosely woven and because it is difficult to control

**FABRIC SELECTION AND PREPARATION
FOR CUTTING**

both fabrics well during the bonding operation; actually, tentering problems are multiplied because the two layers may both be poorly tentered in opposite directions. The problem is magnified because they cannot be straightened without breaking the bonding seal.

The permanence of the bond is a major consideration. The quality of the adhesive material itself varies. If two fabrics are not compatible and if they have not had the same care in finishing to control shrinkage, the bond can be broken by wear or by washing or dry cleaning. If the two layers become separated by washing or cleaning, the fabric finisher (not the dry cleaner) is at fault. There is no way the customer can judge the permanence of the bond with complete accuracy before purchase, and so there is no assurance of long-lasting satisfaction from any bonded fabric.

Laminated fabrics are comparable to bonded fabrics in that they are composed of two layers which act as one; the underlayer is a sheet of foam laminated to a great variety of top-layer fabrics. This is done by use of an adhesive or by heating the foam before lamination to create a self-seal. The latter method is used more frequently because it offers better resistance to washing and dry cleaning. The foam backing eliminates stretch, and for this reason laminated fabrics offer more shape retention than bonded fabrics. Although these fabrics are used commonly for ready-to-wear raincoats and coats, they are rarely available on the yard goods market.

An evaluation of blends

Blends are fabrics made of a combination of two or more fibers. Natural fibers may be blended (silk with wool, cotton with linen), or a natural fiber may be blended with a synthetic (wool with nylon, silk with polyester), and synthetics can be blended with each other. Blends make it possible to gain the advantages of certain properties of both fibers and so achieve a combination of characteristics not present in any one fiber. Blends are, in general, less expensive than their "pure-breed" counterparts because the manufacturer uses a minimum amount of the more expensive fiber to produce the maximum desirable characteristics in the finished fabric. The manufacturer can, by varying these percentages, scientifically control the characteristics of the finished fabric; for example, he can make a fabric with the hand of a natural fiber and with the additional strength and easy-care qualities of a synthetic. He can create these characteristics to the degree he desires by balancing the percentages of the component parts.

Blends in suiting- or coating-weights are appropriate for tailoring purposes; many instructors advise students to purchase a good-quality blend in preference to a poor-quality wool at the same price. However, the worker must understand that the fabric will have characteristics of both fibers and that she will need to experiment to see how these combined characteristics work together to influence construction, pressing, cleaning, etc.; obviously, the fiber which makes up the greatest percentage will influence decisions most significantly. In doing any work that is influenced by the fiber content, the worker should read suggestions for both fibers and suspect that any one of the suggestions about any one of the fibers may be applicable to her fabric. For example, the polyesters cannot be straightened if they are poorly tentered, but wools which have not been given easy-care finishes can be corrected. When purchasing a wool-polyester blend, the worker should suspect that the polyester content may prevent straightening, and therefore she should not purchase a poorly tentered fabric if the quality of tentering will adversely affect the appearance of the costume.

All readers are familiar with the popular blend of cotton and dacron (one of the best is 35 percent cotton, 65 percent dacron), which is so successful for easy-care blouses and summer dresses. This fabric is ideal for the lining of a washable suit to be constructed by sewing rather than tailoring methods, because it will be compatible with the washable fabric of which such a suit would be made.

Blends of suiting and coating weights are usually a combination of wool with one of the synthetics (polyester, acrylic, nylon); they provide some of the warmth and hand of wool with the crease resistance, strength, and shape retention of the chemical fibers at a lower cost than a comparable quality of 100 percent virgin wool.

Another desirable blend is a fabric made of a small percentage of silk fibers combined with polyester fibers. It results in a very desirable fabric with some of the subtle sheen and elegance of silk combined with the easy-care, easy-wear characteristics of the polyester. These blends are wise choices for a tailored costume, if the worker takes into account the qualities of both fibers when making decisions about construction and pressing methods.

General suggestions

Choose a fabric which adapts readily and well to tailoring processes Review the desirable characteristics on page 18. This suggestion is especially applicable for those who will be working in a classroom situation, where time required and experience gained are important issues. There is much to learn in a limited time, and fabrics which are difficult to handle distract from basic learning experiences and require more than the available time.

Buy top-quality fabric in the desired price range This is not to say the fabric must necessarily be expensive. A good-quality blend, a polyester, or a cotton suiting may prove to be a wiser choice than a low-quality wool. Review the discussion in "Fabric (Texture and Texture Combination)" on page 25 with particular attention to the cost-comparison chart on page 26. Resist being influenced to buy less yardage than the amount stated on the yardage chart.

Consider wise economy measures Preshrinkage costs can be all but eliminated by selecting one of the washable fabrics and washing and machine drying it at home; this is possible even if the finished costume will be dry-cleaned.

Linings and supporting fabrics play a major role in the success of the tailored costume; but, if costs must be pared, it is generally wiser to economize on these, rather than on the suiting or coating fabric. Although they must be of good quality and must keep pace in appearance and durability with the major fabric, they need not be expensive. Synthetic lining crepes are available in a wide price range and make excellent linings. Special underlining and interfacing fabrics are quite costly, the more so because many are woven in narrow widths. To reduce costs, standard blouse and dress fabrics (less expensive, or woven in wider widths, or both) can be substituted for a special-purpose supporting fabric. Inexpensive muslin in an appropriate weight and hand makes an excellent supporting fabric.

Shop for other fabrics which will be a part of the costume Before making a definite decision, it is well to survey the market for other fabrics which will be a part of the total costume. Any contrasting fabric required, such as the lining fabric and companion blouse and dress fabrics, should be considered at this time. It is unwise to buy a tweed in tones of plum and red, no matter how lovely, without being sure that harmonizing colors are available for go-with fabrics.

Suiting and coating fabrics

It is not possible to evaluate all the great variety of fabrics which might be chosen for a tailored costume. This section is confined to brief statements of problems which influence decisions on some of the most popular types of suiting and coating fabrics.

Napped and pile fabrics These must be cut with a one-way layout, which usually requires more fabric than other types of layouts. If one-way layouts are not included on the pattern, it will be necessary to make a special layout to figure yardage require-

ments before purchasing fabric; directions are given on page 53. Napped and pile fabrics must be pressed very carefully to prevent crushing of the pile or flattening of the nap; crushed velvets require less care because of their surface interest. Any of these fabrics will have a tendency to crush under wearing conditions in areas where abrasion will occur, but the crushed velvets will not reveal the ravages of wear as much as the others. All construction will be obvious, and construction irregularities will be magnified; this is especially true of pile fabrics, although the surface interest of crushed pile helps to hide imperfections. Detailed directions for working with these fabrics appear on page 495.

Fake furs These present the problems of all napped or pile fabrics (see above) as well as the complications of heavy or thick fabrics (see below). In addition, they offer unique problems of their own. If there is a prominent design (zebra stripes, etc.), and if that design is large (and it is likely to be), these fabrics will require more yardage than is stated in the yardage chart and, depending on the size of the design units, may require considerably more yardage. Construction is slowed in several ways. Basting must be tediously done in such a way that long yarns (or "hairs") are not caught in with the machine stitching. After seams are stitched, yarns which have been caught in the stitching must be carefully lifted out. These and other special problems of working with these fabrics appear on page 495.

Thick, heavy coatings These are best made into simply cut designs with a minimum of seams because seams will necessarily be very bulky. In some cases it is wise to eliminate some structural seams of the pattern (see page 253). Cutting will be more time-consuming because many of these should be cut one layer at a time (or on an open layout) to ensure accuracy on both thicknesses. Their very weight and bulk will continue to slow progress; they are more difficult to control and support at the machine, the ironing board, etc. Pressing is more difficult because the worker must exert great pressure to flatten seams without matting surface fibers and causing a shiny, slick ridge in thick seam areas.

Knitted fabrics Good-quality double knits in wool or polyester (or a blend of these) adapt very well to tailoring and are a wise choice for students with limited experience. These fabrics are very stable, and there is no reason to anticipate problems with stretching. Work is speeded because they do not ravel; this is a great advantage for the novice or the person who lacks patience. Bulky sweater knits are less stable, and they will tend to stretch during construction and later under wearing conditions; this tendency can be controlled adequately with firm underlinings and interfacings. Some of the most loosely woven sweater knits are bonded to a more stable backing for greater stability; read "An Evaluation of Bonded Fabrics" on page 71 before selecting one of these. Sweater knits are most appropriate for loosely fitted, sweater-type jackets or coats and for easy-flowing capes. They are not recommended for fitted skirts but they can be used for skirts with some style fullness. Many of the knits will be made of polyesters or acrylics; see the following paragraphs.

Polyester double knits The customer is accustomed to choosing these partially (or perhaps largely) for their washability; this is less of an advantage in a tailored costume because the finished garment must be dry-cleaned. However, the washability feature is an asset because pre-shrinkage costs can be reduced by washing

and machine drying at home and because the finished costume can be easily spot-cleaned with soap and water. These double knits come in wider widths (58 to 60 inches, 66 inches); and if the yardage chart does not include these widths, it pays to delay purchase until a special layout can be made to figure the exact yardage needed. Depending on the shape of the particular pattern pieces involved, the saving may be modest, but it is more likely to be significant.

The quality of tentering is a major concern because poor tentering cannot be corrected; review "The Quality of Tentering and Its Implications" on page 63. Examine the fabric carefully from a distance of several feet. Many of these knits have a subtle woven-in design, hardly visible at close range, which will be evident in the finished costume. If the design is not positioned at a perfect right angle to the long edges of the fabric, the direction of the crosswise design will adversely affect visual satisfaction under wearing conditions. Any fabric with a visible crosswise design (woven-in design, plaid or striped fabric, and fabrics with heavy slubs) must be tentered very well because it must be cut in the condition it is when purchased. *Before purchasing,* test to see that the quality of tentering is excellent.

Plaid, checked, and crosswise striped fabrics The many problems of estimating yardage requirements and of cutting and sewing these fabrics are covered in detail in Chapter 11. These fabrics require additional time, effort, and patience at every stage of construction, and therefore are not wise choices for the student who must complete a costume in the limited time allowed in a tailoring class. Two major problems are these: (1) They will require more fabric than that stated on the yardage chart, and although the amount of extra fabric can be estimated, it cannot be estimated with complete accuracy. To ensure sufficient yardage the customer should make an ample estimate or buy fabric which is in good supply at the store, so that she can purchase more if it becomes necessary. (2) The quality of tentering is of utmost importance. If the fabric is a woolen which has not been given easy-care finishes, it can be straightened and there will be no problem. However, if it is a washable wool or a polyester, poor tentering cannot be corrected; this means it will be impossible to match crosswise lines in poorly tentered fabric and the garment will appear to be askew on the figure (see fabric *b* in Figure 4-1, page 63). It is a mistake to assume that fabric with crosswise lines which slant a mere $\frac{1}{2}$ inch from selvage to selvage (a $\frac{1}{2}$-inch variation) will be acceptable; this is enough to prevent matching at seams.

Fabrics with very small checks, and fabrics woven or knitted with very small geometric designs which give the appearance of tiny checks, present unique problems. They will not require more yardage than is stated on the yardage chart, but they will require more time when basting and sewing. Some of them are especially difficult because the checks or designs are so small that it is almost impossible to match them, and yet, after seams are stitched, the mismatch becomes obvious when viewed from a distance. If this happens, the mismatch must be corrected; if the check is very tiny, this may have to be done by tedious trial and error.

Before selecting a plaid, checked, or striped fabric, the student who will be working in a classroom situation should read the detailed directions on page 474 to 495 to decide if she will have the additional time and patience these will require.

NOTE: **The above statements and similar ones in preceding pages are not intended to discourage the use of plaids, checks, and stripes or to suggest that it is advisable to avoid difficult fabrics under all circumstances. On the contrary, the experienced person will (and should) enjoy the challenge of working out problems; and the person who sews for a hobby and who therefore does not work under time deadlines will (and should) prefer fabrics which require more thought, care, and concentration.**

Fabrics with a diagonal weave
These fabrics are discussed in "Twills" on page 502. Diagonal weaves do not create as many problems as the consumer is led to believe; a note which reads "Design not suitable for diagonal weaves" appears on a large percentage of the yardage charts, implying that these present great problems. Actually, this note appears on many patterns which can be cut from diagonal weaves. This is not to say that the inexperienced person can afford to ignore the note. Students working in a classroom situation should ask the instructor to evaluate the design to be used; very possibly, the instructor will decide that a diagonal weave can be used.

SELECTION OF LINING FABRICS

The two methods which can be used for lining skirts or pants should be evaluated before purchasing the lining fabric. One is more elegant than the other (as well as more difficult and time-consuming), and the experienced sewers who choose that method may wish to choose a more decorative fabric that will be worthy of the extra effort and will keep pace with the elegance of the construction method. Those who choose the simpler method may want to select a staple lining fabric for functional purposes only. Read "An Evaluation of Lining Methods" on page 339 before selecting the lining fabric.

Purposes of lining

Understanding the several purposes or functions of the lining makes it possible to make a wiser selection of the fabric that will best serve those functions for each particular costume.

To add to the aesthetic appeal of the costume The aesthetic appeal of the lining is obviously a pertinent issue in jackets and coats because it is visible under wearing conditions. The fact that the dress or skirt lining will be visible only to the wearer does not diminish the need for considering beauty when selecting lining fabrics.

To provide greater comfort Any scratchy, rough fabric (such as wool tweed) will be less irritating to the skin if lined with a soft, smooth fabric. Those who are allergic to certain fibers can wear fabrics made of these fibers comfortably if the entire garment is lined.

Linings for jackets and coats which will be slipped on over sweaters and other rough or fuzzy fabrics must necessarily be silky smooth.

To prevent wrinkling The layer of lining fabric acts as a cushion to reduce creasing as it is worn or folded for packing; under these circumstances, the lining doubles as an underlining.

To prevent stretching If the skirt lining is a firmly woven fabric which will not stretch appreciably, it will help prevent woolens, crepes, and knits from stretching with wear. Any garment or any portion of a garment which will fit close to the body will retain its shape better if lined with a firm fabric of proper weight and texture. Under these circumstances the lining serves as an underlining as well.

General suggestions

These suggestions are applicable when selecting the traditional type of lining which is used for most suits and coats. The considerations are necessarily quite different when selecting novelty linings (quilted for extra warmth, fake fur for design interest, etc.); see page 81 for a discussion of these. If a thick, bulky lining fabric will be used, special consideration must be given to pattern size; review "Reevaluate All Circumstances Which May Influence Size" on page 47 before selecting one of them.

Select a lining that will be subordinate to the fabric of the garment It is very important that the lining be lighter in weight and of a softer hand, so that it will not dominate the character of the major fabric. The wool suit or coat should look and act like wool; for example, if a lightweight wool were lined with a stiffer, heavier lining, the resulting costume would take on the character of the heavier and stiffer of the two fabrics. By this rule, taffeta is a poor choice for the lining of most costumes, and yet many sewers buy taffeta because they have seen it used so frequently in ready-to-wear costumes. Taffeta is used by the ready-to-wear manufacturer not because it is ideal for the purpose but because it is inexpensive and easy to work with in the factory.

There are exceptions to this important general rule. If the lining will be in a very heavy fabric (fake fur) for a particular design effect, it will possibly be heavier than the fabric of the garment, and the resulting problem must be dealt with. If the lining will serve the additional purpose of building a silhouette (to support the lines of an A-line skirt, for example), it must be a dominant fabric.

Choose a lining that is pleasant to the touch A good lining is a smooth, soft fabric, whether it is silk, cotton, or rayon. The feel of the lining is important in skirts, jackets, and coats, and the smooth, somewhat slick lining gives a more pleasurable sensation than one with a fuzzy, sticky surface.

The lining fabric, ideally, should not be rough and fuzzy, so that it will hang freely on the body. The skirt lining must not adhere to a girdle or a slip, and the jacket or coat must slip on easily over any fabric or sweater that might be worn with it. For this reason, the smooth and slick man-made fabrics, especially rayon, make excellent linings. Cotton and silk sheath-lining fabrics tend to cling more readily.

Select a lining fabric with the durability to keep pace with the garment Replacement of the lining of a jacket or coat and of the skirt or pants is possible, but it is a time-consuming process which might better be avoided. It is a foolish economy of time and money to buy a low-quality lining that will shred and pull out at the seams in one season of wear. The thin, sleazy sheath lining offered at minimum prices on the market is acceptable for lightweight garments, but will not withstand the kind of wear given to the typical tailored garment.

A good test of wearing qualities can be made in the store before purchase. Scrape a fingernail hard against the threads near the cut or torn edge at the end of the piece; then hold the fabric up to the light to see whether the threads have shifted and separated noticeably. If the threads have shifted out of line to any great extent under this kind of pressure, the fabric will not wear well and is not worth the time and effort that go into the tailored garment. This test will make the shortcomings of the sleazy sheath linings obvious; a slightly more expensive fabric will withstand the test much better.

Be sure the lining will keep pace aesthetically with the garment The obviously cheap lining is a very expensive mistake, for if the lining cheapens a $50 suit to the $25 level (and it can do just that), the lining is actually very expensive.

The aesthetic and durable qualities of the lining become more important when there is to be a companion piece to match. A blouse or dress requires a higher-quality fabric than might otherwise be used for a lining; in this case it is better to favor the companion piece when making fabric choices. When a companion piece is involved, the fabric must be durable enough to withstand the most severe wearing conditions because the weaker link of the costume will limit the value of the stronger link.

Test the lining with the fabric of the garment If the lining is to be of a contrasting color or in a design of several colors, the color may show through loosely woven fabrics, especially if they are light in weight and color. The darker color of a print underneath a lightweight fabric in a light color may cast a muddy, spotty appearance over the garment.

NOTE: **The complete interfacing, handled like an underlining discussed in connection with the construction of the jacket or coat, solves this problem. The addition of an extra layer of supporting fabric under the major fabric will prevent lining colors from showing through, and therefore lining possibilities are increased.**

Buy a lining heavy enough to hide inner construction The lining fabric must be sufficiently heavy in weight to hide the raw edges and construction details inside the jacket or coat. These unattractive details will show through lightweight fabrics more readily; light-colored linings should be placed over the fabric to test the effect. A lightweight lining can be underlined to make it opaque enough to hide inner construction, see page 439.

Give special consideration to skirt linings If the lining is to control stretch (as in the straight skirt), put pressure on the fabric in both lengthwise and crosswise directions by pulling it firmly against the hands. Pebbly crepes, although attractive in a jacket or coat, will stretch more readily than more firmly woven flat fabrics.

The skirt lining need not match the jacket lining, and although it must be as durable, it need not be as beautiful and may therefore be less expensive than the jacket lining. Perhaps there is a certain pleasure for the wearer as she dresses if all linings match, but a less costly skirt lining is a wise economy and is recommended if the jacket or coat lining will be expensive.

Select a practical lining but be sure it is interesting The lining must serve a functional purpose, but one must guard against choosing a fabric that is so practical and functional that it becomes uninteresting. Linings can be replaced (the lining patterns should be saved for the lifetime of the tailored garment), and perhaps an unusual, even impractical, lining is the wisest choice if it provides the perfect accent. What is more, a new lining can give renewed zest to the costume, and many women will enjoy having a change in a few years.

Buy extra fabric if the Hong Kong finish is used The Hong Kong finish, a novel method of finishing seams and hems in skirts and unlined jackets and coats, requires the use of matching bias strips of lining to replace the usual seam binding. A unique way of finishing inner edges of front and neck facings makes the finish adaptable to the lined jacket or coat. Directions for finishing seams and hems appear on page 287, and directions for finishing facing edges in lined garments are given on page 470.

It would be well to study those pages at this time and to decide now whether this method will be used; extra lining fabric will be required if the Hong Kong construction is chosen and will not be required for traditional construction methods. Because of the very delicate nature of the finish, piecing seams in the bias strips must be avoided whenever possible. Ideally, the bias strips should be almost a yard long; ¾ yard of extra lining fabric would provide enough extra strips to bind all seams in a skirt, do the skirt hem, and finish the jacket and facing edges with a minimum of piecing. If, however, the skirt and jacket linings are different fabrics, about ¾ yard of each will be required.

Lining fabrics

A great variety of fabrics will serve the functions of the lining, and the role each costume will play in the wardrobe will determine the wise balance between aesthetic and practical considerations.

Lining fabrics for traditional tailored costumes which will be dry-cleaned

The choice of these is extensive because they need not be limited to fabrics which must be dry-cleaned; washable linings can be used in costumes which will be dry-cleaned.

For the skirt or pants The lining for these must be durable to withstand the stress of wearing; this is especially true of pants linings and linings for snugly fitted skirts. The lining fabric may be the same as that used for a matching jacket or coat (this adds a touch of elegance) if it is a firmly woven fabric which will withstand hard usage. On the other hand, it can be a durable but less expensive fabric than the coat or jacket lining. One of the attractive underlining fabrics (Siri, for example) can serve as a skirt lining; but it is not as attractive as other linings, and although it looks very lovely when judged as an underlining, it loses some of its appeal when compared with typical lining fabrics. China silk is often used for skirt linings, but it tends to adhere

to undergarments, a disadvantage which must be considered. China silk is not durable enough to use for lining pants. Crepe-back satin feels and looks very luxurious, and if it is supple, it is appropriate for elegant cocktail and dinner skirts. Probably the wisest choice for skirt or pants linings is one of the many lightweight blouse or dress crepes (rayon, nylon, polyester, or silk) which are available in a wide range of colors and designs.

For the jacket or coat Special lining fabrics (many in a twill weave) are available; these have a certain functional appearance which makes them most appropriate for casual tailored costumes. Crepe-back satin (very supple fabric with a satin face) is an ideal lining for elegant costumes. Brocades can be chosen for cocktail or dinner costumes if they are very supple. Most readers will select one of many lightweight blouse and dress crepes (of rayon, nylon, polyester, or silk) because these are appropriate and available in many colors and designs in a wide price range.

For warmth without weight or bulk, fabrics with a Milium backing are the choice of many women. Some of these have the functional appearance of the special lining fabrics mentioned above, but a few very lovely ones have the appearance and hand of a crepe-back satin. The effectiveness of this lining as compared with the conventional lining is difficult to judge; consumer reaction is colored by the freedom from bulky linings and the subconscious thought that it is supposed to be warmer. This is the only "warm" lining fabric that is sufficiently light in weight to be combined with medium-weight (suiting) fabrics.

Lining fabrics for washable costumes that will be laundered at home Washable costumes should be sewn rather than tailored because it is important that con-

struction be minimized. Most of these costumes will be made of polyester double knits; and usually skirts and pants are not lined, because they will wash more effectively if there is a minimum of construction. Furthermore, a lining is not required to prevent stretching (they retain their shape) or to prevent seams from abrasion (the knits will not ravel). If for some reason the worker wishes to line the skirt or pants (to gain experience or to add extra body), she may choose an attractive underlining fabric or a very lightweight blouse or dress fabric in one of the easy-care fabrics (supple nylon, polyester crepe, or a cotton-dacron blend, etc.).

For the jacket or coat The wisest choice of a lining fabric for a washable costume is a very lightweight dress or blouse crepe in an easy-care fabric of nylon, polyester, or a cotton-dacron blend. The lining must be one that will not require pressing, for it is difficult to press a finished costume properly after it is lined.

Special-purpose linings The lining may be a fabric quite different from one with the characteristics usually expected of a lining. If it is to provide extra warmth, it may have a Milium back; any other fabric that will add warmth will be thicker, bulkier, and in general more dominant than is usually considered appropriate. Similarly, if the lining is to provide unique design interest, its fashion appeal must outweigh practical considerations. In general, these special-purpose linings are heavier, thicker, or stiffer than is ideal. Being heavier and thicker, they will dominate the costume, influencing and altering the appearance of the major fabric. Their bulk and thickness will have the effect of adding many pounds to the figure, and it is possible the wearer will require a different size pattern than her true size; review the section "Reevaluate All Cir-

cumstances Which May Influence Size" on page 47 before purchasing a heavy, dominant lining fabric.

For design interest or a unique effect For the sake of high fashion, all general rules of selection may be ignored provided that the worker has the time, experience, and ability to handle the complications which will arise. The lining can be too stiff, or too sheer, or too thick and heavy *if* the worker has the ability required to indulge in fashion above practicality. For example, simulated furs and stiff brocades do not lend themselves easily to lining purposes, but they can be used by the experienced worker if they create the desired fashion effect.

For extra warmth A Milium lining will add some warmth; but if warmth is a major concern, the lining fabric will necessarily be bulkier and heavier. The finest of the warm linings is Sun-Bak satin, which looks like a lovely satin on the face and has a wooly backing which adds great warmth. There are some quilted linings on the market; most of them are made of a relatively inexpensive satin or taffeta with a fuzzy cotton backing and quilted in a very simple design. Any conventional lining fabric can be quilted to a layer of warm wooly fabric at home, and if the worker desires, she can do the quilting by hand in an intricate design that will add elegance to the costume. If a layer of warm fabric is quilted (or simply basted) to the lining sections before seams are joined, the process is the same as underlining sections of the garment; directions appear on page 303.

It must be understood that any lining which is backed with a warm wooly layer

will be considerably bulkier than a traditional lining. After these heavy linings are inserted, the garment will seem considerably
smaller (particularly in the sleeves), and
this fact must be considered when the pattern size is decided. If this type of lining will
be used, the pattern should probably be
one size larger than the true size of the
wearer.

The following discussion is included as
background information which professionals should understand. There is another
method of handling interlining fabrics for
added warmth which results in somewhat
less bulk and so can be considered a better
method than combining the lining and interlining to act as one (as shown on page
303). Interlining fabrics can be cut from
lining pieces (with certain modifications
to reduce bulk) and inserted into the garment as a separate operation. Seams of the
interlining are hand-sewn to seams of the
garment, and then a traditional lining is inserted in the usual way. This method of construction has not been included in this text,
because so few readers wish to spend the
extra time a separate operation requires.
The fact that interlining fabrics are not readily available on the market (even in well-
stocked fabric departments) is proof that
few customers wish to use them, and it follows that most home sewers use their sewing hours for suits or between-season coats
and purchase their heavy coats ready-
made.

SELECTION OF SUPPORTING FABRICS (UNDERLININGS AND INTERFACINGS)

The supporting fabrics play a backstage
role, but if the fabric of the garment or the
nature of the design calls for support, these
fabrics (along with the additional construction details they require) take on great significance. The fact that their purposes are
varied, and that their choice is dependent
on the great variety of fabrics with which
they will be combined, creates a need for
a wide selection of supporting fabrics and
causes confusion in the minds of those who
sew. This confusion is further nurtured by
some variety in construction methods. The
extra expense and additional time and complications of construction discourage some
workers, and as a result all too many home
sewers avoid using supporting fabrics; this
is unfortunate because if their need is indicated, they are essential to the success of
the garment. The imaginative use of underlinings and interfacings will result in truly exciting improvements in the quality of home
sewing.

A full grasp of the differences between
underlining and *interfacing,* the terms used
to classify the supporting fabrics (in the
yard goods department and on the instruction sheet), will dispel confusion. The differences between the two are dependent
on the weight and body of the supporting
fabric itself, the purpose for which it is intended, and (as a result of the purpose) the
construction techniques required.

*Interfacing is the term used to describe
heavier supporting fabrics with more stiffness or greater body.* Because the fabric
is heavy, it is intended to serve the purpose
of preventing stretch and adding body to
only portions of the garment, to support
exaggerated silhouettes, and to act as a
cushion to bulky seams. If the term *interfacing* appears in the yardage chart, con-

struction details will show the supporting fabric used in only portions of the garment and yardage amounts will be relatively low.

Underlining is a term used to describe supporting fabrics much lighter in weight or with less body than typical interfacing fabrics. Because of the subordinate nature of underlining fabric, it is intended to add some (but not great amounts of) additional weight and body to the entire garment, control stretch somewhat, and prevent wrinkling. If the term *underlining* appears in the yardage chart, yardage amounts will be comparable to the yardage required for the entire garment and construction methods will be involved with combining two layers of fabric to act as one in entire sections of the garment.

Purposes of supporting fabrics

Understanding the several purposes or functions of the supporting fabrics makes it possible to make a wiser selection of the fabric that will best serve those functions for each particular costume. The purposes follow.

To control stretch in the entire garment or in those portions which must withstand stress If a loosely woven fabric is used for any unit of the costume which will fit snugly, the entire unit should be underlined with a supporting fabric of appropriate weight. The same supple fabric will not require a supporting fabric throughout if there is style fullness involved. For example, if a skirt or a jacket is gathered to a yoke, only the yoke portion will require a supporting fabric to control stretch.

The entire front edge of the jacket or coat (or the edge of any unit which will be buttoned) must be interfaced to enable it to withstand the strain of frequent buttoning.

To add extra body to the fabric of the entire garment to change and enhance the character of the fabric When supporting fabrics are chosen with imagination, the hand and character of any fabric can be altered so that its uses can be extended and multiplied. For example, a lightweight woolen which looks lovely in a skirt may be too light and supple for effective use with a matching jacket. But if the jacket is completely underlined with a supporting fabric of substantial weight, the fabric will take on the hand and characteristics expected of a dressmaker jacket.

To add body and stiffness to certain areas of the garment Collars and lapels, cuffs, band trims, pocket flaps, and some pockets are examples of design details which require interfacings to create the trim, flat, somewhat stiff character expected of them. Belts and waistbands are examples of details which need very firm, stiff interfacings to create the proper character and also to withstand the great stress of wearing conditions.

Interfacings in collars and lapels serve an additional purpose that is unique to tailoring. The interfacing is pad-stitched to the under-collar and lapel area in such a way that the two layers act as one and at the same time are molded and shaped to the contours they will take on the figure.

To add stiffness and body to support silhouette lines A collar with an exaggerated stand, a wide flaring cuff, and a fitted jacket with molded rounded hips are examples of design features which require a firm foundation of supporting fabric to maintain the desired silhouette.

To act as a cushion for bulky seams
The extra layer of supporting fabric between the outside fabric and bulky encased seams keeps bulk from pressing through to form an unattractive ridge along finished edges. These bulky encased seams appear in the most prominent areas because they are along the faced edges of collars, lapels, cuffs, etc.—on units which are deliberately planned to gain attention. Interfacing is essential in any area where bound buttonholes will be made because it will cushion and hide the imprint of the bulky pleat of the buttonhole.

NOTE: **As an aid to better understanding of the functions of supporting fabrics, glance through directions for their construction before making the final purchase. Directions for underlining skirts and pants appear on page 339; and directions for using interfacings and underlining in jackets and coats (several alternatives are explained) appear on pages 353 to 366.**

Selection is influenced by the purpose to be served and the construction method to be used

The diversity of purposes for which supporting fabrics may be used and the extent to which support and control are needed are dependent on the nature of the fabric and the type of design. It becomes obvious that the type, character, weight, stiffness, color, and body of the supporting fabric are major considerations. The selection of supporting fabrics, the extent to which they will be used, and the construction methods to be employed are decisions which must necessarily be made with discrimination and imagination.

The one consideration of greatest importance in the selection of these fabrics is that of subordination versus domination. *The supporting fabric should be in almost all cases a fabric subordinate in weight and body to the fabric of the garment; it must add the desirable supporting characteristics without changing the character of the fabric greatly.* The one exception to the above statement has to do with the need to maintain silhouette lines which stand away from the body; to serve this purpose the supporting fabric must dominate (stiffer, firmer, with more body) the fabric of the garment. *Supporting fabrics must enhance the fabric of the garment and give it characteristics slightly (but not radically) different from those it alone possesses.* If the character of the fabric is altered radically, the effect will not be pleasing, as illustrated by the following examples:

If the purpose of the supporting fabric is to prevent stretching, it must be firmly woven and its weight and strength determined by the amount of strain it must withstand and the weight of the fabric it must control. Therefore, the *interfacing* fabric for a belt or waistband must be stronger and stiffer than the *underlining* fabric used for the entire body of the garment, which will get less strain during wearing. Heavy pellon (stiff and board-like in character) is an effective interfacing for a belt but a very poor choice for underlining a garment, because in an entire garment its stiffness would make the wearer uncomfortable and also because it would dominate and alter the character of the fabric.

If the purpose of the supporting fabric is to add body and weight, it must have characteristics compatible with those of the fabric of the garment. For example, wool crepe is limp and pliable by nature, and these are the qualities for which it is chosen. If a very heavy, stiff *interfacing* fabric (such as hair canvas) is used to add body to the entire garment, the effect will be unrealistic and disturbing because the soft fabric will take on the character of the dominant supporting fabric, a character entirely foreign to its nature. By contrast a lightweight, soft, drapable *underlining* fabric used with wool crepe will add body to the entire garment without changing the character of the limp wool; the effect will be pleasing, for the wool will look and behave as expected but will be improved by the additional weight and body which will appear to be a part of the wool itself.

If the purpose of the supporting fabric is to add body or stiffness to certain portions of a garment, the need for support in the particular unit must be considered along with the character of the fabric. For example, a cuff 5 inches wide will need greater support than one that is 1½ inches wide, and a stand-up collar will need greater support than a softly rolled Peter Pan collar. A wide cuff made of wool crepe demands more support than the same cuff made in a suiting fabric, but the greater support for the wide cuff in limp fabric must be provided by a supporting fabric that is not radically different from the fabric; in other words, the cuff in wool crepe should not be supported by stiff canvas but rather by a crisp, somwhat stiff fabric which will provide adequate support while retaining some of the characteristics of crepe. Under these circumstances it is better to use a double layer of a compatible supporting fabric than one layer of a dominant supporting fabric.

If the purpose of the supporting fabric is to maintain an exaggerated silhouette, a dominant supporting fabric will be needed even though it will alter the character of the fabric. In this case the supporting fabric should be only as dominant as necessary to create the effect: the idea of using two layers of a less dominant supporting fabric in preference to one layer of a more dominant fabric should be considered.

Modify general rules to serve the demands of each costume It is understandable that some confusion results from the need to consider the diverse purposes of supporting fabrics and the extent to which support is needed for each particular fabric and pattern design. The woman who sews must understand general rules thoroughly and be able to apply them to each individual costume with discrimination and imagination.

In general; interfacing fabrics are used to (partially) interface a garment and underlining fabrics are used to (completely) underline a garment. While the definitions of underlinings and interfacings (page 82) seem decisive on the surface, there are additional considerations of weight of fabric and design of the garment. The fact that the two are classified by weight and body is complicated by the fact that there can be no distinct line to separate lightweight supporting fabrics (underlinings) from those classed as heavy (interfacings); consequently, the whole group of supporting fabrics of medium or average weight and body can be used interchangeably for interfacings or underlinings, depending on the weight of the fabric and the demands of the design. Study the following statements carefully. Hair canvas is a very stiff *interfacing* fabric which should be used (as per definition) only for interfacing portions of a garment. Siri, batiste, and voile are typical *underlining* fabrics which should be used (as per definition) to underline an entire garment. But cotton percale (or a fine muslin pillowcase) can be considered midway between the two in weight and body and therefore it can be used to *interface portions of a garment in lightweight fabrics such as*

*wool crepe, or it can be used to underline
an entire garment made of suiting or coating fabrics.*

For the above reasons, the classification
of supporting fabric (interfacing or underlining) in the yard goods department is of
no great importance to the consumer as
she makes a choice for a particular use;
rather, the issue is one of selecting an appropriate supporting fabric to serve the
purpose for which it is intended with a particular fabric in a specific design. An appropriate fabric may be chosen from the collection of special interfacing and underlining
fabrics, or it may be any inexpensive fabric
with the qualities necessary for the intended
use. The selection chart for supporting fabrics (opposite page) lists dress and blouse
fabrics which make excellent underlinings and interfacings, and many of these
are effective and less expensive than special
supporting fabrics. Muslin is a very inexpensive fabric, and since it is available in a
great variety of weights, it is a most versatile supporting fabric. Old sheets and pillowcases make excellent supporting fabrics
because the differences in wear in certain
areas result in a variety of weights within
the one unit.

Yardage amounts The yardage chart
will include the amount of yardage required
for the design because the pattern company must assume that the customer will
buy supporting fabrics for just one pattern
at a time. However, experienced sewers
and those who sew frequently will find it
advantageous to keep a good supply of a
variety of interfacing and underlining fabrics on hand; old sheets and pillowcases
and scraps of dress fabrics which can serve

supporting purposes can be added to the
collection. An ample home supply of supporting fabrics in several weights will provide the following advantages: Long-term
expenses will be less because small units
for one costume can be cut from scraps
of another, fabrics can be tested with a
variety of supporting fabrics to determine
the best effect, and several different supporting fabrics can be used in one costume
to serve unique and divergent needs in
various units of the design.

The word *optional* usually follows any
mention of interfacings and underlinings in
the yardage chart and on the instruction
sheet. The pattern company adds this word
because some fabrics (such as the polyester knits) do not require supporting fabrics to the extent that other fabrics do and
because beginners may wish to eliminate
them to simplify first projects. Unfortunately
many customers interpret optional to mean
that it makes no difference one way or the
other, and this is not true. If the fabric or
the design or both call for a supporting
fabric, it is absolutely essential to use one
for couturier results. *Use of supporting fabrics is optional only if the fabric and the
design do not require them.*

Quite often the yardage amount for a
complete garment underlining is greater
than that for the fabric of the garment itself,
leading customers to suspect that yardage
amounts are inaccurate. The differences
are simply a result of different widths; supporting fabrics are usually offered in narrower widths—27 inches (for hair canvases), 36 inches, and 45 inches. If the
width of the underlining fabric and the fabric for the garment are the same, yardage
amounts will be very comparable, with
the amount for the underlining usually being
slightly lower. Yardages for (partial) interfacings are always relatively low.

SELECTION CHART FOR SUPPORTING FABRICS

	Lightweight fabrics: wool crepe, cotton, suitings, brocades, etc.	**Medium-weight fabrics: typical suitings in wool, polyester or linen, corduroy and velvets etc.**	**Heavyweight fabrics: coating fabrics, fake furs, etc.**
Underlinings: For adding body to the entire garment	Muslin of a sleazy quality **In colors:** Batiste, lawn, or voile in appropriate weights Organdy or silk organza SiBonne, Siri, Touché, and Undercurrent—soft finish	Lightweight muslin **In colors:** Heavier weights of lawn, batiste, voile, organdy, or organza SiBonne, Siri, Touché and Undercurrent—crisp finish	Light- to medium-weight muslin **In colors:** Fine cotton percale, 35% cotton—65% Dacron blends
Interfacings: For adding body and stiffness to portions of garment	Lightweight, loosely woven muslin Worn sections of used sheets and pillowcases **In colors:** Voile in firm weights, fine cotton percale, 35% cotton—65% Dacron blends	Medium-weight muslin Medium-weight sections of used sheets and pillowcases Lightweight hair-canvases **In colors:** Cotton percale	Heavyweight muslin Firm sections of used sheets and pillowcases Medium to heavyweight hair canvases **In colors:** Indian Head, Kettle Cloth

Test the supporting fabric with the major fabric Whether the supporting fabric is selected in the store or from a home supply, testing it with the fabric to be used for the costume is very important. In the store the clerk will allow the customer to take the length of fabric she has purchased to other displays in the department to help her in selecting appropriate supporting fabrics. For underlinings (to add additional body to the entire garment), single layers of several different underlining fabrics can be tested with a single layer of the fabric for the garment to compare various effects; the layer of underlining fabric should add desirable body without radically altering the character of the fabric for the garment. For interfacings (to add body to portions of the garment) single layers of several different interfacing fabrics should be tested with two layers of the fabric for the garment because, in most cases, interfacings are used in areas and units which will be composed of two layers of the fabric for the garment (collars, lapels, etc.).

The advantage of using more than one supporting fabric in one garment will be evident as several supporting fabrics are tested. For example, a somewhat firmer underlining fabric may be chosen for jacket or coat pieces and a limper one may be selected to add less body to skirt or pants pieces. Similarly, a very stiff interfacing fabric may be best for a wide contour belt, while a more supple interfacing is more appropriate for the rolled collar in the same costume.

The color of the supporting fabric is an issue in loosely woven fabrics and in fabrics that are very light in weight. Test one layer of the fabric over the supporting fabric to experiment with color effects. Many of the special underlining and interfacing fabrics are offered only in white or black. In many cases these are entirely suitable, but in other cases the color of the supporting fabric must be comparable to, but not necessarily identical to, the color of the fabric. Testing several colors under the fabric will reveal subtle improvements in the depth of colors.

The care and upkeep of the finished garment must be considered, and for the sake of this the supporting fabric must have wear and care qualities similar to those of the fabric of the garment. If the finished garment will be washed and if it is made of fabric which will require no ironing, the supporting fabric must necessarily be chosen from the easy-care group. Supporting fabrics must be preshrunk under the same conditions that the finished garment will undergo; this is of paramount importance because the two must act as one in the finished garment.

Underlining fabrics

SiBonne, Super Siri, Touché, and Undercurrent These are trade names of special underlining fabrics currently on the market. All are available in at least two weights—one soft and more pliable and the other firm and crisp. They are offered in a full range of fashion colors as well as black and white. All have a smooth surface with a subtle sheen, which makes them comfortable next to the skin and visually attractive. Underlining fabrics made of polyester are also available.

Cotton lawn, voile, organdy, and silk organza These, all available in fashion colors, are dress fabrics which can serve as underlinings. Lawn and voile are very similar to the soft types of special under-lining fabrics and organdy is comparable to the crisp types. These fabrics will wrinkle when washed unless they have been treated with an easy-care finish.

Interfacing fabrics

The selection of interfacing fabrics is possibly wider than that of underlining fabrics. Those listed below are examples from a wide market.

The hair canvases These are special interfacing fabrics which are given stiffness and body by the addition of hair fibers; the type and percentage of hair fibers influence the stiffness and body of the fabric. The basic fabric may be made of cotton, rayon, or wool fibers or a combination of these. The weight and hand of these fabrics vary greatly, making them very versatile. They are not used with washable garments but are recommended for use with wool and other fabrics of similar weight and character; they are excellent for use with suiting and coating fabrics. All-wool hair canvas is costly, but its pliable qualities make it ideal for molding units such as collars, cuffs, and lapels when a soft, natural roll is desired.

A 100 percent polyester woven inter-facing This is available, and one can expect the polyesters to become increasingly popular for interfacing as well as underlining fabrics.

Indian Head and cotton percale These are dress fabrics which can be used for interfacings when circumstances demand a colored fabric (with loosely woven fabric, for example); special interfacing fabrics are available only in white, black, and neutral beiges and grays.

Muslin This inexpensive cotton fabric is the most versatile supporting fabric because it is available in many grades and weights. Some muslins of sleazy quality are limp and fine enough to use for underlinings, but the more typical weights are more appropriate for use as interfacings; they vary from a medium weight (rather comparable to cotton percale) to a very firm weight (comparable to a lightweight canvas or duck). Muslin is not treated with easy-care finishes and so it is not appropriate for costumes that will be laundered.

The nonwoven interfacings These have struck the public fancy, and all too many consumers buy them without considering other possibilities. This is a serious mistake because these are dominant fabrics which will cause the unit of the costume to take on the character of the interfacing rather than the fabric. There are varieties that are somewhat more pliable (with what is called a "bias feature"), but no interfacing of the nonwoven type is sufficiently pliable for interfacing shaped areas of the garment. The use of nonwoven interfacings is limited to those circumstances where a dominant interfacing is required to build an unusual silhouette or to provide maximum strength for stiffening belts and waistbands. They are also appropriate when a flat, firm effect is required, as in band cuffs or band trims.

Interfacings with an adhesive back, which can be bonded to the fabric of the garment by pressing, are available in woven and nonwoven types. All the fusible interfacings offer these advantages: basting can be eliminated and, when pressed together, the two fabrics truly act as one.

There are disadvantages similar to those of bonded fabrics (see page 71): the bond may break with wear and cleaning and the interfaced area becomes somewhat less pliable. Adhesive interfacings are recommended only for interfacing small units in quickly constructed, utilitarian garments. A fusible interfacing can be used effectively in a tailored costume provided it is basted and shaped into wearing position before it is permanently pressed in place.

NOTE: **The supporting fabrics described above were classified into interfacings and underlinings to point out their most typical uses—but it is important to understand that they are all adaptable to a variety of uses. In the chart on page 87 note that lightweight interfacing fabrics can be used as an underlining with heavier-than-average fabrics.**

SELECTION OF MUSLIN FOR THE TEST COPY

Because of the expense and time that go into the tailored costume, a test copy of the jacket or coat (and for some figures, the skirt or pants) is made in muslin to test pattern alterations, to solve problems of fitting, and as practice for new and difficult construction details. Muslin is traditionally used for test or sample garments because it is inexpensive, is firmly woven, and can be purchased in several weights.

The most important consideration in the selection of fabric for the test copy is the matter of suitable weight and body. The weight and character of the test fabric should be similar to those of the fabric to be used in the garment. The muslin for a jacket and a skirt or pants should be medi-um to heavy in weight; the muslin for a coat should be heavy in weight, and if the fabric to be used is especially thick and heavy (a true coating), muslin may not be heavy enough and a lightweight canvas, pillow ticking, or duck is a better choice.

Muslin can be purchased in a bleached (pure white) or unbleached condition (somewhat yellowish). The unbleached type is recommended for use in test copies because it is less expensive and serves the purpose as well. Muslin is so inexpensive that there is no need to do a special layout to figure yardage amounts. Make a generous estimate of yardage. These estimates, based on 36-inch fabric, should be ample: for a skirt, 2 yards; for pants, 3 yards; for a suit jacket, 3½ yards; for a full-length coat, 5 yards.

Other firmly woven fabrics, similar in weight to the fabric to be used for the garment, may be used. In addition to duck, ticking, and canvas for use in coats, fabrics similar to heavy percale, Indian Head, and Tarpoon Cloth may be used for the suit jacket or skirt. If a more decorative fabric is used, the test copy may possibly, but not always, be made up into a serviceable garment; for example, the sample coat made of attractive ticking might be salvaged for a house coat or beach coat. However, the reader must understand that she may need to cut into the test copy if unusual fitting problems arise and that it may not be in condition to be used later. The use of these more expensive fabrics is not recommended; unbleached muslin is the wisest choice under most circumstances.

PREPARING FABRIC FOR CUTTING

Basic terms

Several terms which will be used frequently throughout the construction process should be memorized before work begins; they are illustrated in Figure 4-3.

Selvage The selvage is the finished edge of the fabric running lengthwise on the bolt of fabric. There is a selvage on both lengthwise edges of woven fabric. The selvage is woven differently, with stronger threads than the rest of the fabric.

Lengthwise threads These are the threads running parallel to the selvage. The lengthwise threads are stronger as a rule than the crosswise threads, and for this reason garments are cut in such a way that lengthwise threads run lengthwise on the body. The words "straight of material," "straight of fabric," and "lengthwise grain" are used on the pattern to designate the direction of the lengthwise threads. Woven fabrics will not stretch when pulled in a lengthwise direction.

Crosswise threads These are the threads running at right angles, or perpendicular, to the selvage. These threads are usually slightly weaker than the lengthwise threads, although they will not stretch appreciably. Sometimes the layout will show a pattern piece laid so that the straight-of material line lies in a crosswise direction. This is done only on pattern pieces where maximum strength is not required or to create a particular effect in striped fabric.

True bias True bias is the diagonal of a perfect square of fabric. The bias line makes a 45-degree angle with the lengthwise and crosswise threads. The outstanding characteristic of the bias line is its elasticity. Any

diagonal line on the fabric is bias and will stretch somewhat, but the maximum amount of stretch and give is obtained only with the true bias line.

General suggestions

Fabric flaws Before preshrinking the fabric, inspect it carefully for flaws; although the fabric was examined before purchase, it should be even more carefully scrutinized at this time. If there is a serious flaw which cannot be avoided when cutting, the fabric can be returned to the store for a complete refund. If there are little flaws (a heavier thread, a loose end of yarn, etc.), mark each flaw with a pin. Later, just before cutting, be sure these areas are marked with a pin on the uppermost thickness of fabric, so that they are visible while the pattern is pinned in place. Most insignificant flaws

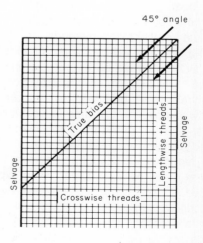

FIGURE 4-3 Basic terms illustrated.

can be avoided when cutting; or, alternatively, the pattern can be placed so that the flaw will appear in an inconspicuous area in the finished costume.

Special problems If the fabric has a design which must be balanced (markings on simulated fur, woven-in designs on polyester knits, etc.), or design lines which must be matched (plaid, stripes, etc.), the fabric will have to be folded for cutting in a way that will make balancing and matching possible; it will not necessarily be folded with selvage edges together. Before preparing these fabrics for preshrinking and cutting, see pages 474 to 477.

Selection of preshrinking method
Most suiting and coating fabrics should be preshrunk by dry cleaning at a professional dry-cleaning establishment or in a coin-operated machine, depending on how the finished costume will be cleaned. However, because there are many washable suiting and coating fabrics available on the current market, it becomes necessary to re-evaluate preshrinking methods.

If a costume will be tailored (if all tailoring techniques will be employed), the finished costume must be dry-cleaned, whether or not the fabrics in the garment are washable. If a costume is washable, it must also be "pressable"; and a truly tailored garment, with its many layers of fabric molded together, cannot be pressed properly at home by an amateur (even experienced home sewers are amateurs when compared with professional dry cleaners). For this reason, fabrics for a tailored costume should be preshrunk professionally. Typical suiting and coating fabrics (appropriate and recommended for tailored costumes) and many lining fabrics are not washable fabrics and must necessarily be preshrunk by dry cleaning.

If a washable fabric will be used for any one of the fabrics in a tailored garment, it can be preshrunk at home even though the finished costume will be dry-cleaned. For example, polyester, nylon, or acrylic fabrics in suiting and coating weights and in lining and blouse weights can be preshrunk by washing and drying at home. Washing and drying in the automatic dryer causes more shrinkage than dry cleaning (machine drying is responsible for most of the shrinkage), and therefore it is entirely safe to preshrink these fabrics at home and to have the finished costume professionally dry-cleaned.

Ideally everything which will be a part of the finished garment should be preshrunk; certainly this is true if the finished garment will be washed (if the suit or coat will be sewn rather than tailored). *All linings must be preshrunk,* and it is a foolish economy of both time and money to fail to treat the lining exactly like the major fabric for the garment. *Zippers and cotton twill tape must be preshrunk.* It may not be necessary to preshrink supporting fabrics, and probably will not be, if the finished costume will be dry-cleaned and the supporting fabric is made specifically for that purpose. As a safety measure, it is well to preshrink these fabrics; if they are washable, they can be processed at home even if the finished costume will be dry-cleaned.

The decision to preshrink decorative trims must be an individual one, based on the circumstances of each costume. If the finished costume will be washed (if it will be sewn rather than tailored), trims must be washable and must be preshrunk. Many trimming accents should not be preshrunk by washing, because preshrinking would adversely affect their appearance.

It is a wise precaution to have them pre-shrunk by the professional dry cleaner.

The steps and order of procedure differ slightly for fabrics which can be straightened and those which cannot be straightened. Prepare the fabric by following the steps in one of the following two sections.

To prepare fabrics which can be straightened

Poorly tentered fabrics which have not been given easy-care finishes can be straightened to correct off-grain variations and *they must be evened and straightened prior to preshrinking and cutting;* these fabrics include quality woolens which have not been bonded or treated with easy-care finishes. If these fabrics can be straightened (if the lengthwise and crosswise threads are not locked permanently into position by the high pressure and temperature of the resin treatments), they must be properly aligned before cutting or they will tend to correct themselves in the finished garment, causing the garment to twist on the figure. The steps of preparation are as follows:

1 Even fabric If the fabric has been torn from the bolt, the torn edges follow along crosswise threads. If it has been cut from the bolt, it must be evened by cutting along a crosswise thread. This should be done by the easiest and quickest of several methods.

Clipping into a selvage and then tearing the fabric is the very easiest and quickest method, but one should use caution because some fabrics do not tear well; in some fabrics the lengthwise threads snag and distort to damage the fabric. This method is not acceptable for most suiting and coating fabrics, and it must always be pretested on scrap fabric. Fabrics made in a plain weave usually tear well, whereas the novelty, jacquard, and satin weaves will be damaged by tearing.

Very loosely woven fabrics, fabrics with a woven crosswise stripe (such as a stripe or plaid), or fabrics with some prominent crosswise threads (such as some novelty weaves) can be evened very quickly by cutting along a visible crosswise thread. These threads in a loosely woven fabric (even in a plain color) are quite easy to follow, although results may not be entirely flawless; raveling out a few threads will correct slight errors.

In some more firmly woven fabrics, the crosswise threads can be followed quite well if the fabric is held up to the light by an assistant. One can see the threads better and, with care, can cut along the threads with reasonably accurate results. The errors can be corrected by raveling out excess threads. This method is not a wise choice unless the threads can be readily seen.

The most time-consuming method but the one that is entirely safe for any fabric is the following: clip into the selvage near the cut edge of the fabric through a single thickness. Pull out a crosswise thread and continue pulling it until it puckers up the fabric. Then cut along this puckered line. Ravel out another thread and continue across the width of the fabric. This procedure is easy or difficult depending on the nature of the threads. A strong, smooth crosswise thread in a loosely woven fabric can be pulled for perhaps half the width before it breaks; a weak, sticky, wooly thread in a tightly woven fabric may break when the puckered line is only ½ inch long.

**2 Straighten poorly tentered fabrics
to correct fabric grain** Open up the
fabric to full width and place it on a table;
crosswise and lengthwise lines should be
at right angles to each other and the entire
piece should form a rectangle with square
corners, as shown in Figure 4-4. The flaws
of tentering will show up readily in contrast
to the square corners of the table, as illustrated by the three examples of poorly
tentered fabrics pictured in Figure 4-5.

The flaw shown in sketch *a*, with crosswise threads slanting across the entire
width, is most common. Sketch *b* shows an
example of fabric in good condition in some
areas only. Sketch *c* shows crosswise
threads out of line, changing direction at
the center line where the fabric was folded.
By pulling along bias lines in the direction
required (study the arrowed lines in the
sketches), the crosswise threads can be
properly aligned.

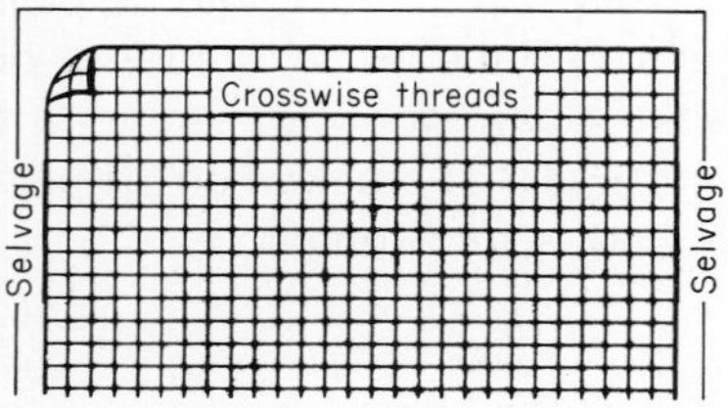

Note that crosswise threads are out of
line in the entire length of the fabric (inexperienced persons tend to think the problem is only at the ends or the corners),
which means the entire length must be
straightened. Move along about 6 inches
between each bias line and always pull in
the true bias direction for maximum results.

If the fabric is very firmly woven or very
poorly tentered, the process may have to
be repeated several times. Some fabrics
require considerable pressure, and if they
are in the wider widths it is helpful for two
persons to work together at opposite selvages; take care that fingernails do not cut
into the fabric.

Place the fabric on the table top to check
progress; when the piece is rectangular, as
shown in Figure 4-4, the straightening process is completed. If the fabric has not been
improved (if it is still in the original shape or
if, after a few minutes, it creeps back to
the original shape) it is a fabric that cannot
be straightened and must be cut as purchased (see the directions accompanying
Figure 4-6). If the fabric was in very poor
condition when work began, it can be
brought into a rectangular shape but it may
not lie flat and smooth on the table; it may
appear "bubbly" or diagonal ripples may
appear. These will be corrected when the
fabric is washed or dry-cleaned, because
when fabric is wet, threads settle more readily into proper position; this is the reason
the straightening process precedes preshrinking.

*FIGURE 4-4 Lengthwise and cross-
wise threads properly aligned for cutting.*

3 Select the layout Find the one that will be used for the view, size, type of fabric (napped, etc.), and fabric width.

4 Place the fabric on a table and fold it, right sides together, in proper position for the layout that will be used The edges must be basted rather than pinned so that the fabric can be put through the preshrinking process; basting stitches can be quickly done with long (1-inch) stitches. Fabrics which were originally in very poor condition may appear more bubbly or diagonal ripples may appear for the first time when the fabric is folded for cutting; preshrinking will correct this condition.

5 Preshrink fabric (and underlinings, interfacings, zipper, tapes, trims, etc.) Do this under the identical conditions to be used for the finished garment (by hand or machine washing and line or machine drying, or by dry cleaning in a coin-operated machine or by a professional dry cleaner). Instruct the cleaner to put the fabric through the complete dry-cleaning process; if he is instructed to preshrink fabric, he may steam-press it only, and this is not adequate because additional shrinkage will result when the fabric is completely wetted and cleaning chemicals are employed. Ask the cleaner to avoid pressing in a sharp crease at fold edges.

Some supporting fabrics which have not been given easy-care finishes will require pressing; do not press in a crease along the fold edge.

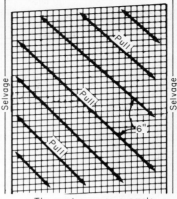

a The most common example

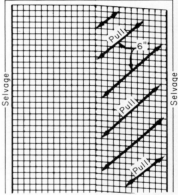

b A portion is in perfect condition

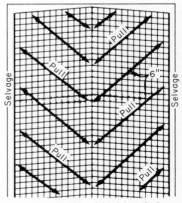

c Fabric could be folded lengthwise and two layers stretched at once

FIGURE 4-5 To correct fabric grain in poorly tentered fabrics.

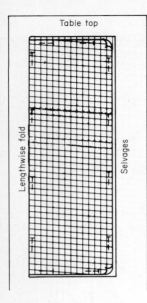

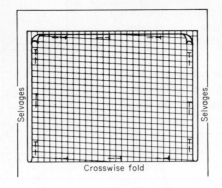

a A fabric that cannot be straightened which was cut from the bolt on lines parallel to long edges of the bolt—note loss in yardage if fabric is poorly tentered

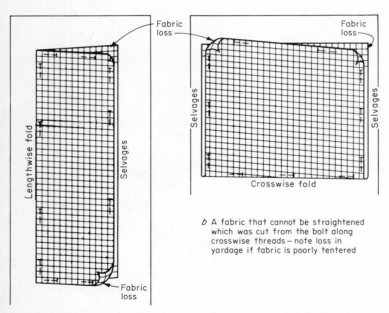

b A fabric that cannot be straightened which was cut from the bolt along crosswise threads—note loss in yardage if fabric is poorly tentered

FIGURE 4-6 *To prepare fabrics which cannot be straightened.*

To prepare fabrics which cannot be straightened

Fabrics which have been given easy-care finishes (permanent-press, crease retention, etc.) and the polyesters cannot be straightened to correct off-grain variations and must therefore be cut in the condition in which they were purchased; there is no value in attempting to straighten them. These fabrics are not necessarily poorly tentered but they are usually not perfectly tentered. The examples in Figure 4-6 show fabrics that are very poorly tentered, as an aid to illustrating problems more effectively. The steps of preparation are as follows:

1 Preshrink fabric (and underlinings, interfacings, zipper, tapes, trims, etc.) Do this under the identical conditions to be used for the finished garment (by hand or machine washing and line or machine drying or by dry cleaning in a coin-operated machine or by a professional dry cleaner). Instruct the cleaner to put the fabric through the complete dry-cleaning process; if he is instructed to preshrink fabric, he may steam-press it only, and this is not adequate because additional shrinkage will result when the fabric is completely wetted and when cleaning chemicals are employed. Instruct the dry cleaner to avoid pressing a crease at the fold line, for the crease may remain permanently.

If these fabrics will be preshrunk by washing, pressing will not be necessary (usually) and it is well to avoid it if possible. If the fabric requires pressing, do so before it is folded; if fold edges are pressed, the crease may remain permanently.

2 Select the layout Find the one that will be used for the view, size, type of fabric (napped, etc.), and fabric width.

NOTE: **If the fabric is a knit, before proceeding see sketch *b* in Figure 4-7 and the accompanying text.**

3 Place the fabric on a table and fold it, right sides together, in proper position for the layout that will be used If the fabric has been cut from the bolt on lines parallel to edges of the bolt as shown in sketch *a* of Figure 4-6, it will fold easily into a rectangular shape, as shown. If it has been cut from the bolt along a crosswise thread as shown in sketch *b,* manipulate (pat, smooth, and shape) the fabric to bring selvage edges together, but do not attempt to force cut edges together. The cut edges will fall together only if the fabric has been perfectly tentered; otherwise they will fall in lines similar to those illustrated. If the fabric buckles and diagonal ripples appear, shift the fabric and allow it "to do what it wants to." When the fabric is flat on the table, pin along all edges, using as many pins as are necessary to control edges (crepes and filmy sheers will require more control).

**FABRIC SELECTION AND
PREPARATION FOR CUTTING**

Special problems

Very supple fabrics Fabrics such as lining, blouse, limp sheers, Banlon, and fine crepes will require extra control to keep them in a rectangular shape for cutting. Sketch *a* in Figure 4-7 shows a method of

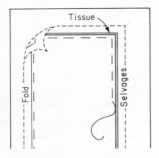

a Very limp pliable fabric held in proper position by pinning or basting to a sheet of tissue

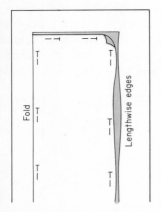

b Knit fabrics may not be rectangular, and lengthwise edges may not be straight lines

FIGURE 4-7 Special problems.

controlling these fabrics by pinning them to a piece of tissue paper; the tissue will be cut along with the fabric and discarded later.

Knit fabrics These usually do not have firm, straight lengthwise edges like the selvages in woven fabrics. These fabrics, which include polyester single and double knits of all quality and price levels, may have quite irregular lengthwise edges and the width may vary as much as 2 or more inches in different areas; see sketch *b* in Figure 4-7. These problems must be handled in the best way for each particular length of fabric by folding the fabric with the long, lengthwise edges lined up in the way that proves most satisfactory under the circumstances. When placing on pattern pieces, measure all straight-of-material lines from the straight fold line, disregarding the irregular lengthwise edges.

Chapter 5

PREPARATION OF PATTERN AND PATTERN ALTERATIONS

Preparing the pattern for cutting and making pattern alterations are basically the same for tailoring projects and sewing projects; and, as always, they necessarily delay the exciting business of cutting. However, careful attention to these details will result in tremendous savings in time and disappointment throughout every subsequent step of the tailoring process and will also ensure a finished costume of higher quality. It is true that pattern alterations require concentrated thought and careful work and that this is discouraging to some. But it is important to keep in mind that fitting corrections are far more difficult to execute and, of greater significance, that *fitting cannot remedy major problems if the pattern has not been properly altered before cutting.* Unless a muslin test copy is made, fitting must be limited to relatively subtle and minor adjustments.

MUSLIN TESTING INFLUENCES DECISIONS THROUGHOUT THE TAILORING PROCESS

Muslin-testing units of the costume before cutting provides multiple advantages by affording the following opportunities: (1) To evaluate the design as a whole—the lines themselves, total proportions, and the comfort and appeal of the costume to the wearer. Pretesting allows one to make major design changes to meet individual needs and tastes or, in the rare cases when the design proves to be unsatisfactory, to select another pattern before major expense is involved. (2) To test the accuracy and effectiveness of pattern alterations. (3) To do major fitting at a time when it is possible to make *any* correction that is indicated. (4) To transfer these fitting corrections to pattern alterations and so to revise and perfect pattern alterations before cutting fabric. (5) To test design features for placement and proportions with the subsequent advantage of doing intricate construction details in a different order than is otherwise possible. For example, after the placement of buttons and pockets has been carefully decided, these intricate details can be done more easily and accurately before the major pieces are assembled into a bulky mass. (6) To practice new and difficult construction details, a great advantage for the novice or the person who lacks confidence. (7) As a result of all these advantages, to ensure a finished costume of higher quality than would otherwise be possible.

Influences on pattern alterations
Points 2, 3, and 4 above explain that pattern alterations will be done in two steps: before the muslin is cut and, later, when fitting changes can be transferred to additional pattern alterations. This necessarily influences decisions when the initial pattern alterations are being made. If no test copy is made, the worker must make every decision very cautiously, and if in doubt, she must play it safe by being sure she has sufficient size and length. By contrast, if a muslin test copy is made, little problems can be temporarily delayed, to be decided upon after the test copy is fitted. For example, if measurements indicate that a mere 1-inch addition in width might be needed in a certain area, the extra inch *must be added* to the pattern if no test copy will be made. With a test copy if the amount involved is very small, the addition *need not be made* as a preliminary pattern alteration, but can be made later, after the muslin fitting.

The initial alterations should not be treated lightly; on the contrary, it is important that they be as accurate as possible. There will be many subtle issues to consider when the test copy is fitted; and because fitting is difficult, the fewer problems to be solved then, the better. Resolve to do an effective job now in the hope that there will be no additional changes after the muslin is fitted; do all major and obvious alterations at this time and anticipate making only subtle, small alterations in the follow-up steps after fitting the muslin test copy.

There is another way that making a test copy influences pattern alterations. If no test copy is made, pattern alterations are made on all corresponding pattern pieces at the same time; in other words, if a jacket is lengthened, the facings, interfacings, and lining pieces should be lengthened a corresponding amount immediately. But if a test copy is made, alterations are made on the major structural pieces only; then, after these alterations have been tested and perfected in the muslin test copy, corresponding pattern pieces are altered accordingly at that time.

Value of muslin-testing all units of the costume The body curves in the upper torso area vary greatly from figure to figure; and because the curves are pronounced, corresponding pattern pieces are intricately shaped. Add to this the fact that many design features are concentrated in the upper half of the figure, and it becomes apparent that the jacket or coat must be muslin-tested. By contrast it is not as necessary to muslin-test a skirt (provided it is cut amply to allow for fitting corrections) because it is cut in simpler lines, body curves are less intricate, and it usually has fewer complicating design features. However, it does not follow that any unit which fits the lower torso is relatively simple to fit; pants create great problems because, as most readers realize, pants and feminine curves are not entirely compatible. Therefore, it is as essential to muslin-test pants designs as it is to test jackets and coats.

Because a tailoring project is a learning experience—a means of reaching higher professional levels—muslin-testing *all* units of the costume is recommended. This test is written with the assumption that all units, including skirts, will be pretested. Chapter 6 (page 216) includes many effective fitting techniques which cannot be done except on a muslin copy; high standards of fit cannot be attained in any other way.

There are circumstances under which the muslin copy loses its value. If the figure is so average in size and shape that patterns and ready-made garments fit perfectly (the "straight-size" figure), there is no need to test the pattern for size and fit. If the figure is average in length as well as size, design features and proportions will be attractive. If the design is a simple one in basic lines (completely "safe," nothing to dislike), there is little reason to test its appeal to the wearer. And of course, the person with much experience needs no practice on construction details.

BASIC PREPARATIONS

1 Sort out the pattern pieces and place them in logical piles—skirt pieces, jacket or coat pieces, lining pieces, etc., together. Separate those pieces which are not required in the view to be used and put them back in the envelope. There is a statement or list of pattern pieces for each view on the layout side of the instruction sheet. Check this list very carefully.

2 Pattern pieces should be pressed with a warm iron to remove the creases; this makes for more accurate cutting. Pattern pieces should be hung over a hanger as soon as they are pressed and should not be folded again until after the fabric is cut.

3 Any pattern piece which is not cut on the fold has a straight-of-material line indicated. This straight-of-material line will be placed on the lengthwise threads of the fabric. It is indicated with a printed line about 5 to 10 inches long. It will be advantageous later if this line is as long as possible. Place a yardstick along the line and extend the straight-of-material line to the edges of the pattern on all pattern pieces, as shown in Figure 5-1.

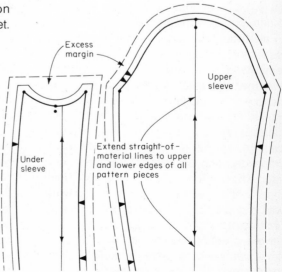

Excess margin

Upper sleeve

Under sleeve

Extend straight-of-material lines to upper and lower edges of all pattern pieces

FIGURE 5-1 Extend grainlines.

4 The excess margin of tissue, which is merely an aid in accurate cutting in the manufacturing process, need not be trimmed away; it will fall away as fabric is cut, and as a general rule one should not take time to trim it away. If the margin is very wide in a few areas, quickly trim close to the cutting line; this will make it easier to pin pattern pieces together for testing on the figure. The margins are shown in broken lines in Figure 5-1, and for the sake of clarity will not be pictured hereafter.

5 When working in a room with a group of friends or in a classroom, each worker should record her name on all pattern pieces.

Anticipate probable figure problems

Make a tentative list of figure problems which have been evident in the past; this list will be revised as scientific tests are made, but as work progresses it will serve to alert the individual (and an assistant or instructor) to trouble areas. Figure problems (which are simply variations from the average) can best be anticipated by comparisons with and knowledge of the average figure. An ability to recognize the average figure (size at various levels, contours, posture, etc.) is a tremendous advantage when deciding on pattern alterations and later when solving fitting problems. While those who have had an opportunity to work with a great number and variety of figures (instructors, professional dressmakers) have a great advantage, any woman who sews can become better acquainted with the average figure by the following means:

1 Study the body measurement charts to see comparative measurements at the various levels of the body; study the entire chart (not just one size) to see that *the average figure of any size has certain characteristics.* For example, examine the chart for the misses' figure type (page 51) and note that the average figure, in any one of eight sizes listed, has a bust measurement 8½ to 9 inches larger than the waist and a hip measurement 10½ to 11 inches larger than the waist. By comparing individual measurements with standard measurements, certain obvious figure irregularities will be revealed and the first problems can be recorded on a tentative list of expected pattern alterations.

2 Consider the fitting problems encountered in the past with home-sewn garments (from unaltered patterns) and with ready-to-wear. Ready-to-wear costumes, like patterns, are made for the average figure; and although the garments from all manufacturers are not uniformly sized (as patterns are), the general interpretation of the average figure is quite universal. If most ready-to-wear garments are too tight at the hips, not curvaceous enough at the bust, or too long-waisted, etc., record those problems on a tentative list.

3 The more subtle characteristics of the average figure (posture, typical contours, etc.) are more difficult to recognize. A dummy in any size (ideally a size in the middle range) made to standard body measurements (not a fashion dummy) reveals these characteristics most accurately; a basic dart-fitted dress, cut of heavy brown paper, taped together at the seamlines and dartlines and supported with side and center lines perpendicular to the floor, will serve as an adequate substitute. Members of the class of any size who are perfectly fitted with unaltered patterns or ready-to-wear can serve as examples of the average figure. By studying the shape and posture of these average figures, one can become sensitive to one's own figure irregularities and can add more subtle points ("my shoulders are more round than average," "my hips are flatter than average," etc.) to a tentative list of anticipated problems.

Body measurements

Two measurement-alteration charts are included: a skirt chart adaptable to shorts and pants (page 108), and a jacket or coat chart (page 107). A copy of the appropriate chart should be made for each garment to be constructed. The classroom teacher can mimeograph additional copies and make up additional charts for other types of garments to better serve the comprehensive needs of her students.

Select the appropriate chart and record body measurements in parts 1 and 3. Record standard body measurements from the chart on the pattern envelope in the designated column in part 2.

See Figure 5-2. Body measurements should be taken over the undergarments that will be worn with the costume. The tape measure should be held flat against the body for a snug but not tight measurement. The tape should be parallel to the floor. Whether someone assists with these measurements (recommended) or the individual takes her own measurements in front of the mirror, measurements will be accurate only if the body is viewed from the side to check the position of the tape in both the front and back. An assistant should work at eye level for even more accurate results. The 3-inch hipline is especially difficult to measure because of the rounded contours in this portion of the body; be very careful that the tape does not slip up in the back.

The length of the torso (from shoulder to

crotch) varies greatly in figures; most people are aware of any problems they may have in waist length but many are less sensitive to variations in length from the waist to the fullest part of the hip. By measuring the fullest part of the hip on the figure and recording the measurement from that level to the waist, the pattern can be altered for irregular figures with torsos longer or shorter than the average. Patterns in the shorter figure types (half-size, junior petite, miss petite, and young junior-teen) are made for figures with the fullest part of the hips at the 7-inch level, and pat-

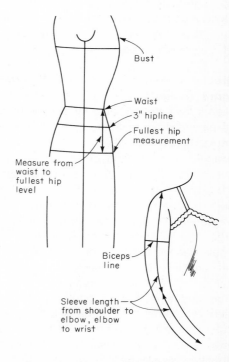

FIGURE 5-2 To take body measurements.

terns in the longer figure types (misses', women's, and juniors) are made for figures with the fullest measurement at the 9-inch level.

The biceps line is measured at the level of the base of the sleeve cap (see it pictured on sleeve patterns in Figure 5-5), and this is usually the fullest part of the arm as well. The length of the sleeve can be measured as an aid to anticipating problems of length; however, this test is less effective than testing the sleeve pattern itself on the arm because it is difficult to determine exact shoulder and elbow positions on the figure. Those who realize that the length of their arms varies greatly from the average may wish to take this measurement as an extra test; more reliable scientific tests will be made later.

Special measurements for individual figure irregularities These should be taken if they are indicated by the needs of the particular figure or the design. For example, space has been allowed on the measurement-alteration chart for a thigh measurement if a pants or shorts pattern is used; this measurement is important for those with heavy thighs, the more so if hip measurements are not correspondingly large. The following examples of figure irregularities will illustrate the possible need for additional individualized measurements: the calf if this measurement is large and a slim-fitting pants pattern is used, the midriff if this area is a problem and a snugly fitted pattern is used, and the lower arm if it is unusually large and a slim-fitted sleeve pattern is used. Space for recording these measurements can be added to either of the measurement-alteration charts.

Measurements at some levels can be eliminated for some figures and for certain designs For example, the person with very thin legs need not record a thigh measurement because she has no problem in that area, and the person with average-sized arms need not measure the biceps line of the sleeve. A great amount of style fullness in the design at the level where a figure problem exists tends to eliminate the problem, although *small amounts of style fullness definitely do not eliminate problems.* For example, the person with a roll of flesh at the 3-inch hipline will have no problem with a pattern for a full, all-around gathered skirt (two or three widths of fabric), but she must test the pattern if there are only a few gathers at the waist and the lines of the skirt are otherwise as straight and slim as a dart-fitted skirt.

Measurements can be updated by taking new measurements for each new costume This is especially important for those who sew infrequently, because figures can change without a revealing weight change. Figures of teen-age girls change quite rapidly, and the figures of adults are influenced by changes in activity, in posture, loss of height (with age), etc. Obviously changes in weight call for new measurements, the more so because the loss or gain will not usually be spread evenly over the entire body; a mere 5 pounds is serious if it occurs in one place. Changes in weight often exaggerate the same old problems because they tend to occur in problem areas; for example, the person whose bust is larger than average will probably have a greater bust problem if she gains weight, and the person with large hips will probably gain much of her extra size in the hips.

USE OF THE MEASUREMENT-
ALTERATION CHARTS

Nothing is more essential to success than a thorough understanding of sizing and of the three components of size: body size, livability (or fitting ease), and style fullness. If the expense were not prohibitive, several pages of information, given earlier when pattern sizing was discussed, would be repeated in this chapter. Before proceeding, the reader must review that information; studying it even more carefully this second time (and again just before fitting) will ensure a better understanding of these pertinent facts. One reference is the section titled "Sizing Standards of the Pattern Fashion Industry" on pages 36 to 43. The discussion of livability and style fullness and the sketches in Figure 3-1 and 3-2 are especially important. A second reference is the section titled "Pattern Selection — Size, Figure Type, Design" on pages 43 to 45 "A Critical Reevaluation of Bust Size" on page 46 is pertinent to subsequent steps of procedure.

Measurement-alteration charts are effective tools for use with basic designs which fit close to the figure — in other words, they are valuable for designs composed basically of size for the body and an allowance for livability or fitting ease, with little or no style fullness. It is impossible to plan a chart that will (in all parts and in every way) serve the needs of every conceivable design which may have style fullness in any one or all of several units. So it must be understood that the charts have limitations. However, they are valuable for two reasons: They are effective for use with the type of garment most readers will make most often and with the very type of garment which reveals fitting problems most readily. This is not to say that the charts have no value for use with designs containing style full-

ness; on the contrary, parts 1 and 2 are adaptable to any type of design. In very complicated designs with varying allowances for style fullness, part 3 (measurements of the pattern pieces) will not be useful; but fortunately the style fullness in the design will largely eliminate the need for these tests because the extra allowances will accommodate all but very exaggerated figure irregularities.

Ideally, the beginner will have worked with a simple basic design for the first several projects. By keeping a record of the alterations made on the first several costumes and making any revisions indicated during fitting, required alterations can be worked out scientifically; thereafter, for more complicated projects, the required alterations can be made without relying as heavily on measurement-alteration charts.

The charts are divided into three parts, as follows:

Part 1 Some measurements having to do with width or size can be checked by comparison with the body measurement chart on the pattern envelope. The chart includes body measurements for the bust, waist, and fullest hip level.

Part 2 Pattern measurements having to do with length and proportion are checked, not really by measurement, but by pinning the pattern together and testing it on the figure. This method is never used as a test for width or all-around size because the pattern appears to be smaller than it actually is, widthwise, when tested on the figure.

Part 3 Certain important measurements in width and all-around size must be made by measuring the pattern pieces because no comparable measurement is stated in the measurement chart; the 3-inch hipline and the biceps line of the sleeve are the most common examples.

Comparisons with the standard body measurement chart (Part 1 in the charts)

Alterations in total width or all-around size are determined by comparing recorded individual body measurements with the standard measurements for which the pattern was made. Select the standard body measurements from the proper size grouping on the body measurement chart of the pattern and record them in the appropriate column. Record required alterations by underlining "increase" or "decrease" and stating the amount in inches. *It is, of course, essential to alter the pattern to allow extra size when it is needed, but it is not necessary to decrease the pattern by pattern alteration because it can be easily taken in during fitting.* A special note in the charts states that waist measurements should not be decreased by pattern alteration. These problems can easily be taken care of during fitting, and the extra waist size provides several advantages which will become evident during the first fitting sessions.

The amounts of livability stated in the measurement-alteration charts are minimum amounts, and those who prefer a somewhat looser fit (for comfort or appearance) should allow for an extra inch of livability at each level on the figure. When estimating the amount of livability required for the all-important decision of width or overall size, keep in mind the psychological effect created by the way clothing fits. A snug fit on a large figure makes the figure look larger by revealing every curve and making it appear the person has gained weight since she made the costume; slightly more livability is much more flattering on fuller figures. By contrast, a loose fit on a very thin figure makes it appear the person has lost more weight; thin people are wise to use the minimum amounts stated in the charts and to consider taking in seams during fitting if a somewhat tighter fit is indicated.

If an alteration in length from the waist to the fullest hip level is indicated, complete that alteration before proceeding to part 2 in the charts; any change in the torso area will affect the total length of the garment, which will be determined in part 2.

NOTE: These findings will be reevaluated later. If an alteration is indicated to increase or decrease pattern pieces in width, the alteration can be done in one of two ways, depending on the needs of the individual figure. The two alternatives are discussed in "Tests for Figure Problems Involved with the Subtle Issue of Shape" on page 117.

MEASUREMENT-ALTERATION CHART FOR JACKETS AND COATS

PART 1. Check the following by comparing individual measurements with those stated in the body measurement chart

	Individual body measurements	Body measurements listed in chart	Alteration required
Bust			Increase or decrease? _____
*Waist			Increase? _____ (do not decrease by pattern alteration)
Fullest hip level			Increase or decrease? _____

* These measurements need not be taken if the jacket or coat is rectangular or boxy but they must be taken if the waist is in any way fitted, no matter how slightly.

PART 2. Check the following by pinning the pattern together and testing on the figure

	Alteration required
Front waist length (level of waistline markings on pattern)	Lengthen or shorten above waist? _____
Position of underarm or French dart	Raise or lower? _____
*Back waist length (level of waistline markings on pattern)	Lengthen or shorten above waist? _____
Total sleeve length (with hem allowance pinned in place)	Lengthen or shorten? _____
Position of elbow dart	Raise or lower? _____
Length of jacket or coat (with hem allowance pinned in place)	Lengthen or shorten? _____
Position of pockets	Raise or lower? _____

* These measurements need not be taken if the jacket or coat is rectangular or boxy but they must be taken if the waist is in any way fitted, no matter how slightly.

PART 3. Check the following by measuring the pattern pieces

	Individual body measurement	Measurement required	Measurement of pattern	Alteration required
*3-inch hipline		Your body measurement plus at least 2 inches is _____		Increase or decrease? _____
Biceps line of of sleeve		Your body measurement plus at least 2 inches is _____		Increase or decrease? _____

* These measurements need not be taken if the jacket or coat is rectangular or boxy but they must be taken if the waist is in any way fitted, no matter how slightly.

MEASUREMENT-ALTERATION CHART FOR SKIRTS, PANTS, AND SHORTS

PART 1. Check the following by comparing individual measurements with those stated in the body measurement chart

	Individual body measurement	Body measurements listed in chart	Alteration required
Waist			Increase? _____ (do not decrease by pattern alteration)
Fullest hip level			Increase or decrease? _____
Length from waist to fullest hip level		9″ below waist for misses', women's and junior figure types, 7″ below waist for other figure types	Lengthen or shorten? _____

PART 2. Check the following by pinning the pattern together and testing on the figure

	Alteration required
Length of garment (with hem allowance pinned in place)	Lengthen or shorten? _____
For pants or shorts, retest length of crotch seam	Lengthen or shorten? _____

PART 3. Check the following by measuring the pattern pieces

	Individual body measurement	Measurement required	Measurement of pattern	Alteration required
3-inch hipline		Your body measurement plus at least 1″ is _____		Increase or decrease? _____
Thigh measurement 2 inches below croctch (for pants or shorts only)		Your body measurement plus at least 2″ is _____		Increase or decrease? _____

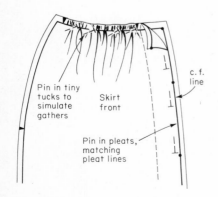

Jacket
back

Clip to seamlines
at neck edges

Turn under seam
allowance, lap
seamlines, and pin

Fold facing
to inside
along
foldline

Jacket
front

c. f. line

Pin in
darts

Pin up hem
allowance

Pin in tiny
tucks to
simulate
gathers

Skirt
front

c. f.
line

Pin in pleats,
matching
pleat lines

FIGURE 5-3 *Pin pattern pieces together for testing on the figure.*

Tests on the figure (Part 2 in the charts)

Pin sections of the pattern together

This is done as shown in the examples in Figure 5-3. Testing can be more effectively done by testing small units at a time. Make no attempt to pin an entire costume together unless the lines of the design demand it. Pin the skirt or pants unit together, test on the figure, and record all findings in the measurement-alteration chart. Do not pin sleeves into the jacket or coat (unless the sleeve is cut in one with the major pattern pieces). Pin sleeve sections together, test and record findings, and then proceed to test the jacket or coat. Pin seams and darts in place by turning under one edge on the seamline or dartline and lapping it to the corresponding line as shown. If the piece includes a self-facing, turn it to the inside along the fold line, as shown in the jacket front. If the neckline is high, clip into the seamline so the pattern can be properly fitted on the figure. If the design is cut in slim lines with little or no style fullness, do not pin side seamlines together; if these seams are pinned, the pattern will not reach around the figure to allow center lines to fall in proper position.

If there are pleats (see the skirt front), crease along a pleat line, fold it in place as indicated on the pattern, and pin it down to the level to which it will be stitched; pin in style tucks in the same manner. If there are gathers, fold in or crush in tiny little tucks until that edge measures the same as the corresponding seamline (the gathered edge in the skirt front between the notches must be the same length as the corresponding edge of the waistband). For help in assembling pieces, follow the order of construction on the instruction sheet. Pin up hem allowances on all pattern pieces; if no hemline is indicated, look for a note stating the width of the hem allowance.

Remember that tests on the figure are used for deciding issues of length or levels of darts and trimming lines (pocket position, lines for band trims) and other matters of proportion, but figure tests are not suitable for judging total width or all-around size.

Tests on the figure should be done over the undergarments to be worn with the costume. For greatest accuracy, an assistant is needed. As an aid to indicating waist position accurately, wrap a piece of twill tape or grosgrain ribbon very snugly around the waist so it will support pattern pieces. The lower edge of the tape indicates the waist position.

To locate units on the figure for testing To test units on the upper torso, have an assistant locate units on the figure, being sure the shoulderline of the pattern (usually a shoulder seam, but it may be a line indicated on the pattern piece) is placed on top of the shoulder. Secure the pattern in place by pinning through the bra straps at the shoulder and by using one pin through the bra itself near the center front and center back.

To test units on the lower torso, place the waist seamline of the pattern along the lower edge of the tape, with center lines falling at the center of the figure. Support the unit with a few pins through the tape at the waistline and one pin through the girdle or panties near the center front and back at about the hip level.

To test separate sleeve units, slip the sleeve on the arm and attempt to locate the seamline of the sleeve cap at about the position of the armhole seam in the finished garment. It must be understood that having to estimate that position creates an unavoidable margin of error, but the error will be slight and can be corrected during fitting.

Test for skirts and pants Be sure hem allowances are pinned up along the hemlines and that units are supported at the waistline.

1 Study the pattern lines on the figure to see that the fullest part of the pattern falls at the level of the fullest part of the hips. This matter was taken care of in part 1 of the chart; and if a change was indicated, the alteration should have been done before proceeding with these tests. Study the effect to see that the amount of alteration is correct; if it is not, revise it at this time. The fullest, most shapely hip curve on the pattern should be at a level of the corresponding curve on the figure, and the fitting darts should end at a level just slightly above the fullest part of the hips so as to create shape where it is required.

2 If the fullest hip level of the pattern is in proper position on the figure, the crotch level in pants should be correct. In typical pants designs (in which the level of the crotch is visible as the garment is worn), the crotch seam should fall about 1½ inches below the body test by tucking the pattern between the legs or by comparing measurements with a favorite pair of pants in the wardrobe. However, if the crotch seam will be hidden from view by a feature of the design, the garment will be more comfortable if the crotch seam falls somewhat lower. The seam must fall several inches below the body if the design is a one-piece garment (top and pants combined in a jump suit) to allow extra length for comfortable sitting. Designs in which the crotch seam will be hidden from view and can fall somewhat lower on the body are culottes with center pleats (or an overlap or partial-skirt feature), very full gathered or flared culottes or pants, and pants which will be worn with long tunic tops and jackets.

3 To decide on the length of the garment, study the effect to see that the length is fashionable and flattering to the figure. Experiment with various lengths at this time. Record the alteration required on the chart by underlining "lengthen" or "shorten" and stating the desired increase or decrease. Be sure to allow sufficient length; the garment can easily be shortened later. One word of warning: if the skirt or pants will be cut of plaid, checked, or crosswise striped fabric, the finished length must be very accurately established at this time; see cutting directions for these fabrics on page 480.

4 If there are small units of design (pockets, flaps, etc.) test them for placement and proportions at this time; refer to directions on the opposite page.

NOTE: **Keep the skirt sections pinned together for additional tests which will indicate figure problems having to do with the subtle issue of shape; these problems, along with similiar ones which may be evident in the jacket or coat, are discussed on page 117.**

Tests for the sleeve unit Slip the sleeve on the arm and have an assistant support it with the seamline in the sleeve cap in the armhole-seam position.

1 If the sleeve is fitted, shape is created either with an elbow dart or with shaping in seams. For comfort and appearance, maximum shaping must be located at the elbow level on the figure. Bend the arm slightly to reveal the elbow position better. Indicate the required alteration by underlining "raise" or "lower" and stating the amount in inches.

By shortening the pattern in the area above the elbow, shaping will be located higher on the figure; by lengthening the pattern above the elbow level, it will be at a lower level.

2 Pin up the hem allowance or, if there is a cuff, pin it in position. Study the total length of the sleeve. If it is a long sleeve, it should end at the bend of the wrist when the arm is held close to the body at waist level. If it is a free-hanging sleeve, the issue is one of personal preference and pleasing proportions on the figure. Record changes in the "alteration required" column.

Tests for the jacket or coat As an aid to studying proportions accurately, test jacket patterns over a skirt (or pants) comparable in lines and length to the one which will be worn with the jacket. Test full-length coat patterns over a dress about the length of most garments which will be worn with the coat; the coat should be at least 1 inch longer than those garments.

1 Test the waist level on the figure and make any alteration required to bring the waist level of the pattern to the proper level on the figure before proceeding with tests for overall length. With the pattern supported properly at the shoulder and with center lines centered on the figure, smooth the pattern over the front and bust area. Differences in length will vary somewhat from center to side, but it is the difference directly below the bust which is most revealing; record any difference in the column titled "alteration required" on the measurement charts by underlining "shorten" or "lengthen" and stating the amount in inches. Go through a comparable test on the back, comparing and recording the differences between the waist markings and the lower edge of the tape in the area below the shoulder blades. Do not expect that alterations will be identical in the front and back; they are frequently different, and some figures may even require that one piece be shortened and the other lengthened.

Very careful and accurate alterations for correcting waist length are absolutely essential in fitted garments with snug-fitting waists; in these designs, variations of ¼ inch are significant. By contrast, the position of the waist is of no consequence in completely boxy garments. However, many inexperienced sewers encounter serious problems because they do not test and correct the waist position in semi-fitted garments like the jacket shown in Figure 5-5. The subtle shaping at the waist in these garments must be located properly on the figure and alterations for correcting waist length are definitely required; a variation of ¼ inch will not be as significant if the garment is semi-fitted, but the waist level cannot be ignored even if the garment is fitted only slightly.

2 Darts create shape for body curves. The bust dart, which fits the most pronounced curve of the figure, must be very accurately located to produce shape very close to the bust point. The tips of darts indicate the position where shape will be created and the tip must be located near (but not exactly at) the high point of the curve, with the dartline pointing to the high point of the curve. Estimate the difference between the level of the darts and the bust level on the figure and record the alteration on the measurement chart by underlining "raise" or "lower" and stating the amount in inches.

3 To decide on the length of the garment. study the effect to see that the length is fashionable and flattering to the figure. Experiment with various lengths at this time. Record the alteration required on the chart by underlining "lengthen" or "shorten" and stating the desired change. Be sure to allow sufficient length; the garment can easily be shortened later. One word of warn-

ing: if the jacket or coat will be cut of plaid, checked, or crosswise striped fabric, the finished length must be very accurately established at this time; see cutting directions for these fabrics on page 480. Complete any alteration required before proceeding to the next test.

4 Check the position and level of small design units and details to see that they create attractive proportions on the figure. Band trims, pockets, or pocket flaps, and other decorative design details are located on the pattern at the most attractive position and level for the average figure; therefore, they will not be ideally positioned if the pattern has been altered for a tall or short figure. If any unit has been shortened, pocket positions and trimming lines will probably need to be raised, and conversely, if the unit has been lengthened, they may need to be lowered. Experiment by moving triming pieces to the level which creates the most flattering proportions on the particular figure and make a note to move the pattern lines and markings accordingly.

NOTE: **Keep the pattern sections pinned together for additional tests which have to do with the subtle issue of shape; these tests are discussed on page 117.**

Tests made by measuring pattern pieces (Part 3 in the charts)

These tests are not required for all individuals, but they are of paramount importance for those with certain special figure problems. Because measurements at some levels are not included in the standard body-measurement charts, tests must be made by measuring the pattern pieces. In every case, problems at these levels will not necessarily be revealed by any other measurements; for example, a person may need no alteration at either the waist or the fullest hip level, and yet she may require a sizeable alteration at the 3-inch hip level.

Pattern pieces are measured to determine the *finished size of the garment—the size of the garment after seams and darts are sewn and pleats and tucks, etc., are held in place.* Some typical patterns are shown in Figures 5-4 and 5-5. In the sketches, the seam allowances, darts, and pleats have been shaded to point out portions of the pattern that are not a part of the *finished size;* pay close attention to the arrowheads in all sketches.

In preparation for taking measurements, place the pieces on the table in proper order with corresponding seamlines close together, as illustrated in the two complete skirt patterns in Figure 5-4 and the two-piece sleeve and jacket pieces in Figure 5-5; pattern pieces are illustrated in a similar logical order in a chart on the instruction sheet. Note that measurements do not include seam allowances, darts, pleats, or any extension beyond center lines (illustrated by the back skirt pleat in Figure 5-4 and the jacket front in Figure 5-5).

The 3-inch hipline A variety of figure irregularities can create problems at this level: plump figures with pads of fat directly below the waist in either the front or back or both, figures with a "pot" tummy, and thin figures with prominent hipbones are examples.

Figures 5-4 and 5-5 illustrate examples of basic garments with typical fashion details. The basic principles are illustrated on the two complete skirt patterns. The lower sketches in Figure 5-4 illustrate that when small amounts of style fullness are involved in a close-fitting skirt, the style fullness must be folded in before taking measurements. Loose pleats (somewhat like fitting darts) which are held in by the waistline seam or stitched down only an inch or so below the waist must be folded in place and allowed to form a dart-like pleat ending at the level indicated on the fashion sketch. Gathers (which substitute for fitting darts) should be crushed and tucked in place, allowing them to taper off at the level indicated on the fashion sketch. Note that the 3-inch measurement is taken with the style fullness folded in; in this way, one is assured of sufficient body size and livability allowance while retaining style fullness to create the proper design effect.

The biceps line of the sleeve The problem of heavy upper arms is most prevalent among older women, although it is not necessarily confined to that group. Women with larger-than-average arms in an all-around way, those with pads of fat in the back only, and very muscular, athletic women may encounter problems of inadequate sleeve size or width.

Figure 5-5 illustrates the basic principles of measurement on a typical one-piece sleeve; the biceps line is at the level of the seamline at the underarm and is perpendicular to the straight-of-material line. When

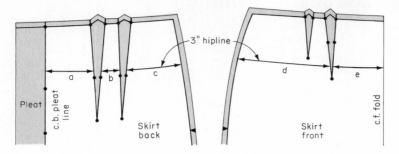

Segments a + b + c + d + e, doubled = finished size

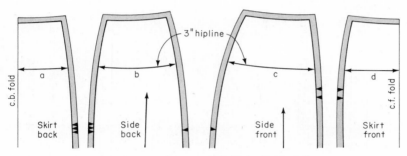

Segments a + b + c + d, doubled = finished size

When style fullness of
loose pleats, tucks, or
gathers is involved, take
measurement with style
fullness folded in.

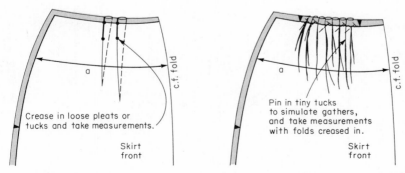

Crease in loose pleats or
tucks and take measurements.

Pin in tiny tucks
to simulate gathers,
and take measurements
with folds creased in.

Line a, doubled = finished size of front skirt   Line a, doubled = finished size of front skirt

FIGURE 5-4   *To measure a pattern at the 3-inch hipline.*

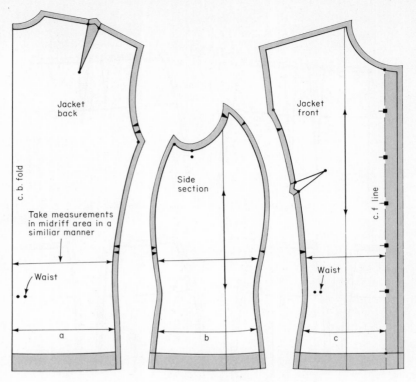

Jacket
back

c. b. fold

Take measurements
in midriff area in a
similiar manner

Waist

a

Side
section

b

Jacket
front

c. f line

Waist

c

Segments a + b + c, doubled = finished size

To measure the 3 - inch hipline of jackets or coats.

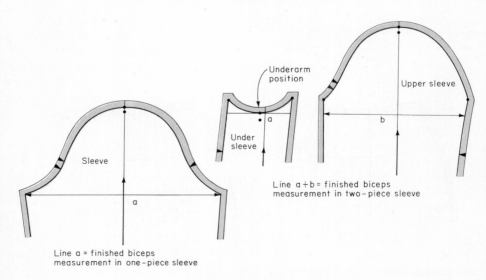

Sleeve

a

Line a = finished biceps
measurement in one - piece sleeve

Underarm
position

Under
sleeve

a

Upper sleeve

b

Line a + b = finished biceps
measurement in two - piece sleeve

To measure the biceps line of the sleeve.

FIGURE 5-5   To take pattern measurements.

working with a two-piece sleeve, draw the line on the under-sleeve section first and then establish the line at the corresponding level on the upper-sleeve section, as shown.

Individual problems Women with large thighs should go through similar tests when working with shorts or pants patterns. Measure the thigh about 2 inches below the crotch and take a corresponding pattern measurement. The livability allowance should be at least 2 inches. Record the required alteration in the space allowed on the charts.

Additional measurements can be taken wherever individual figure problems are anticipated. The woman with a roll of fat above the waist should make similar tests in the midriff area, allowing a minimum of 2 inches for livability in addition to her body size; the method of measurement is illustrated in Figure 5-5. The woman with a larger lower arm should make tests at that level if the sleeve is closely fitted, allowing a minimum of 1 inch for livability in addition to her arm size.

Tests for figure problems involved with the subtle issue of shape

In part 1 of the charts, individual measurements were compared with the standard body measurements of the pattern and the necessary changes were recorded in the "alteration required" column. Alterations in width of pattern pieces (circumference of the figure) can be made in two distinctly different ways, and the choice of the most effective method is dependent on the individual figure. If the figure is quite average in shape but is larger or smaller in an overall way (front, back, and all-around), the alteration must be made on the front and back units of the pattern. For example, the figure with slightly fuller-than-average

hips (about 2 inches) usually has extra padding in both the front and back and requires an equal amount of extra width in both the front and back units of the pattern. "Alterations to Change the All-Around Width or Size of the Pattern" on page 144 are appropriate for this type of problem.

By contrast, the curves of the figure may vary from the average; if the figure requires a change in width at the bust level, the problem is usually centered on the shape of the bust curve itself—in other words, the problem exists in the front of the figure only. Review "A Critical Reevaluation of Bust Size" on page 46. Because bust curves vary more from figure to figure than other body curves, bust alterations are most often required in the front only; directions in "Alterations to Create More Shape for Larger-than-Average Curves" on page 163 and "Alterations to Create Less Shape for Smaller-than-Average Curves" on page 193 are effective for this type of problem. There are other figure irregularities which require a change in shape of one unit; for example, the figure with protruding hips requires a major alteration in the back only, where the problem originates.

In general, if the curves of the figure are quite average, alterations are made in an overall, all-around way by altering the front and back units, and if a curve of the figure differs from that of the average figure, the alteration is made on the one unit where the problem curve appears. The choice of method can best be decided by comparing the figure with the straight-size, average figure; review "Anticipate Probable Figure Problems" on page 102. The following tests on the figure will help to decide ten-

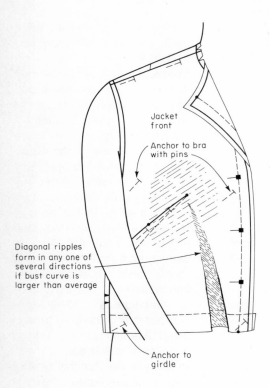

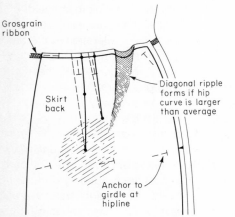

*FIGURE 5-6 Pattern tests to study the shape
of body curves.*

tatively on the best method; after the muslin
test copy is fitted, the decision can be revised, if necessary.

See Figure 5-6. Pin units together but do
not pin side seamlines together unless there
is a considerable amount of style fullness
involved. Support pieces in the proper
position with center lines centered on the
figure and with shoulder and waistlines
located properly. Anchor the pieces to the
figure, adding extra pins to anchor jacket
or coat pieces in the shoulder area and
along the hipline and to anchor skirt or
pants pieces along the hipline and side
edge.

**If curves of the figure are quite aver-
age** In this case, all outside edges of the
pattern will lie smoothly over the body; this
indicates that any alteration in width (or
circumference) should be made by altering
both the front and back units of the pattern
according to directions on page 144. Add a
note to the measurement charts to designate the alteration for "both front and back."

**If curves of the figure are smaller or
flatter than average** In this case, all
outside edges of the pattern will lie smoothly
over the body, but the pattern will stand
away from the high point of the problem
curve because the body curve does not fill
out the shape created by the pattern; this
indicates that any alteration in width (or
circumference) should be made in the unit
where the problem curve exists according
to directions on page 193. Add a note to
the measurement charts to designate the
alteration for "front only" or "back only."

**If curves of the figure are larger or
more curvaceous than average** In
this case, all outside edges of the pattern
will not fit snugly to the figure and diagonal
ripples will appear as illustrated in Figure

5-6. The sketches show patterns on a figure with a larger-than-average bust and a larger-than-average hip curve (probably a result of protruding hips caused by faulty posture); these are two of the common problems. The ripples may appear in one or more directions, but they will always radiate from the high point of the larger-than-average curve. The ripple in the pattern is a sure indication that the body curve is more curvaceous than average, because the ripple forms into a dart and thus tends to create additional shape to fit the curvaceous figure. This indicates that the alteration in width (or circumference) should be done according to directions on page 163. Add a note to the measurement chart to designate the alteration for "front only" or "back only."

INTRODUCTION TO PATTERN ALTERATIONS

If a pattern is purchased in the correct size and figure type, pattern alterations can be kept to a minimum. The alterations included here are those which (1) are required most frequently and (2) can be executed without danger of destroying the accuracy of the pattern. When making pattern alterations it is wise to play if safe. This does not mean that it is wise to cut a pattern far too large or too long, but it does mean that it is far better to make it a little larger and a little longer when making first projects and before individual needs are accurately established. Many women resist adding size to a pattern, often insisting they will not need it (a statement rarely fortified by fact). This is such a foolish mistake; it is so much better to add some size to the pattern as a safety measure and then baste the muslin copy, if desired, along the original seamline of the pattern. If a test copy or a garment is too small when basted for a fitting, it takes

two or three times more effort and time to make it larger than it takes to fit in a garment that is too large. The saving in time is only one issue; if seams in a finished garment are let out, it is not as serviceable.

Keeping records of pattern alterations and their effectiveness is the way to perfect individual requirements. If this is done for several garments, accurate requirements will be established to such an extent that one need not go through any of the pattern measurement steps.

Many people consider pattern alteration confusing and difficult because they make the mistake of thinking of each alteration as a separate problem, unrelated to any other. *There are several types of alterations (to alter length, to alter width, to create more or less shape, etc.), but the basic rules or principles of each type of alteration can be applied and modified for use on a great variety of designs and on any unit (skirt, jacket, sleeve, etc.) of those designs to correct the figure irregularities (or combination of figure irregularities) of the individual.* The secret to success is in understanding basic rules or principles thoroughly and applying them to individual problems of figure and design. One must train oneself to use the very logical basic principles innovatively.

The alterations in this chapter are organized under several types (to alter length, to alter width, etc.). The principles or rules are explained on basic, relatively simple pattern pieces, and it is important to master these rules before undertaking the alteration of more difficult or complicated patterns. Following the presentation of basic rules, a group of other pattern pieces (different units of the garment, different designs, or different types of garments) are shown altered in a similar manner; it is hoped this presentation of material will suggest possibilities for application and will enable the reader to apply basic principles creatively.

Basic rules

Basic rules are illustrated in the pattern pieces for a bolero (including facing and lining pieces but not including the sleeve pattern) in Figure 5-7. The alterations pictured (to add length and to correct the pattern for square shoulders) will be explained later; it is not important at this time to understand the alteration itself—concentrate on the basic rules involved.

1 When alterations are illustrated in a text or on the instruction sheet, only the major pattern pieces are pictured (the front and back bolero pieces in the sketch, for example). *The first basic rule: All corresponding pieces must be altered to correspond with the alterations on the major piece.* See the shoulder edges of the facing and lining pieces and note that they have been altered like the major pieces; corresponding pieces have been altered at the lower edge like the major pieces. To ensure accuracy, work should proceed in the following order: First alter the major pieces and verify results by testing on the figure; then baste and fit the muslin test copy and revise the alterations on the major pieces if corrections are indicated; then alter the corresponding pieces in the same manner. Place the altered piece flat on the table and place all corresponding pieces over it with corresponding cut edges even and make identical alterations on all corresponding pieces. By stacking the pieces together again,

work can be verified for accuracy. One word of caution: It is easy to forget very small and narrow pieces or small design units such as band trims, etc. Sort through all the pattern pieces to be sure every piece, no matter how small, is altered like the major pieces.

2 Additions or extensions on the pattern (the addition to shoulder height and the addition in length shown in the sketch) are shown with diagonal lines in all sketches in this chapter. They are made by adding a strip of paper to the edge and taping it in place with "Magic" transparent tape. Use several small lengths of tape about 1 inch long—never one long strip. The alteration is then drawn on the extension strip and the excess paper trimmed away (sketches show the alteration after excess paper has been trimmed off).

The second basic rule: Additions or extensions should be made by taping an extension strip to the edge involved. It is a temptation to use the extra margin for sketching in additions or extensions on the tissue pattern; this is not a wise practice for several reasons. The margin is not a consistent width and it will not always be wide enough on all edges. The greater danger is that one is so accustomed to cutting along the darkest, most prominent line of the pattern that one may not notice a light pencil line on the margin. If the margin is used for these additions, use a ball-point pen and quickly sketch in extra shading lines to make the addition very prominent.

3 *The third basic rule: Altered patterns must have the same character as the original pattern piece.* They will not be identical, of course, but the general outline and the appearance of altered lines must be such that the pattern looks very comparable to the original. Compare the outlines of the altered pattern pieces in Figure 5-7 with the originals to see that the original character has been retained; for example, the

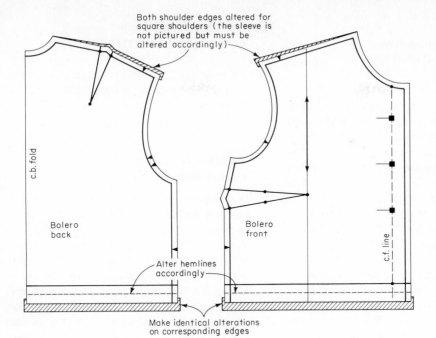

Both shoulder edges altered for square shoulders (the sleeve is not pictured but must be altered accordingly)

c.b. fold

Bolero back

Bolero front

c.f. line

Alter hemlines accordingly

Make identical alterations on corresponding edges

First alter major pattern pieces

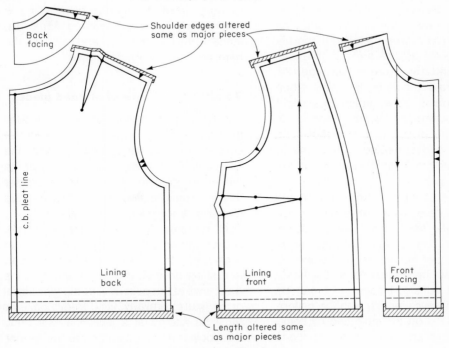

Shoulder edges altered same as major pieces

Back facing

c.b. pleat line

Lining back

Lining front

Front facing

Length altered same as major pieces

Then alter all corresponding pieces

FIGURE 5-7 Basic rules of pattern alteration.

character of the original cutting lines at the lower edges was that they were ruler-straight and perpendicular to center lines on the pattern, and the altered lines have the same character. See the lengthened skirt pattern in Figure 5-8. The original curved character of the cutting line on the skirt has been retained; the altered line, measured an equal distance from that line, has the same curved character.

4 Pattern alterations often slightly distort one or more edges of a pattern, as will be apparent in the first and most simple-to-execute group of alterations. The distortions are unavoidable and, with experience, the worker will learn to expect them. They are not mistakes but they must be corrected. *The fourth basic rule (actually an extension of the third rule): Correct distortions on altered patterns to give the altered line the same character as the original line.* See sketches *b* and *d* in Figure 5-9 on page 124, which picture one type of distortion. When the jacket front is altered in length, a slight distortion appears on any line which is not parallel to the grainline. The distortion is evened out and corrected with a line in character with the original, as shown in the dashed line in sketch *d*.

5 *The fifth fundamental rule: The altered pattern must be perfectly flat (flat as a piece of paper), like the original pattern piece.* If the pattern buckles even slightly, the alteration has been inaccurately done and the pattern cannot be pinned flat to the fabric for accurate cutting. Inaccuracies can be avoided by always working with the pattern smooth and flat on the table and by being sure that taped-on additions or insertions allow the pattern to remain flat.

TWO METHODS OF ALTERING LENGTH

There are two methods of altering pattern length; the choice, an important one, is dependent on the shape of the pattern pieces involved.

To alter the length of rectangular pieces

See Figures 5-7 and 5-8. If the pattern piece is rectangular or nearly rectangular in shape near its lower edge, it can be altered by merely adding to or trimming from the lower edge, as shown in the bolero pieces in Figure 5-7 and the skirt pieces in Figure 5-8. The piece need not be perfectly rectangular; the slight curve at the lower edge of the skirt pattern illustrated does not keep it from being considered nearly rectangular. This method is very simple to execute, involving merely establishing a new cutting line measured an equal distance from the original, and moving the hemline accordingly, as shown.

To alter the length of shaped pieces

The jacket pattern in Figure 5-8 illustrates the proper method of altering the length of shaped pieces. If pieces are shaped, the alteration must be made in the body of the pattern in order to preserve the character of the original pattern lines. This method also allows for altering the pattern at any level required for the individual figure. Jacket and coat pieces must be altered in such a way that the waist level of the pattern shifts position in such a way that the waist level of the pattern is at the waist level of the figure; similarly, fitted sleeve patterns must be altered at a level that will bring the elbow level of the pattern to the proper level on the arm. Note that the total length

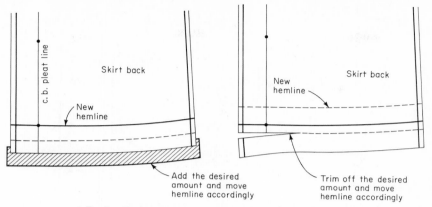

c.b. pleat line

Skirt back

New hemline

Add the desired amount and move hemline accordingly

New hemline

Skirt back

Trim off the desired amount and move hemline accordingly

a To alter the length of rectangular or nearly rectangular pieces.

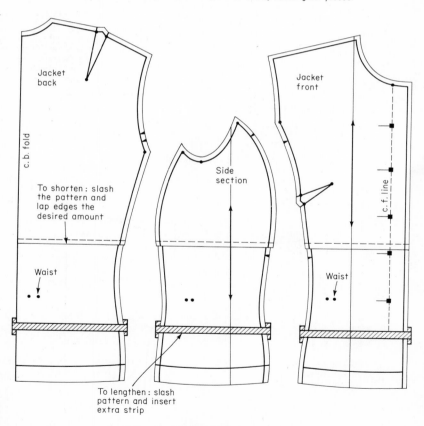

Jacket back

c.b. fold

To shorten: slash the pattern and lap edges the desired amount

Waist

Side section

Jacket front

c.f. line

Waist

To lengthen: slash pattern and insert extra strip

b To alter the length of shaped pieces.

FIGURE 5-8   *To alter the length of shaped pieces.*

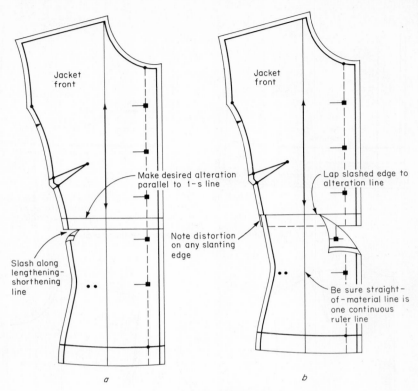

Jacket front

Make desired alteration parallel to ↑–s line

Note distortion on any slanting edge

Slash along lengthening–shorthening line

Jacket front

Lap slashed edge to alteration line

Be sure straight–of–material line is one continuous ruler line

a

b

To shorten shaped pattern pieces.

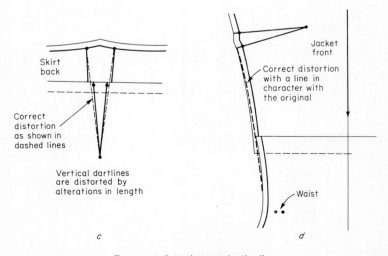

Skirt back

Correct distortion as shown in dashed lines

Vertical dartlines are distorted by alterations in length

Jacket front

Correct distortion with a line in character with the original

Waist

c

d

To correct distortions on slanting lines.

FIGURE 5-9   *Basic rules for shortening shaped pattern pieces.*

of jacket pieces in Figure 5-8 has not been changed (it could be lengthened if the figure required more length); the pattern has been shortened above the waist to correct the waist level and lengthened below the waist by the same amount. The alteration illustrated has served one purpose only: to correct the waist level.

Because the jacket pieces pictured are not intricately shaped below the waist (they are nearly rectangular), any alteration in length, especially if it is small, could be made by the method recommended for rectangular pieces.

To establish lengthening-shortening lines on shaped pieces A lengthening and shortening line appears on most shaped pattern pieces; this line usually appears at right angles to the center line or the straight-of-material line. There are a few exceptions (the sleeve portion if the sleeve is cut in one with the major pieces, for example) when it is drawn in a logical position which is not at right angles to center lines or grainlines. If the pattern must be altered in an area where no alteration line is indicated, establish a sensible, logical line either at right angles to center lines or straight-of-material lines or in some other logical position.

To shorten shaped pieces The basic rules are illustrated in Figure 5-9. See sketch *a*. Draw a line parallel to the lengthening-shortening line on the pattern to mark off the desired decrease in length. The lines must be parallel to ensure that the straight-of-material line in the altered pattern will be in proper position for cutting. Slash along the lengthening-shortening line and lap the cut edge to the remaining line, matching grainlines in the two segments as shown. Check with a yardstick to see that the two segments of the grainline form one continuous ruler-straight line. Tape in place.

Note the distortion at one edge of the pattern in sketch *b*. Any line on the pattern which is not parallel to the straight-of-material line will be slightly distorted when the pattern is altered in length; the front edge which is parallel to the straight-of-material line will not be distorted. The distortions are usually slight, and they become more obvious if the pattern line is very slanted or the alteration is very large. These distortions are not mistakes, but they must be corrected by evening out the line to make it in character with the original pattern line. See the enlarged view of the jacket front pattern in sketch *d*. The heavy dashed line between the dart level and the waist corrects the distortion with a line comparable to the original. Although the original line may appear to be ruler-straight, it may be very slightly curved, in which case the corrected cutting line should be drawn in a similar slight curve.

See sketch *c*. If the pattern is shortened in an area where there are vertical darts, the dartlines will be slightly distorted and must be corrected with lines which retain the character of the original lines. If the dartlines were ruler-straight, they should be corrected with ruler lines, as shown in the sketch; if the dartlines were originally curved, the corrected lines should be curved. Note that the dart markings at the pattern edge and at the dart tip are retained; any markings between those two levels will be slightly out of line and must be shifted over to the corrected lines (not illustrated).

**PREPARATION OF PATTERN
AND PATTERN ALTERATIONS**

Figure 5-10 pictures other pattern pieces shortened by following these basic rules which can be applied (at any level) to any shaped pattern piece.

To lengthen shaped pieces The basic rules are pictured in Figure 5-11. See

sketch *a.* Slash the pattern along the lengthening-shortening line. Draw parallel lines on a strip of paper to mark off the desired increase in length; the lines must be parallel to ensure that the straight-of-material lines in the altered piece will be in proper position for cutting. Tape the upper section of the pattern over the insertion strip, matching the cut edge to a ruler line. Place a ruler along the straight-of-material line and extend that line on the insertion strip.

See sketch *b.* Mount the lower section

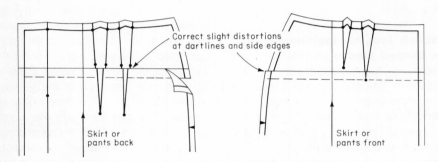

To shorten skirt or pants pieces for the figure with a short torso.

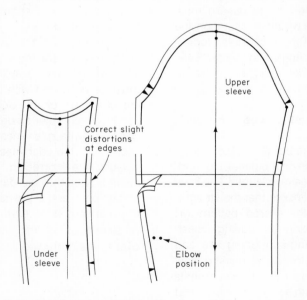

To shorter a two-piece sleeve for the figure with a short upper arm.

FIGURE 5-10 Basic principles applied to other shaped pieces.

on the insertion strip, placing the cut edge along the remaining ruler line and matching the straight-of-material lines in the position shown. Check with a yardstick to see that grainlines in the two sections form one continuous ruler-straight line. Tape in place. Note the distortion at the slanting edge of the pattern in sketch *b*. Any line on the pattern which is not parallel to the straight-of-material line will be slightly distorted when the pattern is altered in length; note that the front edge, which is parallel to the grainline, is not distorted. The distortions are less obvious to the eye when the pattern is lengthened (rather than shortened), but they are there and must be corrected; the correction is shown in a heavy dashed line on the sketch. Read the text accompanying sketches *c* and *d* in Figure 5-9 for additional instructions.

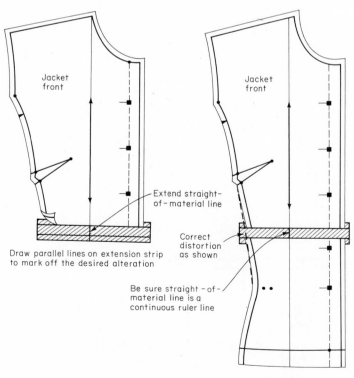

FIGURE 5-11 Basic rules for lengthening shaped pattern pieces.

Figure 5-12 pictures other pattern pieces lengthened by following basic rules which can be applied (at any level) to any shaped pattern piece.

Apply basic rules of both methods, combining methods to solve specific problems of figure or design The figure and design problems shown in Figure 5-13 illustrate applications of the basic principles. Problem *a* pictures a shaped pattern piece altered differently at two different levels; it is included to point out that the arm may be longer than average in one

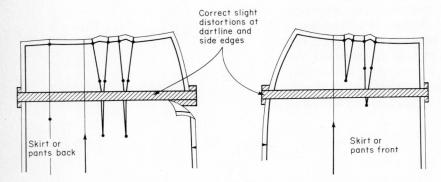

Correct slight distortions at dartline and side edges

Skirt or pants back

Skirt or pants front

To lengthen patterns for the figure with a long torso.

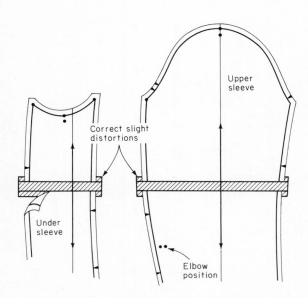

Upper sleeve

Correct slight distortions

Under sleeve

Elbow position

To lengthen a two-piece sleeve for the figure with a long upper arm.

FIGURE 5-12   Basic principles applied to other shaped patterns.

segment and shorter than average in the other.

Problem *b* shows a similar problem, but in this case, because the upper part of the piece is shaped and the lower part is rectangular, both methods of altering length have been employed on one pattern piece. This figure has a long torso and the pattern must be lengthened (by the method appropriate for shaped pieces) to bring the full hip level of the pattern into proper position on the figure. After this alteration is made, tests on the figure reveal that the skirt must be shortened; this indicates that the figure

has a long torso and short legs. The excess is shown trimmed from the lower edge and the hemline raised accordingly by the simpler method appropriate for rectangular pieces. A short pleat is included to illustrate an additional correction necessary to ensure sufficient pleat length when a skirt pattern is shortened by trimming from the lower edge. The length of the extension

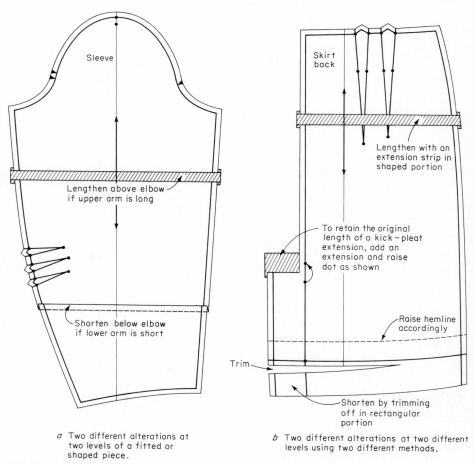

Sleeve

Lengthen above elbow
if upper arm is long

Shorten below elbow
if lower arm is short

Skirt
back

Lengthen with an
extension strip in
shaped portion

To retain the original
length of a kick—pleat
extension, add an
extension and raise
dot as shown

Raise hemline
accordingly

Trim

Shorten by trimming
off in rectangular
portion

a Two different alterations at
two levels of a fitted or
shaped piece.

b Two different alterations at two different
levels using two different methods.

FIGURE 5-13 *Apply basic principles of both methods to solve specific problems of figure, design, or both.*

for a vent closing in jackets and coats is adjusted the same as the pleat extension illustrated.

Problem *c* in Figure 5-13 is included to point out that each design must be studied carefully to determine which of the two methods is most effective. This problem further illustrates that knowing and understanding basic rules will enable one to re-

vise rules under certain circumstances. The jacket pieces shown are rectangular in shape and, according to the basic rule, can be altered to the lower edge as shown in the jacket back. But the proportions of the design lines on the jacket front would be destroyed if the total alteration were made at the lower edge; therefore part of the front alteration is made above the style line, using the method for shaped pattern pieces. Note that the total increase on the jacket back equals the combined alterations on the jacket front sections.

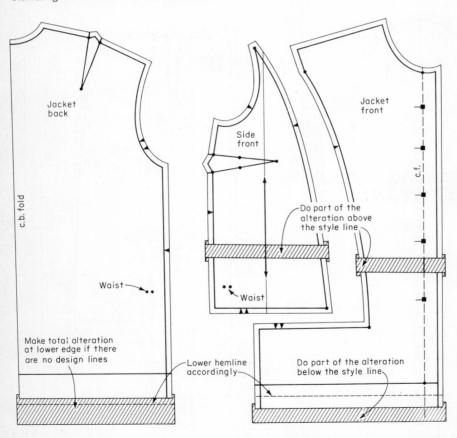

c To retain pleasing proportions created by design lines (pockets, band trims, etc.), alter the pattern piece at two levels in both shaped and rectangular pieces.

FIGURE 5-13 Continued

To adjust the waist level in fitted and semi-fitted jackets and coats

Adjusting the waist level of the pattern to the proper level on the figure is of great importance when there is no waistline seam through which slight fitting corrections can be made. The shaping in the waist area is important even in designs that are only slightly fitted, and it is of paramount importance in snugly fitted designs with nipped-in waists. The pattern should be carefully adjusted to the figure by pattern alteration before the muslin test copy is made, but because great accuracy is necessary, the alteration will very probably need to be revised after the test copy is fitted. Because of this need for perfection, if for no other reason, a muslin test copy is always required for a snugly fitted garment.

Figure 5-8 on page 123 pictures a semi-fitted jacket, shortened an equal amount in all sections of the pattern. An identical alteration on all pieces is quite simple, offering no greater problem than that of any other shaped piece; the alteration is done by basic rules shown in Figure 5-9 and 5-10. The person who requires an equal alteration is one with quite average curves and posture, who varies from the average only in length of torso. Basic rules for lengthening shaped pieces are shown in Figure 5-11.

Because so many varied figure irregularities influence length in the upper torso, only those few persons with almost perfectly shaped figures will require identical alterations for front and back waist lengths. Three major figure irregularities create the need for different alterations in front and back waist lengths. They are:

The nature of curves in the front and the back Larger-than-average curves (large cup size or rounded shoulders) require more length while smaller-than-average curves (small cup size, flat shoulders) require less length.

Posture A very erect posture adds length to the front of the figure and shortens the back, while a sagging posture creates the opposite effect. Consequently a person with a very small cup size and erect posture may require more length in the front while the person with a large cup size and a sagging posture may require less front length and more back length.

The level or position of the waistline itself The waist of the average figure, for which patterns and ready-made garments are made, is almost horizontal, dipping down slightly (about ½ inch) in the front. But individual waist positions vary; some dip more than ½ inch toward the front, some are perfectly horizontal, while others vary greatly from the average by dipping toward the back. This irregularity alone (even if body curves and posture are average) creates the need for different alterations in waist length in the front and the back. Posture may influence the waist level also; a "hips forward" or "hips under" posture tends to cause the waist to dip in the back, while a "hips protruding" posture has the opposite effect. Waist-level irregularities can be easily detected by placing a tape snug around the waist and viewing the figure from the side.

One person may have one or all of these three diverse figure irregularities in various combinations, and so it follows that *many people will require different alterations in front and back waist lengths; only those few with both average curves and average posture will require identical front and back alterations.*

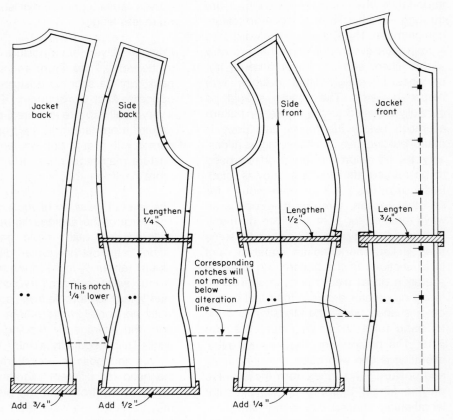

Jacket back

Side back

Side front

Jacket front

Lengthen 1/4"

Lengthen 1/2"

Lengten 3/4"

Corresponding notches will not match below alteration line

This notch 1/4" lower

Add 3/4"

Add 1/2"

Add 1/4"

Problem *a* Total variation from front to back: 3/4".

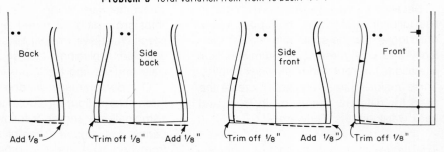

Back

Side back

Side front

Front

Add 1/8"

Trim off 1/8"

Add 1/8"

Trim off 1/8"

Add 1/8"

Trim off 1/8"

Alternative method of evening off lower edges.

FIGURE 5-14 *Basic principles of altering waist length varying amounts in front and back.*

To alter waist length a different amount in the front and back

Problem a—Basic principles   Figure 5-14 pictures pattern pieces for a snugly fitted jacket in typical princess lines; this is the type of design in which the waist level of the pattern must be very accurately located on the figure. Problem *a* shows a total variation of ¾ inches from front of back. The figure for which this alteration is planned is of average length in the back but is longer in the front because of a larger-than-average bust curve, a very erect posture, or a waistline which dips more than is average in the front (or a combination of these). Differences in the waist level are not sudden and sharp; they occur in a gradual way. By altering the various sections in a series of small, even "stairsteps," the alterations can be made to create a smooth transition from front to back. To determine the amount of the "stairstep," use the following formula; it is effective for every type of pattern and every type of alteration. *The total amount of variation from front to back divided by the number of corresponding seams equals the variation (the "stairstep") from one piece to another.* In this example, the total variation of ¾ inches divided by three sets of corresponding seams requires ¼-inch "stairsteps."

Each piece must be altered with a parallel insertion in order to retain the proper direction of the grainline. Grainlines in the two segments of altered pieces must form one continuous ruler line when the alteration is completed.

The length of corresponding seamlines must be equalized; the alteration has caused a variation in their length equal to the size of the "stairstep." This can be most easily done by adding extensions at the lower edges as shown in the upper sketch. This is a simple correction and one that is entirely safe; it may not be entirely accurate on the figure, but it can be easily adjusted later as the hem is hung. The alternative method shown in the lower sketch is not recommended; it will possibly be more accurate on the figure, but it is not as safe, and the extra effort is hardly worth the advantage.

Note that corresponding notches below the alteration line will no longer match; they will miss each other by the amount of the "stairstep" (in this example, ¼ inch). One of the corresponding notches could be moved to correct the discrepancy; however, no correction is necessary, provided that the worker understands that notches should not be matched below the alteration lines as seams are joined. Because the length of seamlines has been equalized by corrections at the lower edges, corners at the lower edge of seams can be used as matching points when joining seams. When working with a full-length coat, notch positions should be corrected as an aid to better control of long seams for basting.

There is another slight discrepancy which can be ignored as a pattern alteration because it is so easily corrected as seams are basted. Waist indentations on corresponding seams will not match perfectly—they will miss by the amount of the "stairstep." A simple paper sample will prove that this inaccuracy can be ignored. See Figure 5-15. Place two identical pieces of notepaper together and cut one long edge in lines similar to the shaped lines of the pattern, as shown. Shift one piece down the amount of variation on the pattern (¼ inch in the example shown) and pin upper and lower edges together as shown. Hold the sample up to the light to see the resulting difference in waist levels. When the seam is basted with the deepest indentation midway between the two levels of indentation on the pattern pieces, the problem is easily solved.

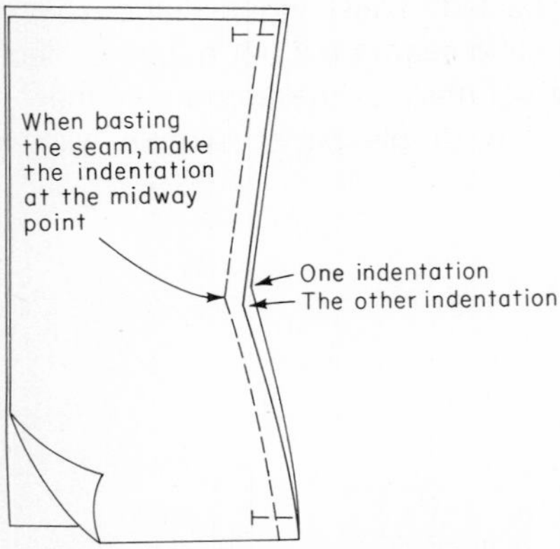

Problem b This example in Figure 5-16 illustrates that basic principles can be applied to other alterations but that they may require certain modifications. Problem *b* shows a total variation from front to back of 1 inch; the figure for which this alteration is planned is an average length in front but is shorter than average in the back. This alteration is done by basic principles with but one exception: a total variation of 1 inch divided by three sets of corresponding seams does not allow for equal "stairsteps." This problem is included to show that the alterations should be done in the best way possible under the circumstances. The "stairsteps" should be as even as is possible; in the example shown, a good solution is two ⅜-inch variations and one ¼-inch variation.

Problem c This example in Figure 5-16 is included to show that a figure may require two different alterations in length in the front and back. Under these circumstances, the alterations must be added together to determine the total variation from front to back (shortening the front ½ inch and lengthening the back ½ inch produces a total variation of 1 inch). The three-piece jacket with two sets of corresponding seams illustrates the effectiveness of the formula for determining the size of the "stairstep": a 1-inch total variation divided by two sets of seams equals the ½-inch "stairstep" illustrated.

When basting the seam, make the indentation at the midway point

One indentation
The other indentation

FIGURE 5-15 Paper test sample.

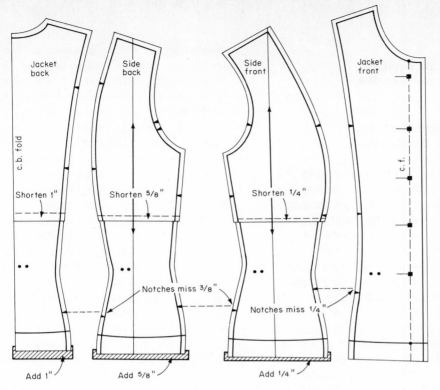

Jacket back

Side back

Side front

Jacket front

c.b. fold

c.f.

Shorten 1"

Shorten 5/8"

Shorten 1/4"

Notches miss 3/8"

Notches miss 1/4"

Add 1"

Add 5/8"

Add 1/4"

Problem *b* Total variation from front to back: 1".

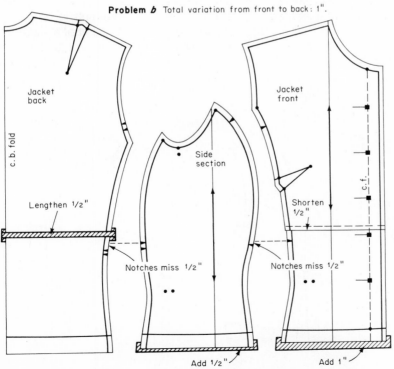

Jacket back

Side section

Jacket front

c.b. fold

c.f.

Lengthen 1/2"

Shorten 1/2"

Notches miss 1/2"

Notches miss 1/2"

Add 1/2"

Add 1"

Problem *c* Total variation from front to back: 1".

FIGURE 5-16 Basic principles applied.

THE PRINCIPLE OF DART FITTING—A GUIDELINE

Flat pieces of fabric are shaped to fit intricate curves of the figure with seams and darts. The typical darts shown in sketch *a* of Figure 5-17 are a means of removing wedge-shaped areas and thereby creating shape at the tips of the darts. Basic fitting darts are usually composed of converging ruler lines, but dartlines may be curved to better fit and reveal body curves. The curved under-bust dart pictured with dartlines curving outward (thereby removing more fabric) will cup in under the bust like the curve of the figure to better reveal the shape of the lower portion of the bust. The curved dart in the skirt front with dartlines curving inward (thereby removing less fabric) will fit the curve of the figure better in that area.

Seams appear in the garment for two purposes: to provide design interest or to provide design interest while at the same time creating shape for body contours. A seam composed of two ruler lines joined together provides only a line or division for design interest. The shaped seamlines shown in the designs pictured in sketch *b* of Figure 5-17 are pinned together at certain points to reveal wedge-shaped areas very similar to darts. When these seamlines are joined, shape will be created exactly as shape is created when dartlines are stitched. These shaped seamlines provide a "dart-fitting-in-a-seam." Notice that the lower edge of the skirt yoke is a prominent curve, while the corresponding edge of the skirt back is only slightly curved. If corresponding seamlines are not identical, shape will be created when the seam is joined. Dart fittings are hidden in most seams. Consider the fit of a shift dress compared with that of a dart-fitted dress with a waistline seam or the figure-hugging fit of a set-in sleeve compared with the fit of a sleeve cut in one with the major pieces of the garment.

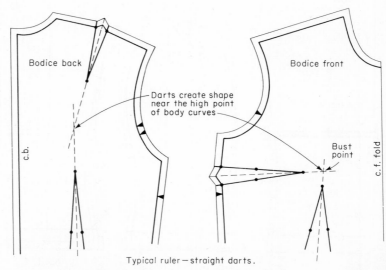

Bodice back

Darts create shape near the high point of body curves

Bodice front

c.b.

Bust point

c.f. fold

Typical ruler—straight darts.

a Darts (straight or curved) create shape.

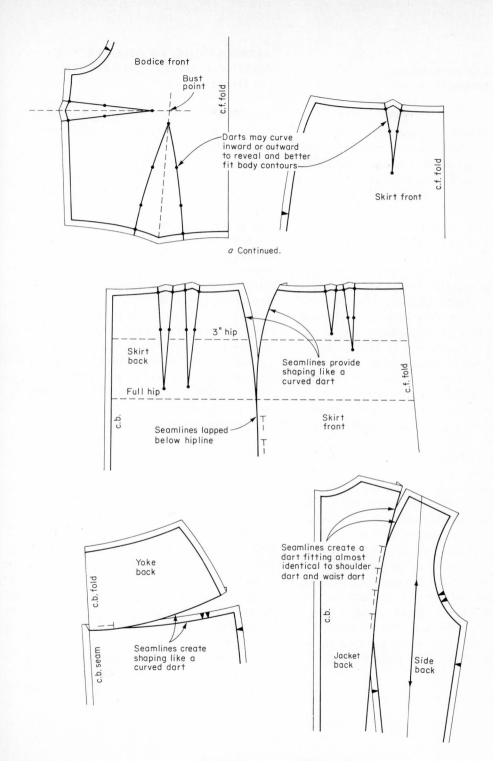

Bodice front

Bust point

Darts may curve inward or outward to reveal and better fit body contours

c.f. fold

Skirt front

c.f. fold

a Continued.

3" hip

Skirt back

Full hip

Seamlines provide shaping like a curved dart

c.f. fold

c.b.

Seamlines lapped below hipline

Skirt front

Yoke back

c.b. fold

c.b. seam

Seamlines create shaping like a curved dart

Seamlines create a dart fitting almost identical to shoulder dart and waist dart

c.b.

Jacket back

Side back

b Dart fitting incorporated in a seam.

FIGURE 5-17   *The principle of dart fitting—a guideline.*

A figure-revealing, close-fitting effect is possible only with many seams and darts to create subtle shape in all the many areas where the figure is curvaceous.

The principle of dart fitting: A dart (or a dart-fitting-in-a-seam) creates shape at the tip of the dart, and the amount of shape created is determined by the size of the angle formed by the dartlines — the wider the dart (or larger the angle), the greater the shape created. The darts in Figure 5-17a will create shape at the tips and provide shape in the area where the figure is curvaceous. The principle applies as effectively to dart fittings in seams. Shape will be created at the point where the seamlines begin to spread apart, or, in other words, at the tip of the dart-fitting-in-a-seam.

Because wider darts create more shape and narrower darts create less shape, any pattern alteration which changes the width of the dart (or the dart-fitting-in-a-seam) will result in a different shape than the original pattern, which fit the average figure. In doing pattern alterations, the worker must be sensitive to her figure irregularities and make alterations in such a way as to provide shape at the proper place and in the proper amount to correspond to her body contours. The principle of dart fitting is obviously involved with any alteration on darts and with any other alteration which changes shape; in less obvious ways, it is involved with alterations to change all-around width or size of pattern pieces.

ALTERATIONS TO CHANGE THE POSITION, LEVEL, OR LENGTH OF DARTS

Figure 5-18 shows a simple alteration to change the direction of a dartline Thus a different design line is created which may be more appealing to the individual or more flattering to her particular figure. The example shown is a popular one because many women feel that a more slanting dart is uplifting and figure flattering. This alteration does not change the position of the tip or the width of the dart and therefore the altered pattern will fit exactly like the original — in other words, it will fit the average bust curve.

Sketch a shows the desired line; it must begin at the tip of the original dart and slant toward the side seam. Pin the pattern together and test on the figure; experiment by placing a pencil at various angles to compare lines on the figure. Slash along the desired dartline to the tip of the dart. Fold out the original dart as shown in sketch b and tape it securely in place (it no longer exists); the new dart with an identical angle forms automatically. Tape in an extension strip and mark new dots as shown. Each dart requires its own unique jog; *the jog is composed of the cutting lines required to ensure that dart edges will be even with the seam edge when the dart is stitched and pressed in the proper direction.* To create a proper jog for the new dart, pin in the new dart as shown in sketch c. The pattern will take shape and this step can be most easily done by working at the corner of the table, with the tip of the dart at the corner. Trim along the cutting line at the side edge with the dart folded in. Sketch d shows the altered pattern with its distinctive jog.

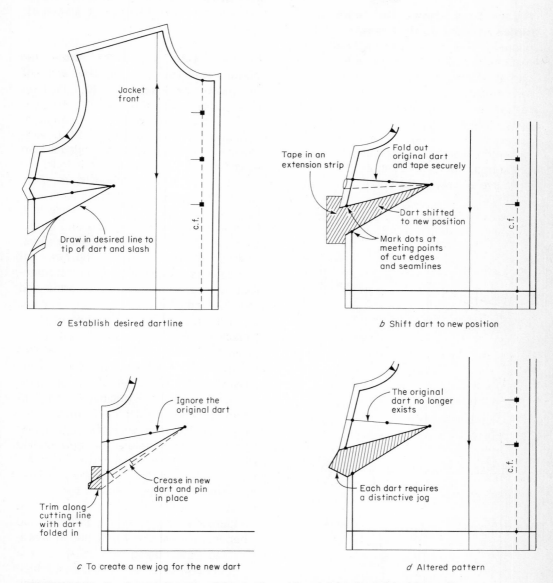

FIGURE 5-18   To alter the direction of the dartline while retaining the original tip position.

Figure 5-19 shows the basic principles of altering dart length Draw a ruler line through the center of the dart and mark the desired new dart tip. Draft in a new dart as shown in the dashed lines; retain the original dots near the edge of the pattern. Darts of the proper length for the figure create shape near the high point of the curve involved. Longer darts, with tips closer together and closer to the high point of the body curve, concentrate shape near the curve and reveal the curve better, while

shorter darts provide more generalized shape. This alteration does not change the dart in any other way, and therefore the pattern will fit essentially like the original; the pattern will fit average body curves and will simply reveal curves to a greater or lesser extent.

Figures 5-20 and 5-21 show the basic rules for altering the level of horizontal or French darts The level is raised or lowered in a similar way; the dart is shown in a lower position in Figure 5-20 and a higher position in 5-21. Draw a line through the center of the original dart as shown in the *a* sketches; this indicates the bust level of the average figure. Construct a line parallel to that center line at the proper bust level for the individual. Draft in a dart of equal width and length as shown; the original dart no longer exists. Tape on an extension strip; the new dart will require a new jog and the vertical seamlines will have been slightly distorted and must be corrected.

Pin in the new dart as shown in the *b* sketches and note that cut edges of the pattern have been distorted (more evident in Figure 5-21). The new vertical seamlines must have the character of the originals. The character of the original seamline in Figure 5-20 was a ruler line formed by the vertical cutting lines when the original dart was folded in; therefore the new cutting lines must form a straight line when the new dart is folded in. The corrected lines are shown as dashed lines in the sketch.

The character of the original seamline in Figure 5-21 was a smooth, gradual curve when the original dart was folded in; therefore the new cutting line must form a smooth curve when the new dart is folded in. The corrected lines are shown as dashed lines in the sketch. By trimming along the corrected cutting line with the new dart folded in, the distortion is corrected and

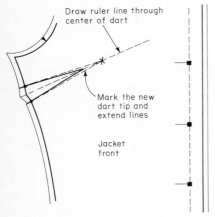

Draw ruler line through center of dart

Mark the new dart tip and extend lines

Jacket front

a To lengthen darts.

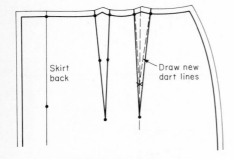

Skirt back

Draw new dart lines

b To shorten darts.

FIGURE 5-19 *To alter dart length.*

a proper jog for the new dart is provided, as shown in the *c* sketches. The new darts create the same shape as the original dart (the proper amount for the average figure), but the altered pattern will provide shape at a different level to meet the demands of the individual figure.

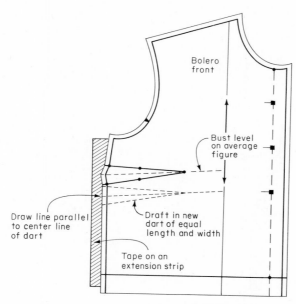

Bolero
front

Bust level
on average
figure

Draw line parallel
to center line
of dart

Draft in new
dart of equal
length and width

Tape on an
extension strip

a Move dartlines to the desired position

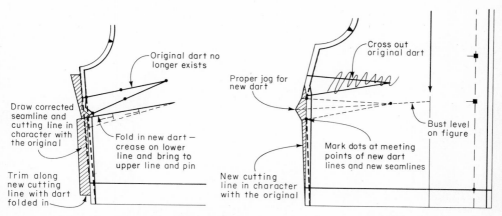

Original dart no
longer exists

Draw corrected
seamline and
cutting line in
character with
the original

Fold in new dart —
crease on lower
line and bring to
upper line and pin

Trim along
new cutting
line with dart
folded in

Proper jog for
new dart

Cross out
original dart

Bust level
on figure

New cutting
line in character
with the original

Mark dots at meeting
points of new dart
lines and new seamlines

b Establish new seamlines and cutting lines

c Altered pattern

FIGURE 5-20 *Basic rules for altering the level of horizontal or French darts.*

**PREPARATION OF PATTERN
AND PATTERN ALTERATIONS**

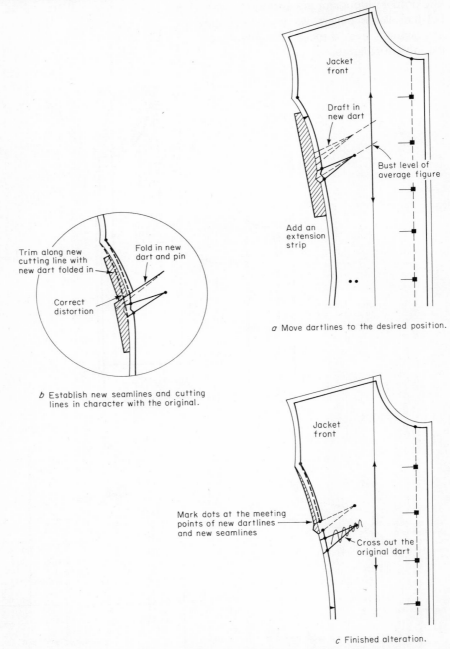

Jacket front

Draft in new dart

Bust level of average figure

Add an extension strip

a Move dartlines to the desired position.

Trim along new cutting line with new dart folded in

Fold in new dart and pin

Correct distortion

b Establish new seamlines and cutting lines in character with the original.

Jacket front

Mark dots at the meeting points of new dartlines and new seamlines

Cross out the original dart

c Finished alteration.

FIGURE 5-21   *Basic principles applied to a pattern with vertical seamlines.*

Figure 5-22 shows basic principles applied Sketch *a* illustrates a dart drafted to a new position and shortened in the same operation. The dart nearest the center is drafted over toward the side edge to create proper shape for a figure (usually very thin) which is flat in front but has prominent hipbones; the dart is shortened to create shape at the level of the hipbone.

The narrow darts in the front skirt do not require prominent jogs; the jogs have been exaggerated in all skirt patterns for illustrative purposes. On a full-size pattern it is usually not necessary to add an exten-

sion strip to make corrections. Fold in the new dart. If the waist seamline is greatly distorted, make corrections as shown in the *b* sketches of Figures 5-20 and 5-21; if it is not distorted, trim off the very slight jog of the original dart.

Any change in the position of the shoulder dart will distort the shoulderline and require correction as shown in sketch *b*.

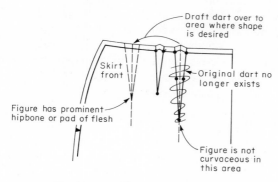

a To change position and alter length in one operation

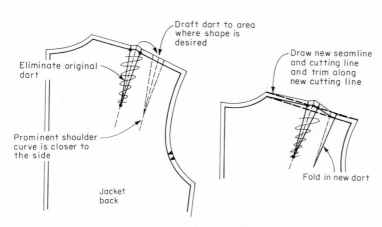

b Shoulder dart drafted to new position

FIGURE 5-22 Basic principles applied.

The character of the original shoulderline
was that it was composed of two ruler
lines which formed one continuous ruler
line when the original dart was folded in;
the new shoulderline must have the same
character. An extension strip will not be
required. Fold in the new dart and draw
a new ruler line from corner to corner as
shown; by trimming along the new cutting
line with the dart folded in, the distortion
will be corrected and a proper jog for the
new dart will be provided.

Like the preceding alterations on horizontal darts, these alterations create the
same shape as the original dart (the proper
amount for the average figure), but the
altered pattern will provide shape in a
different area to meet the demands of the
individual figure.

ALTERATIONS TO CHANGE THE ALL-AROUND WIDTH OR SIZE OF THE PATTERN

Review "A Critical Reevaluation of Bust
Size" on page 46 and "Tests for Figure
Problems Involved with the Subtle Issue of
Shape" on page 117. If an alteration in size
is required, there are two alternatives: (1) To
change the size according to the alterations in this section by changing the all-
around size of both the front and the back.
(2) To alter size within the body of the
pattern piece, changing size and shape
in one unit only. All alterations in this section
alter size in both the front and the back for
the figure which is larger or smaller than
average in an overall, all-around way.

The difference between one size and
another is approximately 2 inches at all
levels on the figure; the addition of ½ inch
at each underarm edge of the front and
back provides a total of 2 inches in all-

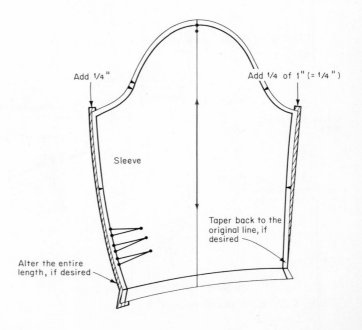

Add ¼"

Add ¼ of 1" (= ¼ ")

Sleeve

Taper back to the
original line, if
desired

Alter the entire
length, if desired

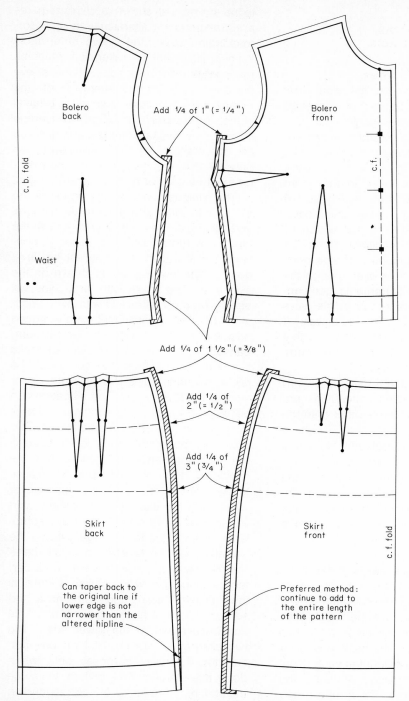

Bolero
back

Add ¼ of 1" (= ¼")

Bolero
front

c. b. fold

c. f.

Waist

Add ¼ of 1 ½" (= 3/8")

Add ¼ of
2" (= 1/2")

Add ¼ of
3" (3/4")

Skirt
back

Skirt
front

c. f. fold

Can taper back to
the original line if
lower edge is not
narrower than the
altered hipline

Preferred method:
continue to add to
the entire length
of the pattern

FIGURE 5-23   Basic rules for altering all-around width or size.

around size (½ inch on the front plus ½ inch on the back equals 1 inch at each of the two sides). Any reader who has consistently added ½ to the entire underarm edges *including the bust level* should move up to the next size; and by the same token, the person who has taken in the entire underarm seams ½ inch *including the bust level* should move down one size. It is important to understand that a size-12 pattern with ½-inch additions along the total length of the underarm seams does not fit as well as a size 14 even though the total all-around measurements are approximately the same; in subtle little ways the altered pattern fits less effectively. It is important to buy the proper size so that alterations can be held to a minimum, *especially at the bust level.*

This is not to say that an altered pattern is inferior to the original; alterations are entirely effective at all levels other than the bust level. Alterations at the bust level have been included in the problems illustrated in this section, but they are in every case limited to 1 inch. Changes of 1 inch at the bust level are necessary for persons of in-between sizes, and alterations of more than 1 inch at the bust indicate the need for a different size pattern.

Figure 5-23 shows basic rules The pattern has been altered for the figure which requires an additional inch at the bust level, 1½ inches at the waist level, 2 inches at the 3-inch hipline and 3 inches at the fullest hip level. The basic rule: Alter a quarter of the total amount at each (front and back) underarm edge. Because the bust level is so close to the armhole, any change at that level must be carried on up

to the armhole, as shown, and this requires a corresponding alteration on the corresponding piece (the sleeve or armhole facing). Note that the alteration must be made at the armhole edge of the sleeve (to correspond to the alteration on the bolero) but it may taper back to the original at the sleeve hemline if the arm is average in size. The two alternatives are pictured on one pattern for illustrative purposes only; when doing this alteration, one method must be used at both underarm edges.

The alterations at the side edges of the skirt, are identical above the fullest hip level and alternate lines are shown below the hipline. In most cases it is better to continue the alteration at the fullest hip level down to the lower edge, as shown on the skirt front. The figure with large hips will usually be more attractive with extra width at the hemline because that extra width will help make hips appear smaller by comparison. Furthermore, it is safer to make the additions because the seam can be taken in during fitting if less width is desired at the lower edge. The alteration can be tapered back to the original width at the lower edge, as shown on the skirt back, providing the width of the lower edge is not narrower than the altered width at the hipline. Fold the hemline up to the hipline to be sure that the hemline is as wide or wider than the altered hipline. Many skirt patterns (like the one shown) are somewhat wider at the lower edge, and so the alteration can be tapered in at the hemline. However, any pattern based on a perfect rectangle below the hipline is identical in width at the hipline and the hemline, and so any addition at the hipline must be continued down to the lower edge. The two alternatives are pictured on one pattern for illustrative purposes only; when doing this alteration on a pattern, the same method must be used on corresponding edges of the front and back.

Figure 5-24 shows basic rules applied to corresponding pieces Once the major pieces are altered, every other piece which fits to it or over it must be altered in a corresponding way. The alteration shown is the same as the one in Figure 5-23.

Consider the pocket and band trim; the alterations on those pieces correspond to the alteration on the skirt at the level where these small units will be applied. The best way to ensure accuracy is to place these

pieces along the markings on the skirt and copy the skirt alteration through to the smaller units.

The waistband requires an application of basic principles. Because it is one piece, there are no seams at the side edges; the side position is indicated by dots on the

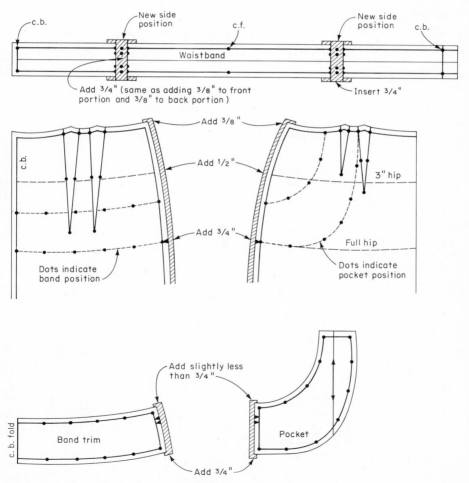

FIGURE 5-24 · Basic rules applied to corresponding pieces.

pattern. The pattern must be slashed at the two side positions indicated and an extension strip inserted; the addition must equal the total addition made on the underarm edges of the front and the back. The new side position, located at the center of the extension, completes the alteration; by adding a total of ¾ inch at the side position, ⅜ inch has been added to the front and ⅜ inch to the back, thereby corresponding with the skirt alteration.

Two methods of altering all-around width or size

The basic rules were illustrated in Figures 5-23 and 5-24 by using one of two possible methods for altering all-around width or size; the method used (alteration made at the pattern edges) is referred to as *method 1* in Figures 5-25, 5-26, and 5-27. Method 2 (alteration made within the body of the pattern piece) is shown in the same sketches and can be done by following the same basic principles. Both methods are included because the two are often equally effective, and the worker can use the one she prefers. But, more importantly, each method is more effective than the other under certain

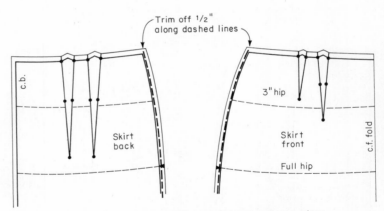

Method 1: To decrease all−around size at underarm edges

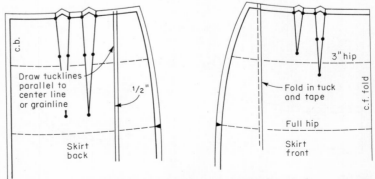

Method 2: To decrease all−around size using a tuck

FIGURE 5-25   Two methods of decreasing all-around size or width.

circumstances, and the worker must be able to use either method when the need arises.

Figures 5-25 and 5-26 illustrate the two methods Each figure shows a total alteration of 2 inches, which is ½ inch or a quarter of the desired alteration at each underarm. Figure 5-25 shows basic rules

for decreasing width. With method 1, the excess is trimmed with the pattern edge. Almost identical results can be achieved with method 2 by drawing lines parallel to

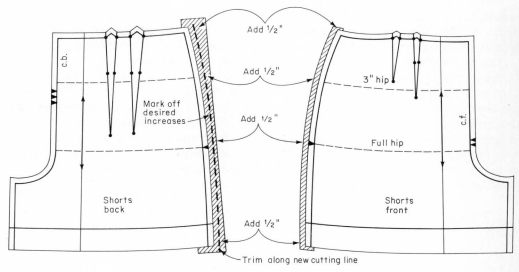

Method 1: To add all —around size at underarm edges

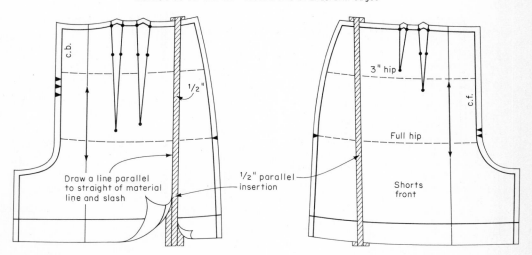

Method 2: To add all — around size with an extension strip

FIGURE 5-26   *Two methods of adding all-around size or width.*

the center line or grainline to mark off the desired decrease (in the example, ½ inch) and then slashing and lapping out the excess; this is the same technique used for shortening shaped pattern pieces.

Additions are shown in Figure 5-26. The insertion strip shown in method 2 is inserted by the same technique used for lengthening shaped pattern pieces.

The two methods produce very nearly identical results in the particular alteration chosen for these illustrations; the choice between the two is entirely dependent on the preference of the worker or the instructor. The two methods are equally effective, producing identical results but only because the alteration is identical at the waist, 3-inch, and full hip levels.

Figure 5-27 shows basic rules for altering different amounts at different levels on the figure Basic rules for both methods are shown in such a way that comparisons can be easily made. For illustrative purposes, method 1 is shown on the back sections and method 2 on the front sections. Study the two alternatives carefully to understand the subtle differences in fit; then select the method that produces best results for the individual figure. Use that method on both sections of the pattern when doing the actual pattern alteration.

Few figures require identical alterations at all levels; far more figures require different amounts at each level, as shown in the examples in Figure 5-27. Because greater alterations cause complications, the illustrations are presented as follows: sketch *a*—basic rules for small alterations, sketch *b*—an explanation of the complications caused by larger alterations, and sketch *c*—basic rules for larger alterations.

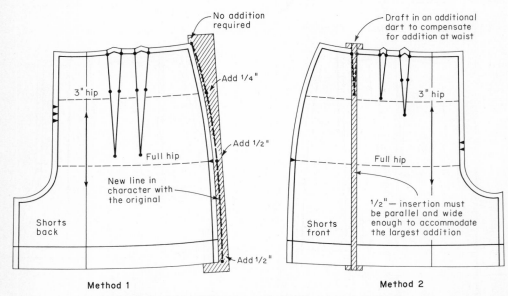

a Basic rules for altering different amounts at different levels on the figure for changes of a total of 2 inches or less (½ inch or less at each underarm).

Sketch a—basic rules for making alterations of a total of 2 inches or less (or ½ inch or less at each underarm) at the hipline The example pictured is for a figure which requires an additional 1 inch at the 3-inch hipline and 2 inches at the full hipline with no change required at the waist level. When

151
**ALTERATIONS TO CHANGE THE ALL-
AROUND WIDTH OR SIZE OF THE PATTERN**

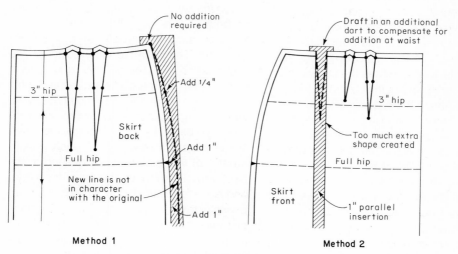

b Large alterations point out weaknesses of both methods — neither alteration is acceptable.

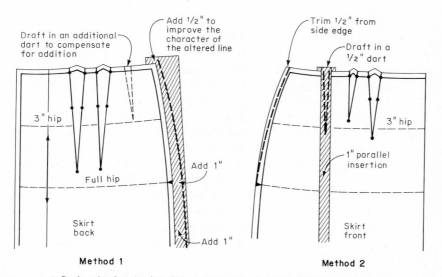

c Basic rules for altering different amounts at different levels for changes of more than a total of 2 inches (more than 1/2 inch at each underarm).

FIGURE 5-27 *Basic rules for altering different amounts at different levels on the figure; an evaluation of the alternative methods.*

**PREPARATION OF PATTERN
AND PATTERN ALTERATIONS**

using method 1, the additions are marked off at the underarm edge (a quarter of the total amount on each side edge). When using method 2, additions must be made on parallel lines, and therefore the insertion must measure the largest amount required at any one level—in this example ½ inch (a quarter of the total 2 inches desired at the hip level). This increases the size at all levels and makes the pattern too large at the waist; to correct this, draft in a dart the width of the insertion as shown, ending the dart at a level where the figure has shape (prominent hipbone or pad of flesh). These are the general rules, and both methods produce very comparable results. However, results are not identical. To show the subtle differences, two basic principles discussed earlier must be employed: (1) The altered line must have the character of the original, and (2) the principle of dart fitting must be applied (page 136). The side edge in method 1 is not identical to the original because the curve between the waist and hip levels is somewhat sharper, but it is *in character* with the original because the change is not great. Refer to the skirt pieces in sketch *b* of Figure 5-17 to see that by adding width at the hipline and making the side seamline more curved, the dart-fitting-in-the-seam has been increased. By using method 1, the skirt will have more shape at the hip level directly at the side. Method 1 will be very effective on the figure with extra pads of flesh near the side and with average curves in the front and back.

By contrast, method 2 creates no extra shape near the side edge because the character of the side seamline is identical to the original. By this method, extra shape is created by the additional dart, and that

shape is located a few inches in front and in back of the underarm seam. Method 2 will be very effective on the figure with pads of flesh (or prominent bones) at about the 3-inch hip level and with average curves at the side.

Sketch b emphasizes the differences between the two methods and the weaknesses of both Large alterations point out differences and weaknesses in any pattern alteration. The example pictured is for the figure which requires an additional 1 inch at the 3-inch hipline and 4 inches at the full hipline with no change required at the waist. When using method 2, additions must be made on parallel lines; therefore, the insertion in this example must be 1 inch wide (a quarter of the total 4 inches desired at the hip level). This makes the waist too large, and an additional dart is shown to compensate for the increase. The alterations pictured have resulted in sufficient all-around width or size for the figure but because the alteration is large, both methods have resulted in exaggerated changes in shape and neither alteration is acceptable.

The new side seamline in method 1 is not in character with the original; the curve between the waist and the hipline is far more curvaceous than the original. The dart fitting in the seam has been greatly increased and this will create exaggerated shape all concentrated at the hip level directly at the side; few if any figures have corresponding shape in that area. By contrast, method 2 results in exaggerated shape all concentrated a few inches from the side edge; few if any figures have as much corresponding shape in that area. This example points out the need to modify general rules when making larger alterations.

Sketch c—basic rules for making alterations of a total of more than 2 inches (more than

½ inch at each side edge) at the hipline
By modifying the basic rules used for smaller alterations, extra width can be obtained and the resulting changes in shape made in such a way that they will better conform to body curves. When using method 1, add some width at the waist level even though the figure does not require it; add about half of the amount that is added at the hipline. The side edge is still somewhat more curvaceous than the original, and this will create some extra shape (dart-fitting-in-the-seam) at the seamline, directly at the side edge. To compensate for the extra width at the waist, draft in a dart as shown. The dart will create shape a few inches from the side edge. The figure with a normal waist that is 4 inches larger than average at the hipline is curvaceous and needs extra shape; this alteration distributes the shape in several places where most figures of this type have corresponding shape.

The modification shown in method 2 results in an identical distribution of the extra shape. By drafting in a dart about half the width of the insertion and trimming the remaining excess (½ inch in this example) from the side edge, extra shape has been distributed in several places where most figures of this type have corresponding shape.

Evaluation of the two methods The two methods of altering all-around width or size are equally effective on skirts, shorts, and pants if they are executed properly with due attention to the shape of the individual figure; when working with most pattern designs, the choice between the two can be based on personal preferences. Review the series of sketches to understand the following conclusions better.

When identical alterations are made at all levels (Figures 5-25 and 5-26), results of the two methods are identical.

When different (but small) alterations are made at various levels (sketch *a* in Figure 5-27), results are slightly different because method 1 results in somewhat more shape at the side of the figure and method 2 creates somewhat more shape a few inches in front or in back of the side position.

When different (but large) alterations are made at various levels (sketch *c* in Figure 5-27), results of the two methods can be considered identical; study the sketches carefully to see that both methods have been modified to distribute the additional shape at the same several areas on the figure.

Each method has advantages over the other under certain circumstances. These will become apparent in the following section when these principles are applied to a variety of patterns; in some cases there can be no personal choice, for only one method will be effective. One outstanding example is a limitation on the use of method 2 (use of insertion strip or tuck): it cannot be used on units which fit the upper part of the torso (blouses, jackets, coats). When the pattern is increased by a parallel insertion or decreased by a parallel tuck, the pattern is altered for its full length and therefore the alteration would increase or decrease width in the shoulder area. Any increase or decrease in the shoulder area is serious, because a change of about ⅛ inch makes the difference between one size and another; a change of ½ inch would consequently make the garment several sizes larger or smaller at the shoulders.

Figure 5-28—Basic principles applied Alterations in width made at the pattern edges will usually require corrections to bring the altered line in character with the original. The required alteration is shown marked off on the back sections in dashed lines and the finished alteration, with lines in character with the original, is shown on the front sections. This is the way to proceed: First mark off the alteration as required (shown on the back section), then study the altered line to see if it is similar enough to the original to be considered in character, and then make necessary corrections before completing the alteration (shown on the front section).

Problem *a* shows the alteration for a figure which is very curvaceous at the 3-inch hipline but is average in size at all other levels. It is obvious that the alteration as marked off is not in character with the original. The corrected line shown on the skirt front is in character with the original, even though it looks quite different. The original line was a slight curve to the fullest hip measurement and a ruler-straight line below that level; the altered line has the same character, and it looks different only because the fullest hip measurement of this particular figure is at a higher level on the figure. The addition at the side edge of the waist, compensated by an additional dart, will create extra shape in the area where this type of figure is more curvaceous. If the alteration at the 3-inch hipline is great, it may be necessary to add some extra width at the lower hipline to keep the altered line

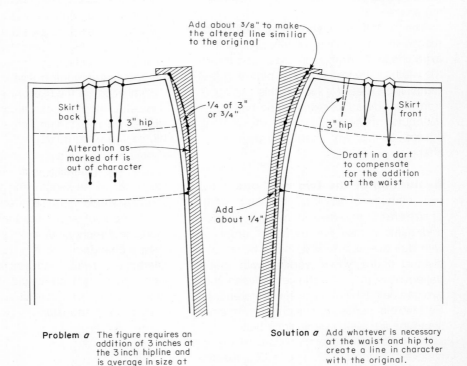

Problem *a* The figure requires an addition of 3 inches at the 3 inch hipline and is average in size at all other levels.

Solution *a* Add whatever is necessary at the waist and hip to create a line in character with the original.

FIGURE 5-28 Basic principles applied.

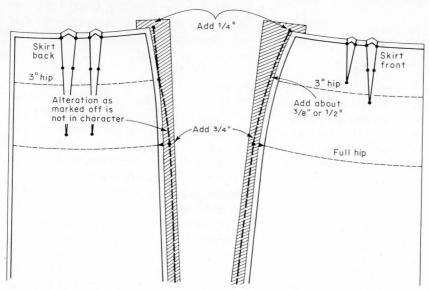

Add 1/4"

Skirt
back

3" hip

Alteration as
marked off is
not in character

Add 3/4"

Skirt
front

3" hip

Add about
3/8" or 1/2"

Full hip

Problem b The figure requires a
1 inch addition at the
waist and a 3 inch
addition at the full
hipline and is average
in size at the 3 inch
hipline.

Solution b Add whatever is necessary
at the 3 inch hipline to
create a smooth curve.

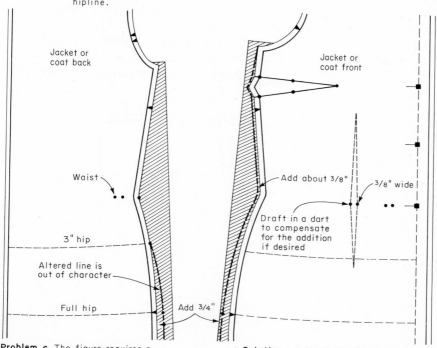

Jacket or
coat back

Jacket or
coat front

Waist

Add about 3/8"

3/8" wide

3" hip

Draft in a dart
to compensate
for the addition
if desired

Altered line is
out of character

Full hip

Add 3/4"

Problem c The figure requires a
3 inch addition at the
full hipline and is average
at all other levels.

Solution c Add at other levels to
improve the character
of the cutting line.

in character (about ¼ inch if the addition is ¾ inch as shown). This extra size is an advantage because it will help to camouflage the figure irregularity. This method is superior to the alternate method in this problem because a parallel insertion (¾ inch wide) would add far too much extra size at the lower hip level.

Problem *b* requires only a slight change between the waist and hipline to bring the altered line into proper character. The additional size at the 3-inch hip level will help camouflage the figure irregularity.

Basic principles apply to garments with no waistline seam, as shown in problem *c*. The altered line, as marked off, is not in character between the waist and the hip; the correction, which adds extra size in the upper torso, is in character with the lines of this type of garment. The additional size at the waist need not be compensated with a dart in a loosely fitted garment if the wearer prefers a looser fit at the waist. If a more fitted effect is desired, the additional size at the waist can be compensated by drafting in a dart, as shown.

Figure 5-29—Basic principles applied to pieces that do not have a seam at the underarm position These examples point out the advantages of method 2 (insertion strip or tuck). The one-piece skirt pictured has a curving dart at the underarm position to replace an underarm seam. To alter the pattern, draw a line through the center of the dart and slash along the line. Compare this alteration with the identical one pictured in Figure 5-23 to see the general principles applied. In Figure 5-23, the cutting line was moved, and this automatically moved the seamline a corresponding amount; in this alteration the change is made directly on the dartline, which serves as a seamline in this design.

The two-piece sleeve has no seam at the underarm, and dots indicate the underarm position. They appear on the under sleeve. Compare the two alterations pictured with the two pictured on the sleeve in Figure 5-23 to see that the alterations are identical.

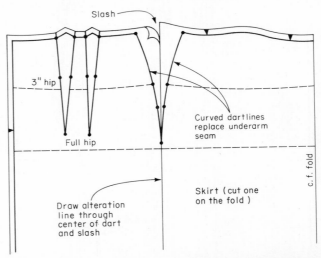

FIGURE 5-29 *Basic principles applied to pieces with no underarm seam.*

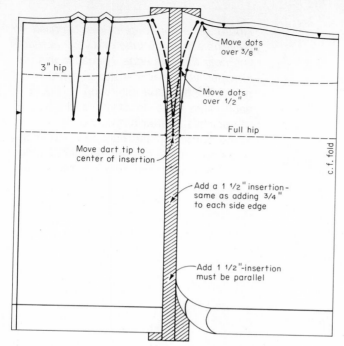

3" hip

Move dots
over 3/8"

Move dots
over 1/2"

Full hip

Move dart tip to
center of insertion

c.f. fold

Add a 1 1/2" insertion -
same as adding 3/4"
to each side edge

Add 1 1/2"- insertion
must be parallel

Problem: Figure requires additions of 1 1/2 inches at the
waist, 2 inches at the 3 inch hipline, and
3 inches at the full hipline.

Compare with the identical skirt alteration in Figure 5−23.

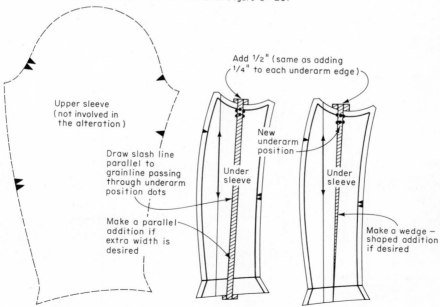

Upper sleeve
(not involved in
the alteration)

Add 1/2" (same as adding
1/4" to each underarm edge)

Draw slash line
parallel to
grainline passing
through underarm
position dots

New
underarm
position

Under
sleeve

Under
sleeve

Make a parallel
addition if
extra width is
desired

Make a wedge −
shaped addition
if desired

Compare with the identical sleeve alterations in Figure 5−23.

Figure 5-30—basic principles applied to patterns with more than one vertical seamline near the side edge Because this pattern has two seams instead of the usual one, half the usual alteration is made at each seam edge; in other words, instead of adding a quarter of the desired amount to the corresponding edges of one seam, one-eighth of the desired amount is added to the corresponding edges of two seams.

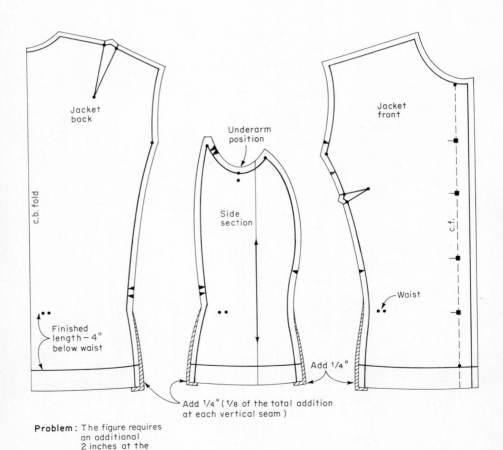

Jacket back

Jacket front

c.b. fold

Underarm position

Side section

c.f.

Waist

Finished length – 4" below waist

Add 1/4"

Add 1/4" (1/8 of the total addition at each vertical seam)

Problem: The figure requires an additional 2 inches at the 4 inch hipline.

FIGURE 5-30 *Basic principles applied to a garment with more than one vertical seam near the underarm position.*

INTRODUCTION TO ALTERATIONS FOR CURVES WHICH DIFFER FROM THOSE OF THE AVERAGE FIGURE

The alterations to create more shape for larger-than-average curves (page 163) and those to create less shape for flatter- or smaller-than-average figures (page 193) are more difficult to execute and perfect than any others which will be encountered, but they are the most rewarding as well. Their great value lies in the fact that they solve a problem which cannot usually be solved by fitting alone—in other words, a problem which cannot usually be corrected in a ready-to-wear garment or one cut from an unaltered pattern. Curves which vary from average require more or less shape and more or less width or length (or both) at the very position where the problem curve exists. These curves therefore require an alteration which passes over the high point of the curve involved. Designs which have no seams through which fitting can be done *must* be altered before cutting, if the curve is either larger or smaller than average; designs with a seam which passes over the problem curve *must* be altered if the curve is larger than average to ensure sufficient width for fitting.

These alterations are difficult to perfect because variations in shape cannot be measured and stated in scientific terms. Problem curves need more or less shape and more or less width or length (or both), but the question of how much shape and how much extra width and length (or both) can only be answered by testing in muslin. The altered pattern can be figure-tested with some degree of success but the only reliable test is to alter the pattern, test the alteration (by making and fitting a muslin copy) and then perfect the alteration. For this reason, if for no other, the person with problem curves should always make a muslin test copy before cutting a garment of expensive fabric.

The alterations to create more shape for larger-than-average curves (page 163) are given in great detail because they are required more frequently and because they can be illustrated more effectively. Alterations to create less shape for smaller-than-average curves are done in the same way— but in reverse. Any reader who has a problem curve, large or small, should first study the entire section for larger-than-average curves, where fundamental principles are explained in detail; then, if her curves are smaller than average, she should turn to that section and follow those directions, applying principles already learned.

Important review Before proceeding, carefully review the following: "A Critical Reevaluation of Bust Size" on page 46, "The Principle of Dart Fitting" on page 136, and "Tests for Figure Problems Involved with the Subtle Issue of Shape" on page 117.

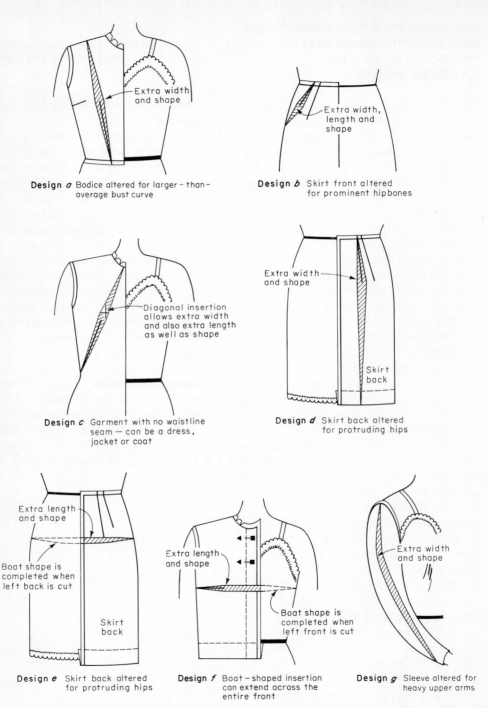

Design a Bodice altered for larger – than – average bust curve

Design b Skirt front altered for prominent hipbones

Extra width and shape

Extra width, length and shape

Diagonal insertion allows extra width and also extra length as well as shape

Design c Garment with no waistline seam — can be a dress, jacket or coat

Extra width and shape

Skirt back

Design d Skirt back altered for protruding hips

Extra length and shape

Boat shape is completed when left back is cut

Skirt back

Design e Skirt back altered for protruding hips

Extra length and shape

Boat shape is completed when left front is cut

Design f Boat – shaped insertion can extend across the entire front

Extra width and shape

Design g Sleeve altered for heavy upper arms

FIGURE 5-31 Basic principle: Curves which differ from the average require a boat-shaped alteration passing over the high point of the curve.

The basic principle of fitting curves which vary from average

Figure 5-31 shows a collection of patterns with shaded boat-shaped areas which are insertions in the pattern to create more shape and more width or length (or both) for curves which are larger than average; similar boat-shaped areas are lapped out of the pattern for curves which are flatter- or smaller-than-average. Do not attempt at this time to understand the alteration itself; simply study the sketches to understand why the alteration is effective. Note that in every case the finished alteration is boat-shaped and except for the sleeve is centered over a dartline. A boat-shaped alteration is the secret to fitting any curve which differs from the average. In the illustrations, the boat shape builds out to a maximum width at the level of the high point of the curve and tapers back to the original at other edges. The direction of the alteration is dependent on the direction of the dart involved. Alterations on vertical darts change the shape and width (designs *a* and *d*); alterations on diagonal darts change the shape, the width, and also the length (designs *b* and *c*); and alterations on horizontal darts change the shape and length (designs *e* and *f*).

It is important to understand the significance of the boat-shaped alteration, so that these principles can be applied to other, more complicated designs. The sketches do not show shape; but in every case the width of the dart will be increased in the alteration process, making the altered pattern more shapely than the original. Consider design *a;* note that the insertion ends at the shoulder and waist and that the width of the insertion, like the curve of the larger-than-average bust, gradually builds out to the fullest width at the bust level. Study the other designs to see that, in every case, the insertion builds out almost exactly like the larger-than-average curve of the figure.

The sleeve and skirt designs are included to show that basic principles can be applied to any unit of the pattern. The sleeve alteration is closely related but not identical to the others pictured; unlike the others, it does not involve a dart at the center of the "boat."

If a garment will hang free from the body (the skirt back in design *d*) and will not be attached to a corresponding piece, the insertion can be parallel below the level of the curve; when alteration is done in this manner, extra shape is created, and in addition extra width (which may help to camouflage the figure irregularity) will be added below the curve. The skirt alteration shown in design *d* can be done as pictured if no extra width is desired at the hemline, or it can be altered with a parallel insertion below the hipline if extra width is desired below the hip level. Both alterations are explained in Figure 5-35 on page 169.

The basic principle: curves which differ from average require a boat-shaped alteration passing over the high point of the curve. The principle can be effectively illustrated in the classroom with three patterns for a basic, snug-fitting dress, all purchased in the same size. Alter the bodice front and skirt back of one for curves smaller than average and another for curves larger than average. When darts are pinned in, compare the two altered patterns with the pattern made for the average figure by testing them on the figure or holding them with outside edges together. The changes in shape will be evident, and it will be obvious these alterations are very effective.

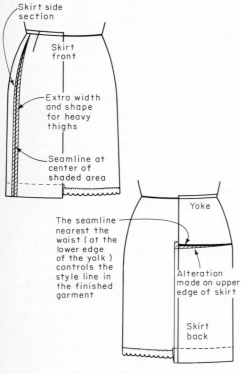

Skirt side section

Skirt front

Extra width and shape for heavy thighs

Seamline at center of shaded area

The seamline nearest the waist (at the lower edge of the yolk) controls the style line in the finished garment

Yoke

Alteration made on upper edge of skirt

Skirt back

Compare with design *e*, Figure 5–31.

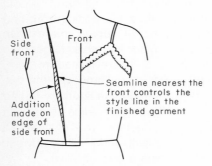

Side front

Front

Addition made on edge of side front

Seamline nearest the front controls the style line in the finished garment

Compare with design *a*, Figure 5–31.

FIGURE 5-32   Boat-shaped alterations made at seamlines.

Boat-shaped alterations made at seamlines that pass over or very near the high point of body curves
The principles of providing extra shape and width or length (or both) for larger-than-average curves remain constant, but they must be modified for application to a great variety of designs, not all of which will have darts and seams in the same position as those in simple basic patterns. Dart-shaping can be incorporated in a seam; design interest and variety are frequently achieved by seamlines which replace dartlines. Princess-line designs are excellent examples of the use of vertical seams to replace dartlines; yokes are examples of the use of horizontal seams to replace dartlines.

The altered patterns pictured in Figure 5-32 reveal boat-shaped additions at pattern edges very similar to the insertions made within a pattern piece, as illustrated in Figure 5-31. In these sketches, the extra shape and width or length are obtained by making additions along pattern edges which pass over or very near the high point of the curve involved. The princess-line skirt pictured has vertical seams on either side of the side-seam position. By adding half the desired increase on each of the two corresponding front edges, the boat-shaped addition will provide extra width and shape for heavy thighs. Similar additions made on the two corresponding back edges provide extra width and shape for protruding hips.

Compare the skirt with a yoke with design *e* in Figure 5-31 to see that the shaded areas are similar in shape and location and therefore provide comparable extra shape and length. Compare the princess-line bodice with design *a* in Figure 5-31 to see their similarity.

Whenever a basic principle is applied to a new design, little techniques must be worked out for effective application to the particular design. For example, note that half the total addition was made at each corresponding edge of the princess-line skirt (the seamline is in the center of the shaded area), whereas the entire addition is shown on only one seam edge in the other two designs. The difference has to do with the effect of style lines in the finished garment. In some designs which feature seamlines replacing dartlines, one of the two corresponding seamlines controls the style line in the finished garment, and any alteration on that controlling seamline would adversely influence the effect. In those designs the entire alteration must be made on the seamline which does not influence the style line when the garment is worn. For example, if the skirt yoke were parallel to the waistline in the original pattern, any addition on the lower edge of the yoke would make the yoke uneven; the entire addition on the upper edge of the skirt section does not influence the style line.

Application of basic principles The best training for the student is to see altered patterns pinned together and tested on the figure for which they were altered. The sketches in Figure 5-31 can be used as a guideline when working with more complicated designs. Study these sketches, seeing where the boat-shaped insertion is required, and then decide how a similar boat-shaped alteration can be made in other pattern designs. In the following discussion, basic principles are covered in detail on simple designs, and then these principles are applied (and sometimes modified) on more complicated pattern designs as an aid to showing how similar results can be attained on a great variety of pattern designs.

To recognize figure problems This is the time to think of all the various fitting problems encountered in the past with garments made from unaltered patterns

or with ready-to-wear, and to study all body curves for variations from the average. The indications that curves are larger than average, stated below, and those for smaller-than-average curves on page 193, will be evident when the pattern is pinned together and tested on the figure; these indications of misfit show up prominently in ready-to-wear garments in the wardrobe and in garments made from unaltered patterns.

ALTERATIONS TO CREATE MORE SHAPE FOR LARGER-THAN-AVERAGE CURVES

Indications that curves are larger than average Figure 5-6 on page 118 and the accompanying text point out that figure tests made with the pattern pinned together will reveal variations in body curves. The unaltered pattern pictured in that sketch does not hug the figure if the bust curve is larger than average; and, similarly, any pattern piece tested on any area of the figure with larger-than-average curves will buckle or protrude and will reveal similar diagonal ripples. The diagonal ripples which are a sure indication of larger-than-average curves are "trying to be darts"—to create more shape for the curvaceous figure. The ripples are more pronounced in the bust area because bust curves vary in size more than other curves of the figure; however, diagonal ripples will form around *any* larger-than-average curve, and the worker must look for the slightest indication of them.

Larger-than-average bust (cup size) Review Figure 5-6 and the accompanying text on page 118.

Protruding hips When viewed from the side, the side seamlines of a straight fitted skirt will not fall in a proper plumbline but will swing toward the back (toward the larger-than-average curve). There may be some evidence of diagonal ripples leading from the high point of the curve diagonally downward toward the side-hemline corner or upward toward the waist-side corner. The skirt will not hang in a plumbline at the center back but will jut out in the back.

Prominent hipbones or stomach When viewed from the side, the side seamlines of a straight fitted skirt will not fall in a proper plumbline but will swing toward the front (toward the larger-than-average curve). Diagonal ripples may appear leading from the high point of the curve downward toward the side-hemline corner or upward toward the waist-side corner. The skirt will jut out at the center front as it does on a pregnant woman.

Round shoulders or prominent shoulder bones Diagonal ripples will form in any direction very much like those pictured radiating from the bust in Figure 5-6. They will usually be less prominent because shoulders do not vary greatly from the average.

Heavy upper arms The sleeve will be too tight at the biceps line because there will not be sufficient width to allow for at least 2 inches of livability or fitting ease, and ripples may form from the biceps line diagonally upward toward the sleeve cap.

Estimate the amount of spread or extra width or length required to create sufficient shape to correspond to body curves In any alteration made in the dart position, the pattern will be slashed and spread apart to allow for a boat-shaped insertion or addition; the amount of spread at the level of the high point of the curve allows extra length or width (and in some cases both), but just as important, it increases the width of the dart, making the garment more curvaceous. The amount of spread is the pertinent issue, and this is difficult to determine with absolute accuracy. In every curve, two factors are involved—the curve itself and the posture of the individual; and the ambiguous subtleties of posture are difficult to recognize. An estimate (an educated guess) must be made and the altered pattern must be tested on the figure. This test will reveal obvious misfits, and the alteration can be revised. But 'the paper-pattern test is not sufficient for high standards of fit, and the estimated alteration must be muslin-tested for predictably good results.

These basic facts apply to alterations made at seamlines. If a seamline is involved, the addition (which corresponds to the spread mentioned above) is made at the pattern edges.

The following estimates of the amount of spread required at the bust level reveal the influence of posture. They are included as helpful guidelines (only) for deciding on the initial alteration, with the understanding that the estimated alteration will be muslin-tested. The amounts of spread, estimated below, are the amounts required at the bust point of the half pattern—in other words, the spread required for one side of the figure.

For an A cup If the posture is normal, no alteration will be required, but it the posture is very erect or the rib cage unusually well-developed a ¼-inch spread may be required.

For a B cup If the posture is normal, probably no alteration will be required, but if the posture is very erect or the rib cage unusually well-developed, a spread of ¼ inch to as much as ¾ inch may be required.

For a C cup If the figure has a sagging posture, probably no alteration will be required. For a C cup with normal posture a spread of ½ inch may be required and, if the posture is very erect or the rib cage well-developed, a spread of as much as 1 inch may be needed.

For a D or E cup Here some spread will be necessary even if the posture is very poor. If the figure has an average posture, a spread of ¾ inch will probably be required, and if the posture is very erect, as much as 1½ inches will be needed. In the author's experience (with well over a thousand figures), only one person required a spread of 2 inches, but many with larger cup sizes required 1¼ or 1½ inches additional spread.

Because other curves of the figure are not classified into sizes, it is more difficult to state estimates; but it is well to keep in mind that the amount of spread will not be as great for other curves simply because other curves do not vary as greatly as bust curves. For round shoulders and for protruding hipbones, the spread will rarely exceed ¼ to ½ inch, but it may be as great as ¾ inch for exaggerated problems. For a protruding stomach or protruding hips, the amount of spread may vary from ½ inch to as much as 1 inch and will exceed 1 inch only for exaggerated problems.

Keep in mind that the primary purpose of the alteration is to increase the spread to create a wider dart for the more curvaceous figure. The spread may result in addi-

tional width or additional length or both (depending on the direction of the dart involved), but that is of secondary importance at this time; the amount of spread for greater shape is the issue for the initial alteration, regardless of the direction of the dart. In other words, the figure which requires a spread of ½ inch to create the proper shape to correspond to a body curve requires approximately the same spread on any dart (vertical, horizontal or diagonal) which will fit that curve.

Alter the pattern and test on the figure Using the estimate decided upon, alter the pattern piece according to directions in the following sections. Then pin all darts and test the altered pattern on the figure. Note the boat-shaped insertion and compare it with a similar design in Figure 5-31. The altered pattern should hug the body along all curves and all edges, and there should be no remaining evidence of diagonal ripples. If there are still indications of insufficient shape, make a new estimate and revise the alteration, allowing for a greater spread, and retest on the figure. If the pattern stands away from the high point of the curve, too much shape has been added; revise the alteration by allowing less spread and retest on the figure.

Muslin testing Testing the paper pattern piece is not adequate if the pattern will be used for an important costume or will be cut of expensive fabric. Evidences of misfit will be revealed in the muslin test copy and the alteration may require some revision; the techniques of fitting and perfecting the alteration are covered in detail in Chapter 6.

Keep records Making estimates, experimenting, revising alterations, and making the muslin test copy are very time-consuming processes, and it is important to shorten and simplify them as soon as possible. All these procedures can be greatly simplified and many (including the muslin test) can be eliminated if careful records are kept for the first several garments. For example, a person may use a ¾-inch spread on a vertical bust dart for her first project and discover with experience on several garments that a ⅝-inch spread is the better solution; soon she can alter all vertical bust darts ⅝ inch and eliminate all testing. Having made this discovery, she can be assured that a ⅝-inch spread will be very adequate regardless of the dart involved—the amount of spread remains quite consistent. However, with experience, little refinements will result in improvements. For example, the same person may find that a ½-inch spread at the bust level is somewhat better if the alteration is done on a diagonal or French dart, and that a ¾-inch spread is more effective for horizontal darts. By keeping records of the alteration and making notes of its effectiveness for several garments, this tedious alteration can eventually be done quickly and simply with predictably effective results.

Alterations for larger-than-average curves in the lower torso

Basic principle of slashing and spreading darts Figure 5-33 illustrates basic principles on a skirt front (above-the-knee length). These principles can be applied to any dart in any pattern piece; the alteration is simpler in basic skirts like the one pictured because they have fewer complicating design details than jackets and coats. Basic principles remain constant regardless of the pattern piece involved, but they must be modified somewhat with each pattern and design.

Work must be done carefully along ruler lines, so that the altered pattern will not buckle and will remain absolutely flat for accurate cutting. The technique is shown in great detail with steps listed in chronological order in Figure 5-33. Study these sketches and the accompanying text very carefully; other alterations in this series will be covered with less detail.

Step 1 Draw a ruler line through the center of the dart to be altered. In this case, the dart nearer the center front is altered for the figure with a curvaceous stomach; the dart nearer the side edge could be altered in like manner for the figure with a prominent hipbone or pad of flesh in that area.

Step 2 Slash along the ruler line to the lower edge of the pattern. If the slash ends at the seamline (as in Figure 5-34), it should be made only to the seamline and should not extend to the cut edge as it does in a pattern with a hem allowance.

Step 3 Draw a ruler line on a strip of paper and tape one slashed edge carefully to that line. If these lines are not taped accurately along the ruler lines, the pattern will buckle and will not lie flat for accurate cutting.

Step 4 Mark off the estimated increase at the high point of the curve (the tip of the dart), and draw a second line on the insertion strip as shown. Note that the ruler lines slant so that they are farther apart at the waistline; in other words, if the pattern is spread about ½ inch at the hip level, it will spread to perhaps ¾ inch at the waistline, increasing the width of the dart by ¾ inch at its base.

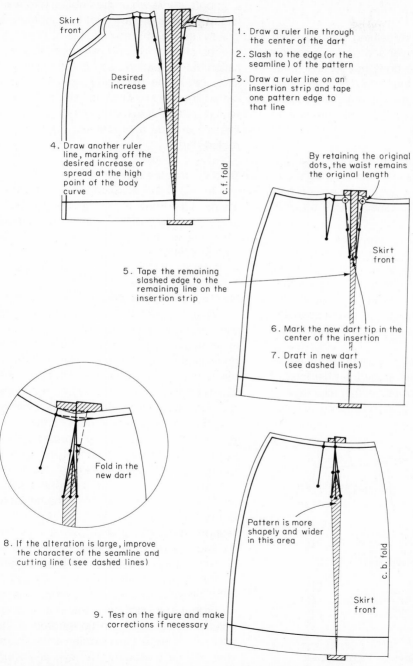

Skirt
front

Desired
increase

1. Draw a ruler line through
   the center of the dart
2. Slash to the edge (or the
   seamline) of the pattern
3. Draw a ruler line on an
   insertion strip and tape
   one pattern edge to
   that line

4. Draw another ruler
   line, marking off the
   desired increase or
   spread at the high
   point of the body
   curve

c.f. fold

By retaining the original
dots, the waist remains
the original length

Skirt
front

5. Tape the remaining
   slashed edge to the
   remaining line on the
   insertion strip

6. Mark the new dart tip in the
   center of the insertion

7. Draft in new dart
   (see dashed lines)

Fold in the
new dart

8. If the alteration is large, improve
   the character of the seamline and
   cutting line (see dashed lines)

Pattern is more
shapely and wider
in this area

c.b. fold

Skirt
front

9. Test on the figure and make
   corrections if necessary

FIGURE 5-33   Basic principles of slashing and spreading darts.

Step 5 Tape the remaining slashed edge to the remaining ruler line on the insertion strip. If the pattern does not lie absolutely flat on the table, the ruler lines have not been followed accurately; make corrections at this time by lifting the tape and shifting the pattern slightly.

Step 6 Mark the tip of the new, wider dart at the center of the insertion on a level with the original dart tip. By centering the new dart tip, the new dartlines will be equal in length.

Step 7 Draw new dartlines (shown in heavy dashed lines in all sketches of this series) from the new tip to the original dots at the seamline. By using the original dots at the seamline, the length of the seamline has not been changed at the waist.

Step 8 Fold in the new dart along the corrected dartlines and study the character of the seamline involved. If the alteration is large (more than ½ inch on long darts or more than ¼ inch on short darts), the seamline may be noticeably distorted. The character of the waistline seam is that it formed a smooth curve when the original dart was folded in. If the dart width is increased greatly, the seamline will angle at the dartline, as shown. To improve the character, flatten out the pattern, add on an extension strip, refold the dart, and sketch in corrected lines as shown. Trim along the corrected cutting line with the dart folded in; this will provide a proper jog for the corrected dart.

Step 9 Test the altered pattern on the figure to see if the additional shape corresponds to the body curve. If it does not, separate one section of the pattern, draw a new ruler line on the insertion strip (allowing for a greater or lesser spread), and proceed as before.

Basic principles applied Figure 5-34 shows a diagonal dart altered for the figure with prominent hipbones. Because the dart is in a diagonal direction, the slash line ends at the side seamline rather than at the hemline. Whenever this happens, the slash is made to the seamline and not to the cut edge because in this way the original length of the seamline is not changed and remains the length of the corresponding seam to which it will be joined. Refer back to Figure 5-33; slashing through the hemline directly to the cutting line adds a slight amount to the measurement of the hemline, but because it will not be seamed to a corresponding piece, a slight addition is not a disadvantage when a hem is involved.

When a slash is made and the pattern is spread out, both edges are distorted; if the alteration is small, the distortion is so slight that it will not be visibly out of character and therefore can be ignored. If the alteration is large, the distortion at the seamlines will be obvious to the eye and must

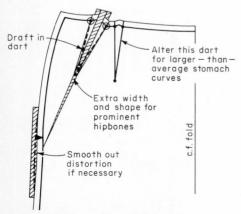

Draft in dart

Alter this dart for larger — than — average stomach curves

Extra width and shape for prominent hipbones

c.f. fold

Smooth out distortion if necessary

FIGURE 5-34 *Basic principles applied.*

be corrected. See step 8 in Figure 5-33, which shows the waistline (which has become angular) corrected with a smooth curve in character with the original seamline. The seamlines in Figure 5-34 at the waistline and at the side edge will both be distorted if the alteration is sizable. The waist should be corrected the same as in step 8 in Figure 5-33. If the side seamline dips inward, correct the distortion as shown in Figure 5-34.

Figure 5-35 shows basic principles applied to create additional shape and width for protruding hips. Sketch *a* shows a full-length skirt altered exactly like the short skirt in Figure 5-33. If there are two darts in the skirt, either may be altered; the choice is determined by the location of the larger-than-average curve on the figure. In some

figures the high point of the hip curve is nearer the center and in others nearer the side. If the figure irregularity is exaggerated, both darts can be altered; for example, if the dart must be spread ¾ inch at the hip level, it is advisable to slash both darts, spreading each ⅜ inch so that neither dart will be too pointed to fit the hip curve smoothly. The alteration in sketch *a* has maintained the original width at the lower edge and is acceptable only in certain patterns. *The lower edge must be as wide as or wider than the altered hipline;* fold the pattern to bring the lower edge up to the hip

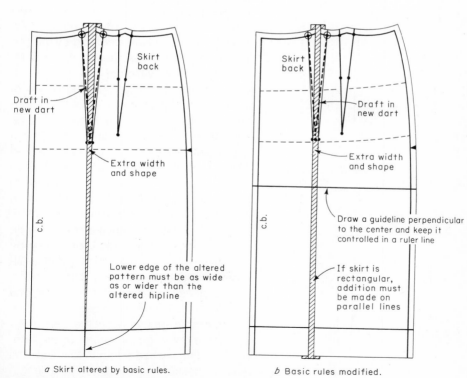

a Skirt altered by basic rules.   *b* Basic rules modified.

FIGURE 5-35 *Basic principles applied to vertical darts.*

level and compare widths. If the altered hip-line is wider than the lower edge, use the similar alteration shown in sketch *b*.

Sketch *b* shows the basic alteration modified in such a way that the extra width at the hipline is added on parallel lines, increasing the width at the lower edge by the same amount. This method must be used if the pattern (before alteration) is

rectangular below the hipline; this method can be used with any skirt design if the individual desires extra width at the lower edge.

The guideline shown in sketch *b* is necessary when a pattern will be slashed and completely spread apart; the guideline, made perpendicular to the center line (or the grainline) and then controlled to remain ruler-straight in the altered pattern, keeps the two parts of the pattern in proper position to each other.

The parallel insertion has resulted in a modified boat-shaped addition. The familiar boat shape (half of a boat) is created above the level of the body curve. A parallel insertion can be used if the edge will fall free from the body and will not be joined to a corresponding seam.

To create a new dart where there is no existing dart If the figure is curvaceous at a place where there is no dart provided, a new dart can be created by modifying the basic rules illustrated in Figure 5-33. See Figure 5-36, which shows a skirt back with only one dart. If the figure has a pad of flesh a few inches below the waist, another dart is required to fit the problem curve. Test the pattern on the figure and mark the high point of the problem curve (marked *x* in the sketch). Establish the desired dart-line; it can be in any direction—diagonal, as shown, or parallel to the existing dart, if desired. Continue the ruler line until it touches the edge of the pattern; this may be the side edge, as illustrated, or it may be the lower edge if the additional dart is almost parallel to the existing dart.

The alteration differs from the basic one only in the way the new dart is marked. Note that dots are marked at the base of the dart at the meeting point of the waist seamline and the slashed edge; in this way, the waist seamline retains its original length when the dart is folded in.

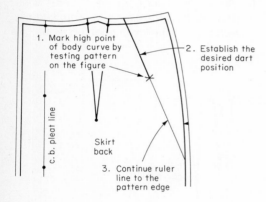

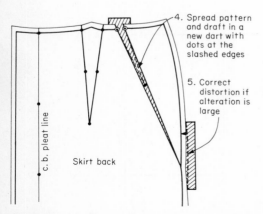

FIGURE 5-36 *To create a new dart where there is no existing dart.*

Horizontal alteration adds shape and length for protruding hips Protruding hips require more shape and more width or length, and ideally they require both width and length. A vertical alteration is often adequate for figures which are only slightly more curvaceous than average; but if the figure irregularity is great, more length is required as well. The best solution for curvaceous figures is to combine vertical and horizontal alterations, as will be seen in Figure 5-38.

Refer to design e in Figure 5-31. When a boat-shaped alteration is made horizontally, the "boat" reaches from side to side, being completed when two sections of the skirt or pants are cut of fabric.

The alteration shown in Figure 5-37 is somewhat different from preceding ones, but it is closely related because it results in the same boat-shaped insertion and in an accompanying increase in dart width. The alteration is the same for any type of garment—pants, shorts, or skirt. It is equally necessary and effective in all types of costumes, but the person with protruding hips will be more aware of its influence on wearing comfort in pants or shorts; she is aware of the need for extra back length because pants or shorts pull too tightly in the crotch when she sits and the waistband becomes uncomfortable as it tugs down to provide the extra length her figure needs.

It will be necessary to experiment and muslin-test the alteration to determine the amount of extra length required for the figure. It is not unusual for this type of figure to require as much as 1 inch of extra length. A proper amount of extra length will provide both comfort and attractive fit in pants or shorts, and in skirts it will prevent the skirt from jutting outward at the back and will allow side seamlines to hang in proper plumblines (side seamlines of skirts swing toward the back if the pattern is not altered for this type of figure).

Draw slash lines at the level of the longest dart as indicated in sketch a. Note the area circled in sketch b; the upper section nearest the center must be separated from the remainder of the pattern in order to control

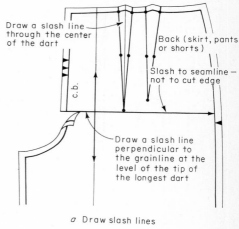

a Draw slash lines

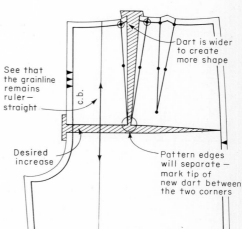

b Alteration completed

FIGURE 5-37 *Horizontal alteration adds extra length and shape for protruding hips.*

grainlines properly along ruler-straight lines. Note that the pattern is lengthened along parallel lines between the center line and the tip of the dart and that the familiar boat shape is created between the dart tip and the side seamline. These procedures have created a wider dart, as shown. A new dart must be drafted in as usual, with the tip located at the center of the insertion and the lines returning to the original dots at the waist; the new dartlines are not illustrated in order to simplify the sketch.

Combine horizontal and vertical alterations for the ideal solution Any figure which is very curvaceous (and especially a figure with posture irregularities which cause exaggerated problems) requires more shape and both extra width and extra length; the best solution, therefore, is to combine the two alterations, obtaining extra width with a vertical alteration and extra length with a horizontal alteration. See Figure 5-38. The two alterations are combined by simply altering the pattern in one direction and then altering the already-altered pattern in the other direction; it makes no difference which one is done first. Note that because the horizontal alteration will involve the dart nearer the center, it should not be used for the vertical alteration. The vertical alteration can be done in either of two ways; by altering one of the existing darts as in sketch b, Figure 5-35, or by creating a new dart the same as in Figure 5-36. The choice is dependent on the figure irregularity and the location of the curve on the figure. If the figure has protruding hips and also a pad of flesh near the side edge, the creation of a new dart, as illustrated here, will solve both figure problems.

After the vertical alteration is made, proceed with the horizontal alteration (the same as in Figure 5-37), by slashing through the already-altered pattern as though it had not been altered.

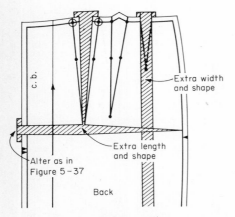

Draft in a dart to create shape and compensate for the addition at the waist

End the dart at the level where the figure is curvaceous

c.b.

Back (skirt, pants or shorts)

Complete vertical alteration to add width and shape.

Extra width and shape

c.b.

Alter as in Figure 5-37

Extra length and shape

Back

Do a horizontal alteration on the altered pattern to add length and shape.

FIGURE 5-38 Vertical and horizontal alterations combined are the ideal solution for exaggerated curves.

Basic principles of making boat-shaped alterations at pattern edges

Figures 5-33 through 5-38 and the accompanying text reveal that alterations which change shape and width or length (or both) can be made in two ways: by slashing and spreading an existing dart or by slashing and spreading and then

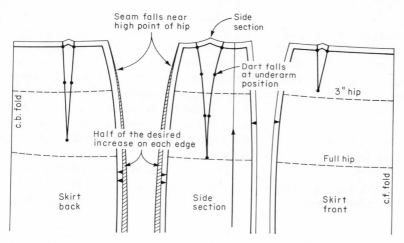

Boat — shaped addition on each side back seam for protruding hips.

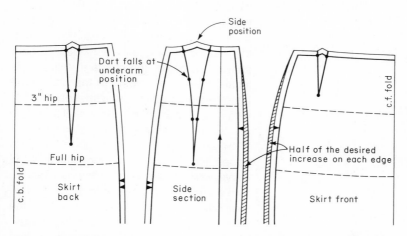

Boat — shaped addition on side front seams creates extra width and shape for heavy thighs.

FIGURE 5-39 Boat-shaped additions made at vertical seamlines that pass over or near the high point of curves.

creating an additional dart. The alteration must be made in the place where the problem curve exists; if that curve is in a position where there is no seam in the pattern, it must be made within the body of the pattern piece, as illustrated in Figures 5-33 through 5-38.

The same type of alteration can be made at the pattern edges if the seamline passes over or near the high point of the body curve. Seamlines in these positions replace dartlines and provide a dart-fitting-in-a-seam; princess-line designs employ this type of fitting.

The skirt pattern shown in Figure 5-39 is shaped by darts and also by vertical seamlines near the high point of body curves. Note that a wide curving dart creates shape in the side position and that

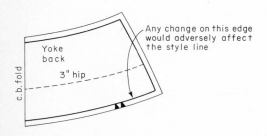

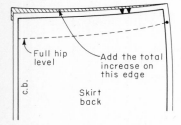

To create extra length and shape for protruding hips

FIGURE 5-40 Boat-shaped additions made at horizontal seamlines that pass over or near the high point of body curves.

the two vertical seams are a few inches on either side of the side position — close to the hipbones and thighs in front and close to the hips in the back. Any one of the three darts pictured can be altered to create extra shape and width by following the basic principles outlined in Figure 5-33. However, if the seamlines pass over or near the problem curve of the body, the alteration can be done at the outside edge of the pattern. The upper sketch shows an alteration which is comparable to the one shown in sketch *b*, Figure 5-35; the familiar boat shape appears above the level of the problem curve and the addition is made on parallel lines below the curve. See the altered pattern on the figure in Figure 5-32. This alteration is very effective to provide extra width and shape for heavy thighs. Note that one half of the desired increase is made on each corresponding edge. This is acceptable in this design; but, as will be seen in Figure 5-40, in some designs the entire addition must be made on only one of the corresponding edges.

The lower sketch in Figure 5-39 shows an identical alteration made at the back seamlines to create extra shape and width for protruding hips. Compare this alteration with the one shown in sketch *b*, Figure 5-35, to see their similarity. The difference in the results is only in the location where shape is created; the shape in this one is located somewhat closer to the side of the figure. Also compare this alteration with the vertical alteration in the upper sketch of Figure 5-38; the two are almost identical.

In any alteration made at the pattern edges, the addition at the high point of the curve, which tapers back to the original pattern edge (at the waistline in these skirt alterations), creates more shape because the dart-fitting-in-the-seam has been increased; this has the same effect as making a dart wider.

The horizontal alteration shown in Figure 5-40 creates extra shape and length for protruding hips. See the altered pattern on the figure in Figure 5-32 and compare it with design *e* in Figure 31; both result in a boat-shaped alteration reaching from side to side on the figure. Note that in this case the addition is made on only one of the two corresponding pattern edges. In some designs this must be done in order to maintain the original design line. Note that the lower edge of the yoke is parallel to the waistline; if an addition were made on the yoke edge, the yokeline would dip in the center, greatly affecting the design.

Refer back to the alterations in Figure 5-39. They, too, altered the position of the style lines of the design because the style line of the altered pattern is somewhat more curvaceous. However, in those skirt designs the style line was not adversely affected because its general character (curved above the hipline, hanging in a plumbline below the hip level) was not changed. The altered line is in character but just slightly more curvaceous. By contrast, a change in the yokeline in Figure 5-40 (from being parallel to the waist to dipping in the back) would greatly change its character.

Alterations for larger-than-average bust curves

Before beginning work Study the entire section for alterations in the lower torso beginning on page 166. Basic principles were explained in detail on skirt patterns because they have fewer complicating design details; the same type of alteration is more difficult on jacket and coat patterns where design features are concentrated. In addition, curves in the upper torso, especially bust curves, vary from the average more than other curves of the figure.

The cross references mentioned in the foregoing pages are repeated here to emphasize the importance of pooling all information relative to the problems of fitting

curves. They are: "A Critical Reevaluation of Bust Size" on page 46, "Tests for Figure Problems Involved with the Subtle Issue of Shape" on page 117, "The Principle of Dart Fitting—a Guideline" on page 136 and "Estimate the Amount of Extra Width or Length Required" on page 164.

Before deciding on alterations for the bust curve, study all information in this entire series. This is important because the ideal solution (especially for large alterations) requires a combination of alterations which should not be attempted until all are thoroughly understood.

The sketches in this series picture relatively short jackets to conserve space on the page. The alterations are done in the same manner on overblouses and coats. Any alteration which requires a vertical slash and spread is more difficult to handle in a coat only because of the greater difficulty in controlling longer lines; the altered pattern, therefore, will be flat for accurate cutting. Take great care to control the pattern along ruler lines.

Basic principles of slashing and spreading darts Figure 5-41 pictures a jacket (or coat) front with a shoulder dart altered by the basic rules outlined in detail in Figure 5-33. It is important to compare each new problem with a similar problem; this is the best way to learn to apply principles to the ever-changing circumstances which will be encountered with each new design. Note that the distorted cutting line at the lower edge is corrected in sketch *a;* distortions are obvious if the original cutting line is ruler-straight, but the curved lower edge of the skirt in Figure 5-33 did not reveal a distortion (although it was there). *If the distortion is visible, it must be* *corrected.* Sketch *b* shows the new dart drafted in. Strips of paper are shown taped to the shoulder edge in preparation for correcting a distortion which will be visible.

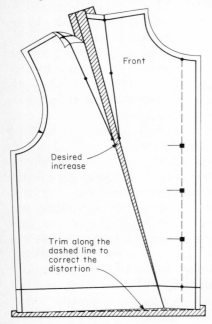

Front

Desired
increase

Trim along the
dashed line to
correct the
distortion

a Basic alteration.

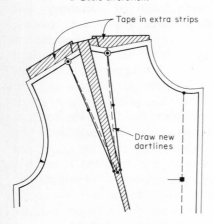

Tape in extra strips

Draw new
dartlines

b Draft in new dart.

See sketch *c.* Fold in the new dart. The original cutting line at the shoulder edge was composed of two ruler-line segments which became one continuous ruler line when the original dart was folded in. This alteration has caused the two segments to angle. Draw a new ruler line, as shown, and cut along this line (dashed line) with the dart folded in; by so doing, a proper jog is formed for the new dart. See the finished pattern in sketch *a,* Figure 5-42.

This vertical alteration adds shape and width and as the distortions at the shoulder and lower edges are corrected, a small amount of extra length as well. Note that the extra length is provided above and below the high point of the bust curve — exactly where more length is needed to span a larger-than-average curve.

Basic principles applied Sketch *a* of Figure 5-42 shows the finished shoulder-dart alteration made by following the basic rules. Sketch *b* shows a comparable alteration done by modifying basic rules; compare these two with the altered skirts in Figure 5-35. The choice between these two methods is dependent on the figure involved; the extra width at the lower edge of

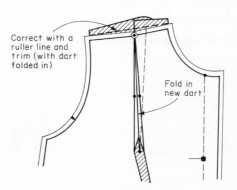

Correct with a
ruler line and
trim (with dart
folded in)

Fold in
new dart

c Correct distortion at seamlines.

FIGURE 5-41 Basic principles of slashing and spreading darts for larger-than-average bust curves.

sketch *b* will be an advantage if hips are larger than average and will also help camouflage a curvaceous bustline.

The guideline in sketch *b,* Figure 5-42, is necessary when a pattern will be slashed and completely spread apart; the guideline, made perpendicular to the center line (or the grainline) and then controlled to remain a ruler line in the altered pattern, keeps the two parts of the pattern in proper relation to each other.

An alteration on a shoulder dart does not influence the front-facing pattern. However, alterations on diagonal or horizontal darts do involve the facing. See Figure 5-43. As the boat-shaped insertion tapers off to the seamline at the neck edge, extra width is added to the pattern and the facing must be altered accordingly, as shown.

Note that the original lines of this French dart were slightly curved to reveal the bust curve better. Draw in new dartlines in character with the original lines. Because in previous patterns dartlines were ruler-straight, the new dartlines were drawn with a ruler. By drawing new dartlines in character with the original, one retains the effect the designer intended; however, if one does not wish to reveal the bust curve, these new dartlines can be made ruler-straight.

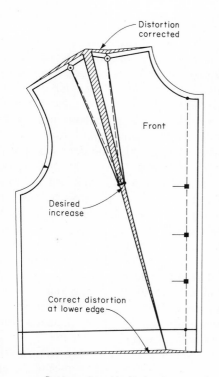

a Pattern altered by basic rules.

FIGURE 5-42 Basic principles applied.

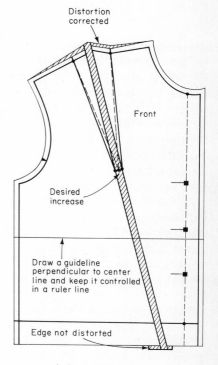

b Basic rules modified.

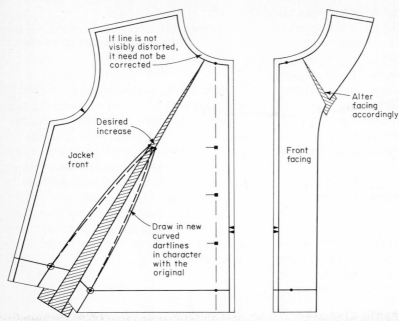

Labels within figure:

If line is not visibly distorted, it need not be corrected

Desired increase

Jacket front

Draw in new curved dartlines in character with the original

Alter facing accordingly

Front facing

FIGURE 5-43 *Basic principles applied.*

Alterations on horizontal darts Figure 5-44 pictures a double-breasted design with a horizontal underarm dart. Because a double-breasted design laps over the center front (often several inches) any increase in length gained with a horizontal alteration must be made on parallel lines. The same boat-shaped alteration will result, but in this case the "boat" is completed when the two fronts are cut of fabric. It extends from side to side across the figure and allows extra length over the bust and also between the high points of the bust curves. The slash follows the center line of the dart and need not be (very probably will not be) perpendicular to the center line or the grainline. The two parts of the pattern are in proper relationship to each other when grainlines and center lines in the altered pattern are controlled in one continuous ruler line. Draft in the new dart in the usual manner. Alter the front facing accordingly. If the facing is cut in one with the

major piece, the alteration is simplified, as shown. If there are buttons and buttonholes below the level of the alteration, they must be respaced. To correct the distortion at the side edge of the pattern, see Figure 5-46 and the accompanying text.

This alteration must be done on parallel lines if the design is double-breasted, as shown in Figure 5-44, and it can be done the same way in single-breasted designs. The alternative method detailed in Figure 5-45 is appropriate for single-breasted designs only. Compare the two to see that in Figure 5-44 the boat shape reaches from side to side and allows extra length at the center of the figure and that in Figure 5-45 the boat shape extends from side to center, tapering off at the finished front edge and allowing no extra length at the center of the figure. The more complicated alteration in Figure 5-45 is difficult to execute because it distorts so many lines on the pattern. Even so, many persons will prefer it when working with single-breasted designs. If the alteration will not be large (½ inch or less) and if the figure is well-controlled to create pronounced cleavage, no extra length is required at the center and this alteration will be more effective than its alternative. By contrast, the figure with a massive but not shapely bust (little cleavage) requires the extra length at the

center, which the side-to-side "boat" provides. To correct the distortion at the side edge, see Figure 5-46.

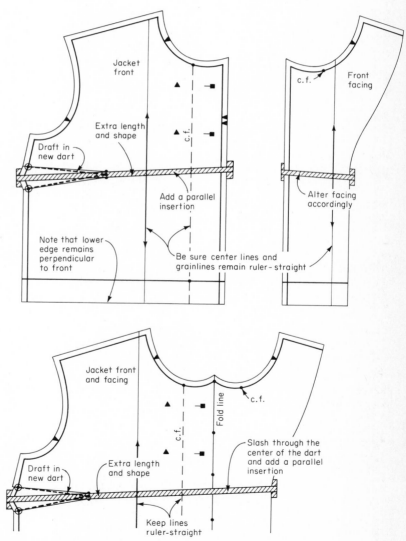

FIGURE 5-44 Horizontal alteration done on parallel lines.

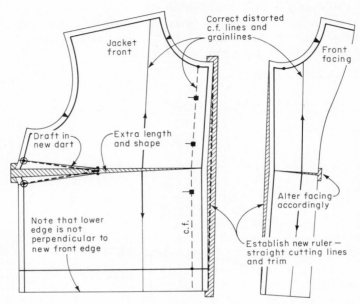

Correct distorted
c.f. lines and
grainlines

Jacket
front

Front
facing

Draft in
new dart

Extra length
and shape

Note that lower
edge is not
perpendicular to
new front edge

c.f.

Alter facing
accordingly

Establish new ruler —
straight cutting lines
and trim

a Jacket with separate facing

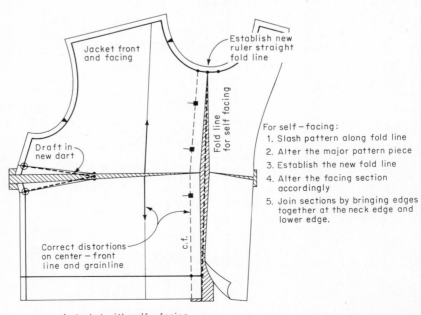

Jacket front
and facing

Establish new
ruler straight
fold line

Fold line
for self facing

Draft in
new dart

Correct distortions
on center — front
line and grainline

c.f.

For self – facing:
1. Slash pattern along fold line
2. Alter the major pattern piece
3. Establish the new fold line
4. Alter the facing section
   accordingly
5. Join sections by bringing edges
   together at the neck edge and
   lower edge.

b Jacket with self – facing

FIGURE 5-45 *Alternative method for single-breasted designs only.*

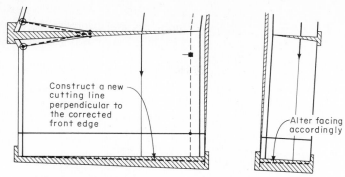

Construct a new
cutting line
perpendicular to
the corrected
front edge

Alter facing
accordingly

c Additional step required for boxy designs that will be cut in plaid
or fabric with a prominent crosswise thread or design

FIGURE 5-45 *Continued.*

Exaggerated distortions at pattern edges Whenever a dart is slashed and spread, there will be a slight distortion at the pattern edge; it is revealed when the new dart is folded in and the character of the altered line is compared with the character of the original. See similar distortions in step 8, Figure 5-33 and sketch *c*, Figure 5-41. These distortions are exaggerated by large alterations and short darts. Because horizontal darts are the shortest darts, the distortions will be greater for these, as shown in Figure 5-46. The side edge of a boxy garment formed a continuous ruler-straight line when the original dart was folded in; any alteration will cause the line to angle. To correct it, tape on an extension and fold in the new dart. Construct a new ruler line as shown and cut along this new cutting line (dashed line) with the new dart folded in; this will provide a proper jog for the new dart. Note that the corrected line allows another boat-shaped addition which provides extra width in the bust area. This is an advantage because horizontal alterations provide only extra shape and length.

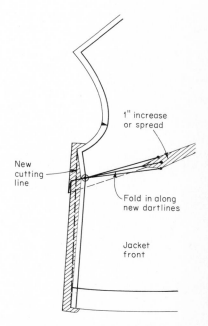

1" increase
or spread

New
cutting
line

Fold in along
new dartlines

Jacket
front

FIGURE 5-46 *Distortions are exaggerated by large alterations, by short darts, and by long pattern pieces.*

Basic principles applied Figure 5-47 pictures a pattern in which portions of the front and back are combined to form a side section. The style line is a few inches from the bust curve, and the dart to create shape at the high point of the bust curve is very short (usually 2 or 3 inches long). If the alteration is small (⅜ inch or less), the side section need not be altered. If the alteration is large, another alteration can be combined with this; it is shown in sketch *a* of Figure 5-52.

The very short dart will distort the pattern edges considerably, as shown in sketch *b*. Draw a new cutting line, forming a smooth curve which conforms to the character of the original seamline.

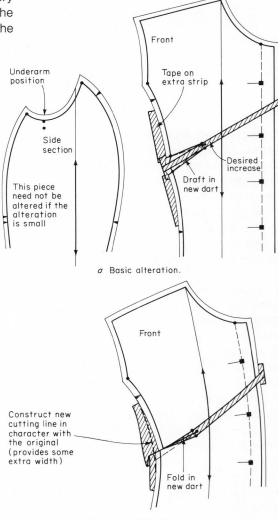

a Basic alteration.

b Correct distortions.

FIGURE 5-47 *Basic principles applied.*

To create a new dart where there is no existing dart The basic principles of slashing and spreading the pattern to create more shape and width or length (or both) can be slightly modified to create a new dart; by this method shape can be provided to correspond to individual body curves. Review Figure 5-36 and the accompanying text.

Although irregularities of the individual figure are usually responsible for a need for additional darts where no dart existed in the original pattern, *fashion may magnify problems and may even create the need for additional shape, and therefore for additional darts, for the figure that is quite average.* Examples are relatively rare, but one outstanding example will serve as an excellent illustration. In the late 1960s and early 1970s, fashion dictated a "no dart" look at the bust. The problem was grave because the bust curve is the most pro-

nounced on the figure. Although these designs usually (not always) included some slight shaping in the general area of the bust, the amount of shape was not adequate for average bust curves and the shape was not created directly at the high point of the curve. As a result, average curves appeared larger than average and larger-than-average curves were exaggerated; the need for a dart was very evident.

The pattern pieces shown in Figure 5-48 are typical of the no-dart type. The curved style line is located several inches from the high point of the bust curve. Although there is some dart fitting in the seam, it is slight, and the seam is not located sufficiently

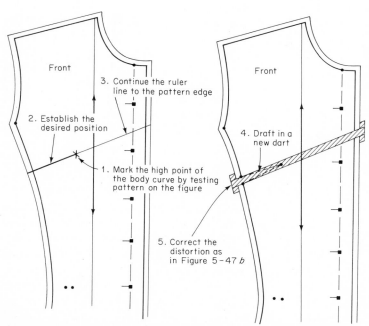

FIGURE 5-48 *To create a new dart where there is no existing dart.*

close to the bust curve to effectively provide shape for the bust. Creating a new dart is very similar to increasing the width of an existing dart, as will be evident by comparing this alteration with the one pictured in Figure 5-47.

Pin the pattern pieces together and test on the figure to see the effect of the no-dart fitting and to look for evidence of diagonal ripples; they will appear on all figures except those with very small bust curves. Mark the bust point on the figure and establish the position of the new dartline; a line that slants upward, as shown, is flattering

to most figures. Slash and spread the pattern in the usual way; the amount of spread will usually be greater than the same figure requires on a pattern which already includes the standard dart shaping at the bust. Complete the alteration in the usual manner (see Figure 5-47) with one exception: Mark off the dart width with dots at the meeting point of the seamline and the slashed edges, as shown.

This dart must be basted before stitching because there may be adjustments during fitting. The original pattern may (or may not) have been made with a small amount of ease between the notches on the front; ease between these notches creates a slight amount of shape, comparable to (but more generalized than) the shape created by a dart. During fitting, the fitter will have the option of retaining the ease along with the new dart or of increasing the width of the dart to include the generalized shape created by the ease.

Basic principles of making boat-shaped alterations at pattern edges
Review the section under this heading on page 173 and "Boat-shaped Alterations Made at Seamlines That Pass Over or Very Near the High Point of Body Curves" on page 162.

In making alterations for bust and shoulder curves, the entire alteration is made on only one of two corresponding pattern edges. In this type of design, one of the two seams controls the style line in the finished garment (by being the line visible to the eye), and any alteration on that edge would adversely affect the design. See the two pieces in Figure 5-49; the line over the bust of the front piece will be visible as the garment is worn, and it will control the corresponding edge of the side section, which will not be visible.

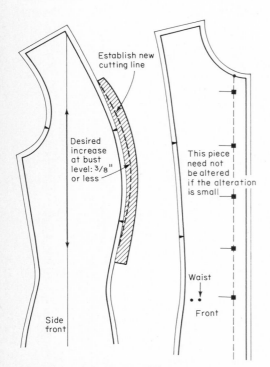

FIGURE 5-49 *Small boat-shaped alterations made at vertical seamlines that pass over or near the high point of the bust curve.*

Small alterations A small alteration (⅜ inch or less) is shown in Figure 5-49. The familiar boat shape, which tapers off a few inches above and below the bust level, is created by drawing a new cutting line in character with the original. The side front-piece will be marked for ease between the notches, as shown. The new cutting line is slightly longer than the original, which means that there will be slightly more ease when the seam is joined. This will present no problem if the alteration is small and the fabric eases well. If the fabric is not pliable, an additional step, shown in the following sketch, will be necessary.

Large alterations   If the alteration is large, both front pieces must be altered as shown in Figure 5-50; the sketch shows a 1-inch increase in width at the bust level of the side section. Compare it with the alteration in Figure 5-49 to see that the new cutting line for larger alterations tapers back to the original over a longer span; this is necessary to preserve the character of the original line. It also serves to add some width over a larger area to correspond to the greater expanse of the fuller bust. The new cutting line is considerably longer than the original, and this is an advantage because the fuller bust requires extra length. But it means that the front piece must be altered accordingly.

The difference can be scientifically measured by comparing the measurements of the seamline (not the cut edge) of the original pattern with the seamline (not the cut edge) of the altered pattern. But this is difficult to do accurately; and since this problem requires muslin testing, the better solution is to estimate the increased length on the front and make corrections if necessary after fitting the muslin test copy. The increase in length of the seamlines is slightly less than the increase in width. Estimate a solution (using measurements in this example as a guide) and anticipate making corrections on the muslin copy and perfecting the alteration later.

It may be helpful to know that of the hundreds of figures the author has worked with, the largest alteration was an extra 2 inches in width on the side front and an extra 1½ inches in length on the front. The woman had a large, matronly bustline and an erect posture which exaggerated her figure irregularity. By contrast, many figures require an additional 1 inch on the side front and an extra ¾ inch in length on the front, as illustrated.

Horizontal alterations   Figure 5-51 shows a yoke seam near the bust level. The entire boat-shaped alteration must be made on

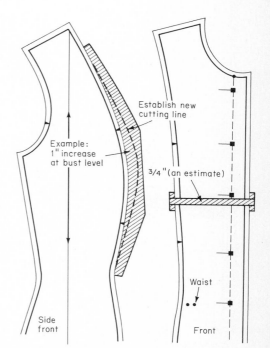

FIGURE 5-50 *Large boat-shaped alterations made at vertical seamlines that pass over or near the high point of the bust curve.*

the upper edge of the front because any addition at the lower edge of the yoke would adversely affect the design line. Two solutions are shown. The new cutting line shown in dashed lines creates a "boat" reaching from side to center and is effective for small alterations. The cutting line shown in a dotted line is required for larger problems; it provides a "boat" which extends from side to side on the figure.

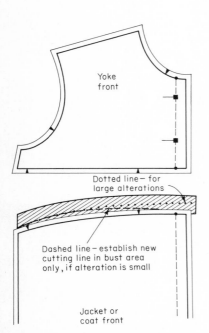

Yoke front

Dotted line— for large alterations

Dashed line—establish new cutting line in bust area only, if alteration is small

Jacket or coat front

FIGURE 5-51 Boat-shaped alteration made at horizontal seamlines that pass over or near the high point of the bust curve.

Combine vertical and horizontal alterations for the ideal solution

Larger-than-average curves require extra shape and both extra length and width; it follows, then, that a combination of vertical and horizontal alterations is the ideal solution. The larger the curve, the greater the need for both length and width. This is done simply by doing first one alteration and then the other; it makes no difference which is done first.

Sketch *a* in Figure 5-52 shows a combination of slashing and spreading a dart in the front for extra shape and length combined with an addition to the pattern edge of the side front for extra shape and width. Compare it with sketch a in Figure 5-47 to see that this solution is better for the very curvaceous figure.

Sketch *b* shows a shoulder dart slashed and spread for extra shape and width (the same as in sketch *b*, Figure 5-42). Then the already-altered pattern is slashed horizontally and spread and a new dart created; this provides additional shape and length for the very curvaceous figure.

When combination alterations are used, both alterations add extra shape; therefore each alteration is smaller than a single alteration would be. For example, the figure which requires a 1-inch spread if there is just one dart will probably require about a ½-inch spread on each of two alterations.

Alterations for rounded shoulders or prominent shoulder blades

Review "Before Beginning Work" on page 175. All the alterations for larger-than-average bust curves can be made in the same way for larger-than-average shoulder curves, although they are less complicated on back patterns (fewer design lines). These alterations are further simplified by the fact that back curves do not vary from the average as much as bust curves (ex-

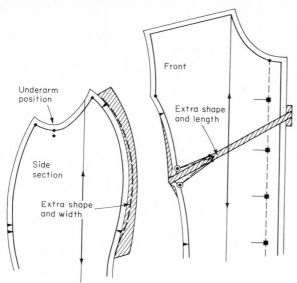

Underarm position

Side section

Extra shape and width

Front

Extra shape and length

a Compare with Figure 5–47 *a*.

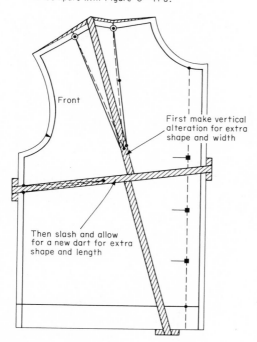

Front

First make vertical alteration for extra shape and width

Then slash and allow for a new dart for extra shape and length

b Compare with Figure 5–42 *b*.

FIGURE 5-52   *Combine vertical and horizontal alterations for the ideal solution for exaggerated curves.*

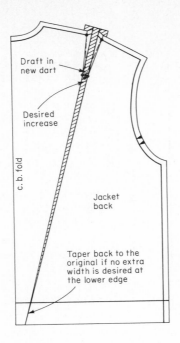

a Shoulder dart altered by basic rules.

Draft in new dart

Desired increase

c. b. fold

Jacket back

Taper back to the original if no extra width is desired at the lower edge

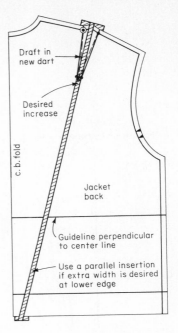

b Basic rules modified.

Draft in new dart

Desired increase

c. b. fold

Jacket back

Guideline perpendicular to center line

Use a parallel insertion if extra width is desired at lower edge

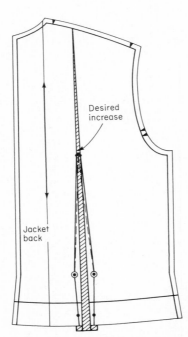

c Waist dart altered by basic rules.

Desired increase

Jacket back

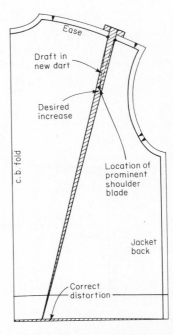

d To create a new dart where there is no existing dart.

Ease

Draft in new dart

Desired increase

c. b. fold

Location of prominent shoulder blade

Jacket back

Correct distortion

FIGURE 5-53 *Basic principles applied to back patterns—for rounded shoulders or prominent shoulder blades.*

cept in the crippled figure). For example, a 1-inch bust alteration (even 1½ inches) is not unusual, and by contrast a ½-inch alteration at the shoulder level can be considered sizable: many shoulder problems are solved with a ¼-inch alteration. The smaller alterations create insignificant distortions at the pattern edges, often being so slight they are not visible and need not be corrected.

Basic principles of slashing and spreading darts Figure 5-53 pictures jacket back patterns altered by slashing and spreading the pattern for extra shape and width in the shoulder area. Sketch *a* shows the basic alteration which increases the dart and provides extra width; note that the boat shape reaches from the shoulder to the lower edge, allowing no extra width at the lower edge. Sketch *b* shows a modification to allow extra width at the lower edge; this is the wiser choice if hips are larger than average. Compare the two sketches with the two in Figure 5-42; they are identical.

Sketch *c* shows a jacket pattern which is slightly fitted at the waist. The alteration is essentially the same, resulting in a "boat" which reaches from the shoulder edge to the waist level. The new dart retains the original dots at the waistline; the jacket will therefore fit exactly like the original except in the shoulder area.

Sketch *d* pictures a new dart where no dart existed in the original pattern. Note that the shoulder edge is marked for ease between the notches; this means that it is slightly longer than the corresponding edge of the front. The ease creates shape in the shoulder area, but the shape is more generalized than the shape created at the tip of a dart. The figure irregularity pictured here is a prominent shoulder blade, located closer to the armhole than it is in the average figure (the dart is usually centered on the shoulderline). To create a new dart, test the pattern on the figure and mark the

high point of the body curve. Then draw the desired dartline and slash, allowing for the increase desired. Mark the new dart, as shown. See a similar problem in Figure 5-36. This alteration can be done on parallel lines (similar to sketch *b*) if extra width is desired at the hip level. See a similar alteration in Figure 5-48; although that one is made horizontally and this is made vertically, the two are done in an identical way.

Basic principles of making alterations at pattern edges Figure 5-54 shows jacket or coat pieces for a princess-line design. When a style line passes over or very near the high point of the body curve, the alteration is done at the pattern edges.

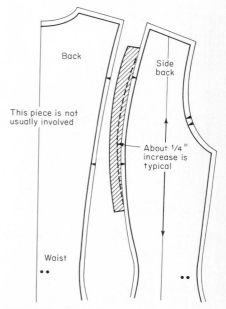

Back

Side back

This piece is not usually involved

About ¼" increase is typical

Waist

FIGURE 5-54 Basic principles applied.

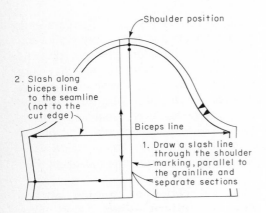

2. Slash along
biceps line
to the seamline
(not to the
cut edge)

Shoulder position

Biceps line

1. Draw a slash line
through the shoulder
marking, parallel to
the grainline and
separate sections

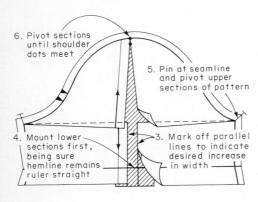

6. Pivot sections
until shoulder
dots meet

5. Pin at seamline
and pivot upper
sections of pattern

4. Mount lower
sections first,
being sure
hemline remains
ruler straight

3. Mark off parallel
lines to indicate
desired increase
in width

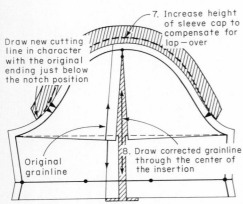

7. Increase height
of sleeve cap to
compensate for
lap — over

Draw new cutting
line in character
with the original
ending just below
the notch position

Original
grainline

8. Draw corrected grainline
through the center of
the insertion

FIGURE 5-55 Alteration for short sleeves or
boxy sleeves of any length.

It is done in the same way for any larger-than-average curve. Compare this sketch with Figure 5-49; they are identical. Review the text accompanying Figures 5-49 and 5-50.

An increase of ¼ inch (rarely more than ½ inch) will be adequate to solve most figure problems. The new cutting line will be slightly longer than the original and will therefore increase the ease on the side section as the seam is joined. If the alteration is small and the fabric is pliable, this will cause no problem. For larger alterations that may be required for a crippled figure, the back pattern will have to be lengthened the same as the front section was lengthened in Figure 5-50.

Alterations for larger-than-average upper arms

These alterations increase the width of the sleeve at the biceps line for large upper arms without increasing the length of the seamline at the sleeve cap appreciably.

The greatest problem of large arms is the need for extra width or all-around size, and although large arms are more curvaceous than average, the issue of shape is less important. The alterations shown in Figures 5-55 and 5-56, like others in this series, involve slashing and spreading the pattern and the use of a boat-shaped insertion; but, unlike most of the preceding alterations, these do not involve a dart. For this reason, they do not necessarily influence the amount of shape created (some do, others do not).

Alteration for short sleeves or boxy sleeves of any length See Figure 5-55. The sketches show a short sleeve to conserve space on the page; the alteration is done in an identical manner on a boxy sleeve of any length.

Follow the seven steps that are outlined

on the sketch, proceeding in chronological order. By mounting the lower sections to allow for a parallel insertion (steps 3 and 4), the sleeve is made wider at the hemline, which is an advantage for a short sleeve or any boxy sleeve. However, extra width at the lower edge of a long, fitted sleeve is not attractive; therefore, this alteration is used only with short sleeves, boxy types, and sleeves designed to flare or to gather to a cuff.

Steps 5 and 6 show the technique necessary to bring the pattern edges together at the shoulder position so that there will be no extra ease at the armhole. Note that this forces pattern edges to lap over each other at the biceps line, thereby shortening the sleeve cap. The length of the sleeve cap must be returned to the original, as shown in step 7 (If anything, larger arms require more height). The increase in height must equal the amount of lap-over at the biceps line; study the corrected line carefully—it must retain the character of the original curve in the cap area.

Basic principles applied Sketch *a* in Figure 5-56 shows a similar alteration on a long, fitted sleeve. The sketch pictures a one-piece sleeve, but it is done in an identical manner if the sleeve is cut in two sections; in that case, only the upper sleeve section is involved in the alteration.

If the sleeve is fitted, the basic alteration must be modified to add extra width for the upper arms while retaining the original width at the lower edge. Begin by drawing one line on an insertion strip and marking off the desired amount of increase at the biceps level on either side of that line. Proceed, pivoting sections from the corners of the seamline and the biceps line as shown. As in the boxy sleeve alteration, compensate for the lap-over at the biceps line by adding height at the sleeve cap as shown.

See sketch *b*. If the sleeve is cut in one with the major sections of the pattern, the desired increase must be divided between the front and back sections. Therefore half of the desired increase is added to the shoulder edge of the front and half to the shoulder edge of the back. Note that the addition begins at the shoulder position marked on the pattern. If the sleeve is short, the addition should continue to the lower edge as shown. If the sleeve is long and if no additional width is desired at the wrist, the addition can be tapered back to the original line at the lower edge. By pinning the altered front and back patterns together, the boat-shaped alteration will be visible, and it will be evident that it has resulted in extra width and also extra shape.

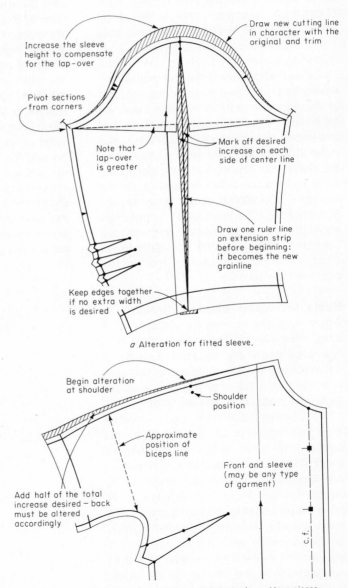

Draw new cutting line in character with the original and trim

Increase the sleeve height to compensate for the lap-over

Pivot sections from corners

Note that lap-over is greater

Mark off desired increase on each side of center line

Draw one ruler line on extension strip before beginning: it becomes the new grainline

Keep edges together if no extra width is desired

a Alteration for fitted sleeve.

Begin alteration at shoulder

Shoulder position

Approximate position of biceps line

Front and sleeve (may be any type of garment)

Add half of the total increase desired – back must be altered accordingly

c.f.

b Alteration for sleeves cut in one with the major pattern pieces.

FIGURE 5-56 Basic principles applied.

ALTERATIONS TO CREATE LESS SHAPE FOR SMALLER-THAN-AVERAGE CURVES

The basic principles stated and illustrated with great detail in the foregoing section can be applied *in reverse* to alterations which will decrease shape (as well as width or length or both) for smaller-than-average curves.

The basic principle: Smaller-than-average curves require a boat-shaped decrease passing over the high point of the body curve. This type of decrease, being widest at the high point of the curve and returning to original lines at the pattern edges, decreases the width at the level of the curve and creates less shape for the smaller-than-average curve. The decreased area is shaped exactly like the increases shown in Figures 5-31 and 5-32. Decreases are more difficult to illustrate because they are formed by edges of the pattern lapping over each other; they will be evident when darts are pinned in the altered pattern and when the altered pattern is held up to the light or figure-tested over a dark slip. Before using these directions, be sure to understand the basic principles written and illustrated in great detail for larger-than-average curves.

Two quite common figure irregularities result in smaller-than-average curves and both are largely dependent on posture; some people have a very erect posture which results in smaller- or flatter-than-average shoulder curves, and the "debutante slouch" posture (with hips pushed forward and tucked under) results in flat hips. In addition to posture problems, some figures do not have average rounded contours of flesh and so are boyishly flat and straight.

Indications that curves are smaller than average   When the pattern is tested on the figure, all edges of the pattern will settle to the body but the pattern will stand away from the high point of smaller-than-average curves. The required decrease in shape and width or length can be estimated by pinching in the excess in the form of a tuck directly over the high point of the curve —the total width of the tuck is the amount of decrease required.

The direction of side seamlines in a skirt indicates irregularities in hip and stomach curves. These lines hang in proper plumb-lines on the average figure, but if the curve is larger than average, the seam swings toward the larger-than-average curve, and *if the curve is flatter than average, it swings away from the smaller-than-average curve.* Therefore if hips are flat in the back, the side seam swings toward the front.

Alterations of this type are usually relatively small   Alterations on back darts are always smaller than those made on bust darts because back curves do not vary as greatly from figure to figure as bust curves. A lap-over or decrease of $\frac{1}{4}$ to $\frac{1}{2}$ inch will be a typical alteration of this type. This amount of lap-over at the level of the high point of the curve will result in a somewhat greater decrease in the width of the dart involved; if the lap-over at the shoulder level is $\frac{1}{4}$ inch, the width at the dart base will be decreased by about $\frac{3}{8}$ inch.

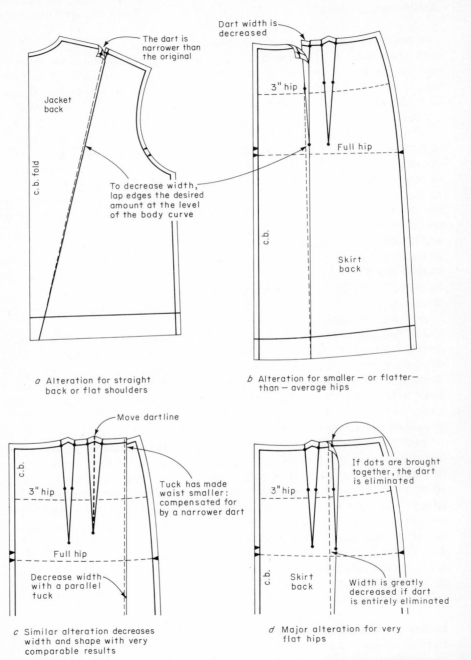

The dart is narrower than the original

Jacket back

c.b. fold

To decrease width, lap edges the desired amount at the level of the body curve

a Alteration for straight back or flat shoulders

Dart width is decreased

3" hip

Full hip

c.b.

Skirt back

b Alteration for smaller — or flatter — than — average hips

Move dartline

c.b.

3" hip

Tuck has made waist smaller: compensated for by a narrower dart

Full hip

Decrease width with a parallel tuck

c Similar alteration decreases width and shape with very comparable results

3" hip

If dots are brought together, the dart is eliminated

c.b.

Skirt back

Width is greatly decreased if dart is entirely eliminated

d Major alteration for very flat hips

FIGURE 5-57   To decrease the width of vertical darts for less width and shape for smaller-than-average or flatter-than-average curves.

Alterations for smaller- or flatter-than-average back curves

Vertical alterations to create less shape and width for smaller-than-average back curves See Figure 5-57. Sketch *a* shows the alteration for flat or straight shoulders; compare it with the one for rounded shoulders shown in sketch *a* of Figure 5-53 to see that alteration applied *in reverse* for the opposite figure problem.

Draw a ruler line through the center of the dartline, extending it to the seamline or to the lower edge if there is a hemline. Slash along the line to the seamline or to the lower edge if there is a hemline, as shown here. Now, instead of spreading the pattern apart (as for larger-than-average curves), lap one slashed edge over the other to decrease the width by the estimated amount (the total width of the little tuck made when it was tested on the figure). Note that this results in a narrower dart. The new dart must be drafted in (not illustrated to simplify the sketch); mark the tip of the new dart on a level with the tip of the original dart, at the midpoint of the lap-over, and use the original dots at the seamline.

Sketch *b* shows the same alterations applied to one of the darts in the skirt; either skirt dart can be altered depending on the needs of the particular figure. Compare this alteration with the one for protruding hips shown in sketch *a*, Figure 5-35, to see that alteration applied *in reverse* to the opposite figure problem.

Compare sketch *c* with sketch *b* to see another solution to the same problem resulting in an almost identical alteration. Make a parallel tuck the full length of the pattern, marking off the decrease desired at the hip level. The tuck has made the waist smaller by the same amount, and the waist size can be returned to the original by drafting over one line of one of the darts (move the dartline nearer the side edge) to com-

pensate for the decrease. This results in a narrower dart that will create less shape. The parallel tuck has resulted in less width at the hipline and the hemline, while the alteration shown in sketch *b* retains the original width at the lower edge.

Sketch *d* shows an alteration very similar to the one shown in sketch *b*, which results in the elimination of one of the skirt darts, thereby decreasing the shape in the back skirt by approximately half. If the pattern edges are lapped over until the two dots marking the width of the dart are brought together, the dart is entirely eliminated. This is a major alteration because the decrease in width at the hip level will be approximately 1 inch on the half-figure pattern; however, figures with very straight postures or those with very slim, boyish lines may require such a major alteration.

**Horizontal alteration to create less
shape and length for flat hips** See
Figure 5-58. Draw a ruler-straight slash line
at right angles to the center line or grainline, passing through the tip of the longer
dart as shown. Mark off the desired decrease by drawing the lower line in two segments — keep the lines parallel between the
center line and the tip of the dart and then
taper the lower line so the two meet at the
seamline. Draw a slash line through the
center of the dart. Slash along the slash
lines. Lap the horizontal slash line over to
the remaining line; center lines and grainlines will remain ruler-straight and the width
of the dart will be decreased as the vertical

slashed edges lap over each other. Compare this alteration with the corresponding
one for protruding hips in Figure 5-37 to
see those principles applied *in reverse* for
the opposite figure problem.

When figure problems are exaggerated,
best results can be achieved by combining
horizontal and vertical alterations; the combination will result in less shape, less width,
and also less length. For example, do the
vertical alteration shown in sketch *c* or *d*
in Figure 5-57, and when it is completed,
do a horizontal alteration on the already-
altered pattern. Keep in mind that each alteration decreases the width of one dart;
therefore, when the combination is used,
the amount of each alteration must be smaller than each would be if it were to be used
alone. See the combination alteration in Figure 5-38 and apply those principles in reverse to this opposite problem.

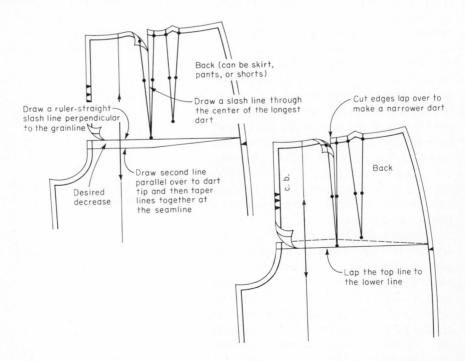

FIGURE 5-58   *To create less length and shape for smaller- (or flatter-) than-average
curves in the hip area.*

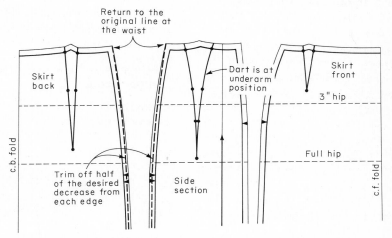

Return to the
original line at
the waist

Skirt
back

Dart is at
underarm
position

Skirt
front

3" hip

Full hip

c.b. fold

Trim off half
of the desired
decrease from
each edge

Side
section

c.f. fold

To decrease width and shape for flat hips; compare with Figure 5-39.

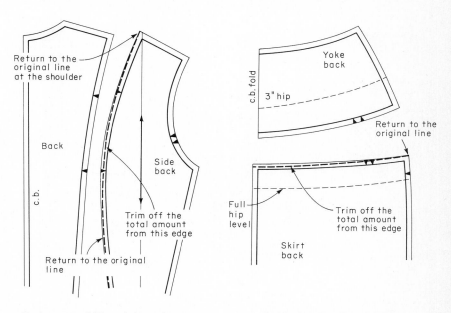

Return to the
original line
at the shoulder

Back

Side
back

c.b.

Trim off the
total amount
from this edge

Return to the original
line

c.b. fold

Yoke
back

3" hip

Return to the
original line

Full
hip
level

Trim off the
total amount
from this edge

Skirt
back

To decrease width and shape for
straight shoulders; compare with
back alteration in Figure 5-49.

To decrease length and shape
for flat hips; compare with
skirt alteration in Figure 5-40.

*FIGURE 5-59 Boat-shaped alterations made at seamlines—to create less shape for
smaller- (or flatter-) than-average curves.*

Basic principles of making boat-shaped alterations at pattern edges
The pattern can be altered to create less width or length and less shape by trimming off a boat-shaped portion of the pattern along seamlines that pass over the high points of body curves; these seams replace darts, and the dart fitting is incorporated in the seam. Before proceeding, review the discussion given under this same heading on page 173. Figure 5-59 shows three patterns altered for smaller-than-average back curves; compare them with the corresponding sketches for larger-than-average curves to see principles applied in reverse for the opposite figure problem.

Alterations for smaller-than-average upper arms

People with thin upper arms need not necessarily alter sleeve patterns, because in

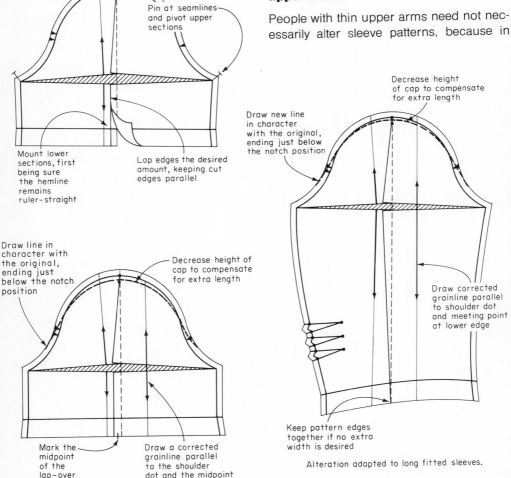

Pivot upper sections until shoulder dots meet

Pin at seamlines and pivot upper sections

Mount lower sections, first being sure the hemline remains ruler-straight

Lap edges the desired amount, keeping cut edges parallel

Draw new line in character with the original, ending just below the notch position

Decrease height of cap to compensate for extra length

Draw corrected grainline parallel to shoulder dot and meeting point at lower edge

Draw line in character with the original, ending just below the notch position

Decrease height of cap to compensate for extra length

Mark the midpoint of the lap-over

Draw a corrected grainline parallel to the shoulder dot and the midpoint of the lap-over

Keep pattern edges together if no extra width is desired

Alteration adapted to long fitted sleeves.

Basic alteration for boxy sleeves.

FIGURE 5-60   *To decrease width and shape for thin upper arms.*

some cases an unaltered sleeve better camouflages the figure irregularity. This may be true in a long, fitted sleeve where the excess size simply adds to the amount of livability and makes the arm appear more average in size. In other words, there is no reason why the amount of livability in the sleeve cannot be greater than it is on the average arm if the effect is attractive on the figure. If the arm is only slightly smaller than average, an alteration is not usually necessary. If, however, the arm is very slim and the sleeve is short and boxy, the sleeve will appear much too wide and the arm even thinner by comparison. Here an alteration becomes necessary.

Typical alterations are detailed in Figures 5-60 and 5-61. Review the comparable alterations for heavy upper arms in Figures 5-55 and 5-56 to see those principles applied *in reverse* for this opposite problem.

SHOULDER ALTERATIONS

Three major types of figure problems

Three distinctly different problems may

occur in the shoulder area. One is involved with the amount of shoulder curve and the prominence of the shoulder blade in the back. It is remedied by creating the proper shape in the back pattern, as discussed in the foregoing sections. Another concerns the width of the shoulders from side to side. Shoulders may be wider or narrower than the average in proportion to bust size; the terms *broad* and *narrow* are used to describe irregularities in width. The third is the degree of slant of the shoulderline (from neck to armhole); the shoulderline is termed *square* when it is less sloping than average and gives a square, boxy appearance; it is termed *sloping* when the line slants downward toward the armhole more than average. Proper fit in the shoulder area is always an important issue, and it is more important if the garment falls free from the body with its entire weight supported and controlled by the shoulder-line (boxy coats or jackets, shift dresses, etc.).

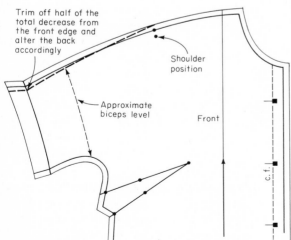

Trim off half of the total decrease from the front edge and alter the back accordingly

Shoulder position

Approximate biceps level

Front

c.f.

FIGURE 5-61 *Basic principles applied to garments with sleeves cut in one with the major pieces.*

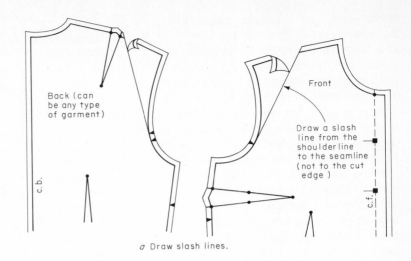

Back (can
be any type
of garment)

c.b.

Front

Draw a slash
line from the
shoulder line
to the seamline
(not to the cut
edge)

c.f.

a Draw slash lines.

To alter shoulder width

The width of the shoulders is determined by the location of the armhole line, which is the armhole seam if the garment has a sleeve or the seamline (the finished edge) if the garment is sleeveless. The ideal location of the armhole line is difficult to establish because there is no well-defined line on the figure to indicate a precise division between shoulders and arms. The ideal location can be stated as follows: *The armhole line should be located in such a way that the sleeve is comfortable and provides proper freedom of movement and, at the same time, creates a pleasing dividing line between the shoulders and arms.* If the garment is sleeveless, the armhole line must be visually attractive, revealing neither too little nor too much of the bare arm.

Women with very wide or very narrow shoulders are well aware of their figure irregularities, but those with slight problems (¼ inch or less on each half of the figure) may be unaware that a small alteration would be helpful. Shoulder width can be adjusted during fitting; shoulders can be narrowed quite easily at that time, and they can be made wider (by about ¼ to ⅜ inch)

by letting out some of the seam allowance on the garment sections. Therefore those women who anticipate only slight problems may decide not to alter the pattern and to make corrections when fitting the muslin copy. However, if one suspects her shoulders are wider than average, it is wise to alter the pattern to provide additional width; any excess width can be removed during fitting. After fitting one garment with a set-in sleeve, record the fitting corrections so that adjustments can be made more easily and quickly by pattern alteration in the future.

The amounts of alteration in shoulder width are relatively small—¼-inch alterations will be required by many, a ½-inch alteration can be considered large, and an alteration of as much as ¾ inch is most unusual. Relatively large alterations have been used in all sketches to slightly exaggerate problems for illustrative purposes.

To increase shoulder width for broad shoulders Follow the directions in Figure 5-62. Note in sketches *a* and *b* that the slash line is made to the seamline (not to the cut edge), so that the alteration will not change the length of the armhole seam. Note the

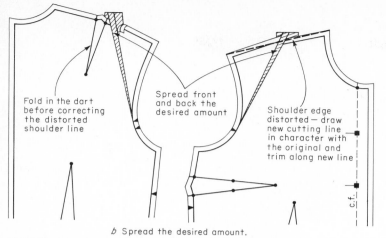

Fold in the dart
before correcting
the distorted
shoulder line

Spread front
and back the
desired amount

Shoulder edge
distorted — draw
new cutting line
in character with
the original and
trim along new line

b Spread the desired amount.

FIGURE 5-62   To increase shoulder width for broad shoulders.

distortion on the front shoulder in sketch *b*; the diagonal slash has resulted in increased height and the new cutting line compensates for the increase. When correcting the distorted seamline on the darted back shoulderline, fold in the dart before establishing the new line and trim along the established line with the dart folded in place.

An alteration of shoulder width does not influence the sleeve because this alteration simply brings the armhole seam of the garment to a position where the sleeve will hang or fit properly.

The basic principles can be applied to other designs as shown in Figure 5-63. The back pattern (not illustrated) must be altered   accordingly.

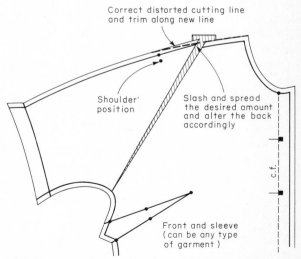

Correct distorted cutting line
and trim along new line

Shoulder
position

Slash and spread
the desired amount
and alter the back
accordingly

Front and sleeve
(can be any type
of garment)

FIGURE 5-63   Bašic principles applied to a pattern with the sleeve cut in one with the major pieces.

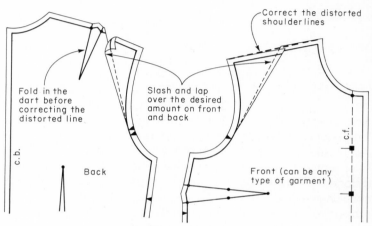

Correct the distorted
shoulder lines

Fold in the
dart before
correcting the
distorted line

Slash and lap
over the desired
amount on front
and back

c.b.

Back

Front (can be any
type of garment)

c.f.

a To decrease shoulder width.

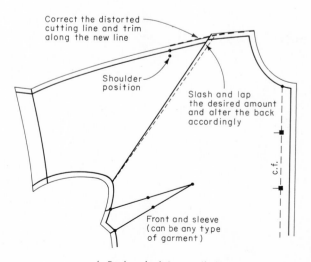

Correct the distorted
cutting line and trim
along the new line

Shoulder
position

Slash and lap
the desired amount
and alter the back
accordingly

Front and sleeve
(can be any type
of garment)

c.f.

b Basic principles applied.

FIGURE 5-64 *To decrease shoulder width for narrow shoulders.*

To decrease shoulder width for narrow shoulders   Sketch *a* in Figure 5-64 shows directions for narrowing the shoulderline. Study Figure 5-62 and the accompanying text to understand underlying principles better; the principles are applied *in reverse* for this opposite figure problem. Sketch *b* shows the identical alteration on another type of pattern; compare this alteration with the one shown in Figure 5-63.

To alter the slant of the shoulderline

Two different figure irregularities can create a shoulder slant more square or more sloping than that of the average figure for which the pattern was made; see Figure 5-65 and compare the broken lines which illustrate the figure problem with the solid lines showing the contours of the average figure. As the illustrations and captions indicate, the problem may be located near the armhole or at the neck edge, and it follows that the alteration must be done where the problem occurs.

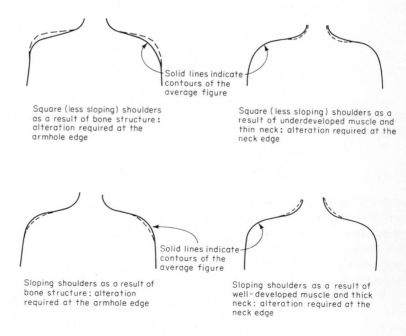

Solid lines indicate contours of the average figure

Square (less sloping) shoulders as a result of bone structure: alteration required at the armhole edge

Square (less sloping) shoulders as a result of underdeveloped muscle and thin neck: alteration required at the neck edge

Solid lines indicate contours of the average figure

Sloping shoulders as a result of bone structure: alteration required at the armhole edge

Sloping shoulders as a result of well-developed muscle and thick neck: alteration required at the neck edge

FIGURE 5-65   Shoulder-slant irregularities are created by two distinctly different figure problems.

Indications of square (less sloping) shoulders If shoulders are square as a result of bone structure near the shoulder, any ready-to-wear garment or one made from an unaltered pattern will reveal diagonal ripples between the armhole end of the shoulderline and the bust. If the square shoulders are a result of underdeveloped muscle near the neck and a thin neck, garments stand away from the body in that area. Both problems are easily recognized and distinguished from each other.

Indications of sloping shoulders If shoulders slope more than average as a result of bone structure near the shoulder, any ready-to-wear garment or one made from an unaltered pattern will reveal diagonal ripples originating at the neck end of the shoulderline and slanting diagonally downward, forming a ripple at the armhole edge near the notch positions. If they slope as a result of muscle development near the neck and a thick neck, the neckline of the garment will be too tight and there will be diagonal ripples leading from the neck end of the shoulderline to the bust. Both problems are easily recognized and distinguished from each other.

Note: All alterations in this section involve drawing new front and back shoulderlines in character with the original lines. Keep in mind the character of the original back shoulderline; the two segments form a ruler-straight line when the shoulder dart is folded in. Therefore whenever there is a back shoulder dart, fold in the dart, make the correction, and then trim along the new cutting line with the dart folded in. To simplify sketches this step is not shown; only the completed alterations are illustrated.

Basic rules for altering the pattern at the armhole edge for square shoulders See Figure 5-66. Sketch *a* shows the alteration on the major pieces. The desired increase is made on the corresponding shoulder edges of the front and back; the example pictures a ½-inch increase in height. This alteration is simple to execute, but it is complicated by the fact that several corresponding pieces are involved, as shown in sketch *b*. This alteration will influence the sleeve because the shoulderline has been increased in height and the sleeve cap must be raised accordingly. *Note that the increase on the front and on the back is the same as the increase on the sleeve cap* (each has been increased ½ *inch in the example illustrated*). By adding the same increase in height to the front edge, the back edge, and the sleeve cap, all edges have been raised the same amount and, at the same time, corresponding seamlines have been lengthened by approximately the same amount. For example, the total length of the armhole seam of the garment has been increased 1 inch with the addition of ½ inch on the front and ½ on the back shoulders; the increase of ½ inch in the height of the sleeve cap has resulted in an increase of approximately 1 inch in the total length of the new seamline of the sleeve as well.

The corresponding alteration on front and back neck facings is very small. It is important to alter all corresponding pieces (no matter how small the pattern piece or how small the alteration) to ensure smooth-fitting facings in all types of fabrics.

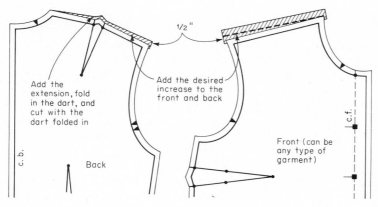

Add the
extension, fold
in the dart, and
cut with the
dart folded in

Add the desired
increase to the
front and back

1/2"

c. b.

Back

Front (can be
any type of
garment)

c.f.

a Alter the major pieces

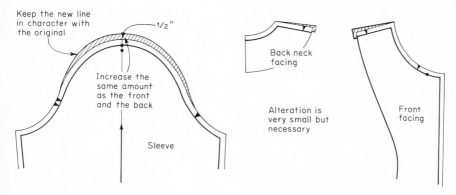

Keep the new line
in character with
the original

1/2"

Increase the
same amount
as the front
and the back

Sleeve

Back neck
facing

Alteration is
very small but
necessary

Front
facing

b Alter corresponding pieces accordingly

FIGURE 5-66   *Basic rules for altering the pattern at the armhole edge for square (less
sloping) shoulders.*

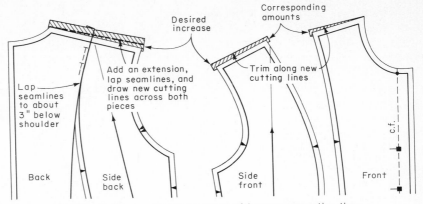

Lap seamlines to about 3" below shoulder

Desired increase

Add an extension, lap seamlines, and draw new cutting lines across both pieces

Corresponding amounts

Trim along new cutting lines

Back

Side back

Side front

Front

c.f.

a Basic principles applied to a pattern with seams separating the shoulderline into segments.

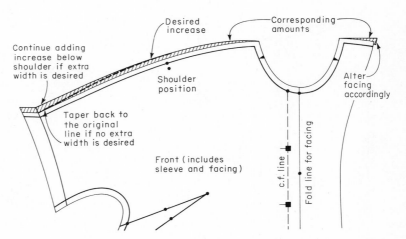

Desired increase

Corresponding amounts

Continue adding increase below shoulder if extra width is desired

Shoulder position

Alter facing accordingly

Taper back to the original line if no extra width is desired

Front (includes sleeve and facing)

c.f. line

Fold line for facing

b Basic principles applied to a pattern with the sleeve and facing cut in one with the major piece (alter the back accordingly).

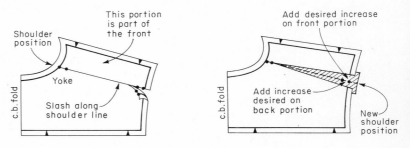

Shoulder position

This portion is part of the front

Add desired increase on front portion

c.b. fold

Yoke

Slash along shoulder line

Add increase desired on back portion

c.b. fold

New shoulder position

c Basic principles applied to a pattern with no shoulder seam.

FIGURE 5-67   *Basic principles applied—to alter the pattern at the armhole edge for square shoulders.*

Figure 5-67 shows the same alteration on other types of patterns and illustrates that when design lines influence or complicate circumstances, basic principles apply equally effectively. Sketch *a* shows pattern pieces with seams crossing the shoulder seam. The technique of doing the alteration is shown on the back pieces and the finished alteration is pictured on the front pieces. Corresponding pattern pieces are altered the same as in Figure 5-66.

Sketch *b* pictures a front pattern with the sleeve and the facing cut in one with the major pattern piece; the back pattern and back neck facing must be altered accordingly. The alteration on the neck facing is done in the same way on separate facings and on facings cut in one with the major pieces.

Sketch *c* shows a yoke pattern (similar to the yoke in men's shirts) in which there is no shoulder seam—in other words, a front and back yoke combined in one pattern piece. The shoulder position is indicated on the pattern with dots, as shown. Slash and spread the pattern along the shoulderline and make the increases on an insertion strip as shown. Keep in mind that the desired increases for both the front and the back must be included; for example, the person who requires a ½-inch increase on a pattern with typical shoulder seams must spread the pattern a total of 1 inch and mark the new shoulder position at the center of the insertion. Corresponding sleeve and facing patterns are altered the same as in Figure 5-66.

Basic rules for altering the pattern at the neck edge for square shoulders
See Figure 5-68. Sketch *a* shows the alteration on the major pieces. The desired decrease is made on the corresponding shoulder edges of the front and back; the sketch shows a ⅜-inch decrease in height as an example. The alteration is simple to execute, but it is complicated by the fact that several corresponding pieces will be involved. The sleeve will not be involved in this alteration, because no change is made at the armhole edge. Sketch *b* shows the front and back neck facings altered accordingly.

Any alteration at the neck edge will influence the collar pattern and require a corresponding alteration. Sketch *c* shows a typical collar; the shoulder position is marked with dots, as shown. The under collar pattern must be altered accordingly. Draw tucklines on either side of the shoulder position, marking off the decreases made on the front and back edges; in the example shown, each neck edge on the major piece was decreased ⅜ inch and therefore the tucklines in the collar are ¾ inch apart.

Figure 5-69 shows the same alteration on other types of patterns and illustrates that when design lines influence and complicate circumstances, basic principles apply equally effectively. Sketch *a* pictures a front pattern with the sleeve as well as the facing cut in one piece; the back pattern and back neck facing must be altered accordingly. The alteration on the neck facing is done in the same way on separate facings and on facings cut in one with the major pieces. The collar patterns are altered the same as in Figure 5-68.

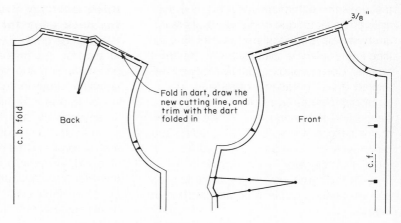

Fold in dart, draw the
new cutting line, and
trim with the dart
folded in

Back

Front

c. b. fold

c. f.

3/8 "

a Alter the major pieces.

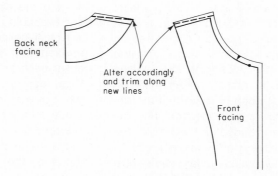

Back neck
facing

Alter accordingly
and trim along
new lines

Front
facing

b Alter facings accordingly.

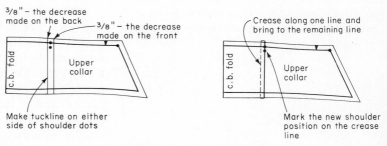

3/8 " – the decrease
made on the back

3/8 " – the decrease
made on the front

c. b. fold

Upper
collar

Make tuckline on either
side of shoulder dots

Crease along one line and
bring to the remaining line

c. b. fold

Upper
collar

Mark the new shoulder
position on the crease
line

c Corresponding alteration on collar.

*FIGURE 5-68   Basic rules for altering the pattern at the neck edge for square
shoulders.*

Sketch *b* shows a yoke pattern (similar to the yoke in men's shirts) in which there is no seam at the shoulder—in other words, a front and back yoke combined in one pattern piece. The shoulder position is marked on the pattern with dots as shown. By drawing lines on either side of the shoulder position to mark off the desired decrease and creasing in a wedge-shaped tuck as shown, the alteration is completed. Corresponding collar and facing patterns are altered in the manner shown in Figure 5-68.

The examples do not include a pattern (like the typical princess-line garment) with seams crossing the shoulder seam; refer to the technique illustrated in sketch *a* of Figure 5-67 to see how basic principles can be applied to patterns in which the shoulder-line is separated into segments.

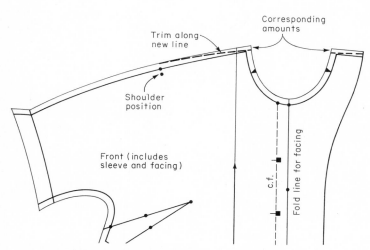

a Basic principles applied to a pattern with the sleeve and facing cut in one with the major piece (alter the back accordingly).

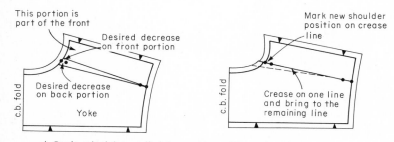

b Basic principles applied to a pattern with no shoulder seam.

FIGURE 5-69   *Basic principles applied—to alter the pattern at the neck edge for square shoulders.*

Basic rules for altering the pattern at the armhole edge for sloping shoulders See Figure 5-70. Sketch *a* shows the alteration on the major pieces. The desired decrease is made on the corresponding shoulder edges of the front and back; the example pictures a ⅜-inch decrease in height. This alteration is simple to execute,

but it is complicated by the fact that several corresponding pieces are involved, as shown in sketch *b*. This alteration influences the sleeve because the shoulderline has been decreased in height and the sleeve cap must be lowered accordingly. *The decrease in height of the sleeve cap is the same as the decrease on the front and back (each has been decreased ⅜ inch in the example illustrated).* By making the same decrease on the front edge, the back edge, and the sleeve cap, all edges have been lowered the same amount and, at the

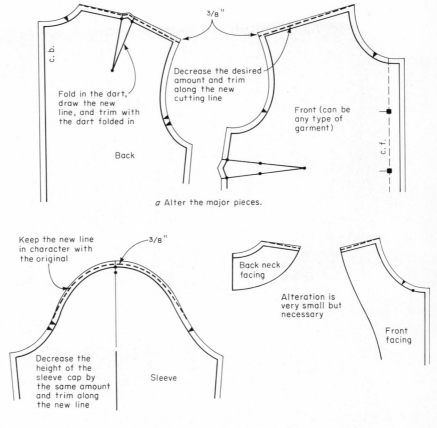

a Alter the major pieces.

b Alter corresponding pieces accordingly.

FIGURE 5-70 *Basic rules for altering the pattern at the armhole edge for sloping shoulders.*

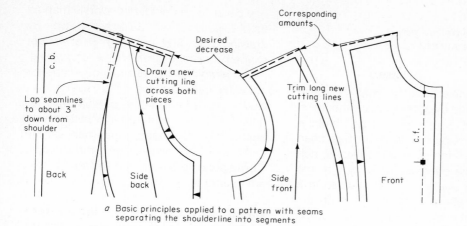

Corresponding amounts

Desired decrease

c. b.

Draw a new cutting line across both pieces

Lap seamlines to about 3" down from shoulder

Trim long new cutting lines

c. f.

Back

Side back

Side front

Front

a Basic principles applied to a pattern with seams separating the shoulderline into segments

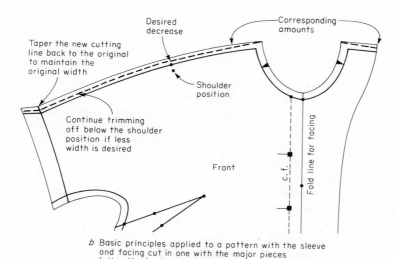

Desired decrease

Corresponding amounts

Taper the new cutting line back to the original to maintain the original width

Shoulder position

Continue trimming off below the shoulder position if less width is desired

Front

c. f.

Fold line for facing

b Basic principles applied to a pattern with the sleeve and facing cut in one with the major pieces (alter the back accordingly)

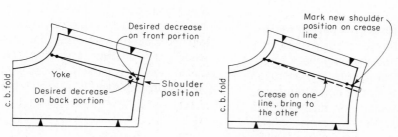

Desired decrease on front portion

Mark new shoulder position on crease line

c. b. fold

Yoke

Desired decrease on back portion

Shoulder position

c. b. fold

Crease on one line, bring to the other

c Basic principles applied to a pattern with no shoulder seam

FIGURE 5-71 *Basic principles applied—to alter the pattern at the armhole edge for sloping shoulders.*

**PREPARATION OF PATTERN
AND PATTERN ALTERATIONS**

same time, corresponding seamlines have been shortened by approximately the same amount. For example, the total length of the armhole seam on the garment has been decreased ¾ inch by making two ⅜ inch alterations; the decrease of ⅜ inch in the height of the sleeve cap has resulted in a decrease of approximately ¾ inch in the total length of the armhole seamline of the sleeve.

The corresponding alteration on front and back neck facings is very small. It is important to alter all corresponding pieces (no matter how small the pattern piece or how small the alteration) to ensure smooth-fitting facings in all types of fabrics.

Figure 5-71 shows the same alteration on other types of patterns and illustrates that when design lines influence or complicate circumstances, basic principles apply equally effectively. Sketch *a* shows pattern pieces with seams crossing the shoulder seam or, in other words, shows a pattern in which the shoulderline is separated into segments. The technique of doing the alteration is shown on the back pieces and the finished alteration is pictured on the front pieces. Corresponding sleeve and facing patterns are altered in the manner shown in Figure 5-70.

Sketch *b* pictures a front pattern with the sleeve as well as the facing cut in one piece; the back pattern and the back neck facing must be altered accordingly. The alteration on the neck facing is done in the same way on separate facings and on facings cut in one with the major pieces.

Sketch *c* shows a yoke pattern (similar to the yoke in men's shirts) in which there is no seam at the shoulders—in other words, a front and back yoke combined in one piece. The shoulder position is marked on the pattern with dots, as shown. By drawing lines and creasing in a wedge-shaped tuck, the alteration is completed. Remember that the desired decrease for both the front and the back must be included; for example, the person who required a ⅜-inch decrease in a pattern with typical shoulder seams must mark off the tucklines ¾ inch apart at the armhole edge. Corresponding sleeve and facing patterns are altered as in Figure 5-70.

Basic rules for altering the pattern at the neck edge for sloping shoulders
See Figure 5-72. Sketch *a* shows the alteration on the major pattern pieces. The desired increase is made on the corresponding shoulder edges of the front and back. The alteration is simple to execute but it is complicated by the fact that several corresponding pieces will be involved. The sleeve will not be involved in this alteration, because no change is made at the armhole edge. Sketch *b* shows front and neck facings altered accordingly. It is important to alter all corresponding pieces (no matter how small the piece or how small the alteration) to ensure smooth-fitting facings in all types of fabrics.

Any alteration at the neck edge will influence the collar pattern and require a corresponding alteration. Sketch *c* shows a typical collar; the shoulder position is marked with dots, as shown. The under-collar pattern must be altered accordingly. Slash the pattern and allow the total increase made on both the front and the back; for example, if the shoulder is raised ¼ inch on the front and ¼ inch on the back, the total increase on the collar must be ½ inch.

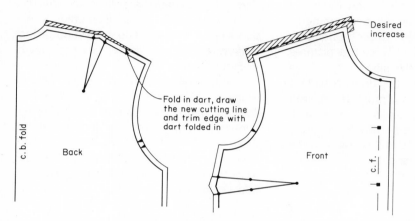

Fold in dart, draw
the new cutting line
and trim edge with
dart folded in

Back

Front

Desired
increase

c. b. fold

c. f.

a Alter the major pieces.

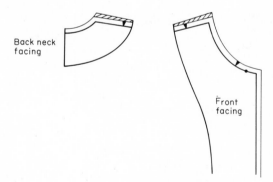

Back neck
facing

Front
facing

b Alter facings accordingly.

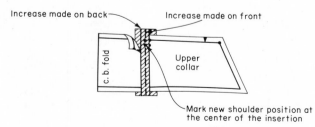

Increase made on back

Increase made on front

c. b. fold

Upper
collar

Mark new shoulder position at
the center of the insertion

c Corresponding alteration on collar.

*FIGURE 5-72   Basic rules for altering the pattern at the neck edge for sloping
shoulders.*

Figure 5-73 shows the same alteration on other types of patterns and illustrates that when design lines influence or complicate circumstances, basic principles apply equally effectively. Sketch *a* pictures a front pattern with the sleeve as well as the facing cut in one piece; the back pattern and back neck facing must be altered accordingly. The alteration on the neck facing is done in the same way on separate facings and on facings cut in one with the major pieces. The collar patterns are altered the same as in Figure 5-72.

Sketch *b* shows a yoke pattern (similar to the yoke in men's shirts) in which there is no seam at the shoulder—in other words, a front and back yoke combined in one pattern piece. The shoulder position is marked on the pattern with dots, as shown. Slash and spread the pattern the desired amount and make the addition on an insertion strip. Corresponding collar and facing patterns are altered in the manner shown in Figure 5-72.

The illustration does not include an example of a pattern (like the typical princess-line garment) with seams crossing the shoulder seams; refer to the technique illustrated in sketch *a* of Figure 5-71 to see how basic principles can be applied to patterns in which the shoulderline is separated into segments.

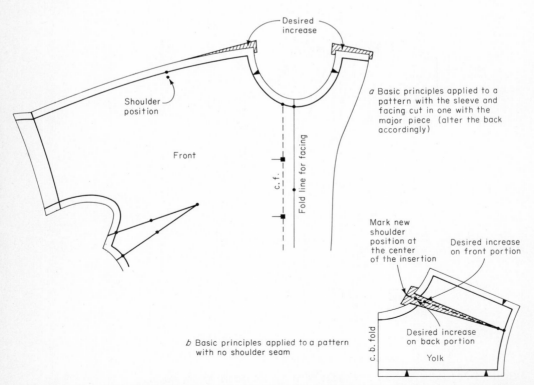

FIGURE 5-73   *Basic principles applied—to alter the pattern at the neck edge for sloping shoulders.*

Special note to instructors and experienced readers: The possibilities of altering patterns can be greatly expanded by the knowledge and use of flat pattern design methods. If one understands how to make a pattern, she can make quite complicated and comprehensive changes on the commercial pattern by using it in much the same way the professional pattern maker uses a basic pattern for making commercial pattern designs. *Flat Pattern Design* (Bane, McGraw-Hill, New York, 1972) is written with major emphasis on using pattern-making methods to strengthen and expand pattern alteration possibilities. The unique presentation of material (the technique shown first on a basic pattern in the way the professional pattern maker works and then the principles applied to a variety of commercial pattern designs) will allow the instructor or the experienced worker to make accurate major changes in the design.

CORRESPONDING ALTERATIONS FOR LINING PATTERNS

If separate lining pieces are included with the pattern, alterations must be made on the lining patterns. These alterations should not be made immediately; alteration of the structural pieces should be tested in muslin before alterations are made on lining pieces.

Back-lining patterns are simple to alter because the dart arrangement is identical to that in the jacket pieces. But the dart positions in lining front patterns are not always identical to those in the jacket or coat sections, so it is often difficult to alter these pieces in an identical manner. For example, the lining pattern included with the commercial pattern may have a shoulder tuck or dart that does not appear in the garment, or there may be a tuck in the lining in the

position where a dart appears in the garment. It is difficult to make identical pattern alterations on pieces that do not have identical darts and seams. If the lining pattern is very different or if very complicated pattern alterations were made, it is simpler to make a new lining pattern than to alter the existing one. This can be done by copying the portions of the already-altered major pattern pieces; see page 445.

Chapter 6

FITTING THE MUSLIN TEST COPY

Fitting is the most difficult step in the construction sequence because figure irregularities may occur in infinite combinations and each problem may differ slightly with each design. Fitting problems must be seen to be solved effectively; they cannot be mastered from written directions alone. There are many variables: the figure, the fabric, the design, and the performance expected of the garment. It is not possible to write directions that will encompass every problem which will be encountered by every reader; at best, written directions can only explain general principles on relatively basic designs. Basic principles must be applied by each individual and each instructor.

Fitting is further complicated by the fact that major corrections in size, length, and shape cannot be done after the garment is cut in expensive fabric. A muslin test copy allows for major changes and additions because radical changes can be done on the muslin test copy, much as they are done when altering the pattern. It is important to understand that fitting corrections and pattern alterations are comparable and that the two, one in paper and the other in fabric, require the same thought processes. Eventually all fitting corrections made on the muslin copy will be transferred to the pattern as pattern alterations. Before attempting any fitting correction, review the comparable pattern alteration; the directions

in the following pages include cross references to pattern alterations in Chapter 5.

Important review Before beginning work, carefully review and study all the information relative to problems of fitting the individual figure. They include the comprehensive information on sizing on pages 36 to 53, "Muslin Testing Influences Decisions" on page 99, and "The Principle of Dart Fitting—a Guideline" on page 136.

CUTTING, MARKING, AND BASTING

If the muslin copy is to serve all purposes well, it must be made with high standards of accuracy. One must guard against the tendency to be careless; the tendency does exist because the worker realizes that she will not wear the garment and that she is working with inexpensive fabric.

Cutting Only major pieces of the jacket or coat and the skirt or pants are used for the test copy. Interfacing and lining pieces will be altered later, after all fitting corrections have been transferred (in the form of pattern alterations) to the major pieces.

Pieces are cut in the usual way, although certain concessions can be made. If necessary to save yardage, piecing is possible provided that the seam will not complicate construction details or adversely affect the design. Some pieces can be eliminated; for example, if there are pockets hidden in a seam, one of the two pockets is sufficient for practice in construction. However, if there are several visible pockets or pocket flaps, all must be cut to study their combined effect on the design and on the figure.

It is advisable to add some extra size to the pattern if there may be a need for some extra size and if the pattern was not altered before cutting the muslin, or if a garment will hug the body for a very trim effect (slim-fitting skirts, fitted jackets, coats with nipped-in waists, etc.). In these cases it is well to cut 1 inch beyond the cutting line of the pattern at the side edges (the edges which will be at the side when the garment is worn). If this addition is made, copy the seamline of the pattern on the muslin so that the seam can be basted on the proper line. For example, if an extra 1-inch allowance is added, the seam must be basted in a 1⅝ inch width for the first fitting.

To transfer pattern markings Transfer all pattern markings to the muslin with pencil (recommended) or with a tracing wheel and carbon. If a lead pencil is used, draw in the shape of the marking (triangle, square, large or small dots). Colored pencils, one for each shape of marking, can be used. Ruler lines (for darts and center lines) can be drawn on the muslin as an aid to accurate construction.

Basting The test copy can be basted by hand or machine as the worker desires. Machine basting should be done with the longest stitch on the machine and with no back-stitching at the ends of darts or seams. If numerous corrections are anticipated, it is well to use thread in a contrasting color, which will be easier to remove.

Use a shorter stitch (12 to 15 stitches per inch) for doing intricate construction

details such as collars and welt pockets. These design details are seldom changed during fitting, and the regulation stitch length will result in greater accuracy for practicing complicated construction.

The muslin test copy must look much like the finished garment, but it is not a truly finished garment because only the necessary construction points are completed. Interfacing, tape, and padding stitches are not needed; buttonholes can be pencil lines or slashes in the fabric; buttons can be devised of circles of cloth or paper; and top-stitching can be indicated with pencil lines. However, all structural parts of the garment must be basted with accuracy. It is necessary to follow through the order and directions on the instruction sheet and supplement them with the more detailed directions in the text. Intricate construction details, such as gussets (page 398), and the typical tailored collar (page 407), should be followed very carefully from the text to gain full benefit from practice of construction. Pressing seams in the proper direction before proceeding to the next step is as important as it would be if the garment were to be worn. All directions and sketches in Chapter 9 include the interfacing, tape, and padding stitches, and the worker must simply skip sentences involved with those details and concentrate on the basic construction.

If there are points to be reinforced (points that will be clipped or slashed before being seamed), the instruction sheet will include one of two methods of reinforcement. Read "Reinforcing Corners" on page 261 for more detailed discussion and directions, and if the circumstance calls for a very secure reinforcement (method 2), use a scrap of fabric on the muslin copy; reinforced corners are difficult to handle, and practice is required.

Do not try on the garment or attempt to fit any section or feature of it until the entire muslin copy has been completed. Even if there are obvious corrections to be made, the entire garment must be complete before it will hang properly on the body; for example, the collar greatly influences the fit of the entire shoulder area.

Turn up hems along the hemline as indicated on the pattern and pin in place temporarily. Press the finished muslin copy well. Pin in shoulder pads if they will be used. Be sure to have the center-front line clearly defined on the outside of the garment on both right and left fronts; use a marking-basting line or a pencil line.

PREPARATION FOR FITTING

Both persons involved with the fitting must know, before the fitting, what to expect during fitting and, in a general way, the solution to problems of misfit. Both persons, then, should study the remainder of this chapter before any fitting is undertaken.

The person to be fitted should wear the bra and foundation garment she will wear with the costume as well as any other item of clothing (blouse and skirt or dress, as the case may be) similar in line to the garments which will be worn with the costume. Shoes similar in design and heel height to those which will be worn with the garment will aid in giving a more accurate picture of the total effect. And for a psychological advantage, the person to be fitted should look her best and should comb her hair in a style similar to the style she will wear with the costume; a casual, wind-blown coiffure can detract from a sophisticated design while an appropriate hair arrangement will enhance the costume.

There is no reason why the fitting must proceed in the exact order presented in this text. There *is* reason to avoid disappointment and discouragement by correcting large, obvious errors of fit immediately. The total length of the garment often needs the most obvious correction, and so this may be the right place to begin and there is no reason why shifting the position of a pocket or changing the width of the collar or lapel cannot be the first step.

Put the garment on right side out and do all fitting from the outside. Fitting is more difficult to do with the garment right side out, but it is done in this way because the two sides of the figure can be fitted independently of each other, if the figure requires that kind of attention. However, it is much easier to fit skirts or pants wrong side out, and if the figure is balanced, there is no reason why this cannot be done. Of course, the fitted garment should be tested right side out on the figure before permanent fitting decisions are made.

Factors which influence fit

Figure problems In general, figure faults of the larger-than-average figure are minimized by a slightly looser, easier fit. A psychological effect is created by the garment which is too tight on a large figure —the observer has a feeling the person has gained more weight, and so she appears larger than she really is. Unfortunately, all too many large persons have a very different opinion; so many think they must make a garment tighter than average to make their figures look trim. This is not true; rather, the garment which fits with slightly more freedom gives a subtle effect that the wearer has lost weight recently. This principle can be applied to a particular part of the body; if any part of the body (the bust, the thighs, etc.) is larger than average, the best way to hide the fault is to allow more size than average during fitting. However, the person who is too thin will appear to have lost still more weight in a garment that is fitted with great freedom. Most thin persons will look much better in a trim fit.

A person who lives at a high tempo, who moves more quickly than a less active person, must have greater freedom in fit.

Type of fabric The type of fabric has a bearing on the way a garment should be fitted. Very heavy fabrics must not be fitted too tightly or they will feel too binding; fabrics which are stiff and wrinkle seriously (cotton suitings, for example) do not lend themselves to snug-fitting garments, but if they are used for that type of garment, they must be fitted more loosely (with slightly more size for livability) to reduce wrinkling. Limp, flexible fabrics such as double knits can be fitted more snugly and still be confortable to wear.

Design and purpose The design dominates the whole fitting sequence. If a pattern has been purchased in the proper size, the pattern company will have allowed the proper amount of freedom for movement and the extra size for style fullness. Review "Sizing Standards of the Pattern Fashion Industry" on page 36. The design influences the purpose of the garment, of course. In general, costumes for active sports are fitted with more freedom than street clothes, and cocktail and dinner suits are often fitted quite snugly because the figure-revealing quality of a snug fit is in

good taste in the evening. The costume which will be worn often and over extended periods of time must be fitted with slightly more freedom than one worn for occasional short periods of time.

Learn to be critical

It is so easy to decide that a garment fits and let it go at that to avoid time-consuming fitting and basting alterations. But one of the greatest advantages of fashion sewing is the individual fitting one can achieve; it is foolish to decide it is good enough as is; be critical. Take time to experiment and see if fitting corrections improve the effect; try more than one solution and compare results. Keep in mind that a superbly fitted garment enhances the figure by camouflaging figure faults. No step in the construction process is more rewarding.

The number of fitting sessions

Although experienced persons are capable of fitting an entire costume in one or two fitting sessions, the number of sessions can and should vary with the variety and magnitude of figure problems and with the experiences of the fitter (who will do the techniques) and the wearer (who will baste the fitting corrections). *If problems are complex and if one or both of the workers is relatively inexperienced, more sessions are recommended.* Most readers who are tailoring a first costume will prefer to fit the skirt or pants and jacket or coat at separate fitting sessions, although eventually the two units must be studied together to make final decisions. Fittings for each unit can be broken down into several sessions; although this requires more time, problems are more easily understood and more accurately solved when approached one or two at a time.

FITTING THE SKIRT OR PANTS

Most sketches in this series show a strip of grosgrain ribbon, lapped over the waist edges, acting as a waistband to support the garment during fitting. The ribbon should be wrapped quite snugly around the figure (somewhat tighter than a waistband) for better support. The lower edge of the ribbon will settle to the waistline of the figure; it should be pinned in place with its lower edge along the seamline at the waist. Its position will probably be changed during fitting; see examples in Figures 6-4 and 6-5. For illustrative purposes, the sketches show a narrow ribbon (⅜ to ½ inch wide), so that cut edges will be visible above the ribbon.

Professional standards of fit The woman who aspires to professional results in her home-sewn wardrobe must be as sensitive to high standards of fit as she is to quality construction. These standards are difficult to achieve because one so seldom has an opportunity to observe them; what one does see (even in professional shows) are costumes made to fit the average figure on figures which vary from the average in any number of ways. In fact, all too many persons with figure irregularities, large as well as small, are so accustomed to the way made-for-the-average clothes fit that they have come to accept poor fit and actually no longer see the flaws. Under the guidance of an instructor, they must learn to recognize their many figure problems (perhaps for the first time) and to adopt more demanding standards.

Briefly stated, the standards are as follows: The weight of the skirt or pants should fall from the waist; it should not be supported by the hips but instead should rest easily over the hips. It should fall freely below the hip level; it should not cup in below the hips to reveal body contours. Under most circumstances, pants should not cup in below the hip level, although if a figure-hugging effect is desired in knit or stretch fabrics, pants can be as figure-revealing as desired. Center lines and side seamlines (as viewed from the side) should fall in plumblines on the figure. These standards will be expanded and clarified as fitting techniques are presented in the following pages.

Make tentative decisions concerning overall size or width

Be sure the garment is large enough before proceeding. If it is too tight, rip out seams immediately to prevent stretching. If a ripple of fabric forms just below the waist, encircling the entire figure, the garment is too tight at the hip level; rip out the side seams in the hip area to allow the garment to settle down over the hips. If a ripple forms in the front or back only, one of two problems exists: (1) Curves in that area are larger than average and more shape or length or width is required in that one unit only (see page 228); or (2) the waist level of the figure dips more than is average in that area (see page 232). As fitting begins, it is helpful to have sufficient size to work with; ideally the garment should be somewhat too large, especially at the waist. It is a very simple operation to take out excess size as a final step, after other, more difficult, fitting has been finished.

Although the experienced person is able to judge size by observation alone, many may need the extra help of a few generalizations which apply to garments with no style fullness. Pinch out the excess fabric not required for body size; the amount which can be pinched out is the amount of livability in the garment. A straight, fitted skirt with no style fullness should have the following minimum allowances for livability or fitting ease: 1 inch at the 3-inch

hip level and 2 inches at both the 7- and 9-inch hip levels. Livability amounts can be increased, if desired, to allow for greater comfort in utilitarian garments, for more freedom of movement for active sportswear, or for the purpose of camouflaging figure irregularities. Shorts and pants (in fabrics other than knit or stretch fabrics) will be more comfortable as the wearer sits if they are fitted somewhat looser. It must be understood that the livability or fitting-ease requirements stated above do not allow for style fullness, which varies with each design. The inexperienced person can compare the style fullness in a particular garment with a similar and favorite one in her wardrobe by pinching out the excess in the latter for comparison.

Extra size at the waist is a great advantage during fitting, and one should expect to make changes in waist measurement. During fitting, the waist size can be corrected to correspond to the demands of the individual figure; it can be changed by taking in or letting out side seams (which changes shape in the seam position) or by taking in or letting out darts (which changes shape in the dart positions). In this way, fitting can serve the dual purpose of adjusting waist size and, at the same time, creating proper shape for individual body curves.

**SPECIAL NOTE CONCERNING KNIT GARMENTS
Part of the appeal of a knit costume lies in its soft, somewhat clinging or molded lines on the figure—in other words, a knit fabric is enhanced if it must stretch slightly over body curves. This is especially true of pants, shorts, dresses, and blouses; to a lesser degree, it is true of jackets and coats as well. As a muslin copy is fitted, it is not possible to make final decisions**

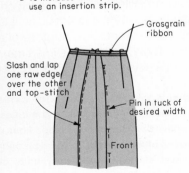

a To increase width, let out seams or
use an insertion strip.

b To decrease width, take in seams or
slash and lap out excess.

*FIGURE 6-1 To change overall
size or width.*

on overall size; one cannot predict how a particular knit fabric will react or what its effect will be on a particular figure. The test copy should be fitted as it would be for any other fabric, although it can be fitted somewhat smaller (perhaps 1 inch) than it would be if a woven fabric were to be used. Later, when the knit fabric is cut and basted, the costume can be better evaluated in the light of the particular knit on the particular figure. After the garment is cut and basted, it should be fitted again, and the worker should anticipate that seams may need to be taken in slightly.

To change overall size or width
Seams can be let out in the usual way if there is sufficient seam allowance; this is the only possible solution if a muslin test copy is not made. Sketch *a* in Figure 6-1 shows the use of an insertion of muslin to allow extra size, possible when a muslin test copy is made. This is the same as the pattern alteration (method 2) in Figure 5-26 on page 149. Refer to that sketch and add the strips in an identical manner. Estimate the required increase. Slash the muslin on the grainline in the area between the darts and the side edge. Draw parallel lines on the insertion strip to mark off the desired increase, and top-stitch the raw edges over the ruler lines. When a slash is made along the grainline of the muslin, it will appear as a curved line on the figure, as the sketch shows.

The simplest way to decrease width is to take in seams, and this is the best solution if the decrease will be relatively small. If a muslin copy is made and if the alteration is large, the slash-and-lap method shown in sketch *b* is the better solution. This is done like the pattern alteration shown in Figure 5-57 on page 194. Draw parallel ruler lines along the grainline in the area between the darts and the side edge, marking off the desired decrease. Slash along one line and top-stitch the raw edges over the remaining line. When a slash is made along the grainline of the muslin, it will appear as a curved line on the figure, as shown.

To bring the fullest hip level of the pattern to the hip level on the figure

The techniques shown in Figure 6-2 are possible only if a test copy is made. If the garment is cut in fabric, the torso area of both skirt or pants can be lengthened by lengthening darts and reshaping side seamlines. The torso area of skirts (already cut in expensive fabric) can be shortened by shortening darts and reshaping side seamlines; but in pants, the garment must be lifted up on the figure and the entire waist area reshaped.

Sketch *a* in Figure 6-2 shows the torso lengthened with an insertion strip; this is done the same as the pattern alteration shown in Figure 5-12 on page 128. Rip out darts and seams in the torso area. Slash along the crosswise grainline of the muslin. Draw parallel lines on a strip of muslin to mark off the desired increase and topstitch the raw edges along the ruler lines. Rebaste darts and seams.

Sketch *b* shows the torso area shortened. Pin in a parallel tuck to bring the full hip level to the proper position. This is done like the pattern alteration shown in Figure 5-10 on page 126. Rip out darts and seams in the torso area. Draw ruler lines (the width of the tuck) on the crosswise grainline of the muslin. Slash along one line, lap the raw edge to the remaining line, and topstitch. Rebaste darts and seams.

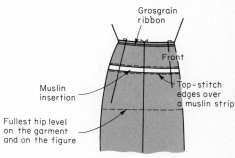

a To lengthen the torso area.

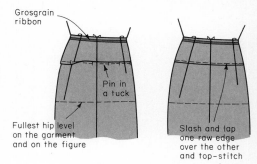

b To shorten the torso area.

FIGURE 6-2   *To bring the fullest hip level of the pattern to the hip level on the figure.*

Study the direction of all vertical lines from front, back, and side views

Figure 6-3 shows a basic skirt on the figure with vertical lines hanging in proper plumblines. Center lines must hang perpendicular to the floor; but, as shown in the front-view sketch, the side edge of a skirt may slant out (as in an A-line skirt) unless the skirt is a perfect rectangle below the hip level. When viewed from the side, the side seam must hang in a plumbline, and if there is no flare (or style fullness) involved, lines at the front and back edges must hang in plumblines also. The fitter can best recognize irregularities of line direction by studying the figure from a distance of several feet.

Changes in line direction are difficult because they require intricate fitting and because they cannot always be completely rectified by fitting unless a test copy is made. A person who has these problems should make a muslin test copy in order to make the major changes required by pattern alteration in the future; serious problems can be completely solved only by pattern alteration. Small irregularities can be corrected by fitting, but large problems can only be improved, not completely corrected, after the garment is cut in good fabric.

To test the direction of center lines
See Figure 6-4. Center lines hang in proper plumblines on a well-balanced figure, but they slant or swing to one side on an unbalanced figure. *Center lines always swing to the side of the figure which is larger or more curvaceous or to the side with a longer leg (which causes a greater hip curve).* By lifting the skirt up on the oppo-

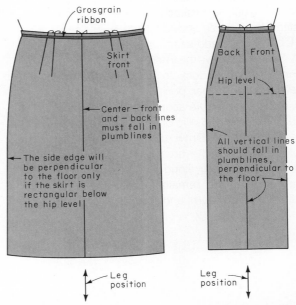

FIGURE 6-3 Vertical lines must fall in plumblines on the figure.

site side as shown, center lines can be straightened. When this is done, there will be excess size at the hip level on the smaller side of the figure; the excess should be taken in, but it is well to fit that side somewhat loosely so as to camouflage the figure irregularity. Place pins along the lower edge of the ribbon to mark the corrected waistline and later replace the pins with marking basting. The corrected waistline must have the character of the original; the original resulted in a smooth curved line along the waist edge, and the corrected line must make a smooth transition from one side to the other even though the two sides will be different.

To test the direction of side seamlines

See Figure 6-5. If body curves are larger than average in the front or back or if the posture is such that it creates irregular body curves, *the side seamline will slant or swing toward the larger-than-average*

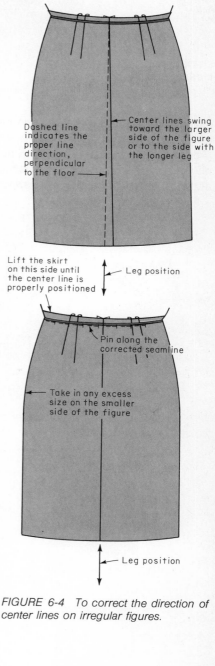

Center lines swing toward the larger side of the figure or to the side with the longer leg

Dashed line indicates the proper line direction, perpendicular to the floor

Leg position

Lift the skirt on this side until the center line is properly positioned

Pin along the corrected seamline

Take in any excess size on the smaller side of the figure

Leg position

FIGURE 6-4   To correct the direction of center lines on irregular figures.

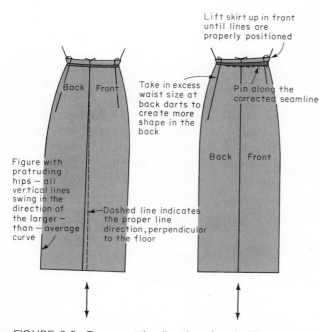

Lift skirt up in front until lines are properly positioned

Back   Front

Take in excess waist size at back darts to create more shape in the back

Pin along the corrected seamline

Back   Front

Figure with protruding hips — all vertical lines swing in the direction of the larger — than — average curve

Dashed line indicates the proper line direction, perpendicular to the floor

FIGURE 6-5   To correct the direction of vertical lines as seen from the side view.

*curve and the entire skirt will swing in the
same direction, so that all vertical lines
(from side view) will be affected.* Study the
plumbline and leg position in the left sketch
and notice that the entire skirt swings to-

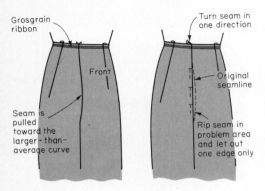

*FIGURE 6-6 To perfect the character of verti-
cal seamlines.*

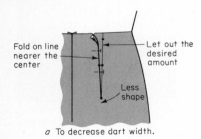

a To decrease dart width.

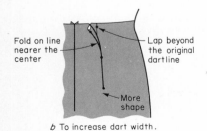

b To increase dart width.

*FIGURE 6-7 To   change   dart
width.*

ward the back, forcing the lower edge up
in the back.

The problem illustrated is one of protruding hips, and it can be completely
solved by a major fitting correction which
will create more shape, length, and width
for the larger-than-average curve. This
solution is possible if a muslin test copy is
made; see Figures 6-10 and 6-11 and the
accompanying text if the figure irregularity
is exaggerated.

If a muslin test copy is not made, large
corrections are not possible. Small corrections can be made by lifting the skirt up
in the front, as shown. This will create excess size at the waist, and it should be distributed along the waist as the figure demands; in the example shown, excess waist
size should be taken in at the back darts,
if possible, to gain the advantage of creating extra shape in the area of the larger-
than-average body curve.

An alternative solution is to allow the
garment to drop in the back; see Figure
6-14 and the accompanying text.

**To perfect the character of vertical
seamlines** See Figure 6-6. If a seam
curves or wobbles at any level, it is distorted
by—pulled in the direction of—a larger-
than-average body curve. The example
shows a seam pulled toward the front; the
problem may be larger-than-average hipbones or stomach curves. The seam would
curve toward the back at the same level
on a figure with an extra pad of fat at that
high hip level. If a seam is distorted, rip
bastings in the problem area and turn the
seam allowance in one direction as shown;
the seam will spread apart to reveal the
correction needed.

These corrections are confined to the
small amount that can be safely let out at
the seam (about ⅜ inch) if a test copy is
not made; if a test copy is made, the edge
can be extended with a scrap of muslin.

Another method of gaining extra width or size for a larger-than-average curve is to let out dartlines and pin in shorter darts along curved lines, as shown in Figure 6-7.

To alter the width, length or location of darts

Because darts create shape to fit body curves, they frequently require fitting corrections. Even very small changes will be rewarding, and both workers should look for ways of changing darts so that the shape they create will better conform to individual curves of the figure.

To alter dart width See Figure 6-7. When changing the width of the dart, rip out the existing dart and fold along the dartline nearer the center, thereby making the change on the line nearer the side. By retaining the line nearer the center, the proportions of the original design are retained and the corrected dartline remains the same distance from the center and will match other design lines in the costume. Sketch *a* shows a dart let out so that it will create less shape in the area directly below its tip. Sketch *b* shows a dart widened by lapping the line nearer the center beyond the remaining dartline; this will create more shape in the area directly below its tip. Mark the new dartline with pencil (on a test copy) or with marking basting (if no test copy is made) and rebaste the darts in the usual manner.

To alter dart length and character To alter dart length, rip out the existing dart and shape in a new dart, allowing it to fall in place on the figure; it will tend to shape itself, with its tip at the proper level on the figure. Dart length is changed during fitting as it is in pattern alteration; see Figure 5-19 on page 140. Figure 6-8 shows this simple alteration, as it is basted.

The character of a dartline can be changed from ruler-straight to curved, if desired. This correction is often required on front darts for the figure with rounded contours directly below the waist; many patterns will have a curved dart in this position. Any dart can be curved if the contours of the figure are rounded in the area over which the dart will fall.

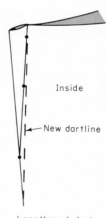

Lengthened dart

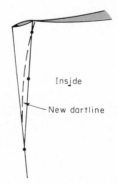

Shortened and rounded dart

FIGURE 6-8 To change darts as the garment is basted.

Alterations for larger-than-average curves

To change the location of a dart An existing dart can be ripped out and made narrower or completely eliminated and replaced with another dart in a different location. See Figure 6-9, which shows the original dart ripped out and moved toward the side; this alteration eliminates shaping near the stomach area and moves it over to create shape for prominent hipbones. The thin, boyish figure often requires no shape near the front but does require shape for hipbones, which are often more prominent on a slim figure. The new dart can be located in the position that is most appealing on the figure; the diagonal line pictured is often the most flattering. The new dart need not be the length or the width of the original; it should be the length and width that creates the proper amount of shape at the particular level required for the individual figure.

If vertical lines (when viewed from side view) do not hang in plumblines on the figure but slant toward the front or the back, the problem is one of curves which differ from the average and the simple correction in Figure 6-5 will not be adequate. However, these figures, no matter how curvaceous, can be perfectly fitted if a muslin test copy is made.

Fitting corrections for curvaceous figures are the most difficult because there is need for more shape and also more width or length (or both). If the curve is large, extra fabric is required (widthwise or lengthwise or both) in the one unit where the curve exists. Corrections are difficult because the fitter must do two operations in one (obtain more shape and also more length or width) and because she must fit the front and back independently of each other and then put the two together again in proper relationship to each other.

To create extra shape and width Figure 6-10 pictures the technique of fitting the front and back units independently of each other; note that the entire side seam has been ripped and that the two units are shown pinned at different levels (see the uneven edges at the waist and lower edge).

An important fitting concept is involved in this type of correction. The sketches show how to gain more shape and width in the front unit (only) to fit the figure which is curvaceous in the front (full stomach or very heavy thighs); the same techniques can be applied to the back to fit protruding hips. Before proceeding, it is important to understand why the two units must be shifted into new positions, with waist and lower edges no longer meeting; concentrate on the waistline edge of the front.

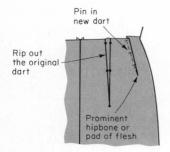

Pin in
new dart

Rip out
the original
dart

Prominent
hipbone or
pad of flesh

FIGURE 6-9 To change dart location to conform to body curves.

When an extra dart is pinned in, the edge is forced into a sharper curve, and it "wants" to move up on the figure; pin a dart in a piece of paper to see the influence of a dart. Since the problem exists in only one unit, the correction is involved with that one unit and has nothing to do with the other unit. When side seams are ripped, the edge with an extra dart will move up automatically, and it should be allowed to move. Smooth the unit being fitted over the figure, and anchor it in place with pins. Then smooth the remaining unit into position and pin the new seam in place.

Sketch *a* in Figure 6-10 shows the only possible solution if no test copy is made. If there is sufficient fabric at the waist, an extra dart can be pinned in to give extra shape in the one unit. But the amount of available width is limited to the amount which can be let out from the seam; lapping the back edge over the front only ⅜ inch leaves a ⅜-inch seam on the front and allows an extra ¼ inch of width only. This will be of some help, but it is not adequate for many figures. Sketch *b* shows the same fitting correction as it can be done if a muslin test copy is made; by slashing the muslin skirt and inserting a strip of any desired width, major problems can be corrected.

To create extra shape and length

Larger-than-average curves require more length as well as width; if the curve is very prominent, the need for extra length will be evident. Refer to Figure 6-5 on page 225. Larger-than-average curves force the side seamline to swing toward the larger-than-average curve; actually, the entire skirt swings toward the larger-than-average curve. If hips protrude, the skirt juts out from the figure at the back, indicating the need for extra length which will allow it to fall in proper plumblines. In pants, the need for extra length is obvious because the waist tugs down in the back.

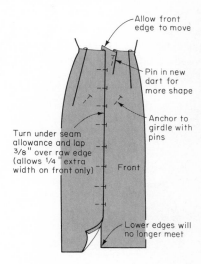

Allow front edge to move

Pin in new dart for more shape

Anchor to girdle with pins

Turn under seam allowance and lap ⅜" over raw edge (allows ¼" extra width on front only)

Front

Lower edges will no longer meet

a If skirt is cut of good fabric.

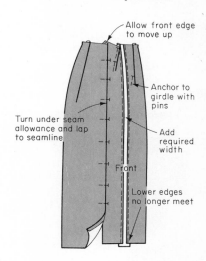

Allow front edge to move up

Anchor to girdle with pins

Turn under seam allowance and lap to seamline

Add required width

Front

Lower edges no longer meet

b If skirt is cut of muslin.

FIGURE 6-10 To create extra shape and width for larger-than-average curves.

Sketch *a* in Figure 6-11 shows the method of gaining extra length for prominent curves. Slash the muslin test copy along the crosswise grainline, at the level of the longest dart, as shown. Pin in a scrap of muslin, allowing it to take the boat shape illustrated. Study the figure at some dis-

tance to see that vertical lines have been brought into proper plumbline position, and make additional corrections if necessary. After the proper amount of length has been decided, rip the longest dart and alter the muslin copy exactly as the pattern is altered in Figure 5-37 on page 171. Rebaste darts and test again on the figure.

Combine vertical and horizontal alterations for exaggerated problems
Review the section with a similar heading on page 172 and see a corresponding pattern alteration in Figure 5-38. The fitting technique is shown in sketch *b,* Figure 6-11. Doing the horizontal alteration shown in sketch *a* and a vertical alteration similar to the one shown in Figure 6-10, makes it possible to obtain the extra shape this type of figure requires and also to gain additional length (as well as width) to span the larger-than-average curve.

Alterations for flatter- or smaller-than-average curves

If vertical lines (when viewed from side view) do not hang in plumblines on the figure but slant toward the front or back, the problem is one of curves which differ from the average. In most cases, problems of line direction exist because the seams slant in the direction of larger-than-average curves, but smaller-than-average curves cause changes in line direction as well; vertical seams slant away from the smaller-than-average curve.

It is difficult to make major changes for figures with curves which vary from the average because there is need for less shape and also less width or length (or both). The fitter must do two operations in one (decrease shape and also length or width) and must fit the front and back independently of each other and then put the two together again in proper relationship to each other.

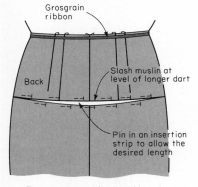

a To create extra shape and length for protruding hips.

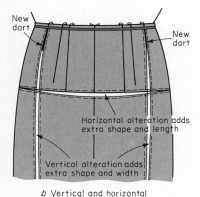

b Vertical and horizontal alterations combined.

FIGURE 6-11 *Alterations for exaggerated problems.*

To create less shape and width Figure 6-12 shows the technique of fitting the front and back units independently of each other. Note that the entire side seam has been ripped and that the two units are shown pinned at different levels (see the uneven edges at the waist and lower edge).

An important fitting concept is involved in this type of correction. The sketch shows how to decrease shape and width in the back only for the figure with flat hips; the same techniques can be applied to the front. Before proceeding, it is important to understand why the two units must be shifted into new positions, with waist and lower edges no longer meeting; concentrate on the waistline edge of the back. When a dart is decreased in width or eliminated entirely, the edge straightens out, and it "wants" to move down on the figure; pin a dart in a piece of paper to see the edge curve and then remove the dart to see the edge straighten. Since the problem exists in only one unit, the correction is involved with that unit and has nothing to do with the other unit. When side seams are ripped, the edge with the altered dart will move down automatically, and it should be allowed to move. Smooth the unit being fitted over the figure and anchor it in place with pins. Then smooth the remaining unit into position and pin the new seam in place.

The alteration pictured can be done even if no muslin test copy is made. Decrease the width of a dart or eliminate a dart. Then turn under more than a ⅝-inch seam to decrease width the desired amount and lap that edge to the seamline on the remaining edge.

To create less shape and length Flatter- or smaller-than-average curves require less length as well as width. If curves are flatter than average, the entire garment swings away from the problem curve. On the figure with flat hips, the entire skirt will swing toward the front. In pants, the waist

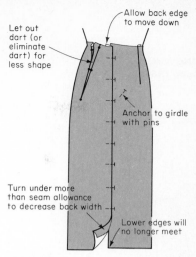

FIGURE 6-12 *To create less shape and width for flatter- or smaller-than-average curves.*

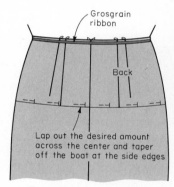

a To create less shape and length for flat hips.

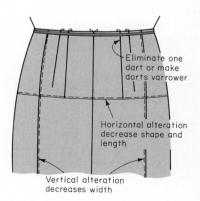

b Vertical and horizontal alteratios combined.

FIGURE 6-13 *Alterations for exaggerated problems.*

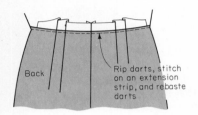

a Add the extension.

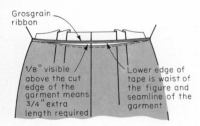

b Lap ribbon in place.

c Correction seen from side view.

d Fitting correction transferred.

FIGURE 6-14 To extend upper edges.

edge rides up above the waist level of the figure or the pants bag in the seat, and the need for less length is obvious. The major correction required is not possible unless a muslin test copy is made.

See sketch *a* in Figure 6-13. Pin a boat-shaped tuck along the crosswise grainline at the level of the longest dart, as shown. Study the figure at some distance to see that vertical lines have been brought into proper plumbline direction and make additional corrections if necessary. After the proper amount of decrease has been decided, rip the longest dart and alter the muslin copy exactly as the pattern is altered in Figure 5-58 on page 196. Rebaste darts and test again on the figure.

Combine vertical and horizontal alterations for exaggerated problems
See sketch *b* in Figure 6-13. Doing the horizontal alteration shown in sketch *a* and a vertical alteration similar to the one shown in sketch *b* of Figure 6-1 makes it possible to decrease shape and also decrease length and width.

Make corrections at the waistline

To extend upper edges If any fitting corrections have caused the waist of the garment to move down on the figure, so that there is not ample seam allowance or sufficient length at the waist level, extend the upper edge of the muslin copy with an extension strip, as shown in Figure 6-14. The problem illustrated shows extra length in the back skirt for larger-than-average hip curves.

Rip out darts and seams in the problem area, top-stitch the raw upper edge over a strip of muslin, and rebaste, as shown in sketch *a*. Wrap the grosgrain ribbon around the waist as in sketch *b*. Note that if ⅛ inch of the extension is visible below the ribbon, the total amount of the correction is ¾ inch—⅛ inch plus the original ⅝-inch seam allowance. Sketch *c* shows the figure from side view, and sketch *d* shows the corresponding pattern alteration.

Workers are often confused when making this type of correction. For example, if they see ⅛ inch of the extension visible below the ribbon, they are apt to make a ⅛-inch pattern alteration. To avoid confusion, mark the original seamline on the muslin (⅝ inch below the cut edge) with pencil in a contrasting color; then, after the corrected seamline is marked, the differences between the two can be more easily recognized.

Make improvements Both workers should anticipate the need for very small fitting adjustments at the waist. After all other major fitting has been completed, work for greater perfection at the waist.

The advantage of allowing some excess size at the waist has been stressed in several previous steps, and even at this stage some excess size is advantageous. After the garment is cut of fabric and basted, it will be fitted again; and it is a simple operation to take in darts and seams slightly if the need arises at that time. Allow at least ¼ inch excess size for each quarter of the figure— in other words, allow for ¼ inch of ease on each side of the front and back.

Establish the seamline at the waist and make a temporary waistband guide See Figure 6-15. Cut a strip of pellon about 1 inch wide to act as a temporary waistband guide. Wrap it around the figure over the waist edges and pin it in proper position; it must be snug enough to support the weight of the garment and long enough to be comfortable for many hours of wearing. The lower edge of the pellon indicates the waistline of the figure and

therefore the proper seamline of the garment. Mark along the seamline with pencil or marking basting, as shown.

The temporary waistband will be used for all subsequent fittings and also as a guide when preparing the permanent waistband. To establish matching points, mark the waistband as follows:

For a side-opening zipper Mark the position of the front left end and the lapline on the back end. Mark the right side position. Do not mark center positions; they will be measured and marked later when the permanent band is prepared.

For a back-opening zipper Mark the position of the left back end and the lapline on the right back end. Mark the side positions. Do not mark the center front; it will be measured and marked later when the permanent band is prepared.

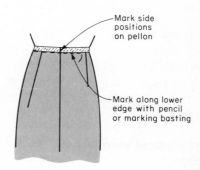

FIGURE 6-15 *Establish the seamline at the waist and make a tempo- rary waistband guide.*

Tentatively decide issues on length and total proportions

Experiment with various lengths and establish the desired hemline. This is a temporary decision because the total proportions of the costume must be studied after the jacket or coat is fitted; some change in length may be indicated at that time.

If there are pockets or trimming bands, study their effect and experiment by placing them at various levels to observe their influence on proportions.

Transfer all fitting corrections to the pattern

Alter the major pattern pieces to conform to the fitting corrections; these may be new pattern alterations, or they may be additions or revisions on alterations made earlier. There will be few corresponding pattern pieces in a skirt or pants; review Figure 5-24 on page 147 when altering smaller pieces. Test the waistband pattern with the pellon strip to be sure it will be of ample length.

FITTING THE JACKET OR COAT

Review the introductory pages of this chapter from page 216 through page 220. Review the special note for knit fabrics on page 47.

Professional standards of fit It is not possible to establish standards which will be applicable to all jacket and coat designs, because they vary greatly in overall size, depending on their purpose and their in-tended effect. Before proceeding, carefully review and study "Reevaluate All Circumstances Which Influence Size" on page 47 to 52. By considering the influences of the fabric and the type of costume, workers prepare themselves to set up fitting standards for each costume.

Make tentative decisions concerning overall size or width

Some fitters tend to fit the muslin test copy so that its overall size gives the effect desired in the finished costume. One must avoid fitting too snugly at this time because the thickness of suiting and coating fabrics (especially in hem and facing areas) and the additional bulk of supporting fabrics and linings will tend to decrease the overall size of the finished costume. It is important to allow sufficient size when fitting the test copy; a good general rule is to fit in such a way that the test copy is at least 1 inch larger at all levels than the desired finished size of the costume; knit fabrics are an exception, as explained on page 47. After the garment is cut in fabric, it should be basted and fitted again; at that time it is a simple matter to take in seams slightly.

The tailored garment, fitted or boxy, must hang from the shoulders without being supported at any other level on the figure, because if it is too tight at any level it will ride up, creating unattractive horizontal ripples. If horizontal ripples form at any level, rip vertical seams below that level before proceeding. In a boxy or semi-fitted costume, horizontal ripples indicate that the garment is too tight at the hip level. In snugly fitted costumes, small horizontal ripples above the waist may indicate that the waist is too tight; but if ripples are pronounced, they indicate that the garment is too long-waisted.

Because the pattern was purchased in the proper bust size, there should be no adjustments in overall size at that level. Changes in overall size are made at vertical seams, most of which lead to the armhole, and therefore changes made at the bust level must be made on the sleeve as well; these changes greatly influence the intricately cut lines of the armhole and the sleeve. If it appears that the test copy is a size too large or too small, it is wiser to buy a new pattern in the proper size than to attempt such radical fitting corrections.

Changes in overall size cannot be made by one method used in skirts (as in Figure 6-1, page 222), because that method involves a parallel correction for the entire length of the garment. This cannot be done, because even a very slight change in width in the shoulder area is a great change; about 1/8 inch is the difference in shoulder width between one size and another. Changes in size should begin below the bust level and be done by taking in or letting out vertical seams. If seams must be let out more than 1/2 inch, rip the seam and top-stitch the raw edge over a strip of muslin (the technique is shown at the waist edge in Figure 6-14), and then let out the amount required.

To bring the waist level of the garment to the waist level of the figure

If the garment is fitted or semi-fitted, the waistline must be at the proper level on the figure, or else the entire garment will look unattractive. See sketch a in Figure 6-16. If the garment is too long-waisted in both front and back, pin in a parallel tuck all around the figure to bring the waist to the proper position. Then alter the muslin like the pattern alteration shown in Figure 5-9 on page 124. Rip out darts and seams below the bust level. Draw ruler lines (the width of the tuck) on the crosswise grain of the muslin. Slash along one line, lap one raw edge to the remaining line, and top-stitch. Rebaste darts and seams.

Sketch b in Figure 6-16 shows the waist lengthened an equal amount in the front and back. This is the same as the pattern alteration in Figure 5-11 on page 127. Slash along the crosswise grain of the muslin. Draw parallel lines on a strip of muslin to mark off the desired increase and top-stitch the raw edges over the ruler lines. Rebaste darts and seams.

To alter waist lengths different amounts in the front and back See "To Adjust the Waist Level in Fitted or Semi-fitted Jackets and Coats" on page 131 and review the type of pattern alteration required if waist length must be altered differently in the front and back. This can be done on the muslin copy exactly as it is done by pattern alteration. Sketch c in Figure 6-16 shows an example of the fitting technique; it is identical to the pattern alteration in Figure 5-14 on page 132. Note that lower edges are no longer even; this will be corrected when these fitting changes are transferred to the pattern.

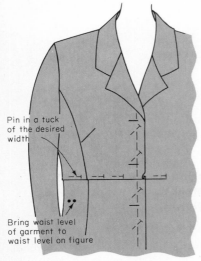

Pin in a tuck
of the desired
width

Bring waist level
of garment to
waist level on figure

a To shorten waist length.

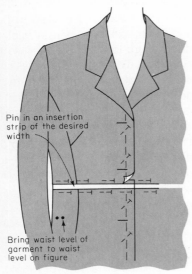

Pin in an insertion
strip of the desired
width

Bring waist level of
garment to waist
level on figure

b To lengthen waist length.

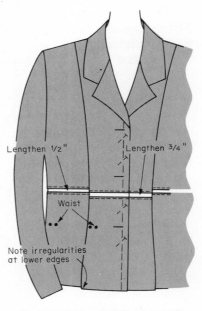

Lengthen ½"   Lengthen ¾"

Waist

Note irregularities
at lower edges

c To alter waist length different amounts
in the front and back.

FIGURE 6-16 To bring the waist level of the garment to the waistline of the figure.

Study the direction of vertical lines from front, back, and side views

When working with a long coat or jacket, review the material under this heading on page 224; the principles explained there on skirts are applicable to jackets and coats.

Study the direction of center lines

When viewed from the front or back, these lines must hang in plumblines on the figure; if they do not hang in proper vertical position, one of two figure irregularities is responsible. In most cases a slanting center line indicates that one shoulder is higher than the other; the center lines slant toward the side of the higher shoulder. This problem will be encountered frequently (many persons have a variation of almost ½ inch). The best solution is to work with shoulder pads, adding extra thickness to the underside of one pad to increase the height of the low shoulder; alternately, padding can be removed from the pad on the side of the high shoulder. Another solution is to fit the two shoulders independently, but this tends to point out rather than conceal the problem.

In some cases center lines may slant because one bust curve or one shoulder curve is larger than the other. If bust curves differ, the best solution is to pad the bra on one side. An extra pad made of Dacron quilt batting, covered with a soft fabric and tacked to the inside of the bra cup, will balance the bustline; laundering will be no problem if the pad is quilted with hand stitches and tacked securely in place. If one shoulder curve is slightly larger than the other, it may be best to ignore the problem; but if the variation is great (as in a crippled figure), the only solution is to fit the two sides independently of each other.

When viewed from side view A fitted garment follows the contours of the figure to the hip level and must hang in plumblines below the hip level. A boxy garment must hang in plumblines below the bust level. If side seams slant and the entire garment appears to swing toward the front or back, it is a matter of body curves which are not average. Lines swing in the direction of the larger-than-average curve or away from the flatter- or smaller-than-average curve. If bust curves are larger than average, a boxy garment swings toward the front, giving a maternity-wear effect. If boxy garments swing to the back, the problem may be one of rounded shoulders or prominent hips. Directions for fitting irregular curves appear on pages 238 through 242.

To alter width, length, or location of darts

Review "The Principle of Dart Fitting—A Guideline" on page 136. Detailed directions for fitting darts appear under this heading on page 227; the principles explained there on skirts are applicable to jackets and coats.

Because bust curves are the most pronounced curves on the body, and because they vary greatly from one figure to another, they require careful fitting; expect to make changes. The bust dart should point to the high point of the bust curve, ending about 1 to 1½ inches from the high point. Slight changes will result in great improvements. Raising or lowering a horizontal dart a mere ¼ inch or changing the line of an underarm dart (as shown in the pattern alteration in Figure 5-18 on page 139) may greatly improve the total effect.

Alterations for larger-than-average curves

Before proceeding, review the entire section under a similiar heading on pages 163 to 191. The sketches in this series picture bust curves; rounded shoulders are fitted in the same manner. Larger-than-average curves require extra width or length (or both) and extra shape to conform to body curves. Amounts can be estimated before the pattern is altered, as explained in "Estimate the Amount of Spread or Extra Width or Length" on page 164. When the muslin copy is fitted, diagonal ripples leading in any direction from the high point of the body curve are a sure indication that the curve requires more shape and width or length or both. This may be a new correction if the pattern had not been altered, or it may be an increase on a pattern alteration made previously. The purpose of the fitting techniques in this series (Figures 6-17 to 6-20) is to determine the proper amount of spread required for the body curve. These fitting corrections are similiar but not identical to the corresponding pattern alterations. All sketches show the test copy slashed and an insertion strip pinned in place; but note that the slash is near (but not directly through) the dartline. When these changes are transferred to the pattern, the slash line will pass through the center of the dart (as in all corresponding alterations in Chapter 5), but for fitting purposes it is simpler to slash near the dart without disturbing the dart itself. In each case, as in the corresponding pattern alteration, the fitting results in a boat-shaped insertion or addition passing over the high point of the body curve.

The extra spread created by all corrections of this type is determined by the amount required to make telltale diagonal ripples disappear and, in the case of horizontal or diagonal darts, the amount required to allow the garment (when viewed from the side) to hang in plumblines below the bust level (in boxy garments) or below the hip level (in fitted garments).

To create extra shape and length
Figure 6-17 shows techniques of creating more shape and length in horizontal or diagonal darts. Sketch *a* shows the boat-shaped insertion reaching from side to side on the figure; the boat shape must extend across the entire front in double-breasted designs, whereas it may extend from the side seam (or a style line near the side) to the front edge, as in sketch *c,* on single-breasted designs.

Slash the test copy either slightly above or slightly below the dartline, slashing almost to the seamline at the side. Pin the upper section over the insertion strip. Then allow extra spread or length and pin the remaining section in place. Compare this fitting with the alteration in Figure 5-44 on page 178.

In single-breasted designs, fitting corrections and corresponding pattern alterations can be done in two different ways; review an evaluation of the two on page 179. Sketch *b* shows the insertion reaching across the entire front; sketch *c* shows the alternative method, with a boat shape reaching from the style line to the center. Slash the muslin close to the dartline, slashing almost to the seam. Pin the upper section over the insertion strip. Then allow the proper amount of spread at the high point of the bust and test out both methods pictured. Figures with pronounced cleavage will be better fitted by the method shown in sketch *c;* massive, bulky figures are better fitted with the method shown in sketch *b*. Compare these corrections with the pattern alterations in Figures 5-44 and 5-45 on pages 178, 180, and 181.

If there is no existing horizontal dart, slash the muslin exactly as it is shown here and pin in a similar boat-shaped insertion. To alter the pattern, use this amount of spread and create a new dart as in Figure 5-48 on page 183.

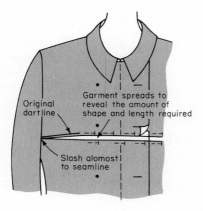

Original dartline

Garment spreads to reveal the amount of shape and length required

Slash alomost to seamline

a To fit double-breasted designs.

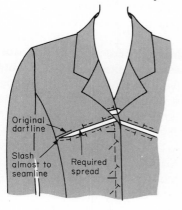

Original dartline

Slash almost to seamline

Required spread

b To fit single-breasted designs.

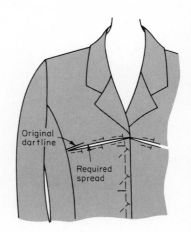

Original dartline

Required spread

c Alternative method for single-breasted designs.

FIGURE 6-17   *To create extra shape and length.*

To create extra shape and width See sketch *a* in Figure 6-18. Vertical darts are altered to create extra shape and width exactly as horizontal darts were handled in Figure 6-17. Two alternatives are shown in sketch *a*. The true boat shape on the left of the sketch allows extra width but retains the same size at the hemline. The modified boat on the right side allows extra width at the hemline to help camouflage the bust curve or to give extra size for full hips.

The same type of boat-shaped addition is shown on a princess-line design in sketch *b*; in this case, extra width is gained by letting out (or in other words, adding to) the edge of the side section. The extra spread required is the measurement between the original seamline on the side section (shown in dotted lines) and the seamline on the front section. The identical pattern alteration is shown in Figure 5-49 on page 184.

If there is no existing vertical dart, slash the muslin as shown in Figure 6-19 and pin in a similiar boat-shaped insertion. To alter the pattern, use this amount of spread and create a new dart by applying the principles shown in Figure 5-36 on page 170; the new dart can be a shoulder dart or an under-bust dart, as desired.

Combine vertical and horizontal alterations for exaggerated problems
If a curve is much larger than average, it requires a considerable amount of extra shape and both extra width and extra length. Study the two examples shown in Figure 6-20 and apply these principles to other designs. Sketch *a* shows both corrections on a princess-line design. First do the vertical alteration to add some shape and width, as in sketch *b*, Figure 6-18. Letting out the seam increases the length of the seamline on the side section; if that seam is lengthened appreciably, the cor-

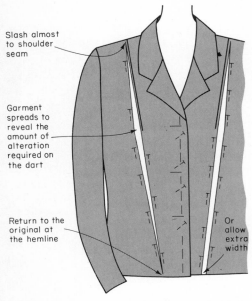

Slash almost to shoulder seam

Garment spreads to reveal the amount of alteration required on the dart

Return to the original at the hemline

Or allow extra width

a To gain shape and width by altering a vertical dart.

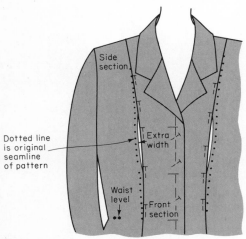

Side section

Dotted line is original seamline of pattern

Extra width

Waist level

Front section

b To gain shape and width by letting out vertical seams.

FIGURE 6-18   To create extra shape and width.

responding seam on the front must be lengthened accordingly. This fitting correction is identical to the pattern alteration in Figure 5-50 on page 185.

Sketch *b* shows a design with one underarm dart to which an additional shoulder dart has been added. This fitting correction is similiar to the one shown in sketch *b* of Figure 5-52 on page 187. First alter the muslin to make the existing dart wider and more shapely; this allows extra shape and length. Then slash the muslin and create a new dart for extra shape and width.

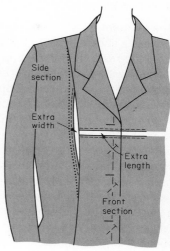

a Combined alteration in a princess-line design.

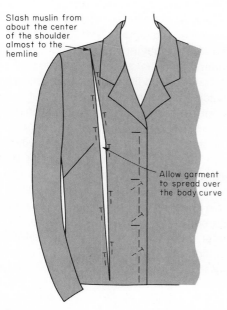

FIGURE 6-19 *To create a new dart for extra shape and width.*

b Combined alterations in a dart-fitted garment.

FIGURE 6-20 *Combine vertical and horizontal alterations for exaggerated problems.*

Alterations for flatter-or smaller-than-average curves

When the garment stands away from body curves, this is a sure indication that it is too shapely and too wide or too long (or both) for the figure with slim, boyish lines. The fitting technique is shown on a horizontal bust dart in Figure 6-21, but it is done the same way for all darts, vertical or horizontal, in the front or in the back. This correction is rarely required in front because a padded bra eliminates the problem more easily and appealingly. To correct this type of problem, pin in a boat-shaped tuck, beginning and ending the tuck at the edges of the garment and making it widest at the high point of the body curve. Then use the width of the tuck as a guide to make a corresponding pattern alteration. The most typical alteration of this type is for straight, flat shoulders; it is shown in sketch a, Figure 5-57, on page 194.

Pin in a boat-shaped tuck
to decrease shape and length

FIGURE 6-21 To fit flatter- or smaller-than-average curves.

In princess-line garments, a similiar boat-shaped decrease can be made by ripping the seam in the area of the curve and taking in the seam on the side section while retaining the original seamline on the center section. The operation is simply a reverse of the one shown in sketch b, Figure 6-18.

Shoulder alterations

Review "Three Major Types of Figure Problems" on page 200. Before altering the width of the shoulder, study the fashion sketch carefully. In some seasons a dropped armhole is fashionable and a garment with a slightly dropped armhole seam (⅜ to ½ inch) may appear at first glance to be too wide in the shoulders.

To alter shoulder width Review the section under this heading on page 201. If the muslin test copy is not wide enough at the shoulder, the shoulder area will feel binding to the wearer, she will not be able to use her arms freely, and the sleeve may reveal diagonal ripples leading from the underarm to the center of the sleeve cap.

The required fitting correction, shown in sketch a of Figure 6-22, is identical to the pattern alteration in Figure 5-62 on page 200. Slash the muslin from the shoulder almost to the armhole seam and pin in a strip of muslin, allowing sufficient extra width to eliminate all evidence of diagonal ripples in the sleeve and to allow the armhole seam to fall in the proper position on the body. This technique can be applied to other designs as well; a similiar pattern alteration is shown on a design with a sleeve cut in one with the major piece in Figure 5-63 on page 201.

If the muslin copy is too wide at the shoulders, pin in a temporary boat-shaped tuck, extending it about 4 inches below the shoulderline in the front and back, as shown in sketch *b*. .Make the tuck wide enough at the shoulder to bring the armhole seam into proper position on the body. Then, using the width of the tuck as a guide, slash and alter the muslin the same as the corresponding pattern alteration shown in sketch *a*, Figure 5-64, on page 202. Sketch *b* in Figure 5-64 shows the same alteration on a design with a sleeve cut in one with the major pieces.

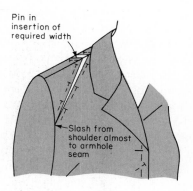

Pin in insertion of required width

Slash from shoulder almost to armhole seam

a To lengthen shoulderline for broad shoulders.

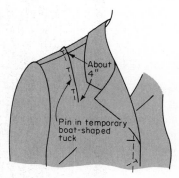

About 4"

Pin in temporary boat-shaped tuck

b To shorten shoulderline for narrow shoulders.

FIGURE 6-22 To alter shoulder width.

To alter the slant of the shoulder   Review the section under this heading on page 203, paying particular attention to Figure 5-65 and the accompanying text. The pattern alterations shown on pages 203 to 215 are more comprehensive than the fitting techniques here; the fitting techniques include only corrections made at the armhole edge. If the slant of the shoulder must be changed at the neck edge, do the fitting by following the pattern alterations in Figure

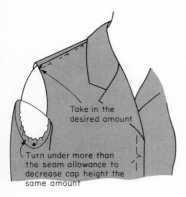

a To fit sloping shoulders.

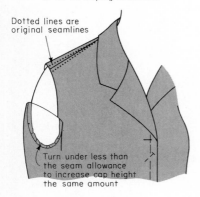

b To fit square shoulders.

FIGURE 6-23   To change the slant of the shoulderline.

5-68 and 5-69 (for square shoulders) and Figures 5-72 and 5-73 (for sloping shoulders).

To change the slant of the shoulder at the armhole edge, see Figure 6-23. Sketch *a* shows the upper part of the armhole seam ripped and the shoulder seam taken in for sloping shoulders. The height of the sleeve cap must be changed accordingly. For example, if the seam is taken in ¼ inch on the front and back edges, the cap must be shortened ¼ inch. To do this, turn under the seam allowance plus ¼ inch (⅞ inch) at the center of the cap and gradually taper back to the original seamline at the notch level. Then lap and pin the sleeve to the seamline at the armhole edges to test the effectiveness of the change. The identical pattern alteration is shown in Figure 5-70 on page 210, and the principles are applied to other types of designs in Figure 5-71.

Sketch *b* shows the shoulder seam let out for square shoulders. The height of the sleeve cap must be changed accordingly. If the seam is let out ⅜ inch on the front and back edges, the cap must be altered ⅜ inch. To do this, turn under ⅜ inch less than the seam allowance (¼ inch) at the center of the cap and gradually taper back to the original seamline at the notch level. Test the effectiveness of the change on the figure. The corresponding pattern alteration is shown in Figure 5-66 on page 205, and the principles are applied to other types of designs in Figure 5-67.

Sleeve alterations

To alter sleeve width   The sleeve must have at least 2 inches of livability at the biceps line when tested under actual wearing conditions—over the blouse, sweater, or dress with which it will be worn.

Sketch *a* in Figure 6-24 shows the sleeve slashed and a boat-shaped insertion pinned in place for the figure with heavy arms; note that the insertion is widest at the biceps line. This correction is similiar but not identical to the required pattern alteration. *The sole purpose of this fitting is to determine the amount of extra width required; the pattern alteration is done quite differently, as shown in Figure 5-56 on page 192.*

It is usually not necessary to alter a full-length sleeve for thin arms because if the sleeve is not changed, the arms often tend to look more average in size. If it is necessary to decrease the width of the sleeve, pin in a boat-shaped tuck, beginning and ending at the sleeve edges and making the tuck widest at the biceps line. Then alter the muslin accordingly by following directions in Figure 5-60 on page 198.

To alter sleeve length The shaping of a fitted sleeve (which is created by a dart or by dart-fittings-in-seams) must conform to the elbow level of the figure. To test length, bend the arm and bring it to the waist level. In this position the lower edge of

a full-length sleeve should rest at the bend of the wrist. If the shaping for the elbow is at the proper level, the sleeve will feel comfortable to the wearer. If it is too high or too low, the sleeve will bind and feel too constricting.

See sketch *b* in Figure 6-24. First make corrections to bring the elbow level into proper position. Lengthen or shorten the sleeve above the elbow by pinning in an insertion or pinning in a tuck. Then test the total length and make necessary corrections in the lower part of the sleeve. The example shown pictures a sleeve lengthened above the elbow and shortened below the elbow to illustrate that arm length can vary in many ways. To do this type of pattern alteration, see Figures 5-10, 5-12, and 5-13, beginning on page 126.

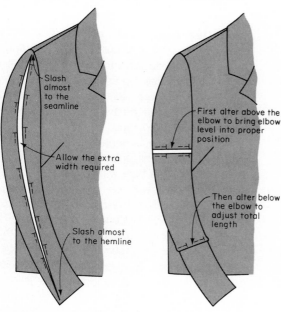

Slash almost to the seamline

Allow the extra width required

Slash almost to the hemline

First alter above the elbow to bring elbow level into proper position

Then alter below the elbow to adjust total length

a To increase sleeve width.

b To alter sleeve length at two levels.

FIGURE 6-24   Sleeve alterations.

Evaluate design features

Small changes in design features—in their size, placement, or style lines—help to enhance the facial features and figure of the wearer, to personalize the costume, and to make it more appealing to the individual. This is the time to experiment; do not assume that a novice cannot improve on the work of a professional designer. The designer is, of course, more knowledgeable and talented, but he or she designed for hundreds of customers with average figures; the home sewer is working with one particular figure, face, and personality, and this gives her a tremendous advantage.

SPECIAL NOTE FOR INSTRUCTORS AND EXPERIENCED READERS It is possible to make radical changes in the design with complete accuracy and safety if one has a knowledge of flat pattern design methods. Those who wish to do more comprehensive and creative redesigning may wish to obtain a copy of *Flat Pattern Design* (Bane, McGraw-Hill, 1972). This text is unique in that design principles are presented first on basic patterns (as the designer works), and then the principles are applied to redesigning commercial patterns.

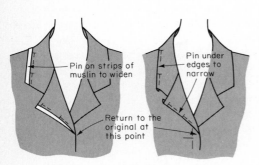

a To change the width of collars and lapels.

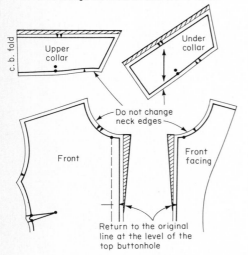

b Pattern alteration to widen collar and lapels.

FIGURE 6-25 To alter the width of collars and lapels.

To alter the width of collars and lapels The techniques of changing the width and design of collars and lapels, shown in Figures 6-25 and 6-26, can be applied to pockets, belts, band trims, etc. The width of the collar and lapel has a marked effect on facial features and apparent neck size. A small delicate face or a thin neck may be enhanced by a narrower collar, while a face with heavier features or a thick neck will take on more pleasing proportions with a wider collar and lapels. See Figure 6-25. Sketch *a* shows the methods of changing collar and lapel width. The changes are shown on only one side of the sketch, to illustrate the marked change in effect. When doing this fitting, first test out the effect on one side of the figure and then make the correction on both sides before coming to a final decision. Note that changes are made at the outside edges of the collar; no change should be made at the neck edge, because the neck edge, which will be seamed to the garment, is intricately cut.

The sketches show both the collar and the lapel area altered approximately the same amounts, but there is no reason why both must be altered the same. Work for the effect desired. Perhaps the wearer will like the effect when only the collar or only the lapel is altered, or she may prefer to alter both but in different amounts.

Note that corrections on the lapel do not extend below the roll line; in this way the change involves only the lapel. It is possible to make changes in width below the roll line of the label, but they would involve a change in button size: see "Decide on Button Size and Placement" on page 248 before making any change below the roll line. The level of the roll line is controlled by the placement of the top button, and any change in the length of the roll line changes the width of the collar and lapel. For this reason it is well to consider button size and placement (page 248) when making changes on the collar and lapel.

Sketch b in Figure 6-25 shows the pattern alteration for widening the collar and lapels, and the principles can be applied when making collars and lapels narrower. Four pattern pieces are involved if the pattern has two collar patterns and a separate facing. The change shown on the lapel is not possible if the garment has a self-facing unless the entire front edge is extended; see sketch b in Figure 6-28, which shows a pattern with a self-facing widened down the entire length of the front. This makes the extension for buttoning wider, and therefore a larger button may be required. Likewise, if a pattern is narrowed for the entire length of the front, a smaller button will be required.

To redesign style lines and labels It is possible to make radical changes in the design lines of collars and lapels and also in the design lines of pockets, flaps, and belts. Sketch *a* in Figure 6-26 shows a

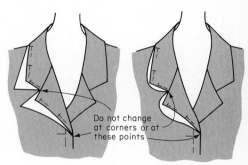

a Styles can be changed radically.

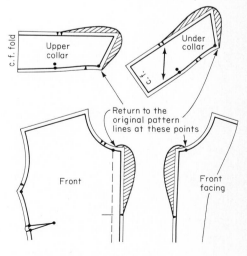

b Pattern alteration.

FIGURE 6-26   *To redesign style lines of collars and lapels.*

basic tailored collar redesigned to create very different effects. The changes are shown on only one side of the sketch, to illustrate the marked differences. When redesigning style features, first test out the effect on one side of the figure and then make the correction on both sides before coming to a final decision. Note that no change is made at the corner where the collar meets the lapel and that the change does not extend below the roll line of the lapel.

The sketches show both the collar and lapels changed; when the collar is redesigned, a similiar change on the lapels is usually indicated. However, there is no reason why both must be changed; work for the effect desired.

Sketch *b* shows the pattern pieces of a typical tailored pattern altered for a change in collar design. The lines of the collar can be changed in any type of pattern. However, this type of change on the lapel line, which requires an addition that is not made on ruler lines, cannot be done on a pattern with a self-facing unless an additional change is made; if the lapel area will be shaped in curved or pointed lines, the pattern with a self-facing must be converted to one with separate facings.

Study the effect of pockets, belts, and other design details All applied design details can be changed in width, size, or placement; and they can also be redesigned if this is desired. Experiment with the size of pockets; the width of belts, flaps, and trimming bands; and their placement. These changes affect the proportions and therefore greatly influence the appeal of the costume on the individual figure.

Button placement and size

Button placement The top button controls the effect of the lapel and collar area. If that button is moved up, the lapel is smaller and narrower, and the collar is narrower and rides up somewhat higher on the neck; the woman with delicate facial features and a thin neck may prefer this effect. If the top button is moved down, the lapel is wider and the collar is somewhat wider and does not ride up as high on the neck; the woman with heavier facial features or a thick neck may prefer this effect. A word of caution when working with snugly fitted garments: there must be a button close to the bust level and exactly at the waist level in fitted costumes (buttonhole markings on the pattern will be placed properly); if the position of buttons is changed during fitting, it may be necessary to add an extra button

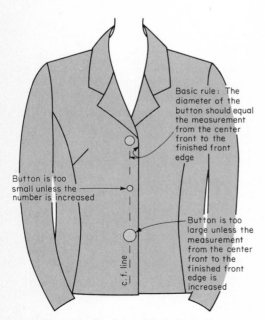

Basic rule: The diameter of the button should equal the measurement from the center front to the finished front edge

Button is too small unless the number is increased

Button is too large unless the measurement from the center front to the finished front edge is increased

c. f. line

FIGURE 6-27 To determine button size.

(if the top buttonhole is moved up) or eliminate one button (if the top buttonhole is moved down) when respacing buttonholes.

The number and placement of buttons is largely a matter of design; it is entirely possible that the flavor of the entire design is achieved with one oversized button or, alternatively, with many very small buttons which would be considered too small under ordinary circumstances. In general, typical suits and snugly fitted coats have buttons spaced approximately 4 inches apart.

Button size The size and number of buttons vary with the design of the costume; but in general the size of buttons for a typical suit is approximately ⅝ to ¾ inches, and the size of buttons for a typical coat is approximately 1 to 1¼ inches. The number and size of the buttons, as recommended by the designer, usually appear in the list of notions on the envelope. If the size is not stated, it is a simple matter to determine the appropriate size; see the single-breasted design in Figure 6-27. The diameter of the button should equal (approximately) the measurement from the center front line to the finished front edge; this effect is shown in the top button. It is obvious that the middle button is too small; however, a smaller button can be used if extra ones are added. A button that is too large cannot be used effectively, as the sketch shows, because it comes too close to the finished front edge, creating a disturbing effect; however, it can be used if the pattern is altered to increase the measurement from the center front to the finished front edge.

Experiment with button size and placement by cutting circles of cloth or paper to simulate buttons. Read "Selection of Button Size and Design" on page 382. Color or mark the circles to simulate the type of button which will be used and test

out different sizes and numbers before coming to a final decision. Once this decision is made, buttons should be purchased immediately; they will be needed before buttonholes are made, and they are done early in the construction sequence.

To alter the pattern for use with larger buttons See Figure 6-28. Sketch *a* shows the alteration on a pattern with a separate facing; sketch *b* pictures the same

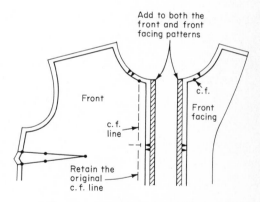

a For a pattern with a separate facing.

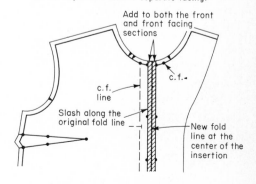

b For a pattern with a self-facing.

FIGURE 6-28 *To increase the front extention for larger buttons.*

change on a pattern with a self-facing. The addition made on the front and on the facing (or the facing section) must equal the difference between the diameter of the button which will be used and the size of button for which the pattern was made. Measure the diameter of the button to be used and compare it with the measurement on the pattern from the center front line to the finished front edge. Then make an addition on both edges involved. Note that this increases the width in the lapel area as well; this is advantageous because a wider lapel will create more pleasing proportions if a larger button will be used.

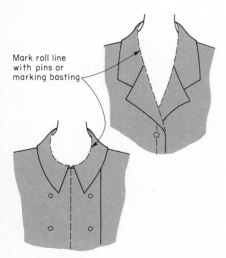

Mark roll line with pins or marking basting

FIGURE 6-29 To mark the roll line of collars and lapels.

Mark the position of buttonholes If buttonhole markings are accurately established at this time and recorded on the pattern, the worker has a great advantage because buttonholes can be made on one easily managed section before the entire garment is assembled.

Establish the roll line on the collar and lapels

Several of the most rewarding tailoring techniques have to do with molding and shaping the collar and lapels. The effectiveness of these techniques depends on molding and shaping these units in the lines they will take on the figure—in other words, molding and shaping them along proper roll lines. Because these techniques will be done before the entire costume is assembled, it is important to mark the roll lines in the muslin copy and transfer those lines to the pattern, so that they can in turn be transferred to the fabric. These lines are already marked on some patterns; but if the position of the top button has been changed during fitting, the roll lines must be corrected.

To do this, match center front lines and pin the front edges in place, as shown in Figure 6-29. Be sure to pin directly through the top button marking if there is a lapel. Smooth the upper collar over the under collar and then mark the roll line with pins. Remove the garment and replace the pins with a marking-basting line. Then transfer these lines accurately to the corresponding pattern pieces.

Make decisions on length and total proportions

Test the jacket or coat with the skirt or the type of dress with which it will be worn; in every way attempt to simulate actual wearing conditions. Experiment with various lengths and, in the case of a suit, with the length of the skirt as well as the jacket. Since under most circumstances the length as decided at this time can be revised somewhat when the hem is hung in the finished garment, for most costumes it is better to allow a slight amount of extra length now. However, if the costume will be made in a large plaid or any fabric with a wide crosswise stripe, hemlines must be accurately established at this time; refer to the discussion of these fabrics on page 480 to see the importance of having the hemline permanently established before the fabric is cut.

At this final fitting, study the total effect with particular attention to the effect which pockets, flaps, and other applied design features have on total proportions. Experiment by placing these units at different levels to see if their placement has been influenced now that the hemline has been established.

Recommended hem allowances Hem allowances for tailored garments are quite standard unless some unusual feature of the design calls for an unusual hem width. Most patterns will have the following hem allowances: 1½ to 2 inches for jackets (depending on their length), 1½ inches for sleeves, and 3 inches for full-length garments. If the hem allowance on the pattern varies greatly from these amounts, there is a sound explanation; for example, if a jacket or sleeves feature slits in the seams, the hem allowance many have been made wide enough to extend above the slit opening, thereby serving as a facing to finish off the edges.

At this time, be sure hem allowances are adequate; see "Factors Influencing the Width of the Hem" on page 332. When the hem is put in the finished garment, these amounts can be adjusted to the demands of the fabric and the figure.

Transfer all fitting corrections to the major pattern pieces and alter other pieces accordingly

Now that all fitting is completed, it is important to inspect the garment very carefully and make an accurate list of all corrections. This is a difficult step because some of these corrections will be new and must be made as new pattern alterations, while others may be revisions of pattern alterations made earlier. This work is further complicated by the fact that only the major pieces of the pattern were altered before making the test copy; now all pieces—interfacings, linings, etc.—must be altered accordingly. Special directions for altering lining patterns appear on pages 215 and 252.

Carefully make all changes on the major pieces by doing a pattern alteration which corresponds to the fitting correction. When this is done, place corresponding pieces over the major piece with corresponding cut edges even, as shown in Figure 6-30. The sketch shows a simple alteration of shoulder and lower edge on the major piece. When the corresponding pieces are positioned in this way, the need for corresponding alterations can be easily seen.

If the fitting corrections and the pattern alterations on the major pieces are very complicated, it may be simpler to make new patterns for these small pieces than

to alter the existing ones. For example, one could make a new facing pattern by simply tracing the shoulder, front, and lower edges of the front pattern piece and establishing the width of the new facing pattern from the original pattern. This would not be advisable for the simple alteration shown here, but it would be wise for a complicated change like those shown in Figure 5-45 on pages 180 and 181.

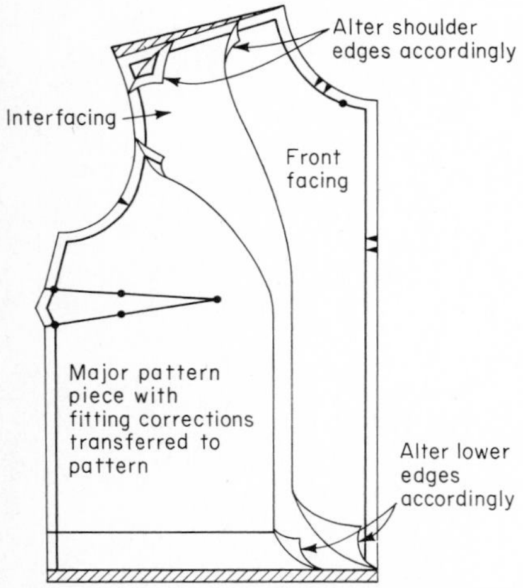

Corresponding alterations on lining patterns If the pattern includes a pattern for the lining, the pattern piece may be 1 inch or more shorter than the major piece; the lining pattern need not be as long as the major piece, because it will be turned up at least ½ inch above the hemline in the garment and, if it will be attached to the garment rather than free-hanging, the hem allowance need not be as great. *These shorter lining patterns are accurate and properly made, but they are made in minimum lengths in order to economize on lining yardages.* As a precaution, it is well to add some extra length, even if it is no more than ½ inch. See "Tests for Length" on page 447 before proceeding. Depending on the pattern alteration involved, front linings may be very difficult to alter like the major piece. This is especially true if the major piece has been altered for a curve larger or smaller than average; that type of alteration requires a major change in the dart, and the front lining cannot always be altered the same way, because it may not have a dart in the same position. For example, a jacket or coat often has an underarm dart which changes shape and length when altered for curves which vary from average. However, if there is a separate lining pattern, it may have (usually does have) a shoulder dart which, if altered, would create more shape and more width, rather than length. If corresponding alterations on the lining pattern will be extensive,

FIGURE 6-30 *Corresponding pattern alterations.*

it will be much simpler to make new lining patterns; directions appear on page 445.

To eliminate seams There are a few seams in the pattern which can be eliminated, if desired. For example, *if a center back seam is ruler-straight and also parallel to the grainline, it can be eliminated by placing the pattern on the fold.* Turn under the seam allowance, tape it in place, and mark the fold edge (the original seamline) for placement on the fold of the fabric. This can be done for the following reasons: to eliminate bulk in heavy coatings; to avoid disturbing the design lines in fake furs, etc; or to avoid matching an additional seam in plaid fabrics.

The center back seam of the under collar can be eliminated by making a new complete pattern. Fold a piece of tissue paper and place the fold line along the seamline (not the cut edge) at the center back. Cut along the cutting line of the collar and transfer all pattern markings to the new pattern; be sure to record the grainline from the original pattern piece.

Figure 6-31 shows how to combine the front and front facings pattern into one pattern piece, thereby eliminating the bulky seam at the finished front edge. This is a very helpful suggestion provided the larger pattern piece will fit into the layout satisfactorily. This can be done to eliminate the great bulk in an encased seam when working with heavy fabrics. It is also helpful when working with polyesters which will be laundered because it will prevent puckering along the finished front edge.

Sketch *a* shows that the pieces can be combined very easily if the two edges are ruler lines; lap the original seamlines for a total lap-over of 1¼ inches and tape the pieces together. The original seamlines become the fold line for the self-facing.

If the lapels are shaped as shown in sketch *b*, the pattern pieces can be com-

bined, but the design of the lapel will not be the same and the lapel will be narrower. Under ordinary circumstances, it is not wise to destroy the very design lines that added character to the costume; and yet, if very heavy fabric such as fake fur will be used, it may be better to sacrifice the design interest for the advantage of eliminating bulk. To do this, place a ruler along the seamline of the front edges and extend the line into the lapel area. Then proceed as shown in sketch *a*.

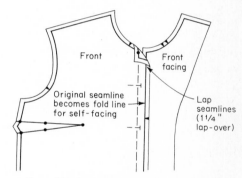

a To combine front and front facing patterns.

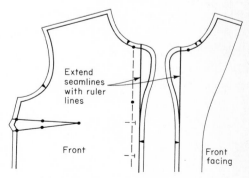

b Preliminary step if lapels are shaped.

FIGURE 6-31 To eliminate the seam at the finished front edge.

To add seams A seam allowance can be added to any edge of the pattern planned for cutting on a fold. If this will be done, it should be done at this time as a pattern alteration by taping a ⅝-inch extension to the edge. A seam may be necessary when working with a fabric narrower than any of the widths included in the layouts. There are several reasons why one might prefer a seam rather than a fold at the center lines in skirts. Persons with wide hips will find that seams which divide the figure at the center lines have a slimming effect. A seam at the center back of a skirt is some slight help in preventing loosely woven fabrics from stretching with wear. For some, a seam at the center back is recommended because it allows for a center back zipper. A back zipper has two distinct advantages over a side zipper. First, it is much easier to insert, because the center line is straight and usually cut on the lengthwise grain; the edges, therefore, will not stretch during manipulation as much as the curved side edges. Second, anyone who changes size frequently or who anticipates a weight loss which will require that the finished skirt be altered will prefer a back zipper; with it, the side edges can be altered without complication.

Chapter 7

FUNDAMENTALS OF CONSTRUCTION AND PRESSING

The information in this chapter covers the clothing construction techniques which will be used most frequently in tailoring and is included here for review and easy reference. It is not possible to cover all fundamental details in a specialized tailoring text, and inexperienced readers may wish to obtain a copy of *Creative Clothing Construction,* 3d ed. (Bane, McGraw-Hill, 1973), which covers fundamental techniques and basic information more comprehensively.

The best way to use this chapter effectively is to become well-acquainted with its contents and then to refer to these directions just before beginning work on a particular detail. This information, then, should be a supplement to the instruction sheet of the pattern and to the directions in other chapters of this text.

LAYING OUT AND CUTTING

Although the most efficient method is to cut all fabrics in one long cutting session, most workers prefer to cut the major fabric first and to delay cutting other fabrics (underlinings, linings, etc.) until they are needed in the construction sequence. For this reason, the directions below are limited to general suggestions; additional directions are interspersed throughout the text. Directions for cutting fabrics which require special attention (plaids, fake furs, twills, etc.) are included in the appropriate sections of Chapter 11. Other cutting directions and their page references are:

underlinings for skirts and pants—page 304

supporting fabrics (underlinings and interfacings) for jackets and coats—page 359

linings for jackets and coats—page 443

interlinings for extra warmth—page 449

If the fabric has not been prepared for cutting (preshrunk, evened, and straightened) see "Prepare Fabric for Cutting" on pages 91 through 98.

Basic rules

1 If the fabric will be folded, it is usually better to fold the right side inside because in this way pattern markings can be more easily transferred to fabric. The fabric *can* be folded with the right side outside, and it is better to do so when the fabric has any type of design (distinctive weave, large design, etc.) which must be matched or balanced during cutting. If a combination layout will be used and if the combination includes a crosswise layout, cut the crosswise portion last. If a single-thickness layout is used, place the fabric right side up on the table.

2 Select the pattern pieces that will be needed for the view to be used and put any

**FUNDAMENTALS OF
CONSTRUCTION AND PRESSING**

pieces that will not be needed back in the envelope. A list of pattern pieces required for each view appears on the instruction sheet. Separate the pieces for cutting in various fabrics—the pieces of the garment, pieces to be cut in contrasting fabric, lining pieces, interfacing pieces, etc.

3 Following the placement plan of the layout selected, first quickly place pieces in position on the fabric. Note the shape of the pieces as shown in the layout and pay

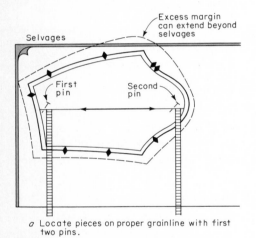

a Locate pieces on proper grainline with first two pins.

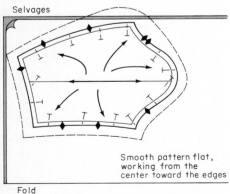

b Pin pattern flat to fabric.

FIGURE 7-1 To position a pattern and pin it in place.

attention to the position of notches to be sure pieces are positioned properly. Note the straight-of-material line and place it approximately parallel to the fold or selvage edges. Position large pieces first and then fit in the small pieces.

Each pattern piece has been separated on the layout so it can be easily distinguished; this is a sketching technique used solely for purposes of clarity and does not indicate that the pieces should be separated as they are placed down. Each pattern piece should be placed as close as possible to other pattern pieces on the layout.

4 Check to see that each piece required has been included and also be sure to allow for cutting each piece the proper number of times; some pieces (collars, cuffs, flaps, etc.) may appear more than once on the layout. In the classroom situation, the instructor may wish to check the student's work at this stage before she has spent too much time; she will want to check the perfected layout later as well.

5 Perfect the layout by carefully following the detailed directions in the sections that follow.

Measuring straight-of-material lines and pinning on the pattern

The straight-of-material lines are placed on the pattern in a position to ensure maximum wearing qualities and to obtain the desired effect. They were drawn very scientifically by an expert pattern maker; it is very important to the success of the finished product that these lines be placed to fall on the lengthwise threads of the fabric. Measure with an L square or a ruler as shown in sketch *a*, Figure 7-1; measure from the extended straight-of-material lines and place a pin at the upper and lower edge of the pattern. Place fold lines accurately along the fold of fabric.

When the straight-of-material lines have been pinned in place accurately, more pins must be added to hold the whole pattern in place. Pins should be placed close to the cutting line (no more than ½ inch away) and approximately at right angles to the cut edge (sketch *b*). The number of pins depends on the contour of the pattern piece and the nature of the fabric. More pins are needed on curved edges than on straight edges; more pins are needed on slippery fabrics than on firm, stiff fabrics. In general, pins placed every 3 or 4 inches will prove satisfactory. It is important to lay the pattern flat on the fabric with no bubbles that will result in inaccuracies; smooth the pattern with the fingers by working from the center toward the edges as shown and pinning from the center to the edges (note the position of the pinheads).

Place pattern pieces on the fabric as economically as possible. The excess margins (which simply allow pieces to be cut more quickly and accurately in the manufacturing process) are not a part of the pattern and will be trimmed off as the pattern is cut. Therefore these margins can extend beyond the selvage and fold edges as shown in sketch *a*, Figure 7-2. Margins can lap over each other and can lap over another pattern piece, as shown. The darkest line on the pattern is the cutting line, and pattern pieces should be placed as close as possible to all edges of the fabric and to each other without overlapping the cutting lines.

Cutting techniques

Keep the fabric as flat on the table as possible during cutting; shears are recommended (in preference to scissors) because the handle is positioned to allow for cutting without lifting the fabric from the table. Never use pinking shears for cutting out because they are difficult to handle easily (the more so on curved edges) and therefore their use results in inaccurate cutting; the problem is magnified by the

jagged cutting line, which is, itself, less accurate than the clean-cut edge possible with shears or scissors.

See Figure 7-2. Using long slashes, cut carefully and accurately along the cutting line of the pattern (or on the altered pattern line), cutting the notches out into the margin as shown. Notches cut out into the margin show up more prominently during

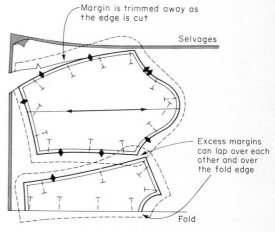

a Cut along cutting lines, cutting notches out into the margin.

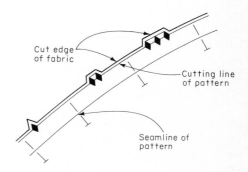

b Enlarged view showing method of cutting groups of notches.

FIGURE 7-2 Cutting the fabric.

construction and also allow the seam allowance to remain intact in case it becomes necessary to let out seams.

The excess margin falls away as each edge is cut, as shown in sketch *a*. Sketch *b* shows an enlarged view of the proper way to cut groups of notches. Most patterns show a little line across the notch tips to indicate that the notches in a group need not be cut separately; the width of the notch indicates the number of notches in the grouping and distinguishes groups of notches from single notches, as shown.

NOTE: If the fabric is very thick and heavy (coating, simulated fur, camel's hair), it may be impossible to cut two layers at one time. Each thickness can be cut separately by slipping the scissors between the two layers of fabric, cutting one thickness on one edge, cutting the second thickness on that edge, and proceeding.

Proper care of pieces during construction

During the interim between cutting and the time construction has progressed to a point where the garment can be hung on a hanger, every attempt must be made to keep the fabric in good condition and prevent wrinkling. In a classroom situation (or in a crowded home situation) pieces can best be stored between work sessions by hanging sections over a hanger. There is one exception; very heavy fabrics should not be hung over a hanger until after the pattern has been removed. Those working at home and fortunate enough to have a spare bedroom can place pieces flat on a bed or any long flat surface.

TRANSFERRING PATTERN LINES TO FABRIC

The tailored garment can be marked with chalk lines, with tracing wheel and carbon, or with tailor's tacks. Tailor's tacks are recommended because they are very secure in wool fabrics, because they are the only method of marking that marks both the right and the wrong sides of the fabric, and because they can be made in contrasting colors to denote different sizes and shapes of markings. Certainly if one is using a Vogue Paris Original or International Couturier pattern, this method must be used because the complicated design lines and the four sizes and shapes of markings used by Vogue can be very confusing unless they are distinguished by contrasting colors. Center lines, particularly center-front lines in the buttoned-front jacket or coat, must be clearly marked with a marking-basting stitch made with a contrasting color of thread.

The following suggestion for saving time in making tailor's tacks is included for the competent, experienced person only; the novice would be wise to skip over this paragraph. If one understands patterns so well that she can predict the use that each pattern marking will serve before she encounters it in construction, this suggestion has merit. If the garment will be completely underlined, dartlines and seamlines for any construction which will be done from the wrong side of the fabric can be drawn on the interfacing or underlining with a pencil. For this reason, there is little value in marking the fabric for the garment with tailor's tacks along those same construction lines. If the reader can understand the various uses each pattern marking will serve, she can save time by tailor-tacking only those points which will be needed on the right side or on both sides and marking simple darts with a pencil line on the interfacing or underlining only. While this suggestion can indeed save the experienced person a great deal of time, if one is in doubt it is far better to mark all points with tailor's tacks.

STAY-STITCHING

The person experienced enough to undertake a tailoring project has had experience in stay-stitching, understands the purposes of staying cut edges of the pattern, knows how to stay-stitch, and understands which edges must be stay-stitched. Directions for stay-stitching appear in all basic clothing construction books. This section will be confined to problems that might arise in the tailored garment.

Several factors influence the need to stay-stitch (1) The nature of the fabric itself is the dominant consideration. Some fabrics are very stable and need not be stay-stitched because they are woven in a firm, close weave. Other fabrics (spongy woolens, single knits, and very heavy fabric which stretch from the stress of their own weight) are not stable and must be stay-stitched. (2) The fiber content of the fabric may be responsible for some stretching; for example, wool fibers are more elastic than cotton or linen fibers. The polyesters (even if they are knitted or are very limp and crepey) are not as likely to give or stretch during construction. (3) The grainline along the particular cut edge involved is a major consideration. Fabrics will not stretch in the lengthwise and crosswise direction; stretch occurs on any edge that is true bias or somewhat bias. Therefore, only certain edges of each fabric section require stay-stitching. (4) The construction method is a consideration. If the garment will be underlined (and many tailored garments are completely underlined or interfaced), the need for stay-stitching is diminished. When underlining sections are basted to sections of the garment, the basting stitches help prevent stretching and, in addition, an extra firming effect results from combining two layers. (5) The ability of the individual is a factor. The novice, who will work longer on each construction detail and who has not learned to handle fabric properly, must stay-stitch to compensate for her inexperience. The experienced person who knows a certain elusive "something" about handling fabric can control very stretchy fabric well and may have no need for stay-stitching.

Very heavy coating fabrics create unusual stretching problems Although stay-stitching may be strong enough to control vertical seamlines, the extreme weight of some coatings creates a need for greater control on those curved edges which will get great strain during

construction and on edges (the same curved edges) that are responsible for size (or width) in the very important shoulder area. Stay-stitching will do very little to control the curved neck edge or shoulderline if extremely heavy fabrics are used. See Figure 7-3. After the fabric has been marked with tailor's tacks and center lines have been marked, baste ¼-inch-wide cotton-twill tape to neck and front shoulder edges on the right side of the fabric, as shown. This tape is a temporary aid and will be removed as soon as the edge is stitched to another. The tape should be placed about ⅛ inch inside the seamline (in the body of the garment, not in the seam allowance) so that the seam can be basted and stitched without catching in the tape. The ends of the tape should be trimmed off about ⅛ inch from any cross seamline, as illustrated at the back shoulderline. The tape should be pinned first, and the edge should be tested on the corresponding pattern edge to be sure that it has retained the original length. Figure 7-3 does not picture tape on the back shoulder edge because the dart must be sewn in before tape is used on that edge.

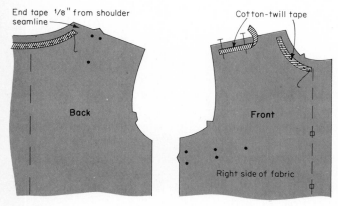

End tape ⅛" from shoulder seamline

Cotton-twill tape

Back

Front

Right side of fabric

FIGURE 7-3   To control stretching of heavy fabric temporarily.

REINFORCING CORNERS

There are points of construction which require a clip directly down to the seamline before the seam is joined. The seamline must be reinforced at this point before clipping to prevent weakness and eventual raveling and ripping. Such points include the tip end of a gusset opening, the corner of the shoulderline and neckline seam in a collar cut in one with the major piece, and other points too numerous and varied to mention. Reinforcing corners is the very first step in the construction sequence if the garment will not be underlined. If the garment will be underlined or completely interfaced, corners are reinforced as soon as the supporting fabric is basted in place.

Vogue patterns contain a great number of these clip points, and the more intricate the pattern, the greater their number. This is a basic construction detail, so basic that the pattern may not stress it. But if directions for clipping are given, the points must always be reinforced by one of two methods, even if it is not mentioned on the instruction sheet. These points are reinforced before any basting is done on the garment. Go through the entire instruction sheet and look for all the points that are clipped or slashed before a seam is sewn, for it will save a great deal of time to do all reinforcing during the same session at the machine. Think about the wear each point will receive, take the fabric into consideration, and then choose one of the two methods of reinforcement shown in Figure 7-4.

Simple method of reinforcement

See sketch a. This is suitable for points that will not get a great deal of wear and pull as the garment is worn and for fabrics that do not ravel. An example of a point that will not get a great deal of wear is the point

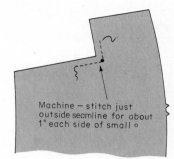

a Simple reinforcements for points that will get little stress and for fabrics that do not ravel.

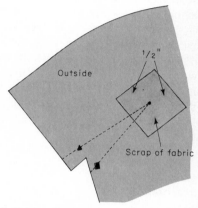

b Secure reinforcement for points that will get stress in fabrics that will ravel.

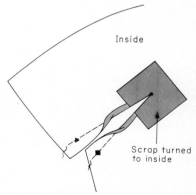

c The reinforcing scrap acts as seam allowance in an area where there is little seam allowance available.

FIGURE 7-4 Methods of reinforcing corners that will be clipped before seams are joined.

which will be under the collar in a collar cut in one with the major piece, as pictured. Use a short stitch at the machine (seventeen to twenty-two per inch) and machine-stitch just outside the seamline for about an inch each side of the marking, stitching directly through the marking. Be careful to make a distinct point (do not retrace any stitches) because a cut must be made to within 1/16 inch of that point. The point can now be clipped; however, it is well to avoid making the clip until just before the seam will be joined. In fabrics that do not ravel at all, such as felt, double knits, or napped coatings, this method of reinforcement can also be used for points that will get considerable wear.

**Very secure method
of reinforcement**

See sketch *b*. This method will be used more often, for it is required for points which will get strain when the garment is worn and for fabrics that ravel. The outstanding example of a point that will get tremendous strain is the slashed opening for a gusset. An extra scrap of fabric is used for reinforcement; this fabric will not be visible in the finished garment and it is well to use a lighter-weight, closely woven fabric. Lightweight underlinings, organdy, or sheath lining fabrics are appropriate. Place the scrap of fabric (about a 2-inch square) right sides together over the point to be clipped or slashed in such a way that at least 1/2 inch of the scrap extends beyond the seamline as shown in the sketch. Pin in place.

Caution: A common mistake is to place

this scrap on the wrong side of the fabric; it must be placed on the right side in order that it can turn to the wrong side later.

Use a short stitch (seventeen to twenty-two per inch) at the machine and machine-stitch along the seamline, making a distinct point at the marking. Be very careful not to retrace stitches, because a cut must be made directly to the marking. When this point is clipped, the scrap of fabric is turned to the inside and serves as seam allowance at the point where there really is no seam allowance, as shown in sketch *c*. It is well to avoid making slashes of this sort until they are required in the construction process.

BASTING

The need for basting is not diminished by the fact that major fitting was done on the muslin test copy. By basting at this time, it will be possible to make subtle fitting changes to take care of the influence of the fabric weight and thickness; it is necessary to test the effect of fabric bulk on overall size. Basting serves other purposes as well. An important function of basting is to hold pieces securely in position to prevent slippage as seams are stitched; this is especially helpful when working with thick, spongy coating and suiting fabrics. The fact that tailored garments (especially jackets and coats) are often completely underlined or interfaced means that seams will be more bulky, creating a greater need for secure basting stitches. The limp, often slippery fabrics used for linings require basting for proper control at the machine.

Basting may serve as a guideline for top-stitching and to mark center lines. Basting is an essential aid to pressing. Pleat lines and finished edges of collars and lapels, etc., must be basted in preparation for pressing. It is well to use silk or nylon thread for basting edges in preparation for pressing because these finer threads will not leave a prominent mark on the fabric.

Figure 7-5 includes directions for the most common basting stitches. Basting is done with a single thread, and there is no circumstance under which it is advisable to use a double thread. Security and strength depend on two factors: the length of the stitch and the frequency with which the thread is reinforced with smaller, firm back stitches.

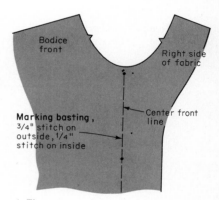

Even basting stitches, 1/4 inch long, reinforced frequently — for fabrics that are difficult to control and for edges that will get strain during fitting

Uneven basting stitches, longer and reinforced less frequently — for fabrics that are easily controlled and for edges that will fall free from the body

a Basting stitches — even and uneven.

Bodice front

Right side of fabric

Marking basting, 3/4" stitch on outside, 1/4" stitch on inside

Center front line

b The purpose of marking basting is to reveal a line prominently.

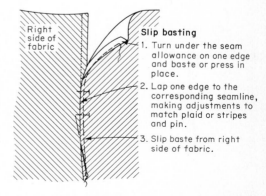

Right side of fabric

Slip basting

1. Turn under the seam allowance on one edge and baste or press in place.
2. Lap one edge to the corresponding seamline, making adjustments to match plaid or stripes and pin.
3. Slip baste from right side of fabric.

c Slip basting is an aid to matching stripes or plaid.

FIGURE 7-5 *Basic basting stitches.*

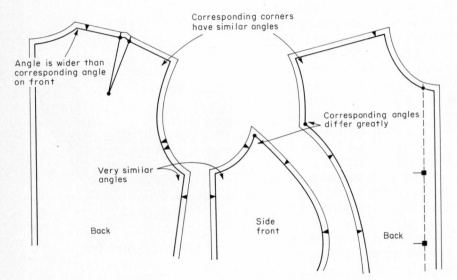

Corresponding corners
have similar angles

Angle is wider than
corresponding angle
on front

Corresponding angles
differ greatly

Very similar
angles

Back

Side
front

Back

a The angles of corresponding corners influence the proper position
for pinning seams.

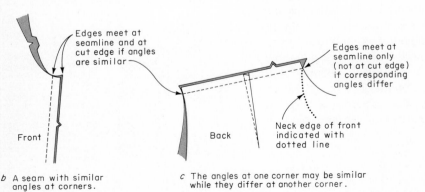

Edges meet at
seamline and at
cut edge if angles
are similar

Edges meet at
seamline only
(not at cut edge)
if corresponding
angles differ

Neck edge of front
indicated with
dotted line

Front

Back

b A seam with similar
angles at corners.

c The angles at one corner may be similar
while they differ at another corner.

*FIGURE 7-6   To position seams properly, match the ends at the seamline (5/8 inch
in from the cut edge). Understand that corners extending beyond the seamline may
or may not match.*

Preparation for basting

The most fundamental principle of assembling sections of a garment is illustrated in Figure 7-6; it has to do with the length of seamlines. Sketch *a* shows the pattern pieces for a design with a princess-type seam in the front. Study the angles of corresponding corners. The angles at the side seamline and the shoulder end of the shoulderline are almost identical, while the angles at the neck edge of the shoulderline differ. The corresponding corners at the armhole of the front and side-front sections are very different. When sections are joined, identical corners will cause no problems, but corresponding corners that differ greatly often confuse even the experienced worker. Note the dots at the corners where the seamlines meet. Because these corners complicate the construction process, the pattern should include dots which can be tailortacked for matching. Vogue patterns always include dots at this type of corner, but some other patterns do not. If the angles at corresponding corners differ and if dots are not marked on the pattern, add a dot at the corner of seamlines and transfer it to the fabric with tailor's tacks.

Sketch *b* shows the underarm seam joined. Because the angles are very similar, the edges at the end of the seam meet at the seamline and also at the cut edges as shown. There are many seams of this type in garments with very basic design lines. Sketch *c* shows the shoulder seam joined; note the neckline end of the seam where the angles of the corresponding corners differ slightly. *In this type of corner the edges meet at the seamline only and the cut edges of corners do not match each other.* The seam is properly joined; it is of no importance whether or not the cut edges of corners match because they are part of the seam allowance only and not a part of the finished garment.

Sketch *a* in Figure 7-7 (page 266) shows an enlarged view of the armhole corners of the front and side-front sections in which angles differ greatly; it is this exaggerated problem which may confuse the experienced person as well as the novice. Edges must meet at the seamline so that other seamlines which cross the seam will form a continuous line, as shown in the finished seam in sketch *a*. If one corner extends, trim it off even with the cut edge; the corner is simply a part of the seam allowance and has nothing to do with the finished garment. Sketch *b* illustrates the importance of matching seam ends at the seamline by showing a serious mistake; these corners have been matched at the cut edges with the result that the corresponding dots and notches do not match. The view of the seam when joined and pressed open reveals the full extent of the error.

The general rule for positioning seams which will be joined: Match the ends of the seamline so that the ends of the two corresponding edges meet at the seamline ($^5/_8$ *inch in from the cut edge*). This rule will serve for all seams; if the angles of corners are identical, cut edges at the corners will also match, and if angles are not identical, cut edges will not (and should not) match.

Proper method of pinning seams

See sketch *a* in Figure 7-8. All seams or darts must be pinned before basting. The pins should be placed at right angles to the line to be basted because they will better control the seam and allow the seam to bend and give as it is basted. In addition, one can baste across the pins without re-

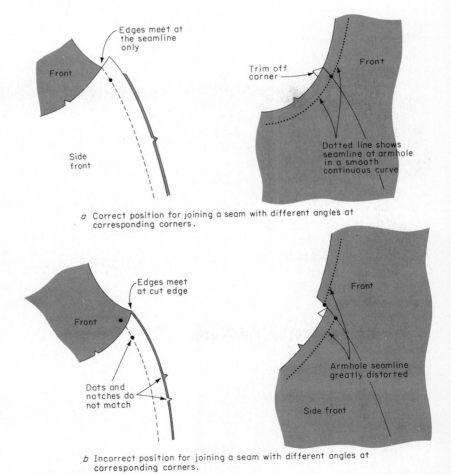

a Correct position for joining a seam with different angles at corresponding corners.

b Incorrect position for joining a seam with different angles at corresponding corners.

FIGURE 7-7 To position seams properly.

moving them and later remove them all at one time; this is a very small saving in time but it adds up to great savings on an entire project. The pin should catch only a few threads of fabric directly at the seamline to control the fabric well at the very place where control is needed. Compare the length of the pin in Figure 7-8 with the amount of fabric caught up by the pin.

With cut edges perfectly even, first pin one end and then the other; then match any points (notches or dots) and pin in between these established points. Place patterns with long edges flat on a table to pin them properly. In sketch a, the ends of the seam and the notch positions are pinned first, and later other pins added in between those points. The number of pins varies, and it is no virtue to use too many. A good rule is to use only the number required to hold the seam securely and keep cut edges even. For a long, straight seam in firm fabric, pins every 4 inches are sufficient, but for an intricately curved seam in slippery fabric, pins every 2 inches or even every inch may be required.

Many corresponding seams are identical in character; sketch a of Figure 7-8 shows identical ruler-straight edges. Many curved edges may be identical in character as well. These seams are easy to pin properly with cut edges perfectly even. Sketch b shows a type of seam that is more difficult to work with. To assemble seams that are different in character, the shorter cut edge (the concave curve) must be clipped to release it and allow it to take the shape of the longer cut edge. Make clips into the seam allowance before attempting to pin the edges together; clips of 3/8 inch are sufficient for fabrics that are not stiff, while 1/2 inch clips will be required for stiff fabrics. The greater the difference in character of the two corresponding lines, the greater the need for releasing the cut edges of the shorter one.

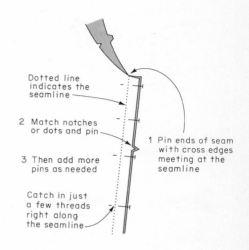

Dotted line indicates the seamline

2 Match notches or dots and pin

1 Pin ends of seam with cross edges meeting at the seamline

3 Then add more pins as needed

Catch in just a few threads right along the seamline

a Proper method of pinning a seam in preparation for basting.

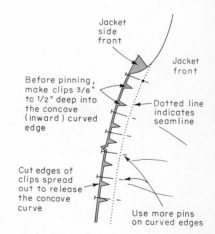

Jacket side front

Jacket front

Before pinning, make clips 3/8" to 1/2" deep into the concave (inward) curved edge

Dotted line indicates seamline

Cut edges of clips spread out to release the concave curve

Use more pins on curved edges

b If two seam edges are not identical in character, clip the concave curve (the inward curve) to allow it to take on the character of the convex curve.

FIGURE 7-8 *The proper method of pinning seams.*

**FUNDAMENTALS OF
CONSTRUCTION AND PRESSING**

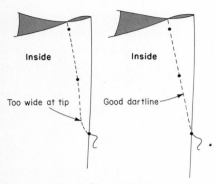

a Example of ruler-straight dartline

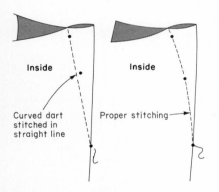

b Example of curved dartlines

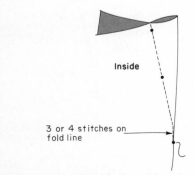

c To improve stitching of both straight and
curved dartlines

FIGURE 7-9 To stitch darts.

Basting and stitching darts

The experienced woman can further improve her work by employing the proper
method of basting and stitching darts. A
most common error is shown in sketch
a, in Figure 7-9. Many darts are composed
of ruler-straight lines, as shown, and the
most common error is that of basting and
stitching in a way that makes the dart too
wide at the tip. A good dartline retains the
ruler-straight character all the way down to
the tip, which results in a smooth fit over
body contours. Sketch *b* pictures a similar
problem. In this case, the dartlines curve,
becoming even slimmer at the tip, and a
typical mistake is to stitch the curved dart
in a ruler-straight line. Sketch *c* pictures
a subtle technique that can be used on any
dart to create a very smooth, molded effect
over figure curves. A dart with straight lines
is pictured, and it is stitched in straight lines,
but note that the stitching is brought to the
fold edge about ¼ inch above the dart
tip so that the last few stitches are right on
the fold edge. This technique is not used
in basting because of its intricacy; a bit of
practice will enable one to make this improvement as the dart is machine-stitched.

EASING IN FULLNESS AND GATHERING

*Easing in fullness and gathering are both
processes by which the longer of two corresponding seamlines is worked into the
shorter seamline; the difference between
the two is a matter of the amount of extra
length or fullness involved. Small amounts
(½ inch of extra length to be worked into
a 4- or 5-inch span) are called "ease" while
large amounts (4 or 5 extra inches to be
worked into a 4- or 5-inch span) are considered gathers. Gathers are obvious and
visible as the garment is worn because the*

fabric is puckered into the seam with very tiny little tucks that give the typical gathered effect. By contrast, there are no puckers in an eased seam if it is done properly and so (ideally) ease is not visible.

Easing in fullness

Easing is a process by which yarns of the fabric are crowded together more closely than they were spaced as the fabric was woven. Some fabrics can be eased in more easily than others because they are woven loosely, with space between yarns to allow for some shifting and crowding of the yarns.

Directions appear in Figure 7-10. The sketches show a back shoulder edge eased to the front; if the back shoulder is eased (rather than darted) the amount of extra length is approximately ½ inch to be worked into a span of about 4 inches; therefore, this is a typical example of easing in. Two additional suggestions: Catch pins through just a few threads, directly along the seamline, and use small secure basting stitches to better control the ease. These suggestions are increasingly useful if the fabric does not ease in readily or if greater amounts of ease are involved.

Gathering

Gathering stitches must be perfectly even in length. The best way to ensure even gathers is to stitch by machine. However, hand stitches are needed when very heavy fabrics must be drawn up into a very small area because in that case a longer stitch than is possible on the machine is required. If hand stitches are used, take the greatest care to make them even.

Gathering stitches must be as short as possible and yet long enough so the fabric can be drawn up to the proper length. The gathering stitch must be longer than the stitch used for sewing seams because

only then is it possible to draw up the fabric by pulling a bobbin thread. Small stitches make tiny, even gathers; long stitches draw up so much fabric that the result is a tucked effect. For gathering purposes, the machine can be set to sew with from eight and up to twelve stitches per inch, depending on the fabric used. The heavier and stiffer the fabric, the longer the stitch must be. It is well to test-stitch a scrap of fabric to determine what length of stitch to use.

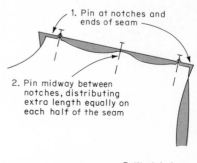

1. Pin at notches and ends of seam

2. Pin midway between notches, distributing extra length equally on each half of the seam

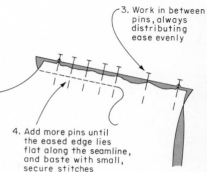

3. Work in between pins, always distributing ease evenly

4. Add more pins until the eased edge lies flat along the seamline, and baste with small, secure stitches

FIGURE 7-10 Directions for easing in fullness.

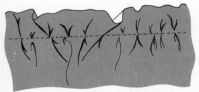

a A single row of gathering does not control fabric well.

b Gathers properly controlled.

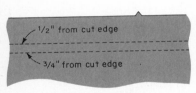

½" from cut edge

¾" from cut edge

c General rule: Place rows ⅛ inch on each side of the seamline (see one exception stated in text).

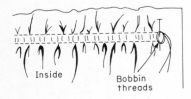

Inside

Bobbin threads

d To hold threads temporarily.

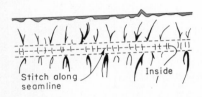

Stitch along seamline

Inside

e Two rows control the gathers at the seamline.

FIGURE 7-11 Directions for gathering.

The stitches should be made in such a way that gathers fall at right angles to the seam and are very well controlled. Sketch *a* in Figure 7-11 pictures one row of gathering pulled up. Note that some of the gathers fall at right angles to the seam and at other points the gathers fall every which way; there is not sufficient control at the seamline. Excellent control is achieved with a double row of stitches as shown in sketch *b;* if both bobbin threads are pulled up at the same time, it is possible to keep the gathers in line and to make sure they fall at right angles to the seamline.

Gathering stitches should be placed to control the fabric best for stitching; the best control is needed at the seamline. The general rule is stated in sketch *c*. By following the directions pictured, the two rows will be ¼ inch apart, which is close enough to control the fabric well. If there is a ⅝-inch seam allowance, the gathering rows are placed ½ and ¾ inch in from the cut edge, as shown.

There is an important exception to the rule given above, and it has to do with the lower row of stitches. There are some fabrics (satin is an example) in which needle punctures show after stitches have been removed. Pressing will remove needle punctures in most fabrics. The fabric must be tested to determine if needle marks will disappear with pressing. *If the needle marks remain after the fabric is pressed, all gathering stitches must be kept in the seam allowance. In that case, put one row of stitches on the seamline and the other ¼ inch outside the seamline.*

When the bobbin threads have been pulled up the desired amount, wind them around a pin. This will hold the gathers until the seam is basted (sketch *d*).

If the general rule can be followed, the stitching will fall between the two rows of gathering stitches. Sketch *e* illustrates perfect control at the seamline. The lower row of threads will show from the outside of the garment, and can be easily removed by pulling the bobbin thread.

MACHINE STITCHING

It is assumed that workers who are undertaking a tailoring project have mastered the use of the machine. The information here is limited to general suggestions and the special problems which will be encountered with typical suiting and coating fabrics.

General suggestions

1 Before stitching, each seam must be properly pinned and basted. The basted garment must be fitted and corrections made and tested before stitching.
2 Prepare several units for stitching before going to the machine. Much time can be saved with fewer trips to the machine. Arrange a pile of pieces so that similar jobs can be done at one time. For example, do the machine gathering on all pieces before changing the length of stitch for another type of work.
3 Certain equipment will be needed at the machine, and it should be well arranged on the right end of the machine top and ready for use. Necessary equipment is a box of pins or filled pincushion, a needle and basting thread, gauges, scissors (preferably small ones) for clipping threads, scraps of fabric, and the instruction sheet (folded for convenient use).
4 Always test-stitch with the machine to check threading, the size and condition of the needle, the balance of tension, and the length of stitch. Remember that each fabric makes a different demand on the machine, so adjustments may be needed.

Always test-stitch under circumstances identical to those under which the stitching will be done; use the same number of thicknesses of fabric and supporting fabric as the seam of the garment will have. Test-stitching will save much time and trouble, so do not neglect to do it each time the machine is adjusted. Test-stitching becomes increasingly important with technological advances in the textile industry. The new fabrics, woven to create new, exciting effects and often made of new fibers that react differently from the old favorites, demand experimentation and innovation throughout the construction sequence.
5 Examine each seam before sewing to determine if one edge of the seam will be more difficult to manage than the other. Curved, clipped, bias, gathered, and eased edges require more care than a flat, straight edge, so the four types of edges mentioned are "difficult." Always keep the more difficult edge uppermost when stitching to better control it. Usually corresponding seams have a similar character, and in that case it does not matter which edge is uppermost. Keep the bulk of the garment to the left of the machine whenever possible.
6 Support the weight of the fabric well. Small pieces will lie on the machine top very nicely, but large heavy units (such as an almost completed coat) need extra support to keep them from falling away from the machine and causing too much strain on the needle. A chair drawn up to the machine will help support fabric well. Always adjust fabric so that a portion of the seam (6 or 12 inches, depending on the seam) is in a position to be stitched, stitch that

portion, and then adjust another segment of the seam. Intricate seams must be stitched in shorter segments (2 or 4 inches) than straight seams. Never try to stitch more than a 1-foot segment before adjusting the fabric again. If the fabric is well supported and adjusted at the machine, it is possible to sew a straight seam with just the slightest touch of a finger to guide the fabric. Pulling and tugging at the fabric while the machine is in motion causes an uneven, wobbly stitching line.

7 The machine will operate at several speeds. An intricate seam should be stitched slowly, and it is well to have the right hand poised near the big balance wheel when intricate stitching is required; most people find it helpful to stop or slow down the machine by controlling the balance wheel with the hand. If the machine has a speed control, set the control on slow speed for intricate seams, top-stitching, etc. A long, straight seam can be stitched at top speed, and the increased speed actually helps make a smooth, even stitching line if the seam is straight and free from complications. Everyone should acquire perfect control of the machine at high or low speeds. Although it is more difficult to keep proper control at the lower speeds, it is possible to practice until one can go so slowly that stitches can be counted.

8 The presser foot will act as a measuring guide. Both prongs are ¼ inch wide in some machines and in others one is ¼ inch and the other ⅛ inch wide. Many machines have additional guidelines marked on the machine plate. A cardboard gauge notched for special measurements is a valuable measuring aid.

Special problems

Because of their sponginess and thickness, suiting and coating fabrics tend to push out of line at the machine; the top layer pushes forward. Basting stitches must be firm and reinforced often. If the problem is especially serious, cross bastings will be very helpful (see sketch *a* in Figure 7-12). The pressure on the machine foot can be adjusted to compensate for the extra bulk passing beneath it. If a rolling pressure foot is available for the machine being used, test its effectiveness with thick, spongy fabrics, pile fabrics, fake furs, etc.

If a seam must be stitched across another seam in very thick fabrics, the machine may not move forward or "climb up" to the thicker level at the cross seam. Lifting the machine foot, moving the fabric forward slightly, and then releasing the foot will help the machine operate through the thicker area.

Novelty weaves with long floats of exposed yarns or loops create an additional problem. The floats of thread or loops may catch in the machine foot. A strip of tissue paper placed over the seam edge and fed into the machine with the fabric will prevent this problem.

Pile fabrics present similar problems because of their thickness, and fur fabrics present all the problems of pile fabrics plus a few additional ones. When basting and stitching seams in fur fabrics, push the pile away from the seam and try to get stitches down to the backing without catching any of the hair-like fibers. If fibers are caught in the stitching, they can be pulled free by lifting them out with a pin.

Lining fabrics are delicate and easily snagged with a slightly dull needle or pin. A test-stitching should be done prior to stitching lining sections; possibly a new needle or one in a smaller size will be required. In the school laboratory situation, the student must test-stitch each time she uses the machine for lining fabrics; another student, using less delicate fabric, may have damaged the needle without being aware of it.

Many lining fabrics are so flat that additional pressure on the machine foot is required. Even so, often the seam will pucker slightly, making it seem that the thread tension is too tight, and yet adjustment of the tension may not help. The problem is simply that the fabric is too thin for the machine to accommodate well. Placing slight pressure on the fabric (in other words, holding the fabric somewhat taut) as it passes through the machine will solve the problem.

Pin-basting lining fabrics should be avoided because although the machine will ride over pins, often the needle is damaged slightly in the process and will snag the fabric. If lining fabrics are pin-basted, the pins must be removed before crossing them with the machine.

Most lining fabrics made to add warmth combine the problems created by thick fabrics (like wool) as well as those of delicate lining fabrics.

TOP-STITCHING

When a design requires top-stitching effects, the top-stitching becomes part of the design and is extremely important to the ultimate success of the garment. It is well worth the great amount of experimentation that is necessary to obtain the desired result. If directions call for edge-stitching, the effect is not intended to be particularly striking, and regular sewing thread may be quite satisfactory. However, if top-stitching is ¼ inch or more from the edge, it is intended as part of the design and should be done in such a way that it is attractively conspicuous.

Choice of thread The pattern usually suggests buttonhole twist for top-stitched effects because of its high luster and its thickness. Buttonhole twist will be used for the top thread only. It is the ideal choice, but the limited number of colors available makes it necessary to consider alternative solutions. The high luster of silk thread makes it the next logical choice, although the range of colors is somewhat limited in many small stores. If it becomes necessary, mercerized thread must be used because appropriateness of color is more important than luster. The special thread available for use with knits and polyesters can be used for top-stitching. It does not have high luster but it has great elasticity which will help prevent puckering.

Test-stitching Tests must be done through the proper number of fabric thicknesses. Ideally, several test seams should be stitched to allow experimentation in width from the seam edge and to test the appearance of the stitching itself. In most designs, subtle adjustments in width to please individual tastes are acceptable.

One must be inventive in order to obtain the desired result. The nature, weave, and design of the fabric will demand a variety of solutions. The length of stitch, usually longer than that used for seams, can vary greatly. The tension of the thread may need adjustment because more tension (without drawing up the edge) will make stitches sink into the fabric and create a more conspicuous indentation.

Silk thread and mercerized thread are not as thick and heavy as might be desired, although they are usually quite effective in flat fabrics (wool gabardine, worsteds, etc.). If the fabric is spongy or in a novelty weave, top-stitching done with these threads may not be as conspicuous as desired. Another row of stitching can be placed directly on top of the first, provided great care is taken to stitch directly over the first row; this is so difficult that it is almost impossible to do a perfect job. However, if the fabric has great surface interest, if it is in a fairly dark color, or if it is composed of several colors, as in a tweed, little inaccuracies will not be evident, and this idea may prove to be very effective.

If the machine has holders for two spools

of top thread, two threads can be threaded through the needle for a more conspicious top-stitched line. Be sure to test-stitch before proceeding; the tension of the machine will very probably need some adjustment under these circumstances.

A suggestion of limited applicability is to use a very narrow zigzag stitch with stitches so close together that they give a solid-line effect. This technique is recommended if top-stitched effects are an important part of the design and if the fabric is so heavy and tweed-like that more orthodox methods will not give the desired conspicuous effect. The bight of the zigzagged stitch should be very narrow ($\frac{1}{32}$ or $\frac{1}{16}$ inch), and the stitch length should be as fine as is required to give a very slim, solid line. Because such stitches would be difficult to remove if the line were not perfect, it is well to obtain a perfect line of straight top-stitching first and then use it for a guide, stitching over it with the zigzag stitch.

Control of fabric The seam should be carefully pressed in the proper direction before work is begun. Sketch *a* in Figure 7-12 pictures the method of basting edges for top-stitched details. Because the machine pushes the fabric out of line (more so with more layers of fabric), basting stitches must be very small and firm. The sketch shows two rows of basting, $\frac{1}{16}$ inch on each side of the line to be top-stitched. Reinforce with firm back stitches as often as necessary to hold the fabric securely. By basting each side of the line desired, excellent control is achieved, and the short, firm stitches can be more easily removed. Firm cross bastings are a further protection against inaccuracy in very spongy fabric.

Sketch *b* shows the use of a small cardboard gauge as a guide for top-stitching at the machine. If desired, a basted guideline for stitching can be used.

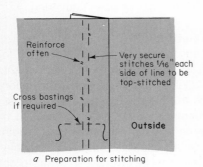

a Preparation for stitching

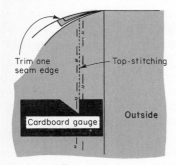

b Top-stitching

FIGURE 7-12 To top-stitch.

Special problems The three thicknesses of fabric which result when a seam is pressed in one direction pad the stitches and help to achieve an attractively conspicuous effect. If top-stitching is required in areas where there is no padding or where there is a variation in padding, the resulting stitches will not be consistently conspicuous. Figure 7-13 illustrates this problem with a top-stitched dart. The problem arises because the dart narrows down at the tip, so that stitches in the upper part of the dart are padded with two thicknesses of fabric, but are padded with only one layer in the tip area. The solution is to cut scraps of matching fabric and baste them in a position on the inside to pad the top-stitching; be sure that raw edges just meet each other, as shown. As soon as the dart is top-stitched, excess fabric can be trimmed close to the stitching.

This idea is applicable to any top-stitching problem in which more padding is desired for a greater indentation at the stitched line. A narrow strip of fabric can be basted the full length of any seam to provide extra padding for stitches, and if it is then trimmed close to the stitching, no great amount of bulk results.

CLIPPING SEAMS AND NOTCHING OUT FULLNESS

There are two types of seams. *Structural seams* are those that join major sections of the garment (side seams, underarm seams of sleeves, shoulder seams) and will be visible from the wrong side of an unlined garment. If the seams will be visible in the finished garment, they will also be subject to friction as the garment is worn and will tend to ravel; for this reason, major structural seams should remain the full ⅝-inch width.

Encased seams are those that will be hidden from view and protected from friction in the finished garment. They include seams at the finished edges of collars, cuffs, facings, trimming details, etc., and seams of the hem or the facing that will be covered when the hem or facing is in place. Because these seams will not get wear, they can be trimmed to a narrower width to decrease bulk (discussed in detail in the fol-

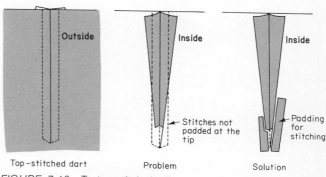

Top-stitched dart   Problem   Solution

FIGURE 7-13   To top-stitch dartlines.

lowing section). Many of these seams are curved (neck edge, collar edges) and must be clipped or notched so they will lie flat at the edges of the finished garment.

Clipping seams and notching out fullness are very simple techniques; unfortunately even those who are experienced have difficulty understanding when and how to use clipping and notching effectively. Figure 7-14 pictures a very helpful

illustrative sample. Make a paper sample similar to the one shown in sketch *a* to simulate a collar, pocket flap, etc. The combination of a convex curve, a point, a ruler line, and a concave curve will serve to illustrate the various reasons for notching, clipping, and trimming corners. Sketch in a pencil line to indicate the seamline; if this were an actual collar, two edges would be joined and then the collar would be turned right side out with the finished edge along the seamline, somewhat as it is shown in sketch *b*. Begin by attempting to turn under the seam allowance. It will be immediately evident that the edges

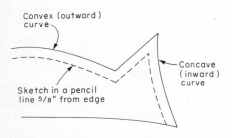

a Paper sample to simulate collar, cuff, pocket flap, etc.

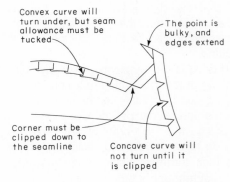

b Turn under the edges along the pencil line: the need for clipping, notching out, and trimming points is evident.

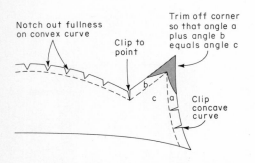

c Trim the corner, clip to the inner point and into the concave curved edge, and notch out fullness on the convex curved edge.

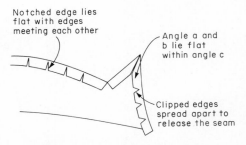

d Seam allowance turns under easily when properly prepared.

FIGURE 7-14   A paper sample reveals the reasons for notching out fullness, clipping seams, and trimming corners of encased seams.

cannot be turned under until the point is clipped. Similarly, the concave curve will not turn until clips are made. The ruler line turns under easily and lies flat and the convex curve turns under with little wedge-shaped tucks. The point is very bulky (four layers at the point) and the edges extend as shown.

Sketch *b* reveals the basic reasons for notching and clipping. *If the cut edge of the seam is longer than the area over which it will lie in the finished garment (as in convex curves), the extra length must be notched out. If the cut edge of the seam is shorter than the area over which it will lie (as in concave curves), it must be released by clipping.* See sketches *c* and *d* and note that the notched edges move toward each other when the seam is turned under and the clipped edges spread apart.

Note the shaded area of the point in sketch *c* and see the general rule for trimming corners of encased seams. The trimmed edges meet each other (two layers instead of four) in sketch *d* because the two angles in the seam allowance equal the angle of the finished point of the collar.

Experiment with paper samples until the reasons for trimming corners, clipping, and notching out fullness are thoroughly mastered.

REDUCING BULK IN SEAMS

To stagger or grade seam widths See sketch *a* in Figure 7-15. When two seam edges will lie over each as they do in encased seams, the edges should be trimmed to a narrower width and the widths should be graded or staggered so the thickness does not create a ridge along the finished edges. The concave curved edge in sketch *a* shows general rules for trimming edges of encased seams. The sketch includes an interfacing, making a total of

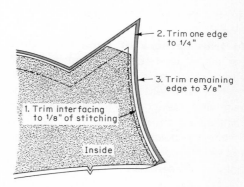

a Trim encased seams, staggering or grading the edges to prevent a bulky ridge along finished edges.

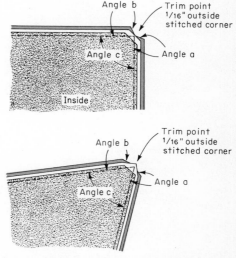

b General rule: Trim points of encased seams so that the angles between the stitching line and the trimmed edge (the angles of the seam allowance) equal the angle between the stitching lines.

FIGURE 7-15 *To stagger or grade seams and trim corners of encased seams.*

three layers of fabric; note that the corner of the interfacing was trimmed off before the seam was stitched (directions on page 371). The proper order is listed; always trim the narrower widths first.

To trim corners of encased seams See the general rule illustrated in sketch *b* (similar to the simple sketch in Figure 7-14). It is necessary to trim close to the point while leaving a slight amount so the point will not ravel at the tip; trim 1/16 inch beyond the point in closely woven fabrics and slightly more (an ample $1/16$ inch) if the fabric ravels seriously.

Figure 7-16 shows clipping and notching on a seam which has been trimmed; the seam should be trimmed first, and then notched and clipped.

To trim corners of cross seams See three alternatives in Figure 7-17. When one seam (or a dart) crosses another seam, the area is necessarily bulky, and it becomes more bulky as the cross seam is pressed open. Trimming out one layer of fabric results in remarkable improvement. All three suggestions are effective; the method shown in sketch *b* results in less stiffness and bulk and is recommended for the type of fabrics used for tailored garments.

To distribute bulk in darts See Figure 7-18. A dart pressed in one direction will

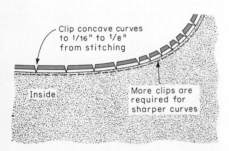

a Trim seam and then clip concave curved edges.

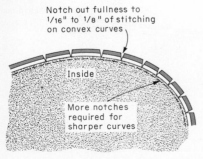

b Trim seam and then notch out fullness on convex curved edges.

FIGURE 7-16 *To clip seams and notch out fullness on encased seams.*

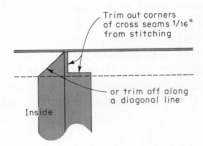

a Two methods of trimming corners of cross seams after the seam is stitched.

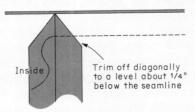

b Preferred method of trimming corners — trimming done before the cross seam is stitched

FIGURE 7-17 *To reduce bulk by trimming corners of cross seams.*

create three thicknesses of fabric in the area in which it lies. If the fabric is heavy, this will result in an unattractive bulkiness which is even thicker, because a fold edge is more bulky than two cut edges. If a dart measures ½ inch wide when folded (or ⅜ inch wide in thick fabrics), it should be slashed and pressed open. It can be slashed down to a point where the fold edge of the dart is about ¼ inch from the stitching

line; this means there will be a seam allowance of ¼ inch at the narrowest point. In wide darts, this will be quite close to the tip, but in narrow darts it will be quite a distance from the tip. A little diagonal clip through one edge will allow the dart edges to be pressed open and the tip to be pressed in one direction.

If a dart is very wide, trim ⅝ inch from the stitching line of the dart and proceed as above.

Although small darts are not usually slashed because of the narrow seam allowance, their bulk does create problems. Figure 7-19 shows three possibilities of

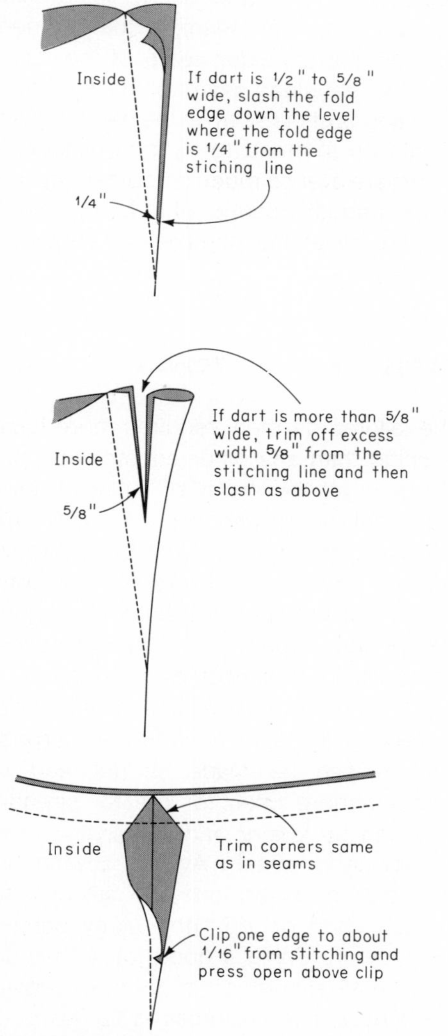

Inside

If dart is ½" to ⅝" wide, slash the fold edge down the level where the fold edge is ¼" from the stiching line

¼"

If dart is more than ⅝" wide, trim off excess width ⅝" from the stitching line and then slash as above

Inside

⅝"

Inside

Trim corners same as in seams

Clip one edge to about ¹/₁₆" from stitching and press open above clip

FIGURE 7-18 Slash darts and press open to distribute bulk.

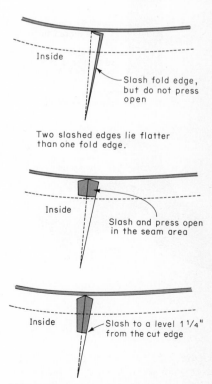

Inside

Slash fold edge, but do not press open

Two slashed edges lie flatter than one fold edge.

Inside

Slash and press open in the seam area

Inside

Slash to a level 1¼" from the cut edge

FIGURE 7-19 Very narrow darts can be slashed in fabrics that do not ravel.

decreasing their bulk in fabrics that do not ravel; it must be understood that the seam allowance of a narrow slashed dart may be only ¼ inch at its widest point. The third suggestion is the most effective (if the fabric is appropriate), because slashing and

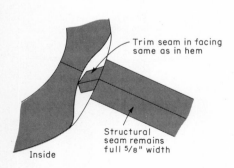

a To decrease bulk in hems.

b To decrease bulk in any area where there is more than one seam.

FIGURE 7-20 *To reduce bulk by staggering or grading the width of corresponding seams.*

pressing open for 1¼ inches distributes the bulk in the seam allowance and in the area covered by the cross seam when it is pressed open.

To reduce bulk by staggering the width of corresponding seams See Figure 7-20. The idea of staggered seams can be applied to the situation where one structural seam lies under another, as is the case in the hem. The identical situation exists when a facing seam lies directly under a structural seam in the garment, such as the shoulder seam of the facing and the shoulder seam of the garment. Both edges of the seam in the hem or facing should be trimmed to ⅜ inch; staggered seams are ever so much smoother because of the gradual tapering off of bulk. A notch cut directly at the hemline, as shown, is very helpful.

BASIC HAND STITCHES

The tailored garment requires more hand-stitching than any other construction project, and yet the secret of success lies in the inventiveness with which a few stitches are used. The worker must think through her own problem and vary her interpretation of basic stitches with each problem.

The four types of stitches described here will solve almost every purpose of hand sewing because each can be modified somewhat to serve a particular purpose. Stitches can be made shorter and reinforced more often for greater strength; they can be longer and looser for an inconspicuous effect. Avoid "sewing the style out" of a garment with stitches that are too short or too tight. Many persons feel they are doing a good job if they use very small stitches, but on the contrary, the beauty is being impaired for no good reason; in most cases hand stitches do not have a heavy job to do. A far better practice is to make hand stitches as long and as loose as they can possibly be and still hold the edges securely enough. Easy, "lazy" stitches will make the construction less obvious and result in more professional standards.

Use the basic hand stitches innovatively For best results, the worker should modify and adapt the basic hand stitches to each particular use and to the fabric involved. The length of stitches, the frequency of reinforcing stitches, the tautness of the thread, and the placement of the stitch in relation to the edge involved can serve to expand a few basic stitches into a great variety to solve every hand-sewing problem. Each solution should reflect a wise balance between the security required to do the job and the slight play required to keep stitches invisible.

The directions for doing a particular stitch and the position in which work is held allow for convenient hand position, ease, and speed of construction. Most workers will quickly discover the advantages of using the accepted methods. But if proper methods are tested over a period of time without success, the worker can devise her own methods and hold her work in the position she prefers provided that her innovations result in acceptable construction standards and are not too time-consuming. There is no reason why one should be burdened by being textbook right on insignificant issues.

An aid to left-handed workers The left-handed person is accustomed to reversing directions as she works, but she frequently has difficulty in learning complicated hand stitches; and a right handed instructor finds it difficult to demonstrate with her left hand. A simple trick is for the right-handed instructor to demonstrate by facing the left-handed student; she can use her right hand, which will be directly across from the student's left hand, making it possible for the student to continue working in the direction most convenient for her.

Four basic hand stitches

The three basic stitches illustrated in Figures 7-21 and 7-22 and the blind stitch (not illustrated) can serve almost every hand-sewing need with modification in the length of stitch, the frequency of reinforcing stitches, the tautness of thread, etc. For all hand work, a single thread is used and the stitch that is taken into the garment (the stitch that may be visible as the garment is worn) must be very small, catching in just a thread or two of the fabric. The stitch taken into the hem or facing can be somewhat larger; and all reinforcing stitches, which are taken in the hem or facing layer only, can be quite secure.

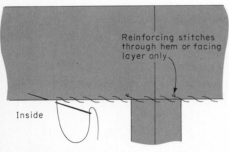

a Whipping or overhand hemming stitch.

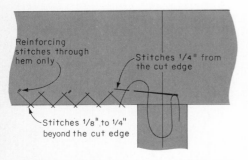

b Catch—stitch allows for some shifting or play.

FIGURE 7-21   Basic hand stitches.

The whipping or overhand hemming stitch   This stitch, shown in sketch *a* of Figure 7-21, is often called a "slip stitch." Work progresses from right to left. The length of stitch can vary greatly from a scant ¼ inch for securing narrow (¼-inch-wide) hems or narrow bias facings to a length of ½ or ⅝ inch for securing wider hems. The stitch can be used on any turned-under edge which has been finished in any way (top-stitched or finished with binding, etc.) and can be used on raw edges of fabrics that do not ravel and do not require a finish.

It is a very secure stitch because it encases the edge; therefore it is recommended for utilitarian garments which will get hard wear and require frequent laundering. However, because the edge is encased and held quite firmly to the garment, there will be a tendency for the bulky ridge to show, making the hem more conspicuous than the others pictured. This stitch is included here because it may be used on blouses and go-with pieces; the catch stitch and tailor's hemming stitch will better serve tailoring purposes.

The catch stitch   This stitch, shown in sketch *b,* is the only basic stitch in which work progresses from left to right; however, note that the needle points toward the left, just as it does in the other stitches. Stitches can vary from ¼ inch apart to ½ inch apart, depending on the security required.

To do a stitch which allows for a small amount of shifting or play, take a small stitch, ¼ inch from the hem or facing edge, then move along for the desired length of stitch and take a tiny stitch into the garment about ⅛ inch from the cut edge of the hem or facing, and proceed. There is an additional little technique: Each time a stitch is made, place the thread under the tip of the needle, as shown, for a more attractive and elastic stitch. This stitch is less secure in that the edge is not held firmly to the garment; because stitches are made ⅛ inch from the cut edge, the edge can move and shift slightly. This stitch is used for securing raw edges (edges of interfacings or underlinings and hems in fabrics that require no finish). It is quite inconspicuous because of the play and because the cut edge is not held flat against the garment.

To do a stitch which allows for more shifting or play, place stitches ¼ inch beyond the cut edge of the hem or facing. They will not hold the edge as firmly but the extra play will help to keep stitches inconspicuous.

The tailor's hemming stitch This stitch, shown in two steps in Figure 7-22, has many advantages, and it can, if the worker desires, be adapted to serve almost every hand-hemming need. It can be used on a raw edge or on an edge finished in any way; it is pictured with the Hong Kong finish in Figure 7-27. First baste the hem to the garment with stitches ¼ inch below the hem or facing edge; make the row parallel to the hem edge because the hem will be folded back along the basted line and this line will control the placement of hand stitches. Fold the hem or facing to the outside, allowing the free edge to extend about ¼ inch. Take stitches into the hem or facing and into the garment, placing stitches ⅛ to ¼ inch in from the edge as shown.

The stitch can be used for many purposes by varying the tautness of the thread and the length of the stitch. It can be done with long, loose stitches to serve the purposes of catch stitching. It can be done with small stitches, frequently reinforced, for a secure hem in utilitarian garments. It is ideally suited to typical hemming purposes when an easy stitch about ½ inch long is required. It is well to experiment

with this stitch and use it as frequently as possible. It has the great advantage of being the most invisible stitch because the bulky finished edge is free from the garment. In addition, because stitches are hidden from view on the inside, it is attractive and stitches cannot be pulled or snagged if the garment is given hard wear.

The blind stitch This stitch (not pictured) is used when a hand stitch is needed on a finished seamline and the construction requires the most inconspicuous stitch.

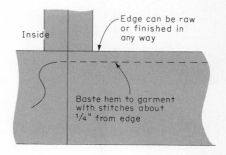

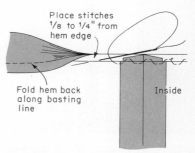

FIGURE 7-22   The tailor's hemming stitch.

This stitch is used for securing the pleat of a bound buttonhole, for sewing in shoulder pads, and for other purposes too numerous to mention. The stitch is done from the right side of the garment, with a single thread in matching color.

The stitches are usually placed right in a seam. Working from right to left, bring the needle up through the seam from the wrong side. Then take the smallest back

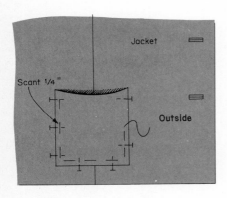

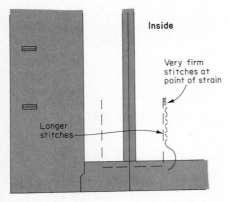

FIGURE 7-23   *To apply design details by hand.*

stitch possible (just a thread or two) in the seam and slip the needle under the seam. Do not pull stitches too tight. Then bring the needle up again along the seamline and repeat. The length of the stitch varies with its uses from ¼ to ½ inch.

A special problem

Very often design details (pockets, flaps, and trimming details) are applied by hand because a top-stitched effect is not desired for the particular design. Even if edges of the pocket or other detail are to be top-stitched for a decorative effect, the results will be more accurate if the top-stitching is done on the detail before it is applied to the garment by hand. Details such as pockets and flaps must withstand great strain during wearing and the slip stitch, which is usually recommended, will not be adequate. The suggestion given in Figure 7-23 results in invisible stitches which are as strong as machine stitches and which can, in fact, be made even stronger.

Pin and then baste the detail firmly in the proper position with stitches a scant ¼ inch from the finished edge; examine the result to be sure it is in perfect position. Work from the inside. The edge of the pocket extends ¼ inch from the visible basting stitches, and so stitches taken in the area just ⅛ inch outside the basted guideline will fall just inside the finished edge of the pocket and will be invisible from the outside. Care must be taken that the stitches go through only one layer of the pocket or detail. Take small hand stitches at right angles to the edge for maximum security, as shown; the stitches can be longer and less firm in areas of less strain, as shown.

In most cases the result will be excellent, and the detail will look as if it "just grew," but in heavy fabrics the finished edge may need additional slip stitches made from the outside to hold the heavy edge to the garment. In this case the slip stitch can be inconspicuous because it is not required for strength.

NOTE: **Padding stitches (another type of hand stitch) will be used for shaping the collar and lapel areas of the jacket or coat. They will be described in detail as they are required during construction.**

SEAM AND HEM FINISHES

The purposes of a seam finish are to finish raw edges to prevent raveling if the seam will be exposed to friction as the garment is worn and to improve the appearance of the inside of the garment. Although there have been times in fashion history when the appearance of the inside was of major importance, the current trend is to use the simplest type of seam with the least amount of additional bulk and stiffness (a plain seam with no finish is the least bulky) and to use the simplest, flattest seam finish that will prevent fraying. The inside of the garment is not neglected; current construction methods favor a neat, uncluttered look that is attractive in its simplicity. Eliminating unnecessary seam finishes or using the most simple finish that will prevent fraying improves the appearance of the garment on the outside by creating less bulk and preventing a distracting, overconstructed appearance.

As a general rule, seam and hem edges are allowed to remain raw in tailored garments because they will be hidden from view and protected from friction by a lining. The need to finish these edges is dependent on whether or not a lining will be used and, if so, how it will be handled. Because seams are finished early in the construction sequence, it is important to make a deci-

sion on lining methods immediately. Study the information on skirt and pants linings on pages 339 to 350, evaluate the alternatives on page 344, and decide how the lower edge of the lining will be handled.

If the skirt or pants will not be lined In unlined garments, the need for seam finishes depends on the fraying quality of the fabric. Closely woven fabrics and double knits (in wool or polyester) will not need to be finished. Loosely woven fabrics can be finished by the simplest and least bulky method that will prevent fraying; or, for a couturier touch, the attractive Hong Kong finish is recommended.

If the skirt or pants will be lined by the simpest method The standard method of lining skirts or pants (with the lining handled like an underlining) leaves raw edges exposed. If this method is used, a seam finish may be very necessary because the lining fabric may fray more than the major fabric. Under these circumstances, the seam finish should be functional but also attractive; the Hong Kong finish, with binding made of scraps of the lining, is recommended.

If the couturier or shell method of lining is used If this method is used and the lining is attached to the garment at the hem, seams and hems should remain raw, for they will be protected from friction. However, if the lining is not attached at the lower edge but falls free from the garment, seams in loosely woven fabrics may require a simple finish. Hem edges of all fabrics, whether or not they fray seriously, are usually finished by an attractive finish

**FUNDAMENTALS OF
CONSTRUCTION AND PRESSING**

because they are so near the lower edge and may be revealed under certain wearing conditions; the Hong Kong finish is recommended.

If a jacket or coat will not be lined In this case seam and hem edges should be finished to provide a more attractive effect. The Hong Kong finish is recommended.

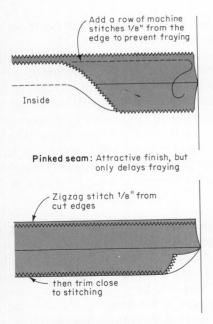

Add a row of machine stitches ⅛" from the edge to prevent fraying

Inside

Pinked seam: Attractive finish, but only delays fraying

Zigzag stitch ⅛" from cut edges

then trim close to stitching

Zigzagged seam finish

FIGURE 7-24 Seam finishes with a minimum of bulk serve most purposes.

Seam finishes which create little bulk and can be done quickly

See Figure 7-24. Pinking the cut edges gives an attractive finished look, but pinking only delays (it does not prevent) fraying; the delaying action may adequately control raveling in fabrics which have only a slight tendency to ravel. A row of machine stitches as shown will help prevent raveling. Seams can be pinked to add a finished look to fabrics which really need no finish.

The zigzag seam finish, possible with a machine with the zigzag feature, is a versatile finish which has largely replaced the two traditional seams shown in Figure 7-25. The finish is versatile because adjustments on the length and width of the stitch make it possible to control fraying to the degree desired and to control additional bulk and stiffness as well. By controlling the width of the zigzag (from $\frac{1}{16}$ to $\frac{1}{4}$ inch), the stitches will encase as many threads as are required to prevent fraying. By controlling the length of stitch (from a zigzag comparable to the points of a pinked edge to a solid line or band of stitches), the seam can be made more or less secure and more or less stiff and bulky. Although this finish may be considered less attractive than the two traditional seams it has largely replaced, it is less bulky and stiff than either of them and so it is preferred for use with fabrics that ravel appreciably.

The hand-over-cast seam is comparable to the zigzag seam. It is more time-consuming and less functional than the zigzag finish but it creates less of a ridge (less bulk) and it has the great advantage of allowing the seam to remain limp and supple.

These finishes and the very elegant Hong Kong finish shown in Figure 7-26 are currently favored by most professionals in the home-sewing field and by most designers of ready-to-wear as well.

Traditional seam finishes which result in bulky construction

See Figure 7-25. The turned-under-and-stitched seam and the traditional bound seam are both finishes that will prevent serious raveling. The turned-under-and-stitched finish is acceptable for use with lightweight fabrics, while the bound seam is preferred for heavier fabrics. Both finishes stiffen the seam with rows of machine stitching close to the seamline. Note that the bound seam requires rayon bias seam binding; cotton binding is much too heavy and straight bindings are stiffer than the bias type. These seam finishes are attractive if they are carefully done. The top-stitched finish results in an attractive seam about ⅜ inch wide. The bound seam can be allowed to remain the full width or can be trimmed narrower before it is encased; the binding is ¼ inch wide in the finished seam. These secure finishes have been largely replaced by the machine zigzag finish and the Hong Kong finish.

The Hong Kong finish is very attractive and functional with little additional bulk

See Figure 7-26. This finish is so elegant that those who do fashion sewing frequently use it when no finish is required, just to add a couturier touch. Its attractiveness is largely dependent on the narrow width of binding possible with this construction; the binding in a traditional bound seam is ¼ inch wide while this binding is only ⅛ inch wide, and the difference is tremendous. The narrow width is possible because the binding is not turned under on the underside (as in the traditional bound seam); this results in one less thickness of binding, which seems insignificant but is a great improvement.

The binding can be made of purchased

rayon bias seam binding (with the creases pressed out), but other choices will result in a more elegant effect. Bias strips of very lightweight underlining fabric are ideal, and the effect will be enhanced if the garment is underlined with the same fabric. Similarly, if a lightweight lining fabric will be used and handled as if it were an underlining, bias strips of the same lining fabric will be attractive. It is important that the

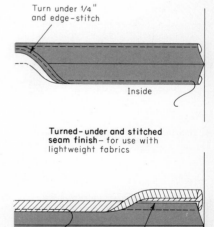

Turn under ¼"
and edge-stitch

Inside

**Turned-under and stitched
seam finish**– for use with
lightweight fabrics

Encase cut edges with
rayon bias seam binding

Traditional bound finish– for
use with heavier fabrics

FIGURE 7-25 Two traditional seam finishes that have been largely replaced by less bulky construction.

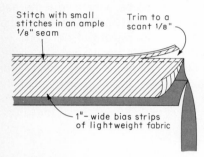

Stitch with small
stitches in an ample
1/8" seam

Trim to a
scant 1/8"

1"-wide bias strips
of lightweight fabric

a Stitch binding to cut edges of seams.

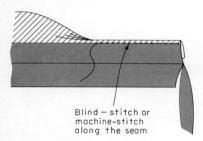

Blind – stitch or
machine-stitch
along the seam

b Encase raw seam edge with binding.

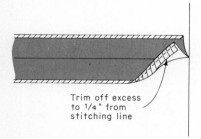

Trim off excess
to 1/4" from
stitching line

c Trim off excess binding, leaving the edge raw
on the underside of the seam.

FIGURE 7-26 The Hong Kong
seam finish is both attractive and
functional, with little bulk.

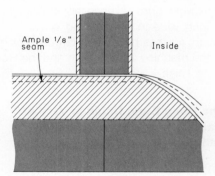

Ample 1/8"
seam

Inside

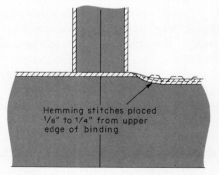

Hemming stitches placed
1/8" to 1/4" from upper
edge of binding

FIGURE 7-27 The Hong Kong finish
can be adapted to finishing hem and
facing edges.

strips be cut on the bias of a limp, light-weight fabric so that the finish will create a minimum of additional bulk and stiffness.

See sketch a. Stitch the binding with small stitches (about fifteen to twenty stitches per inch) because the seam will be trimmed very close to the stitching. Stitch in an ample ⅛ inch seam (or slightly wider) and then trim the seam down very close to the stitching; in this way the row of stitching can be more accurate than is possible if the original stitching is done very close to the cut edge.

See sketch b. Roll the binding over the seam (snug but not tight) and hold it in place with machine or hand stitches placed directly in the seamline (stitches will be almost invisible.) Results will be more attractive and the seam more supple if the binding is held in place with blind stitches done by hand.

See sketch c. Trim the excess binding on the underside to about ¼ inch from the row of stitches. This edge remains raw; it will not ravel because it will be protected by the seam and because fabric does not ravel on the bias.

Figure 7-27 illustrates the Hong Kong finish applied to hem edges (replacing the traditional ½-inch-wide hem binding) for a very delicate, attractive finish. It can be used to finish facing edges as well. The hand stitches to secure the hem are placed an ample ⅛ inch under the finished edge (specific directions appear on page 283), and the total effect is most attractive and delicate.

FUNDAMENTALS OF PRESSING

Pressing is as important as the quality of construction to the ultimate beauty of a garment. Indeed the professional presser in a manufacturing establishment is one of the highest-paid workers, more highly paid than the operator who sews the garment. There are many tricks to the pressing trade, each one easy enough to do at the proper stage during construction. A knowledge of pressing will do a great deal toward making the home-sewn garment meet and surpass the high standards of exclusive ready-made garments.

Avoid the dangers of overpressing Pressing flattens fibers; and overpressing (too often, too hard, too hot) will weaken the fabric, flatten it, and eventually make it shiny. Overpressing means that the fabric has been pressed with too hot an iron, with too great a pressure, or too many times.

Pressing can be kept to a minimum by handling the fabric properly at every stage in the construction process—by hanging sections on a hanger or placing them on a large flat surface as soon as they are cut, by hanging the assembled garment on a hanger as soon as it is basted, and by keeping the fabric smoothed out and as flat as possible on the table or at the machine as work progresses.

Test-press each fabric to determine the most effective procedures One must know at what temperature to set the iron, the amount of moisture required to make seams and edges flat, and the amount of pressure needed to give a flat finish without harming the appearance of the fabric. Because today's market is replete with the greatest variety of fabrics, because new fibers and fabrics are introduced every season, and because many of the new fabrics are made of a combination of two or more fibers, it is impossible to predict with true accuracy how a fabric will react to pressing. *Testing is of utmost importance.*

Tests must be made on the fabric as it will be handled during construction; seams, pleats, darts, and the still heavier encased

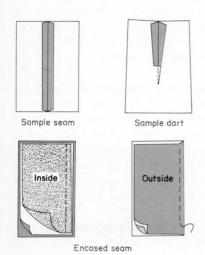

Sample seam   Sample dart

Inside   Outside

Encased seam

FIGURE 7-28 To test pressing methods.

seams will require different techniques to produce a flat effect without harming the fabric. Figure 7-28 shows samples of fabric prepared in the various ways it will be handled during construction. The encased seam, composed of two layers of fabric and one layer of interfacing, must be stitched and the seam edges staggered and basted in preparation for testing. If the garment will be underlined or interfaced, the test sample should be handled in an identical manner.

Always test on a scrap of fabric large enough so that half of it can be pressed while the other half is left as purchased as a standard for comparison. For example, if moisture spots the fabric, it will be more noticeable if half of the scrap is in its original condition. If moisture shrinks the fabric, it will be easily detected by a puckered line between the pressed area and the original. Changes in the color and appearance of

the fabric can be seen more accurately this way. Test several methods to determine which is best for each particular fabric.

Tests for pressure and moisture The pressure on the iron can vary from a slight tap to maximum pressure, with the worker leaning heavily on the iron and using a great amount of body weight. Some heavy, wiry wools will require tremendous pressure to force seams and darts to lie flat, while lightweight dress woolens and polyester knits will require little pressure. Examine the pressed seam or dart on the right side; it must be consistently flat and inconspicuous.

The amount of moisture required will vary greatly; there must be sufficient moisture to press the seam open without shrinking the fabric. For some fabrics, the degree of moisture from the steam iron will be too great and must be reduced by the use of a dry press cloth. Heavy and wiry fabrics may require more moisture than is obtainable with a steam iron; if so, a dampened press cloth must be used with the iron.

Despite the advertising claims that a press cloth is not required with a steam iron, the surface of the fabric will be somewhat flattened by the slick iron; a press cloth is required for high-quality tailoring. It may be entirely dry for some purposes or truly wet for others. Dampen the press cloth by soaking the entire cloth and then wringing it out. Then press over the entire area of the cloth (for consistent moisture) until the proper degree of moisture remains.

More pressure and moisture will be required to press darts and seams flat than to press wrinkles from fabric; even more pressure and moisture will be required to press a firm edge on heavier encased seams and folded edges.

Tests for surface appearance Examine the test samples in a strong light to determine whether the surface of the fabric has been adversely affected by pressing. Fibers may be flat, and seam ridges may appear somewhat shiny. This is an indication that the pressure was probably too great, but if these flaws appear even if less pressure is applied, correct them with a "touch-up" on the right side of the fabric. First hold the steam iron about 1/8 inch above the fabric, allowing steam to escape; the flattened fibers may be loosened and picked up by the released steam. For more serious problems, use the same technique with a press cloth (almost wet) over the fabric.

The heavy edges of encased seams must be basted before pressing and later, when basting threads are removed, marks of the thread may be imprinted in the fabric. Touching up on the right side of the fabric (with the steam iron held slightly above the fabric and with or without a dampened press cloth, depending on the degree of the imprint) will remove thread marks.

Adapt pressing techniques to the demands of each fabric It is important to test-press on scraps of fabric before pressing any garment, and *the need for test pressing is magnified by the continuing technological advances in the textile industry.* Exciting new fabric offerings made of entirely new fibers woven in imaginative new ways and finished with one or more new finishing processes (as well as long-forgotten old favorites enjoying a revival) have unknown qualities that must be discovered by testing. The fact that fabrics can be made of blends of two fibers to gain the advantages of both (for example, a polyester blended with wool to combine the easy-care qualities of the polyester with the warmth and feel of wool) complicates the issue and makes it impossible to predict the most effective method of pressing. Test-pressing with a scrap of sufficient size so that a part is left

unpressed (as a standard for comparison) is absolutely essential.

Pressing directions are included for some of the special fabrics discussed in Chapter 11. Consider these general suggestions but use them with caution; do not assume that general directions in a text are consistently reliable for every fabric available on the market. The more exciting the market offerings (and fabrics become increasingly imaginative each year), the greater the need for testing techniques.

Check the condition of the iron before each pressing session Before pressing, the condition of the iron must be tested, a step that is more necessary in the school laboratory, where many persons use one iron. Be sure the steam iron is adjusted to the steam setting, and if there might be water in the iron, be sure the iron is plugged in and that the water has turned to steam. Leakage of water from the iron, with subsequent spotting of the fabric, is almost always the result of careless working habits. A small amount of water replenished as needed will serve the purpose; use the recommended amount when filling the iron. The iron may leak if too much water is used.

If the iron does not slide easily over the ironing surface, check the condition of the plate. If it has been used for a fabric that has a great amount of sizing or if it has been used at too high a temperature on some synthetic fabrics, a crust of burned matter will have formed and must be removed.

The use of a press cloth is very important The press cloth must be made of an unsized fabric because sizing sticks to the iron and burns. The weight of the press cloth should be similar to the weight of the fabric—a heavy press cloth is needed for heavy fabrics, and a lightweight press cloth for lightweight fabrics. The press cloth may be dry for some fabrics, particularly if the steam iron is used, and it may be damp (with varying degrees of dampness) for other fabrics. A press cloth may be dampened by one of two methods: (1) A wet sponge can be rubbed on the press cloth until the desired amount of moisture is achieved, or (2) the press cloth can be dipped in water, wrung out, and then pressed until the desired dampness is attained. Notice that the word damp is used; a wet press cloth is seldom used because it may shrink fabric. Some fabrics can take more moisture than others before shrinking occurs—this must be tested on a scrap of fabric. The press cloth must be uniformly damp so that no part of the fabric will shrink more than any other part. Sometimes fabric must be shrunk (described on page 294), and then the press cloth must be very wet.

Do major pressing on the wrong side —do only touching up on the right side Always press on the wrong side of the fabric. The original appearance of the fabric is retained if the iron is not placed on the right side of the fabric. And of course seams and darts are not revealed on the right side and can be pressed properly only from the wrong side. A certain amount of touching up will be necessary on the right side of the fabric, but it should be very little.

Several thicknesses of the press cloth (two, three, or even four) should be used when pressing on the right side of the fabric, because this will create steam without leaving a print of the iron. Unattractive marks of the iron show on wool or pile fabrics more readily than on other fabrics, so great care must be taken when pressing these fabrics. It is an excellent idea to use a large scrap of the wool of the garment for a press cloth on that garment to prevent a shine.

Allow some of the moisture to remain in the fabric after it has been pressed Pressing until all moisture is removed from the press cloth causes the fabric to dry out and become deadened. This suggestion is especially important for wool fabrics. When pressing, lift the press cloth occasionally to allow steam to escape. Damp fabric will muss and wrinkle easily, so it is essential to hang up that section of the garment and allow it to dry by natural means before working with it again. Plan to work on some other unit of the garment for 15 minutes or more while the fabric dries.

Press each seam as work progresses There is no more important rule for pressing than this: *Press each seam before crossing it with another.* First of all, pressing each seam as work progresses makes for easier construction. And certainly pressing can be done more effectively and more easily while the garment is in small sections.

The initial pressing of the garment (as soon as the seams are stitched) should take a considerable length of time; about half an hour may be required to do an excellent job on a skirt. By contrast, final pressing of the skirt may take only a matter of minutes.

Special problems

To remove marks of basting threads

When an edge such as the fold edge of a pleat or the edge of a collar is folded under, the basting threads must be left in until light pressing is done. Heavy basting threads will press a mark into the fabric which will be noticeable when the bastings are removed. These marks can be prevented by using a fine cotton or silk thread for basting such edges. Thread marks can be removed from most fabrics by using several thicknesses of a damp press cloth on the right side of the fabric and holding the iron against the press cloth with the entire weight of the iron supported by the hand. The steam from the press cloth will remove the marks.

To press seams See Figure 7-29. Always press seams together and flat first, as shown in sketch a. This flattens out the stitching line and makes it easier to press the seam open later.

Sometimes the seam allowance will press through and cause an unattractive ridge or line; this will happen most often with wools and other heavy fabrics. The mark of a seam can be prevented by slipping strips of paper (ticker tape is convenient to use) under the seam before pressing, as shown in sketch b.

A lapped or top-stitched seam should be pressed before it is stitched and again after it is stitched and the bastings have been removed. It is a good idea to press the edge that will be lapped as soon as it is basted under and before it is basted to the other piece; a better, straighter, more accurate line can be achieved in this way.

Keep seams ruler-straight on the board. If a seam is pressed in a wobbly line, that inaccurate line may be retained and the seam may never hang properly on the body.

Use a tailor's ham to press curved seams

such as those in the hip region of a slim sheath skirt (sketch c). Darts, too, are better pressed over a tailor's ham because a curved, molded line is desired at the tip of the dart. By pressing over a rounded surface, those portions of the garment that will fit a curve on the body are molded and shaped to conform to the figure.

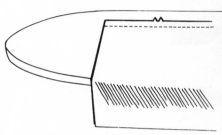

a First press seam flat, then open.

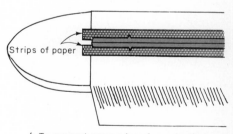

b To prevent seam edges from showing prominently on the right side.

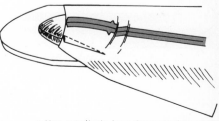

c Use a tailor's ham for pressing curved areas.

FIGURE 7-29 To press seams.

To press gathers, darts, tucks, and pleats See Figure 7-30. Fabric should be pressed before it is gathered. Then, if it is handled carefully and hung on a hanger when not in use, that area of the garment

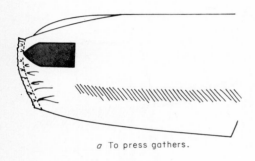

a To press gathers.

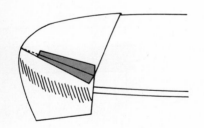

b To press darts and tucks.

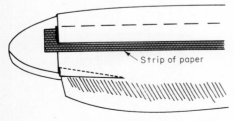

Strip of paper

c To prevent pleat edges from showing prominently on the right side.

FIGURE 7-30 To press gathers, darts, tucks, and pleats.

will require little if any pressing. If it must be pressed, let the gathered edge curve around the end of the ironing board, smooth out one area, and press with the tip of the iron pointing toward the gathered edge (sketch *a*).

Most darts will be pressed open. If they are small and will be pressed to one side, the instruction sheet states or illustrates the direction in which darts and tucks should be pressed. The general rule is: *Press vertical darts toward the center front or center back and press horizontal darts down.* However, there are exceptions to the rule, depending on the design, and they will be stated on the instruction sheet.

Place the tip of the dart or tuck at the end of the ironing board so that one area of the piece is flat on the board while the rest of the piece hangs off the board, as shown in sketch *b*. This will enable one to press the dart right up to its tip. Use the tailor's ham for pressing darts that should be molded to fit a curve of the body.

The entire length of the pleat should be basted before pressing is done; it is impossible to get an accurate, true line without basting. The thickness of a pleat will mark through to the right side of the garment and cause an unattractive ridge or line, particularly in heavy fabrics. This can be prevented by inserting a strip of paper (any plain paper but never printed newspaper) under the fold of the pleat before pressing (sketch *c*).

Press to within 6 inches of the lower edge and remove bastings. The 6-inch unpressed edge will make the hem easier to put in. When the hem has been finished and pressed, baste the remaining fold edge of the pleats and press.

To shrink out fullness See Figure 7-31. If an edge has stretched or if an edge must be eased to another edge (such as the back shoulder to the front shoulder or the front skirt to the waistband), the fullness can be shrunk out so that it is not noticeable, provided the fabric will respond. Fabric will shrink with the application of a great deal of moisture, so a press cloth must be used, and it should be as wet as possible for best results. The iron is held against the press cloth with the weight of the iron supported with the hand because steam and heat, rather than pressure, are required. After the fullness has been shrunk out (and it may require more than one processing), press the fabric in the usual manner.

It is necessary to shrink out the fullness of an eased hem. The lower edge of such hems is a curved line. The problem is to shrink the hem without shrinking the layer of fabric directly underneath the hem; this means that a cushion of some sort must be inserted between the hem and the garment. A piece of cardboard about 8 inches long and 4 inches wide, cut in a curved line similar to the hemline, will serve the purpose nicely (sketch *a*). Slip the shaped cardboard under the hem as shown in the sketch and proceed to shrink out the fullness as described above.

If two edges of different lengths must be joined together, one edge must ease to the other. Although this easing is necessary for a beautiful fit, the edge should not look gathered; if the fullness is shrunk out, the fit will be retained but the edge will be flat and smooth. Gather the longer edge and draw up the gathers to the desired length. Place the edge over the tailor's ham and smooth out the garment until it curves around the cushion (sketch *b*). Then proceed to shrink out the fullness as described above.

This technique can be used to solve many other problems with fabrics which, like wool, respond well to shrinking. For example, the unattractive bowed-out appearance of a skirt stretched from hours

of sitting can be improved by shrinking. Place the skirt flat on the board; allow the stretched area to ripple up on the board as it did on the figure. Using a very wet press cloth, go through the shrinking process; it may have to be repeated often, but gradually the ripples will settle down to the board, and the skirt can be pressed flat.

The final pressing Because all seams, darts, and edges—actually all portions of the garment—have been pressed well during construction, there is little to do

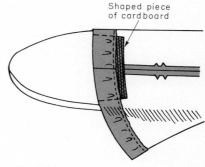

Shaped piece of cardboard

a To shrink out fullness in hems — to shrink out fullness in only one of two layers of fabric

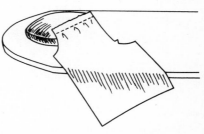

b To shrink out fullness in one layer of fabric

FIGURE 7-31 *To shrink out fullness.*

in the way of final pressing. The main purpose of a final pressing is to remove the folds and wrinkles caused in working with the garment. Many of them will fall out if the garment is allowed to hang for a few hours after it is finished. Pressing should follow the general suggestions given earlier

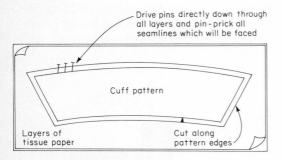

a Cut the desired number of guides.

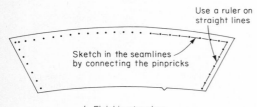

b Finishing touches.

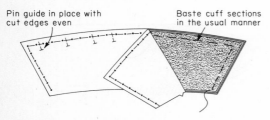

c Follow lines on the guide when facing the cuffs.

FIGURE 7-32 *To prepare and use a stitching guide.*

and the method which has proved best for the particular fabric.

For those costumes that will play leading roles in the wardrobe, professional pressing when the garment is finished is well worth the cost. The large-area irons and the pressure and steam control available at the professional establishment result in a more finished appearance. The cost is relatively nominal.

AIDS TO ACCURACY

Many decorative details are quite simple to do, but they can lower the quality of a garment if they are not accurately done; for example, facing a Peter Pan collar is very simple, but facing it so the two curved ends, which appear so close together, will be identically curved is not simple. Similarly, a patch pocket with rounded edges is simple to stitch in place, but it is not easy to make both curved corners identical or to make four patch pockets with eight identical curved corners. The very fact that features such as collars, cuffs, pockets, and band trims are small units is largely responsible for problems of construction; the slightest inaccuracy is magnified on any small unit. The pattern is accurate; if fabric is cut perfectly along the pattern lines and if seam allowances are perfectly accurate, there will be no inaccuracy. However, it is almost impossible to avoid slight cutting irregularities and variations in seam widths. It is important to realize that a $\frac{1}{16}$-inch mistake on a band with a finished width of $\frac{3}{8}$ inch is a serious mistake that will be very obvious.

The construction of any small unit can be greatly simplified and the effect greatly improved by taking precautions to guarantee accuracy at every stage in the construction sequence.

Make tissue copies to use as stitching guides for faced details

A tissue copy of the pattern piece, with seamlines sketched in and perfected before work proceeds, is a most helpful stitching aid. The tissue guide is pinned over the unit and the pencil lines act as a guide for stitching. After the seam is stitched, the paper, which is weakened by the machine stitches, can be easily lifted or ripped away from the seam. Although tissue stitching guides are simple to make, work must progress in an order that will result in accuracy for the particular unit; the three examples in Figures 7-32 to 7-34 illustrate slight differences in techniques and working order.

To prepare two or more identical guides See Figure 7-32. Sketch *a* shows a cuff pattern on two layers of tissue to make two separate stitching guides for facing the two cuffs. To transfer the seamline of the pattern to both layers of the tissue, drive a pin directly down through all layers and continue making pinpricks every ½ inch along the entire seamline. The sketch shows three pins as a means of illustrating the technique, but under actual working conditions one uses a single pin to pinprick the entire seamline.

Sketch *b* shows the tissue stitching guide spread out. The pinpricks will be visible; connect the pinpricks with a pencil line as shown. Because the pinpricks were made through two layers at once, the two cuffs will be identical. Examine work and correct any slight irregularities in the curve. Sketch *c* shows cuff sections (and the interfacing layer, if one will be used) basted together and prepared for stitching in the usual manner. Pin the stitching guide over the cuff sections, cut edges even, and stitch along the pencil lines on the guide.

The need for stitching guides is even greater if the style line is intricate and if several identical details are involved See Figure 7-33. The sketches show a pocket flap with an intricate style line (convex curve, concave curve, and a point) that must be identical on both halves of the flap. Sketch *a* shows the method of making both halves identical. After one stitching guide is completed, use it to cut and pinprick additional copies, as shown in sketch *b*. This flap design illustrates the great advantage of stitching guides; without them, it would be difficult to stitch both halves of one flap in identical curves, it would be all but impossible to stitch two flaps, identically, and if there were four flaps, as in the sketch, even experienced and talented workers would have difficulty.

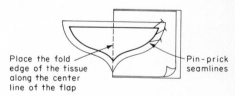

Place the fold edge of the tissue along the center line of the flap — Pin-prick seamlines

a Cut one stitching guide.

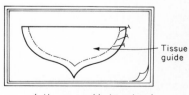

Tissue guide

b Use one guide to cut and pin-prick additional copies.

FIGURE 7-33 *To prepare stitching guides for units with intricate style lines.*

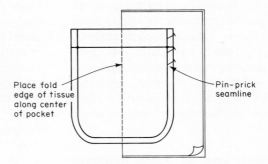

Place fold
edge of tissue
along center
of pocket

Pin-prick
seamline

a Cut one stitching guide and use it to cut
and pin-prick others.

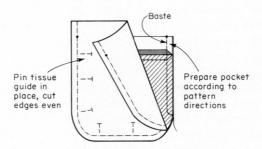

Baste

Pin tissue
guide in
place, cut
edges even

Prepare pocket
according to
pattern
directions

b Lined pockets are handled the same as
faced cuffs.

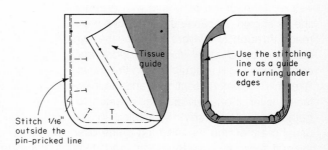

Tissue
guide

Use the stitching
line as a guide
for turning under
edges

Stitch 1/16"
outside the
pin-pricked line

c For unlined pockets.

FIGURE 7-34   *Stitching guides for patch pockets.*

To prepare stitching guides for patch pockets See Figure 7-34. Sketch *a* shows the method for making both halves identical. After one stitching guide is completed, use it to cut and pin-prick additional copies (as shown in sketch *b* of Figure 7-33).

Sketch b—lined pockets These are faced, and the stitching guide is used as it is for any faced unit (same as the cuff in Figure 7-32).

Sketch c—unlined pockets These are handled somewhat differently. In these pockets the seam allowance will be turned under and the tissue guide used to put in a guideline for turning under the edges. Using the pencil lines (which indicate seamlines) as a guide, stitch ⅟₁₆ inch outside the pencil line. Then turn under and baste the edges of the pocket along the seamline, with the stitching guide lines ⅟₁₆ inside the fold as shown.

To ensure accuracy when applying trimming bands

Trimming bands, whether they are parallel strips or shaped sections at the neck and armhole edges, must be perfectly even in width when finished. Because these bands are narrow, the slightest cutting irregularities or variations in seam width will be magnified. The suggestions included in Figures 7-35 and 7-36 emphasize the wisdom of concentrating on finished width rather than on the width of seam allowances.

Trimming bands cut in parallel lines

See Figure 7-35. Sketch *a* shows a parallel band with wobbly cutting lines deliberately exaggerated to emphasize the principle of correcting flaws. Turn under the seam allowance on one long edge, but, at the same time, follow the grain of the

fabric and concentrate on making a ruler-straight line. This means that the seam allowance is the proper width *in general* but that slight cutting irregularities are corrected by allowing some variation in seam width. Sketch *b* illustrates a most important technique. Rather than measuring and turning under the seam allowance on the remaining edge, *measure the finished width of the band pattern* (the width between seamlines) and make a cardboard gauge of the proper width. Then use the gauge as a guide and baste under the remaining edge, working from the right side of the band and paying no attention to the seam allowance. The seam allowance will be the proper width in general, but if there were cutting irregularities, there will be some variation in its width.

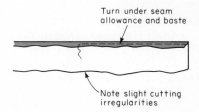

Turn under seam
allowance and baste

Note slight cutting
irregularities

a Baste under one edge, correcting cutting errors.

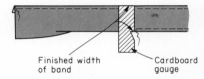

Finished width
of band

Cardboard
gauge

b Measure the finished width of the band when basting under the remaining edge.

FIGURE 7-35 *To ensure accurate parallel lines on trimming bands.*

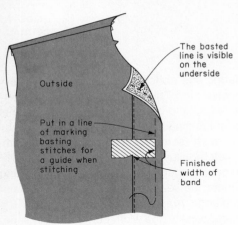

The basted line is visible on the underside

Outside

Put in a line of marking basting stitches for a guide when stitching

Finished width of band

a Secure one edge of the band and measure the finished width to mark remaining seamline.

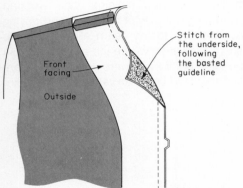

Stitch from the underside, following the basted guideline

Front facing

Outside

b Join facings to band and neck edges, following the basted guideline.

FIGURE 7-36   To ensure accuracy when one edge of an applied band is caught in a seam.

Applied trimming bands caught in with a seam on one edge   See Figure 7-36 . Slight cutting and stitching irregularities can be corrected in a similar manner by applying one edge of the band to the garment and then measuring the finished width of the band to mark a basted guideline on the remaining edge that will be caught in with the seam. Sketch *a* shows a ruler-straight band with one edge basted under and stitched to the garment. If the garment will be interfaced, the interfacing would not include the seam but would be cut all in one piece; this means that the first seam is not visible from the underside. As the seam is stitched (see sketch *b*) the facing covers the seam on the right side and so the original seam is hidden from view on both sides. To ensure accuracy, work must progress in the order illustrated. Measure the finished width of the band pattern (the distance between seamlines) and make a cardboard gauge of the proper width. Using the gauge, put in a row of marking-basting stitches (hand or machine) parallel to the finished edge of the band; make the stitches from the right side through the band and the interfacing (if one will be used) so they are visible from the underside, as shown. When the facing is joined to the front and neck edge, stitch from the underside, following the basted guideline as shown in sketch *b*.

Chapter 8

TAILORING THE SKIRT OR PANTS

Most skirts and pants are very simply designed, while more interesting details are reserved for the jacket or coat. This is unfortunate if much of the time the jacket will be worn open or the skirt and blouse will be worn without the jacket. The suit should be a distinctive, important costume, with or without the jacket. Little details can create desirable interest if they do not dominate the details of the costume or give a cluttered look. In general, these details should be confined to the area under the jacket. The details must be compatible with the character of the jacket and also the blouse.

Several ideas are pictured in Figure 8-1; note that each has a different character, from the tailored plaid blouse with matching belt to the elegant velvet and rhinestone combination. Both visible and concealed waistbands are shown; either waistband may be used in any skirt or pants design. Fabric combinations should be used imaginatively. For example, the cummerbunds pictured may match the major fabric or the blouse fabric or contrast in color and texture to both; the plastic-leather belt section pictured may create interest through mere contrast in texture, or it may be more striking in a contrasting color. A nice idea, which is not pictured, is simply to make the skirt waistband of the blouse fabric; this has a tendency to make the skirt and blouse look somewhat more like a dress. A purchased leather belt is a very simple way to add a finished touch to the costume.

Choices of construction methods influence the work sequence

The directions in this chapter could be simple and brief if it were possible to say "this is the one way to do it." But each fabric and each design makes demands on construction methods, and in addition, each person has her preferences, which must be taken into account. Alternative construction methods are given for several details of the skirt and pants. The choices of methods and an evaluation of each appear in several sections of this chapter. Making these pertinent decisions before beginning work will simplify and speed construction processes. Study the entire chapter at this time, paying particular attention to the evaluations of various construction methods. Decide the following matters:

1   The need for an underlining.
2   The need for seam finishes. This is influenced by whether or not the garment will be lined; and, if it will be lined, by the choice of lining method.
3   The type of zipper construction, the length of the zipper, and the placement of the zipper (side or center seam).
4   The type of construction for the waistband or waistline casing; and, if a casing will be used, the advisability of modifying the pattern for a more fitted effect.
5   The type of hem finish. This is influenced by whether or not the garment will be lined; and, if it will be lined, by the

choice of lining method and the way the lower edge of the lining will be handled.

6 The advisability of lining the garment; and, if it will be lined, by which method. If the couturier method is chosen (as recommended), whether to attach the lining to the hem of the garment or to allow it to hang free.

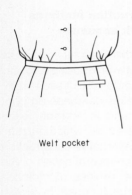

Welt pocket

Belt to match blouse

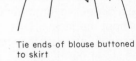

Tie ends of blouse buttoned to skirt

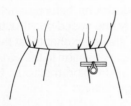

Bound pocket with loop and button closing

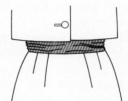

Contrasting cummerbund worn with bolero blouse

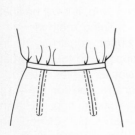

Top-stitched darts

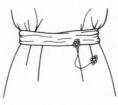

Velvet cummerbund with rhinestone pins and chain

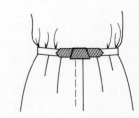

Sections of purchased plastic leather belt stitched to waistband or matching belt

FIGURE 8-1 *Accent details for basic skirts and pants.*

Techniques of presentation This chapter is organized in the most logical sequence for most basic skirts and pants designs. If the garment will be underlined or lined by the simplest method (with the lining caught in with seams, the same as an underlining), the underlining (or lining) sections are always basted in place as the first step of construction—before units of the garment are basted together. The information on underlinings includes cutting directions and construction details; as work proceeds, those who make underlined garments will need to refer back to this special section. Underlinings are not pictured in the remaining sections of the chapter.

The zipper may be in a side position or in a center back position. The construction of the zipper is essentially the same regardless of its position. Each sketch in the zipper series is marked "front" (or "left back") and "back" (or "right back"); the sketches therefore are applicable to either position.

Directions for linings are organized in one section of the chapter, and linings are not pictured in other sketches. If the simplest method of lining is used, it is handled like an underlining and does not complicate construction in any substantial way once structural seams are stitched and trimmed. If the couturier method is chosen (as recommended), some details are done after the zipper is inserted and before the waistband or waistline casing is finished, and others are done after the hem of the garment is finished; special notes point out the proper order of work.

Muslin testing influences decisions

Review the section with a similiar heading on page 99. It is assumed that a muslin test copy was made, as recommended, and that major fitting was done before cutting the garment. In this chapter, the section titled "Basting and Fitting" on page 309 is

very brief; if a test copy was made, fitting at this time is confined to small changes which simply take care of the influence of fabric on fit and other subtle corrections.

If a muslin test copy was not made, major fitting must be done at this time; refer to the appropriate sections of Chapter 6. *Caution: Some of the radical fitting corrections pictured in Chapter 6 can be done only on a test copy.* In most cases, directions include alternative solutions for fitting a garment already cut in good fabric, but the worker must understand that it may not be possible to achieve perfect fit if a test copy was not made.

Review "Make Decisions on Length and Total Proportions" on page 250. Although directions in this chapter include finishing the hem, the effect of skirt length on total proportions cannot be ignored. If a muslin test copy was not made, delay finishing the hem of a skirt and decide on its length later, when it can be tested with the jacket.

DIRECTIONS FOR UNDERLINING SKIRTS AND PANTS

An underlining is not required in most skirts and pants made of typical suiting-weight fabrics, and most readers will prefer to eliminate this step (and therefore the bulk of the underlining) when using firm, medium-weight fabrics. However, there are circumstances under which an underlining is desirable: (1) If the design of the skirt is such that it needs support (the bell silhouette or the A-line skirt), an underlining will give added weight and will, if it has a degree of stiffness, aid in supporting the silhouette; (2) if the figure is more curvaceous than the typical "suit" figure, an underlining, if it is lightweight but slightly crisp, will stiffen the fabric slightly so that it lies more smoothly over rounded contours; (3) if the fabric is of a lighter weight than is desirable for the design (dress woolen used for a dressmaker suit), the addition of an underlining will add apparent weight to make the fabric perform satisfactorily; and (4) if the fabric is too limp or too spongy for the intended purpose, a slightly stiff underlining will improve its character and help to prevent stretching.

To cut underlining sections

Cutting layouts for underlinings may not be pictured on the instruction sheet; if they are not, the instructions will call for cutting underlinings exactly like the major pattern pieces. Although this is not wrong, the few modifications shown in sketch *a* of Figure 8-2 are recommended because they result in less bulk in some areas which do not require extra body. The shaded portion of the pattern designates the area to be underlined.

If the pattern edges are composed of seams or center-fold lines, cut the underlining sections exactly like the pattern piece. If there is a pleat that will be stitched down, cut the underlining in such a way that extra

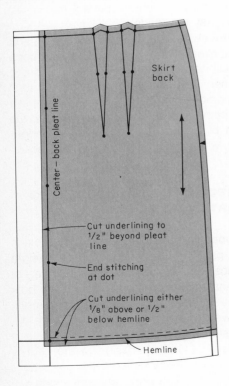

a Method of cutting underlining from a pattern with a stitched-down pleat.

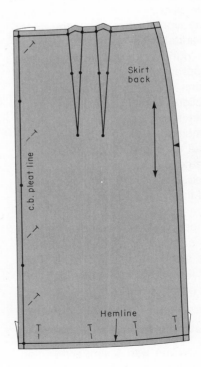

b To prepare pattern pieces for cutting underlining sections.

FIGURE 8-2 *To cut skirt or pants underlinings.*

bulk will not be added in the pleat area. If the underlining is cut to ½ inch beyond the stitching line of the pleat, as shown, it will be caught in with the stitching and will be secure without increasing bulk in the pleat area. Caution: if there is a loose, free-hanging pleat which will not be stitched in place and will hang free from the waistline, the pleat area must be underlined; the underlining, therefore, should be cut exactly like the pattern piece.

There is no need for extra body in the hem area, and if the underlining sections are cut shorter than the major pieces by either method pictured, the hem will be flatter. For most skirts and pants it is better to cut the underlining sections about ⅛ inch above the hemline; this is recommended if the fabric is of suiting weight. If the fabric is very limp (requiring a limp underlining), there may be an advantage in cutting the underlining about ½ inch below the hemline. Then when the hem is folded up, the extra layer will give a desirable firming effect for a better crease at the hemline. If in doubt, cut the underlining ½ inch below the hemline; if the extra layer creates too much bulk after the hem is turned up, the underlining layer can be trimmed to a shorter length at that time.

Sketch b shows the pattern piece prepared for cutting; simply fold under and pin the edges of the pleat and hem which will not be cut of underlining.

Construction techniques

Transfer pattern markings to the underlining sections Most of the construction on simply designed skirts and pants is done from the inside of the garment; therefore pattern markings, marked on the underlining sections, are more helpful than tailor's tacks made in the major fabric. Before removing the pattern piece, mark dots for darts with a pencil. After the

pattern is removed, draw any ruler-straight dartlines or seamlines with a light pencil line. Sketch a in Figure 8-3 shows the darts and the pleat line marked with ruler lines. Any straight seamlines (such as the side seam below the notch level) can be drawn in pencil for stitching guidelines, if desired.

Press center-fold creases from both fabrics before combining corresponding sections The underlining fabric and the fabric of the garment must act as one in the finished garment, and great care must be taken to see that both are absolutely flat before they are basted together.

To combine sections of the garment and underlining Place the garment sections right side down on the table and place underlining pieces over them right side up. See sketch a in Figure 8-3. Pat and smooth pieces in place, bringing cut edges together at seam edges. There will be slight differences in the two pieces due to unavoidable cutting irregularities. Do not force cut edges even; place cut edges together but concentrate on keeping pieces flat. Smooth from the center toward the outer edges and pin from the center toward the sides (note the position of pinheads in the sketch). Use as many pins as necessary to control the two layers well for basting. If any edge of the underlining extends beyond the edge of the garment section, trim off the excess underlining fabric.

Baste all edges in place with stitches placed about ⅜ to ½ inch in from the cut edges, as shown in sketch b; avoid basting directly along seamlines so bastings will not be caught in with machine stitches and can be more easily removed. Work as quickly as possible; stitches need not be perfectly even but they must be small enough to control the edges well.

Baste through the center of dartlines as shown in sketch *b;* shorten the stitches near the dart tip and baste slightly beyond the dart tip as shown. These stitches are especially important because they hold the two layers together so they can act as one as the dart is stitched; darts are more difficult to stitch in underlined garments because of the additional layer of fabric.

To secure edges that will not be caught in with stitching lines Most of the edges of the underlining for a basic skirt or pants will be caught in with stitching lines. One exception is at the pleat line of a stitched-down pleat; the edge of the underlining must be secured below the point where the stitching for the pleat ends. See sketch *a*, Figure 8-3. Make a ¾-inch clip at the level where the stitching will end and turn under ¾ inch below the clip. Secure this edge to the fabric of the garment with hand stitches, as shown in sketch *b*, catching in just a thread of the fabric; these stitches must be invisible from the outside for they will fall right along the pleat edges.

The lower edge of the underlining will

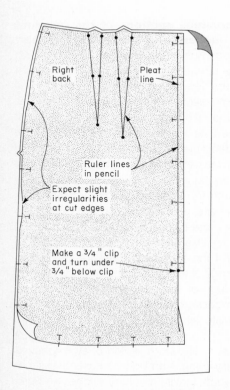

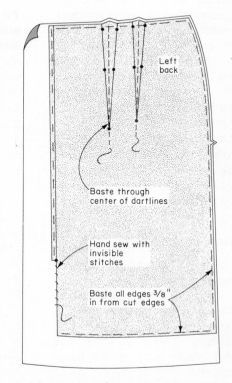

a Pin flat on a table with cut edges even.   *b* Baste along cut edges and through dartlines.

FIGURE 8-3 *Underline units before seams are joined.*

not be caught in with stitching and may need to be secured with hand stitches. It is better to baste these edges at this time, and if it becomes necessary to secure them, to do so when the desired hemline has been permanently established. If the underlining is cut to about ⅛ inch above the hemline. the lower edges will not need to be secured later with blind stitches.

Consider the two fabrics as one and baste the sections together in the usual manner In general, an underlining does not complicate construction and fitting procedures except in two ways:

Basting stitches must be made shorter and secured more frequently with back stitches. This is so because four layers of fabric are involved; firm, secure basting stitches will help prevent layers from pushing out of line at the machine. Test-stitch on four layers to determine the proper pressure on the presser foot; the pressure should be reduced somewhat.

Darts in underlined garments must be handled in a special way. This is shown in Figure 8-4. The problem is to see that the stitching ends at the proper level on the fold edge of the fabric for the garment. Because there are two layers and the more important layer is not visible as the darts are basted and stitched, the stitches must end at the level of the dart point but slightly in from the fold edge of the underlining, as shown. When basting the darts, test to see where stitches must end on the inside (the underlining side) to make sure that they end at the proper level on the right side of the garment. If both fabrics are very sheer, stitches ending a mere 1/32 inch from the fold may be effective, but in most dress-weight fabrics, stitches must end about 1/16 inch from the fold on the inside. In suitings and coatings, this measurement must be about ⅛ and in very heavy coatings, it may be as much as 3/16 inch.

After seams and darts are stitched, stagger the edges to reduce bulk The amount of trimming is dependent on the weight of the two fabrics involved and the raveling qualities of the underlining fabric. See Figure 8-5. The width of the underlining seam should always be trimmed narrower than the full seam width of the

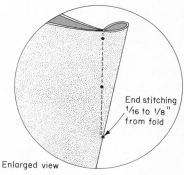

End stitching
1/16 to 1/8"
from fold

Enlarged view

FIGURE 8-4 *To stitch darts in underlined garments.*

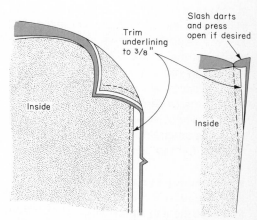

Trim underlining to 3/8"

Slash darts and press open if desired

Inside

Inside

FIGURE 8-5 *Stagger seam edges to reduce bulk in seams and darts.*

garment layers; in this way seam edges are staggered for a flatter seam. The sketch shows underlining seams trimmed to ⅜ inch from the stitching; a ⅜-inch seam allowance on these edges is sufficient to withstand the stress of wearing and, because they will be protected by a wider seam allowance when the seam is pressed open, they will not ravel appreciably. These edges can be trimmed to about ¼ inch if the underlining fabric is firmly woven and if the garment is loosely fitted or the seam is located in a portion of the garment which will get little stress under wearing conditions. The appearance from the inside of the garment will be improved by trimming some width from the underlining layers of seams.

If excess bulk is trimmed from dart areas, the garment will not be as "finished" and attractive from the inside. However, darts pressed to one side are very bulky (the more so with two additional layers of underlining fabric), therefore the need to reduce bulk in dart areas is great. Darts can be slashed and pressed open as shown in Figure 8-5 and the underlining edges trimmed in the same way as seams, but this will necessarily leave raw edges exposed on the inside. This is not a disadvantage in most garments, but there are circumstances when it might be wiser to allow darts to remain bulky; for example, in an unlined jacket, raw edges at darts would be unattractive and it would be wiser to allow them to be somewhat bulky.

Hems require special handling The lower edge of the underlining was basted to the garment in a preliminary step. Before measuring the hem, remove these bastings to allow both layers of fabric to hang "as they will" on the figure. Additional steps are required when measuring and finishing the hem of an underlined garment, as shown in Figure 8-6. Sketch *a* shows a row of pins about 5 inches above the hemline. The assistant who hangs the hem should place one hand inside the skirt and pin the underlining to the skirt, allowing it to hang in a natural manner; see the technique pictured in Figure 10-16 on page 458. The hem is then measured in the usual way, with pins catching through both layers of fabric.

See sketch *b*. Slip a magazine under the portion being worked on; this prevents pins and stitches from catching in additional layers of fabric and makes it possible to keep the two layers (fabric and underlining) flat and smooth in the hem area. Baste along the upper pin line and remove the pins. Control the fabrics to be flat and smooth below the basted line as work progresses.

Although the underlining was cut accurately, it may not be exactly the right length now that the hemline has been permanently established. The sketches illustrate how to correct the length of the underlining; the example shows an underlining ⅛ inch above the hemline, and this step is done in the same way for the underlining which will extend ½ inch below the hemline. Using the measured pin line as a guide, mark a pencil line along the desired cutting line. Carefully trim along this line, with the rounded blade of the scissors next to the garment to prevent accidentally cutting the fabric.

If the underlining is too short, it does not have to be lengthened for most fabrics. However, if the fabric of the garment is so light in weight or color that a shading difference is evident where the underlining ends, an extension must be added. See sketch *c*. Cut a bias strip of underlining fabric of the required width. Lap the strip over the lower edge of the underlining, slip one hand under the underlining layer, and hand sew the two edges together.

If the underlining is cut to ⅛ inch above the hemline, it need not be secured to the garment, for it will hang properly in place. However, if it is cut ½ inch below the hemline (to make a firmer and more pronounced crease in limp fabrics), the lower edge must be secured as shown in sketch d. Hand sew the underlining to the garment directly along the desired hemline; a good method is to work from the right side, making blind stitches along the desired hemline. When the hem is turned up, these stitches will not be visible, because they will fall in the crease of the hem.

BASTING AND FITTING

If a muslin test copy was not made, this is the time to baste the garment for a fitting and to go through the directions in Chapter 6. Keep in mind that some of the more radical corrections shown in that chapter cannot be done now that the pattern has been cut in fabric.

If a muslin test copy was made, it is well to baste and fit again at this time. There will be no major problems, but this extra

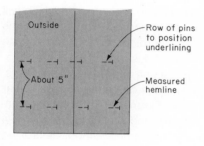

a Extra step when measuring hemline.

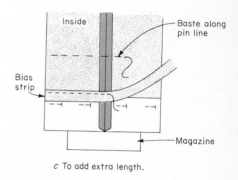

c To add extra length.

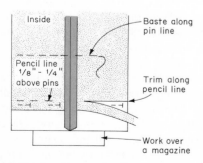

b To trim off excess length.

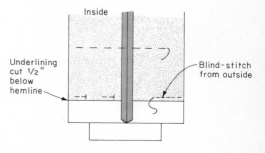

d To secure lower edge.

FIGURE 8-6 *Additional steps for finishing the hem of underlined garments.*

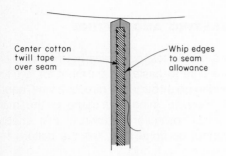

Center cotton twill tape over seam

Whip edges to seam allowance

a Flat, quite secure reinforcement for seams.

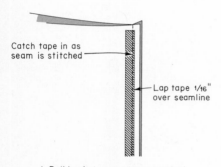

Catch tape in as seam is stitched

Lap tape 1/16" over seamline

b Bulkier but more secure method for utilitarian garments.

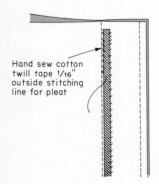

Hand sew cotton twill tape 1/16" outside stitching line for pleat

c To reinforce a pleat line.

FIGURE 8-7 To reinforce seams with cotton twill tape.

fitting will allow for the subtle little changes that make for perfection. If the fabric is very different from the muslin used in the test copy (for example if it is much bulkier, or if it is a knitted fabric which should mold over the figure), this final fitting session is especially important.

REINFORCING SEAMS WITH TAPE

Narrow cotton twill tape (¼ to ⅜ inch wide) is applied to some seams in a tailored garment to prevent edges from stretching and to stiffen certain edges in a jacket or coat. The tape must be preshrunk (by washing) because it shrinks as much as 1 inch or more per yard. Because skirt seams are usually more attractive if they are pliable and lie limply over body contours, the use of tape is limited to those seams which will get great strain under wearing conditions (pleat seams, crotch seams) and to use with spongy fabrics.

The tape can be applied in several ways, depending on the demands of a particular costume. See Figure 8-7. In skirts, the center back seam and the heavy seam of a pleat can be reinforced without destroying the free-flowing lines in the skirt. The crotch seam in pants should be reinforced, especially if the pants will be snugly fitted and made of loosely woven fabric.

The method shown in sketch *a* is recommended for high-quality tailored garments. After the seam is stitched and pressed (and a seam finish applied if one will be used), pin and baste cotton twill tape over the seamline, as shown. Do not stretch the tape when applying it but simply center it over the seam, patting and smoothing it in place. Hand whip both edges in place, controlling stitches to catch through the seam allowance only. This method results in a very flat seam that is sufficiently secure for most purposes.

The method shown in sketch *b* should not be used in high-quality tailoring; it is a stronger reinforcement favored for utilitarian garments. The fact that the tape is caught in with the seam makes for great strength but also creates more bulk (the seam will not press as flat). Note that the tape is not centered over the seam; if it is placed $\frac{1}{16}$ inch over the seamline, the two edges of tape will not fall in the same position and so will be staggered when the seam is pressed open.

See sketch *c*. The stitching line for a pleat will get great strain during wearing, and it should be reinforced, as shown, if the fabric is spongy. Note that the tape is placed just inside the stitching line, in the pleat area, so that hand stitches will fall in the pleat and can be made very secure. The two cut edges of the seam will not be pressed open but will remain in the position shown. Because the seam edges will also stretch under the strain of wearing in loosely woven fabrics, tape can be lapped over the two edges and machine-stitched in place (this is not illustrated).

Because tape will stiffen as well as strengthen, it can be used to solve unique problems. For example, if there is a hollow in the figure at about the 7-inch hip level, tape can be applied to the short segment of seam in that area to stiffen the seam and create a smoother line.

ZIPPER CONSTRUCTION

Study all general information (through page 317) before beginning work. The zipper, like buttonholes and other deceptively simple little details, greatly influences the total effect of the costume; if it is done improperly, even those who do not sew will be aware of its imperfections.

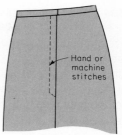

Regulation zipper

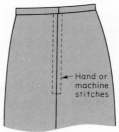

Slot-seam zipper

Invisible zipper

Visible zipper

FIGURE 8-8
Methods of zipper construction.

An evaluation of methods

The regulation and slot-seam methods are used for most garments; the two can be considered almost equally appropriate, but there are subtle differences which influence choices. Although the zipper is a relatively insignificant detail, fashion sometimes favors one method over the other. Four methods are illustrated in Figure 8-8.

Regulation method In this method, one opening edge laps over the other, completely covering the zipper, and only one row of stitches (hand or machine) is visible; the stitches are made ½ to ⅝ inch from the finished edge.

This method is appropriate for all openings and is generally preferred. Although it is somewhat more difficult and more time-consuming to do, it has three great advantages. The zipper is completely hidden from view. Many find it easier to put in one row of stitches ½ inch from the fold than to do two rows closer together, as is necessary in the slot-seam method. Its greatest advantage is that it can be basted in and tested on the figure before stitching is done; this is especially helpful for side-opening edges in fitted skirts and pants which are curved and may require corrections before stitching.

Slot-seam method As the name implies, seam edges are brought together at the center of the zipper teeth and are held in place with two rows of hand or machine stitches placed ¼ inch from each edge. This method is used for short openings (as in the sleeve) and can be used for other openings as well. It is considered less appropriate for side openings than for back openings. Because there is no lap-over, the teeth of the zipper may be visible. However, that disadvantage must be balanced by an advantage; because there is no lap-over, the zipper is less bulky, and therefore this method may be preferred for very heavy or thick fabrics. This method is somewhat simpler than the regulation method, although irregularities are slightly more evident when rows of stitches are so close together. The usual method of construction does not allow for testing on the figure before stitching; for this reason it is better to use this method on straight edges—the curved side edges over the hips are more likely to stretch and require correction before stitching.

"Invisible" method This method must be used only with invisible zippers. It requires a special presser foot, different from a regulation zipper foot. When the zipper is inserted, the opening edges look very much like a pressed-open seam; if insertion is done well, the only evidence of the zipper will be the tiny tear-drop pull. This method is excellent for use with pile fabrics or other thick novelty fabrics which are crushed by rows of stitches. Because the invisible zipper is somewhat less flexible and more difficult to open and close, this method should be confined to front or side openings (it is difficult to adjust in the back without help) and to use with pile fabrics.

Visible method This is simply a method by which the zipper is inserted in such a way that the teeth are exposed. It is used only when the zipper serves a design purpose, such as a fashion accent on pockets. Often the zipper will be further accented with a contrasting color, a prominent decorative pull, and exaggerated by large teeth.

NOTE: To conserve space for comprehensive directions for the regulation and slot-seam method used for the great majority of garments, directions for the invisible and visible methods are not included. Directions for the invisible method are included in the zipper package. Directions for the visible zipper differ with the design; they are included on the instruction sheet.

Factors which determine choices

Fabric Choose flexible-coil types of zippers for limp fabrics and use metal types for heavier fabrics and for very functional costumes. Use the type with polyester tapes for washable garments. Use the invisible type for fine velvets.

Construction method If the slot-seam method will be used, choose a flexible-coil type, preferably fabric-covered, because if the zipper teeth show through the slot, this type is less conspicuous. Choose either type if the regulation method will be used. If the invisible method is used, the zipper must be the invisible type.

Color The color should match or harmonize with the color or colors in the fabric. If the fabric includes several colors, an individual judgment must be made; the zipper can match the dominant color or it can match the lighter of the colors if the fabric is so light in weight or color that darker colors would show through the fabric and be seen as a cloudy or muddy line.

Length The level where the skirt or pants zipper ends influences proportions in a subtle but significant way. It should end at or slightly above the hip level; if it ends higher or lower, the mistake is obvious even to those who are not usually sensitive to proportions. When deciding zipper length, consider both the requirements for dressing and the effect of its length on proportions; favor functional considerations in utilitarian garments and aesthetic considerations in fashion garments.

Skirt and pants zippers will look most attractive if they are 7 inches long, and this length is sufficient to allow a person with an average figure to slide the garment over her hips. Some patterns suggest the 9-inch length, not because it looks as attractive but because that length allows women with small waists and large hips to slide the garment over curvaceous hips. Those with large hips *must use the 9-inch length for shorts and pants;* these same women can use the more attractive 7-inch length in skirts if they are willing to slip skirts over their shoulders. The person with an average figure has no need for the extra length, and if the pattern suggests a 9-inch length, she should use the more pleasing 7-inch length. Short women should avoid the 9-inch length if at all possible, especially in seasons when short skirts are fashionable.

General rules

Carefully study this entire section as a preliminary step and refer back to these details as construction progresses.

1 If the regulation method is used for a side opening, the front edge laps over the back. For back-opening zippers, the lapover can be in either direction. Most designers favor lapping the left back over the right, and for that reason the directions in this text are written and illustrated for a left-over-right lap-over in the back.

2 The zipper edges are basted in place and, for regulation zippers, will be fitted

Regulation zipper — inconspicuous
hand stitches

Slot-seam zipper — prominent hand
stitches

FIGURE 8-9 Zippers finished with hand stitches.

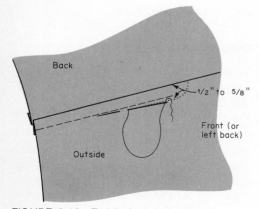

FIGURE 8-10 To blind-stitch the zipper.

before they are stitched. These basting stitches must be very secure (small, ¼-inch stitches reinforced every ½ inch or so) so that the heavy edges are held securely and will not slip during stitching and fitting.

3 Side-opening zippers require more care during construction because the side opening is often a curved line and has a tendency to stretch. It is assumed the opening edges have been stay-stitched if the fabric is loosely woven, and if they have not, they should be stay-stitched before proceeding.

Two flaws in construction may appear after the zipper is basted and tested on the figure, and both are more apt to occur in the hip area of a side-opening garment. One is that the garment may stand away from the body as if it were too large at the level where the zipper ends. This frequently occurs on the figure with a little hollow at the 7-inch hipline. The solution is to make a slight correction in the stitching of the side seam; beginning 2 or 3 inches below the opening, gradually taper in the side seam about 1/16 to 1/8 inch. Then insert the zipper and retest on the figure.

The most common flaw is that the basted-in zipper creates a ridge or ripple (appears to "poke out") right at the end of the zipper. This is a sure sign that the opening edges have stretched as they were basted to the zipper. The solution is to rip out the basting stitches and allow the fabric to ease up on the zipper to counteract the stretch. Curved side edges are more easily stretched than straight edges, and a suggestion for preventing stretch is included in the directions. However, straight opening edges can be stretched in supple fabrics, knits, and any fabric cut on the bias. If the garment tends to ripple or poke out where the zipper ends, the problem is one of stretch and can be remedied by easing the fabric up on the zipper.

4 The permanent stitches may be done

by hand or machine. Contrast the effect of machine stitching in Figure 8-8 with hand stitches in Figure 8-9. Hand stitches are less conspicuous, appear less functional, and add a couturier detail. Hand work requires little if any additional time, and many find this is the simpler way because little irregularities are less obvious. The stitches are spaced ¼ inch apart. They can be done with fine sewing thread so they are hardly visible or made deliberately prominent by using buttonhole twist. Hand stitches can be done so that the zipper is very secure; therefore hand stitching need not be confined to elegant costumes.

See Figure 8-10. Fasten the thread securely in the zipper tape and then bring the needle to the outside. Take a small back stitch and then slip the needle under all thicknesses and bring it up to the right side, spacing stitches ¼ inch apart. Take another small back stitch and proceed. Secure the stitches as frequently as necessary by passing the needle through to the underside and taking several small stitches in the zipper tape. Then bring the needle back to the right side and proceed. The stitches should be reinforced about every inch or two, but they can be reinforced every ½ inch if the garment will get great stress under wearing conditions.

A great variety of effects can be achieved. By using fine thread, very small back stitches, and allowing the stitches to be firm but not taut, the stitches will be almost invisible. By using buttonhole twist, a slightly longer back stitch, and pulling the thread tight enough to make an indentation in the fabric, stitches will be more prominent.

5 Stitching at the machine is an important step because this part of the construction is visible. Some general rules are illustrated in Figure 8-11.

Always machine-stitch from the bottom up to prevent pushing the fabric into a ripple at the lower end. Note in the case

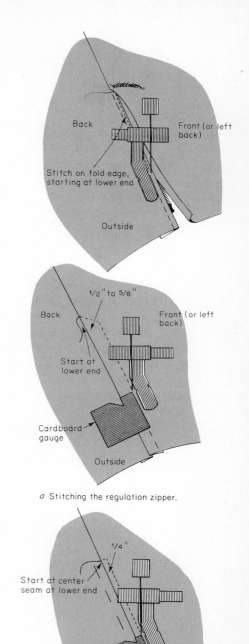

a Stitching the regulation zipper.

b Stitching the slot-seam zipper.

FIGURE 8-11 *Techniques for machine stitching.*

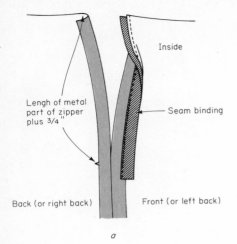

Lengh of metal part of zipper plus 3/4"

Inside

Seam binding

Back (or right back)

Front (or left back)

a

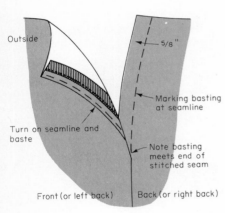

Outside

5/8"

Marking basting at seamline

Turn on seamline and baste

Note basting meets end of stitched seam

Front (or left back)

Back (or right back)

b

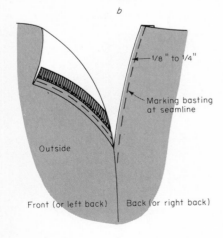

1/8" to 1/4"

Marking basting at seamline

Outside

Front (or left back)

Back (or right back)

c

FIGURE 8-12 *Regulation method—preliminary steps.*

of the slot-seam zipper (sketch *b*) that this means the zipper must be stitched in two operations rather than in a continuous stitching.

A zipper foot must be used, and the adjustable foot, which can be moved from one side of the needle to the other, is recommended. Notice in sketch *a* that the foot is on the left side of the needle as the back edge is stitched and on the right side as the front edge is stitched. The zipper foot must be away from the teeth of the zipper. Because the zipper foot has only one prong, it is slightly less steady than the regular stitching foot. It is well to test-stitch to get the feel of the zipper foot.

Test-stitch to check length of stitch and tension of the machine. Be sure there is sufficient thread on the spool and bobbin before proceeding.

The zipper must be stitched from the outside, but by turning the garment wrong side out, the stitching can be done more easily on the right side. There is no sketch to illustrate this position, but when the garment is turned wrong side out, it will be obvious how this simplifies machine stitching on the top side.

The zipper should be zipped up while machine work is done because this keeps the whole area in better control.

Notice that a cardboard gauge is used to ensure even top-stitching. Many people find this is a greater help than following basting lines. The gauge must be held firmly in position before stitching; it cannot be moved while the machine is moving. It is a good idea to practice stitching with the gauge to learn how it can best be handled; remove the top thread from the needle and practice on the garment for best results.

Notice in sketch *a* that the front edge of the regulation zipper is flipped up so the stitching is placed right along the fold of fabric on the back edge, just 1/16 inch from the fold. Notice that this machine stitching falls inside the marking-basting line; thus the stitching will not show when the garment is worn.

Regulation method

All sketches are labeled for the front and back pieces for a side-opening zipper, and the captions "right back" and "left back" are included for back-opening zippers. Read all preceding information in this chapter. The zipper is put in when all seams and darts have been stitched and pressed and before the waistband is applied.

Preliminary steps See sketch *a* in Figure 8-12. If the usual visible waistband will be used, the opening edges must be ¾ inch longer than the coil or metal portion of the zipper, as illustrated in the sketches. Make adjustments on the seam if necessary. If an inner or concealed waistband will be used, the opening edges must be 1½ inches longer than the coil or metal part. If a waistline casing will be used, the upper end of the zipper will be placed ½ inch below the waist level; therefore the length of the opening edges must be adjusted accordingly.

If the seam has been let out, there will not be sufficient seam allowance on the front edge; the ⅝-inch allowance is a minimum. If necessary, extend the seam allowance as follows:

Cut a piece of seam binding ½ inch longer than the opening. Lap it ¼ inch over the raw front edge and stitch it in place with stitches very close to the edge of the binding. The seam allowance on the back edge will be wide enough.

See sketch *b*. Turn the front opening edge to the inside along the seamline and baste in place. Press. Run a marking-basting line along the seamline of the back.

See sketch *c*. Turn under the back-opening edge ⅛ inch (or ³⁄₁₆ to ¼ inch in spongy or heavy fabrics) beyond or outside the seamline and baste in place. Press. Hold work in the position shown in this sketch and see that it looks just like the sketch; the marking basting, designating the seamline, will be visible.

Finishing steps See sketch *a* in Figure 8-13. The location of the upper end of the zipper is dependent on the waistline finish. For the traditional waistband, place the tab ¾ inch below the upper cut edges as shown in the sketches. For an inner or concealed band, place the tab 1½ inches below the upper cut edges. For a waistline casing, place the tab ½ inch below the waist level.

Lap the back-opening edge over the zipper with the fold edge close to the zipper teeth. This is a very helpful trick for side-opening zippers: Hold the zipper and the garment in the position it will take on the body. From the waist down, the body curves outward, and the zipper and garment must curve that way too. Study the particular curve of the body, and then hold the zipper in that curve and pin the back edge in place. Because the side edges of the garment are often bias, there is a great danger of stretching the opening edges. To avoid stretching the edges, it is a good idea to ease the garment slightly (perhaps ⅛ inch) while pinning it. Baste the edge with small, firm stitches.

If, when the garment is fitted, there is a ripple directly below the zipper, return to this step and rebaste, easing up the fabric even more as it is pinned to the zipper.

See sketch *b*. Lap the front edge over the zipper so that the fold edge (which is the seamline) meets the marking-basting line on the back (which is the seamline). Notice that the front laps over the back and hides the zipper completely. As in the back, hold the garment and zipper in the position it

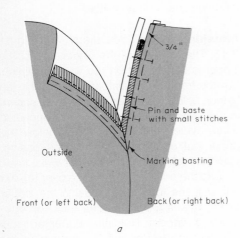

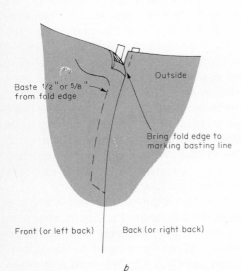

FIGURE 8-13 Regulation method—finishing steps.

will take on the body (an outward curve if it is a side-opening zipper) and pin the front edge in place. Baste with firm, small stiches about ½ inch from the seamline. Have the stitches take a diagonal direction at the lower end.

Fit the garment. See that the zipper lies flat on the body. The most common defect of zipper construction is the formation of a ripple at the lower end. This means the opening edges have stretched. If this happens, rebaste the zipper, easing the garment as needed.

Review points 4 and 5 on page 314 and do permanent stitches by hand or machine as desired.

Slot-seam method

Study the general information from the beginning of the chapter through page 317. The zipper is put in when all seams and darts have been stitched and pressed and before the waistband is applied.

See sketch a in Figure 8-14. If the usual visible waistband will be used, the opening edges must be ¾ inch longer than the coil or metal portion of the zipper, as illustrated in the sketches. Make adjustments on the seam if necessary. If an inner or concealed band will be used, the opening edges must be 1½ inches longer than the coil or metal portion. If a waistline casing will be used, the upper end of the zipper will be placed ½ inch below the waist level; therefore the length of the opening edges must be adjusted accordingly.

From the inside, pin the opening edges together and baste along the seamline with small, firm hand stitches or, better still, with a long machine stitch. Press the seam open.

See sketch b. Place the zipper on the inside of the garment with the right side of the zipper to the wrong side of the garment. Place the tab end of the zipper at the proper level: ¾ inch down from the cut edge for a traditional waistband, 1½ inches down from the cut edge for an inner band, or ½ inch below the waist level for a waistline casing. Pin the zipper in place, carefully centering the seamline over the teeth.

From the outside, baste the zipper in place with stitches about ¼ inch from the seamline. Use small, firm stitches.

Review points 4 and 5 on page 314 and do permanent stitches by hand or machine. Remove the basting stitches to release the opening edges. Test on the figure. If corrections are required, the permanent stitches must be removed and replaced later after corrections have been made.

SPECIAL NOTE: If the couturier or shell method of lining will be used, see "Construction Details—Couturier or Shell Method" on page 342 and do the preparatory steps (Figure 8-31) at this time. Also finish the free edges over the zipper (directions in either Figure 8-32 or Figure 8-33) before applying the waistband or finishing the waistline casing. Once the waistline and zipper edges are in place, the lining does not complicate the waistband or waistline casing in any way; the two layers simply act as one, and construction proceeds in the usual way. Linings are not pictured in the waistband and waistline casing series of sketches. However, seamlines and dartlines will be visible and can be matched to corresponding positions on the waistband; they simply show as single lines rather than the triple lines visible in an unlined garment.

WAISTBANDS AND WAISTLINE CASINGS

The traditional waistband should look flat, firm, and somewhat stiff, and it must prevent stretch under the stress of wearing. The waistline can be finished with an inner

or concealed waistband which prevents stretching as effectively but need not be as stiff because it is narrower and will hold its shape more easily. The fashion for pants

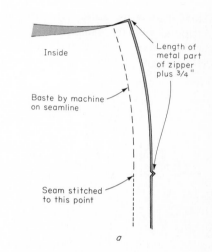

a

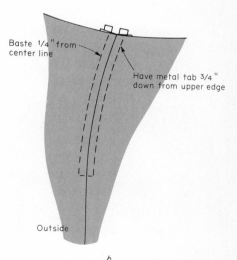

b

FIGURE 8-14   The slot-seam method.

suits is responsible for another type of finish—a waistline casing for elastic, comparable to the finish on pajama pants.

An evaluation of methods

The interfaced waistband   This is most often included with the pattern directions because it is the simplest and quickest method for visible waistbands; the pattern directions are given in sufficient detail and will not be included in this text. This method is not recommended for fashion sewing; it is a bulky construction (in all but lightweight fabrics) and furthermore most interfacing fabrics will not prevent buckling and stretching in a snugly fitted waistband. The method is used in most ready-to-wear, not because it is best but because of the speed and ease of its construction.

The stiffened waistband   This, shown in sketch a of Figure 8-15, is strongly recommended for all visible waistbands in high-quality fashion garments. The degree of stiffness can be controlled by the stiffen-

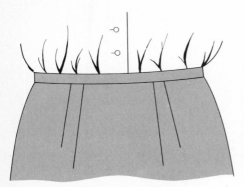

a Traditional stiffened waistband gives a somewhat tailored effect.

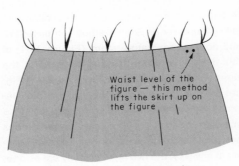

Waist level of the figure — this method lifts the skirt up on the figure

b Inner or concealed waistband gives a dressier effect.

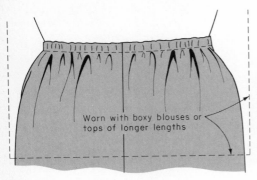

Worn with boxy blouses or tops of longer lengths

c Traditional casing with no dart fitting and no zipper opening.

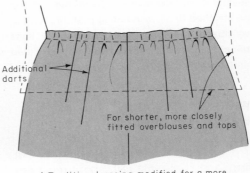

Additional darts

For shorter, more closely fitted overblouses and tops

d Traditional casing modified for a more fitted garment.

FIGURE 8-15 *Construction methods evaluated.*

ing material and by increasing the number of layers. It will retain its shape and will never stretch. Being trim and flat, it provides a firm base for adding decorative belts, etc. Like all quality construction, it requires additional time; but the extra minutes are well rewarded.

A visible band, which must necessarily look somewhat functional, gives a more tailored or casual effect than the inner band described below. However, the width of the stiffening will influence the effect of a visible waistband; a narrow (¾ inch) band will give a delicate and more decorative effect for elegant costumes, while the traditional width (1½ inches) is appropriate for utilitarian uses.

The inner or concealed waistband
This, shown in sketch b of Figure 8-15, is made of a strip of grosgrain or decorative ribbon turned to the inside and tacked to seams. This method creates less bulk than other methods; therefore it is a wise choice for use with unusually heavy fabrics. Contrast the effect of this band with the visible band; the skirt looks less functional, so this method is appropriate for very softly tailored garments. See the dots which indicate the waist level of the figure. The inner band is made of narrow ribbon which should not exceed ¾ inch in width. When the ribbon is turned to the inside, the lower edge of the ribbon will rest along the waist of the figure and therefore the skirt will be lifted above the waist level on the figure. If wide ribbon is used, the skirt is forced up too high on the figure.

Waistline casings These are made by turning under a self-facing at the waistline edges and inserting elastic in the casing. The typical waistline casing is shown in sketch c. Usually the garment has no dart fittings and there is no need for a zipper opening because the waist is large enough

to slip over the hips. The area between the waist and the hips is therefore somewhat bulky, but that is no disadvantage if a boxy hip-length top or jacket will complete the costume. Commercial patterns (and ready-to-wear pants) are made for this type of casing because of its simple construction.

Sketch d pictures the same type of garment modified to include some dart fitting; note that some (but not all) of the fullness has been eliminated with darts. The area between the waist and the hips is less bulky and looks slimmer; consequently a shorter, more fitted blouse or jacket can be worn. Directions for modifying the typical pattern and doing the additional construction details required are included in Figures 8-22 through 8-24. A zipper will be required if these modifications are made.

In addition to being easy and quick to construct when used with pants or shorts, the elasticized casing is an aid to comfort. It allows pants or shorts to slide down from the waist when the wearer bends or sits, thereby providing the extra length needed to prevent strain on the fabric. By modifying the typical pattern for the trimmer effect shown in sketch d of Figure 8-15, it is possible to extend the uses of casings and gain the advantage of comfort in a greater variety of designs.

A waistline casing need not be hidden; the casing and the puckered effect of the elastic is not unattractive, and it can provide fashion interest. For example, a visible casing used with a gathered skirt adds a novel touch to a standard design.

The stiffened waistband

To determine the finished width Experiment with strips of fabric and consider the effect of the waistband on proportions of the design and the figure. The usual 1½-inch width is appropriate for functional and casual costumes, while a narrow width (as narrow as ¾ inch) is very attractive for

Single layer of pellon.

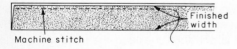

Folded layer of pellon.

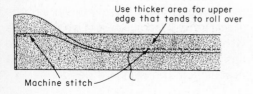

A suggestion for wider belts.

FIGURE 8-16 To decide on the degree of stiffness and prepare the stiffening strip.

elegant costumes. Because the band will rest at the waist and extend above, the person who is very curvaceous directly above the waist will be more comfortable in a narrow band, while those with slim midriffs can wear wide bands comfortably. If the skirt is very heavy because of style fullness added for gathers or pleats, a wider (1½ to 2 inches) waistband will give better support; in addition, the waistband must be fitted more snugly (made slightly shorter) when it must support greater weight.

To determine the degree of stiffness required Heavy pellon or lightweight beltings are the best stiffening materials. Pellon is recommended because it provides the necessary body and can be handled more easily; belting is more difficult to pin and baste. See Figure 8-16. The stiffening strip can be a single or double layer, depending on the amount of stiffness desired. The lower sketch shows a way of adding extra stiffness to the upper half of a wide band where buckling is apt to occur; the lower half will be thickened by the seam as the band is stitched to the garment.

To prepare a stiffening strip Cut a strip of stiffening about 4 inches longer than the waist (it will be trimmed accurately later) and mark off parallel lines for the desired finished width; allow sufficient width for a single or double layer as desired. If more than one layer is used, fold the stiffening and stitch edges together as shown in Figure 8-16.

To determine the length and establish matching points See Figure 8-17. The waistband must have an overlap on one end. This overlap, if put on the back edge of the waistband, will lap under the front edge and will result in a clean line as shown in the upper sketch; this is the preferred method. The extension can be put on the front edge of the band, which will result in the effect shown in the second sketch; the line at the side edge is not as clean, and although this method is not wrong, it is not recommended. For a back-opening skirt, the extension is added to the right back for a left-over-right lap-over.

The waistband can be fastened with skirt hooks, which add no detail at all to the outside of the garment and which result in an uncluttered look that is always appropriate. The waistband can be fastened with buttons, as illustrated, to achieve the desired effect.

Finished edges of the waistband can be top-stitched ¼ inch from all edges if desired. Compare the upper sketch with others in Figure 8-17 to see that top-stitching is most appropriate with casual costumes.

The length of the waistband can be determined and matching points established in three ways: by transferring markings from the commercial pattern, by perfecting measurements on the temporary waistband (prepared when the garment was muslin-tested), or by preparing a waistband at this time. Persons who have not altered the waist of the pattern or made any fitting changes at the waist can mark the length and establish matching points by transferring markings on the commercial pattern to the stiffening strip. However, very few women will have made no changes at the waist, and it must be understood that if any change was made at the waist (no matter how small), every matching point will have been affected. For this reason, the method shown in Figure 8-19 will be more accurate for the great majority of figures.

Review "Establish the Seamline at the Waist and Make a Temporary Waistband Guide" on page 233. Those who did not make a temporary guide earlier must do this fitting at this time, using the permanent stiffening strip (as prepared in Figure 8-16).

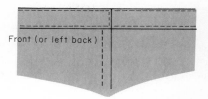

Extension for lap-over on back edge of waistband — preferred method

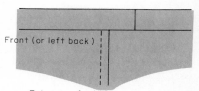

Extension for lap-over on front edge of waistband — acceptable but not recommended

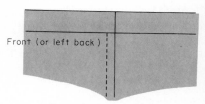

Fastening with skirt hooks — safe choice for any use

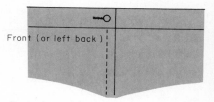

Fastening with machine — worked buttonhole and button for tailored garments

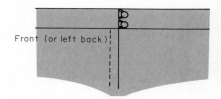

Fastening with loops and buttons for decorative effects

FIGURE 8-17 Construction alternatives.

See Figure 8-18. Wear the blouse or sweater to be worn with the costume as shown. Wrap the prepared strip around the waist to a snug but comfortable posi-

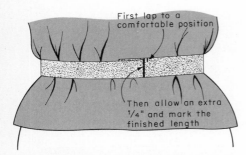

Lap the stiffening strip around the figure to determine the desired finished length.

FIGURE 8-18 *To establish the length of the waistband stiffening.*

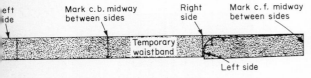

a For a side-opening zipper – to establish center positions.

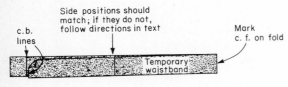

b For a back-opening zipper – to perfect measurements.

FIGURE 8-19 *To perfect measurements on the temporary waistband.*

tion (think of comfort over several hours) and then allow an extra ¼ inch (or as much as ½ inch if the fabric is bulky and there are pleats or gathers in the garment); the extra allowance allows for the thickness of fabric as the band is applied, and after it is applied it will feel as it did before the extra allowance was added. Put the garment on the figure and pin the band over the waistline of the garment; adjust ease in such a way that all vertical lines fall in plumblines. Mark matching points according to directions on page 233.

To perfect measurements on the temporary waistband Figure 8-19 gives directions for perfecting measurements on a side-opening or back-opening garment. After these measurements are perfected, the temporary band can be used as a permanent band if it is in good condition and is the desired width; alternatively, it can be used as a guide in preparing the permanent waistband.

Sketch *a* pictures a waistband for a side-opening garment. The two left-side positions and the right-side position were marked when the muslin copy was fitted. Center lines must be located midway between the two sides; to do this, fold one side position over to the other, as shown, and mark the center positions on the fold edge. Mark the center back position in the same way.

Sketch *b* pictures a waistband for a back-opening garment. The center back positions and the side positions were marked when the muslin copy was fitted. The center-front line must be located midway between the center-back lines; to do this, fold the band with center-back lines matching as shown, and mark the center front on the fold edge. The marks for the side positions should fall in the same position; but they probably will not fall perfectly in position, because they were not measured

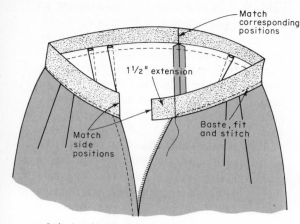

a Stitch stiffening over the waistline edge, matching corresponding points.

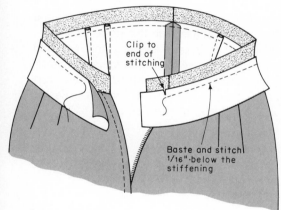

b Baste and stitch fabric over stiffening strip.

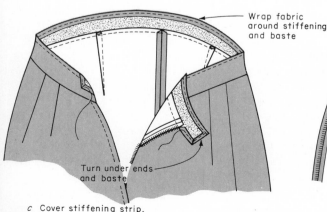

c Cover stiffening strip.

d Finish underside with ribbon.

FIGURE 8-20 To apply and cover a stiffened waistband.

accurately when the muslin copy was fitted. If they miss slightly, as illustrated, establish the permanent side positions midway between the two lines (note the position of the arrow).

Construction details See Figure 8-20. Insert the zipper before applying the waistband. If the couturier or shell method of lining will be used, insert the lining before applying the waistband. See sketch a. Lap the stiffening over the waistline edge, placing the lower edge along the seamline; match side and center positions. Baste in place and test on the figure before stitching; make any fitting corrections indicated. Stitch the stiffening to the skirt with stitches very close to the lower edge.

Cut a strip of fabric about 2 inches longer and 1 inch wider than the stiffening. Place the fabric band over the garment, right sides together, allowing it to lap just ½ inch over the lower edge of the stiffening as shown in sketch b; allow a seam allowance at each end for turning under edges.

Baste and stitch just below the edge of the stiffening. Clip to the end of the stitching at the lapline as shown.

See sketch *c*. Wrap the fabric snugly around the stiffening and baste under all remaining edges. If top-stitching is desired, top-stitch ⅛ to ¼ inch from all edges of the waistband at this time.

To finish the raw inside edges, use a strip of grosgrain or decorative ribbon about ¼ inch narrower than the waistband as shown in sketch *d*. Holding the band in a curve similar to the curve of the figure, pin the ribbon under the band and whip it to the seam allowances. Fasten the band with skirt hooks.

The inner or concealed waistband

The width of the ribbon band This should not exceed ½ to ¾ inch for reasons stated on page 321. The band should be made of a very firm-quality ribbon (grosgrain or decorative) because it must prevent stretching; a strip of lightweight pellon can be stitched to the underside to strengthen the ribbon if desired.

To determine the length and establish matching points Follow directions in Figure 8-19 with the one exception shown in sketch *a* of Figure 8-21. Allow an extra 2 inches at each end of the ribbon for turning under and hemming the ends. Turn under and hem the extra allowance at each end before applying the ribbon to the garment. The sketches show a side opening, but the ribbon can be marked for a back opening if desired.

Special directions for placement of the zipper Details are included in the zipper directions. The zipper must be placed somewhat lower to allow sufficient space for turning under the ribbon. If the couturier or shell method of lining will be used, insert the lining before applying the waistband.

Construction details See sketch *b* in Figure 8-21. Lap the ribbon to the seamline on the garment, matching corresponding side and center positions. Baste in place and test on the figure before stitching; make any fitting corrections indicated. Stitch the ribbon to the garment with stitches close to the edge.

Turn the ribbon to the inside, rolling the seam about ⅛ inch to the inside as shown. Pressing may keep the band in place, but usually it is wise to tack it to vertical darts and seams as shown. Hand sew the front end in place with invisible stitches. Fasten the band with a skirt hook.

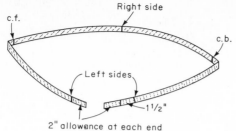

a Cut ribbon and establish matching points.

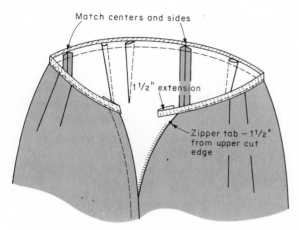

b Stitch ribbon to waistline edges,
corresponding points matching.

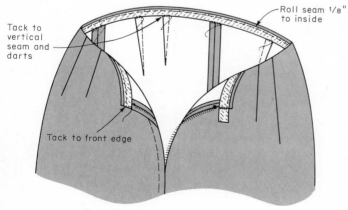

c Turn ribbon to inside and tack into place.

FIGURE 8-21   The inner or concealed waistband.

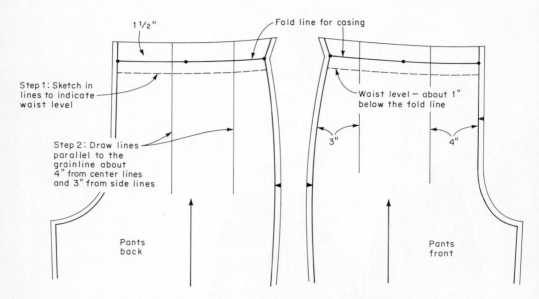

a Typical pattern with no dart fitting — zipper not required.

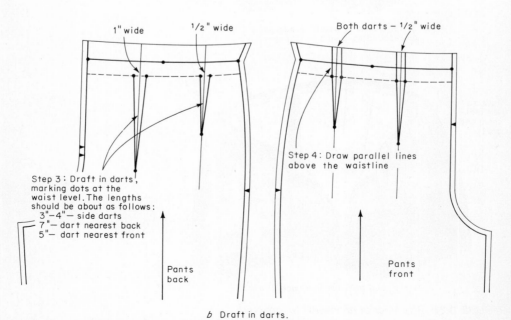

b Draft in darts.

FIGURE 8-22 *To modify the traditional pattern for a more fitted effect.*

Waistline casings

The typical pattern for a garment with a waistline casing is shown in sketch *a* in Figure 8-22. There is little shaping in the pattern above the hipline and the excess fullness at the waist is gathered in by the elastic. Note the waistline level shown in a dashed line; the pattern will have some marking to indicate the waist level. The extra height above the waist level allows for the width of the casing (usually about 1 inch) and for a self-facing of the same width plus an additional ½ inch for a turn-under.

To modify the traditional pattern for a more fitted effect   See Figure 8-22, sketch *b*. By drafting in darts to eliminate some of the excess width in the area above the hip level, elasticized casings can be used in a greater variety of garments; see "Waistline Casings" on page 321. Follow the steps illustrated in the sketches. The width of the darts indicated stated in step 3 will not *and should not* result in a snug-fitting garment; some fullness will remain to be held in with the elastic and to give a slightly eased effect (as in sketch *d* in Figure 8-15) The darts are spaced differently than they would be if they were to be visible as the garment is worn; this spacing distributes the shape well on the figure and removes the excess fullness in a way that results in smoother lines under a blouse or jacket.

See step 4. By drawing the dartlines parallel above the waist level, the casing will fit perfectly flat when folded under. Because darts have decreased the waist measurement, the garment will require a zipper. Mark a point on the side seamline where the stitching must end to allow for a zipper (not illustrated); the zipper tab must be placed about ½ inch below the waistline level, so measure from that position and allow for a zipper of the desired length (7 inches is ample). The zipper can be inserted in the center-back or the center-front seam if desired.

Construction techniques See Figure 8-23. The suggestions illustrated can be used with traditional or dart-fitted garments. Sketch *a* shows darts slashed and pressed open in the casing area. Top-stitch all cut edges in place as shown, then trim off any excess width by trimming very close to the stitching; this will keep edges in place and make it easier to slide elastic through the casing.

The inner edge can be handled in two ways shown in sketches *b* and *c*; in either case the finished width of the casing should be about ¼ inch wider than the elastic to be used. Use a zigzag stitch if possible, although the stitching can be done with a standard machine stitch.

NOTE: **In the traditional casing, a short opening for inserting the elastic is left free as the casing is stitched; after the elastic is inserted, the free edges are then secured by hand. If the garment will be fitted and have a zipper opening, the elastic is inserted through the ends of the casing as shown in Figure 8-24.**

Additional steps for a fitted garment with a zipper opening See Figure 8-24. Cut a strip of elastic several inches longer than will be required to reach around the body. One end of the elastic will be used as an extension (like the extension for overlapping the traditional waistband) and should be covered with fabric. Cover one end for a length of about 1½ inches as shown in sketch *a*. Insert the elastic through the casing, allowing the covered end to extend 1 inch beyond the back edge (for a side-opening zipper) or beyond the right back edge (for a back-opening zipper). Stitch that end securely in place. Pull the elastic

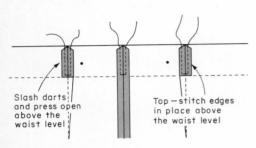

Slash darts and press open above the waist level

Top—stitch edges in place above the waist level

a To keep seams in place as elastic is inserted.

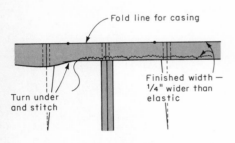

Fold line for casing

Turn under and stitch

Finished width — ¼" wider than elastic

b Turn under raw edges if fabric ravels.

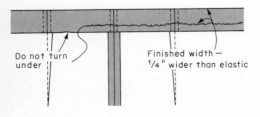

Do not turn under

Finished width — ¼" wider than elastic

c Leave the edges of the casing raw if fabric is knitted.

FIGURE 8-23 Construction techniques.

through the casing and test on the figure to determine the proper length. Then securely stitch the elastic to the front opening end, as shown, and trim off the excess elastic. Fasten the casing with a skirt hook.

To control fullness at the waist and prevent the elastic from buckling Elastic has a tendency to buckle with extended hard use. To prevent this and to keep the fullness controlled properly on the figure, the elastic can be tacked to the casing at several points. After the casing is finished and skirt hooks are in place, put the pants on the figure and adjust the ease or gathers to best fit body curves. View the figure from side view and adjust gathers so that the side seamlines hang in plumblines; pin. Then adjust the ease or gathers so that center lines are located properly on the figure and pin. If no ease or gathers is desired near the center of the figure, smooth the fabric along the casing for approximately 3 inches on each side of center lines and place pins at those points; this keeps fullness controlled on the sides of the figure and is more flattering to most figures. Tack the upper and lower edges of the elastic to the casing at these control points. This can be done with firm hand stitches or with machine stitches.

HEM FINISHES

The finished length of all units of a costume and the width of the hem itself greatly influence the success of the costume. Hastily made decisions and careless construction will be very evident, and the worker must guard against a tendency to relax standards when the garment is so nearly finished. The inexperienced often underestimate the length of time required to do a professional hem; the hem may take less than an hour in a straight skirt (especially if it will

be a hem with raw edges), and it may require several hours in a circular skirt finished with a binding. Regardless of the time required, the hem is worthy of thoughtful decisions and careful work. Study all general information through page 334 before beginning work.

General information

Factors influencing the finished length The length of the costume is often the most easily recognized characteristic of fashion; therefore, those who do

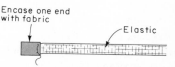

a Encase one end of elastic to form an extension for lapping.

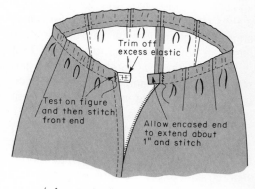

b Insert elastic and stitch securely.

FIGURE 8-24 *Additional steps for a casing with a zipper opening.*

must be somewhat longer to create pleasing proportions. Test several lengths and study each one carefully before making a final decision.

couturier sewing must honor current fashion to a certain extent; this is especially true in seasons when only one length is fashionable. The subtleties of fashion cannot be ignored even in seasons when fashions are permissive. For example, the fashions of the early 1970s, characterized by the greatest variety of lengths in the history of fashion, were not as permissive as they appeared. For example, the full-length dress was ankle-length and not floor-length, as full-length dresses are in other seasons. Similarly, ankle-length pants, popular until about 1972, were outdated by 1973 when fashionable pants were one or two inches longer and many were designed to drag along the floor. Other factors must be considered, and although individual decisions may differ slightly from current fashion, the difference must not be so great that the costume loses its fashion appeal.

The finished length of the costume can be adjusted to create more pleasing proportions on the figure. A longer length makes the torso look longer and therefore slimmer, but this advantage must be balanced against the fact that the longer length makes legs appear shorter. Similarly, shorter lengths must be studied for their effect on both the torso and the legs. Test out several lengths, carefully studying the effect of each one, and make the final decision not on just one figure irregularity but on overall proportions.

The lines of the design influence length to some extent. In general, flared, gathered or pleated skirts can be somewhat shorter than straight skirts. Designs with long, unbroken, vertical lines can be somewhat shorter, while designs with prominent horizontal lines (band trims, skirt yokes, etc.)

Factors influencing the width of the hem Fashion and precedent set certain standards. There are logical and scientific reasons why hems are made a certain width; the designers of quality ready-to-wear must consider the same factors, and therefore many of them use approximately the same hem width. And so, in a way, certain widths become fashionable. There is another way that fashion enters the picture: hem widths should be in good proportion to the total length of the garment (the hem in a bolero jacket is not as wide as the hem in a skirt of midcalf length), and so hems are narrower when very short skirts are fashionable than when skirts are long.

The type of fabric makes certain demands. One of the purposes of the hem is to add weight to the garment to make it hang well; therefore it follows that a wider hem will create more weight for the garment made of lightweight fabric. In general, heavy fabric requires hems up to ½ inch narrower than the average widths stated on page 251 and lightweight fabric demands hems up to ½ inch wider than average.

The type of garment is a factor. The particular type of garment calls for a certain hem width simply because of precedent based on all the factors mentioned in this section.

The height of the wearer is a consideration. If the hem is to create good proportions with the total length of the garment, a slightly wider-than-average hem width can be used for the tall girl and a slightly narrower-than-average hem width for the short girl. A good general rule is this: Plan for a hem of (approximately) average width; however, the person who is 5 feet tall can make her hems about ½ inch narrower than average, and the person who is 5 feet 9 inches tall or taller can add about ½ inch to hem widths.

The recommended hem allowances stated on page 251 are estimates based on the figure of average height (about 5 feet 6 inches tall). These rules are good guidelines, but each problem must be given individual consideration. The discerning person must keep up with trends on the high-quality ready-to-wear market.

SPECIAL NOTE: **If the couturier or shell method of lining will be used, the lower edge of the lining must be pinned up in a fairly wide hem so that it will be out of the way; it should not be visible as the length of the garment is established. The assistant who measures the hem must take care not to catch in the lining as she works. Later, when the hem in the garment is finished, the lower edge of the lining will be measured and turned up in a separate operation.**

Hanging or measuring the hem Wear the undergarments and shoes that will be worn with the costume. Before putting on the garment, turn up the hem allowance and pin in place. This length may not be correct, but it will help to establish the desired length. Put the garment on and be critical of the length. Test other lengths by turning up slightly more or less hem (do not measure—this is just an estimate). The hem will be measured by this estimated line.

The hem can be measured with a yardstick, an L square, or a pin marker; the pin marker is recommended. Have an assistant hang the hem. She should test along the estimated hemline and find a "happy medium" hemline (the estimated hem will not be entirely accurate). Ideally the assistant should work at eye level; the best method is for the assistant to sit and the wearer to stand on a table.

Pins should be put in every 4 or 5 inches for a straight skirt and every 3 or 4 inches for a flared skirt. It is of no advantage to use more pins, and there is an added danger that a longer length of time spent will result in less accuracy because the wearer gets weary and unsteady.

The measured hemline must be tested for appearance. The garment can be taken off and the wearer can pin up the hemline and then dress again, or the assistant can pin up the hem as she finishes her work. This latter method is really easier unless the skirt is very full or flared or the hem is very wide. In either case, put pins in at right angles to the hemline so that the hem falls in a limp, natural manner, and use a sufficient number of pins to keep the hem in the proper position.

Be critical—look for optical illusions
The hemline of skirts must appear to be parallel to the floor, but the fact that it has been measured parallel to the floor is no assurance it will look even. *And the important issue is that the hemline must* look *even.* Sometimes, for elusive reasons of figure or posture or design, a garment which really is parallel to the floor appears uneven. If this happens (and it does frequently), the optical illusion must be corrected.

Frequent optical illusions are these: (1) The garment may look longer in the back, beginning a few inches in front of the side seamlines; this may be the result of posture or a result of fullness in the back—a pleat, etc. (2) Whenever a garment has concentrated fullness of pleats or gathers (no matter where that fullness is), it has a tendency to look longer in that area. (3) The garment may look longer on one side if the wearer has one leg longer or one hip larger than the other; this garment may need a correction in both front and back for a few inches on either side of the side seamline (the correction may extend as far as the center-front and center-back lines).

No matter what the illusion, correct it by making an estimate of the amount of correction required and testing the results. Figure 8-25 shows the method of correction; the illustration is one of apparent extra length in the back. Note that the original line of measuring pins is retained as a guide; note also that the line of correction is gradual and eventually returns to the original (in this case in the front area). Now test on the figure to see whether the hem appears even; continue testing until the hem appears parallel to the floor before proceeding.

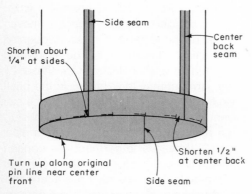

Side seam

Center back seam

Shorten about 1/4" at sides

Shorten 1/2" at center back

Turn up along original pin line near center front

Side seam

FIGURE 8-25 Use the measured pin line as a guideline when correcting optical illusions.

Hem with raw edges

NOTE: **Study all general information on the preceding pages before beginning work. If the garment is underlined or if the lining is caught in with structural seams (like an underlining) see "Hems Require Special Handling" on page 308. If there is a seam on the inner edge of a pleat, see page 337. If a skirt buttons all the way down to the hemline, the front corner is handled the same as in jackets and coats. If there is not adequate length for a standard hem, see "To Face the Lower Edge" on page 337.**

Recommended uses   This finish is quick and simple to do and has the great advantage of adding no extra bulk. Because there are no machine stitches or binding involved, the hem will retain the elasticity of the fabric, will not pucker, and will therefore be inconspicuous. It is recommended for unlined garments if they are made of fabrics which do not ravel (wool and polyester double knits, etc.). It is the wisest choice for lined garments of any fabric if the lining will be attached to the garment at the hemline; the lining will protect raw edges, and fabrics which would ravel under other circumstances can be left raw. If the lining will hang free from the garment, a bound hem (Hong Kong finish) is the better choice.

Construction details   See Figure 8-26.

Step 1   Turn up the hem along the measured pin line and perfect the line as pins are placed at right angles to the fold edge. Baste 1/8 inch from the fold edge with 1/2 to 3/4 inch-long stitches to hold the hemline in a secure position.

Step 2   Make a cardboard gauge the desired width of the hem. With chalk or pencil, put a marking line on the hem parallel to the fold edge. Trim 1/8 inch from the marking line as shown.

Step 3 For flared or circular garments only. Machine-stitch as shown, using a long stitch. Put a pin through one of the bobbin stitches every few inches and draw up the edge slightly by pulling out loops of thread as shown. This will draw in the upper edge of the hem; adjust the ease and pull up the thread until the hem fits flat to the garment. As the hem is hand-hemmed, the loops can be tucked underneath. This gathering line must remain in the hem.

Step 4 Pin the upper edge of the hem flat to the garment. Baste ¼ inch from the raw edge. Directions for doing the tailor's hemming stitch appear on page 283.

SPECIAL NOTE: If the couturier or shell method of lining is used, the lower edge of the lining is finished at this time; see page 350.

Bound hem—the Hong Kong finish

NOTE: See the note on the opposite page before beginning work.

Recommended uses Review the evaluation of the Hong Kong finish on page 287 and see the construction techniques in Figures 7-26 and 7-27. This is the most attractive of the bound finishes; however, rayon bias seam binding can be used in the traditional way, if desired. Bound hems are necessarily more bulky than hems with raw edges; even so, the hem must be bound in unlined garments made of fabrics which will fray and in garments which will be lined by the couturier method if the lining is not attached to the garment at the hemline. The bound hem can be used simply to add a touch of elegance to any unlined costume, even if the fabric does not ravel.

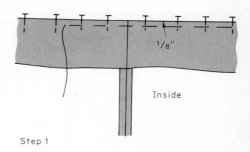

1/8"

Inside

Step 1

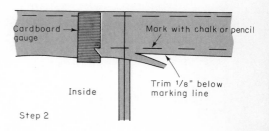

Cardboard gauge →

Mark with chalk or pencil

Trim ¹/₈" below marking line

Inside

Step 2

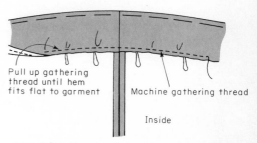

Pull up gathering thread until hem fits flat to garment

Machine gathering thread

Inside

Step 3 (for flared and circular garments only)

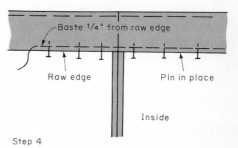

Baste ¼" from raw edge

Raw edge

Pin in place

Inside

Step 4

FIGURE 8-26 *Hem with raw edges.*

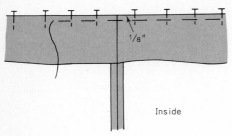

1/8"

Inside

Step 1

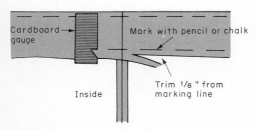

Cardboard gauge

Mark with pencil or chalk

Inside

Trim 1/8" from marking line

Step 2

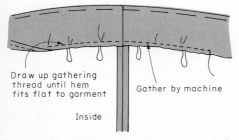

Draw up gathering thread until hem fits flat to garment

Gather by machine

Inside

Step 3 (for flared and circular garments only)

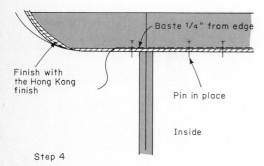

Baste 1/4" from edge

Finish with the Hong Kong finish

Pin in place

Inside

Step 4

FIGURE 8-27 Bound hem—the Hong Kong finish.

Construction details   See Figure 8-27.

Step 1   Turn up the hem along the measured pin line and perfect the line as pins are placed at right angles to the fold edge. Baste ⅛ inch from the fold edge with ½- to ¾-inch-long stitches to hold the hemline in a secure position.

Step 2   Make a cardboard gauge the desired width of the hem. With chalk or pencil, put a marking line on the hem parallel to the fold edge. Trim ⅛ inch from the marking line as shown.

Step 3   For flared or circular garments only. Machine-stitch (with stitches sized at about eight to ten per inch) ¼ inch from the raw edge as shown. Put a pin through one of the bobbin stitches every few inches and draw up the edge slightly by pulling out loops of thread as shown. This will draw in the upper edge of the hem; adjust the ease and pull up the thread until the hem fits flat to the garment. Caution: Avoid drawing up the gathering thread too tightly; as the binding is applied it will have a firming effect which will tighten or draw up the edge slightly more at that stage of construction.

Step 4   The binding is applied to hem edges the same as to seam edges; see Figure 7-26 on page 288 and the accompanying text. Baste the hem in place with stitches ¼ inch from the edge. Directions for doing the tailor's hemming stitch appear on page 283.

SPECIAL NOTE: If the couturier or shell method of lining is used, the lower edge of the lining is finished at this time; see page 350.

Special problems

To hem the area near a pleat seam

Very often a seam will fall at the inner fold of a pleat, as shown in the upper sketch of Figure 8-28. This seam is not pressed open because it must lie flat as it is pictured. However, when the hem is turned up, a seam turned to one side is very bulky. The bulk in this seam, as the reader knows, eventually causes a distortion of the pleat. This construction method decreases bulk and at the same time ensures that the pleat will stay in position for the lifetime of the garment.

Step 1 Press the seam open for about 5 or 6 inches from the lower edge. Trim both edges of the seam allowance down to ⅜ inch in the area below the measured hemline.

Step 2 Return to the hem directions and finish the hem, treating this seam exactly as any pressed-open seam is treated. Clip into the seam directly above the finished hem as shown.

Step 3 Fold the pleat into position. The seam is still bulky, but it has been greatly improved by the preceding steps. As an aid to holding these very thick edges flat and secure during wear and washing or dry cleaning, sew by hand or by machine about ¼ inch from the finished folded edge. Hand stitches will be easier to remove if the hem length is changed; machine stitches hold the edge flatter and are recommended for very heavy fabrics.

To face the lower edge

The faced hem is usually a "make-do" solution to the problem of a garment cut too short or one that must be lengthened because of a change in fashion. On rare occasions the faced hem is used as a design feature to

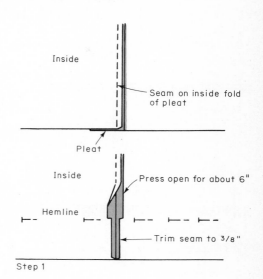

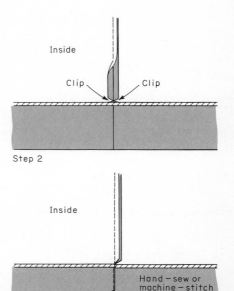

FIGURE 8-28 To hem the area near a pleat seam.

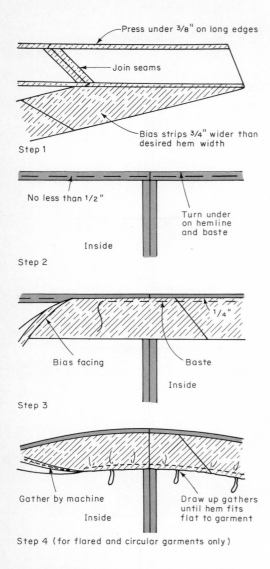

Press under ³/₈" on long edges

Join seams

Bias strips ³/₄" wider than desired hem width

Step 1

No less than 1/2"

Turn under on hemline and baste

Inside

Step 2

Bias facing

1/4"

Baste

Inside

Step 3

Gather by machine

Draw up gathers until hem fits flat to garment

Inside

Step 4 (for flared and circular garments only)

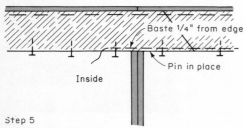

Baste 1/4" from edge

Pin in place

Inside

Step 5

FIGURE 8-29 To face the lower edge.

create a contrasting band of color; an example is the circular skating skirt with a hem faced in contrast to create interest as the skirt flares. Unless the faced hem is required for design purposes, it should be avoided whenever possible. The hem acts slightly differently from the usual fold-edge hem and also looks slightly different simply because a seam is involved near the lower edge and the seam and its extra thickness tend to stiffen the edge.

If the faced hem must be used, the secret to success is to avoid extra stiffness in every possible way. The directions given below result in a hem amazingly like the limp fold-edge hem because stiffness has been avoided in three ways: by cutting the facing strips on the bias, which molds and bends easily; by using a limper fabric for the facing; and by doing all sewing with hand stitches, which are more flexible than machine stitches.

The fabric used for the facing should be subordinate to the fabric of the garment. An underlining or lining fabric in a matching color is ideal for a hem facing. Hem-facing strips are available on the market, cut on the bias and prepared ready for application. Certainly the purchased facing is a convenience, but it is not recommended except for heavier fabrics because it is made of a fairly stiff cotton or relatively heavy and stiff rayon.

See Figure 8-29.

Step 1 Cut bias strips of facing fabric ³/₄ inch wider than the desired hem width. Join the strips to obtain sufficient length for the sweep of the garment. Press under ³/₈ inch on both long edges.

Step 2 Turn up the lower edge of the garment on the measured pin line and baste in place. A turnup of at least ½ inch in width is required.

Step 3 Place the facing strip along the lower edge, with one pressed-under edge ¼ inch from the fold edge of the garment. Pin and baste in place.

Step 4 For flared or circular garments only. Machine-stitch ⅛ inch from the remaining fold edge of the facing with stitches sized at about eight to ten per inch. Put a pin through one of the bobbin stitches every few inches and draw up the edge by pulling out loops of bobbin thread as shown. This will draw in the upper edge of the facing; adjust the ease and pull up the thread until the upper edge of the facing fits flat to the garment. As the hem is hand-hemmed, the loops can be tucked underneath.

Step 5 Pin the upper edge of the facing flat to the garment. Baste ¼ inch from the folded edge, as shown, and secure the upper edge with hand hemming stitches. The long edge of the facing near the hemline should be secured with invisible stitches made by slipping the needle in and out of the fold edge or with the tailor's hemming stitch (page 283).

SKIRT AND PANTS LININGS

Review "Selection of Lining Fabrics" on page 77, with careful attention to the purposes of the lining. It serves aesthetic and functional purposes which may or may not be important to a particular costume. During the decade of the 1960s, linings were considered essential in all types of couturier costumes, and to a certain extent that is still true. However, the increasingly popular polyester knits do not usually require linings for functional purposes, and since the lining adversely affects their desirable elasticity and easy-care characteristics, costumes of

these fabrics are not usually lined unless the lining will be visible, as in jackets and coats.

Pants are not usually lined, because they are in general more functional than skirts and because a lining may possibly make them more constricting. If the wearer must have a lining—for example, if she is allergic to the fabric or if her skin is easily irritated by rough textures—the better solution is to buy one of the separate shell linings available on the market. They are very similar to slips in that they are made of the same supple, smooth fabrics and have elasticized casings. The fact that they are washable and that one shell can be worn with many pants makes them more practical than a lining.

An evaluation of lining methods

The standard method In this, the simplest method, lining sections are basted to sections of the garment and the two handled as one during construction. The construction details are identical to those used for underlinings; glance through the directions on page 301 through 310. The only difference is one of fabric selection; lining fabrics better serve aesthetic purposes because they are smoother to the touch and more decorative than typical underlining fabrics.

In this method the lining serves the purpose of an underlining, preventing stretch and adding body to the fabric more effectively than the alternative method.

Because the lining and garment sections are handled as one throughout the construction sequence, work is greatly speeded and simplified. Seams are basted, fitted, stitched, and pressed as one. Once the lining and garment sections are basted together, the lining will require little additional time and effort. There are continuing advantages because the garment can be easily altered and hem lengths can be changed with a minimum of effort. For all these reasons, this method is used most frequently for dresses, skirts, pants, and shorts at all price levels on the ready-to-wear market.

The advantages of this method must be balanced by several disadvantages. The inside of the garment does not look as finished or as elegant as is possible with the alternative method. Raw seams are exposed, and if the fabric ravels seriously, the seams must be finished in some way which will add additional bulk.

Seams composed of four layers of fabric are necessarily bulky. They cannot be pressed as flat as standard seams and creases will not hold as permanently. The seam may have a tendency to pucker; this is a greater problem with fabrics that pucker at seams under ideal circumstances (the polyesters, permanent-press cotton suitings, etc.).

Hems will be more prominent because in most garments stitches must pass through both layers; stitches through a lightweight lining (only) will not usually support the weight of the hem. Stitches through both thicknesses will make the hem more conspicuous. If the fabric ravels, the hem must be finished by some method which will further stiffen the edge, making it more difficult to maintain a limp and invisible hem.

Both the fabric for the garment and the lining must always be preshrunk under the circumstances that will be used for the finished costume. This is of paramount importance if this method is used; if the two are not preshrunk, results of laundering or dry cleaning can be disastrous.

The couturier or shell method In this method the lining is seamed and handled separately from the garment, like a separate shell. It is the method used for jackets and coats, but it is rarely pictured on the instruction sheet for dresses, skirts, and pants. Therefore the person who chooses it must be able to study fundamental techniques in a text and apply them to the unique demands of each new pattern. Glance through the directions on pages 342 to 350 and compare the finished effect and the difficulty of construction with the standard method.

The greatest advantage of this method is its elegance, and for those who strive for couturier standards, this advantage alone outweighs all other considerations. Although the lining in dresses, skirts, and pants is not visible to the public, the aesthetic appeal of an elegant lining adds much to the wearer's pleasure.

Seams are hidden from view and protected from friction; even if the fabric ravels seriously, seams will not require special finishes which add undesirable bulk. Because the seams of the garment and the lining are handled separately, they can be pressed flatter and creases will be more permanent. If the fabric is one in which seams tend to pucker, this method is the better choice.

In the couturier or shell method, the lower edge of the lining can be attached to the garment or allowed to hang free. If it is attached, hem edges can remain raw even in fabrics that ravel seriously. If the lower edge hangs free, the hem edges are hidden from view and protected from friction; therefore they may not require as bulky a finish as would be necessary with the standard method. In some fabrics merely pinking, zigzagging, or overcasting hem edges is an adequate finish.

This method has disadvantages. It takes more time for stitching, handwork, fitting, pressing; it may almost double the time required to make the garment (no disadvantage to one who sews for the joy of it). It does not control stretch as well as the standard method. Alterations and even changes in length are time-consuming and more difficult to execute. Pressing the finished garment is more difficult to do at home, although professional dry cleaners do an excellent job.

The greatest disadvantage lies in the greater difficulty of the method. Linings for basic dart-fitted skirts, pants, shorts, and shift dresses offer few problems, but intricately cut designs (especially Vogue Paris Original or Couturier designs) may require experience and the ability to innovate. The order of construction is determined by the demands of each intricate design, and the person who undertakes this method must be able to apply basic directions to new and ever-changing, circumstances.

Conclusions The standard method is recommended for inexperienced persons and those who must use quick methods. Results can be considered professional, and certainly this method can be used for all garments except jackets and coats; it is the wise choice for utilitarian garments and less important items in the wardrobe.

The couturier or shell method is recommended for special-occasion costumes and for costumes made of any fabric which puckers at the seams. It is recommended for those who are experienced or for the less experienced who are working under the direction of an instructor. Those who

sew for a hobby or for the joy of creating a "masterpiece" will enjoy the aesthetic appeal of this lining and will welcome the additional hours of sewing pleasure.

To cut lining sections

As a broad, general rule, the lining for a skirt or pants is cut exactly like the structural pieces of the garment, using the same pattern pieces. One exception is shown in Figure 8-30. If there is a pleat and if the pleat will be stitched down to a

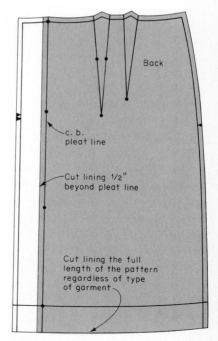

Back

c. b.
pleat line

Cut lining ½"
beyond pleat line

Cut lining the full
length of the pattern
regardless of type
of garment

FIGURE 8-30 To cut linings from major pattern pieces.

level a few inches above the hemline, it is important to reduce unnecessary bulk in the pleat area. This is done by allowing only a ½-inch seam beyond the pleat line, as shown. Caution: If there is a free-hanging pleat that will not be stitched down and will be controlled only at the waistline, the lining must be cut exactly like the pattern.

Construction details—standard method

If the lining will be caught in with seams of the garment, it is handled the same as an underlining; the only difference lies in the selection of a smoother, more decorative fabric for a lining than the one that would be acceptable for an underlining. Follow the directions for underlinings on pages 301 to 310.

Construction details—couturier or shell method

NOTE: The lining shell is prepared and inserted in the garment and the opening edges are sewn to the zipper tape just before the waistband is applied (or the waistline casing finished).

Preparatory steps See sketch *a* in Figure 8-31. The lining must be basted for a fitting, and it is basted in the same way as the garment with but one important exception—and that is if there is to be a side-opening zipper. If there is a side-opening zipper, the opening must be reversed—in other words, in the garment the left side was left open for the zipper, and now, in the lining, the opening must be on the right side. When the lining is inserted into the garment wrong sides together, the opening in the lining will be over the zipper side of the garment. Be sure the opening for the zipper is the same length as in the garment. One cannot assume that the lining will

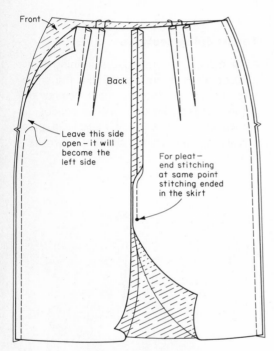

Front

Back

Leave this side
open – it will
become the
left side

For pleat—
end stitching
at same point
stitching ended
in the skirt

a Seam lining sections

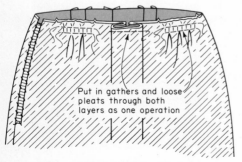

Put in gathers and loose
pleats through both
layers as one operation

b Special directions for loose
pleats and gathers

FIGURE 8-31 Preparatory steps.

fit properly even if it is cut and basted exactly like the outside garment, because the garment may be made of fabric that will stretch (wool, knit, crepe, etc.), whereas the lining will not stretch. If a choice must be made, it is better to allow the lining to be slightly larger (rather than slightly smaller) than the garment, because if the lining is made of the limp fabric recommended, it can be eased into the waistband of the skirt with no difficulty.

If there is a pleat, baste and stitch the seam in the lining to exactly the same point where the stitching for the pleat ends; there should be a pattern marking at that point, but if there is not or if the pleat length in the garment has been changed, check now and make sure that this seam ends exactly where the garment stitching ends.

See sketch *b* in Figure 8-31. If there are loose pleats or gathers involved, the lining must be inserted into the garment and the zipper edge must be finished before the gathers or pleats are laid in because the loose pleats and gathers must be handled in such a way that the garment and lining act as one.

To finish the lining at a regulation zipper opening See Figure 8-32. The lining is inserted into the garment cut edges even and seamlines matching. This is easy enough to do at all points except the zipper edges; at those edges, there are two different seamline positions. *Keep in mind that seamlines in the lining must match seamlines in the garment.*

The sketches are labeled "back" and "front" for the traditional side-opening zipper; in addition, the words "right back" and "left back" indicate the situation for a back-opening zipper.

Step 1 This sketch pictures the garment before the lining is inserted: Notice that the seam allowance on the back opening

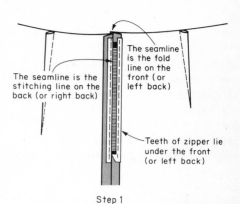

Step 1

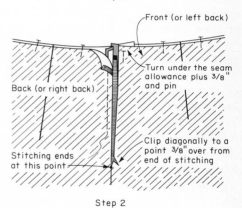

Step 2

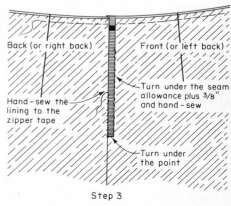

Step 3

FIGURE 8-32 *To finish the lining at a regulation zipper.*

edge is approximately in the position of the stitching line of the zipper; on the front edge the seamline is on the fold edge: Keep this in mind as the lining is inserted. Pull up the zipper and notice that in the regulation zipper construction, the metal or coil part of the zipper lies under the front of the skirt. This means that an opening for the zipper must be made in the front of the skirt lining.

Step 2 Pin the lining in place, seamlines matching and waistline edges even; baste in place. Turn under the seam allowance on the back edge of the lining, lap it to the stitching line of the zipper, and pin in place as shown. Now turn under the seam allowance plus ⅜ inch (a total of 1 inch) on the front edge of the lining and place the lining ⅜ inch over from the fold edge of the garment at the waistline edge and pin in place (this is the same as matching seamlines). In order to turn under the seam allowance plus ⅜ inch, a clip is required in the front section at the lower end of the opening. Make a diagonal clip to a point ⅜ inch over from the end of the stitching at the side seam, as shown. Now the entire front edge can be turned under the width of the seam allowance plus ⅜ inch.

Step 3 Baste the edges in place to the zipper, turning in the little triangular point at the end. Test on the figure to see that the garment fits as it did before. Then whip these edges to the zipper tape with small whipping stitches; be sure to keep these stitches small so the thread will not catch in the teeth as the zipper is used.

To finish the lining at a slot-seam zipper opening See Figure 8-33.

Step 1 This sketch pictures the garment before the lining is inserted. The seamline on both opening edges is on the fold line. Pull up the zipper and notice that in the slot-seam zipper construction, the metal or coil part of the zipper is centered over the seam. This means that an equal opening for the zipper must be made on either side of the seamline of the lining.

Step 2 Pin the lining in place, seamlines matching and waistline edges even; baste. Turn under the seam allowance plus ¼ inch (a total of ⅞ inches) on the opening edges of the lining at the waistline and pin as shown. Make a ¼-inch clip on either side of the seamline to points on a level with the end of the stitching of the vertical seam, as shown.

Step 3 Turn under the seam allowance plus ¼ inch on both opening edges, pin to the zipper tape, and baste, turning in the little triangular point at the end as shown. Test on the figure to be sure the garment fits as it did before. Then whip these edges to the zipper tape with small whipping stitches; be sure to keep these stitches small so that the thread will not catch in the teeth as the zipper is used.

Alternative methods of finishing the lower edge The lower edge of the lining can be attached to the lower edge of the garment or hemmed separately and allowed to fall free. It is important that the lining be handled in such a way that it can act independently of the garment; in other words, it must be allowed to shift without disturbing the lines of the garment. Obviously the free-hanging lining allows for independent play between the lining and the garment, and as work progresses on the attached lining, it will become evident that that method also allows for some shifting. Both methods have advantages which must be weighed against their disadvantages.

In the attached lining, the hem is held in place by sewing the raw edge to the hem of the garment; therefore, no hemming stitches are visible from the lining side. This makes the attached lining more attractive than its alternative. It requires less time and is the simpler method. Handled by this method, the lining is a better protection for seam and hem edges, so that these edges will not require bulky seam finishes even if the fabric ravels seriously. This is a tremendous advantage: it saves time and also improves the appearance of the finished garment. Because the attached lining is hand sewn to the garment, it must be cut exactly like the garment; in other words, style fullness cannot be eliminated in the lining.

These advantages must be weighed against the following disadvantages. Pressing is more difficult because the finished garment must be pressed from the lining side with both layers pressed as one. If seams do not retain creases properly, they cannot be corrected easily. This is the greatest disadvantage for garments that will be laundered at home; professional cleaners handle the problem very well. Because two layers are attached, the lower edge of the garment is somewhat stiffer. The difference is so slight that it is not evident in straight or slightly flared garments if a subordinate lining fabric is used. There would be a difference in a skirt with a great deal of flare, because the folds of style fullness would not be as limp when two layers are combined to act as one. Because of its attractive appearance, this method is recommended except under the following circumstances: if the garment will be laundered at home, if either of the fabrics does not retain a crease well enough so that seams will re-

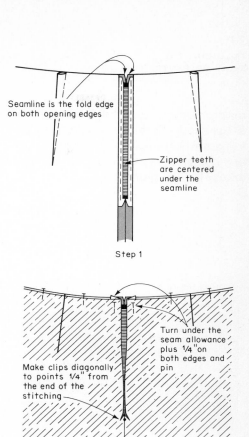

Seamline is the fold edge on both opening edges

Zipper teeth are centered under the seamline

Step 1

Make clips diagonally to points 1/4" from the end of the stitching

Turn under the seam allowance plus 1/4" on both edges and pin

Step 2

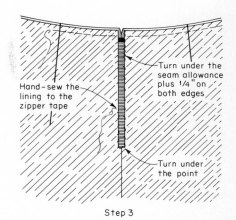

Hand-sew the lining to the zipper tape

Turn under the seam allowance plus 1/4" on both edges

Turn under the point

Step 3

FIGURE 8-33 To finish the lining at a slot-seam zipper.

main properly pressed, if the lining fabric is not supple, if the design features style fullness which must fall in very soft folds, or if (for some reason) the lining is not cut exactly like the garment.

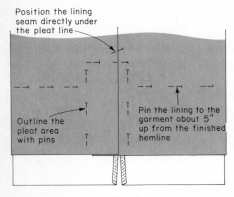

Position the lining seam directly under the pleat line

Outline the pleat area with pins

Pin the lining to the garment about 5" up from the finished hemline

a To position lining.

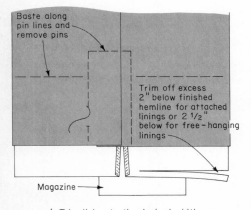

Baste along pin lines and remove pins

Trim off excess 2" below finished hemline for attached linings or 2 1/2" below for free-hanging linings

Magazine

b Trim lining to the desired width.

FIGURE 8-34 Preliminary steps for either method.

The free-hanging lining will solve all the disadvantages of the attached lining. Because it provides for easier access to seams in the lining and the garment, pressing problems are minimized. Certainly it is the better choice for garments which will be laundered at home. Because the lining hangs free, this method is the better choice if the lining fabric is not as supple as a typical lining fabric or if the garment is very flared. It is the only choice if the lining was not cut exactly like the garment. These advantages must be balanced against the following disadvantages. This method requires more time and effort. The hemming stitches in the lining will show prominently in most lining fabrics; as a result, the inside of the garment will not look as attractive. Seams have less protection from friction; if the fabric ravels seriously, seams will have to be finished. Hem edges of both fabrics must be finished in some way, although the hem edge of the garment can remain raw if the fabric is a knit.

Preliminary steps for either method See Figure 8-34. Sketch *a* shows positioning the lining in the garment so that the two layers hang properly. The row of pins pictured control the lining above that level; as work progresses at the lower edge, the worker can concentrate on keeping the two layers flat in the lower few inches of the garment. This step can be done with the skirt well-supported on a skirt hanger or, preferably, with the help of an assistant. Allow the lining to hang down free. Do not pull or tug at it, but allow it to hang as it will. Seams in the lining must match seams in the garment and should be shifted into position. With one hand inside the garment and lining, place a row of pins about 5 inches from the finished edge, matching seamlines, as shown in sketch *a*. Refer to Figure 10-16 on page 458, which shows a jacket on the figure and includes hand positions.

If there is a pleat or split opening, care-, fully position the center seam of the lining over the stitching line of the pleat and put in a rectangle of pins, as shown. Place the pin line close to the pleat or split area (about 1½ inches outside).

See sketch *b* in Figure 8-34. In doing this step (and several other steps in the construction sequence) it is very helpful to slip a magazine under the area, as shown. This will prevent catching stitches in other layers of the garment and prevent mistakes in cutting. The flat working surface makes it easier to keep the two layers smooth and flat.

Baste along the pin lines and remove the pins. The lining must be trimmed parallel to the finished edge of the garment. This can best be done from the outside, as shown. The sketch shows maximum widths. By trimming off 2 inches below the finished lower edge for an attached lining (and 2½ inches from the finished edge for a free-hanging lining) the hem in the lining is made approximately the same width as the hem in the garment; should it become necessary to lengthen the skirt, the lining can be lengthened accordingly. However, the lining need not have a hem of this maximum width. If there is not sufficient fabric, there will be no problems if the lining is only ½ to 1 inch longer than the finished garment. In a flared skirt a narrower hem allows fullness to fall in softer folds.

Finishing steps of construction differ according to the method used. For an attached lining, see the directions accompanying Figures 8-35 and 8-36. For a free-hanging lining, see the directions accompanying Figure 8-37.

Finishing steps—attached method The sketches in Figure 8-35 show a basic skirt. If there is a pleat, the free edges in the pleat area are finished as shown in Figure 8-36.

See sketch *a*. Turn the garment wrong

side out and work from the lining side. Turn up the lower edge of the lining with the fold edge about ¾ inch above the finished edge of the garment. In doing this step, smooth the fabrics in place and keep both layers flat and smooth in the area below the basted line. Pin in place. Baste the layers together with a row of stitches placed about ¾ inch above the lower edge of the lining as shown. Do not press at this time.

See sketch *b*. This step is more easily handled if the garment is held upside down, as pictured. Fold the lower edge of the lining back about ⅛ inch from the basted line and pin. In doing this, keep in mind that

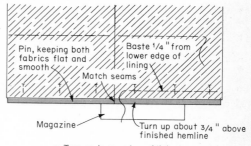

a Turn up lower edge of lining.

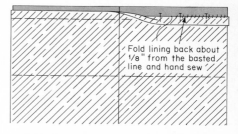

b Hand sew lining to hem layer of garment.

FIGURE 8-35 *Finishing steps—attached method.*

one layer of lining will be sewn to the hem of the garment. Hand sew one layer of lining to the hem layer in the garment, being careful that stitches do not catch through the outside layer of the garment. Stitches should be about ½ inch long and should catch through only a thread or two of each fabric; they can be reinforced every few inches by taking an extra back stitch in the hem layer.

Press a crease in the lower edge of the lining; place the iron just over the fold edge and do not press over the basting stitches. Remove the basting stitches. If the construction has been done in this way, the lin-

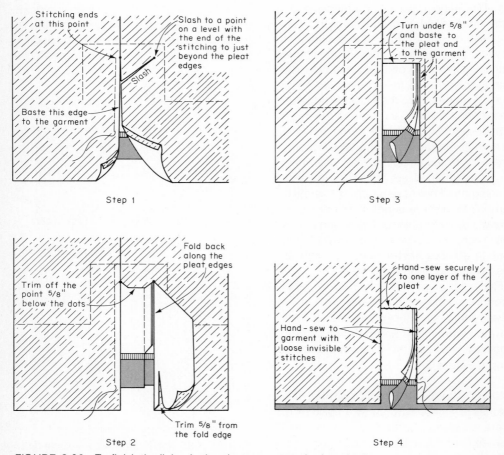

FIGURE 8-36 *To finish the lining in the pleat area—attached method.*

ing can shift without disturbing the lines of the garment. This is not illustrated; test to see how this construction allows for the necessary shifting or play between the lining and the garment.

To finish the lining in the pleat area—attached method See Figure 8-36 and study the finished sketch in step 4 as an aid to understanding what is to be done. The purpose of this construction is to finish the pleat edges in such a way that the pleat area is exposed for movement. A knife pleat, which folds in one direction only, is shown in the sketches; if the skirt has a box pleat, the techniques required are the same, but both sides of the skirt lining are slashed to expose the pleat on both sides of the center line.

See step 1. One turned-under edge of the lining can be basted directly to the skirt because the pleat folds in one direction only (shown on the left side of the sketch).

To expose the pleat, a slash must be made into the lining; it is made to a point on a level with the end of the stitching of the pleat seam, and it must extend to a point just outside the pleat edges. See the finished sketch in step 4 to understand the reason for the position of the slash; the slash must be made to the point that will be the corner of the exposed pleat.

See step 2. Trim off the tip of the triangle of lining fabric, as shown, leaving a ⅝-inch allowance below the end of the stitching. Fold the slashed extension of the lining to the outside, as shown, folding it along a straight line, just outside the finished pleat edges. Pin in place temporarily and trim off the excess lining, leaving a ⅝-inch seam beyond the folded edge.

See step 3. Turn under the remaining raw edges, making a corner at the slashed point, and baste the lining to the skirt. Finish the lower edge of the skirt according to the directions accompanying Figures 8-35.

See step 4. Blind-stitch the lining edges to the skirt, taking great care to make the stitches very inconspicuous on the right side of the garment. These stitches will catch into the skirt fabric, but they need not be strong or secure; catch in just a thread or a portion of a thread of the skirt fabric. Do not use firmer or tighter stitches at the corner.

Finishing steps—free-hanging method
See Figure 8-37. If there is a pleat, hem the free edges of the lining, as shown in sketch *a*. Use the seam allowance, turning under ¼ inch and then turning again for a narrow hem about ¼ inch wide. Keep stitches as small and invisible as possible. When using this method, all hemming stitches will be visible on the right side of the lining and they should be as small and invisible as possible.

See sketch *b*. Turn the garment wrong side out and work from the lining side. Turn up the lower edge of the lining with the fold edge about ¾ inch above the finished edge of the garment. Pin the lining hem in place but keep the lining free from the garment, as shown. Baste about ¼ inch from the lower edge of the lining.

See sketch *c*. The lining hem is finished the same as it is in any garment. The raw edge will have to be finished in some way to prevent raveling and to give an attractive finish. It should be done by the simplest and least bulky method possible. If the lining fabric is limp and supple, turning under the raw edge is the best finish. If the fabric is stiff or heavy, a bound finish may be a better choice. Be sure hand stitches are as inconspicuous as possible. Remove bastings and press.

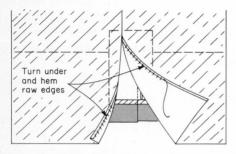

a To finish opening edges at a pleat.

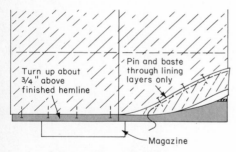

b Turn up lower edge of lining.

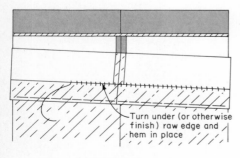

c Hem lining.

FIGURE 8-37 Finishing steps—free-hanging method.

Chapter 9

TAILORING THE JACKET OR COAT

Each jacket or coat design presents individual problems which have been carefully worked out by the writer of the pattern instructions. The fact that techniques presented in great detail in a text are not as explicit and comprehensive on the instruction sheet is in no way a reflection on the quality of pattern directions. They must necessarily be brief; but there is no substitute for them, and a tailoring text should be considered a supplement to them. The worker must follow both—the instruction sheet for specific directions related to the particular design and the text for greater elaboration.

BEFORE BEGINNING WORK

Muslin testing influences decisions

Review two sections with similiar headings—one on page 99 and the other on page 303. The order of construction in this chapter is planned for the most efficient work sequence so that as much detailed work as possible can be done before sections are joined together is one bulky unit. *It is a different order than that on the instruction sheet; and this simpler sequence is possible only if a muslin test copy was made.* If a test copy was not made, pieces must be assembled in the traditional order so that the garment can be fitted before final decisions are made.

The muslin test copy served many purposes: because fitting was done, the garment need not be basted together before work is begun; because the roll line was established on the collar and lapel area, intricate work can proceed in these areas without basting the entire garment together; because the position and size of buttons were decided, buttonholes can be made before the entire garment is assembled; and because proportions of details were studied and corrected, they need not be basted for testing. Consequently, many intricate details can be done when the garment is still in relatively small pieces; for example, the collar and lapel are shaped, pad-stitched, and taped as one of the first steps of construction, and buttonholes are made before the right front is joined to any other section.

If a test copy was not made The first step of construction, whether or not a test copy was made, is the application of underlining and interfacing sections (see pages 353 to 366. After that, those who did not make a test copy must assemble the major pieces, including the under collar and sleeves, and follow the fitting sequence in Chapter 6. See "Assemble Pieces for a Final Fitting Test" on page 366 before proceeding. It must be understood that the techniques in Chapter 6 will be helpful but that some of the more radical changes shown there cannot be done once the garment is cut in fabric.

After fitting has been done, it is possible to regain the advantage of working in the order presented in this chapter. If fitting corrections have been made, record the new seamlines and dartlines with marking basting or tailor's tacks so that bastings can be removed and the pieces separated; later the units can be reassembled by basting along the corrected lines. In other words, by separating pieces after fitting corrections have been recorded, the worker can regain the great advantage of working on smaller units.

If a test copy was made Even so, there is an advantage in basting sections together for a final fitting test, as explained on page 309.

Review fundamental techniques

Chapter 7 was concerned with the fundamentals of construction and pressing which will be used throughout the construction sequence. These techniques will not be explained in great detail in this chapter. It is important for the worker to know the fundamentals so well that she can use them automatically and unconsciously, because she will need to give her conscious thought to the more difficult tailoring principles presented in this chapter. The section titled "Reducing Bulk in Seams" on pages 277 to 280 is especially important because the problem of keeping seams and edges flat and inconspicuous is chronic. Pay particular attention to "Aids to Accuracy" on page 296. The techniques shown in that section can be modified and applied to a

great variety of details which may be encountered throughout the tailoring processes.

The lining can be handled by using a novelty method which involves finishing facing edges with the Hong Kong finish; see details on page 470. There are some slight changes in construction (order and techniques) if the lining will be done by this method. The differences involve finishing the facing and neck edges before inserting the lining; the difference, then, comes in the last steps of construction.

Incorporate suggestions from chapter 11

Chapter II includes specific information for solving special problems. In most cases the problems are created by fabrics which require special handling. The reader who is using one of these must thoroughly understand the special nature of her problems so that she can combine those directions with the basic tailoring techniques in this chapter.

Plan to gain maximum benefits from instructional time

Tailoring requires a great deal of time; and once the fundamentals are understood, much of the hand work is repetitious. The student should not use class time for repetitious tasks—they make excellent "television" jobs. The instructor will use class time to present theory and demonstrate proper techniques; if the student will progress to the point where her initial steps can be checked by the instructor, then the follow-up busywork should be done outside of class hours. For example, basting underlining or interfacing sections in place is time-consuming; but after the basic techniques are mastered, the remainder of this job should be done as an out-of-class assignment. The same is true of pad-stitching the collar and taping seam edges; once the student has mastered the technique, she does not require the instructor's attention.

CONSTRUCTION METHODS FOR SUPPORTING FABRICS

The supporting fabrics—underlinings and interfacings—are essential in tailored garments; without them the garment cannot be tailored. Carefully review "Selection of Supporting Fabrics" on pages 82 to 90. It is important to understand the differences between underlinings and interfacings before attempting to evaluate various construction methods. In brief: underlining fabrics are firm, flat, lightweight fabrics used to add some extra body to the entire garment; interfacings are stiffer, heavier fabrics used to add more stiffness and body to certain portions of the garment.

An evaluation of construction methods

The sketches shown in Figure 9-1 are included for illustrative purposes only; they are simplified sketches planned to show basic differences in methods of construction. Detailed directions appear later in the chapter. The sketches on the left illustrate how the supporting fabrics are cut and applied, and the sketches on the right show basic construction.

Small units of the design (collars, cuffs, pocket flaps, etc.) are not included in the sketches, because these are always interfaced and cutting directions appear on the instruction sheet of the pattern.

The partial interfacing See sketch *a* in Figure 9-1. This is the traditional method of interfacing used almost exclusively until the late 1950s. It is still used for fairly simple

patterns planned for the beginner, although it is not necessarily simpler to do than the other methods. The front interfacing may be cut from the facing pattern piece (in which case it is the shape indicated by the broken line on the sketch), or a separate interfacing pattern may be included (the shaded area) which allows the interfacing to extend over the front shoulder area, as shown. The back interfacing pictured is usually not included in the pattern directions, but it has obvious advantages and can be added, if desired. The bias strip of interfacing extending above the hemline may or may not be included in the pattern directions. A similar strip of interfacing is used at the hemline of the sleeve.

Purpose The purpose of the partial interfacing is to stiffen the front portion of the jacket or coat and to strengthen the shoulder areas to prevent stretching in the areas which get great strain as the garment is worn. The bias strip above hemlines stiffens the hem area for a firm, well-defined edge, and if it is cut ½ inch wider than the hem and placed in the position shown, it cushions the hem and makes it inconspicuous as the garment is worn.

Fabric used The fabric for a partial interfacing is a typical interfacing fabric (muslin or hair canvas, etc.) in a variety of weights to complement various weights of fabric.

Advantages and disadvantages The partial interfacing requires less fabric, of course, and judging by the fact that it is often suggested in easy-to-make patterns, there may be some feeling that it is simpler to construct. This is doubtful, however.

The great disadvantage of this method has to do with the consistency of effect and thickness of the total jacket or coat. See the basic construction on the right in sketch *a*. Note that in the front area, faced and interfaced, there are two thicknesses of fabric and one thickness of interfacing and that the same amount of thickness is present in the hem area. By sudden contrast, there is just one thickness of fabric in the remaining body of the garment. This results in a great difference in thickness, body, and weight within the areas of the garment — a difference which is often obvious because the area that is not faced and interfaced looks limp compared with the stiffer areas. The other methods do not have this disadvantage.

Recommended uses The great disadvantage of this method limits its use for tailored garments; its one advantage, the fact that less fabric is required, is relatively insignificant because the saving is so slight compared with the total cost of a tailored garment. It seems best to reserve this method for use in little dresses and blouses in which additional body throughout the total garment is not desirable. Brief cutting directions are included on page 359; certain suggestions given there (that do not appear on the pattern) will help to make a better transition between the thick and thin areas, thereby improving this method.

Underlining and interfacing combined
See sketch *b* in Figure 9-1. This is the method used almost exclusively in pattern directions. Note that the structural pieces of the entire jacket or coat have been cut of underlining fabric (down to the hem level)

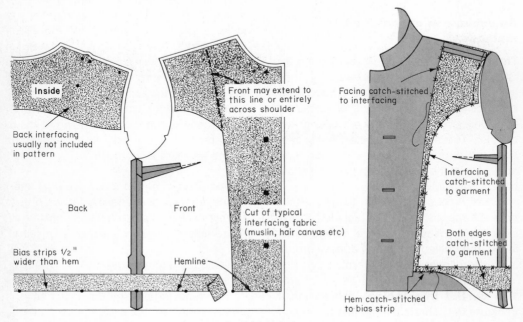

Inside

Back interfacing
usually not included
in pattern

Back

Bias strips ½"
wider than hem

Front may extend to
this line or entirely
across shoulder

Cut of typical
interfacing fabric
(muslin, hair canvas etc)

Front

Hemline

Facing catch-stitched
to interfacing

Interfacing
catch-stitched
to garment

Both edges
catch-stitched
to garment

Hem catch-stitched
to bias strip

a Partial interfacing.

FIGURE 9-1 An evaluation of construction methods.

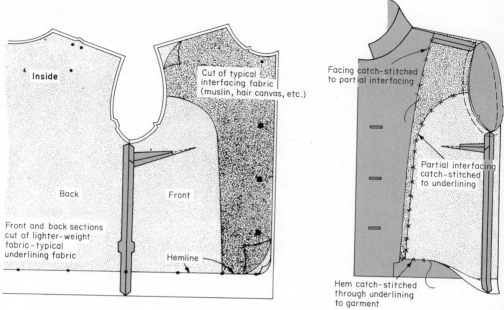

Inside

Cut of typical interfacing fabric (muslin, hair canvas, etc.)

Facing catch-stitched to partial interfacing

Back

Front

Front and back sections cut of lighter-weight fabric – typical underlining fabric

Hemline

Partial interfacing catch-stitched to underlining

Hem catch-stitched through underlining to garment

b Underlining and interfacing combined.

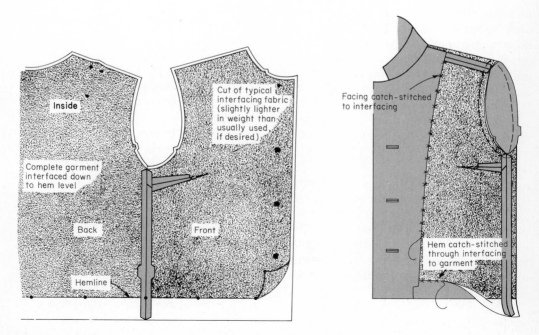

Inside

Cut of typical interfacing fabric (slightly lighter in weight than usually used, if desired)

Facing catch-stitched to interfacing

Complete garment interfaced down to hem level

Back

Front

Hemline

Hem catch-stitched through interfacing to garment

c Complete interfacing, handled like an underlining.

and that it is caught into seams and darts so that the underlining and the fabric of the garment act as one during construction. The pattern includes a separate interfacing piece for the front, extending over the front shoulder area; note that it is exactly like the front interfacing used in the partial interfacing. The sketches shown here and the sketches on the pattern guide sheet show the underlining and interfacing shaded or marked differently so that they can be distinguished. The worker should study the sketches on her instruction sheet to see the plan of shading or marking for that particular pattern. The entire sleeve can be underlined, or it can be handled like the sleeve in the partial interfacing method by using a strip of interfacing at the hemline.

Purpose The purpose of the lightweight underlining is to add a small amount of body to the fabric; it gives the fabric a firmer and perhaps crisper hand, enhancing its appearance and making it more durable. The purpose of the (partial) interfacing of heavier fabric is to stiffen the front portion of the jacket or coat and strengthen the shoulder area for the strain it will receive during wearing.

Fabric used The underlining is cut from a lightweight, typical underlining fabric (Siri, Undercurrent, etc.) in a limp or crisp grade to achieve the desired effect. The fabric for the partial interfacing is a typical interfacing fabric (muslin or hair canvas, etc.) in a variety of weights to complement various weights of fabric.

Advantages and disadvantages The great advantage of this method is that it adds

weight, body, and stiffness to the fabric of the garment. It does not entirely correct the disadvantage (inconsistency of effect and thickness of the total garment) of the partial interfacing. See the basic construction of this method in the sketch on the right. Note that the front edge is composed of two layers of fabric, one layer of interfacing, and one layer of underlining—a total of four layers; the hem area is composed of two layers of fabric and one layer of underlining. By contrast, there are two layers (one of fabric and the other of lightweight underlining) in the remaining body of the garment. This results in some difference in thickness, body, and weight within the areas of the garment—a difference which is less obvious than it would be if the partial interfacing method were used.

Recommended uses This method is excellent, and it is used almost exclusively by the pattern companies and ready-to-wear manufacturers. It is possible that pattern directions will show the underlining cut the full length of the garment to simplify cutting directions. It is shown here cut to the hem level; this is an improvement, because it reduces the bulk in the hem area by one layer. Because this method will probably be pictured on the instruction sheet, there is an advantage (especially for the novice) in choosing it. Make the decision after considering the advantages of the complete interfacing handled like an underlining, and after reading "Conclusions" on page 358.

Complete interfacing handled like an underlining See sketch *c* in Figure 9-1. This method was devised by the author and has been tested for many years in her personal sewing and in classes with all types and weights of fabric and with a great variety of patterns—a total of many hundreds of garments. The results are so satisfying that this method is highly recommended. As a general rule, the author is opposed to recommending methods which are radically different from those on the instruction sheet, because they can confuse the worker to the point where their advantages are lost. However, the complete interfacing is so effective and so simple to do that it is recommended above the other methods which are pictured on the instruction sheet. There are a few circumstances, stated on page 358, when the underlining and interfacing combined (sketch *b*) will be preferred; but in most cases the complete interfacing will give the best results.

Note that the interfacing is caught in with seams and darts; it is, in other words, handled exactly like an underlining, and the only difference is that the fabric is heavier or stiffer (or both) than a typical underlining fabric.

Because the fabric used for the complete interfacing is somewhat heavy (a typical interfacing fabric), it will create more body than an underlining, and the issue of additional body and stiffness in the sleeve becomes an important consideration. The sleeve can be treated in three different ways: it can be completely interfaced by cutting the interfacing to the hemline, according to the general rules given above; it can be underlined (with a lighter-weight fabric than the interfacing in the garment) and cut in the same manner; or it can be treated like the sleeve in the partial interfacing method, by using a bias strip at the hem edge only. All three methods will give an excellent effect; because the armhole seam separates the sleeve from the body of the garment, there is no discernible difference in effect if the body of the garment is interfaced and the sleeve is not. The choice is an individual one, dependent on the preferences and comfort requirements of the wearer. The interfaced sleeve will feel somewhat confining to some active per-

sons; the underlined sleeve will be less confining; and the sleeve interfaced only at the hem edge will give the greatest amount of freedom.

Purpose The complete interfacing serves a dual purpose. It adds body (a greater amount than an underlining would provide) to the entire jacket or coat, and it provides stiffness and body in those areas which are ordinarily stiffened with the partial interfacing.

Fabric used The fabric used will be very comparable to a typical interfacing fabric that would be used in a partial interfacing (muslin or hair canvas, etc.) in a variety of weights to complement various fabrics. Because the complete interfacing serves the dual purposes of an underlining and an interfacing, the fabric should be slightly lighter in weight than a typical interfacing but heavier in weight than a typical underlining fabric.

Advantages and disadvantages The very great advantage of this method is in the consistency of thickness, body, and weight of the total garment; in other words, it corrects the disadvantages of its alternatives. See the almost-finished garment on the right in sketch *c*. Note that the hem and faced area are composed of two thicknesses of fabric and one thickness of interfacing — three in all. By contrast, the difference in thickness in the remaining area is a subtle one because the remainder of the garment is composed of only one less thickness of fabric. When the lining is in place, it will cover this thinner area, so that all areas of the garment will have a very consistent hand and appearance. The other two methods allow for greater differences in feel and appearance in various areas of the garment, and it is because this method corrects these differences that it is so highly recommended.

A comparison of the three methods of construction pictured in Figure 9-1 reveals that the complete interfacing is actually the simplest method and that it requires less time because of the small amount of handwork involved.

It can be considered a disadvantage that this is not the method pictured on the instruction sheet of the pattern. However, because it is handled like an underlining which is pictured there, it is not so different that it is confusing. The choice of a heavier interfacing fabric does add extra weight and body; and if the fabric for the garment is itself unusually bulky (as are thick coatings) or if the wearer demands the freedom of supple, soft garments for personal comfort, this method is not the wisest choice. The evaluation of this method continues in the following section.

Conclusions

For most typical tailored garments, the choice of method for supporting fabrics narrows down to two choices—the underlining and interfacing combined or the complete interfacing. The partial interfacing does have some limited advantages; it is acceptable if the fabric for the garment is unusually heavy or if it has its own backing (as do fake furs and some vinyls). In all other fabrics, some extra body is desirable, and it becomes a matter of deciding how much extra body is required.

Use an underlining and interfacing combined if a complete interfacing would add too much body for the effect desired. If the wearer demands unusual freedom of movement, she will prefer a more supple garment. If the fabric is very lightweight (really too lightweight for a suit or coat) the supporting fabric must not be so heavy that it dominates the fabric, making it appear to be something entirely different from what it is.

Use the complete interfacing for all high-quality tailored garments made of typical coating or suiting weights. Two further advantages are these: (1) If an all-wool hair canvas is used, the interfacing serves the purpose of adding warmth to the entire garment. (2) Because the interfacing is heavier than the underlining used in the combination method, it will hide a lining of a dark color or a gay and even splashy print used with a light-colored garment.

Regardless of the method used Review "Selection Is Influenced by the Purpose to Be Served and the Construction Method to Be Used" on page 84. Supporting fabrics serve many varied purposes; it follows, then, that no one supporting fabric can serve every purpose in any one design. Keep in mind that a variety of supporting fabrics can be used in one garment. The following example will serve to illustrate how to use supporting fabrics imaginatively. To completely interface the body of the garment (front and back), choose an interfacing fabric that is slightly less dominant (less stiff, slightly lighter in weight) than the type of interfacing that would be appropriate for a partial interfacing. For the sleeve, choose a lighter-weight muslin or a firm underlining fabric. For the tailored collar, choose a heavier hair canvas. If there is a trim belt included in the design, choose pellon in an appropriate weight.

NOTE: Many sketches throughout the chapter picture the complete interfacing, but it should be understood that subsequent construction (buttonholes, setting in sleeve, etc.) is done in the same way regardless of the method of construction chosen for the supporting fabrics.

Cutting directions

The instructions on the pattern must be brief to conserve space and must be simple and uncomplicated to be easily understood by the average reader. The directions given below are essentially like those on the pattern, but there are slight differences and improvements which are included here because there is not the same need to conserve space.

NOTE: Collars, cuffs, pocket flaps, etc., are not pictured. They are cut in the same manner for all three methods; directions are included on the pattern instruction sheet.

For a partial interfacing See directions in Figure 9-2. The pattern will probably include a front-interfacing pattern piece (as shown in the shaded area). If the pattern is included, it may be the same width as the front facing pattern; note that the sketch shows this piece ½ inch wider than the front facing. This is advantageous because it allows the interfacing to cushion the cut edge of the facing, creating staggered edges for a better transition in fabric thickness. If the pattern piece for the interfacing is the width of the facing, add a ½ inch extension on the inner edge to make it wider.

If there is no pattern for a front interfacing, make one by placing a sheet of tissue over the front and copying the outlines of

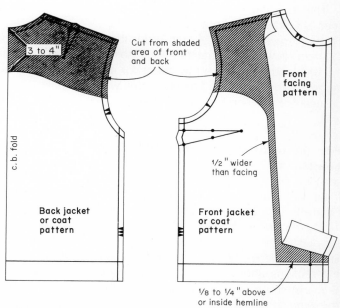

FIGURE 9-2 To cut a partial interfacing.

the front, as shown in the shaded section on the sketch.

Note that the interfacing is cut to a level ⅛ to ¼ inch inside or above the hemline. Cutting the interfacing slightly above the hemline will allow the hem to fold up smoothly. If the fabric is unusually heavy, use the ¼-inch measurement; for most suiting-weight fabrics, use the ⅛-inch measurement.

The pattern does not usually include a pattern for the back shoulder interfacing illustrated. Copy from the back pattern as indicated by the shaded section in the sketch; note that the interfacing is exactly like the garment at the cut edges and that it is cut to a level of about 3 or 4 inches below the neck edge at the center back, curving off at about the notch position at the armhole edge.

The bias strips for strengthening hemlines should be cut from scraps of fabric. These strips should be ½ inch wider than the hem allowance so that they will cushion the hem and stagger the raw edges for an inconspicuous hemline. The bias strips will be used at the hemline of the sleeves as well.

For an underlining and interfacing combined   To cut sections for this method, see Figure 9-2 and the accompanying directions to cut the interfacing sections and see Figure 9-3 to cut the underlining sections.

The pattern will probably give directions for cutting the underlining exactly like the structural pieces of the garment. Cutting the sections shorter, as shown in Figure 9-3, is an improvement. Read details in the following section.

The sleeve can be completely under-

lined to the hem level; or, if the wearer wants less stiffness and body in the sleeve, bias strips at the hemline, like those used in the partial interfacing, can be used.

For a complete interfacing handled like an underlining   Figure 9-3 pictures general rules for cutting underlining sections or pieces for a complete interfacing; and the general principles, shown on basic pattern pieces, can be applied to any pattern piece. The general rules are as follows: use the main structural pieces of the pattern only (do not include facings). Cut pieces exactly like the pattern along all edges with seam allowances, as shown. If the piece is to be cut on a fold, cut the underlining or interfacing on the fold. The only variation in cutting is involved with edges which have self-facings or hems; the self-facing and hem areas should not be underlined or interfaced, to reduce bulk in those areas which will have a double thickness of fabric. To prepare the pattern for cutting, fold under the edges to allow for cutting in one of two ways shown in Figure 9-3.

If the fabric for the garment is of typical suiting or coating weight, see sketch a. Cut the underlining or interfacing to a level ⅛ to ¼ inch above or inside hemlines and fold lines; cutting just inside hemlines or fold lines will allow facings and hems to fold back smoothly. Use the ⅛-inch measurement for most suiting-weight fabrics and use the ¼-inch measurement for bulky coating fabrics.

If the fabric for the garment is lightweight (dress-weight woolen, denim, brocade, etc.), see sketch b. Cut the underlining or interfacing to a level ½ inch below or outside fold lines and hemlines. Cut in this way, a ½ inch edge of the supporting fabric will fold back on itself, creating a double thickness at hem and facings edges to provide a crisper, firmer effect at the finished edges.

The rules stated above can be applied to

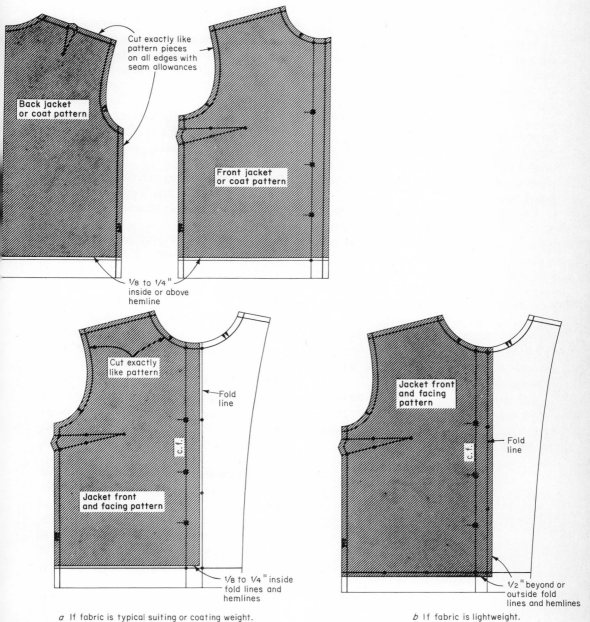

Cut exactly like
pattern pieces
on all edges with
seam allowances

Back jacket
or coat pattern

Front jacket
or coat pattern

1/8 to 1/4"
inside or above
hemline

Cut exactly
like pattern

Fold
line

c. f.

Jacket front
and facing pattern

1/8 to 1/4" inside
fold lines and
hemlines

a If fabric is typical suiting or coating weight.

Jacket front
and facing
pattern

Fold
line

c. f.

1/2" beyond or
outside fold
lines and hemlines

b If fabric is lightweight.

*FIGURE 9-3   To cut underlining sections or pieces for a complete
interfacing, handled like an underlining.*

any pattern shape or design. Most persons have no difficulty understanding the purpose of cutting to a level above or inside a hemline, but many are confused by self-facings and the accompanying fold lines. It will be helpful to think of self-facings as if they were hems and to keep in mind that no matter where a facing and its fold line appear (at the front edge, as shown, or at a pocket edge or at the lower edge of the yoke, etc.), the facing will fold back exactly like a hem.

Alter and adapt general rules to solve special problems. General rules are guidelines that best serve most purposes and most persons, but rules are to be used and followed as appropriate and under some circumstances to be broken. For example, a gusset is a structural piece, but it is very small and because of its position in the garment, there is no advantage in giving it additional stiffness; it need not be interfaced if the wearer would like less stiffness under the arm.

The sleeve can be handled in three different ways, as explained on page 357; it is a structural piece, but it need not always be cut by the general rules.

CONSTRUCTION TECHNIQUES

The supporting fabrics, both interfacings and underlinings, are involved in many technical tailoring details. For example, the lapel area and the collar will be shaped and molded in such a way that the fabric for the garment and the supporting fabric will truly act as one; detailed directions for handling these areas will appear in appropriate sections of the text. The initial steps included in this section are largely involved with basting the supporting fabrics in place in preparation for more detailed work to follow.

Partial interfacing Directions here are very brief, because this is the method covered in detail on the instruction sheet of the pattern. See sketch *a* in Figure 9-1 for an overall understanding of basic principles of construction. Seam edges of the interfacings are caught in with the stitching of seams (front, neck, shoulder, and armhole edges). The inner edge of the interfacing is catch-stitched to the garment. Both edges of the bias strip are catch-stitched to the garment. The fact that the front interfacing and the bias strips are cut ½ inch wider than the facing and hem makes it possible to catch-stitch those edges to the interfacing only, without catching the stitches through to the garment. Note that there is a great deal of hand work involved in this method.

Underlining and interfacing combined Directions here are brief, because this method is a combination of the partial interfacing (covered in detail on the instruction sheet) and an underlining. Directions for handling the underlining are included in Figures 9-4 to 9-6 and the accompanying text.

See sketch *b* in Figure 9-1 for an overall understanding of basic principles of construction. The underlining is basted to the pieces of the garment before any stitching is done so that it is caught in with the stitching of seams on all edges. The inner edge of the interfacing is catch-stitched to the underlining, without catching the stitches through to the garment. The inner edge of the facing is catch-stitched to the interfacing only. The hem is catch-stitched through the underlining to the underside of the garment fabric.

Complete interfacing handled like an underlining

Detailed directions are included in Figures 9-4 to 9-6 and the accompanying text. See sketch *c* in Figure 9-1 for an overall understanding of basic principles of construction. The interfacing is basted to the pieces of the garment before any basting or stitching is done so that it is caught in with the stitching of seams on all edges. The inner edge of the facing is catch-stitched to the interfacing only. The hem is catch-stitched through the interfacing to the underside of the garment fabric. Note that this method, which is highly recommended, requires the minimum amount of hand work.

Initial steps for underlinings or complete interfacings handled like an underlining

The technique of handling supporting fabrics is essentially the same in jackets and coats and in skirts and pants. Work is somewhat more complicated in a jacket or coat because of the complications of shaping the collar and lapel areas and because the greater number and variety of design details in the jacket or coat necessarily demand more time and effort. Before beginning work, it will be helpful to review the more simple techniques included in "Directions for Underlining Skirts and Pants" on pages 303 to 309.

Transfer pattern markings Because much of the construction of basic jackets and coats is done from the inside, pattern markings, marked on the supporting fabric, are more helpful than tailor's tacks in the major fabric. Before removing the pattern piece, mark dots for darts with a pencil. After the pattern is removed, draw any ruler-straight dartlines or seamlines with a light pencil line, as shown in Figure 9-4; these will be an aid to accurate stitching. Curved seamlines can be drawn in pencil for stitching guidelines, if desired. Pencil lines are pictured in Figure 9-4 but are not shown in subsequent sketches.

Press center-fold creases from both fabrics before combining corresponding sections The supporting fabric and the fabric for the garment must act as one in the finished garment, and this is possible only if both fabrics are absolutely smooth and flat before they are combined.

Combine sections of the garment and the supporting fabric

See sketch *a* in Figure 9-4. Smooth the body sections of the jacket or coat on a table with the wrong side uppermost. Place the interfacing or underlining sections on the inside (wrong side) of the garment pieces, cut edges even. Smooth and pat the two together flat on the table. Although seamed edges were cut in such a way that they should fall with cut edges even, little inaccuracies in cutting will result in very slight differences in the cut edges. Do not force the edges together in perfect cut-edges-even position if it seems obvious that there are slight cutting irregularities. Pin all edges in place. Pin along the center-fold lines and along the center of darts, as shown.

Sketch *b* shows the supporting fabric sections properly affixed. The basting must be done by hand and must be firm enough to hold the pieces securely in place; in most cases, stitches about ½ inch long are adequate. By basting ⅜ inch in from cut edges as indicated, the fabrics are well controlled near the seamline, where control is needed, and yet basting stitches will not be caught in with the stitching of the seam itself.

Treatment at dartlines Baste through the center of all dartlines as shown in sketch *b* of Figure 9-4; shorten the stitches near the dart tip and baste slightly beyond

the tip, as shown. These stitches are especially important because they hold the two layers together so that they can better act as one as the dart is stitched. Darts are more difficult to stitch in underlined garments because of the additional layer of fabric, and the problem is magnified right at the tip.

Treatment at fold lines Most of the edges of the supporting fabric will be caught in when seams are stitched. One exception is at the fold line of garments with a self-facing, as shown in Figure 9-5.

Sketch *a* shows the proper treatment if the supporting fabric was cut ⅛ inside the fold line. The edge is basted in the usual manner and then catch-stitched to the garment *up to the level of the top buttonhole.* The stitch must be small and inconspicuous (catching in just a thread or two of the fabric) and be placed to fall right along the fold line. *If there is a lapel, baste along the roll line, as shown, and do not catch-stitch*

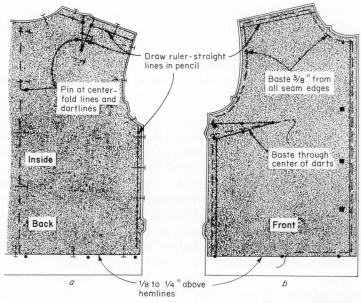

Draw ruler-straight lines in pencil

Pin at center-fold lines and dartlines

Baste ⅜" from all seam edges

Inside

Baste through center of darts

Back

Front

a

⅛ to ¼" above hemlines

b

FIGURE 9-4 *To apply sections of an underlining or a complete interfacing handled like an underlining.*

the edge above the top buttonhole marking. Later, after the lapel area is shaped, this edge will be catch-stitched in place.

Sketch *b* shows the proper treatment if the supporting fabric was cut ½ inch beyond the fold line. The edge is basted in the usual manner and then blind-stitched to the garment *up to the level of the top buttonhole marking.* The blind stitch is done from the right side with very small inconspicuous stitches placed right along the fold line. *If there is a lapel, baste along the roll line, as shown, and do not blind-stitch the edge above the top buttonhole marking.* Later, after the lapel area is shaped, this edge will be blind-stitched in place.

Treatment at hemlines The lower edge of the supporting fabric is basted in place at this time. Later, after the desired hemline has been permanently established, the lower edge can be secured. It is done the same as along fold lines—as shown in sketch *a* or *b,* depending on the cutting plan used. It is not necessary to secure this edge if the supporting fabric was cut ⅛ to ¼ inch above the hemline, but this must be done if the alternative plan is used.

To underline or interface sleeves See Figure 9-6. It requires special handling to combine sleeve sections; they cannot be smoothed out flat on the table because the sleeve takes such a sharp curve on the body. Pieces combined while they are flat on a table are identical in size, and if the sleeve sections were handled this way, the supporting fabric (which must take a sharp inside curve on the arm) would be too wide and would ripple or buckle on the inside of the sleeve. To prevent this, sleeve sections must be handled in such a way that the supporting fabric is narrower than the garment section.

Use a magazine rolled into a tube approximately the size of the sleeve—about

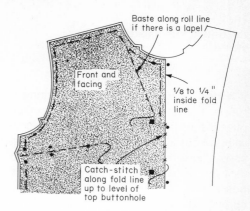

Baste along roll line if there is a lapel

Front and facing

⅛ to ¼ " inside fold line

Catch-stitch along fold line up to level of top buttonhole

a If supporting fabric was cut ⅛ to ¼ inch inside fold lines.

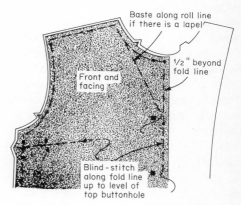

Baste along roll line if there is a lapel

½ " beyond fold line

Front and facing

Blind-stitch along fold line up to level of top buttonhole

b If supporting fabric was cut ½ inch beyond fold lines.

FIGURE 9-5   *Treatment at fold lines.*

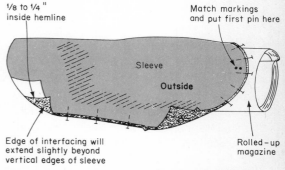

⅛ to ¼ " inside hemline

Match markings and put first pin here

Sleeve

Outside

Edge of interfacing will extend slightly beyond vertical edges of sleeve

Rolled-up magazine

FIGURE 9-6   *Shaping technique for working with a sleeve.*

6 inches in diameter. Fasten it with string or rubber bands. Place the garment sections over the interfacing or underlining pieces with the outside (right side) uppermost, as shown. First match the pattern markings at the cap of the sleeve (and at the underarm position in the under sleeve) and then secure those matching points with the first pins.

Continuing to work over the curved surface, smooth and pat the two fabrics together, and pin the remaining edges in place. This takes care and thought because the edges will not fit with cut edges even. Edges of the supporting fabric will extend slightly beyond the vertical edges of the sleeve, as illustrated in the sketch; they will extend a greater amount if the fabric is heavy. The worker must balance the two sides of each sleeve section. If the supporting fabric extends 1/8 inch beyond one vertical edge, it should extend about the same amount beyond the other. If the two vertical edges are not the same, the two sections are not properly aligned. After the edges are properly pinned, baste in the usual manner and then trim the supporting fabric even with the cut edge of the garment sections.

Miscellaneous details

To baste seams and darts and to stagger seam edges and reduce bulk after seams are stitched, see "Consider the Two Fabrics as One and Baste Sections Together in the Usual Manner" and "After Seams and Darts Are Stitched, Stagger the Edges to Reduce

Bulk," beginning on page 307. The directions in those sections include directions for the structural pieces of the garment only. The collar and lapel area requires special treatment—see "Principles of Shaping the Tailored Garment" on the following page. A suggestion for interfacing belts, welts, and other strip-like, small units of design appears under "Adaptations of the Shaping Principle" on page 376.

ASSEMBLE PIECES FOR A FINAL FITTING TEST

If a muslin test copy was not made, pieces must be basted together for a fitting; follow the fitting sequence in Chapter 6. It must be understood that some of the radical fitting procedures shown in Chapter 6 cannot be done after the garment is cut in fabric; the worker will have to accept the fact that she will not be able to correct certain serious problems at this time.

Even if a muslin test copy was made and fitting corrections were carefully recorded, there is an advantage in basting sections together for a final fitting test under certain circumstances. At this time—for the first time—it is possible to assess accurately the effect of the fabric on fit. The circumstances under which it is very important to go through another fitting test (even if a muslin test copy was made) are: (1) If the fabric is very different (heavier or lighter in weight) than those recommended for the pattern. (2) If the fabric is knitted. Knits will give or stretch somewhat (and they should for the best effect) but the amount and the direction—lengthwise or crosswise or both—of the natural stretch of the fabric could not have been anticipated accurately before this time. (3) If the design fits the body very snugly (nipped in at the waist and trimly fitted at the hipline), because then fabric thickness greatly influences overall size. Under these circumstances the garment must be fitted again. Pin up hemlines, pin the front facing sections into proper wearing position, and be sure center-front lines are lapped over each other before doing this final fitting. Extra layers of bulky fabric in hem and facing areas have a marked effect on overall size.

By contrast, the thickness and character of fabric are not a major concern provided that: (1) the fabric is comparable to those recommended for the pattern; (2) the fabric was taken into consideration at the time the muslin copy was fitted and (as recommended) an allowance was made for its thickness; and (3) the design is one with an ample amount of livability (a boxy jacket or coat) or a considerable allowance for style fullness. Under these circumstances, it is not necessary to do another fitting, although those who demand perfection will still want to make this final test.

PRINCIPLES OF SHAPING THE TAILORED GARMENT

The one thing, more than any other, that distinguishes tailoring from sewing is the shaping and molding that is an integral part of tailoring. And one of the advantages of knowing tailoring is that these shaping principles (if thoroughly understood) can be carried back to sewing, thereby improving the quality of all home-sewn garments.

A simple question will aid in understanding the principle of shaping: Can three wooden boxes, identical in size, be stacked into the area required for one box? This is very obviously impossible unless the boxes are graded in size. Keep this example in mind and consider the identical problem in sewing. In sewing, the "boxes" are fabric rather than wood, and they fit around curved edges rather than square corners, but the problem is identical. Two or more

objects (wood, paper, or fabric), identical in size, cannot be contained in the same area—the one on the inside must be smaller, or it must "give" in some way to decrease its size.

Consider the typical blouse collar, which is composed of two identical layers of fabric and one of interfacing—three boxes of identical size. These three are sewn to the garment and then curve in two ways as the collar rolls over and also bends around the neck. The three layers cannot be contained in the same area, and so usually the interfacing ripples up and a tiny crease is formed, and often the layer which is on the inside curve (the collar facing) creeps out, allowing the facing seam to show on the right side. The problem would not be present if the three layers differed slightly in size, with the one on the outside curve (the top section) being slightly larger than the one in the middle (the interfacing section) and both being slightly larger than the piece on the inside curve (the collar facing).

The wooden boxes and the typical blouse collar illustrate the problem. It is a greater problem in the tailored garment because of the thickness of fabric used for tailoring. Again the example of the boxes will be helpful: If the boxes were made of wood $\frac{1}{4}$ inch thick (like very heavy fabric), they would have to differ greatly in size in order to be contained in the same space, whereas if they were paper-thin (like lightweight fabric), the size differences would not be as great. The very nature of tailoring fabrics demands careful attention to this problem.

Examples of the shaping principle

The problem of shaping is solved by the position in which each edge and each segment of work is held as construction proceeds. *Work must be held in the position it will take when the garment is worn.* The reader has met this problem several times, although the issue has not been discussed in detail. It will be helpful to review certain construction details at this time. Refer back to the directions accompanying Figures 8-12 and 8-14 on pages 314 and 319. The skirt with a side opening was held in an outside curve like the body curve; this allowed the skirt to take the outside curve over the zipper. An example that is very easy to understand is mentioned in the directions accompanying sketch *d* in Figure 8-20 on page 325. Although the sketch shows the skirt turned wrong side out, so that the construction is visible, the directions state that the skirt should be held in wearing position as the underside of the waistband is finished; this allows the waistband to take the outside curve, while the ribbon is shaped to the inside curve. If the ribbon were stretched out flat it would not be as long, by actual measurement, as the waistband stretched out flat, but holding them in this position makes the two the same length.

An example which is comparable to the problems that will be encountered in tailoring appears in the directions accompanying Figure 9-6 on page 366. Because the sleeve takes such a sharp curve on the arm, the supporting fabric for the sleeve must be narrower than the sleeve. By shaping the sleeve sections over a curved surface comparable to the curve of the arm, work is held in proper wearing position.

Shaping the collar

The shaping principle is greatly involved with work on the collar and lapel areas because these areas take sharp curves when the garment is worn and because they are such prominent features of the finished costume.

The commercial pattern for a tailored garment allows for shaping to some extent. This is why the typical suit or coat pattern includes two collar patterns—the under-collar pattern is smaller than the upper-collar pattern, so that it can take the inside curve on the figure. However, it is impossible for the pattern company to solve every problem of size gradations. The worker must solve most of these problems by considering the weight of her own fabric because the pattern company must make the pattern for "average" fabric (usually medium-weight fabric).

Sketch *a* in Figure 9-7 shows the typical collar composed of two pattern pieces. Place the upper-collar pattern over the under-collar pattern with neck edges (notched edges) and center-back lines matching. Note that the upper-collar pattern is slightly wider and longer because the upper collar will take the outside curve on the figure. The amount is about $\frac{1}{8}$ to $\frac{1}{4}$ inch for a suit pattern and about $\frac{1}{4}$ inch or perhaps slightly more for a typical winter coat pattern; the pattern company has estimated the size difference based on the fabric that will be used by most persons. Note that the under collar is cut on the bias as a further aid to folding over and shaping to the inside curve on the figure.

Sketch *b* pictures the one-piece collar pattern in which the upper and under collar are combined in one piece. Usually this pattern is cut on the bias, as shown. When this pattern is folded along the fold line, there may be no size differences between the two halves or the differences in the two halves may not be as great as those stated above; this is because the bias cut allows one half, which will become the under collar, to ease slightly to shape to the inside curve, while the other half, which will become the upper collar, stretches slightly to take the outside curve.

Shaping the two-piece collar See Figure 9-8. Join the center-back seam of the under-collar sections. Trim the seam to ⅜ inch and press open, as shown in sketch a. Join the center-back seam in the interfacing sections, as shown in sketch b. In

order to reduce bulk, this must be a lapped seam. Lap one raw edge of interfacing 1¼ inches over the other (in other words, lap seamlines) and machine-stitch. Trim each seam edge to ¼ inch. Then pin the interfacing to the under collar, neck edges (notched edges) even, as shown in sketch c, and baste the neck edge only.

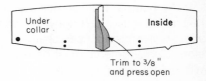

a Join under-collar sections.

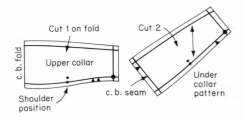

a Typical pattern includes two collar patterns.

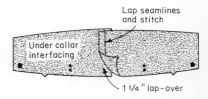

b Join interfacing sections with lapped seam.

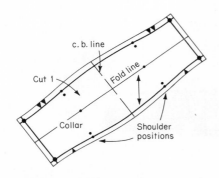

b Upper and under collars combined in one piece

FIGURE 9-7 *Examples of collar patterns.*

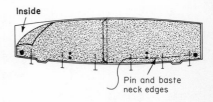

c Baste interfacing to under collar.

FIGURE 9-8 *To prepare interfacing and under-collar sections.*

See Figure 9-9. The roll line of the collar must be marked with a pencil line on the interfacing piece, as shown. Some patterns include this roll line, in which case it can be marked from the pattern. However, if there is a lapel and if the position of the top buttonhole was changed during fitting, the roll line will be slightly different; in that case, it must be marked by taking measurements from the muslin test copy or from the garment as it was basted for a fitting. Corresponding measurements must be carefully taken because no two roll lines are alike. Caution: Remember that seams have been stitched in the muslin test copy, but as yet the under collar has not been seamed, and therefore measurements must be taken to seamlines (not to cut edges).

See Figure 9-10. To shape the collar, hold it in a curve similar to wearing position, with the interfacing taking the outside curve over the under collar. Smooth the two together and baste along the roll line. Holding the unit in wearing position, pin the remaining edges in place, allowing the under-collar edge to extend as it will beyond the interfacing; because both layers were cut from the same pattern, the one taking the outside curve must have more width. The difference will not be great. Trim off the corner of the interfacing to a point about $\frac{1}{16}$ inch inside the seamlines, as shown. Baste the remaining collar edges together with basting stitches $\frac{5}{8}$ inch in from the cut edge of the under collar. Then pin the ends together and keep the unit in this position at all times.

Shaping the one-piece collar See Figure 9-11. The one-piece collar is interfaced to within $\frac{1}{8}$ to $\frac{1}{4}$ inch from the roll line. The interfacing should be basted to the

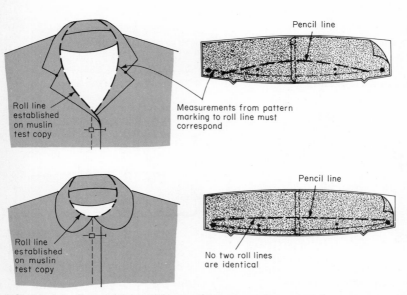

FIGURE 9-9 To establish roll line on the under collar.

half which will become the under collar; determine which half will be the under collar by comparing notches on the collar and neck edge of the garment. The under half of the collar will be sewn to the garment and will be notched like the garment pieces; the upper half will be sewn to the neck edges of the facing pieces. In these sketches a single notch has been used for the garment and the under collar, and a double notch for the upper collar and facing edges; be sure to check each pattern to see the notch system used for that particular pattern.

The one-piece collar is shaped in exactly the same manner as the two-piece collar; see the detailed directions above. The principles are the same, and the extra width of the collar is of no concern in this step of construction.

NOTE: The collar cut in one with the front pattern is shaped much later in the construction sequence—after shoulder and back neck seams are stitched. It is handled in the same way (essentially) as these more typical collars, but it requires that the collar and lapel be shaped in one operation. See Figure 9-13 for details.

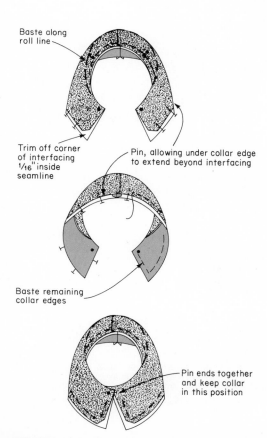

Baste along roll line

Trim off corner of interfacing 1/16" inside seamline

Pin, allowing under collar edge to extend beyond interfacing

Baste remaining collar edges

Pin ends together and keep collar in this position

FIGURE 9-10   To shape under collar and interfacing.

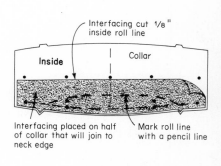

Interfacing cut 1/8" inside roll line

Inside　　　Collar

Interfacing placed on half of collar that will join to neck edge

Mark roll line with a pencil line

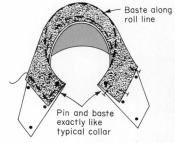

Baste along roll line

Pin and baste exactly like typical collar

FIGURE 9-11   To shape a one-piece collar.

Shaping the lapel area—initial steps

The principles of shaping the lapel area are exactly the same as those for the collar. Remove any bastings in the lapel area. See sketch *a* in Figure 9-12. Establish the roll line of the lapel by taking corresponding measurements from the muslin copy, just as with the collar. The roll line on the lapel is a ruler-straight line which ends at the level of the top buttonhole marking, as shown. The roll line is established in the same manner for the garment with a separate facing or a self-facing, as shown.

See sketch *b*. To shape the lapel, hold it in a position similar to wearing position, folding the lapel to the outside along the

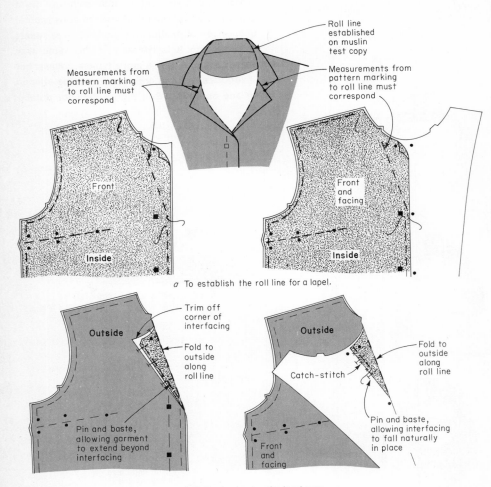

a To establish the roll line for a lapel.

b To begin shaping the lapel area.

FIGURE 9-12 *Shaping the lapel area—initial steps.*

roll line. Garments with separate facings and those with self-facings are shaped in the same manner, as shown. With the lapel in wearing position, pin the remaining edges in place, allowing the interfacing to fall into place as it will. The interfacing will not appear to be as wide as it was originally (will not reach to the cut edge or the fold line) because some of the width was required to bend around the curve. In the garment with a separate facing, trim off the corner of the interfacing, as shown. Baste the interfacing in place. Pin the lapel to the garment to keep it folded to the outside at all times.

If the garment has a self-facing, catch-stitch the free edge of the interfacing in place in the lapel area.

Shaping the collar and lapel area for a collar cut in one with the front

Figure 9-13 illustrates that the collar cut in one with the garment presents shaping problems that are identical to those of a collar and a lapel; the collar and lapel are simply shaped in one operation. The principles are the same, and the detailed directions given above can be adapted to this design. The only difference is that this step is done after the shoulder and neck seams are stitched.

Padding stitches aid in shaping the collar and lapel

Padding stitches are small running stitches made from the interfacing side and caught through the layer of interfacing to the underside of the garment fabric. The stitches are done in such a way that they take a slightly diagonal line, which allows for a certain amount of shifting or freedom in the area.

The purposes of padding stitches are:

(1) to hold two layers of fabric together so that they truly act as one fabric, (2) to aid in shaping the garment by molding the shaped areas together in wearing position, (3) to ensure that the shaped area will retain its shape throughout years of wear, and (4) to stiffen the area for the desired effect. The collar and lapel areas of the garment, where a molded, shaped effect is especially important, must be pad-stitched. The stitches will aid in shaping the garment if they are done while holding the garment in the position it will take when worn. A stiffening effect is required to support the stand of the collar and is often an advantage at corners where a limp fabric might tend to curl.

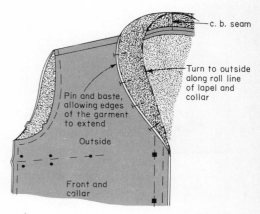

FIGURE 9-13 To establish the roll line and shape a collar cut in one with the front piece.

The length of the stitch, the frequency of rows, and the kind of thread used allow for great differences in results. See Figure 9-14, which pictures a portion of a collar to illustrate the placement of stitches and their purposes. The sketch pictures the collar in a flat position, but the collar should be kept in a shaped position when work is in progress. Note that no stitches are placed in the seam allowances so that the interfacing can be trimmed later for a staggered seam. The area between the neck edge and the roll line is the portion of the collar that will stand at the neckline, and so smaller stitches spaced in narrow rows are used for extra stiffness and body. The portion of the collar that is visible as the garment is worn can have a somewhat softer effect, which is achieved by larger stitches, spaced less frequently. The small area at the corner, which might have a tendency to curl, is stiffened with small stitches. Note that rows of stitches are placed parallel to the roll line as an aid to more effective shaping.

The tautness of the stitch used has an effect on the result. A firm stitch, pulled flat against the fabric, will create more stiffness than a loose, "lazy" stitch. Therefore, the stitch can be held flat in the lower part of the collar and can have greater freedom in the remaining part if a soft, somewhat limp effect is desired.

The padding stitches will make a noticeable change in the hand or character of the fabric—the entire collar will feel much firmer, and the areas with smaller stitches will be definitely stiffer. The kind of thread used also influences the firmness and stiffness of the collar. Silk thread will create less bulk and stiffness than mercerized thread in a utilitarian weight.

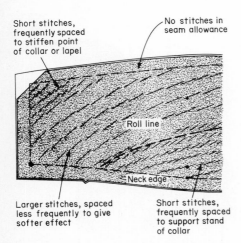

Short stitches, frequently spaced to stiffen point of collar or lapel

No stitches in seam allowance

Roll line

Neck edge

Larger stitches, spaced less frequently to give softer effect

Short stitches, frequently spaced to support stand of collar

FIGURE 9-14 Placement and purposes of padding stitches.

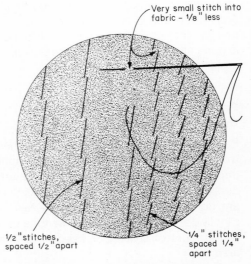

Very small stitch into fabric – 1/8" less

1/2" stitches, spaced 1/2" apart

1/4" stitches, spaced 1/4" apart

FIGURE 9-15 To do padding stitches.

To do padding stitches See Figure 9-15 for general directions. The two lengths pictured are used most frequently, but there is no reason why stitches must be a certain length; they can be longer for a softer effect or as small as ⅛ inch if a great deal of body and stiffness is desired.

A single thread is used, and it should never be knotted but merely fastened with a few short stitches. The position in which work is held can vary with individual preferences, but the position shown, with rows in a vertical position, allows for a very comfortable hand position because the stitch is made at right angles to the row; note that the needle can be held in a comfortable right-to-left position. The fact that the stitch into the fabric is made at right angles to the direction of the row results in the diagonal stitch that is visible from the interfacing side. The stitch that passes through the interfacing to the underside of the fabric should be as small as possible and this stitch does not vary in size, no matter what length of visible stitch is used. The longer visible stitch is merely a result of taking fewer stitches.

NOTE: **Work must be held in wearing position. Refer to the drawings in Figures 9-11, 9-12, and 9-13 and hold the work in the same position while doing padding stitches. The entire collar and the lapel area (between the roll line of the lapel and the finished front edge) should be pad-stitched.**

Pressing as an aid to shaping

Figure 9-16 shows a typical under collar and lapel area, shaped and pad-stitched. The faint lines (parallel to the fold lines of the collar and lapel) indicate rows of padding stiches.

NOTE: **The rows of padding stitches will not appear in the remaining sketches in this chapter.**

The shaped areas should be pressed over a curved surface similar to the curve these areas will take on the body. A rolled turkish towel is excellent as a pressing surface for the collar; tip the iron as required to press over the curve, pressing only very small segments at a time. The tailor's cushion should be used for pressing lapel areas.

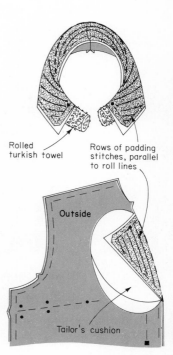

Rolled turkish towel

Rows of padding stitches, parallel to roll lines

Outside

Tailor's cushion

FIGURE 9-16 *Pressing aids in shaping collar and lapel areas.*

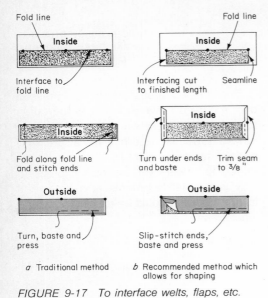

Fold line	Fold line
Inside	Inside
Interface to fold line	Interfacing cut to finished length Seamline
Inside	Inside
Fold along fold line and stitch ends	Turn under ends and baste Trim seam to 3/8"
Outside	Outside
Turn, baste and press	Slip-stitch ends, baste and press
a Traditional method	*b* Recommended method which allows for shaping

FIGURE 9-17   To interface welts, flaps, etc.

Adaptations of the shaping principle

Figures 9-17 through 9-19 show various band-like design features. The way interfacing is applied and the manner of construction of these strip-like details can incorporate the shaping principles. The traditional method of construction is pictured in Figures 9-17a and 9-18a. Note that the interfacing is caught in with the seams and that it will be turned to the inside, forcing it to occupy less space; since it cannot occupy less space, the interfacing will buckle and form a tiny crease or ripple. The recommended construction shown in Figures 9-17b and 9-18b allows for shaping and will result in flat bands. Note that the interfacing is cut to the finished size and that it is not caught in with the end seams. The garment fabric is folded over the interfacing, and finishing is done by hand.

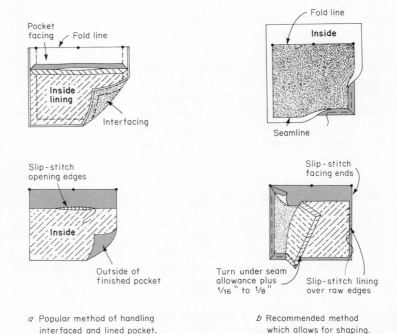

a Popular method of handling interfaced and lined pocket.

b Recommended method which allows for shaping.

FIGURE 9-18   To interface and line patch pockets.

Figure 9-19 pictures this recommended construction adapted to belts. The traditional construction of the belt is very similar to that of the welt or pocket flap pictured in Figure 9-17, with the interfacing caught in with the stitching of the belt seam. By cutting the belt interfacing to the desired width and length, the fabric can be worked over the interfacing for a very flat and attractive effect.

NOTE: **Pellon is an excellent interfacing fabric for any belt, welt, or other striplike design feature. The heavier weights are ideal for belts, and lighter weights can be used if desired for softer effects in welts or pockets.**

Apply principles to other units

The principle of shaping is basically the principle of holding work in wearing position and smoothing layers together rather than working cut edges even; held in this way, edges will not fall with cut edges even, because the piece taking the outside curve must be slightly larger (wider or longer or both). The principle can be applied to any construction detail; sections of the garment will always be smoother if they are combined while in wearing position.

The need for shaping is more pronounced in any unit that will curve sharply when worn; for example, the collar and the lapel roll over in a sharp curve, whereas the entire jacket or coat curves around the figure in a much larger curve. Two units which roll or fold over as sharply as a collar are cuffs and pocket flaps. If these units are held in wearing position (rolled over) while the interfacing is applied and the two sections are faced, they can be smoothed in place and thereby molded into permanent shape.

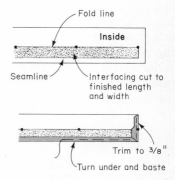

a Belt with seam at one edge - one fold line

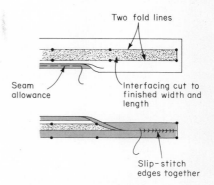

b Belt with center seam - two fold lines.

FIGURE 9-19 Suggestions for interfacing belts.

TAPING THE FRONT AND LAPEL AREAS

Narrow cotton twill tape, available in white or black, is used for several purposes in the tailored garment. The tape must be preshrunk because it shrinks considerably in dry cleaning. It is available in a variety of widths; widths recommended for tailoring purposes are ¼ or ⅜ inch.

The tape serves the following purposes: (1) It strengthens those edges which will get constant strain as the garment is worn (front edges), (2) it strengthens bias lines that will be subject to strain and subsequent stretching (the lapel line), (3) it strengthens slightly bias seams to prevent stretching (shoulder and armhole edges in all garments and the waistline in fitted garments), and (4) it stiffens those edges where a flat,

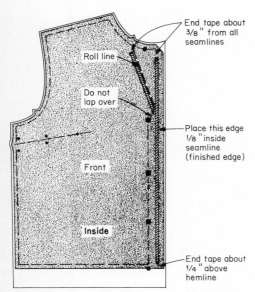

Roll line

End tape about ⅜" from all seamlines

Do not lap over

Place this edge ⅛" inside seamline (finished edge)

Front

Inside

End tape about ¼" above hemline

FIGURE 9-20   General rules for placement of twill tape.

hard line is desirable. The fourth purpose requires some explanation. A flat, hard line is desirable at the finished front edge of the garment (seamline or a fold line); the front edge should look flat and sharply creased, and the addition of twill tape will be helpful. In general, this is the only place where tape is used for this particular purpose in women's tailoring. It is used at many more edges in men's tailoring; for example, it is used at all edges of the collar in men's suits and coats to achieve the very flat, hard-pressed appearance that is desirable in menswear.

NOTE: The taping of shoulder, armhole, and waistline edges (of fitted garments) will be done after the garment has been assembled; directions appear on page 380.

General rules for placement

The general rules appear in Figure 9-20, and adaptations are shown in Figure 9-21. The general rules are:

1 Place the tape ⅛ inch inside the finished front edge (⅛ inch inside the seamline if there is a separate facing or ⅛ inch inside the fold line if there is a self-facing), with the tape placed in the body of the garment, not in the seam allowance.

2 End the tape about ⅜ inch from seamlines (at the neck edge, for example) and from the hemline, as shown. This will allow for seam allowances to turn back with a minimum of bulk.

3 Do not lap over the ends of the tape as the tape at the roll line of the lapel meets the tape at the front edge; the garment must bend over at this point and will need freedom. The tape should be trimmed so that the end just touches the tape at the front edge, as shown.

4 Place the tape just inside the roll line of the lapel, as shown.

Adaptation of general rules

Figure 9-21 pictures several circumstances that might be encountered. Sketches *a* and *b* are concerned with the garment with a self-facing, which might have been interfaced in the two ways pictured. The rules for placement of the tape are exactly the same: the tape is placed ⅛ inch inside the finished front edge, which is, in these examples, a fold line. The only difference is that the stitches which secure the tape will not be exactly the same. In sketch *a,* one edge of the tape will be hand-stitched to the interfacing layer, and the other edge will be secured with stitches placed right along the roll line into the underside of the garment fabric. In sketch *b,* one row of stitches (at the inner edge) will be secured to the interfacing only, while the stitches along the fold line should pass through the interfacing and catch into the underside of the garment fabric right along the roll line.

Sketch *c* pictures the collar cut in one with the garment. The tape is placed ⅛ inch inside the seamline at the front edge according to the general rules. It can extend into the collar area to achieve the effect desired. It can stop at the roll-line level if a very soft effect is desired on the collar edge. It can continue into the lapel area or even extend entirely to the center-back line if a hard-creased edge is desired. The roll line for the collar and lapel should not be taped at this time; it should be taped after the center-back seam is joined so that it can pass across the center-back seam in one continuous strip.

Sketch *d* pictures a curved front edge. The tape is placed ⅛ inch inside the seamline at the front and curved edge according to the general rules; it should end ⅛ inch above the hemline, as shown. The tape must be flat to the garment at the outer curved edge and therefore must be eased in slightly at the inner curve.

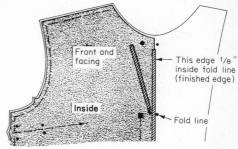

a If interfacing was cut ⅛ to ¼ " inside fold line of self-facing

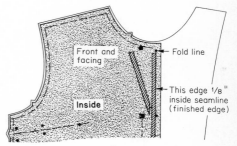

b If interfacing was cut ½ " beyond fold line of self-facing

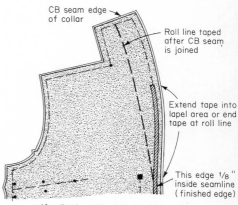

c If collar is cut in one with the garment

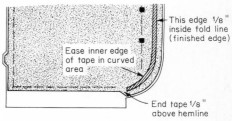

d If the lower front corner is curved

FIGURE 9-21 *Adaptations of general rules.*

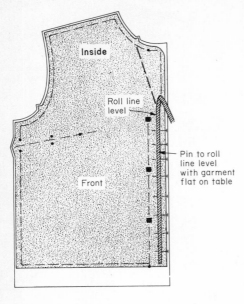

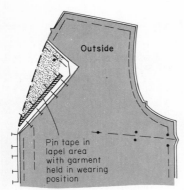

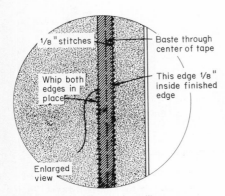

FIGURE 9-22 To apply twill tape.

To apply twill tape

See Figure 9-22. The garment must be held in wearing position as the tape is applied. Pin the tape to the garment between the hemline and the roll line, with the garment flat on a table. Do not pull and tug at the tape, but simply pat it in place along a ruler-straight line. A pencil line at the seamline will be an aid to proper placement. Pin it in place with pins spaced frequently to obtain a perfectly straight line. Then working from the outside with the lapel area held in wearing position, pin the tape over the curve and into proper position. Baste along the center of the tape. The enlarged view shows the tape in proper position along a seamed edge. Both edges must be whipped in place with small (⅛-inch) stitches, as shown, with stitches catching through the interfacing layer only.

TAPING SEAMS AND EDGES OF THE ASSEMBLED GARMENT

For the sake of continuity, these directions are included in this section; but under actual working conditions, the garment will not be assembled until later, after buttonholes have been made.

Figure 9-23 shows additional uses for cotton twill tape. Seamlines which are slightly bias and which will get strain as the garment is worn should be strengthened with tape. After a seam is stitched and pressed open, tape is centered along the seamline, as shown at the shoulder seam in sketch *a*. Reread General Rules for Placement on page 378. Whip both edges in place, catching in the seam thickness only.

The neck edge of a collarless garment will get considerable strain in wearing and will stretch unless it is strengthened with twill tape, as shown in sketch *a*. Tape the neck edge between the center-front lines by easing the tape to fit around the curve (see the directions accompanying sketch *d* in Figure 9-21) and placing the tape ⅛ inch inside the seamline. Whip both edges of the tape in place, catching in the supporting fabric only.

The slightly bias, curving lines at armhole edges should be taped, as shown in sketch *a*. Tape the armhole edge between the notches, as shown, placing the tape ⅛ inch inside the seamline. The armhole edge has a slight curve, so the tape must be shaped and eased to the curve. Whip both edges of the tape in place, catching in the supporting fabric only.

If the sleeve is cut in one with the garment, tape a portion of the shoulder seam, as shown in sketch *b*. The length of the shoulderline is about 5 inches, and it is this portion of the seam that will get strain as the garment is worn.

If the garment is snugly fitted at the waist, there will be a great deal of strain at that level when it is worn. Sketch *c* shows how tape can be used to strengthen the garment. Hold the garment in the curve it will take on the figure and pin the tape along the waist level; this position will ensure that the strain will fall on the tape, rather than on the garment. Tack the tape to vertical seams and fasten one end to the end of the buttonhole scrap, as shown. On the left front, where there is no buttonhole, the tape can extend to the front edge and be tacked to the tape along the front edge.

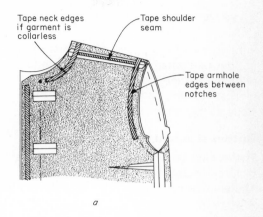

Tape neck edges if garment is collarless

Tape shoulder seam

Tape armhole edges between notches

a

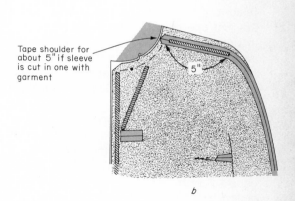

Tape shoulder for about 5" if sleeve is cut in one with garment

5"

b

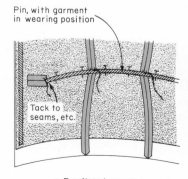

Pin, with garment in wearing position

Tack to seams, etc.

c For fitted garments

FIGURE 9-23   *To apply tape after the body of the garment has been assembled.*

BUTTON SELECTION

If the size and placement of buttons were not decided when a test copy was made, refer to "Decide on Size and Placement of Buttons" on page 248 and do those steps at this time.

Button size and design

The fashion sketch on the pattern envelope pictures a button of the appropriate size. There are several factors to be considered. A large woman can use a larger button than a small woman. If there are many buttons, they must be smaller than if there are just one or two. The button must be in proportion to the length of the edge it is near. For example, the button on a huge pocket can be much larger than the one on a tiny pocket. The designer of the commercial pattern is an expert at such matters of beauty and proportion, so it is well to buy a button comparable in size to the button pictured in the sketch. The gauge for stating button size is forty lines equals 1 inch—for example, a twenty-line button is ½ inch in diameter. The button size is usually stated in the list of notions; if it is not, the fashion sketch reveals the approximate size. Cut circles of paper or matching fabric to simulate contrasting or covered buttons and to test the size and number on the figure if this was not decided on the muslin test copy. Experiment with different sizes of circles and numbers of buttons.

It is impossible to offer a complete classification of button types; they are available in infinite variety. Some of the most common types are flat buttons with a shank or eyes (those with eyes are more casual), combination buttons with a decorative rim at the edge, and ball buttons (full ball or half ball). The ball types are most appropriate for use with corded loops; the half-ball type can be used with worked or bound buttonholes, while the full ball is rarely used with traditional buttonholes because it is too easily unbuttoned under the stress of wearing conditions.

Purchased buttons The design of the button is largely a matter of personal choice. If the buttons are to serve a strictly utilitarian purpose (for example, those on the front of a blazer jacket) they should not be too unusual; if there are many buttons, an unusual design will give an overdecorated effect. If, however, there is only one button, its purpose is decorative and it can be of an elaborate design. If purchased contrasting buttons are to be used, it is well to take the jacket or coat front (or a scrap of comparable size) to the department store so that buttons can be tested under realistic circumstances. If the buttons are sold singly and are not on cards, they can be pinned to the front (or the sample) for a very accurate test. Buttons can add dollars in apparent cost to the garment, and by the same token they can cheapen the costume. The cost should be judged in the light of the total cost of the garment; if the costume investment is about $30, quality buttons will not influence total costs appreciably.

Self-covered buttons The button covered with the fabric of the costume is the frequent choice of the designer of ready-made costumes and the choice of the woman who sews as well. These buttons have great advantages: they are safe choices, for one cannot go very far wrong by choosing any one of the various types on the market. The button will be appropriate in color and texture, and it will harmonize with the garment. There is little or no chance of over-decoration. They look professional but they are not particularly striking and so are a wise choice for a row of several buttons of utilitarian function; yet they are pretty and attractive, and so they do add a nice touch to the design. And they are very much less expensive than a high-quality purchased button.

Metal frames are available at notions counters for covering buttons at home. The alternative is to have them professionally covered by the department store or Singer shop. Most professionals agree that it is wiser to have these buttons covered because the large machines used professionally get a much better grip on the fabric than one can at home, and the buttons will be more serviceable. It takes just a few days to have the buttons covered, and a little planning ahead will enable the woman who sews to have the more sturdy buttons without having to delay finishing her costume. Actually, the button-covering kits cost almost as much as professionally covered buttons; this fact is surprising to many persons who assume that doing it at home is always more economical.

Professionally covered buttons are available in a large variety of designs that add subtle interest to the costume. Study Figure 9-24 to see the infinite variety of effects that can be achieved by the style of the button, the choice of fabric, and perhaps the use of contrasting thread or a decorative rim. In each case these are subtle effects that will not overdecorate the costume, even if there are many buttons. The chart illustrates the wisdom of choosing something with a little bit of interest in preference to the plain round button. The more interesting buttons cost just a few cents more. These buttons come in many sizes, and in other shapes as well. Square designs often enhance a plaid costume, and the traditional full-ball and half-ball button is the choice for loop-and-button closings.

It is well to have one or two extra buttons covered to replace those which will get constant, heavy use.

After the buttons have been purchased, double check the choice by pinning them to the garment before making the buttonholes. It would be wiser to buy a different button now than to ruin the effect of the costume with the wrong design or size of button.

Plain covered button

Combination button with narrow rim and flat center — can be made all in self fabric or one section can be in contrast

Combination button with wide rim and rounded center — can be made all in self fabric or either section can be in contrast

Saddle — stitched button — stitches can be in matching or contrasting color

Usual combination button with gold or silver metallic cord covering the seam

Button with contrasting rim of metal (silver or gold), plastic (in basic contrasting colors), or white or smoke pearl (sometimes available)

FIGURE 9-24 Examples of designs for self-covered buttons.

nice touch if there is need for just one button. A strap and buckle, replacing buttons and buttonholes, is effective on sportswear.

Button substitutes   The decorative frog used on Oriental costumes can be used in place of buttons, but these frogs should be used sparingly on the costume to avoid an overdecorated effect. A corded strip of self-fabric knotted into a ball-like shape makes an attractive, different button. A half bow of self-fabric, to be pulled through the buttonhole like a button, is a

BUTTONHOLE CONSTRUCTION

Just as buttons are a part of the design, so are the accompanying buttonholes. Buttonholes which primarily serve a functional purpose have an important role to play, and they can be outstanding design features. Usually the buttonhole is func-

Diagonal buttonholes can be sewn by the machine or bound method in matching or contrasting color.

Buttons and buttonholes grouped — made by machine or bound method in matching or contrasting colors.

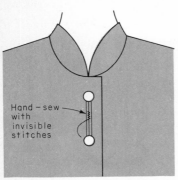

Long, wider–than–usual buttonhole, hand–sewn at the center to make two buttonholes — button or buttonhole or both can be in contrasting color.

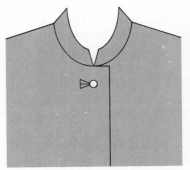

Triangular— bound buttonhole in matching or contrasting color — see another novelty adaptation in Figure 9–34.

FIGURE 9-25   Buttons and buttonholes as a design feature.

tional, and so it is done with matching thread if it is done by hand or machine and with self-fabric for bound, corded, and looped types.

See Figure 9-25 for examples of ways buttons and buttonholes can be used for design purposes. The more unique suggestions pictured must be used sparingly and on simple costumes for the striking detail to be the dominant feature of the design.

Types of buttonholes and appropriate uses

There are two types of buttonholes recommended for tailored garments. One of various types of bound buttonholes is most suitable for the softly tailored effects desired in women's tailoring, and the handworked tailor's buttonhole is reserved for menswear and women's garments that are obviously planned for a man-tailored look. The machine-worked buttonhole can be substituted for the tailor's buttonhole for man-tailored effects, but is not recommended for high-quality tailoring.

The bound buttonhole that is appropriate for most designs can be constructed in a great variety of ways. The one construction that is superior to all others is the two-piece corded buttonhole; this is the construction used by talented professionals on all high-quality ready-to-wear. The rounded lips of this buttonhole are much more attractive than the flat lips of the buttonholes made by all other construction methods. In addition, the stiffer, firmer edge results in a more serviceable buttonhole. However, the construction of a two-piece corded buttonhole is very difficult for most nonprofessionals because it requires great finger dexterity; results are somewhat unpredictable, and a mistake early in the construction process cannot be corrected later. Many persons who can make one beautiful two-piece corded buttonhole find

that making a row of beautiful ones is almost impossible. Because consistently excellent results are so difficult for most people to achieve by that method, the construction included in this text is one which requires less finger dexterity and in which slight mistakes can be corrected at several stages in the construction sequence. The construction includes a corded feature that results in a buttonhole so very like the two-piece one in appearance and serviceability that there is no need to attempt a method that is less predictable.

The bound buttonhole with a cording feature appears on page 387. A novelty construction (related to the bound types) is included on page 392; it is recommended for unusually heavy fabrics (especially fake furs and leathers) and for making buttonholes of decorative shapes. The tailor's buttonhole appears on page 395.

SPECIAL NOTE: **Directions for making two-piece corded buttonholes and loops for buttoned closings are included in the construction manuals prepared by the pattern companies. These directions are also available in greater detail in** *Creative Clothing Construction (Bane, McGraw-Hill, 1973).*

Placement on the garment

Buttonholes are placed on the right front of women's garments for a right-over-left button closing; they are placed on the left front of men's garments. The rule concerning placement of buttonholes on front openings of men's and women's garments is ordinarily very rigid. However, the rule was violated quite frequently in women's wear in the early 1970s; designers featured

**TAILORING THE JACKET
OR COAT**

left-over-right front buttonings on shirt-waists, tailored blouses, and casual coats to emphasize the man-tailored look and to give a certain unisex character which was currently fashionable.

The buttonhole is usually made at right angles to the front edge because this placement will hold the button more securely. If there is a band-type feature at the front edge, buttonholes must be made on the center-front line and parallel to the design feature. Special consideration must be given to the buttonhole placement at this time if these matters were not decided when the muslin test copy was made:

1 If there is a lapel, the upper buttonhole controls the roll line of the lapel—the lapel will fold back at the level of the upper buttonhole. If the lapel line was changed during fitting to allow for a longer or shorter lapel than that planned on the pattern, the buttonhole marking must be moved to the cor-rected level, and all buttonhole markings must be respaced.

2 If the garment is fitted snugly at the waist, there will be great strain at that level, and a button and buttonhole will be required at the waistline; a fastening that is a mere ½ inch above or below the waist will not control garment lines well. If the pattern marking is not exactly on the waistline of the figure, it must be moved to the cor-rected waist level, and all buttonhole mark-ings must be respaced.

3 If the garment is snugly fitted (the typical figure-hugging fitted suit or coat), there will be a buttonhole marking very near the bust level because of the strain at that level as the garment is worn. However, if the design is semifitted or boxy, there may not be a buttonhole marking at the bust level. However, if the wearer is large-busted and if she chooses to fit a boxy garment very snugly, there will be strain at the bust level; in this case, a buttonhole must be placed at that level, and all buttonhole mark-ings may have to be respaced.

4 If the jacket or coat has been length-ened or shortened, some adjustment of buttonhole markings may be required. If the garment is a full-length coat, marking an additional buttonhole or removing one marking may solve the problem. A change in jacket length requires more subtle changes, and probably all buttonhole mark-ings will have to be respaced.

5 There is some confusion about the place-ment of buttonholes on double-breasted designs. This confusion is due to the idea that every button should have a button-hole when in fact most pattern directions suggest buttonholes for only one of the two rows of buttons. The illustration in Figure 9-26 pictures a jacket front; the broken line indicates the center-front line. The worker will proceed with more con-fidence if she understands why most de-signers use only one row of buttonholes. Buttons must be an equal distance from the

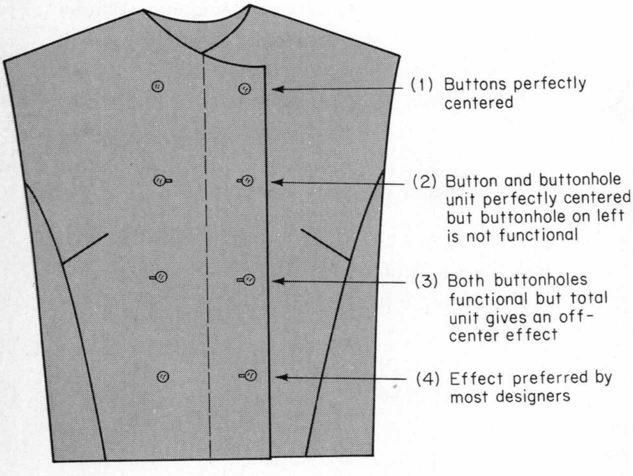

(1) Buttons perfectly centered

(2) Button and buttonhole unit perfectly centered but buttonhole on left is not functional

(3) Both buttonholes functional but total unit gives an off-center effect

(4) Effect preferred by most designers

FIGURE 9-26 Placement of buttons and but-tonholes on a double-breasted garment.

center-front line, as they are pictured. However, both the button and the buttonhole are a part of the total design effect and must be balanced (as balanced as possible) on each side of the center front; the button and the buttonhole make up the design unit.

Buttons pinned in place can be perfectly balanced, as shown at level 1. A unit of buttons and buttonholes can be perfectly balanced if the buttonholes are made in the position illustrated at level 2. However, a buttonhole is functional only if it extends from the button position toward the right half of the figure; if it extends toward the left of the button (as shown in the left half of the sketch), it looks wrong to the eye and will not be functional. Therefore, although a perfectly balanced effect has been achieved, this placement is not acceptable. The unit shown at level 3 is composed of functional buttonholes, but notice the resulting off-center effect. Although this placement is sometimes suggested, it is not a wise choice. The effect at level 4 is the one most favored by designers; although the unit is not as perfectly centered as the units at levels 1 and 2, it is more nearly centered than the unit at level 3. In other words, level 4 pictures the best placement to combine attractiveness and usefulness.

The left front will need the support that buttonholes would give it; it will be supported with large snaps, placed in position directly under the decorative row of buttons.

SPECIAL NOTE: **All types of bound buttonholes are made before the garment is assembled to gain the advantage of working with a smaller section. This is possible only if the number, size, and placement of buttons have been tested either on the muslin test copy or on the garment itself (basted for a fitting). Even if the garment is assembled, bound buttonholes are made before facings are applied. By contrast, the tailor's buttonhole is made after the facings are applied and turned to the inside—as one of the very last steps of construction.**

Bound buttonholes with a cording feature

See Figure 9-27, which shows a section of the finished garment. The finished front edge is a seamline (if there is a separate facing) or a fold line (if there is a self-facing). The sketch shows the facing turned to the inside, as it will be when the garment is finished. The measurement from the finished front edge to the center-front line is an indication of the button size recommended by the designer; buttons should not vary greatly from that recommended size. Note that one end of the buttonhole is about ⅛ inch beyond the center-front line; therefore, a button placed on the

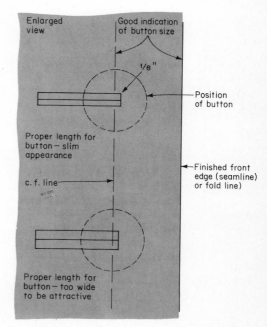

FIGURE 9-27   Standards of appearance.

center line of the left front will fasten in such a way that center-front lines will match.

The buttonhole should be slim in order to give an attractive appearance; a wide buttonhole is too conspicuous. Buttonholes have a tendency to look slightly smaller (in length and width) when finished, and because they should appear to be a scant ¼ inch wide when finished, a good general width for stitching is ¼ inch. Very short buttonholes should be slightly narrower to create similar proportions.

Ways in which buttonholes must be even Buttonholes must be spaced an equal distance apart and they must be even in length and width. In addition, they must be an equal distance from the finished edge. The finished edge is the edge of the garment when it is sewn and finished; this may be a fold line if the garment has a facing cut all in one with the garment, or it may be a seamline if a separate facing piece will be seamed to the garment. In all directions given in this chapter, the term *finished edge* is used and the worker must study her pattern to see whether that means fold line or seamline.

In addition to these four ways in which buttonholes must be even, keep in mind that if there are buttonholes in both the skirt and the jacket, they must be equally spaced and identically sized. To ensure consistency, make the paper patterns for all buttonholes (as in Figure 9-28) at the same time.

The *length* of the buttonhole is determined by the particular button size and need not be the same as given on the pattern. However, if buttons have been chosen wisely, the length of the buttonhole will not vary greatly from that marked on the pattern.

The general rule for determining the length of buttonhole required The length of the buttonhole must equal the diameter plus the height of the button. Test out the rule by cutting a slash in a scrap of fabric and passing the button through it. The button should go through the opening easily with no undue strain on the fabric. The length of the buttonhole as achieved by taking these measurements is the minimum length required; sometimes a buttonhole made this minimum length will appear too short for the button (this is apt to happen with a heavy-looking button and with heavy fabrics) and if it does appear too short, the buttonhole can be made longer than minimum length.

CAUTION: A test buttonhole, perhaps more than one, must be made to determine proper width and length and to discover problems that will arise as a result of the nature of the fabric. Raveling and weak corners are serious problems, and one must know what to expect before work is begun on the garment.

Preparatory steps To ensure accurate measuring of all four ways in which the buttonholes must be even, a paper pattern will be made with the necessary lines drawn on it as shown in Figure 9-28. This pattern will then be pinned in the correct position on the garment, the machine stitching will be done through the paper, and the paper will be torn away. Ticker tape is ideal for this purpose, but any strip of paper 3 or 4 inches wide can be used. Short pieces can be taped together to obtain sufficient length. Cut a piece of paper 3 or 4 inches wide and long enough to cover all buttonhole markings on the pattern.

To make the paper pattern, use the pattern as a guide and transfer the measurements of the buttonhole markings to the strip of paper as shown in sketch *a* of Figure 9-28. Use a ruler, make sure all lines are parallel, measure accurately, and use a fine pencil for best results. By drawing the lines shown in sketch *a*, the buttonholes have been made even in three of the four ways: an equal distance from the finished front edge, an equal distance apart, and equal in length.

Draw another horizontal line about ¼ inch above or below the first line (be consistent—make all lines above or all lines below) to make the buttonholes even in width. See Figure 9-27 for help in deciding exactly how wide they should be. Draw this last line so the buttonhole is in beautiful proportion (sketch *b*).

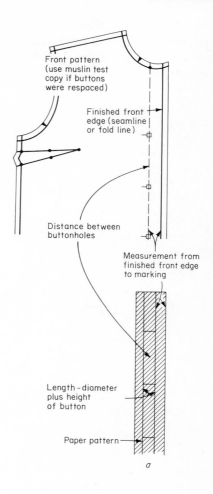

Front pattern (use muslin test copy if buttons were respaced)

Finished front edge (seamline or fold line)

Distance between buttonholes

Measurement from finished front edge to marking

Length-diameter plus height of button

Paper pattern

a

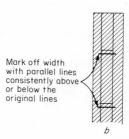

Mark off width with parallel lines consistently above or below the original lines

b

FIGURE 9-28 To make a pattern for bound buttonholes.

Cut 3-inch squares of fabric (preferably on the bias) to be used as the bindings for the buttonholes.

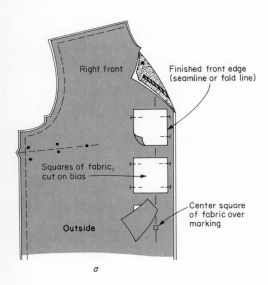

a

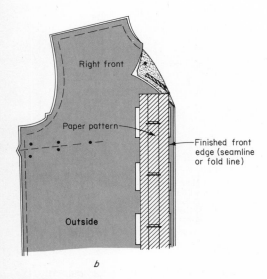

b

FIGURE 9-29 Preparatory steps.

NOTE: If the squares are cut on the bias they can be more easily handled as construction progresses and will not tend to ravel. However, the squares can be cut on the crosswise or lengthwise grain to achieve the effect desired with the fabric. For example, a crosswise striped fabric can be handled with stripes in the squares in a crosswise direction (this will tend to hide the buttonhole) or in a lengthwise direction (this will provide a striking contrast) or on the bias (this will give a subtle contrast of line direction).

Usually the binding squares are of self-fabric, but they can be of a compatible fabric in a contrasting color or texture if desired. See sketch *a* in Figure 9-29. Center a square over each buttonhole marking, with one edge of the square along the finished edge of the garment, as shown. Pin or tape in place with right sides together.

See sketch *b* in Figure 9-29. Place the paper pattern over the squares of fabric; have the long cut edge of the pattern along the finished front edge of the garment and see that the top and lower buttonhole markings on the pattern fall in the same position as the top and lower markings on the garment. Pin or tape in place carefully.

Stitch and slash the buttonholes   See sketch *a* in Figure 9-30. Test the machine for tension, etc. Use matching thread and set the machine to sew about seventeen to twenty-two stitches per inch. Begin stitching the small rectangles at one corner. Count stitches at the ends so that all buttonholes for a garment will have exactly the same number of stitches in width, since a difference of one stitch can make a great difference in the resulting size; leave the needle down in the fabric to pivot at the corners. Double-stitch for a few stitches so that knots will be unnecessary.

Carefully tear the paper pattern away from the stitches. See sketch *b*. Using small sharp scissors, cut down the center of the

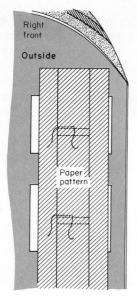

a Stitch over paper pattern.

buttonhole to within ¼ inch of the ends. Then cut diagonally to each corner. Clip the corners directly to the machine threads. If stitches are accidentally clipped, restitch the corner before proceeding. Cut only one buttonhole and finish it before cutting the others.

Now turn the binding through the slash to the wrong side of the garment. It should lie flat with no puckers at the corners. If it does not lie flat, forming a perfect rectangle, turn the binding back to the right side again, and clip into the puckered corner; it puckers only if it has not been clipped to the corner.

Prepare to form lips See Figure 9-31. Turn the garment to the wrong side. Flip up one edge of the binding and notice the small seam. That seam has a tendency to lie toward the buttonhole, but it must be forced to lie away from it as shown. In order

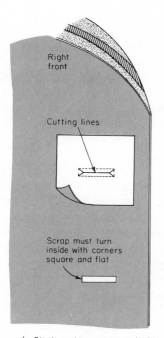

b Slash and turn scrap to inside.

FIGURE 9-30 Construction in progress.

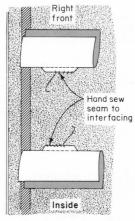

FIGURE 9-31 Prepare to form lips.

to hold the seam in the correct position, press it in the position illustrated or hand sew it to the interfacing, as shown. Pressing is better for fabrics which ravel because hand stitches encourage fraying; hand stitches hold the seam more securely and help make the following steps easier to do.

Standards of appearance   Figure 9-32 illustrates the common flaws in buttonhole appearance and the reason that testing is absolutely necessary. In this method with a corded feature, the width of the lips of the buttonhole will be controlled by the size of the cord. The desired effect is a buttonhole with edges almost meeting at the center, as shown in the upper sketch. If the rectangle is too narrow for the size of cord and thickness of fabric used, the edges will bow out, and the resulting buttonhole will

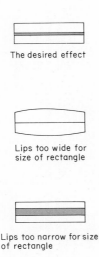

The desired effect

Lips too wide for
size of rectangle

Lips too narrow for size
of rectangle

FIGURE 9-32   Standards of appearance.

be fat and heavy-looking; a thinner cord must be used, or the original rectangle must be made wider. If the edges do not meet each other (see the lower sketch), the cord must be thicker, or the original rectangle must be narrower. Study the test buttonhole, make corrections, and retest before proceeding.

Final details   The advantage of a corded buttonhole is that the lips will be rounded instead of flat and the buttonhole will feel firm and be more serviceable. The two-piece corded buttonhole is the most professional buttonhole, but it is far more difficult to do than this method, and results are less predictable. However, a corded feature included in these directions results in a buttonhole so nearly like the true corded one that there is no need to consider a more difficult and less predictable construction. The cord used for this purpose should be pliable and of a diameter slightly less than $\frac{1}{8}$ inch. Cut the cord in 3-inch lengths.

See sketch *a* in Figure 9-33. Pin one edge of the binding flat against the garment and work with only one lip of the buttonhole at a time. Lay the cord inside the stitching line, as shown; do not attempt to pin it—it must be held in position with the fingers.

See sketch *b*. Working from the right side of the garment, wrap the binding snugly around the cord and, using no pins, blind-stitch along the seam of the buttonhole, encasing the cord; blind stitches should be a scant $\frac{1}{4}$ inch long and should be firm but not tight. This step is easier to do than it sounds because the cord is a great aid in keeping the lip of the buttonhole even in width. When one edge is finished, place a length of cord in the remaining edge and repeat the process.

Hold the lips of the buttonhole together with diagonal basting stitches; pull them only tightly enough to hold the buttonhole in a perfect rectangle, as shown. These stitches should remain until the garment is finished and should be taken out only when it is time to mark the position of the buttons.

See sketch c. From the wrong side, fasten the ends very securely, passing the stitches through both cords and as many thicknesses of fabric as possible without allowing the stitches to show on the outside.

Trim the binding strips to ½ inch from the stitching on the long edges and ¼ inch on the ends as shown. Whip the edges of the binding strip to the interfacing.

NOTE: Much later in the construction process, the facing will be applied; when it is turned to the inside, the buttonhole patches will be covered. Return to the instruction sheet and proceed. When the facing is in its permanent position, finish the underside of the buttonhole as described on page 433.

Novelty method for special uses

This is a method by which binding strips for the pleat or lips or the buttonhole are prepared beforehand (Figure 9-34). The scraps for facing the buttonhole openings are made of a lighter-weight fabric (Figure 9-35). A matching or harmonizing color in an underlining fabric or nylon sheer, etc., is a suitable fabric for facings. Because the facing scraps are light in weight and because the pleats have fewer folds, this buttonhole is considerably less bulky than buttonholes made by any other method, making it ideal for use with heavy or stiff fabrics.

The decorative shapes shown in sketch a of Figure 9-34 reveal two of many possibilities for unique designs that are possible only with this method. If buttonholes will be in striking shapes, they should be used sparingly.

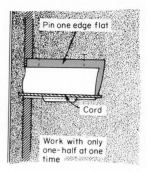

a Place the cord in position

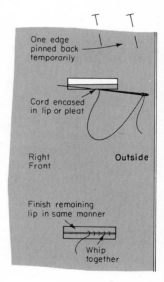

b Form the lips

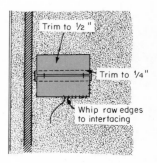

c Trim excess from scrap

FIGURE 9-33 Final details.

Preparatory steps See Figure 9-34. Sketch *a* shows buttonhole designs equally spaced and identically shaped by making a paper pattern and using as many guidelines as are required for the particular buttonhole shape. Prepare the pattern as in Figure 9-28. To prepare the pleat or lips beforehand, cut two bias strips for each buttonhole; strips 2 inches square will be adequate for most buttonholes. If desired the

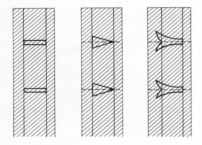

a Make a paper pattern, as in Figure 9 – 28.

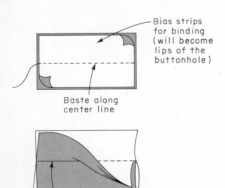

Bias strips for binding (will become lips of the buttonhole)

Baste along center line

Fold strips, wrong sides together, along basted line and press

b Prepare binding strips.

FIGURE 9-34 Preparatory steps—novelty construction.

strips can be cut on the crosswise or lengthwise grain; see the note concerning grain direction on page 390. See sketch *b*. Place two strips right sides together and baste with small firm stitches through the center (the bastings will be removed when construction is completed). Fold each scrap back on itself, wrong sides together, and press as shown.

Finishing steps Following directions in Figures 9-29 and 9-30, pin facing scraps in place, right sides together. Place the pattern in place and stitch around the buttonhole. Sketch *a* in Figure 9-35 shows the buttonholes stitched and the paper torn away. The buttonhole must be slashed through the center and clipped to every corner. Turn the facing to the inside, rolling the seam slightly to the inside, and baste the finished edges of the opening.

See sketch *b*. Center the prepared strips under the opening, pin, and baste in place. The prepared strips must be held in place with invisible blind stitches made directly into the seam. Slide the needle into the fold of the finished edge, catching in both layers of the binding, and bring it up again in the seamline. Take a tiny back stitch and repeat. As an extra precaution to be sure both layers of the prepared strips are held in place, take some extra hand stitches from the underside, catching through both layers of the binding.

Trim off excess width from the underside as in sketch *c* of Figure 9-33. Press from the underside. Remove center bastings to separate the lips.

NOTE: **Much later in the construction process, the facing will be applied; when it is turned to the inside, the buttonhole patches will be covered. Return to the instruction sheet and proceed. When the facing is in its permanent position, finish the underside of the buttonholes as described on page 433.**

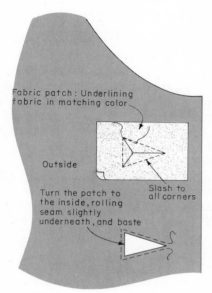

Fabric patch: Underlining
fabric in matching color

Outside

Slash to
all corners

Turn the patch to
the inside, rolling
seam slightly
underneath, and baste

a Follow steps in Figures 9–29 and 9–30.

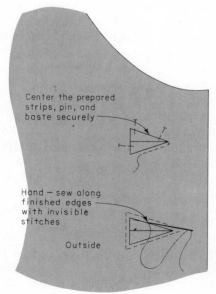

Center the prepared
strips, pin, and
baste securely

Hand — sew along
finished edges
with invisible
stitches

Outside

b Secure the prepared binding strips.

FIGURE 9-35 Finishing steps.

The tailor's buttonhole

This type of buttonhole is done after the facing has been turned to the inside; it can be done just before the lining is inserted or as the very last step of construction. It is included at this time in order to present all buttonhole details in one section of the text.

The tailor's buttonhole gives a man-tailored appearance and it is always used on men's garments. The sketches picture a woman's garment with a right-over-left buttoned closing. Keep in mind that button-holes are done on the left front of men's garments for a left-over-right closing.

Figure 9-36 pictures the finished jacket or coat. The position of the buttonholes should be marked with basting lines or faint chalk lines as shown; this step is quite similar to the making of the paper pattern for bound buttonholes (see Figure 9-28 and the accompanying directions).

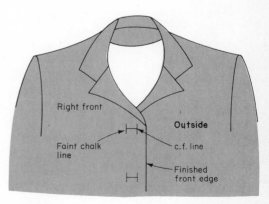

Right front

Outside

Faint chalk
line

c.f. line

Finished
front edge

FIGURE 9-36 To mark the position for tailor's buttonholes.

Construction sequence Figure 9-37 pictures the right front edge of the finished garment with a row of buttonholes in various stages of completion.

Step 1 Mark the position of the buttonholes with basting lines or chalk lines.

Step 2 Machine-stitch with short stitches (about 20 per inch) $\frac{1}{16}$ inch on each side of the marked line and continue stitching around a small circle ($\frac{1}{4}$ inch in diameter) at the center front, as shown. The circle will allow for a larger opening to accommodate the shank of the button and will also allow for radiating stitches, which will better withstand strain during wearing.

Step 3 Slash down the center line with small, sharp scissors. Make several clips to the stitching at the circle, as shown.

Step 4 The thread used for buttonhole stitches should be buttonhole twist. The stitches should be worked over a very small cord as an aid to stiffening and strengthening the opening edges. The cord can be a very heavy cotton thread, similar to a tiny cord, or one or two strands of matching buttonhole twist can be used to serve the purpose.

Thread the cord on a heavy needle, knot one end, and secure the knot a short distance away from the buttonhole (it will be trimmed off later). Stretch the cord across the cutting line for the buttonhole and fasten it in place by wrapping it around the needle, as shown. Using another needle, work buttonhole stitches along one cut edge, encasing the cord in the stitches, as shown.

Step 5 Release the cord and carry it along with the stitches at the end. Radiate the stitches around the circular end, as shown. Stretch the cord flat again and proceed.

Step 6 Trim off the ends of the cord. The sketch shows the finished buttonhole.

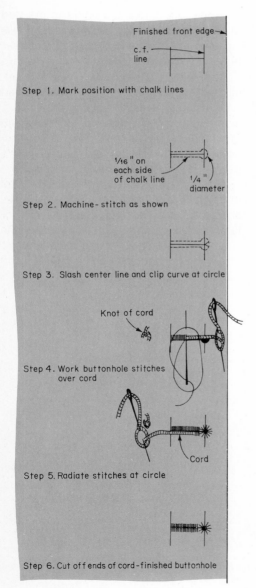

Finished front edge

c. f. line

Step 1. Mark position with chalk lines

$\frac{1}{16}$ " on each side of chalk line

$\frac{1}{4}$ " diameter

Step 2. Machine-stitch as shown

Step 3. Slash center line and clip curve at circle

Knot of cord

Step 4. Work buttonhole stitches over cord

Step 5. Radiate stitches at circle

Cord

Step 6. Cut off ends of cord-finished buttonhole

FIGURE 9-37 The tailor's buttonhole.

ASSEMBLE UNITS OF THE GARMENT

It has been convenient to have units of the garment separated when doing the intricate steps of shaping the collar and lapel, taping seams, and making buttonholes. There may be other construction details which can be done more easily before pieces are assembled in a bulky unit; this will depend on the features of each particular design.

It is assumed that the pieces need not be basted together for fitting purposes; this should have been done on a muslin copy (Chapter 6) or before any work was done (see "Assemble Pieces for a Final Fitting Test" on page 366). However, it is important to baste seams and darts in preparation for stitching. One of the major purposes of basting is to control the layers of fabric so that they will not push out of line as they are stitched. The thick and spongy fabrics used in tailoring, which are combined with extra layers of underlining or interfacing, require quite small and firm basting stitches to keep them in proper control as they pass through the machine.

Basic techniques for underlined or interfaced garments

To stitch darts See sketch *a* in Figure 9-38. Even though basting stitches were placed at the center of dartlines to force the two layers of fabric to act as one, a problem will be encountered at the tips of darts. If the stitching ends directly on the fold edge at the tip of the dart in the usual manner, the stitches will slip off the garment fabric (catching in only the underlining or interfacing) before the tip is reached. Sketch *a*

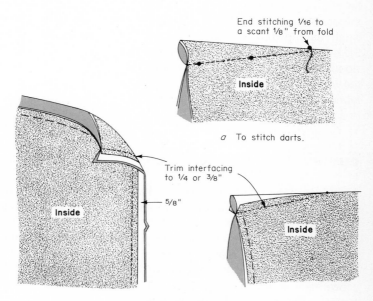

End stitching 1/16 to a scant 1/8" from fold

Inside

a To stitch darts.

Trim interfacing to 1/4 or 3/8"

5/8"

Inside

Inside

b To stagger seams.

FIGURE 9-38 *Basic techniques for underlined or interfaced garments.*

shows the solution. Note that the stitches end—not right at the fold at the tip—but ⅟₁₆ to ⅛ inch from the fold. In very thick fabrics this measurement may be as much as ¼ inch. Make up a test dart using a layer of fabric and interfacing; end the stitches about ⅟₁₆ inch from the fold and examine the effect on the right side. The stitching should end properly at the tip on the outside layer. Make corrections until the proper effect is achieved and then stitch all darts in the same manner.

To stagger seams See sketch *b* in Figure 9-38. The structural seams and darts in underlined or interfaced garments must be staggered to decrease unnecessary bulk; this is done as soon as they are stitched and before they are pressed and crossed with another seam. The supporting fabric should be trimmed to a narrower width, while the structural seam remains the full ⅝-inch width, as shown. Note that both layers of the supporting fabric are trimmed down to about ¼ to ⅜ inch from the stitching line; the wider width is advisable if the interfacing fabric ravels appreciably. Darts are trimmed in a similar manner, as shown.

GUSSET CONSTRUCTION

A gusset is a diamond-shaped or triangular piece set into the underarm area of a garment with a sleeve cut in one with the major pattern pieces. Its purpose is to make the garment fit well and look trim and at the same time provide extra spread for arm movements. A garment with a gusset can be fitted more snugly to the body than a similar design without a gusset. Because of its aid to smart fit, the gusset, in one of

many guises, appears often in highly styled Vogue patterns. Gussets vary in shape or outline, but *their common characteristic is that all are set in along slashed edges of the garment, with the result that the seam allowance on the garment edges varies in width while the seam allowance on the gusset section remains constant.*

The four most common gusset styles See Figure 9-39. The diamond-shaped piece is the traditional gusset and is the most difficult to insert because it has four corners, two of which are set into slashes in the garment. The half gusset is the simplest to do and appears in easy-to-make designs. By cutting two halves for each side, the resulting gusset is very much like the traditional gusset (with the addition of a seam down the center). However, the half gusset is much easier to insert because each half is set in before underarm seams are joined.

A gusset can be combined with a small portion of one of the major pieces, as shown in the two lower sketches. The piece will have a pointed end and will extend to become the underarm section of the garment or an underarm section of the sleeve; notice the markings on the pattern which designate the underarm position. This gusset is easier to insert than the traditional gusset because there is one less sharp corner.

General principles apply to all styles of gussets, regardless of shape or outline In all gussets certain corners are set into slashes in the body of the garment and other corners are set into points formed by the joining of two seams; the most difficult corners to do are those which are set into slashes in the garment. In every illustration used in this chapter, the difficult points are marked with small o's and the easier corners with large O's.

Because the traditional diamond-shaped

gusset with its four corners best illustrates general principles of construction, directions for it are given in great detail. The most difficult step (basting and stitching the seam) is shown in sketch *b* of Figure 9-41, and the same principles are applied to other, simpler gussets in Figure 9-43. The worker must carefully follow the directions with her pattern and use these directions for elaboration and clarification. For example, the pattern markings to be matched will differ from pattern to pattern. Vogue often uses four different marks (a small o, a large O, a triangle, and a square) at the four corners.

Spread out the pattern pieces and study the pattern markings in the gusset area. The main principle to understand is that the pattern piece for the gusset has ⅝-inch seam allowances on all edges (see Figure 9-39), whereas the stitching lines on the garment converge; therefore there is a varying seam allowance on the garment. When the slash is made down the center of the stitching lines, the seam allowance on the garment varies from perhaps ½ or ⅜ inch (maximum width) to no allowance at all at the point. When two edges with different seam allowances are sewn together, they must be sewn with seamlines matching rather than with cut edges even, as one usually sews. This is the principle which so many people do not understand. To repeat: *Gussets are constructed with seamlines matching, not cut edges even.*

Note that gusset lines on the garment look somewhat like darts; mistaking these lines for darts and handling them accordingly is a serious mistake.

SPECIAL NOTE CONCERNING UNDERLININGS AND INTERFACINGS: Under most circumstances it is better not to use a supporting fabric in a small gusset piece; the extra layer adds stiffness and bulk at a place where they are a distinct disadvantage. Note that the diamond-shaped gusset (Figure 9-41) and

the half-gusset (sketch *a* in Figure 9-43) have not been underlined or interfaced. However, if the fabric is very loosely woven and a supporting fabric is needed for extra strength and durability, the gusset sections can be underlined or interfaced. The gusset combined with a portion of the garment (sketch *b* in Figure 9-43) is shown with a supporting fabric because in that case the gusset is a larger piece which is actually a part of one of the structural pieces of the garment.

Traditional
diamond-shaped
gusset

Half gusset —
by cutting two
pieces, it is
identical to
traditional gusset

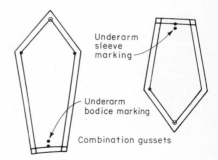

Underarm
sleeve
marking

Underarm
bodice marking

Combination gussets

Combined with
a portion of
the garment

Combined with a
portion of sleeve

FIGURE 9-39 The most common gusset styles.

The diamond-shaped gusset

Preparatory steps See sketch *a* in Figure 9-40. The very first step of construction (before seams are basted) is the reinforcement of the points to be slashed.

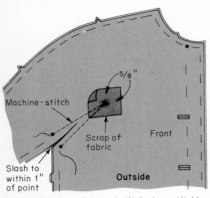

a Reinforce points and stitch along stitching lines.

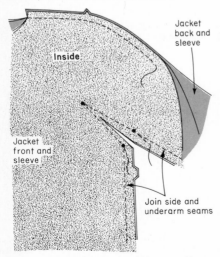

b Join underarm seams of garment and sleeve sections.

FIGURE 9-40 *Preparatory steps.*

Reread "Reinforcing Corners" on page 261. This is done by placing a scrap of fabric on the outside of the garment, allowing it to extend ½ inch outside the stitching lines, as shown. Lining fabric or a lightweight underlining fabric is a good choice; the fabric will not show when the garment is finished. Machine-stitch with short stitches (fifteen to twenty per inch) and with matching thread along the stitching lines, as shown, catching in the scrap of fabric; do not retrace stitches at the point because a slash must be made directly to the point.

Do not slash all the way to the point at this time. It is wiser to cut only partway, to about 1 inch from the point at this time, so there is no chance of the seam fraying while the garment is basted and fitted (these garments are fitted before the gusset is put in). When the fitting is done and the side seams have been stitched and pressed, slash directly to the point of the reinforced lines just before inserting the gusset.

See sketch *b*. This sketch shows another very important step. As the underarm seams of the garment and sleeve are stitched, the stitching must end directly at the marking and must not extend all the way up to the cut edges. Note that the stitches go to the large O and are secured with back-stitching. This is a very common trouble point; the instruction sheet will read, "Join underarm seam below large O." The word *below* is very important, and it is easily overlooked in brief, telegram English terminology. To repeat: Stitch only to the marking at the ends of the underarm seams of the garment and sleeve sections and back-stitch to secure the threads.

To set in the gusset See sketch *a* in Figure 9-41. All the remaining sketches picture the gusset opening as it would look if the arm were raised above shoulder level and the body viewed from the side. Notice that the scrap of fabric turns to the inside and acts as a seam allowance at points which otherwise would have no seam allowance at all. Note the little openings at the ends of the two underarm seams. These openings will act as clips as the gusset is set in; without them, setting in a gusset would be all but impossible.

See sketch *b.* The sketch shows the gusset basted in place; edges should be pinned before basting. The little scrap of fabric, which is a great aid in sewing, covers up some intricate points; therefore the scrap is shown on one point to illustrate how it would look in place and is not pictured on the other side so as to show the construction more clearly. Do understand that a scrap of fabric must be used to reinforce each slashed point.

This drawing illustrates the principle of seamlines matching rather than the usual cut-edges-even construction. Study the sketch carefully (particularly the right half) and notice that the gusset edge, with its ⅝-inch seam allowance, extends beyond the slashed edge with its varying seam allowance. Pull the scrap of fabric to the inside and use it as a seam allowance. Do all subsequent steps (pinning, basting, and stitching) with the garment side uppermost so that the slashed edges are visible. With right sides together and small o's and large O's matching, pin the gusset to the slashed edges, having seamlines matching (not cut edges even). Pin and baste very securely, especially at all corners. With the garment side uppermost, stitch just inside the reinforcing lines from the garment side, leaving the needle of the machine down and pivoting around each corner; all edges can be done in one continuous stitching if the unit is pivoted around the needle.

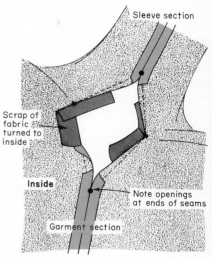

a Reinforcing scraps act as seam allowance when turned to the inside.

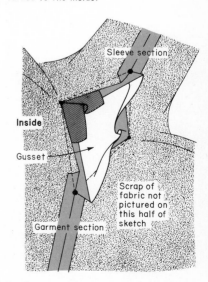

b Set-in gusset with seamlines matching.

FIGURE 9-41 A basic principle of gusset construction: join seams with seamlines (not cut edges) matching.

Finishing touches See Figure 9-42. Trim the edges of the scrap of fabric down to about ¼ inch. Press the seam toward the garment as shown. The gusset is finished and should wear well for most special-occasion clothing. However, even though the slashed points are as secure as they can be made without stiffening the area and calling attention to a functional detail, weakness does exist at these points. To strengthen these points on utilitarian clothing, the gusset seam can be top-stiched from the outside. This will strengthen the points considerably, but the stitching line will make the seam more prominent.

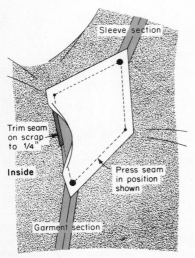

Sleeve section

Trim seam
on scrap
to 1/4"

Inside

Press seam
in position
shown

Garment section

FIGURE 9-42 Finishing touches.

Basic principles apply to other gussets

Construction details for a half-gusset
These are shown in sketch *a* of Figure 9-43; compare this sketch with sketch *b* in Figure 9-41. The point is constructed in the same manner, but the half-gusset piece is set in before the side seams are basted or stitched; notice how much easier it appears. When the two gusset sections have been inserted, the entire underarm seam of the garment, the gusset, and the sleeve are sewn in one easy operation.

Construction details for a combination gusset
These are shown in sketch *b* of Figure 9-43. In this example, the gusset is combined with a portion of the jacket or coat; a gusset combined with the sleeve would be similiar to this, but turned upside down. This sketch compares with Figure 9-41; note how much easier this one is with just one less corner.

Basic principles apply to other unrelated details

The principle of gusset construction is simply the principle of joining seams with seamlines matching, rather than the more usual and simpler method of joining seams with cut edges even. The worker has difficulty with the construction largely because she attempts to work with cut edges even and does not understand the principle of joining by matching seamlines. An additional difficulty arises from the varying seam allowances on one edge and the problems of fraying and weakness if the slashed points are not properly reinforced. The basic principles, covered in great detail in this chapter, are very useful because they can be applied to a great variety of other construction details. The person who wishes to do fashion sewing and will be using Vogue Paris Original or Couturier patterns must master the principles well, because these more intricately cut patterns frequently include details that are handled by matching seamlines rather than cut edges.

THE TAILORED COLLAR

The collar of a suit or coat is constructed very differently from a similar collar on a blouse or dress; it is so different that this is probably the most confusing construction detail encountered in tailoring. Actually, all the steps in the process are simple, but each one must be done with great care and accuracy before proceeding to the next. The collar is attached in a manner which makes it possible to press the neck seams open, thus distributing the great bulk of that seam over a larger area. The directions on the instruction sheet will be essentially like these, but they will be less detailed.

Tests for fabric weight

"Principles of Shaping the Tailored Garment" on page 367 includes an explanation of the differences between the upper-collar and under-collar patterns for a typical tailored garment. The upper-collar pattern is wider than the under-collar pattern so that the upper collar can take the outside curve (over the under collar) as the garment is worn. The average difference in width between the two collars is about ⅛ inch for a suit and about ¼ inch for a winter coat; the pattern maker estimates how much extra width is required for the weight of fabric that most customers will use. If the customer uses fabric in a lighter or heavier weight, the width difference will not be correct for her particular fabric.

The issue of fabric weight can be tested prior to construction, and the collars can

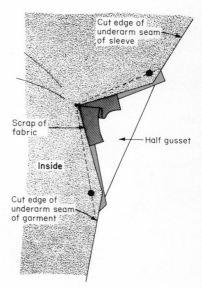

a To insert a half-gusset.

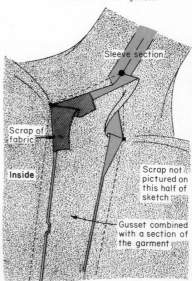

b To insert a combination gusset.

FIGURE 9-43 Apply basic principles to insert other types of gussets.

be corrected at this time. See Figure 9-44. The sketches show the upper-collar piece placed over the under collar (which has been shaped and pad-stitched), pinned with neck edges even, and with the collars held in wearing position. Sketch *a* shows the collars in the proper width, as they will look if the fabric is average in weight. The upper collar should be about ⅛ inch wider than the under collar (when held in wearing position) because after the collar seam is joined and turned to the inside, the seam will be rolled slightly back from the edge.

Sketch *b* pictures a collar cut in fabric that is heavier than average in weight. Note that the upper collar is not wide enough to take the outside curve over the under collar, thus allowing the under-collar edge to extend. Correct this problem by trimming off the excess width on the under collar so that the trimmed edge will be ⅛ inch narrower than the upper collar. To do this, pin the edges together carefully and then trim the under collar even with the upper collar; then, as a last step, trim an additional ⅛ inch from the edge of the under collar.

Sketch *c* pictures a collar cut in fabric that is lighter than average in weight. Note that the upper collar extends more than ⅛ inch beyond the under collar. Correct this problem by trimming off the excess width from the upper collar so that the trimmed edge will extend only ⅛ inch beyond the under collar. Pin the edge carefully before trimming.

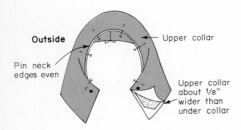

a   Place upper collar over under collar in wearing position.

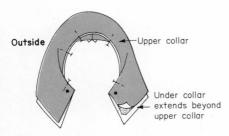

b If fabric is heavier than average.

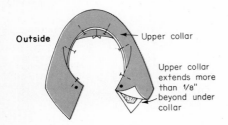

c   If fabric is lighter than average.

FIGURE 9-44   *Test collar for fabric weight.*

Basic problems of construction

Corresponding neck edges of the garment and collar differ See Figure 9-45. The sketches show the front and back pattern pieces pinned together at the shoulderline and collar patterns pinned over them with center lines and neck edges matched at the center back. The basic problem is that corresponding neck edges of the garment and the collar are not identical in character. Sketch *a* shows a typical rolled collar in which the corresponding edges are both curved, but not identically; sketch *b* shows that corresponding edges may differ greatly. When edges to be joined are not identical in character, the problem is solved by clipping into the concave curve of the garment neck edge to release the cut edge so it can take the character of the collar edge. Details are shown in Figure 9-47.

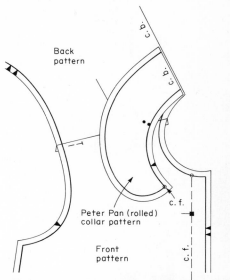

a The neck edge of the garment curves more sharply than the corresponding edge of the collar.

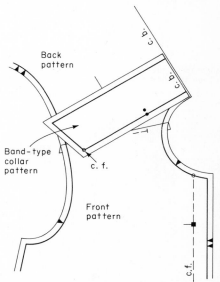

b Corresponding neck edges may differ greatly.

FIGURE 9-45 *The basic problem of attaching collars: corresponding seamlines differ in character.*

The desired effect — a flat "easy" corner.

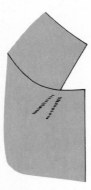

The corner is taut and puckered — one seam has been stitched inaccurately.

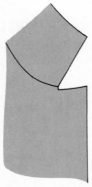

The upper edge of the lapel has been stitched at the wrong level.

FIGURE 9-46 The most common problems at the corner.

Problems at the corner of the collar and lapel See Figure 9-46. The finished collar must fit into the neck edge of the garment, forming a corner that will look smooth and "easy." Note that the curving neckline edge and the extension beyond the collar are on the same level, thereby creating one continuous line.

The most common flaw of construction results in a corner that looks tight and puckered, as shown in the center sketch. This problem is especially troublesome because a slight mistake in stitching can produce a very prominent puckered effect. The following directions are very detailed because of the intricacy involved at this corner; pay careful attention to the enlarged views in Figures 9-52 and 9-53 to eliminate this problem entirely.

Another common flaw is shown in the lower sketch in Figure 9-46. If the curved neck edge and the extension do not appear as a continuous line, the effect is very unattractive. The enlarged view in Figure 9-53 shows the stitching of the extension edge and illustrates that it must be on a level with the stitching of the neck seam.

The upper- and under-collar sections are joined to neck edges in two separate operations The tailored collar construction is different and more difficult because the under collar will be joined to the neck edge of the garment, while the upper collar will be joined to the facing.

Outer edges are joined in three separate operations A problem that is often encountered results from the brevity of pattern directions; the necessarily brief directions for this last step (joining the upper collar and facing to the under collar and garment) sometimes give the impression that this step is done in one operation.

This step must be done in three separate operations: the collar portion in one operation, and then the two facing portions in two separate operations.

Basic principles apply to all types of pattern designs

The most typical tailored garment is one with a two-piece collar and a separate front facing. The garment may or may not have a back facing; if there is no back facing, the lining will finish off the back neck area. However, the reader will encounter many garments that are not as typical: the garment with a one-piece collar and the garment with a front facing cut in one with the garment front are examples. It is important to remember that general principles, explained in connection with the typical garment, can be applied to any design.

The following directions are given in great detail for the typical garment. At crucial points in construction, sketches are included to illustrate how the same construction can be applied to garments of a slightly different cut. Garments that are not typical (combined-section garments) are somewhat more difficult to handle simply because work cannot be done on small units; but regardless of the shape of the pattern pieces, the construction principles remain the same.

Construction sequence

Reinforce and clip neck edges of the garment and facing sections See Figure 9-47. The neck edges of the garment and the facing should be reinforced with machine stitches and then clipped. This step is not usually included in the instruction sheet, but it is an aid to easier

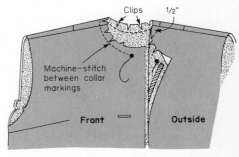

a Machine–stitch neck edge of garment.

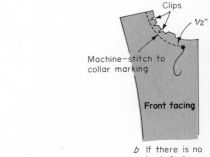

b If there is no back facing.

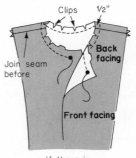

c If there is a back facing.

FIGURE 9-47 Reinforce and clip neck edges.

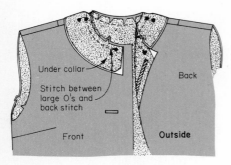

a Join under collar to garment.

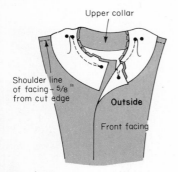

b Join upper collar to front facing.

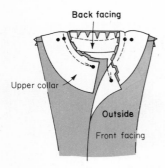

c Join upper collar to neck edges of facings.

FIGURE 9-48   To stitch neck seams—the typical two-piece tailored collar.

construction. The stitches reinforce the neck edge for clipping, and the clips release the seam allowance so that it can "give" and shape to the lines of the collar.

Machine-stitch ½ inch from the neck edge of the garment between the tailor's tacks which mark the position for the end of the collar; use about 15 to 18 stitches per inch and see that the row of stitches is exactly ½ inch from the raw edge, as shown in sketch *a*. Clip to the stitching line. Reinforce and clip the neck edges of the facing sections in the same manner. The separate facing is shown in sketch *b*. If the garment has a back facing, the shoulder edges of the facing should be joined before reinforcing and clipping the neck edge, as shown in sketch *c*.

Join collar sections to garment sections See Figure 9-48 for the basic method of joining collar sections to corresponding garment and facing sections for the typical tailored collar. Figures 9-49 and 9-50 show the same step applied to less typical garments.

The typical two-piece tailored collar See sketch *a* in Figure 9-48. Baste the under collar to the garment, right sides together and cut edges even, with center backs, notches, shoulder markings, and large O's matching. This seam is so thick that very secure basting stitches are required to hold the under collar in place accurately. Notice how the clips at the neck edge of the garment spread out to take the shape of the under collar.

Baste the upper collar to the facing sections in the same manner. If there is no back facing, see sketch *b*. Notches, large O's, and shoulderlines must match; the shoulder marking on the collar should match the seamline at the shoulder edge of the facing. If there is a back facing, see sketch *c*. Baste the upper collar to the entire neck edge, with notches, large O's, and shoulderlines matching.

Check work very carefully before stitching. The measurements from the large O to the front edge at the four corners involved should be equal. If these measurements vary as much as ⅛ inch, correct them at this time. They will eventually become the important lapel extensions, and since they will be so near to one another as the garment is worn, any slight variation will be noticeable.

Stitch these seams as basted, taking the following precaution: the machine stitches must end at the large O and must be secure; backstitch exactly to the large O and then proceed around the neck edge to the other large O and back-stitch.

The two-piece collar on a garment with a self-facing Figure 9-49 shows this same step of construction on a garment with a two-piece collar and a self-facing instead of the typical separate facing. The construction is done in the same manner, and the difference is in the position in which work must be held. Sketch *a* shows the under collar joined to the neck edge of the garment. Note that neck edges are reinforced and clipped before work is begun. Sketch *b* shows the position in which work must be held to join the upper collar to the neck edge of the facings. Note that the under collar has been pulled up so that it stands up at the neck edge. Fold the self-facing to the outside (right sides together) along the fold line. In this position, join the upper collar to the neck edge of the facing, with right sides together and notches and pattern markings matching.

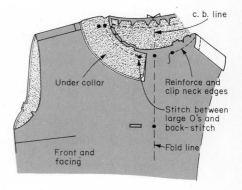

a Join under collar to garment.

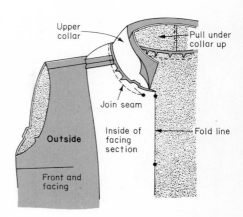

b Join upper collar to neck edges of facings.

FIGURE 9-49 *To stitch neck seams—the two-piece collar on a garment with a self-facing.*

*The one-piece collar on a garment with
a self-facing* Figure 9-50 shows the same
step of construction on a garment with a
one-piece collar and self-facings. The
construction is done in the same manner,
and the difference is in the position in
which work is held. Sketch *a* shows one
collar edge (on the half of the collar that
has been interfaced) joined to the neck
edge of the garment. Note that neck edges
are reinforced and clipped before work
is begun. Sketch *b* shows the position in
which work must be held to join the remaining edge of the collar to the neck
edge of the facings. Note that the collar
has been folded in half (with right sides
together) so that it stands up at the neck
edge. Fold the self-facing to the outside
(right sides together) along the fold line.
In this position, join the remaining edge
of the collar to the neck edge of the facings,
with right sides together and notches and
pattern markings matching.

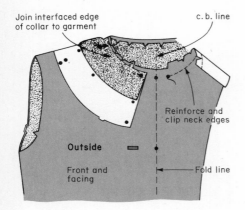

a Join under collar to garment

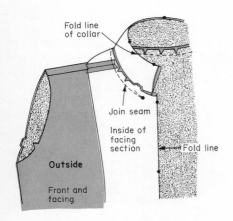

b Join upper collar to facing edges

FIGURE 9-50 *To stitch neck seams—the
one-piece collar on a garment with a self-
facing.*

Trim and press seams The neck
seams are the bulkiest seams in the garment; all unnecessary bulk must be removed from them. After trimming the
interfacing and the bulk from cross seams,
trim the neck seam of the under collar and
garment to about ⅜ inch. Trim the seam
of the upper collar and facings to about
½ inch; these two seams, which will eventually lie on each other, are thus staggered
to reduce bulk.

These seams must be pressed open,
and because they are so curved, this is
difficult to do. It is wise to baste them open
first. See that they lie flat; if they do not,
clip wherever necessary. See Figure 9-51.
Because the garment and under collar
are interfaced, that seam can be whipped
in place with stitches catching into the
interfacing only; this will ensure a seam
that will always remain flat.

Press the seams very well, for this is the last good opportunity to do so. Use a tailor's cushion that is the correct shape for a particular segment of the seam and press small segments of the seam at one time.

SPECIAL NOTE: As work progresses, it is important to hold each unit in wearing position in order to continue shaping and molding the unit. The sketches do not picture the proper position, in order to reveal construction details better. Carefully study the following examples before proceeding. See Figure 9-52. When basting the collar edges, hold work in such a way that the collar rolls over as it will in wearing position, with the upper collar taking the outside curve over the under collar. See Figure 9-53. When basting the front and extension edges for a garment with a lapel, hold work in such a way that the lapel rolls back in wearing position, with the facing taking the outside curve over the lapel area of the garment. Continue to employ shaping principles throughout the construction sequence. See Figures 9-57 and 9-58. The sketches show these steps with the garment turned wrong side out (for illustrative purposes), but these details should be done with the garment right side out, in proper wearing position.

Join outer edges of the collar See Figure 9-52. Pin the upper collar and facings over the under collar and garment, with right sides together and cut edges even, matching notches, large O's, and center lines. All these raw edges must now be basted and stitched, but do this step in three operations—the collar stitching first and then the two front and extension edges.

Before stitching the collar seam, examine the enlarged view very carefully. The collar should be stitched on the seamline, and the stitches should end at the

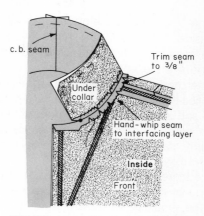

FIGURE 9-51 *Whip the neck seam to the interfacing.*

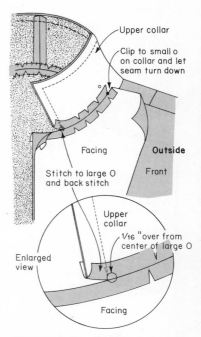

FIGURE 9-52 *Join the outer edges of the collar.*

large O, but if they are placed just 1⁄16 inch outside the large O, as shown (note that the stitching line is not centered in the large O), the corner will turn very much better and will not pucker or appear taut. Notice that the neckline seams are pressed up and are caught in with the stitching of the collar seams. Stitch the entire collar seam, back-stitching at the large O's, as shown.

If there is no back facing, clip the neck edge of the upper collar to the seamline at the shoulder, as shown.

Join facing edges See Figure 9-53. Flip up the seam of the extension edge in preparation for stitching the front and extension edges. Before stitching, examine the enlarged view very carefully. The stitching, as it approaches the large O, must be on a level with the stitching of the neck seam, but should not extend all the way to the end of the stitching of the neck edge. Stitch the front edge, turn the corner and stop stitching, and back-stitch about 1⁄16 inch from the end of the neckline stitching

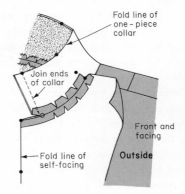

a Join ends of one-piece collar

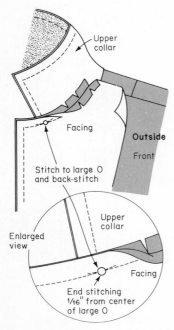

FIGURE 9-53 Join front and extension edges.

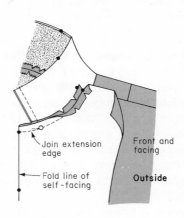

b Join extension edge

FIGURE 9-54 General principles applied to one-piece collar and self-facings.

(note that the stitches do not extend to the center of the large O). This will allow the corner to turn easily and lie flat.

Turn the collar and facing to the inside to see whether the corner of the collar and lapel will turn into a flat, square corner. If it puckers and appears tight, one of the stitchings (the collar or the front and lapel) went a stitch or so too far; a stitch or so must be removed. If the lapel does not make a smooth, even line with the collar seam, the stitching of the lapel was not on a level with the stitching line of the neck seam and must be ripped and moved to the proper seamline.

Apply principles to other designs

Figure 9-54 shows this same intricate step of construction applied to a one-piece collar and a garment with a self-facing. The principles of construction are almost identical. Note that the collar of the garment shown in sketch *a* is identical to that of the typical garment shown in Figure 9-52, with the one exception that there is no seam at the outer edge. Note that the front and extension edges in sketch *b* are identical to those of the typical garment shown in Figure 9-53, with the one exception that there is no seam at the front edge. Follow all directions included with the typical collar, making only these slight changes.

Treatment for front encased seam for garments with a separate facing

The front edge is one of the most prominent lines on the garment, and it is especially important that the front seam be invisible as the garment is worn. The seam will be rolled slightly to the inside before it is pressed, but often after much wear and many dry cleanings, this seam has a tendency to creep out to the edge, creating an unattractive line. The suggestion illustrated in Figure 9-55 will prevent the

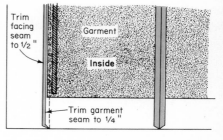

a Trim seam

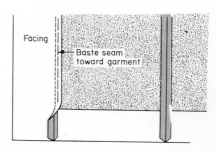

b Baste seam in position

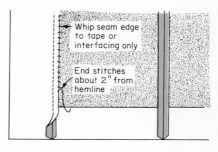

c Whip seam in place

FIGURE 9-55 *Treatment of front encased seam.*

seam from slipping to the outside. The words "to the outside" are very important because this suggestion can be used only on a seam (that will be rolled to the inside) to prevent it from slipping to the outside. The typical garment pictured illustrates that the front edge rolls to the inside from

the roll line of the lapel to the lower edge. From that level upward, the seam is rolled to the outside. Therefore, the construction pictured is done on the front edge only, from the lapel level downward.

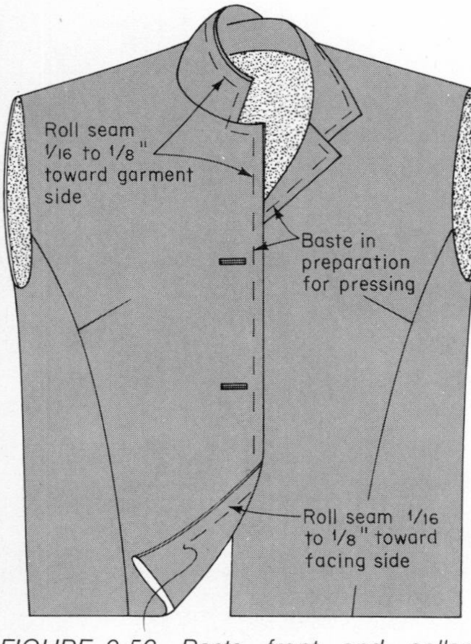

All encased seams must be trimmed in a staggered manner, and ordinarily it does not make a great deal of difference which edge is trimmed to the wider width, although a good general rule is to have the wider seam next to the side that will be uppermost as the garment is worn. The front edge of a tailored garment is an exception to that general rule. The interfacing should be trimmed to $\frac{1}{8}$ inch, as usual. Then the seam edge of the garment should be trimmed to $\frac{1}{4}$ inch from the stitching line, and the seam edge of the facing should be trimmed to $\frac{1}{2}$ inch from the seamline, as shown in sketch *a*.

See sketch *b*. Turn the seam toward the garment (covering the twill tape) and baste it in place from the lapel level down to the hemline. Do not pull the seam tightly against the stitching line, but allow it to fold over easily and naturally; an "easy" roll will force the seam to lie slightly back from the edge (the effect pictured in Figure 9-56). The seam should roll $\frac{1}{16}$ inch from the edge in lightweight fabrics to as much as $\frac{1}{8}$ inch from the edge in very heavy fabrics. Baste a small section of the seam and then turn the facing to the inside to study the effect; if the seam falls too far away from the edge, it must be held more snugly against the stitching line.

See sketch *c*. Whip the seam in place, being very careful that the stitches do not pass through to the garment fabric. The stitches can be caught into the interfacing or into the twill tape. End the stitches about 2 inches from the hemline, as shown. The stitches should begin at the roll line if there is a lapel (or at the neck edge if there is no lapel) and should end about 2 inches above the hemline, as shown.

Roll seam $\frac{1}{16}$ to $\frac{1}{8}$" toward garment side

Baste in preparation for pressing

Roll seam $\frac{1}{16}$ to $\frac{1}{8}$" toward facing side

FIGURE 9-56 *Baste front and collar edges.*

Trim and press seams All seam edges on the outer edges of the collar and lapel are encased seams and must be trimmed in a staggered manner; see "Reducing Bulk in Seams" on page 277.

See Figure 9-56. Turn the facing and the collar to the inside and baste the finished edges in preparation for pressing. The seams must be rolled slightly in one direction or another so that they will be invisible as the garment is worn. Note that the seam at the front edge must be rolled to the inside (the facing side) from the lapel line downward but that the seam in the collar and lapel area must be rolled slightly to the outside (the garment side). The seam should be rolled away from the edge just enough to hide it from view; avoid rolling it so far to one side that it shows an unattractive line on the side that will not be as readily visible.

Secure the roll line of the collar and lapels See Figure 9-57. Holding the garment in wearing position, smooth the upper collar and facing over the under collar and lapel area and pin along the natural roll line, as shown in sketch *a*. The layers should rest easily in place; they should be flat and smooth but not pulled into a taut position. Baste along the pin line and remove pins. See sketch *b*. Fold the facing and upper collar back along the roll line, as shown, and secure the upper layer to the under layer along the roll line with invisible hand stitches that catch into the underside of the collar and facing fabric; this is a further aid to molding and shaping the collar. In certain lightweight fabrics, especially those in plain, light colors, this step must be eliminated because the stitches are noticeable as the garment is worn.

This technique can be used to secure the roll line of cuffs or of sleeve facings that roll back to give a cuff effect.

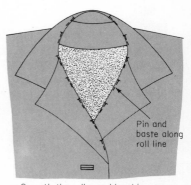

a Smooth the collar and lapel in proper wearing position.

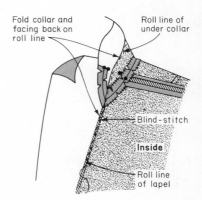

b Hand sew along roll line.

FIGURE 9-57 To secure the roll line of the collar and lapels.

Finish neck and shoulder edges

NOTE: **If the novelty Hong Kong method of
finishing facings and lining is to be used, see
page 470 at this time. Facings and neck edges
will be handled in a manner different from the
traditional method given below.**

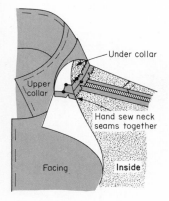

a Hand sew neck seams together.

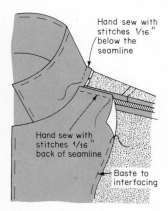

b If there is no back facing,
hand-sew neck and shoulder edges.

*FIGURE 9-58 Finish neck
and shoulder edges.*

See Figure 9-58. The seam of the collar
and facing should be put into place directly
over the seam of the under collar and
garment, with neck seams matching
as shown in sketch *a*. If they miss slightly
(this is possible if the width of the upper
collar was not exactly correct for the weight
of fabric used), it is better to allow them
to miss than to force them to match and
thereby destroy the smooth lines of the
collar. Attach the lower half of the collar
and facing seam to the lower half of the
corresponding seam. By hand sewing the
lower edge of the collar seam to the corresponding seam with stitches close to the
seamline, these stitches can be made to
serve a double purpose; they will mold
the two seams together and at the same
time will aid in keeping the collar-and-
facing seam in a pressed-open position.

NOTE: **The sketches show a garment without
a back facing. If there is a back facing, the
entire neck seam (both front and back) is handled in the same manner. Be sure shoulder
positions match.**

See sketch *b*. If there is no back facing,
hand-sew the raw edge of the collar into
position over the back neck seam with
stitches about 1/16 inch below the seamline.
The back lining will hide the raw edge and
the stitches eventually.

Pin the raw shoulder edge of the front
facing to the garment, matching shoulder
seamlines, as shown. Hand sew the shoulder edge in place with stitches about 1/16
inch back of the shoulder seamline. The
shoulder edge of the lining will hide these
stitches eventually.

Baste the inner edge of facings in place
with stitches through the interfacing layer
only. If there is a lapel, the garment should
be held in wearing position with the lapel
area folded to the outside as the inner
edge of the facing is pinned into position.

These edges will eventually be catch-stitched to the interfacing, but it is well to wait until the hem is completed to do this hand finishing.

THE REGULATION SET-IN SLEEVE

The set of the sleeve plays an important role in the ultimate success of the garment. Perhaps no other step in construction can add so much to, or detract so much from, the final professional appearance of the costume. The directions on the instruction sheet must necessarily be brief, and perhaps this is why setting in sleeves is such a great problem to so many women who sew. Actually it is not difficult if several very simple little techniques are employed. The following directions are written in great detail and should be followed step by step as the construction proceeds.

Typical sleeve patterns

Figure 9-59 shows the three most typical sleeve patterns. The two-piece sleeve will appear quite frequently in patterns for tailored garments because its more intricate cut results in a better-fitting sleeve. The curving lines of the sleeve and the fact that there is ease on one edge of the upper sleeve, as shown, are responsible for the shaping usually created by an elbow dart. Note that neither seam is at the underarm position; the underarm position falls within the under sleeve and is marked with small o's, as shown.

The familiar one-piece sleeve may be either fitted or boxy. The boxy sleeve will not have an elbow dart, and the fitted sleeve may have a dart, or the back edge may have ease to allow for shaping at the elbow.

The biceps line of the sleeve is a line at the base of the armhole curve, as seen most clearly in the one-piece sleeve. The

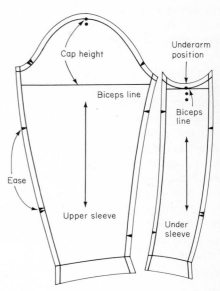

Two-piece sleeve

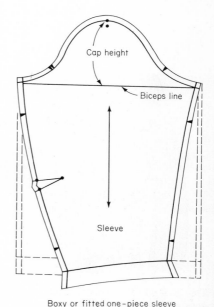

Boxy or fitted one-piece sleeve

FIGURE 9-59 *Typical sleeve patterns.*

biceps line is in an identical position in the two-piece sleeve. It is a line at right angles to the straight-of-material line, beginning at the base of the armhole curve in the under sleeve and extending into the upper sleeve at the same level, as shown. The area above the biceps line is the sleeve cap, and the measurement from the biceps line to the seamline at the shoulder indicates the cap height. The illustrations show a regulation sleeve which has the greatest cap height; this sleeve is used most often because it gives maximum wearing comfort. A sleeve which has a shorter cap height with a somewhat flatter curve in the cap is used for dropped-shoulder effects.

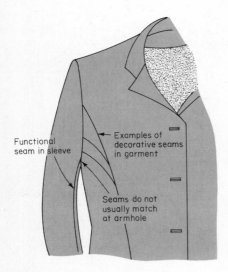

FIGURE 9-60 Functional seams in a sleeve may not match decorative seams in the garment.

The height of the sleeve cap determines the amount of ease in the sleeve The greater the cap height, the more difficult the construction because the sleeve with greater height has more ease that must be worked into the armhole. The regulation sleeve pictured has about 2 inches of ease between the notches, whereas the sleeve for a dropped shoulder-line with a shorter cap height may have as little as 1 inch of ease.

Seams in the sleeve do not always match seams in the garment Many persons are confused by the less familiar two-piece sleeve and have difficulty setting it in. It is not surprising that many women who usually make simple, basic garments (with the underarm seam in the sleeve matching the underarm seam in the garment) have an unconscious habit of matching seams. However, more intricately cut designs, and particularly designs with the two-piece sleeve, frequently have seams that do not match; in these designs there are matching positions that may not be seamlines.

Figure 9-60 illustrates why seams do not necessarily match each other when the two-piece sleeve is used. Some seams are purely functional, while others are purely decorative or serve both a decorative and a functional purpose. *The seams of a two-piece sleeve are functional seams to aid in fitting the sleeve and are placed in a position to hide them from view as much as possible. By contrast, a seam that serves a decorative purpose is placed in a prominent position to give the desired effect.* Because of these conflicting reasons for placement, a functional seam need not match a decorative seam. The worker is often confused by a decorative seam that is very close to the functional seam of the two-piece sleeve, and she tends to think that if the seams are in almost the same position, they should match. It is important to remember that a decorative seam may match the functional seam but that the two may miss each other by as little as ¼ inch or as much as several inches (as in the upper curved line in the sketch).

In all sleeves, notches control the basic position. The underarm positions are another control, but the underarm position may not be a seam. The shoulder position is yet another control, but the shoulder position on the garment may not be a seam. Keep in mind that shoulder and underarm *positions* (not necessarily seams) match.

NOTE: **In the following directions, the illustrations will picture a garment with the usual shoulder and underarm seams, used with a two-piece sleeve. The principles of setting in the sleeve are exactly the same regardless of the lines of the garment. To repeat: Shoulder positions, underarm positions, and notches should be matched, and seams may or may not match.**

Construction sequence

Preparatory steps Some instructors prefer to have students work in ease as the sleeve is pinned in, while others favor the advantages of gathering stitches to draw up the fullnesss. Rows of gathering stitches are very helpful for beginners, for working in greater amounts of ease, and for easing in fullness in stiff fabrics. If gathering stitches will be used, review "Easing in Fullness and Gathering" on page 268.

See sketch *a* in Figure 9-61. Put two rows of machine-gathering stitches in the cap of the sleeve between the notches; place the rows of stitches ⅛ inch on each side of the seamline. Pull up the bobbin threads and attempt to estimate the proper amount of ease; it will never exceed 2 inches (as a total amount) between the notches. Work most of the ease in the

upper portion of the sleeve cap (in the 2 inches on either side of the shoulder marking).

Test the effect by holding the fingers under the sleeve cap (to simulate a shoulder), as shown in sketch *b,* and see that the sleeve looks smooth and molded. It

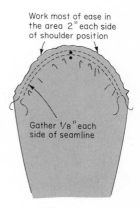

a Draw up ease.

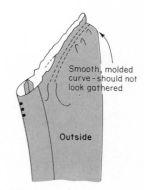

b Test for appearance by holding in wearing position.

FIGURE 9-61 *Preparatory steps.*

should not look gathered, and if it does, it has been drawn up too much. Be sure that it is not drawn up too tightly because if it is, the remaining steps of construction will be more difficult. Do not fasten threads, for this is a temporary estimate; the exact amount of ease will be determined when the sleeve is pinned in the armhole of the garment. It is helpful if this guess is quite accurate, and with experience it is possible to judge the right amount of ease with great accuracy. When making this estimate, keep in mind that too much ease will make construction more difficult than too little ease; when the sleeve is set in, it is simpler to draw the bobbin threads up more than to have to release them.

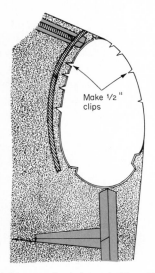

a Helpful suggestion to be used with caution.

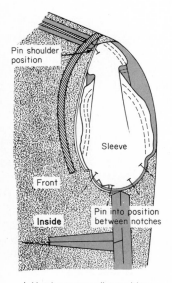

b Match corresponding positions.

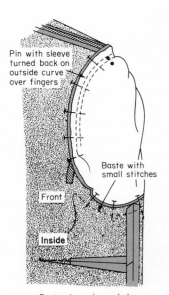

c Baste sleeve in armhole.

FIGURE 9-62 *To set the sleeve in the armhole.*

NOTE: **Some directions suggest drawing up the ease and then shrinking out the fullness before the sleeve is permanently set it. This should be avoided because of the great danger of creating a series of flat surfaces rather than the desired rounded and molded line. If the sleeve is set in properly, it is not necessary to shrink out the fullness.**

Baste and stitch See sketch *a* in Figure 9-62. The armhole line of the garment has a slight inward curve which will be joined to a different curve in the sleeve cap. Clips made into the seam allowance (spaced about an inch apart) along the edges above the notches will release the seam allowance of the garment and allow it to fit more easily to the different curve in the sleeve cap. *This idea is very helpful, but it does prevent letting out the seam for wider-than-average shoulders; therefore, it must not be used unless the sleeve has been prefitted.* The clips are not shown in other sketches in this series (as a caution against using them when the sleeve has not been prefitted) but when work progresses to the construction shown in sketch *c*, the advantages of clips will become apparent; they allow the shorter cut edge of the garment to spread out and better fit the longer cut edge of the sleeve. As soon as the sleeve is basted in and tested on the figure and just before stitching, clip these edges if they have not been clipped previously; the clips make it much easier to stitch the armhole seam accurately. Therefore, clip the edges *before basting* if the shoulderline will not be altered and clip the edges *after basting and fitting* if the shoulderline may be altered.

See sketch *b* in Figure 9-62. Work with the garment turned wrong side out. With right sides together and cut edges even, locate the sleeve in the armhole at four matching points: the underarm position, the two notch positions, and the shoulder

position. First pin the area between and below the notches. The sleeve may be larger than the garment in that area because there is often about ¼ inch of ease between each notch position and the underarm position of the sleeve; it is so slight and so easy to work in that the instruction sheet directions seldom mention it, and the worker may well be unaware of it.

See sketch *c*. This sketch pictures a technique that makes setting in sleeves very much easier. The technique has to do with the way the work is held. Hold the garment and the sleeve in such a position that the sleeve takes the outside curve over the fingers; note that the seam is turned toward the garment for this step. Held in this position, the ease works in so magically that it almost seems to disappear. Adjust the ease, pulling up or releasing the gathering threads as required, being very careful not to draw the sleeve up too tightly. Pin in place, cut edges even. Baste with small stitches that are firm but not so tight that they draw up the garment. Test the seam for tightness by putting the hands into the armhole and gently pulling the sleeve against the hands. If stitches "cut in," the basting stitches are too tight, and the thread should be clipped at several points to release it.

After the sleeve is basted, examine the basted line from the garment side. Because the seam was basted from the sleeve side, there may be slight irregularities on the garment side. If the basted line is not a smooth, continuous curve, rip the stitches in the area and rebaste. Go through this same test after the sleeve is stitched.

Turn the garment right side out and

examine the sleeve. Be sure the garment has not been drawn up and that it does not pucker at the seamline. The upper edge of the sleeve should not look gathered; the eased-in fullness should not be obvious. Fit the garment to test the hang of the sleeve and the width of the shoulderline. Make adjustments if necessary.

Machine-stitch the seam with the sleeve side uppermost for better handling of the eased edge. Stitch over the bastings very slowly and carefully; at this time, careless stitching can create tiny tucks in the sleeve cap. Remove bastings and gathering threads.

NOTE: If the garment will get heavy wear, it is wise to restitch the underarm area to reinforce the seam. Put an additional row of stitches in that area $\frac{1}{16}$ inch outside the original stitching.

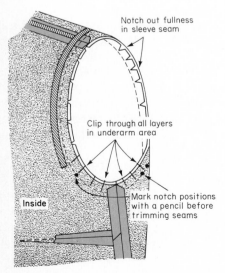

Notch out fullness
in sleeve seam

Clip through all layers
in underarm area

Inside

Mark notch positions
with a pencil before
trimming seams

FIGURE 9-63 Trim seam and clip curves.

Trim seams and clip curves See Figure 9-63. Most structural seams of the garment are not trimmed down in width, but the armhole seam is an exception. It should be trimmed down to a ⅜-inch width so that the sleeve can fall naturally over the shoulder (a ⅝-inch seam allowance would force the sleeve to stand out that far beyond the armhole seam and would make shoulders look too wide). Before trimming this seam, record the notch positions by making pencil dots at the seamline, as shown; these are needed because notch positions in the lining must be matched to them.

The ripples formed in the cap of the sleeve as the seam is turned toward the sleeve make the sleeve cap bulky; to prevent this, notch out the ripples until the seam lies flat and smooth, as shown in the sketch. The seam must be clipped almost to the stitching in the underarm area, as shown; clip about every ½ inch.

In most garments, the armhole seam turns toward the sleeve; refer to the instruction sheet for special directions (under some circumstances, the seam is pressed open). Avoid pressing the seam if it lies in that direction without pressing. If the seam must be pressed, press just the seamline, allowing the iron to extend only about ⅛ inch over the seamline into the sleeve; this will avoid a series of flat surfaces the iron would otherwise create and allows the sleeve to retain a natural roll.

Apply principles to other sleeve designs

A large percentage of all sleeve designs are of the regulation type. They will differ in the amount of ease in the cap (less for a slightly dropped armhole seam), but they are all set in in the same way. It is not possible to give detailed directions for all the many sleeve designs the worker may encounter, but it is possible to apply many of the principles (explained above) to most of the more usual types.

The sleeve with a gathered cap (the puffed sleeve) is handled much like a regulation sleeve. When distributing the gathers above the notches in the sleeve cap, concentrate more fullness in the 2 inches on either side of the shoulder mark-

ing, the same as in the regulation sleeve.

See Figure 9-64, which shows a raglan-type sleeve; this pattern is made by combining the sleeve with a portion of the

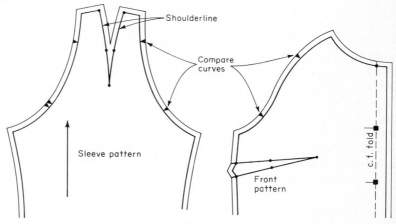

a A sleeve combined with portions from the front and back shoulder area

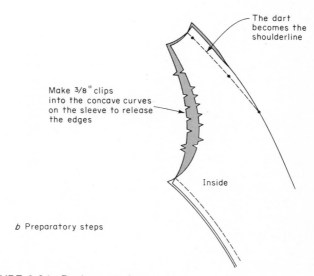

b Preparatory steps

FIGURE 9-64   Raglan-type sleeves.

shoulder areas of the front and back. This type of sleeve is set into the garment rather like an eased-in sleeve, but construction is much simpler because there is very little ease and the longer seam edges are more accessible for hand and machine work.

The curved dartline (with the wedge trimmed out and seam allowances added) replaces the shoulder seam, and the dart extends beyond the shoulderline to end in a smooth curve an inch or so below the shoulder level.

The clips shown in sketch *b* are an aid to easier construction. Note the differences in the curves in the area between the notches on the front and on the sleeve in sketch *a;* the sleeve edge curves inward while the corresponding segment of the seamline on the front curves outward. Whenever edges with different curves will be joined, clips in the concave curved edge will release that edge and allow it to shape more readily to the convex curve, the same as in the regulation sleeve.

SETTING IN SHOULDER PADS

Review "Shoulder Pads" on page 12. The sketches in this section show both round and square pads with one squared-off corner like the typical coat pad. The squared half of the pad must be placed in the front section of the garment, as shown in the sketches. If the pad is triangular in shape, the two halves are identical, and it will make no difference which edge is located in the front.

In general, the square pad is used if there is an armhole seam and a regula-tion sleeve. However, if the armhole seam is a dropped line (deliberately planned to drop below the shoulderline), the round pad should be used.

Square pads for regulation sleeves

See Figure 9-65. Because the pad is thick and probably stiff as well, it is especially important to hold the garment in wearing position as the pad is pinned into place; that position is shown in steps 2 and 3.

Step 1 This sketch is included as an aid to understanding construction details. The pad may extend almost to the neck edge, in which case stitches at the shoulder edge of the facing must be removed so the pad can be placed under the facing. The center line of the pad, a line from the point at the neck edge to about midway between the two ends at the outer edge, should be located at the shoulderline of the garment. Note that the square portion of the pad is placed in the front of the garment. The pad extends ⅜ inch beyond the stitching line into the sleeve. This will give the natural shoulder line that is favored for most fashions. However, the pad can extend any distance into the sleeve to achieve the desired effect; for example, in the middle 1940s, pads extended an inch into the sleeve to give the exaggerated wide-shouldered effect that was fashionable at the time.

NOTE: **The pad may extend beyond the neck seam in some garments with wide necklines; if it does, the tip or point of the pad must be trimmed off.**

Step 2 Working from the outside, locate the center line of the pad under the shoulderline, with the pad extending the desired distance into the sleeve, and place the first pin at the shoulder end of the pad; do not catch through the entire pad thickness with the pin, but simply catch through to the top layer. Again checking to be sure the center line is located on the shoulderline, place the second pin at the neck edge of the pad.

The broken lines indicate the position of the pad and illustrate that the armhole edge of the pad does not follow along the armhole seam in the garment; the edge of the pad will cross the armhole seam in both front and back, as shown. Holding the garment in wearing position, smooth it over the pad and place a pin at each remaining corner, as shown.

Fit the garment to test the effect. See that the pad extends the desired amount into the sleeve; a person with narrow shoulders may want to broaden her shoulderline by allowing the pad to extend a greater distance into the sleeve. See that the garment fits smoothly over the pad; sometimes the corner pins are not in perfect position, causing a little ripple or pucker in the garment. Make all necessary corrections.

Step 3 Working from the outside, blind-stitch the pad in place with stitches about ½ inch long; do not pull stitches tightly enough to make a prominent indentation. Blind-stitch through any seam or dartline that crossed the pad (the shoulder seam, a portion of the armhole seam, and possibly a portion of the back shoulder dart). Stitches need not pass through the entire pad thickness; catch them through the garment to the top layer of the pad.

Reposition the shoulder edge of the facing over the pad and hand sew the shoulder edge to the inside of the pad.

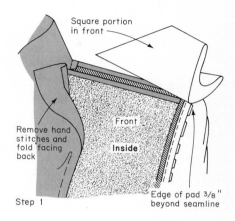

Step 1

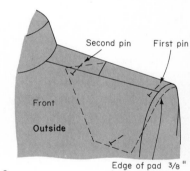

Step 2

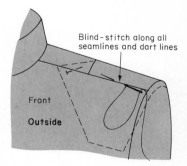

Step 3

FIGURE 9-65 To set in square pads (for regulation sleeves).

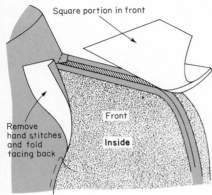

Step 1

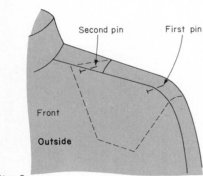

Step 2

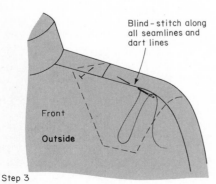

Step 3

FIGURE 9-66 *To set in round pads.*

Round pads for molded shoulderlines

See Figure 9-66. Because the pad is thick and probably somewhat stiff as well, it is especially important to hold the garment in wearing position as the pad is pinned in place; that position is shown in steps 2 and 3.

Step 1 This sketch is included as an aid to understanding construction details. The pad may extend almost to the neck edge, in which case stitches at the shoulder edge of the facing must be removed so the pad can be placed under the facing. The center line of the pad, a line from the point at the neck edge to about midway between the two ends at the outer edge, should be located at the shoulderline of the garment. Note that the square portion of the pad is placed in the front of the garment. The pad must extend into the sleeve section to give the desired effect; it is well to estimate the position and pin the pad in and then make adjustments on the figure until the proper effect is achieved.

NOTE: **The pad may extend beyond the neck seam in some garments with wide necklines; if it does, the tip or point of the pad must be trimmed off.**

Step 2 Working from the outside, locate the center line of the pad under the shoulderline, with the pad extending the desired distance into the sleeve portion of the garment, and place the first pin at the shoulder end of the pad; do not catch through the entire pad thickness with the pin, but simply catch through the top layer. Again checking to be sure the center line is located on the shoulderline, place the second pin at the neck edge of the pad.

Fit the garment to test the effect. See that the pad position results in the shoulder effect desired; a person with narrow shoulders may want to broaden her shoulderline by allowing the pad to extend a greater distance into the sleeve section. Make all necessary corrections.

Step 3 Working from the outside, blind-stitch the pad in place with stitches about ½ inch long; do not pull stitches tightly enough to make a prominent indentation. Blind-stitch through any seam or dartline that crosses the pad (the shoulder seam and a portion of the back shoulder dart). Stitches need not pass through the entire pad thickness; catch them through the garment to the top layer of the pad.

Reposition the shoulder edge of the facing over the pad and hand sew the shoulder edge to the inside of the pad.

FINISHING THE HEM

Two hem finishes are used in tailored garments. The catch-stitched hem, with edges left raw, is used most frequently because it is appropriate for use with the lining that will be attached to the garment. The attached lining is used in all jackets, boleros, and short coats unless some unusual feature of the design requires a free-hanging lining. This finish is used exclusively for sleeve hems. The alternative method finishes the raw edge with seam binding or the Hong Kong finish in those few garments (usually coats) which will have a free-hanging lining. See page 287 for a more detailed evaluation of the attached and free-hanging linings.

Hem width

Patterns for sleeves and jackets give a hem width that is appropriate for the particular garment. The favored hem width for traditional jackets and sleeves is 1½ inches unless some unusual feature of the

design calls for an especially wide hem. The hem allowance given on a full-length coat pattern is approximately (but not exactly) the recommended width. The pattern will probably have a 3-inch hem to allow for some adjustment when the hem is measured. But a 3-inch finished hem is too wide to be attractive; the finished hem width of a coat should be about 2-½ inches. Several factors influence the width of the finished hem of any full-length garment; see page 332.

To establish the desired hemline

The hemline of three-quarter- or full-length coats is measured in the same manner as any other full-length garment, with a line measured parallel to the floor. Above-hip-level jackets are not measured parallel to the floor. They should be turned up along the hemline as indicated on the pattern and corrected on the figure to give the desired effect. These jackets are very often cut somewhat longer in the back for a slightly dipped effect that is very attractive on most figures. Similarly, sleeve length is established by eye rather than by measurement.

The full-length coat should be tried on over a skirt or dress that is the length of the typical garment over which it will be worn. The coat must be at least ½ inch longer than other garments and can be as much as 1 inch or more longer. It should be measured and then pinned into place for testing.

The jacket should be tried on over its accompanying skirt. The hem should be pinned up along the hemline indicated by the pattern. Experiment with jacket length and make corrections, if necessary, to obtain the line that is most flattering for the individual figure.

In many cases, sleeve length, like jacket length, is a matter of personal preference. Three-quarter-length sleeves (or any sleeve that is not full length) should be a length that is most flattering to the whole figure and to the arms and hands. Experiment with sleeve length to obtain flattering proportions. The full-length sleeve allows for less personal choice. A good test is to bend the elbow and bring the arm to about waist level against the body. In this position,

the finished edge of the sleeve should be at the bend of the wrist. With this length as a guide, a slight ⅛-inch variation can be made to please individual tastes.

Make necessary corrections

A test for accuracy See Figure 9-67. Because of the thickness of fabric at the front corner, it is difficult to measure a tailored garment with absolute accuracy. After the desired hemline has been established, the length of corresponding front edges must be tested for accuracy. Pin the right and left front edges together with corners meeting at the neck edge, as shown. Make sure the two edges are the same length by correcting the position of pins at the hemline.

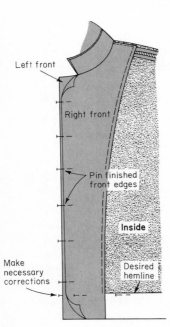

FIGURE 9-67 A test for accuracy.

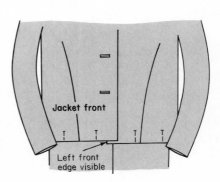

Unattractive effect

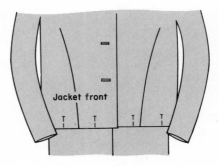

The desired effect

FIGURE 9-68 Make a slight correction at the front corner of the jacket.

Make a slight correction at the front corner See Figure 9-68. The illustrations show a problem that may require a slight adjustment in length, especially on jackets. The right front must lap over the left front. if the two front edges are exactly the same length, the left front may be visible to the eye (at jacket levels, but probably not at full-length-coat levels). The right front of jackets may need to be from a scant ⅛ inch (in lightweight fabrics) to an ample ⅛ inch (in heavier fabrics) longer than the left front. Make this adjustment by lengthening the right front one-half the amount of the desired correction and shortening the left front by a similar amount, gradually tapering back to the desired hemline a few inches from the front edge.

NOTE: **A similar correction may be required on any edge that laps over another edge—vent closings, sleeve closings, etc.**

Make adjustments in the length of the supporting fabric See Figure 9-69. Very often the lower edge of the supporting fabric will not be the proper length (⅛ to ¼ inch above the established hemline), and adjustments in length are necessary. Sketch *a* shows the interfacing the proper length. Sketch *b* pictures trimming off the interfacing if it is too long. Mark a pencil line ⅛ to ¼ inch above the measured hemline. Then slip the pins from the interfacing layer, being sure to replace them in the proper position in the garment. Now carefully trim the excess supporting fabric along the pencil line, being very careful not to cut into the garment; as a precaution, have the rounded edge of the scissors next to the garment.

If the supporting fabric does not reach the hemline, the problem is not serious in most fabrics, provided the difference is not great. However, if the fabric of the garment is so light in weight that a color

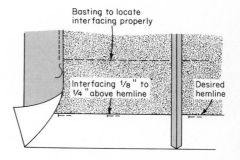

a Supporting fabric cut to proper length.

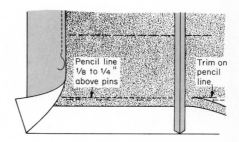

b Trim off excess to shorten.

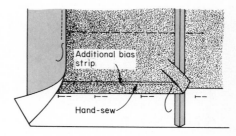

c Add an extension strip to lengthen.

FIGURE 9-69 *Make necessary adjustments in the length of the supporting fabric.*

difference is noticeable where the supporting fabric ends, an extension strip must be added, as shown in sketch c. Cut a bias strip in the required width. Lap the strip over the lower edge, slip one hand underneath the interfacing or underlining layer, and hand sew the two edges together.

Treatment of the front corner

Figure 9-70 illustrates two methods of handling the front corner. Note that the hem is always turned up before the facing is turned back. The thickness of the hem

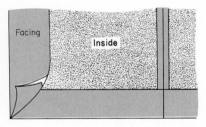

a Garment can be lengthened but front corner will be very bulky.

b Garment can not be lengthened but front corner will be flat and smooth.

FIGURE 9-70 *Methods of handling the front corner.*

and facing in the front corner creates a problem of excessive bulk in a very prominent area. Sketch *a* shows one method of handling the front corner; it results in four thicknesses of fabric and one thickness of supporting fabric that will necessarily be very bulky. This method is used in most ready-to-wear simply because these garments are often altered in length before purchase. *The only advantage of this method over the alternative method is that the garment can be lengthened at a later date.* However, this is a questionable advantage except for children's clothing and strictly utilitarian garments. The tremendous amount of work involved in changing the length of the garment (and the lining) discourages most persons from undertaking the job. Furthermore, results are unpredictable because of the crease that may not press out, because of dust lodged in the hemline that leaves an unattractive line, and because of possible fading of color in the exposed area.

The method shown in sketch *b* is recommended for high-quality tailoring and for most purposes and under most circumstances; all subsequent sketches will picture this method. Note that bulk has been trimmed away and that the two edges have been trimmed to different widths for a flat, staggered effect. The effect is much more attractive, but the garment can never be lengthened.

If there is a separate facing See sketch *a* in Figure 9-71. Make a clip into the hem allowance 1 inch over from the inner edge of the facing. Put a marking-basting line in the facing layer at the desired hemline, as shown. See sketch *b*. Trim away the portion indicated by the shaded area in the sketch (in front of the clip), trimming ¾ inch below the desired hemline of the garment and ½ inch below the hemline of the facing section.

See sketch *c*. Turn up the entire lower edge of the garment along the measured hemline and baste ⅛ inch from the lower edge, as shown; note that the seam at the front edge is pressed open for a short distance. There will still be a great deal of bulk as the pressed-open seam is turned back on itself. Clip the seam open and cut out a little wedge-shaped notch of the seam, as shown. Whip the ¾-inch seam allowance in the garment to the interfacing, as shown.

NOTE: Finish the entire hem before proceeding to the next step. Hem finishes are shown in Figure 9-73. If the novelty Hong Kong method of finishing facing edges and lining is to be used, see page 470 before proceeding to the step shown in sketch *d* of Figure 9-71.

Sketch *d* pictures details that will be done later when the facing edges are finished.

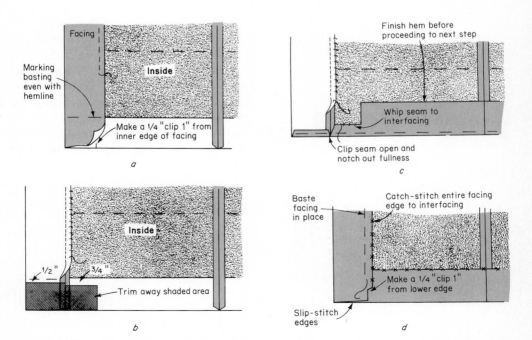

FIGURE 9-71 *Treatment of the front corner for a garment with a separate facing.*

If there is a self-facing In this case follow the detailed directions accompanying Figure 9-71. Work is made somewhat simpler because there is no seam to create extra bulk. Sketch *a* in Figure 9-72 shows the area to be trimmed away. The details in sketch *b* are identical to those in sketch *c* of Figure 9-71.

Hem finishes

The hem can be finished in one of two ways; the choice is dependent on the way the lower edge of the lining will be handled. Review "Alternative Methods of Finishing the Lower Edge" on page 344 and the

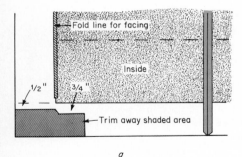

a

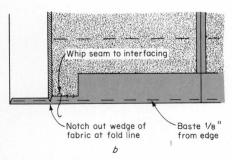

b

FIGURE 9-72 Treatment of the front corner (or vent opening) for garments with self-facings.

section with a similar heading on page 458. If the lining will be attached to the garment hem, the catch-stitched hem, shown in sketch *c* of Figure 9-73, is used. If the lining will be free-hanging, the Hong Kong finish (or another of the bound finishes) is required, as shown in sketch *d* of Figure 9-73.

Construction details for both methods are shown in Figure 9-73. The hem in jackets and coats is done the same as in any underlined or interfaced garment. Review "Four Basic Hand Stitches" on page 280 and "Seam and Hem Finishes" on page 285 before proceeding.

SPECIAL NOTE: A supporting fabric influences the way hemming stitches are made. The stitches will be less conspicuous if they do not catch into the fabric of the garment—in other words, if they catch into the layer of supporting fabric only. However, all too often, the weight of the hem cannot be supported by stitches through the interfacing or underlining layer only, especially on long expanses between seams. If there are several vertical seams (every 4 or 5 inches) stitches can be caught in the supporting fabric only, and tacking the hem to seams will be sufficient to support its weight. If the expanses are great (for example, an entire back cut on the fold) the stitches must pass through the layer of supporting fabric and catch a thread or two of the garment fabric.

Finishing facing edges

Return to sketch *d* in Figure 9-71. Turn the facing to the inside over the hem. Make a ¼-inch clip into the inner edge of the facing about 1 inch from the lower edge, as shown. Baste all edges of the facing in place, turning under ¼ inch below the clip, as shown; this provides a finished edge for that portion of the facing that will be exposed beneath the lining. Slip-stitch (a wiggle-in-and-out stitch) the lower edge of the facing in place, extending the stitches to the clip.

Catch-stitch the entire facing edge in place, with stitches catching into the interfacing or underlining layer only.

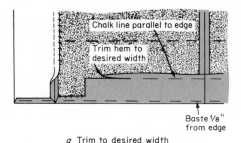

a Trim to desired width

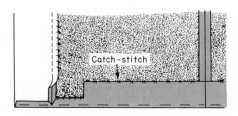

b For flared garments only

c The catch-stitched hem – for the attached lining

d The Hong Kong finish – for the free-hanging lining

FIGURE 9-73 Hem finishes.

FINISHING DETAILS

The tailor's buttonhole

If hand-worked buttonholes are used, they are done at this time. See page 395 for details.

To finish the underside of bound buttonholes

The sequence is shown in three steps in Figure 9-74. Under actual working conditions, one buttonhole is entirely finished before proceeding to the next; this will help to prevent unnecessary raveling after the slash is made.

Step 1 Baste about ½ inch from the buttonhole rectangles, as shown, to be sure the facing is held securely to the garment in proper position. Then from the outside of the garment, stick a pin directly down through the center of the ends of the buttonhole, as shown. These pins will designate the length of the buttonhole marking.

The buttonhole should be the same length and width on the facing side and on the right side; keep in mind the slim proportions of the original buttonhole when doing all steps of construction.

Glance through steps 2 and 3, but do not do them before reading this entire paragraph. As the sketches show, fabric will be cut and must be turned under with very little seam allowance. Raveling is a serious problem, and this step should be tested on scraps of fabric, using the test buttonhole, before work is begun on the garment. When doing these steps on a test buttonhole, be sure the scrap of fabric which acts as the facing layer is cut on the same grainline as the garment facing. In other words, if the slash will be made on a crosswise grainline in the garment, be sure to slash on a crosswise grainline when working with the test buttonhole.

To prevent raveling and to make the remaining steps much easier, clear fingernail polish can be used; it is applied very carefully to just that area underneath the rectangle of the buttonhole. It must be applied lightly so that it does not penetrate through all thicknesses of the fabric. It is easier to do than it sounds, and although it discolors some fabric slightly, if it is applied only under the buttonhole, the stained area will be turned to the inside and will not show. There are no resulting bad effects after washing or dry cleaning, although one should be wary of using this idea with light-colored silks and similar fabrics without pre-testing. Apply the polish and allow it to harden before proceeding to step 2.

Step 2 Cut to within ¼ inch of the pins (through the facing only) and then diagonally to the corners, thus making cuts exactly like those made previously as the buttonhole was made.

Step 3 Turn under the raw edges with the needle and carefully hem the turned-under edges to the binding; pins will not be helpful. Handle this work most carefully because the seam is so small and there are no protective stitches to prevent raveling.

Ideally, these stitches should be inconspicuous, but they must also be sturdy. The edges will be more secure if each stitch is pulled firmly and tightly into the fabric, and the weak corners will be more secure if they are strengthened by one or two diagonal stitches. The stitches must be very small for maximum control of the very small seam and clipped corners. Test this step with scraps of fabric on the test buttonhole to determine how the stitches should be done to allow for the most attractive appearance while serving the necessary utilitarian purpose. Press.

The final pressing

The garment should be finally pressed just prior to inserting the lining. Because all seams, darts, and edges (actually all portions of the garment) have been pressed well during construction, there should be little to do at the final pressing. The main purpose of the final pressing is to remove folds and wrinkles which may have formed

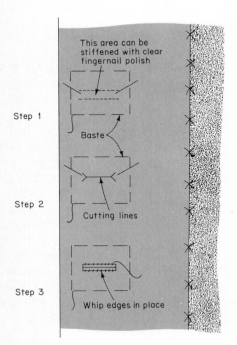

FIGURE 9-74 To finish underside of bound buttonholes.

while the garment was in the final stages of construction. Depending on the nature of the fabric (some fabrics hold a press so well that a final pressing is unnecessary) and the quality of pressing as work was in progress, the final pressing may be a very simple and quick operation.

However, the heavy weight of many fabrics used in tailoring presents additional problems of bulk, and even the most talented and experienced worker may want to have the finished garment professionally pressed. The large-area ironing surfaces and the greater pressure and steam control available in the professional establishment will result in an appearance that is more attractively finished.

Sewing on buttons

Figures 9-75 and 9-76 give general directions for placement, and Figures 9-77 through 9-79 give directions for various types of buttons. Buttons can be sewn in place at this time, or for easier handling while lining the garment, they can be done as the very last step of construction.

To mark the position for buttons See Figure 9-75. Remember that the center-front line of the garment is about ⅛ inch from the end of the buttonhole nearest the front edge and that it is the same distance from the left front edge. As an aid to getting the first button in the proper position, hold the two front edges together, with finished edges even and upper and lower edges even. Then mark the position for the first buttonhole at either the upper or the lower edge by placing a pin through the end of the buttonhole on the center-front line, sticking the pin directly down to the left front of the garment.

Figure 9-76 illustrates how to mark

the position for the remaining buttons. Center-front lines must be matched and all buttons placed along the center-front line so that when the garment is worn,

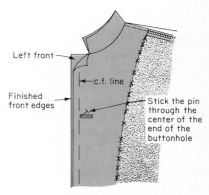

FIGURE 9-75 To mark the position of the top button.

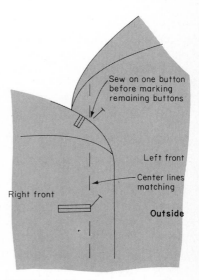

FIGURE 9-76 To mark position for buttons.

the button is at one end of the button-hole. (A word of caution: Many persons think the button should be centered between the two ends of the buttonhole. This is not correct because under the strain of wearing, the button would pull to the end of the buttonhole, and the center fronts would not be in a matching position.)

NOTE: In double-breasted designs, buttons are not placed along the center-front line. Button positions for the two rows of buttons will appear on the pattern. The two rows of buttons are placed an equal distance from the center-front line with center lines matched.

Do not mark the position for all buttons at once because if there is a slight error of placement on one button, many would have to be changed. Mark one position, sew on that button, button it, and then mark the next position and proceed. After sewing on each button, button up the garment and see that each button is properly placed before proceeding to the next.

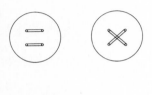

*FIGURE 9-77 Buttons
with four eyes.*

Buttons with four eyes Figure 9-77 shows buttons with four eyes, which can be sewn on in a variety of ways for subtle changes in effect. This type of button is frequently used for tailored garments, in which case the eyes are relatively small. Some large novelty buttons of this type are available with eyes of an exaggerated size. If the button is highly styled with very large eyes, it becomes an important part of the design, and heavier thread will be required. Buttonhole twist will make the stitches more prominent. Sometimes additional stitches made from raveling yarns of the fabric will be needed to create better proportions with the size of the eye. If the buttons are large and the eyes are exaggerated in size (more than $\frac{1}{8}$ inch in diameter), a strip of garment fabric with raw edges concealed can be used in place of thread.

All buttons must have some type of shank The purpose of the shank is to allow for the thickness of the right front when the garment is buttoned, and so heavier fabrics require longer shanks. Most purchased buttons will have a metal shank, and fabric-covered buttons may have a metal or a padded shank; buttons with eyes will require a shank made of thread.

Figure 9-78 illustrates how to sew on buttons with the three types of shanks. In each case, the stitches should pass through the outer layer of garment fabric and the layer of interfacing, but should not be prominent on the facing side. One or two tiny stitches made through all thicknesses (including the facing) will make the button more secure, but most of the stitches should not pass through to the facing side.

When using medium-weight fabrics, the length of the metal shank is such that the shank can be sewn tight to the garment, as shown. However, if very heavy fabric is used, the shank may not be long enough to accommodate the thickness of the right front, and additional length must be obtained with thread, rather like the thread shank shown in the lower sketch. A padded shank offers the same problem because it may or may not be sufficiently long,

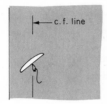

Button with a metal shank

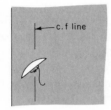

Button with a fabric shank

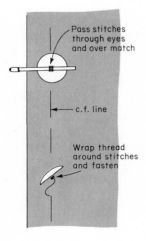

Button with a thread shank

FIGURE 9-78   To sew on buttons.

depending on the thickness of the fabric; it too can be extended with stitches.

For buttons with eyes, hand stitches provide the extra length for the shank. Some method of obtaining extra length must be devised, and several toothpicks or a match will be helpful. Place the match in such a position that stitches must pass over it. Then remove the match and wrap the thread around the stitches, pulling the stitches firmly against the button, as shown in the lower sketch.

To reinforce buttons   See Figure 9-79. Decorative buttons should be reinforced with flat, inconspicuous buttons (on the facing side) in utilitarian garments that will get heavy wear. A reinforcement is absolutely essential if the fabric is very loosely woven or of such a nature (vinyl or suede, etc.) that it can be easily cut with stitches. The reinforcing button is held in place with the same stitches used to secure the decorative button.

Pass stitches over match and through eyes of both buttons

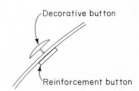

Decorative button

Reinforcement button

FIGURE 9-79   To reinforce buttons for utilitarian garments.

Support for double-breasted closings

The left front edge of the garment with a double-breasted front must be fastened in place to support the weight of the left front and to keep the garment in smooth condition. This is done by sewing snaps directly underneath the row of decorative buttons on the right front; this position will require that snaps be sewn either to the right front facing or to the lining of the right front. Sturdy, large snaps (about ½ inch in diameter) are available on the market. They should be covered with matching fabric (explained below) for a more attractive effect. Sew the flat side of the snap underneath the decorative button on the right front. Before sewing the corresponding snap section to the left front edge, button the garment for its entire length, being sure the left front is in proper position. Mark the placement for one snap, snap that snap, and reposition the two

Cut fabric circles, allowing 1/8" to extend. Gather the outer edge by hand.

Draw up the gathers and fasten the thread securely on the underside.

Sew in place with either the buttonhole stitch (preferred) or overhand stitches.

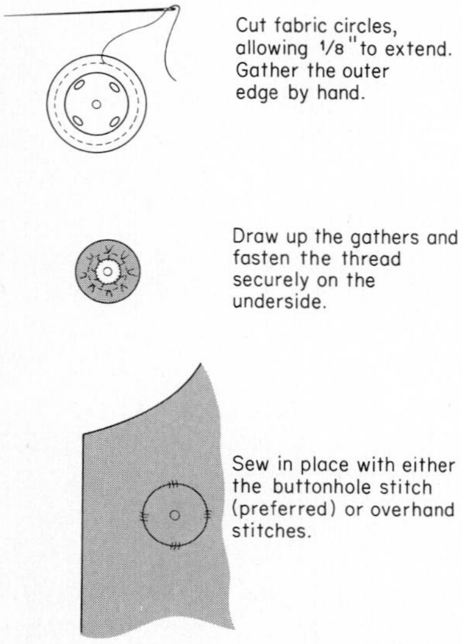

FIGURE 9-80 To cover snaps.

front edges again before proceeding to the next.

To cover and sew on snaps

Snaps are used infrequently on jackets and coats because they are distracting when the garment is unbuttoned. However, there are circumstances of design that make a snap necessary. Snaps for tailored garments should be covered with a lightweight (lining) fabric in a matching color.

The construction details are shown in Figure 9-80. Before beginning work, the worker should understand that snapping and unsnapping will puncture holes that will allow the ball to settle in the socket; these little holes are left raw, and if the fabric frays with prolonged use, the coverings should be replaced. By puncturing a hole in a piece of fabric and inserting the ball through the hole before beginning work, that section of the snap can be covered more easily. The stitches can be made with neat small overhand stitches or with the buttonhole stitch for a more attractive touch.

Hooks and eyes

Hooks and eyes are used infrequently on tailored garments because they are difficult to fasten hurriedly in public and because they are somewhat distracting as the garment is unbuttoned. If this kind of fastening is required, a crocheted thread loop should be used to replace the eye. The hook will be in a less prominent position as the garment is worn, and depending on the fabric, a silver or black hook may not be too prominent. If the fabric is such that either silver or black will be prominent, the hook can be covered with buttonhole stitches made with matching thread.

Chapter 10

JACKET AND COAT LININGS

Before beginning work on the lining, take some time to consider the many decisions that are involved with the lining. Dressmaker details can be added for design interest (see page 440). There are several alternatives in methods of construction to be decided upon (see page 442).

To underline lining sections

Ordinarily lining sections are not underlined, because the lining should be supple and subordinate in character. But there are two circumstances under which it is necessary to underline lining sections; they are (1) if the lining fabric is so light in weight that it will not hide inner construction, and (2) if an extra layer of fabric is desired for extra warmth.

To make the lining sections more opaque If the lining fabric chosen is light in weight and also in color, it may not be opaque enough to hide inner construction. Obviously, it is better to choose a fabric that will hide inner construction, but this is not always possible if the lining matches a blouse or dress or if more typical lining fabric is not available in the desired color. The underlining, if used, should be as supple and light in weight as possible.

The underlining is handled the same as it is for any other layer of the garment with only slight modifications. When cutting the underlining, cut it to about ⅛ inch above the finished hemline of the lining, or wait until the lining is inserted in the coat or jacket and the permanent hemline has been established, and then trim the lining to a level ⅛ inch above the established hemline. It is wise not to underline sleeve sections; and usually it is not necessary, because that portion is rarely visible when the coat or jacket is removed, so that it will not matter if the lining does not entirely hide inner construction.

One problem will be encountered along the front and neck edges which will be sewn by hand to the inner edges of the facing. It is necessary to hold the two layers (lining and underlining) together so that they will act as one. To do this, baste the two layers together with a row of firm, *permanent* basting stitches placed ½ inch in from the cut edge; then when the edge is turned under ⅝ inch, the basting stitches will not show. Trim about ¼ inch from the edge of the underlining to stagger the seam and reduce bulk.

To add extra warmth In this case, the underlining fabric is a thick, wooly fabric that is much heavier and bulkier than a typical underlining fabric. It is handled in the same way as any other underlining with only a few modifications. When cutting the underlining, cut it to a level approximately 3 inches above the finished hemline; cut this way, the lower edge of the underlining will be slightly above the finished hem in the garment and therefore will not add extra bulk in the hem area. The sleeves need not necessarily be underlined if the extra thick layer would make the sleeve too bulky; alternatively, the sleeves can be underlined with a warm layer of fabric that is not as thick as the underlining fabric used in the body of the jacket or coat.

The underlining can be quilted to the lining, if desired. If this is done, the two layers of fabric should be quilted together before the lining pieces are cut because the quilting will pucker up the fabric slightly.

Because of the great bulk involved, it is especially important to trim about ¼ to ⅜ inch from the edges of the underlining layers after seams are stitched. One problem will be encountered along the front and neck edges which will be sewn by hand to the inner edges of the facings. It is necessary to hold the two layers together (lining and underlining), so that they will act as one. To do this baste the two layers together with a row of firm, *permanent* basting stitches placed ½ inch in from the cut edge; then when the edge is turned under ⅝ inch, the basting stitches will not show. Trim about ¼ inch from the edge of the underlining to stagger the seam and reduce bulk.

Consider adding dressmaker touches for design interest

There are many little touches which can be added to the lining for design interest, and the person with a great appreciation for detail will enjoy this subtle method of adding distinction to her costume. Most of the suggestions given below are ideas for finishing the front and neck edges of the lining. The reader should be aware of the emphasis being placed on linings as a source of design interest and should always study the lining techniques used in exclusive ready-to-wear. One of the best sources of lining ideas is the fur coat; the great expense of a fur coat warrants a truly custom-made lining that often includes wonderful details which look very expensive but (for the woman who sews) require nothing more than time and ambition.

Dressmaker details are interesting touches only if they are compatible with the design and the fabric and only if they are used with discretion; as in all matters of design, good taste and judgment are required. Design interest is desirable on a garment with uncomplicated lines in a solid color with a solid-colored lining; it is less desirable when the fabric or the design is very active and interesting. Certain touches lend themselves to a theater suit and would be inappropriate used on a car-coat, for example. In general, the suggestions given are more appropriate for dressmaker suits and coats than for man-tailored garments. Detailed instructions are not given, but each suggestion is relatively simple to do.

Decorative finishes for the front edge

Figure 10-1 pictures methods of finishing the front and neck edges of the lining. The method shown in sketch *a* is probably the most popular because it gives a subtle but very attractive effect. This idea was copied from fur coat linings and is suitable only for fairly heavy garments. The cord (which should be limp and fine) does create a certain amount of stiffness and bulk; therefore, it can be used only on those suiting and coating fabrics which are heavy enough to dominate the stiffness of the cord. The fabric used to cover the cord should be limp and lightweight for a minimum of bulk and stiffness. Cord covered with matching lining fabric gives a subtle and very delicate effect. The cord covering may be in a contrasting color (black coat with a black lining, corded in bright red). The effect will always be subtle, for the width of covered cord should not exceed ⅛ inch.

The cord should be covered with bias strips of fabric; then, instead of basting under the front and neck edges of the lining, the cord is stitched right sides together to those edges. Then the corded edge is basted under and lapped over the facing edges. The hand stitches which secure the finished edges of the lining should be placed along the stitching line in the cord; see the enlarged view in Figure 10-19 on page 461. If the finished edge is not corded, stitches are placed ⅟₁₆ inch under the edge of the lining, as shown; when cord is used, stitches should be placed ⅛ inch under the corded edge, falling in the stitching line.

Sketch *b* shows a decorative stitch used to secure the finished edge of the lining. Because of the very delicate effect, this suggestion lends itself to very feminine and softly tailored garments. The feather stitch is an effective stitch, and it can be placed so that it is more prominent on either the lining or the garment or so that it is equally prominent on both, as shown in the sketch. The thread can match the lining or the garment fabric, or it can contrast to both (gray coat with a white lining, hand-stitched in chartreuse thread).

Sketch *c* shows decorative braid (another idea copied from fur coat linings), which is necessarily stiff and somewhat bulky; the comments concerning the corded effect shown in sketch *a* are true of this suggestion as well. To be truly effective, the braid must be very decorative with a great deal of openwork; a band-

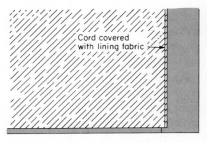

a Front edge of lining corded with matching or contrasting fabric

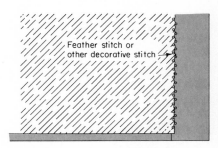

b Front edge of lining secured with decorative hand stitches

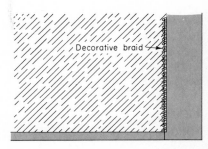

c Decorative braid applied over finished front edge of lining

FIGURE 10-1 *Ideas for finishing the front edge of the lining.*

like braid will not give an attractive effect. There is a simple metallic cord that is only ⅛ inch in diameter and is most effective on some costumes (gray coat with a lighter gray satin lining and silver metallic cord). The braid or decorative cord is applied after the lining is completely finished and

is secured to the front and neck edges with invisible hand stitches. It can be placed over the lining only, as shown in the sketch, or it can cover the front edge of the lining. The braid can match the lining or the garment fabric; because of the decorative nature of the braid, it should not contrast to both fabrics, but should match one or the other.

Other design accents Some imported garments have truly exciting linings which involve the use of padding and quilting, or trapunto work. Some of them have a band of quilting, or trapunto, along the entire front edge that is several inches wide, and others have the decoration extending over the front shoulder area or around the lower front corners as well. It is a very decorative and elegant effect, but it must be used only with heavy suiting and coating fabrics that will not be dominated by its extra bulk, and it must be done by a person who is talented in hand work.

Sketch *a* in Figure 10-2 pictures a bound pocket in the lining. A welt pocket or an interesting patch pocket can be used. Welt or bound pockets can be in the horizontal position shown, and they are equally attractive in a vertical position. Even though the pocket should not be used (at least for nothing more than emergency bus fare), it should be placed in a position that would be convenient. Right-handed persons should have the pocket on the lining on the left front, and it should be at a convenient level between the waist and the hipline. The initials shown in sketch *b* should be placed in a comparable position.

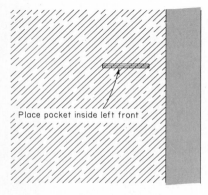

a A bound or welt pocket or an interesting patch pocket is attractive.

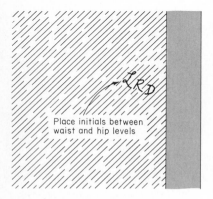

b Hand embroidered or purchased initials give a personalized touch.

FIGURE 10-2 Ideas to add design interest.

Decide on construction alternatives

See "An Evaluation of Lining Methods" on page 450 and decide between the hand and machine methods; the two can be combined. The novelty Hong Kong finish can be used on facing edges (see page 470), and this finish can be done regardless of the construction method used. The · lower edge of the lining can be attached or free-hanging; this should have been decided before the hem in the garment was finished, but that decision can be reversed at this time, if necessary.

The lining is cut in the same way for the hand and machine (or combination) methods of construction. Pay close attention to the cutting directions in the section below. Several suggestions included there do not appear on the instruction sheet, and a few of them are somewhat different from those recommended on the pattern. If heavy lining fabric (Sun-Bac satin, fake fur, etc.) will be used, there is a slight change in cutting directions (see page 449).

CUTTING DIRECTIONS

The commercial pattern will give directions for cutting the lining in one of two different ways, depending on company policy and on the nature of the design.

The pattern may include separate lining pattern pieces for the front and back sections because these sections are cut very differently from the pattern 'for the garment. Vogue patterns always include separate lining patterns (one reason for their higher cost), and the other companies frequently do. However, even if lining pieces are included, certain pieces (such as sleeve and side sections, etc.) that will be cut exactly like garment pieces will not be included. Therefore, the separate lining pieces plus any other pattern pieces pictured in the lining layouts must be used when cutting the lining.

There may be no pattern pieces for the lining, and cutoff lines on certain pattern pieces will indicate cutting lines for the

lining. There will be a cutoff line on the front pattern, and there may be a cutoff line near the back neck edge if there is a back facing; note the position of the dotted lines in Figure 10-4. Not all pieces will have cutoff lines because some pieces should be cut exactly like the garment pieces. Directions for cutting linings appear at two places: on some pattern pieces and in notes and illustrations on the lining layouts. Cutoff lines will be shown in broken lines on the layouts, and a pleat allowance for the back will be obtained by the way the back pattern is placed on the fabric; layout techniques of this method are pictured in Figure 10-8.

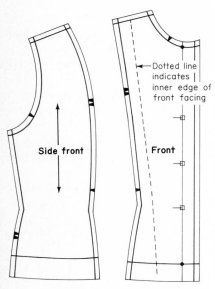

a   Pattern pieces for garment.

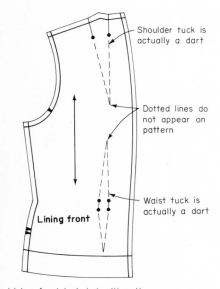

b   Lining front included with pattern.

FIGURE 10-3 A "combination" lining pattern.

Lining pieces included with the pattern

The lining cut from the original pattern by use of cutting lines is identical to the garment in seam and dart location. However, a separate lining pattern made by a professional may be different in shape, and it may have dartlines that are not identical to those in the garment. Figure 10-3 pictures an example of the front-lining pattern included with the pattern for a princess-line garment. Sketch *a* shows the pattern pieces for the garment, and a broken line indicates the inner edge of the facing. The front-lining pattern shown in sketch *b* is a combination piece because it is cut in sufficient width to cover the side front piece and to extend far enough over the front to cover the inner edge of the facing. A dart-like fitting in the lining front provides essentially the same shaping that the shaped seam provides in the garment.

The cut of this lining is superior to that of the lining made by the method shown in Figures 10-4 and 10-5, but this is not a method that should be undertaken by one who is not trained in pattern making. One advantage is that the lining will be more attractive because a seam as close to the front edge as the princess-line seam will result in a very narrow strip. However, if intricate fitting has been done in this seam (very probable in this type of design), making identical alterations on a very different pattern piece is most difficult and often impossible; under these circumstances, it is wiser to make the lining pattern according to the directions accompanying Figures 10-4 and 10-5. The proper fit of the lining is more important than the attractiveness of a seam that is not prominent as the garment is worn.

Note that the lining made by the professional pattern maker has tucks at the shoulder edge (and at the waistline in some fitted designs). The shoulder tuck is actually a dart that is stitched for a short distance only; the tucklines (which do not appear on the pattern itself) are extended in the sketch to illustrate that they converge at a point near the bust level. The tucks are really released darts, and although they fall in place as darts as the garment is worn, they can release with body movements to give a slight amount of freedom in the lining. This advantage is not present if the lining is cut by using the cutting lines on the pattern. This explanation is included as an aid to understanding the lining pattern that might be included with the commercial pattern. The advantages listed do have merit, but the reader should understand that the alternative cutoff-line method is entirely acceptable.

To make lining patterns

It is a very simple matter to make lining patterns by constructing cutoff lines as the professional pattern maker does. Although this is not ordinarily necessary, there are two circumstances under which one might wish to make a lining pattern. In the very simple pattern planned especially for the beginner, there may be no directions for a lining, and yet a lining would be required if this pattern were used for a tailored garment. Another circumstance will be encountered more frequently. If there are very complicated pattern alterations on the original pattern, it is often easier to use a cutoff line on the altered pattern than to repeat intricate alterations on another pattern piece. Making the pattern is a simpler process, and sometimes it is the only way that truly accurate results can be obtained. For example, if a lining pattern piece is a "combination" piece (if one lining pattern covers a seam in the garment, thereby serving as the lining for two sections of the garment) and if intricate fitting has been done on the

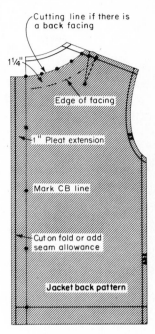

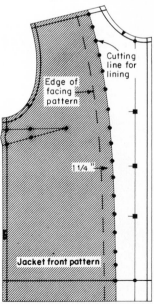

FIGURE 10-4 To make lining patterns for front and back.

seam that does not appear in the lining, it is absolutely necessary to make lining patterns in order to have seams which can be fitted like seams in the garment. Similarly, if an intricate alteration has been made on a dart and if that dart does not appear in the lining pattern (if a separate lining piece is given, dart positions are not always identical to those in the garment), it is essential to make a new lining pattern.

See Figure 10-4. The lining pattern is different from the garment pattern in the front area because of the front facing and in the back section because a pleat must be added; the back lining pattern may be different at the neck edge if there is a back facing. A basic two-piece garment is shown, but the principles illustrated in the sketch can be applied to any design. If there are additional sections in the body of the garment, they are cut from the original pattern piece; sleeve linings are cut from the original pattern pieces.

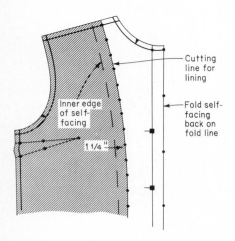

FIGURE 10-5 Principles applied to a garment with a self-facing.

To establish the cutting line on the front This step is shown in Figure 10-4 for the pattern with a separate facing; it is done in the same manner for the pattern with a self-facing, as shown in Figure 10-5. Place the front-facing pattern under the front pattern, front and neck edges even; the inner edge of the facing is shown by a broken line in the sketch. Construct the cutting line for the lining $1\frac{1}{4}$ inches over (closer to the front edge) from the inner edge of the facing; this allows for a $\frac{5}{8}$-inch turn-under on the front edge of the lining and a $\frac{5}{8}$-inch lap-over on the inner edge of the facing. This is the way the professional pattern maker establishes the cutting line that appears on some commercial patterns.

To establish the cutting line on the back neck edge This is done only if there is a back facing on the garment. Place the back-facing pattern under the back pattern, shoulder and neck edges even; the inner edge of the facing is shown by a broken line in Figure 10-4. Construct the cutting line for the lining $1\frac{1}{4}$ inches above (closer to the neck edge) the inner edge of the facing; this allows for a $\frac{5}{8}$-inch turn-under on the lining and a $\frac{5}{8}$-inch lap-over on the inner edge of the facing.

GENERAL RULE FOR ESTABLISHING CUTTING LINES FOR THE LINING: The cutting line for the lining is located $1\frac{1}{4}$ inches over the inner edge of the facing.

To make a pleat allowance at the center back See Figure 10-4. Scotch-tape a strip of paper to the center back of the pattern. Draw a line 1 inch over from the center-back line for the pleat extension. This edge may be cut on the fold if the layout permits, or by adding an additional seam allowance, as shown in the sketch, this edge can be seamed. Mark dots along the center-back line; this line should be tailor-tacked just like any other marked line on the pattern.

Inside image labels: Cutting line for lining / Inner edge of self-facing / Fold self-facing back on fold line / $1\frac{1}{4}$ "

Special suggestions

Before cutting the lining, it is well to give careful thought to pattern alterations. Corresponding alterations on lining pieces should have been done after the muslin copy was fitted (see "Corresponding Alterations on Lining Patterns" on page 215); if they were not done at that time, they must be finished now. If any additional fitting alterations were made in the garment after it was cut in the fabric, these alterations should be incorporated in the pattern before the lining is cut; for example, if a seam was let out in the garment, the lining pattern can be altered so that there will be a full seam allowance in the lining.

NOTE: The suggestions given below differ from the directions included with some patterns. Each suggestion has great advantages, but the reader should understand that her pattern directions are accurate and scientifically correct. The merit of these suggestions lies in their value for individual problems of figure, etc., and in the fact that they are a precaution against mistakes. Read all suggestions before cutting.

Test for length   The lining of a sleeve or a jacket need not be as long as the corresponding pieces of the garment because smaller hem allowances are used and because the finished lower edge of the lining is at least ½ inch shorter than the garment. The hem allowance in the lining of a full-length coat is approximately the same as that in the coat itself, and so coat linings are usually cut as long as the corresponding pieces for the garment. In an effort to save yardage for the customer, commercial pattern companies sometimes (but not always) give directions for cutting the lining pieces for jackets and sleeves in a shorter length. See Figure 10-6. This is done in two different ways. Sketch *a* illustrates how a cutoff line might be used. A note on the pattern may indicate that the cutting line for

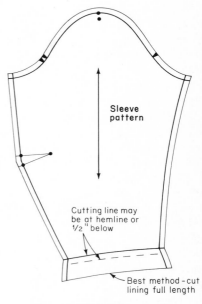

Sleeve pattern

Cutting line may be at hemline or ½" below

Best method - cut lining full length

a Examples of cutoff lines on pattern.

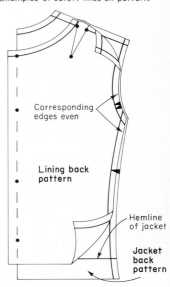

Corresponding edges even

Lining back pattern

Hemline of jacket

Jacket back pattern

b Example of separate lining pattern cut shorter than garment.

FIGURE 10-6   Tests for length.

the lining is at the hemline of the original pattern, or a new cutoff line may be indicated slightly below the hemline. Sketch *b* shows a separate lining pattern cut in a shorter length than the garment pattern. These lengths indicated by the pattern company are correct, provided all work done on the garment is scientific (all seam and hem allowances are accurate) and provided the garment has not been lengthened by even a slight amount.

Insufficient length in the lining results in much more difficulty of construction. *The best and safest rule for the nonprofessional worker is to cut the lining as long as the original pattern for the garment.* If this is not possible because of yardage restrictions, it is well to cut the lining pieces as long as possible. See sketch *a* in Figure 10-6. Cut the lining at least ½ inch below the hemline of the garment, and if possible, cut it ¾ or 1 inch below the hemline. If there is sufficient yardage, cut the lining the full length of the original pattern; some of this length will be trimmed off later, but the extra length will allow for possible mistakes which may have been made or for slight additions in the length of the garment.

See sketch *b.* Place any lining pieces included with the pattern over the corresponding pattern pieces for the garment, corresponding edges even. The sketch shows a quite typical pattern in which the lining pattern extends about ½ inch below the hemline of the garment. Add an extension strip on the lining pattern to make it full length (if there is sufficient yardage) or to extend it to a level at least 1 inch below the hemline.

Cutting the lining for a vent opening
Figure 10-7 pictures the lining-back pattern for a garment with a vent opening. Note that two pieces are to be cut by the pattern piece. However, in the vent area, one layer of fabric is cut very differently from the other layer, as indicated by a cutoff line and a note which usually reads "cutoff line for left side." A glance at the sketches which show how to line the vent opening (Figures 10-25 to 10-28, beginning on page 467) will illustrate that cutting the wrong layer of lining would be a serious mistake. Because it is difficult at this time to determine exactly what "left side" means (whether it is the left back of the lining or the side that will line the left back of the garment), it is not wise to cut one layer of the fabric at this time. Instead, cut both layers the same and tailor-tack the cutting line, as shown. After the lining is positioned in the garment and certain tests are made that will correct little inaccuracies of construction, the proper layer will be cut.

To add a pleat allowance when cutting See Figure 10-8. Pattern companies that do not include pattern pieces for linings make allowance for the back pleat as the pattern is cut from the fabric, with directions on the lining layout, as shown in the two sketches. Sketch *a* shows a method that results in a wedge-shaped or dart-shaped

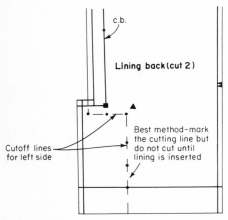

FIGURE 10-7 Cutting the lining for a vent opening.

pleat; this pleat serves the purpose for which it was intended (freedom in the shoulder area), but it is more difficult to baste and press and this method forces the grainline of the lining into a different position from that of the garment. Sketch *b* shows a parallel pleat like the pleat used by those companies which provide a separate lining-back pattern; a slight change in the placement of the pattern on the fabric will transform the wedge-shaped pleat into the parallel pleat pictured.

Suggestions for heavy lining fabrics

Sun-Bac satin, simulated fur, and quilted lining fabrics are so heavy that they frequently tend to dominate the garment fabric; every effort must be made to reduce this bulk. It is wise to eliminate the back

pleat (it serves a good purpose, but it is not entirely necessary) and if possible to eliminate a seam at the back. This can be done by cutting the lining back with the center-back line of the pattern placed on a fold of fabric. If there is a shoulder tuck (see Figure 10-3), it is wise to extend the tuck lines, as shown, and sew the entire dart by machine; a dart is less bulky than the released tuck and can be slashed and pressed open to distribute the bulk. Darts are not usually slashed in lining fabrics, but darts of sufficient width should be slashed and pressed open in these very heavy fabrics.

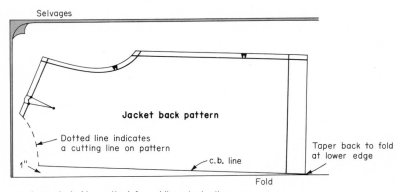

a Less desirable method for adding pleat allowance.

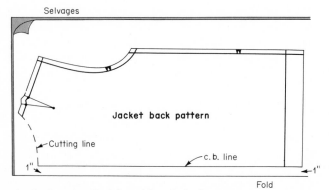

b Preferred method for adding pleat allowance.

FIGURE 10-8 *To add a pleat allowance when cutting.*

AN EVALUATION OF LINING METHODS

There are two methods of lining the tailored garment, and a third, which is a combination of the two, is included in these directions. The two basic methods are the machine and the hand methods. The discussion below will aid in selecting the best method for the particular fabric and design.

In both methods of construction, certain work is done by machine, and certain work is done by hand. Darts, tucks, the center-back seam of a pleat, and vertical sleeve seams are done by machine in both methods. The front and neck edges are done by hand, and the sleeve is set in by hand in both methods. If the lining is attached to the garment at the lower edge, it is done by hand in both methods.

Machine method

In this method, the structural seams of the lining are stitched by machine, so that the body of the lining is assembled before the lining is inserted into the garment. As mentioned above, the sleeve is not set in by machine, but will be attached by hand after the body of the garment has been lined. Details are shown in Figures 10-9 through 10-15.

Advantages and disadvantages This method appears in all pattern directions. It is the method used in all ready-to-wear in all price ranges. This method requires much less time than the alternative method and should be favored over the hand method in most garments. Seams can be pressed open (they must be lapped in the

hand method), and so they create a minimum of bulk.

The disadvantage of the machine method will be better understood after the advantages of the hand method are discussed. One disadvantage has to do with intricate fitting and is a disadvantage only in those fitted garments which are composed of intricate, shaped seams and in garments with many vertical seams.

Another disadvantage of this method has to do with inaccurate construction. The person who has carelessly stitched the garment in irregular seam widths will find that the lining will not fit properly, and the greater the number of seams, the greater the misfit. Careless work is more easily corrected in the hand method.

Because the body of the lining is assembled before it is inserted, it is more difficult to discover the cause of trouble, should it arise. In the alternative method, problems are more easily discovered and solved.

Recommended uses All the disadvantages listed above are not great problems in boxy and semifitted designs. Therefore, this method should be used for full-length coats and jackets cut in straight or slightly fitted lines. This method should be used for all linings that are heavy (heavy-weight satins, simulated fur, or fabrics with thickness added for warmth) to avoid the bulkier lapped seam that must be used in the alternative method. This method can be used for fitted designs (as an economy of time), but results will not be excellent if the worker has been careless and inaccurate.

Hand method

In this method, the structural vertical seams are done by hand, so that each section of the lining is inserted into the garment in a separate operation. Darts, tucks, the center-back seam of the pleat, and vertical sleeve seams are done by machine, as in the machine method of lining. Details are shown in Figures 10-20 through 10-24.

Advantages and disadvantages Because a great deal more time is required for this method and because it does not lend itself to the alterations necessary for all ready-to-wear, this method is never used in manufactured garments. However, there are great advantages, not the least of which is the pride of the wearer.

The great advantage of this method lies in the fact that each section is inserted separately. This means that intricate fitting can be done at each seamline, that inaccuracies can be corrected, and that trouble points can be detected easily in each piece before proceeding to the next. The advantage is of obvious value in fitted garments with more intricate seams and a greater number of seams.

The additional time this method requires will be considered a disadvantage by some readers, but by the many readers who sew for the delight of it, the extra time will mean that much more pleasure and so will be considered an advantage.

The fact that seams done by hand must be lapped seams is a disadvantage because of the problem of bulk. Lapped seams create no problems in typical limp and lightweight lining fabrics, but problems would be encountered with heavy brocades and satin or lining fabrics with extra thickness for warmth; the bulk problem with these fabrics is so great that the machine method should be used.

Recommended uses The hand method should be used for fitted, body-hugging designs (the typical princess-line garment), provided the lining fabric is not unusually heavy and thick. This method can be used in straight, boxy garments if the worker enjoys hand work or if she tends to be inaccurate and anticipates fitting problems.

Combination method

The two methods can be combined in any number of ways to solve individual problems on garments with conflicting demands. For example, vertical sleeve seams are not done by hand, and therefore the garment with a sleeve combined with the body of the garment should be done by the machine method; certainly gussets must be machine-stitched. But a garment with a gusset and with a sleeve combined with the body of the garment might have many intricately fitted seams in the waist and hip area. This garment could be done by the machine method in the shoulder and sleeve areas to a point an inch or so below the gusset, and the remainder of the garment could be done by the hand method.

SPECIAL NOTE CONCERNING ILLUSTRATIONS: Almost all the illustrations in this chapter picture a jacket rather than a coat simply to conserve space. The two garments are lined in an identical manner.

Review "Principles of Shaping the Tailored Garment" on page 367 before beginning work. As work is done on the lining, the garment should be held in wearing position so that the lining pieces are fitted to take an inside curve under the garment. However, all illustrations (in books and on instruction sheets) must necessarily picture the garment turned wrong side out in order to reveal construction details. The worker should study the sketches for the details, but she should hold her own work in wearing position whenever possible.

THE MACHINE METHOD OF LINING

Preparatory steps

Prepare the back sections   See sketch *a* in Figure 10-9. Baste along the center-back line to hold the pleat in place for pressing. This should be done when working with all fabrics except satin or similar fabrics which might be permanently marked by pressing over a basting thread; when working with satin, it is better to hold the pleat in place for pressing. If there is a seam at the back edge, stitch the seam. Stitch darts, etc.

See sketch *b*. The pleat must be pressed in one direction, and although it can be pressed in either direction, it is usually pressed in the direction illustrated.

CAUTION: **The direction of the pleat is very important if there is a vent-back closing, and the direction should be tested before the pleat is pressed; see Figure 10-25 on page 467 before proceeding.**

The basting stitches for the pleat will be removed later, and the pleat must be controlled at two points. The instruction sheet will recommend a bar tack or catch stitches;

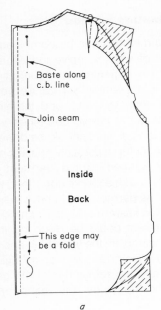

a

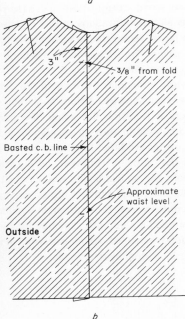

b

FIGURE 10-9 *To prepare back sections.*

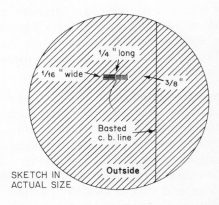

FIGURE 10-10 *The bar tack.*

the bar tack is more serviceable. The position of the tack is shown in sketch *b* of Figure 10-9, and a sketch in actual size appears in Figure 10-10. The tacks should be placed about 3 inches down from the neck edge if there is no back facing and about 1½ inches down from the neck edge if there is a back facing. One is placed at approximately waist level. They are placed about ⅜ inch over from the fold edge of the pleat.

See Figure 10-10. Working from the outside and using a single strand of matching thread, take two or three horizontal stitches in the proper position, making the stitches ¼ inch long and confining them to a 1/16 inch area, as shown. Then encase these stitches with vertical stitches 1/16 inch long, spaced evenly. The resulting effect should be a delicate line that is hardly discernible.

Assemble the body of the lining See Figure 10-11. Stitch darts or tucks in the front-lining sections. Sketch *a* shows an assembled lining for the garment that has no back facing; note that the shoulder edge of the back extends a distance beyond the front edge. Baste under ⅝ inch on the front edge of the lining, but do not press. Join all seams; note that the turned-under edge of the front is caught in the seam at the shoulder edge. Clip the curve at the back neck edge and baste under ⅝ inch on that edge. The shoulder seam should be pressed toward the back, and the re-

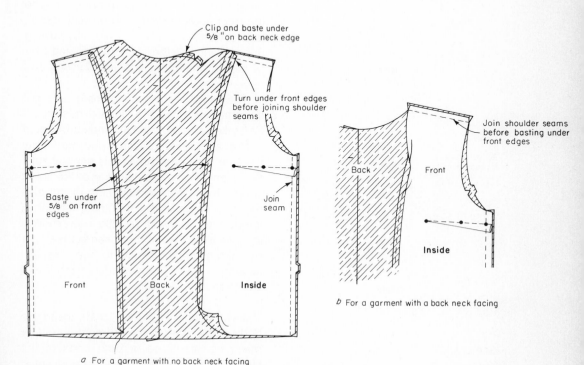

a For a garment with no back neck facing

FIGURE 10-11   To assemble the body of the lining.

mainder of the back shoulder edge pressed in place. Press all other seams open.

Sketch *b* shows this same step for the garment with a back facing. Note that the shoulder edges are identical in length. In this case, join the shoulder seam and press it open and baste under ⅝ inch on the front and neck edges, clipping the back neck curve; do not press.

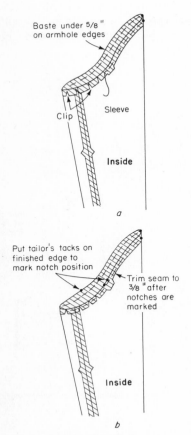

a

b

FIGURE 10-12   To prepare the sleeves.

Prepare the sleeves   See Figure 10-12. Join the sleeve seams, being careful to assemble sections to obtain right and left sleeves. Press the seams open. See sketch *a*. Make ½-inch clips into the curve in the underarm area. Baste under ⅝ inch on the armhole edges, as shown. See sketch *b*. The turned-under seam allowance must be trimmed to ⅜ inch, but before this is done, notch positions must be marked on the turned-under edge. Put tailor's tacks on the edge (shown as dots on the sketch) directly across from the notch positions. Then trim the seam allowance to ⅜ inch.

To insert the body of the lining

The most important thought to keep in mind is that seamlines in the lining must match corresponding seamlines in the garment. The rule of "seamlines matching" also applies at the front and neck edges because (in reality) a seam is involved (the lining to the inner edge of the facing or neck edge), but it is done with a lapped seam by turning under ⅝ inch on the lining and lapping over ⅝ inch on the inner edges of facings and neck edges.

The rule of seamlines matching is a most important one, but the strictest rules must be broken sometimes. Little inaccuracies of cutting and stitching seams and darts may result in a need to break this general rule. For example, the shoulderline of the lining should match the shoulderline of the garment in length, but if the lining is slightly shorter, as a result of little construction irregularities, it would be wiser to break the rule and make adjustment for the irregularity than to force seamlines to match if that would result in a misfit.

See sketch *a* in Figure 10-13. Insert the body of the lining in the garment. Begin by matching seamlines at both ends of the shoulderline. Lap the edge of the lining

⅝ inch over the inner edge of the front taking the following precautions:

1 Catch pins through the facing layer only; do not pin through all thicknesses to the outside layer of the garment. Put in as many pins as are necessary to hold the lining edge in a smooth line because this line is a very prominent one; if the lining fabric is very slippery, pins may be required at 1-inch intervals.

2 The lining should ease very slightly over the bust area, and a simple way to obtain the proper amount of ease is to hold the garment in a position that is opposite to wearing position; in other words, when pinning this area, hold the work in such a way that the lining takes the outside curve over the garment. This will result in approximately ¼ inch of ease when the garment is in wearing position.

3 Note that the garment pictured in sketch *a* has a gradually narrowing facing. Most facings are shaped in this way as far down as the bust level. Some facings continue to narrow to the lower edge, as shown in sketch *a*, while others become parallel below the bust level, as shown in sketch *b*. If the inner edge of the facing is parallel to the front edge, make a cardboard gauge in the proper width and use it to ensure perfection of the line; the finished edge of the lining should lap ⅝ inch over the facing edge, but little irregularities of cutting and construction can be perfected by measuring from the finished front edge. Baste the front and neck edges to the facing layer only, with stitches sufficiently secure to hold the edges in proper position.

The front edge will be sewn with permanent hand stitches after the lower edge is finished, as shown in Figure 10-19.

See sketch *a* in Figure 10-13 to position armhold edges. The raw armhole edges of the lining must be pinned to the armhole of

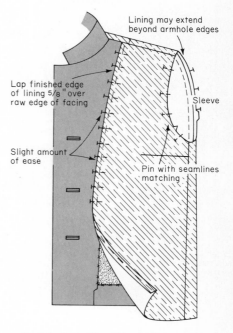

a Pin lining in position with seamlines matching.

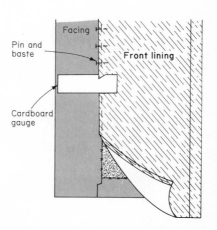

b Check parallel lines for accuracy.

FIGURE 10-13 To insert the body of the lining.

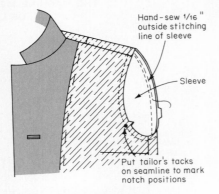

Hand-sew 1/16" outside stitching line of sleeve

Sleeve

Put tailor's tacks on seamline to mark notch positions

a Hand sew to armhole seam— for a garment without shoulder pads.

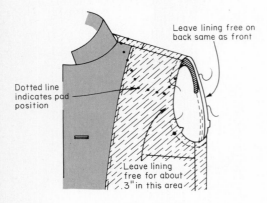

Leave lining free on back same as front

Dotted line indicates pad position

Leave lining free for about 3" in this area

b Hand sew to armhole seam— for a garment with shoulder pads.

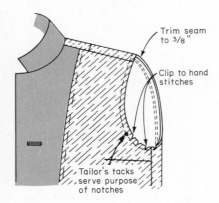

Trim seam to 3/8"

Clip to hand stitches

Tailor's tacks serve purpose of notches

c Trim seam and clip curve.

FIGURE 10-14 To secure the armhole edges.

the garment with seamlines and notch positions matching (the stitching line of the garment armhole to the ⅝ inch seamline of the lining). The directions for setting in regulation sleeves included trimming the seam to a ⅜ inch width. Therefore, if the seam was trimmed at that time, the raw edge of the lining will extend ¼ inch beyond the cut edge of the sleeve seam, as shown. Pin the armhole edges together with seamlines and notch positions matching.

To secure the armhole edges in a garment without shoulder pads See Figure 10-14. Sketch *a* shows the construction for the garment with no shoulder pad, and sketch *b* shows the difference in construction if a pad is used. See sketch *a*. Hand sew the lining to the armhole (permanent stitches that will remain) by working from the sleeve side and placing stitches just 1/16 inch outside the stitching line; stitches should be small and secured frequently with back stitches, particularly in the underarm area. It is important that these stitches be very close to the stitching line of the sleeve because the underarm area of the lining will eventually be clipped (as the sleeve seam was clipped), and the clips must be made to a point very close to the stitching line. The lining seam will be trimmed to ⅜ inch, but before this is done, notch positions must be marked on the seamline. Put tailor's tacks on the seamline directly across from the notch positions.

See sketch *c*. Trim the armhole edges to a ⅜ inch width. If the sleeve seam has not been trimmed, trim all layers of the seam to ⅜ inch. If the sleeve seam has been trimmed, trim off the raw lining edges even with the sleeve seam. Make several clips into the seamline at the underarm area between the notches.

To secure the armhole edges in a garment with shoulder pads Sketch *b* pictures the one construction detail that must be done in a different manner if a shoulder pad is used. The hand stitches which secure the armhole edges must be done in two segments in order to leave a 3-inch span free, as shown. The lining should be left free for a 3-inch span at the transition point between the padded and unpadded portions of the edge, as shown. Therefore, the hand stitches in the upper part will secure the lining to the underside of the pad (not catching through the pad to the garment seam), and the hand stitches in the lower part are done in the usual manner, as explained above. This is a very important detail, for if the stitches were allowed to cross the edge of the pad, the difference in thickness would create a certain tautness that would be apparent from the outside of the garment. Trim the seam and clip the curve, as shown in sketch *c*.

To insert the sleeve lining

Sketch *b* in Figure 10-15 shows this step for the garment with no shoulder pad, and sketch *c* shows the difference in construction if a pad is used.

For a garment without shoulder pads

See sketch *a* in Figure 10-15. Turn the sleeve lining wrong side out and slip it into the garment sleeve, wrong sides together. Pin the underarm area into position by matching the notch positions (marked with tailor's tacks) and the underarm positions; lap the turned-under edge of the sleeve ⅜ inch over the raw armhole edges, thereby matching armhole seamlines and hiding the hand stitches.

The step shown in sketch *b* is the most difficult one because fullness in the sleeve cap must be eased to the armhole, and this is much more difficult with a lapped seam than with a plain seam. The worker must

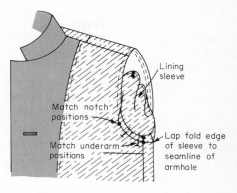

a Position sleeve in area below notches.

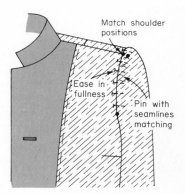

b Position sleeve in cap area —
for a garment without shoulder pads.

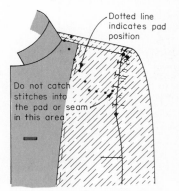

c Position sleeve in cap area —
for a garment with shoulder pads.

FIGURE 10-15 To insert the sleeve lining.

understand that the fullness will be evident and that this portion of the seam will not look entirely smooth and attractive.

Match the shoulder positions and lap the turned-under edge of the sleeve ⅜ inch over the raw armhole edges, thereby matching seamlines and hiding the hand stitches. Pin the shoulder position and then pin the cap of the sleeve in place, easing in the fullness and distributing it properly (review the directions accompanying Figure 9-61 on page 419). Baste the sleeve to the armhole. The sleeve must be sewn to the armhole with hand stitches that are as

attractive as possible and yet secure enough to withstand the strain this seam will receive when the garment is worn. A slip stitch would be most attractive, but the slip stitch will not withstand a great deal of strain. It seems wiser to favor a more utilitarian stitch such as a whipping stitch secured frequently with reinforcing stitches.

For a garment with shoulder pads Sketch *c* in Figure 10-15 shows the one construction detail that must be done in a different manner if shoulder pads are used. Just as the lining was left free from the armhole for a short span in the transition area of the pad, so the sleeve lining must be sewn in such a way that stitches do not catch into the seam of the garment in that same 3-inch span. By lifting up the needle each time a stitch is taken in that area, one can feel that the stitches are catching into the lining layer only.

Finishes for the lower edges

To position the lining See Figure 10-16. Put the garment on the figure, match center fronts, and pin carefully in position. An assistant will be needed. With one hand on the lining side, pin the lining and the garment together with a row of pins placed about 5 inches above the finished edge of the garment; allow the lining and the garment to fall naturally and do not pull at the lining any more than is necessary to shift seamlines into matching positions. If there is a pleat or a vent opening in the garment, additional pins are needed. A vent is handled exactly like the pleat in a skirt; see sketch *a* in Figure 8-34 on page 346. This step is also pictured in Figure 10-26 on page 468.

Sleeve hems are hung in the same manner. After the seams are shifted into matching position, the wearer should bend her arm to waist level close to her body and

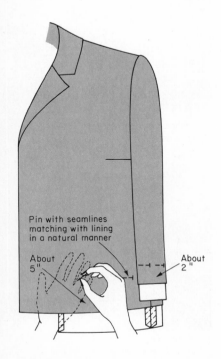

Pin with seamlines
matching with lining
in a natural manner

About
5 "

About
2 "

FIGURE 10-16   To position the lining.

then bring it down to a hanging position; this allows the sleeve lining to settle into wearing position. Then pin the two layers together with pins about 2 inches above the finished edge of the sleeve.

Figure 10-17 shows the lower-edge treatment for all sleeves and for the great majority of jacket and coat designs; this is the lining attached to the lower edge of the garment. Some garments (usually coats with style fullness and with linings that do not have the same amount of style fullness) have free-hanging linings, as shown in Figure 10-18.

For an attached lining See Figure 10-17. Baste through all thicknesses along the pin line, as shown in sketch *a*. Trim the raw edge of the lining parallel to the lower edge of the garment; ideal measurements are 1 inch below the finished edge of the garment for sleeves and jackets and 1½ inches below the finished edge for full-length coats. The lower edge of sleeves and jackets can be finished properly if the lining is only ½ inch longer than the finished edge, but the 1-inch measurement is preferred if there is sufficient fabric.

See sketch *b*. Turn up the lower edge of the lining allowing ½ inch of the garment to extend, and pin the lower edge in place; match seamlines and catch pins into the hem layer only. Measure carefully to be sure the lower edge of the lining is parallel to the lower edge of the garment. Baste ¾ inch above the lower edge of the lining with stitches catching into the hem layer only. Do not press at this time.

See sketch *c*. Roll the fold edge of the lining to the outside, as shown (pin if desired), and slip-stitch one layer of the lining to the hem layer. Be sure that the stitches do not catch into more than one thickness of the lining. Press the crease at the lower edge of the lining and remove the bastings. The lining will hang in the position pictured

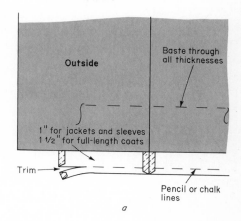

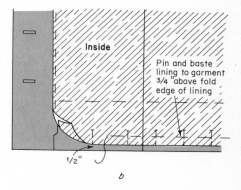

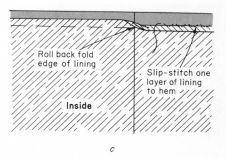

FIGURE 10-17   To finish the lower edge—for an attached lining.

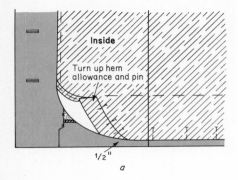

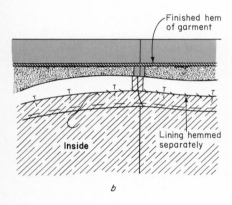

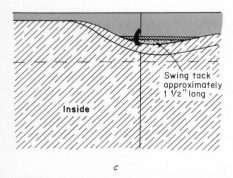

FIGURE 10-18 To finish the lower edge—for a free-hanging lining.

in sketch *b,* but because the stitches are above the lower edge, the lining can shift position without disturbing the lines of the garment.

For a free-hanging lining See sketch *a* in Figure 10-18. Baste through all thicknesses along the pin line, as shown. Trim the lower edge of the lining, as shown in sketch *a* of Figure 10-17, with one exception: allow an extra ½ inch in length (1½ inches for a jacket, 2 inches for a coat) because this will be a regulation hem.

Turn up the lower edge of the lining, allowing ½ inch of the garment to extend, and pin the edge in position with pins in the lining layers only, as shown; do not pin the lining to the garment.

Sketch *b* shows the lining lifted away from the garment and reveals that the garment hem has been finished by one of the bound methods. Hem the lining separately, as shown, using a method appropriate for the fabric. Lightweight linings are best done by turning under and slip-stitching, as shown in the sketch. If the fabric is heavy, a bound hem is a wiser choice.

See sketch *c.* Although this lining requires great freedom because it is usually not as full as the garment, side seams should be fastened together loosely with a swing tack about 1½ inches long. The tack should reach from the lining hem to the garment hem at a level such that it will not be visible when the garment is worn. The tack can be done with a hand crochet stitch or by doing the buttonhole stitch over several strands of thread.

To finish front and neck edges

See Figure 10-19. The front and neck edges are prominent lines as the garment is worn, and because there is relatively little strain during wearing at these edges (especially at the front edge, which is the most prominent), it is important that hand stitches be hidden. Stitches should not show, but because they are more likely to show in thin fabrics, it is usually better to use thread that matches the lining.

Fold the facing to the outside of the garment, as shown. The enlarged view shows the finished edge of the lining extending a scant $\frac{1}{16}$ inch beyond the facing; this position makes it possible to slip the needle into a fold of the lining so that stitches are very close to the fold edge but are hidden from view. After work is finished, remove the bastings and press the front and neck edges. See "Miscellaneous Details" on page 472.

THE HAND METHOD OF LINING

Before beginning work, read the special note on page 451.

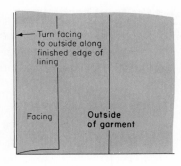

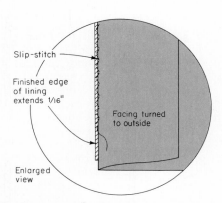

FIGURE 10-19 To finish front and neck edges.

Preparatory steps

Stitch darts, tucks and center-back seam See Figure 10-20, sketch *a*. Baste along the center-back line to hold the pleat in place for pressing. This should

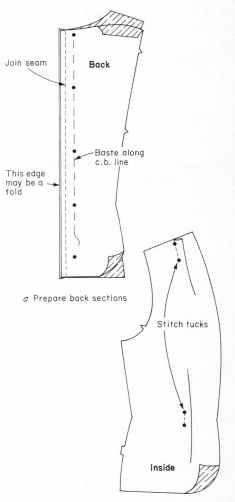

a Prepare back sections

b Stitch darts and tucks in all sections

FIGURE 10-20 Stitch darts, tucks, and center-back seam.

be done when working with all fabrics except satin or similar fabrics which might be permanently marked by pressing over a basting thread; when working with satin, it is better to hold the pleat in place for pressing. If there is a seam at the center-back edge, stitch the seam. Sketch *b* pictures a front-lining section with tucks. Stitch tucks and darts in all sections of the lining.

The pleat should be pressed at this time; see the directions accompanying sketch *b* in Figure 10-9 (page 452) and those with Figure 10-10 for a discussion of the pleat and the bar tacks that will hold it in place.

Baste under the seam allowance on some edges Figure 10-21 shows the preparation of the lining sections for a typical princess-line garment; the sections

are prepared in a similar manner for any type of design. In the hand method, one edge of every seam is turned under, and the corresponding edge is left raw. The edge nearer the front of each section is the one that is turned under; for example, in the side-back section, the side edge is nearer the front, so it is turned under, and the remaining edge, which is nearer the back, remains raw. Note that the back shoulder edge is turned under, while the front edge remains raw. It is well to assemble all lining sections flat on a table in proper order, as shown, before beginning work. Baste under ⅝ inch on the front edge and on the back shoulder and neck edges, clipping the curve on the back neck edge. Then baste under ⅝ inch on one edge of each corresponding seam, as shown. Do not press.

To insert the front sections

The most important thought to keep in mind is that seamlines in the lining must match corresponding seamlines in the

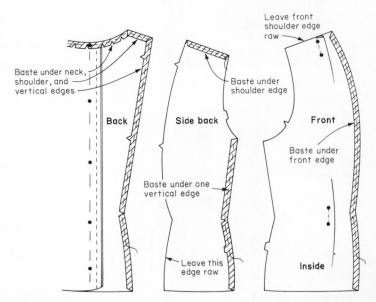

Baste under neck, shoulder, and vertical edges

Leave front shoulder edge raw

Baste under shoulder edge

Back

Side back

Front

Baste under front edge

Baste under one vertical edge

Leave this edge raw

Inside

FIGURE 10-21   Baste under the seam allowance on some edges.

garment. The rule of seamlines matching also applies at the front and neck edges because (in reality) a seam is involved (the lining to the inner edge of the facing or neck edge); it is done with a lapped seam by turning under ⅝ inch on the lining and lapping over ⅝ inch on the inner edges of the facing and neck edges.

The rule of seamlines matching is a most important one, but the strictest rules must be broken sometimes. Little inaccuracies of cutting and stitching seams and darts may result in a need to break this general rule. For example, the shoulderline of the lining should match the shoulderline of the garment in length, but if the lining is slightly shorter as a result of little construction irregularities, it is wiser to break the rule and make an adjustment for the irregularity than to force seamlines to match if that would result in a misfit. In fact, the greatest advantage of the hand method of lining is that it allows one to break rules more easily.

See Figure 10-22 as an illustration of this important point and consider the width of the lining front at the waistline as an example. If all work has been accurate, the lining will lap ⅝ inch over the edge of the facing and will reach to the side edge, so that the raw edge of the lining will be cut edges even with the pressed-open seam in the garment (seamlines matching); the general rule of seamlines matching has been followed, and the results will be perfect *if all work has been accurate.* However, if the front tuck in the lining was stitched just a bit too wide, the cut edge of the lining will not reach to the raw edge of the pressed-open seam without drawing up the garment somewhat; in this case, the rule can be broken easily by allowing the lining to fall along the side edge in the position required for a proper fit. The great advantage of this method is that each seamline can be allowed to fit as required.

Breaking rules must be done scien-

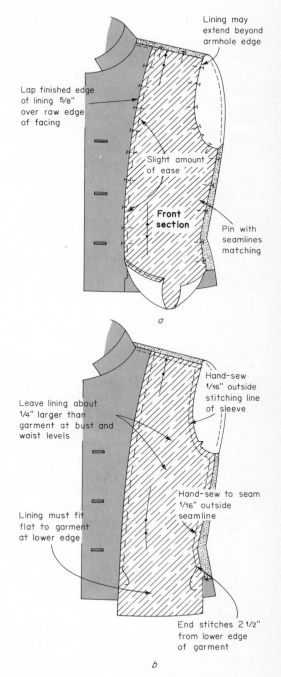

Lining may extend beyond armhole edge

Lap finished edge of lining ⅝" over raw edge of facing

Slight amount of ease

Front section

Pin with seamlines matching

a

Leave lining about ¼" larger than garment at bust and waist levels

Hand-sew 1/16" outside stitching line of sleeve

Lining must fit flat to garment at lower edge

Hand-sew to seam 1/16" outside seamline

End stitches 2 1/2" from lower edge of garment

b

FIGURE 10-22 To insert the front sections.

tifically, however. The worker must understand the general principle involved, she must know the general rule and the reasons why it is effective, and she must look for the reason why the general rule is not satisfactory in her case. Only then is she prepared to break the rule scientifically.

Figure 10-22 shows the front-lining section being inserted into the garment. Both the right and the left fronts should be inserted at the same time, and then adjacent sections, and so on to the back section, which is the last section inserted into the garment.

See sketch *a*. Insert the lining front and begin by lapping the front edge of the lining ⅝ inch over the inner edge of the facing, with seamlines matching at the shoulder. Lap the edge of the lining ⅝ inch over the entire front edge, taking the following precautions:

1 Catch pins through the facing layer only; do not pin through all thicknesses to the outside layer of the garment. Put in as many pins as are necessary to hold the lining edge in a smooth line because this line is a very prominent one; if the lining fabric is very slippery, pins may be required at 1-inch intervals.

2 The lining should ease slightly over the bust area; a simple way to obtain the proper amount of ease is to hold the garment in a position that is opposite to wearing position. In other words, when pinning this area, hold the work in such a way that the lining takes the outside curve over the garment; this will result in approximately ¼ inch of ease when the garment is in wearing position.

3 Note that the garment shown in these

sketches has a gradually narrowing facing. Most facings are shaped in this way as far down as the bust level, and some facings continue to narrow to the lower edge, as shown in these sketches. However, the facing may be parallel below the bustline. If the edge of the facing is parallel to the front edge of the garment, see the directions accompanying sketch *b* in Figure 10-13 on page 455.

See sketch *a* to position the armhole edges. The raw armhole edges of the lining must be pinned to the armhole of the garment with notch positions and seamlines matching (the stitching line of the garment armhole to the ⅝-inch seamline of the lining). The directions for setting in regulation sleeves included directions for trimming the seam to a ⅜-inch width. Therefore, if the seam was trimmed at the time, the raw edge of the lining will extend ¼ inch beyond the cut edge of the sleeve seam. Pin the armhole edges together with seamlines matching.

Pin the side seams together, seamlines matching, and then make tests for proper fit; standards of proper fit are included in sketch *b*. The lining should be just a little larger than the garment at the bust and waist levels, but the lining must be a "flat fit" (must be identical in width to the garment) at the lower edge. Pins can be removed to allow the lining to release or be taken in at the side-seam edge in order to meet these standards of fit. Do not do the permanent hand work shown in sketch *b* before reading the following paragraph.

The great advantage of the hand method is that any problems of fit in one lining section can be discovered before proceeding to the next. To benefit from this advantage, baste the two front sections in place and then test on the figure to see that the garment hangs properly and smoothly. If there are mistakes, they can be corrected now. As each piece is inserted, it should be basted and figure-tested before hand work is done. Thus, because each piece is perfected as work progresses, it is simple to discover and correct problems because they will always be in the last piece inserted.

Hand sew the raw side edge of the lining to the side seam with stitches a scant 1/16 inch outside the stitching line of the seam of the garment. End the stitches and fasten the thread 2½ inches from the lower edge, as shown; this is an important detail, to be explained later. Hand sew the raw shoulder edge of the lining to the shoulder seam of the garment in the same manner.

To secure armhole edges   These edges are treated in the same manner in the hand method and the machine method. The only difference is that the work is done in segments in the hand method: the front armhole is secured at this time, and the back armhole is secured later. Work is more complicated if there is a shoulder pad. See "To Secure Armhole Edges in a Garment without Shoulder Pads" and "To Secure Armhole Edges in a Garment with Shoulder Pads", beginning on page 457.

NOTE: **All the principles and directions given in great detail for the front-lining section should be applied when working with all remaining sections of the lining.**

To insert adjacent sections

Figure 10-23 illustrates details for inserting all adjacent sections. Lap the turned-under side edge to the seamline of the raw edge and pin in place with the upper and lower edges even, as shown in sketch a. Lap the turned-under shoulder edge to the seamline of the raw edge and pin. Pin the remaining raw seam edge to the corresponding seam on the garment, seam-

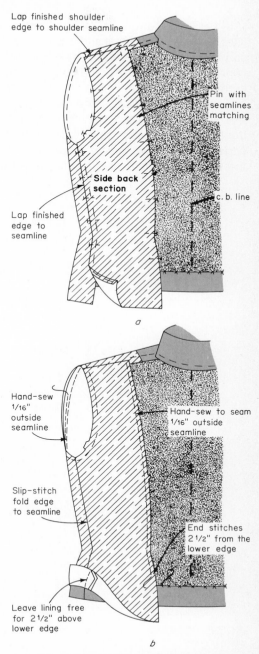

FIGURE 10-23   To insert adjacent sections.

lines matching. Test for fit and make necessary adjustments. Baste both side sections
in place and test on the figure before doing
permanent hand work.

Sketch *b* illustrate some techniques
that are the same as those done on the
front sections; hand sew the armhole
edges and the raw vertical seam edge in
the same manner. A new technique is to

do the hand work on the lapped seam.
This seam should be slip-stitched in place
(see the directions accompanying Figure
10-19 for more details). The side edge of
the front was left free from the garment
for a distance of about 2½ inches from
the lower edge, and now work must be
done in such a way that both edges remain
free from the garment; note the lining edge
flipped up. It is important that the lining
be free from the garment up to a level about
2½ inches above the finished lower edge
.of the garment in order that the lower edge
of the lining can be turned up. Every vertical seam in all lining sections must be
handled in this manner.

To insert back sections

The center-back section, the last section
to be placed in the garment, is shown in
Figure 10-24. All edges of this section
(except the lower edge) have been turned
under and must be lapped ⅝ inch over
the corresponding edges and pinned in
place. Baste, perfecting the fit, and test
on the figure as usual. All edges will be
slip-stitched in place according to the
directions above.

All remaining steps of construction are
the same as those of the machine method
of lining. To insert the sleeve lining, to
finish the lower edge of the lining, and to
finish the front and neck edges, see the
directions on pages 455 to 461.

PROBLEMS OF LINING A VENT OPENING

The vent opening presents several problems because it is a construction detail
in which a small mistake can create a
serious problem. The only differences

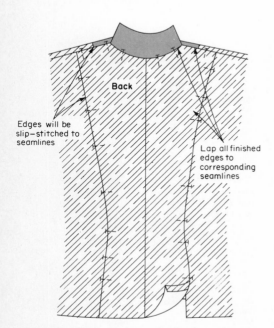

Back

Edges will be
slip−stitched to
seamlines

Lap all finished
edges to
corresponding
seamlines

FIGURE 10-24   To insert the back sections.

between these detailed directions and the brief directions on the instruction sheet are that these include testing suggestions at several stages in construction and that one section of the lining is cut after the lining is inserted (rather than before, as recommended in pattern directions).

Test to determine how to press the center-back pleat See Figure 10-25. Sketch *a* shows the finished vent opening in the garment; detailed directions are not included because this construction is explained in sufficient detail on the instruction sheet. Note that the pleat is pressed in one direction so that one layer of the vent extension becomes a self-facing which is catch-stitched to the garment, while the other edge has been turned under on the seamline. Note that the weight of the vent extension is supported by horizontal stitches ⅝ inch below the upper cut edge. This is usually done by machine, and these stitches must necessarily show on the right side of the garment; if the fabric is not too heavy, they can be done by hand.

The seam and the vent are usually pressed in the direction illustrated; sketches on the instruction sheet picture the proper direction for each individual design.

See sketch *b*. The pleat in the lining must be pressed in a certain direction, depending on the direction in which the vent is pressed. Before pressing the lining pleat, place the back lining in the garment wrong sides together and be sure that the pleat in the lining is pressed in the same direction as the seam and the vent in the garment. Note that both are turned toward the right-hand side of these sketches; had the vent been pressed in the opposite direction, both could be turned in that direction. After this test, press the pleat in the lining and put in the bar tacks.

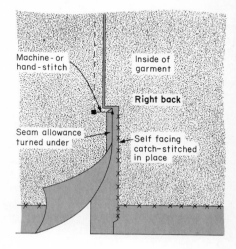

a Finished view of vent back construction.

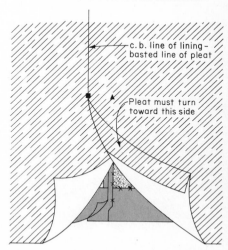

b Lining pleat turned in the proper direction.

FIGURE 10-25 *To determine how to press the center-back pleat.*

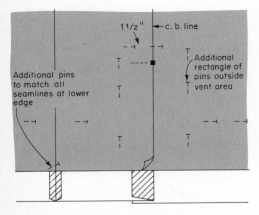

a Pin lining in position on the figure.

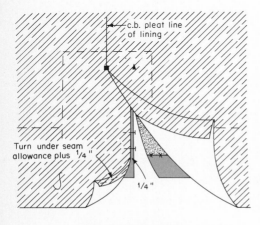

b Pin one edge in position.

FIGURE 10-26 To position the lining in the vent area.

To position the lining in the vent area

See Figure 10-26. Sketch *a* shows the additional pins needed to outline the vent area. First of all, the fold edge of the lining pleat should be placed directly over the stitching line of the garment seam. In addition to the row of pins about 5 inches from the lower edge, pins should be placed right at the lower edge to match all seamlines in the lining to corresponding seams in the garment, as shown. A rectangle of pins, placed about 1½ inches outside the vent area, is needed to locate the lining properly in the entire vent area.

See sketch *b*. Baste along the pin lines, as shown. One edge of the lining extends in such a way that it covers the vent extension. Turn under ⅞ inch (the seam allowance plus ¼ inch) on the raw edge of the lining and lap it over the raw edge of the garment, allowing ¼ inch of the garment to extend, as shown. Pin and baste this edge in place.

To determine the proper cutting line

Study all the directions accompanying Figure 10-27 before proceeding. This is the most difficult step involved with the vent opening because a slash must be made to a precise point and because there is no opportunity to reinforce the point as a precaution against raveling. Furthermore, this is the time when small irregularities of previous construction can be corrected.

A portion of the lining must be cut away. The pattern indicated a cutting line, but (if the cutting directions suggested in this text were followed) the cutting line was tailor-tacked, and the excess lining was not cut away; the cutting line is indicated with a line of dots on the sketch.

The square and triangle shown on the sketch are pattern markings that should match similar points on the garment. Study

sketch *a* in Figure 10-25 to see the position of similar markings on the garment.
The square is at the end of the stitched
seam; the triangle is on a line directly across
from the square, ⅝ inch in from the raw
edge of the self-facing. The point on the
garment marked with a triangle in sketch
a in Figure 10-25 is the point that must
correspond to the slashed corner in sketch
a in Figure 10-27. The markings on the
lining will be almost correct, and they would
be in perfect position if all work done on
the garment had been absolutely accurate.
The sketch shows construction as it would
be if all work had been accurate, but work
should be tested for little irregularities.

The most important step is the slash
shown. Make a slash through the lining
to the pattern marking or to the point that
is directly across from the end of the stitching on the garment and ⅝ inch from the
edge of the self-facing; this is the point
shown with a triangle in sketch *a* in Figure
10-25.

See sketch *b*. A section of the lining
must be cut away, and the cutting line will
be along the tailor-tacked cutting line if all
previous work has been accurate. To test
the cutting line for accuracy, smooth the
lining flat in the whole vent area and fold
the lining to the outside, in such a position
that the fold edge laps ⅝ inch over the
edge of the self-facing, as shown. If all work
has been accurate, the fold edge will be
⅝ inch from the tailor-tacked cutting line,
as shown, but the lining can be adjusted
to whatever position is necessary for a
flat fit on the garment. The proper cutting
line will be a line ⅝ inch from the fold edge
of the turned-back lining.

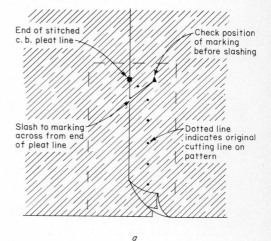

End of stitched
c. b. pleat line

Check position
of marking
before slashing

Slash to marking
across from end
of pleat line

Dotted line
indicates original
cutting line on
pattern

a

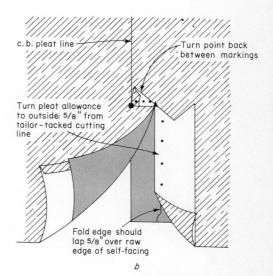

c. b. pleat line

Turn point back
between markings

Turn pleat allowance
to outside ⅝" from
tailor-tacked cutting
line

Fold edge should
lap 5/8" over raw
edge of self-facing

b

FIGURE 10-27 To determine the proper cutting line.

**To secure the lining at the opening
edges** See Figure 10-28. Trim along the
cutting line or the corrected cutting line,
as shown in sketch *a*. Note that the tip of

the triangle has been trimmed away at a
level ⅝ inch below the pattern markings.
Sketch *b* shows the lining edges turned
under and basted over the raw edge of the
self-facing. The hem of the lining should
be turned up and finished before permanent hand stitches are done on these edges.
When the hem is finished, these edges
should be slip-stitched, as shown in Figure
10-19 on page 461. One or two diagonal
stitches placed over the lining edge right
at the slashed corner will help prevent the
corner from raveling.

THE HONG KONG FINISH FOR
FACING EDGES

This is a novelty finish; see it pictured in
Figure 10-30. It differs from the traditional
method in that the inner edge of the facing
is bound with the Hong Kong finish, and

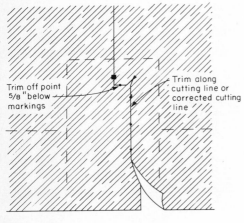

a Trim along cutting line.

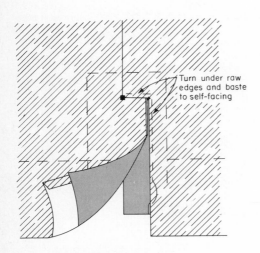

b Baste under remaining raw edges.

FIGURE 10-28 Finishing steps.

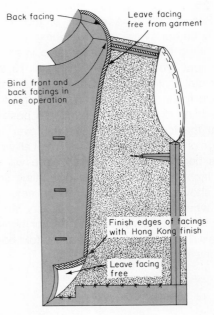

*FIGURE 10-29 To finish facing
edges.*

then the facing edge is lapped over the lining; in the traditional construction, the lining edge laps over the facing. Obviously, this is a subtle change, and yet it does give a very distinctive appearance.

This method is somewhat more expensive because of the extra yardage required for long bias strips to match the lining, it requires somewhat more time, and it results in a certain amount of extra thickness and stiffness at the facing edge. Disregarding the cost factor, which must be considered a disadvantage, the other two points may or may not be disadvantages. The person who sews for pleasure will not object to spending more time, and if the fabric of the garment is sufficiently heavy, the extra stiffness is no more of an issue than a corded edge on the traditional lining. It would be difficult to state that one method is better than the other; both are very attractive. This finish will not replace the traditional one, and yet it is a nice change for the person who has done many linings.

To finish facing edges See Figure 10-29. Note that the corner lower edge has been left free and will be secured later. Directions for doing this finish accompany Figure 7-26 on page 288. If one plans from the very beginning of construction to do this finish, the inner edges of the facings can be finished more easily before the facings are attached to the garment.

To insert the lining Sketch *a* in Figure 10-30 shows the method of inserting the lining. If this method is used, the front and neck edges of the lining are not turned under. As the lining is inserted, the facing edges are flipped up, and the raw edges of the lining are catch-stitched to the interfacing of the garment; be very careful that stitches do not pass through the interfacing

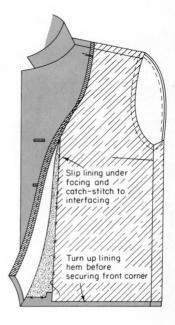

Slip lining under facing and catch-stitch to interfacing

Turn up lining hem before securing front corner

a To insert lining.

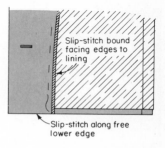

Slip-stitch bound facing edges to lining

Slip-stitch along free lower edge

b To secure facing edges.

FIGURE 10-30   *To insert and finish the lining.*

to the garment fabric. Either the hand or the machine method of lining can be used. The lower edge of the lining is turned up and finished while the facing edges are still free. The sleeve lining is done in the traditional manner.

To secure facing edges Sketch *b* in Figure 10-30 shows the last step of construction. The facing edge is basted in position, and the free lower edge is slip-stitched. The edge of the facing will be slip-stitched to the lining layer only in a manner similar to that shown in Figure 10-19 on page 461. The traditional slip stitch is done a scant $\frac{1}{16}$ inch under the lining edge, but the Hong Kong finish requires stitches about $\frac{1}{8}$ inch back from the finished edge of the facing.

MISCELLANEOUS DETAILS

To cover and attach a garment shield

Purchased garment shields can be used in the tailored garment if they are covered with a layer of lining fabric. The shield can be removed for laundering, and the lining cover can be dry-cleaned or replaced with new fabric if it is badly stained. See Figure 10-31. Cut four sections of lining fabric, using the shield as a guide, as shown in sketch *a*; allow a $\frac{5}{8}$-inch seam beyond the shield edges. Stitch two sections together along the concave curve in a $\frac{5}{8}$-inch seam and clip the curve, as shown in sketch *b*. Place the cover over the shield with the right side of the lining outside and concave curves matching. Turn the remaining raw edges over the shield and baste in place as shown in sketch *c*. Sketch *d* shows the shield in position in the garment. Whip the edges of the shield to the garment, catching the stitches through the layer of lining only.

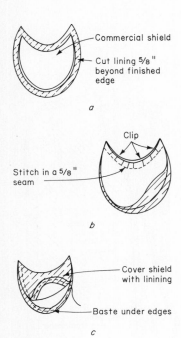

Commercial shield

Cut lining $\frac{5}{8}$" beyond finished edge

a

Clip

Stitch in a $\frac{5}{8}$" seam

b

Cover shield with linining

Baste under edges

c

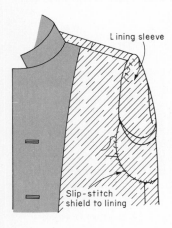

Lining sleeve

Slip-stitch shield to lining

d

FIGURE 10-31 To cover and attach a garment shield.

To insert the Dior chain weight

See Figure 10-32. The chain is used to give additional weight for whatever purpose it might be needed, and therefore it can be used at any position along the hemline of any garment. The extra weight adds desirable weight to lightweight fabrics and also is an aid to controlling straight, boxy lines on curvaceous figures. The chains come in a length suitable for weighting the back of a jacket or coat and will reach across the back and extend a short distance on each side, on an average-size figure. Links can be removed, or more than one length can be used if a different length is required for particular purposes. Center the chain at the center-back line and place it over the garment hem close to the hand stitches which secure the lining and under the fold of lining, as shown. Hand sew through the links with stitches catching into the hem layer only, being very careful that the stitches do not catch through to the outside of the garment.

The fold of lining will cover the chain, but it will peek out as the jacket or coat is removed and will add an attractive professional appearance. The chain should be removed when the garment is dry-cleaned.

To attach a label

See Figure 10-33. Labels provided by fabric or pattern manufacturers or personalized labels can be placed near the neck edge at the center back, as shown, or along the front facing or lining edge. Labels on ready-to-wear are frequently placed near the front in a prominent position that is ideal for advertising purposes, but they do detract from the garment in this position. The center-back position is generally preferred.

The label should be centered over the center-back pleat line and should be placed in a position that creates attractive proportions. If the garment has no back facing, a position about 1½ inches down from the neck edge will be attractive; if there is a back facing, the label will look more attractive placed closer (½ to 1 inch) to the upper edge of the lining. Labels are usually done with catch stitches that pass through the lining layer only; the stitches should be very small and very even. Slip stitches can be used if preferred.

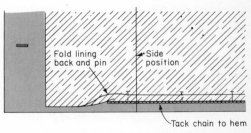

FIGURE 10-32   To insert a Dior chain weight.

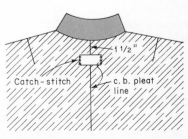

FIGURE 10-33   To attach a label.

Chapter 11

SPECIAL PROBLEMS

EXTRA YARDAGE AMOUNTS ARE REQUIRED FOR MATCHING PLAIDS, CHECKS, AND STRIPES AND FOR BALANCING LARGE DESIGNS

The directions included in this section are confined to estimating yardage amounts; detailed directions for cutting fabrics with large, prominent design units (such as a fake fur with zebra stripes) that must be balanced on the figure appear on page 500 and specific directions for cutting plaids, checks, and stripes appear on page 480. These fabrics require very special attention during cutting because the success of the finished garment is greatly influenced by the way pieces are cut. The novice should avoid these fabrics unless she is working with an instructor.

It is important to understand that extra fabric, over and above the amount stated in the yardage chart, will be required for balancing design units or matching plaids, large checks, or stripes; a note stating this fact appears on every yardage chart. If one view of the design is pictured in plaid, this means that the pattern can be cut effectively from plaid fabric; some patterns cannot be matched with pleasing results. The yardage chart cannot make allowances for balancing design or matching plaid because the need for extra fabric depends entirely on the particular fabric each customer will choose.

The type of plaid (even or uneven) influences yardage amounts; in general, uneven plaids like the one pictured in Figure 11-1 require more extra yardage than even plaids. Even and uneven plaids are compared in detail on page 478. Large plaids or large designs spaced far apart require more extra yardage for matching and balancing than smaller design units. This characteristic of the design is called the repeat. *The repeat is the measurement from a given point on one design unit to the same point on the next identical unit.* The fabrics in Figure 11-1 are shown scaled down from a 54-inch width; a very large repeat of about 10 inches in the crosswise direction and about 11½ inches in the lengthwise direction is shown to exaggerate problems for illustrative purposes.

In addition to the plaid, Figure 11-1 shows a large design intended to suggest a fake fur with a design (such as a zebra stripe) which must be balanced. Some lines in the sketch are darker and spaced systematically, to suggest that there will be a definite design, repeated with regularity. Other lines are sketchy, to point out that design lines are not spaced as mathematically as lines in a plaid; large designs cannot be matched perfectly, and thus the term *balancing* is used.

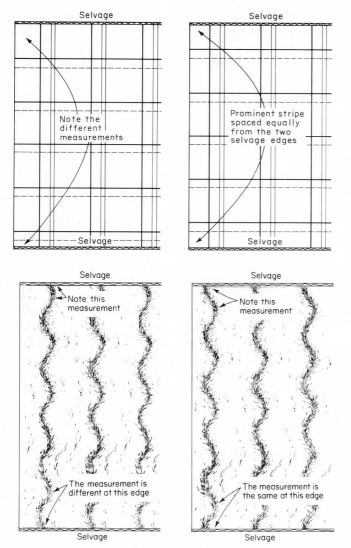

a The way units of design are spaced on the fabric influences yardage requirements.

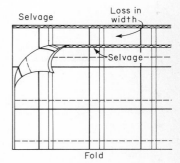

b A loss of usable width results if design units are not centered on the width of fabric.

FIGURE 11-1 Spacing of design units influences yardage requirements.

The fabrics pictured illustrate another reason why the pattern company cannot make allowances for matching plaid or balancing design. Compare the fabrics in sketch a and observe that the spacing of design units from the selvage edges may vary. The evenly spaced designs can be folded for cutting with design units matched on the two layers in such a way that the entire width of fabric is usable. See sketch b; when the unevenly spaced fabrics are folded with design units matched on the

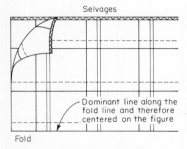

a Evenly spaced plaid with a dominant stripe centered on the width of fabric.

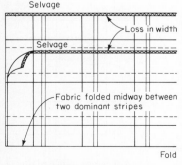

b Usable width may be lost if certain effects are desired.

FIGURE 11-2 Width on evenly spaced designs may be lost if certain effects are required.

two layers, one layer extends and is not usable. If one layer of 54-inch fabric extends 3 inches, the customer will have to use the amounts required for a narrower width as a basis for figuring additional amounts for matching or balancing design units. The alert customer will study the fabric carefully and experiment with various effects before purchase. The issue of usable width influences the cost of the garment, because the narrower width will require more yardage.

There is an additional problem of balancing large design units or matching plaids — a problem that may influence the total cost of the garment by reducing usable width. Figure 11-2 pictures an evenly spaced plaid with the prominent stripe centered on the width of fabric. Sketch a shows the fabric folded lengthwise with selvage edges together; because the design units are evenly spaced from the selvage, the entire width of the fabric is usable. However, the customer may discover by experimenting in the store that the effect is not as attractive with a prominent stripe centered on her figure and may prefer the prominent vertical stripes spaced on either side of the center; refer to sketches on page 481 for a comparison. If she prefers the units spaced on each side of center lines, she will have to fold the fabric as shown in sketch b and, in spite of the fact that the design units are equally spaced from the selvages, there will be a loss of width. In the example shown (exaggerated because of the large repeat), the usable width of 60-inch fabric may be reduced to 54 inches, and the yardage amount stated for the narrower width must be used as a basis for figuring additional amounts for matching or balancing the design.

NOTE The fabric losses illustrated in Figures 11-1 and 11-2 (typical of others that will become evident as work progresses) explain why these special fabrics increase wardrobe costs of home-sewn and ready-to-wear garments alike. Beautifully matched or balanced ready-to-wear costumes are very costly, and, for very logical financial reasons, budget garments are seldom matched and balanced perfectly.

With so many factors influencing the amount of extra fabric required for matching plaid or balancing design, it follows that the yardage chart can only state the amount of fabric required to place pattern pieces on the fabric; each customer must buy an additional amount based on the particular fabric she will use and the effect she wishes to create. At best, she can only make an educated guess, and she must understand· that, depending on circumstances and luck (pattern pieces may just happen to fit well with little loss for matching or balancing on a particular fabric), she may need little extra fabric and she may need much more than she estimates. A wise precaution is to select a fabric in plentiful supply at the store and to cut the pattern as soon as possible so that additional fabric, if needed, will be available.

To estimate the approximate amount of extra fabric required

By studying the layout that will be used, it is possible to estimate the amount of extra fabric required for balancing or matching the crosswise stripes of the plaid or the

crosswise units of the design. To match the crosswise lines in the design, the pattern is moved up or down in a lengthwise direction on the fabric. The layout shown in Figure 11-3 can be used for explaining how to estimate extra yardage amounts for even plaids and for any design that is not a one-way design. The general principles explained on this layout can be applied to a with-nap layout that is appropriate for uneven plaids, one-way designs, and napped and pile fabrics.

Assume that the worker will use this sample layout for cutting a fabric with a 3-inch repeat. Each time pattern pieces are placed in an area (the two skirt sections are placed in the same area), there is a chance that extra fabric will be required for matching. Even at the very left end of the layout, as the first pieces are placed down, there is a chance that some fabric will be lost in order that the plaid unit may be started off right at the waistline. Count the spaces between the units and count one at the beginning end for the number of times extra fabric might be required; in the sample layout, the number is a total of five times. Each time there is a possible need for extra fabric, the amount needed

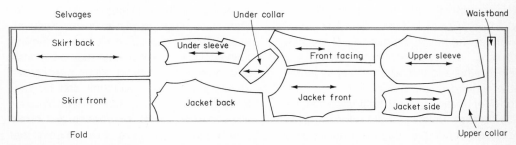

FIGURE 11-3   *A sample layout suitable for use with one-way plaids and designs.*

might be almost as much as the size of the unit of plaid. In this problem almost 3 inches of extra fabric might be needed five times; thus a total of 15 inches of extra fabric is the answer that would be completely safe. However, not that much extra will be needed because it is most unlikely that the maximum amount of extra fabric would be needed each time; sometimes the plaid will fall so that no extra fabric is required. So a good rule is to estimate the maximum amount that might be needed and then buy about half that much extra fabric. In this problem, 7 inches of extra fabric would undoubtedly be sufficient, and so an extra ¼ yard would be a good educated estimate.

It must be understood that the method described above allows for matching the crosswise lines of the plaid or design and that it does not allow for positioning pieces so that lengthwise lines fall in proper position on the figure. There is no way of determining how lengthwise stripes will appear on the figure until pattern pieces are placed on the fabric. For example, note that the jacket front and facing require almost the full width of the fabric. In order to position a certain lengthwise stripe in the desired position in relation to the center-front line of the pattern, it is possible that an entire extra length of fabric will be required; it would be pure luck if the stripe happened to fall in the desired position. The same problem might arise when cutting any piece on the layout. These problems, which may require sizable amounts of extra fabric for matching and balancing lengthwise design units and therefore greatly increased costs, are magnified as the size of the repeat increases. The customer who chooses these fabrics must understand that accurate estimates of yardage for

matching and balancing are not possible, and she must be prepared to buy additional fabric and pay the additional costs if the need arises.

PLAID, CHECKED, AND STRIPED FABRICS

Read the foregoing section for help in estimating the amount of extra yardage (above the amount stated on the yardage chart) needed for matching purposes.

Directions and illustrations in this section are concentrated on matching plaids, which require matching lengthwise and crosswise lines; the information can easily be applied to checks, which are essentially very simple plaids, and to stripes, which require similar techniques but are simpler because they require matching in only one direction.

Recommended work sequence To gain an overall understanding of the problems which will be encountered, carefully study the basic information (to page 490) before beginning work. Then read the special cutting directions on page 491. Decide on the methods which will be most effective for a particular costume and then begin work, referring back to these specific directions as the work progresses.

Types of plaids The two types of plaids are shown in Figure 11-4; assume that each type of line indicates a different width and color of stripe. *An even plaid is one in which each quarter of the unit is identical to every other quarter;* note that lengthwise and crosswise lines in each corner are identical. An even plaid unit can be rectangular so long as lines in each quarter are identical. Plaids or checks are rarely if ever perfectly square units; checks that appear perfectly square are usually somewhat longer than their width because the longer unit is more flattering on the figure.

If the plaid is even, pattern pieces can be laid with the upper edge in either direction (can be turned end for end) because the upper and lower halves of the unit are identical.

Uneven plaids are more interesting because they are composed of a greater variety of stripes, both lengthwise and crosswise, and each stripe may be a different width and a different color; assume that the four types of lines in the sketch indicate four different colors. *Each quarter of the design unit in uneven plaids is different from every other quarter.* Because the upper and lower halves of the unit are different, the plaid must be cut from a with-nap layout, with all pattern pieces laid in one direction (pieces cannot be turned end for end).

Directions and illustrations in this section are concentrated on even plaids. They are somewhat simpler to work with and are the wise choice for first projects. Basic principles can be applied to uneven plaids; see page 490. Read this entire section before beginning work; the section titled "Utilize Line Direction for an Individual Effect" on page 488 will be helpful after an introduction to fundamental rules.

It is not possible to match plaid, checks, or stripes at every seamline on a garment It is important to under-

stand that lengthwise and crosswise lines in the design will not match *(and therefore should not be forced to match)* at every seam in the garment. All lines can be matched in a perfectly rectangular piece (an all-around gathered skirt, for example) but if pattern pieces are shaped to fit the figure, certain seams cannot be matched. *Matching plaid properly becomes a matter of deciding which portion of the garment is most important to the total effect and of favoring that portion and compromising at less important seamlines.* For example, the front influences the total effect more than the back; therefore planning begins at the center front. This point will be clarified in the following discussions. The following list is included at this time to point out several seams where plaid cannot be matched in most designs. The list is not infallible because the design lines of the garment and the width of the plaid unit will influence matching possibilities. As a general rule, the following seams (or segments of seams) will not match in most garments:

Side seams of a fitted skirt can be matched below the hip level, but only cross-

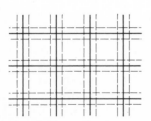

Even plaid — Perfectly square units of plaid or checks are rare.

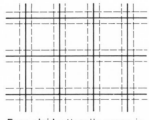

Even plaid — Usually woven in a rectangle, longer in the lengthwise direction.

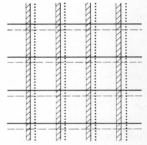

Uneven plaid — Every quarter of the unit is different from every other quarter.

FIGURE 11-4 Even and uneven plaids.

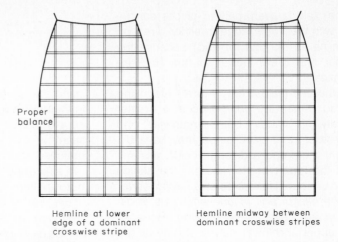

Proper
balance

Hemline at lower
edge of a dominant
crosswise stripe

Hemline midway between
dominant crosswise stripes

Rule 1: The most dominant crosswise stripe should appear in its full width at the lower edge of the garment and, if possible, at other hem edges.

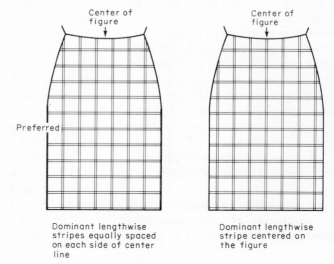

Center of
figure

Center of
figure

Preferred

Dominant lengthwise
stripes equally spaced
on each side of center
line

Dominant lengthwise
stripe centered on
the figure

Rule 2: Two dominant lengthwise stripes should be equally spaced on either side of center lines or one dominant line centered on the figure.

wise lines will match above the hip level; the curve on the front and back skirt above the hip level are not identical and therefore lengthwise lines cannot be equally spaced on each side of the seamline.

Crosswise lines may or may not match at vertical seams in sleeves. They can be matched above the elbow position in a one-piece sleeve, but they will not match below. They can be matched at the front vertical seam of a two-piece sleeve, but they will not (and therefore should not) match at the back vertical seam.

Crosswise lines in the sleeve should be matched to crosswise lines in the garment front at the notch level. However, because the cap of the sleeve is eased, crosswise lines will not match above the

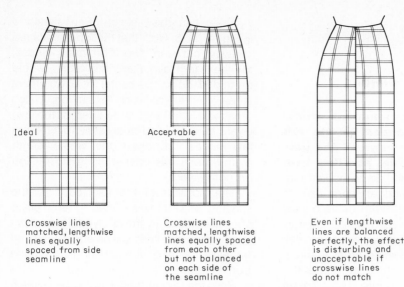

Ideal

Acceptable

Crosswise lines
matched, lengthwise
lines equally
spaced from side
seamline

Crosswise lines
matched, lengthwise
lines equally spaced
from each other
but not balanced
on each side of
the seamline

Even if lengthwise
lines are balanced
perfectly, the effect
is disturbing and
unacceptable if
crosswise lines
do not match

Rule 3: All crosswise lines must match at corresponding vertical seamlines, and dominant lengthwise lines should ideally be equally spaced on each side of vertical seamlines.

FIGURE 11-5 *Fundamental rules for matching plaids, checks, and stripes.*

notch level. Crosswise lines in the back sleeve and back garment will not usually match; in most garments these lines will (and therefore should) miss by about ½ inch. The situation in the sleeve illustrates how the size of the unit can influence the ability to match plaids, checks, or stripes. The mismatch at the back sleeve, usually about ½ inch, will become a perfect match if the fabric is checked in units of ¼ inch. Examine the sleeve in sketch c of Figure 11-8. Note that crosswise lines match at the underarm seam down to the dart level; because of the dart (or ease) on the back edge, the lines cannot match below that level. However, the crosswise lines can match along the entire length of the underarm seam if the sleeve is boxy with no dart fitting or ease at the back edge.

Neither lengthwise nor crosswise lines will match at the shoulderline. They *may* match in small checks, but if lines match at the shoulder it is by pure chance.

The sketches in Figure 11-7 show how style lines (darts and seams) influence

matching possibilities; note that gathers in the skirt of the dress force lengthwise lines closer together in that area so that they cannot possibly match lengthwise lines in the bodice.

These generalized statements serve to emphasize the fact that the worker is not always in control of the situation; *it is important to understand that if one area is favored, the worker necessarily cannot control another.* In matching plaids, all possible lines must be matched for the best effect with that particular plaid, and lines that do not match must be allowed to mismatch; in the eyes of an expert or any discerning person, a mismatch looks right and proper at the seams and segments of seams listed above.

Fundamental rules

Three basic rules are illustrated on the figure in Figure 11-5 and on layout segments in Figure 11-6.

Rule 1: The most dominant cross-wise line should appear in its full width at the lower edge of the garment and, if possible, at other hem edges The dominant line is the line that is most prominent and appears heavier because of its greater width or its darker or brighter color. This heavier line, appearing in full width at the lower edge, creates better balance by providing what appears to be a firmer foundation; compare the two effects shown in Figure 11-5. To be sure that this dominant line will fall at the desired hemline, the hemline is established on the muslin test copy and then transferred to the pattern. If no test copy is made, pattern pieces must be pinned together and the hem length adjusted on the figure carefully and accurately before cutting is done. Mark the desired hemline on the pattern pieces. The skirt pieces are shown in proper position on all layouts in Figure 11-6, with the desired hemline placed along the lower edge of the dominant crosswise stripe to allow its full width to appear in the finished skirt.

Rule 2: Two dominant lengthwise lines must be equally spaced on each side of center lines (preferred), or one dominant line may be centered on the figure Compare the two effects on the figure in Figure 11-5; the difference is subtle in a small sketch (and also in a small plaid on the figure) but in general the preferred plan is more pleasing, especially in large bold plaids. Before cutting, hold the fabric up to the figure and compare the two effects before making a decision. The preferred method is shown in all il-

lustrations in this section. See sketch *a* in Figure 11-6. Note that the fabric is folded midway between two dominant stripes; for the alternative plan, the fabric would be folded along the center of a dominant stripe. To prepare fabric for cutting, match crosswise and lengthwise lines of the two layers carefully and accurately; pins every few inches throughout the whole length of the fabric will ensure accurate cutting on both layers.

The position of the fold controls the spacing of lengthwise lines in any piece cut on the fold; in these layouts the dominant lengthwise lines will be equally spaced on either side of the center in the skirt front because it is cut on the fold.

See the center-back seam in sketch *a:* the seamline is shown in a dashed line. The seamline (not the cut edge) is the center-back line. By placing the seamline of the pattern midway between two dominant stripes, the stripes will be equally spaced on either side of the center back. *When working with plaid, the seamline is the important line involved; concentrate on the effect at the seamline, not at the cut edge.*

Rule 3: All crosswise lines must match at corresponding seamlines if possible and dominant lengthwise lines should ideally be equally spaced on each side of vertical seamlines Compare the sketches in Figure 11-5. The ideal match appears orderly and balanced, while the sketch with crosswise lines unmatched is disturbing. The center sketch, in which lengthwise lines are not equally spaced from the side seamline, is not disturbing, although it is not as pleasing as the ideal match. Depending on circumstances (width and shape of pattern pieces, size of the plaid unit), it is not always possible to have an ideal match, and it may be necessary or wise to use the acceptable

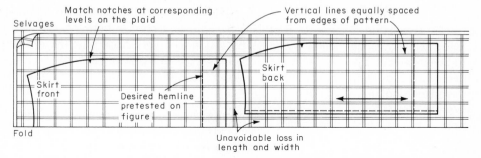

a Skirt sections properly matched by following general rules: this is the ideal effect, but it is possible only if the two sections are identical in width.

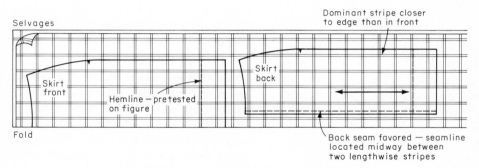

b If the back is narrower than the front (as it usually is), vertical lines cannot be equally spaced on each side of the center back seam and also the side seam.

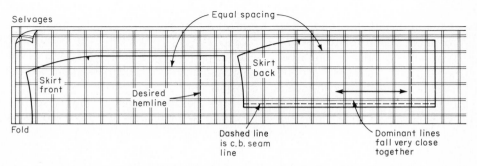

c Alternative solution: If lines are equally spaced on each side of the side seamline, the even spacing of these lines will be disturbed at the center back.

FIGURE 11-6   *Fundamental rules illustrated—matching plaids, checks, and stripes usually requires making compromises.*

plan. The three layouts in Figure 11-6 illustrate factors which will determine the best method; these layouts are used in the following directions to emphasize the fact that the worker is not always in control at every seam.

The sketch *a* layout shows the ideal situation, with pattern pieces placed in such a way that dominant lengthwise lines are equally spaced each side of the center-front and center-back lines. If front and back are favored, the worker lacks control at the side seamline. It so happens that with these particular skirt pieces, lengthwise lines in the front and back fall an equal distance from the side edge and side seam-line; this is possible only if front and back pieces are identical in width; some (but not most) patterns are made with the front and back sections of equal widths to make matching plaids easier.

In most skirt patterns the front skirt is about ½ inch wider (on the half pattern) than the back skirt because in this way the side seam divides the figure more attractively when viewed from the side. See sketch *b,* which shows the more typical pattern with a narrower back skirt. If the worker favors the center front and back, she will be out of control at the side; this layout shows dominant lines equally spaced on either side of the centers, with the result that dominant lengthwise lines are closer to the seam on the narrower back skirt piece. This results in the acceptable plan shown in Figure 11-5.

The worker might make the alternative choice pictured in sketch *c.* In this layout, the front skirt is positioned and then the plaid is matched perfectly at the side seam; therefore the worker is out of control at

the center back. Note that the center-back seamline is quite close to a dominant stripe; two dominant stripes will appear very close to each other on the figure. The worker must study the two effects shown in sketches *b* and *c* and choose between the two. The two stripes very close together in the back may create a pleasing accent or a disturbing "too close for comfort" effect.

NOTE: Attention has been centered on hemlines because the hemline is very important in skirt pieces. It is pointed out in sketch a of Figure 11-6 that when corresponding hemlines are matched, the plaid matches at corresponding notch positions as well. Plaid should always be matched at corresponding notch levels (this is the most fundamental rule of all), and in many pattern pieces, notches serve as the only guide for proper matching.

Rule 4: Separate units of the design must be cut with dominant lengthwise lines matched at the center of the figure and with the approximate spacing between dominant crosswise lines maintained for a smooth transition from one unit to the other This rule is illustrated on the figure in Figure 11-7 and in layout segments in Figure 11-8. Study the information in Figure 11-7. The desired hemline on a jacket or coat should be established on the muslin test copy and then transferred to the pattern. If the garment is a jacket, the level of the jacket hemline must be marked on the front skirt pattern.

The desired length of the jacket will determine whether a dominant crosswise stripe appears at the hemline (Rule 1 states that it should *if possible*). The worker will not know where the jacket hemline will fall until pattern pieces are laid on the fabric. For this pretest, she should determine the desired length; later she can adjust

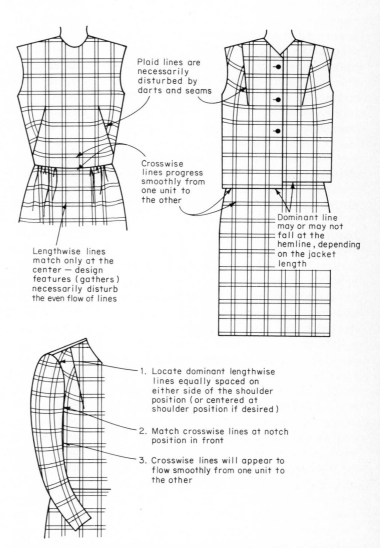

Plaid lines are
necessarily
disturbed by
darts and seams

Crosswise
lines progress
smoothly from
one unit to
the other

Lengthwise lines
match only at the
center — design
features (gathers)
necessarily disturb
the even flow of lines

Dominant line
may or may not
fall at the
hemline, depending
on the jacket
length

1. Locate dominant lengthwise
   lines equally spaced on
   either side of the shoulder
   position (or centered at
   shoulder position if desired)

2. Match crosswise lines at notch
   position in front

3. Crosswise lines will appear to
   flow smoothly from one unit to
   the other

*FIGURE 11-7   Rule 4: Separate units of the design should be cut
with dominant lengthwise lines matched at the center of the figure
and with the approximate spacing between dominant crosswise
lines maintained for a smooth transition from one unit to the other.*

the jacket length to the specifications of a particular plaid if desired. For purposes of balance, it is less important that a dominant stripe appear at the lower edge of jackets; either effect pictured is acceptable, although for large, bold plaids a dominant line at the lower edge will be more attractive. The effect of the plaid must be balanced against the effect of jacket length on the figure; beautifully matched plaid will not compensate for unattractive proportions.

The layout segments in Figure 11-8 are enlarged and pattern seamlines are shown in dashed lines. When matching at seams, attention must be concentrated on the seamline (not the cut edge), and this is increasingly important as matching becomes more intricate.

Sketch a—Dress Note that the bodice and skirt pieces are both cut on the fold; this will ensure that lengthwise lines in the two units will be spaced on either side of the center line. See that the skirt pattern is wider than the bodice (to allow for gathers). Study the notch positions at the waistline edges to see that lengthwise lines will match only in a relatively narrow area near the center front. Concentrate on the seamlines of the two pieces (not the cut edges) and locate them on identical crosswise levels of the plaid at the center front and pin the pattern in place. Follow a dominant crosswise stripe across the bodice and the skirt to see that they do not fall at identical levels on the plaid for the whole width of the pattern; the worker is out of control in the side area because she favored the more important area at the front.

SPECIAL NOTE CONCERNING WAISTBANDS: The sketches show a dress because matching along the shaped edges of a bodice is more difficult than planning how to cut a waistband. The waistband will be stiffened and therefore will not stretch and can be cut on the straight grain or on the bias. If it is cut on the straight grain, it must be cut with vertical lines of the plaid running vertically on the figure, the same as lines fall in the skirt pieces; in other words, it must be placed across the fabric in a crosswise direction, and it cannot be shifted to a lengthwise direction (as can be done with plain fabric). It should be placed so that dominant lengthwise lines in the band match dominant lengthwise lines in the skirt front (the same as the bodice in Figure 11-7), but it must be understood that it will not match any other vertical lines in the skirt; it would be pure chance if it should match dominant lines at the center-back because having favored the front, the worker is out of control in all other areas.

It is better to delay cutting the waistband until all other pieces are cut and then to experiment with scraps of fabric to decide where to position stripes for the best effect. Test out the effect of a bias-cut band. It adds subtle design interest and allows one to avoid the problem of matching; lines in a bias-cut band will contrast with lines in the skirt.

Sketch b—Suit Note the desired hemline, which was pretested and marked on the jacket and also on the skirt section; these lines must appear at identical levels on the plaid. Now that patterns are in place, it is evident that the desired hemline of the jacket does not fall along a dominant crosswise stripe. The worker can decide to retain the desired length (see the right side of the sketch in Figure 11-7), or she can decide to either lengthen or shorten the jacket if she feels it is more important to have a dominant stripe at the hemline than to

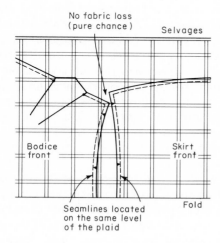

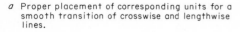

a Proper placement of corresponding units for a smooth transition of crosswise and lengthwise lines.

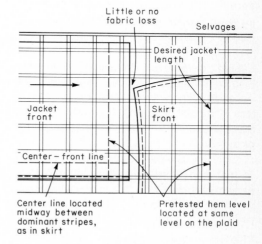

b Proper placement of corresponding jacket and skirt units.

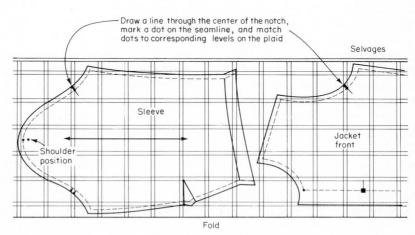

c To match levels of crosswise lines in a sleeve for a smooth transition from one unit to the other.

FIGURE 11-8   *Enlarged sketches to illustrate rule 4.*

retain the hemline as originally established.

The skirt is cut on the fold, but the jacket is not; note that the center-front line of the jacket is located midway between two dominant lengthwise stripes to maintain an even flow of lengthwise lines from the skirt to the jacket.

Sketch c—Sleeve Preferably, dominant lengthwise lines should be equally spaced on each side of the center of the sleeve (the shoulder position); however, a dominant line can be centered at the center of the sleeve if desired.

Only crosswise lines in the sleeve can be matched to crosswise lines in the bodice or jacket front, and the crosswise lines will match only at the notch level in the front only. A subtle point is illustrated here: *crosswise stripes must be matched at the notch level on the seamline (not the cut edge).* Vogue patterns indicate this level with a dot, as shown in the sketch, but the dot is not marked on all patterns. If there is no dot on the pattern, draw a line through the center of the front notch of the sleeve and the garment and mark the point where that line crosses the seamline. When matching levels on the plaid, use the dot on the seamline (rather than the notch on the cut edge) as a guide.

Caution: Having favored the front lines, the worker is out of control at the back sleeve. It should be allowed to fall as it will and should not be forced to match crosswise lines in the back; it may match, but in most patterns and in most plaids crosswise lines will (and therefore should) miss each other by about ½ inch at the notch level of the back armhole seam.

Just as in a jacket, the length of the sleeve can often be adjusted to allow for a dominant stripe at the hemline if such a change will not adversely affect proportions of the sleeve.

Utilize line direction for an individual effect

Although pattern pieces must ordinarily be cut on the grainlines indicated on the pattern, it is possible *under certain circumstances* to utilize grainline direction to gain aesthetic advantages. For example, in work with crosswise stripes, some pattern pieces can be turned so that stripes will fall in the lengthwise direction; a center band trim with stripes in the lengthwise directions will contrast with crosswise stripes in the garment and add a distinctive touch.

In work with plaid or with checks, cutting some pieces on the bias will create a subtle or striking effect (depending on the size and boldness of the plaid or check) as diagonal lines contrast with vertical and horizontal lines. The fact that fabric will stretch in the bias direction must be considered. Many fabrics do not stretch appreciably, many units of the garment will not be adversely affected by stretching, and any unit of the garment which will be interfaced will be supported and controlled by the interfacing. For these several reasons, the possibilities of cutting sections on the bias are many. For example, a sleeve cut on the bias is wonderfully comfortable to wear and will cause no problems in most fabrics. Bias-cut waistbands, which will be stiffened and held in perfect control by the stiffening, give a subtle, pleasing contrast; pockets, collars, and band trims are similar details which will be controlled by an interfacing.

To plan better for cutting a plaid costume, experiment with onionskin paper over the fashion sketch and quickly draw in lines to simulate the plaid to be used. Experiment with various effects before deciding how pieces will be cut. It must be understood that shifting the grain direction on pattern pieces may require extra fabric and therefore it is not always possible, because the pieces that are shifted may not fit into the width of fabric without piecing.

Figure 11-9 shows a sleeve placed on fabric for a bias cut. Essentially the problem is to locate the original grainline of the pattern along bias lines of the fabric; to do this accurately, see directions in the sketch. Construct a line at right angles to the original grainline; mark points on the two lines an equal distance from the corner (see dots in sketch) and draw a line between the two dots. Then construct a line through the square corner, passing through the midpoint as shown. This line bisects the

square angle, forming a 45-degree angle, and it becomes the new grainline.

Position any other piece to be cut on the bias in the same manner. The sketch shows a waistband and an upper collar. When cutting a piece which is cut on the fold (the collar), make a complete-figure pattern (page 493) so that lines of the plaid can be examined through the tissue paper before the pattern is cut. Pay particular attention to lines in the plaid at the front corner of the collar, which will be very prominent in the finished costume. Note that lines of the plaid are identical at the front corner of the sketch. This is possible only with an even plaid and only

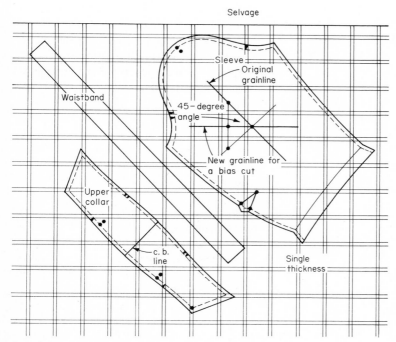

Selvage

Sleeve
Original grainline
Waistband
45-degree angle
New grainline for a bias cut
Upper collar
c. b. line
Single thickness

FIGURE 11-9 To cut sections of the pattern on the bias.

if the plaid is based on a perfect square, like the plaid pictured. Most even plaids are based on a rectangle; and in that case lines cannot be identical in the corners and will be very different if the plaid is uneven. It becomes a matter of placing the pattern in a position to make lines as balanced as possible. Study the lines carefully through the tissue paper and decide if they can be balanced with a pleasing effect. If they cannot, the collar must be cut on the lengthwise grain.

If the collar pattern was made for a bias cut, study the effect in the same way. It is possible that it will have to be cut on the straight grain.

Fundamental rules applied to uneven plaids

Figure 11–10 illustrates an uneven plaid, cut and matched properly according to fundamental rules. Uneven plaids are matched essentially the same as even plaids but are somewhat more difficult because the outlines of each unit are not as easily recognized; see the dots in the front-view sketch. Uneven plaids present three additional problems. The first: *When planning the layout, crosswise lines are matched as usual but it is important to have the heavier (darker, more prominent) half of the unit located nearer the lower edge in every section of the garment.* When the heavier half appears at the lower position of the figure, it gives a more balanced effect; note the greater weight in the lower half of the unit illustrated.

The second problem: *Only the most dominant lengthwise lines can be balanced on either side of centers and vertical seamlines.* Note that the lighter dashed line (less dominant) is not equally spaced on either side of the center line or the side seam. It is this fact that proves most con-

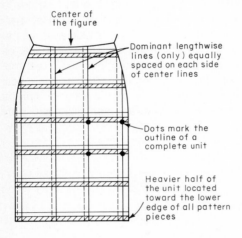

Center of
the figure

Dominant lengthwise
lines (only) equally
spaced on each side
of center lines

Dots mark the
outline of a
complete unit

Heavier half of
the unit located
toward the lower
edge of all pattern
pieces

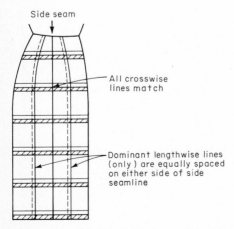

Side seam

All crosswise
lines match

Dominant lengthwise lines
(only) are equally spaced
on either side of side
seamline

FIGURE 11-10 Fundamental rules applied to uneven plaids.

fusing to the inexperienced person; she must train herself to concentrate on spacing only the dominant lengthwise lines and to ignore the less dominant ones.

The third problem: *Many inexperienced workers attempt to cut uneven plaids in such a way that they look more even.* For example, they are disturbed that the less dominant lengthwise lines are not centered on the figure and they therefore attempt to center them. *These lines should appear as they do, consistently on one side of the dominant line,* so that the plaid progresses around the figure with these lines always on the same side of the dominant lines. See the proper effect pictured in the side-view sketch. The worker must train herself to ignore less dominant lines, allowing them to fall as they will.

Uneven plaids must be cut from a with-nap layout Incorporate all directions for folding and cutting by with-nap layouts, beginning on page 496.

Cutting suggestions

When cutting plaid, checked, or striped fabric, work must progress in such a way that dominant stripes (crosswise and lengthwise) appear in corresponding positions on the two halves of the figure. This can be accomplished in two ways: (1) by folding the fabric in a crosswise or lengthwise fold (as required by the pattern layout) with dominant lines carefully pinned together on the two layers, or (2) by cutting complete-figure patterns of tissue paper and placing these complete patterns in proper position on a single thickness layout. Directions for the two methods appear in Figures 11-11 to 11-13.

Evaluation of methods Both methods have advantages and disadvantages and in many cases the decision can be one of personal preference. Cutting on a folded layout requires about half as much time as the alternative method, but it requires a considerable amount of time to locate corresponding lines in the fabric properly before cutting; pins must be spaced every few inches. Even if work is done very carefully, it is almost impossible to locate lines perfectly in the center of a wide expanse of fabric. A suggestion shown in Figure 11-12 corrects errors, but it requires additional time as well. The time and effort are approximately the same if the alternative method is used; it requires almost double the cutting time plus time to cut accurate complete-figure patterns of tissue. Considering time and effort, the two methods are about equal, and the worker can decide which of them she prefers.

Because it is always possible to save yardage with a single-thickness layout, this may be a deciding factor. If the fabric is a very thick coating which cannot be cut accurately on a folded layout, the single-thickness layout is the wiser choice. Glance through the following directions and then decide on the method best suited to each particular project.

To fold even plaid, checked, or striped fabrics See sketch *a* in Figure 11–11. All lines (dominant and subordinate) match in both lengthwise and crosswise directions. The sketch shows a lengthwise fold, but these even fabrics can also be folded crosswise and lines will match properly; in other words, they need not be cut on a with-nap layout. Pin at frequent intervals, matching lines carefully on the two layers.

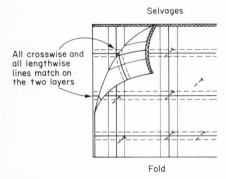

a To fold even plaid, checked, or striped fabrics.

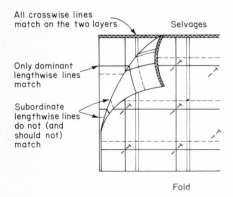

b To fold uneven plaid or striped fabrics.

FIGURE 11-11 To fold fabrics in preparation for cutting.

To fold uneven plaid or striped fabrics
Review "Fundamental Rules Applied to Uneven Plaids" on page 490. Sketch *b* in Figure 11-11 shows the lines in proper position on a lengthwise fold. Note that all crosswise lines (dominant and subordinate) match. But it is very important to understand that not all lines will (or should) match in the lengthwise direction. *Only the dominant lengthwise lines match; note that subordinate lengthwise lines do not match but appear on opposite sides of the dominant lines on the two layers.* Pin at frequent intervals, matching lines carefully on the two layers.

CAUTION: **A crosswise fold is more difficult to work with; the fabric must be folded and then cut along the crosswise fold and one layer shifted into proper position—as in a with-nap layout. Follow directions for a with-nap layout in Figure 11-16 on page 497 and the accompanying test.**

To be sure subordinate lengthwise lines will appear consistently on the same side of the dominant lengthwise lines, place all pattern pieces right side or printed side up. And, as with all with-nap layouts, place all pattern pieces with the upper edges toward one end of the length of fabric.

To achieve greater perfection when cutting on folded fabric Figure 11-12 shows a very helpful technique which can be done only if there is sufficient fabric to allow at least 1 inch of space between pattern pieces on the layout. Even if work is done very carefully, it is almost impossible to match all lines perfectly on the two layers, especially in the center of a wide expanse of fabric. After all pattern pieces have been pinned on the layout, separate sections by cutting about ½ inch to 1 inch beyond the pattern edges, as shown. Then remove the pattern and perfect work by seeing that all lines match on the two layers. Because the cut edges are close to the edge of the pattern, it is possible to locate lines in the fabric with much greater accuracy. Then repin the pattern and cut along the pattern edges.

To work with complete figure patterns on a single-thickness layout See Figure 11-13. To prepare complete figure patterns, fold sheets of tissue paper and cut each pattern piece carefully in tissue, exactly as it will be cut in fabric. Mark grainlines as shown in the skirt back pieces and mark center-fold lines as shown in the skirt front. Label pieces; if two pieces are cut

(if the piece is not cut on a fold), label the pieces "right" and "left" and be sure pieces are reversed for the right and left sides of the figure, as shown in the skirt back pieces.

Follow all rules for matching. Lines of the fabric will be visible through the tissue, and work progresses in essentially the same way. Locate the center line and desired

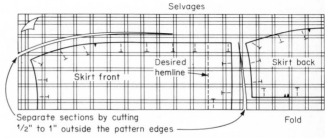

FIGURE 11-12 To achieve greater perfection when cutting on folded fabric.

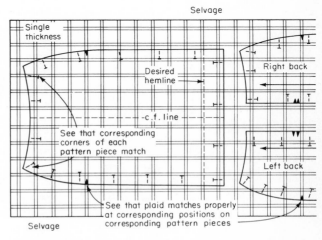

FIGURE 11-13 To work with complete-figure patterns on a single-thickness layout.

hemline in proper position and pin on one half of the pattern. Then pin on the remaining half, taking care to match corresponding levels on corresponding pattern pieces, as shown.

Construction techniques

To prepare seams for basting Seams can be basted in the usual way, or they can be done by slip-basting; either is effective if handled carefully. See sketch *a* in Figure

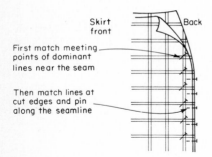

a To prepare to baste seams in the usual way.

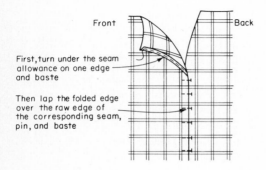

b To prepare for slip-basting seams.

FIGURE 11-14   To prepare seams for basting.

11-14 if seams will be done in the traditional manner. Do not concentrate on the lines at cut edges only. First, carefully match the meeting point of dominant lines a few inches back from the seamline. After they are aligned properly, match lines at the cut edges. Place pins quite close together and catch pins through only a thread or two of the two layers, right along the seamline. Baste by machine or with small, firm hand stitches, reinforced frequently.

To prepare for slip-basting seams see sketch *b*. Turn under the seam allowance on one edge and baste. Then lap the turned-under edge over the raw edge of the corresponding piece. The lap-over should be the width of the seam allowance; but it is more important to examine the lines in the fabric to be sure they are matched in the crosswise direction and that dominant lengthwise lines are equally spaced on each side of the seamline. Baste and remove pins. When slip-basting, use very small stitches and reinforce them frequently.

To prepare for stitching seams After a seam is basted, press it open with just enough pressure to keep it in place; avoid pressing in hard creases. Examine the seam from the right side. See that the crosswise lines are matched perfectly, because even a very slight miss is unsightly. Examine the area on each side of the seamline to see that dominant lengthwise lines are spaced an equal distance from the seamline. Look for little irregularities in the smoothness of the stitching line; if they appear, rebaste those areas. Fit and make corrections before stitching.

Even if the seam has been basted with small, firm stitches, lines have a tendency to slip because the upper layer pushes forward (perhaps about $\frac{1}{16}$ inch) under the pressure of the machine foot. To prevent this, it is well to replace pins at the meeting points of dominant crosswise lines and to stitch over the pins. One can expect to rip small sections of the seam, because the slightest irregularity is very noticeable in these fabrics.

To mark guidelines on underlined or interfaced sections See Figure 11-15. When a section of the garment is underlined or interfaced, the lines of the fabric are no longer visible on the interfaced side; and since this is the side from which the seam is basted and stitched, it is difficult to work accurately along proper lines in plaid, checked, or striped fabrics. If guidelines are made from the right side (with hand or long machine stitches in a contrasting color), the guideline is visible on the underlined or interfaced side. There are many times when a guideline will make it possible to work with more accurate results. For example, the paper pattern for bound buttonholes, which is so helpful with most fabrics, hides lines in the plaid; but if stitched guidelines are used as a substitute for the paper pattern, the lines for the buttonhole will be visible from the interfaced side, and results will be much more accurate. Several suggestions in "Aids to Accuracy" on page 296 involve this same technique.

NAPPED AND PILE FABRICS, INCLUDING FAKE FURS

A very broad use is made of the words *napped fabrics* on the envelope back and on the layouts on the instruction sheet; these words are used to refer to napped fabrics, pile fabrics, and other fabrics (such as uneven plaids and zebra stripes on fake furs) with a one-way design. Napped fabrics are soft wool fabrics which are napped (brushed up) after they are woven. They include suede cloth, broadcloth, and flannel. Pile fabrics are fabrics woven in such a way that cut ends of yarns produce

a furry or hairy effect. Outstanding examples are velvet, corduroy, and velveteen. Both napped and pile fabrics show shading differences depending on the way they are cut. *Velvet and corduroy should be cut so that the pile runs upward in order to achieve a rich effect, while napped fabrics should be cut with the nap running downward.* The nap or pile must run in one direction on a garment, and this means that a special layout (with all pattern pieces laid in one direction) is required; this type of layout requires more fabric.

Pattern selection

If napped textures are included among the suggested fabrics listed on the envelope back, the yardage chart will include napped fabrics, and there will be special layouts on the instruction sheet.

Not all pattern designs can be cut effectively from napped or pile fabrics, and the customer is wise to heed warnings on the yardage chart. If the pattern cannot be cut to enhance these fabrics, a note

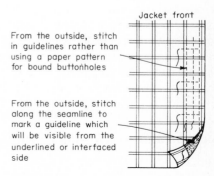

From the outside, stitch in guidelines rather than using a paper pattern for bound buttonholes

From the outside, stitch along the seamline to mark a guideline which will be visible from the underlined or interfaced side

Jacket front

FIGURE 11-15 To mark guidelines on underlined or interfaced sections.

stating "napped and pile fabrics not suitable" will be included on the yardage chart, and these fabrics will not appear in the list of appropriate fabrics.

Napped and pile fabrics are, by their very nature, interesting (and often striking) fabrics which should be allowed to play a dominant role in the costume; design lines should be simple, so that large expanses of fabric are revealed. Furthermore, as a total group, these fabrics present pressing problems which can be minimized by fewer design lines. Delicate, limp, and clinging velvets and striking fake furs must necessarily be cut in simple lines to enhance the fabric as well as to eliminate their greater pressing problems, while velveteen and corduroy are somewhat less interesting and present fewer pressing problems.

The weight and hand of napped and pile fabrics vary greatly, and the character of the fabric influences the choice of pattern designs. Limp velvets should be made in designs that are appropriate for other limp fabrics (flowing lines, soft draping, etc.), while crushed velvets (and to an extent, velveteens and corduroys) have the stiffness and body suitable for suits and coats. The fake furs create exaggerated problems by their bulk in seams and are best suited to simple designs in coats and jackets (capes are an excellent choice). They are very appropriate for little accessory pieces such as vests, sleeveless cardigans, etc.

Selection and preparation of fabric

If yardage amounts for napped fabrics are not included in the yardage chart, see "To Figure Yardage Amounts for Napped or Pile Fabrics" on page 58. If the fabric is plaid, checked, or striped (many corduroys are) or if the fabric has a large design (fake furs in leopard, for example) additional extra fabric will be required; see page 474.

The cost of the fabric is some indication of the magnitude of problems that will arise. The finest, costliest velvets are more delicate; they will be easily marred by dull pins or large needles and will present greater stitching and pressing problems. Fake furs with almost mathematically precise markings that will require careful balancing on the figure or with longer, silkier yarns will require greater care than their less costly counterparts. By contrast, budget-priced corduroy, once it is properly cut, is relatively simple to work with.

Preshrink the fabric (as well as all findings, underlinings, interfacings, and linings) by the method that will be used to clean the finished garment. Most napped or pile fabrics require dry cleaning.

Cutting from a with-nap layout

Napped and pile fabrics, fabrics with a one-way design, and fabrics with an uneven plaid (which is actually a one-way design) must be cut from with-nap layouts. *A with-nap layout is one in which the nap, pile, or design runs in the same direction on the two layers of fabric and in which pattern pieces are all laid in one direction, with the upper edges of all pieces consistently placed nearest one end of the fabric.* Keep in mind that napped fabrics (usually woolens) and fake furs should be cut with the nap or fur running down on the figure and pile fabrics should be cut with the pile running up on the figure. Review "To Figure Yardage Amounts for Napped and Pile Fabrics" on page 58, in which illustrations show pieces properly laid in one direction (as they are pictured on instruction sheets) but do not indicate the direction of the nap, pile, or one-way designs. See the sketches in Figure 11-16 with arrows indicating the direction of the nap or pile; when working with an uneven plaid or a fake fur, assume the arrowhead is the top of the design unit.

In layouts showing a lengthwise fold of fabric, the nap, pile, or design will run in the same direction on both layers of the fabric, as shown, and the only problem is the need to place the upper edges of pattern pieces near one end of the fabric. Problems arise when a crosswise fold is involved. When fabric is folded crosswise, the nap or pile runs in opposite directions on

the two layers; for example, if a sleeve or back skirt pattern were cut from the incorrect layout pictured, the nap, pile, or design would run in opposite directions on the two halves of the figure.

Two additional steps are required to prepare a crosswise-fold layout. First fold the

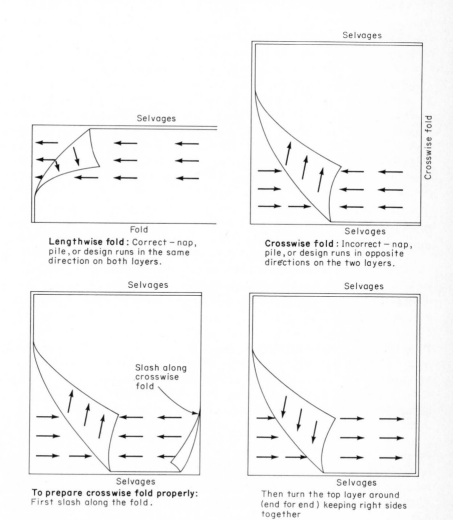

Selvages

Lengthwise fold: Correct — nap, pile, or design runs in the same direction on both layers.

Crosswise fold: Incorrect — nap, pile, or design runs in opposite directions on the two layers.

To prepare crosswise fold properly: First slash along the fold.

Then turn the top layer around (end for end) keeping right sides together

FIGURE 11-16 To fold fabric for with-nap layouts.

fabric in the crosswise direction and slash along the crosswise fold, separating the two layers. Then turn the top layer, end for end, being sure to keep right sides together. Now the nap, pile, or design will run in the same direction on both layers and pieces can be positioned with the upper edges consistently placed nearest one end of the fabric. Shifting the upper layer also allows for the proper matching of an uneven plaid or stripe and for the proper balancing of a one-way design.

Delicate velvets, and to a lesser extent all pile fabrics, are easily marred by large pins and dull needles. When pinning on the pattern pieces, confine pins to the seam allowance and areas between dartlines. Use the finest silk pins, small hand and machine needles, and fine thread throughout the construction process.

Construction and pressing suggestions

NOTE: **See additional suggestions for working with fake furs on the opposite page. Many of those suggestions will be helpful when working with thick, fur-like pile fabrics.**

Interfacings and underlinings Napped and pile fabrics require the same extra body and support as other fabrics of a similar hand, weight, and character (exception: some fake furs do not require an underlining).

Basting This is a necessary step for two reasons. These fabrics (especially the piles) must be basted and carefully fitted before stitching is done; needle punctures may permanently mar pile fabrics if machine

stitching must be ripped out. In addition, napped and pile fabrics tend to shift position under the machine foot and basting stitches must be secured often to control slippage.

Machine stitching This is complicated by the thick, spongy character of many of these fabrics. Experiment on scraps of fabric before proceeding. Many of the following will prove helpful: the rolling presser foot, less pressure on the pressure foot, holding the fabric taut as it passes through the machine, and heavier needles and threads for thick piles and fake furs. Test-stitch and examine results before doing any permanent stitching.

Seams and hem edges must be finished in all unlined pile garments Raveling is not a problem in napped woolens; yarns adhere to each other in napped woolens and edges can remain raw. The problem in pile fabrics is partially one of fraying, but a greater problem is created by little bits of fibers shedding from cut edges; these furry ends will shed off on hair, skin, and undergarments throughout the life of the garment.

Jackets and coats will be lined; and it is wise to line skirts and pants made of pile fabrics, as well. The couturier or shell method of lining protects seams best. If the skirt or pants will not be lined, seams must be bound; see directions for the Hong Kong finish on page 287.

Pressing Napped and pile fabrics require special pressing procedures to keep the nap or pile erect. A needle board, which has a flat surface from which wire points project, is a great help. The needle board is placed on the ironing board, and the napped fabric is placed face down on it. A slightly damp press cloth should be used, and most of the weight of the iron should be supported by the hand; the steam, rather than pressure, accomplishes the desired result. If a needle board is not available (it is an expensive item that is used infrequently) place a scrap of pile fabric right side up on the board. Then place the garment right side down with the two napped surfaces facing each other. Use a heavy, slightly damp press cloth and support the weight of the iron with the hand. Brush the nap lightly while it is still damp to retain the original beauty of the fabric.

Special suggestions for working with fake furs

Incorporate all general information on napped and pile fabrics; these special suggestions are not complete in and of themselves but are, rather, additional techniques which must be combined with those in the foregoing section.

Selection of fabric The density and bulk of the fake furs are a result of the character of the fur-like surface and the weight of the backing. Those with a lightweight, somewhat supple backing are more suitable for novelty linings in heavy coats, while the heavier, firmly woven backings provide the body needed for coats and jackets (the backing acts as an underlining and usually no additional underlining is required). When using very thick fur fabrics, certain sections (for example, the under collar) can be cut of a compatible fabric of a lighter weight such as a medium-weight wool, provided that the contrast of color or texture or both will not adversely influence the design.

Buttons and buttonholes should be avoided—except for fabric loops made of a compatible fabric; decorative hooks, braid loops, and frogs are better fastening devices. Accents of leather are very attractive; portions of leather belts make effective fastenings.

If it is important to the wearer to have buttons and buttonholes, it is possible to make them in most fake furs; see "Buttonholes" on page 501.

Extra yardage is required for balancing large designs The customer must realize that large designs such as zebra stripes (or any other fur marking repeated with regularity) must be balanced on the figure. This will require extra yardage above the amount stated on the yardage chart. See "To Estimate the Approximate Amount of Extra Fabric Required" on page 477. Also, carefully study the first pages of this chapter, beginning on page 474.

Balancing designs is comparable to matching uneven plaids, but it is actually more difficult because although the markings are repeated with regularity, they are not as easily recognized as the design lines in plaids. A fake fur with a prominent design is a project for experienced workers or students who will be assisted by an instructor.

It is not possible to estimate the exact amount of extra yardage which will be required for balancing purposes. The customer can make an estimate, but she must be sure that there is a sufficient supply in the store for later purchase if a need for additional fabric arises. She must understand that the cost of the costume will be greater, perhaps much greater.

See the simulated fur fabric in sketch *a* of Figure 11-1 on page 475. Note that the way the design unit is spaced on the width of fabric influences the amount of usable width. Because the design units are not equally spaced from the selvage in the sketch on the left, there will be a loss of usable width when the design units are balanced. Study sketch *b* to see the effect of this loss in width; the situation is the same for a large design which must be balanced as it is for the uneven plaid pictured. Therefore, the customer must be alert to the width loss she can expect and must buy the amount of fabric for a narrower width, plus an estimated additional amount for balancing purposes.

Cutting To decrease bulk and allow for broad, unbroken expanses of fabric, eliminate as many seams as possible in the pattern before cutting. Any seam that is ruler-straight and parallel to the grainline can be eliminated provided that the width of the fabric will accommodate wider pattern sections. Center-back seams and the front-facing seam can often be eliminated. To eliminate a seam, lap the seamlines of the two pattern pieces (a total lap-over of 1¼ inches from cut edge to cut edge) and pin or tape the sections together.

These fabrics cannot be accurately cut from a folded layout, which requires cutting through a double thickness. See "To Work with Complete-Figure Patterns on a single Thickness Layout" on page 493, and balance the design lines the same as plaid lines are matched, as shown in Figure 11-13.

A continuing problem when working with fur-like fabrics is to avoid a chopped-off look after the seam is stitched; this can usually be handled by lifting caught yarns from the stitched seam (this is explained later). However, if yarns are very long, precautions must be taken when cutting. If there are no design units to be balanced

(as with thick pile, or small designs spaced very close together), the pattern should be placed on the wrong side of the fabric and only the backing layer cut. When cutting from the wrong side, a mat knife or scissors can be used; the mat knife is preferred because it makes it somewhat easier to cut through only the backing layer.

Design units which must be balanced complicate this problem. The pattern must be placed on the right side of the fabric so that the design units are visible. With most fake furs which have short yarns, the fabric can be cut with scissors along the pattern edges in the usual way. However, if there are long yarns (longer than ⅝ inch), cutting in the traditional way may produce the chopped-off effect. To avoid this, proceed in the following order: (1) Place the pattern on the right side of the fabric, balancing the design units. (2) Cut about ½ inch outside the pattern edges. (3) Remove pins and transfer the pattern to the wrong side of the fabric, allowing the ½-inch margin to extend beyond all pattern edges. (4) Cut along the pattern edges with a mat knife from the wrong side, making slashes through the backing layer only.

Underlinings and interfacings There is no need to underline or interface most fake furs, because the backing layer serves as a supporting fabric. However, the character of the backing influences the need for supporting fabrics. If the backing is quite supple, use partial interfacings; and if the backing is knitted, use both underlinings and interfacings.

Basting and machine stitching Use heavier needles and thread of an appropriate weight; the special threads for polyesters are excellent unless the fabric demands a heavy-duty cotton thread. Reduce the pressure on the presser foot or use a rolling presser foot to reduce stitching problems.

When possible, stitch from the upper toward the lower edges of all sections.

While basting and stitching seams, push the pile away from the seam and attempt to place stitches in the backing without catching in many of the hairs; this will prevent the chopped-off look of hairs caught into the seam. Test-stitch to become adept at this technique.

After a seam or dart is stitched, release the yarns which have been caught in the seam; working from the right side, gently lift yarns from the seam with a pin and smooth the fur over the seam, making the seam as inconspicuous as possible.

To reduce bulk After seams and darts are stitched, shear off as much of the fur surface as possible from seam allowances. To reduce the need for pressing and to ensure flatter seams, whip seam and dart edges in place by hand, catching stitches through the backing layer only. Seams handled in this way do not require pressing.

Buttonholes Although it is generally wise to favor other types of fastenings (see page 499), it is possible to make certain types of bound buttonholes in most fur-like fabrics. Construction must be simple to avoid bulk; traditional bound buttonholes are not satisfactory. If buttonholes are desired, use the novelty type for special uses (page 393) or the very simple buttonhole shown in Figure 11-17; test both methods on scraps before making a final decision.

If the novelty method will be used, see Figure 9-34 on page 394. Sketch *b* shows that lips of the buttonhole are prepared and then inserted later under the faced opening. Do not attempt to make the lips from the fur-like fabric; instead choose a flat, firm compatible fabric (such as flannel or wool crepe) in a harmonizing color.

The very simple buttonhole shown in

Figure 11-17 will probably prove most acceptable. Although the boat-shaped opening would not look finished in most suiting and coating fabrics, it is quite attractive in fur-like fabrics because the yarns extend over the edges of the opening, making the opening almost invisible.

Step 1 Cut the facing pieces from scraps of a closely woven underlining fabric or a lightweight interfacing fabric. Stitch in the boat-shaped lines pictured.

Step 2 Slash through the center directly to the ends. Make tiny clips into the curved edges as shown.

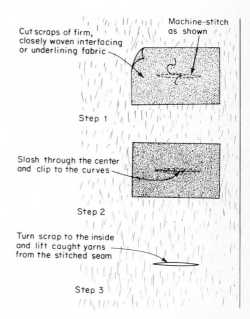

Cut scraps of firm, closely woven interfacing or underlining fabric

Machine-stitch as shown

Step 1

Slash through the center and clip to the curves

Step 2

Turn scrap to the inside and lift caught yarns from the stitched seam

Step 3

FIGURE 11-17 A simple buttonhole effective with fake furs.

Step 3 Turn the scrap to the inside and whip it down to the backing. Yarns will have been caught in the stitching and must be gently lifted out.

When the facing is in place, the underside of the buttonholes is finished in the usual way (page 433); the only difference is that these buttonholes require only a center slash through the facing (no clips to the corners as in rectangular buttonholes), so that the opening on the facing side is boat-shaped, the same as it is on the right side.

TWILL FABRICS

The twill weave is achieved by passing the filling yarn over and under the warp in such a way as to create a diagonal line on the surface of the fabric. In a typical twill, the diagonal lines are unbroken, as shown in the sketches in this series, but the lines can be reversed to create herringbones or broken twills. The following fabrics are examples of twills: serge, surah, denim, whipcord, and gabardine. The diagonal lines may be barely visible from a distance of a few feet (as in gabardine) or may be very prominent. The line will be prominent if coarse yarns are used and still more prominent if the warp and filling threads are two distinctly different colors (for example, black in one direction, white in the other).

These fabrics are no different to sew or tailor from other fabrics, although the longer floats of yarns create more raveling problems, the more so if yarns are coarse (that is, have a low thread count). The major problem has to do with cutting and how it influences the visual effect of the diagonal lines in the finished costume.

Some patterns cannot be cut effectively from twills, because the diagonal lines would be visually unattractive in the finished garment; if the lines are more prominent, problems are magnified. These patterns carry a special note in the yardage chart stating that twills are not appropriate. This note appears very frequently on patterns (more frequently than is absolutely necessary), and customers are so accustomed to seeing it that they have developed what appears to them to be a well-founded fear of twills. Actually, there are few problems in cutting patterns designed in the basic lines of a typical suit or coat. There is usually only one minor problem (easily solved) which will be encountered in the typical costume consisting of a jacket or coat (in straight lines and having a regulation sleeve) and a slim skirt or pants. The single problem in most of these designs has to do with cutting the under-collar sections; it can be easily remedied, as shown in Figure 11-20. And yet this costume may very possibly include the note "Twills are not appropriate."

It is unfortunate that so many patterns carry this warning, because it prevents customers from choosing some of the very attractive twills on the market. The following discussion is aimed at pointing out the relatively few difficulties, so that the knowledgeable customer or the student working with an instructor can anticipate problems and decide for herself if they can be remedied.

The warning note appears on patterns which will create few problems for good and sound reasons; *it should be understood that the pattern company is not wrong to include it.* The pattern is planned for the average customer, who is not able to work out solutions to problems for herself; persons with limited experience need to heed the warning note.

Home sewers anticipate some problems which do not exist It is entirely possible that the note appears more frequently than is necessary because of unfounded complaints directed to the pattern companies; from her experience in the pattern industry, the author believes this is true. Many of these complaints are based on problems which the customer believes exist but which do not actually exist. The following are several examples: (1) Twills do not require with-nap layouts, yet many customers assume they do; when the pattern does not include with-nap layouts, the customer is convinced that the pattern company has made a mistake. (2) Notice in both layouts in Figure 11-19 that the diagonal lines fall in opposite directions on the two layers of folded fabric; this is as it should be. But the average customer, more accustomed to working with checks or plaids, expects the diagonal lines to fall in the same direction on the two layers; if she attempts to line them up in that way, she finds it is impossible and blames her difficulties on the pattern company. Note that in both of the above examples, the customer may be convinced before she begins work that the pattern company has failed her. (3) Most average customers expect the lines to chevron—to reverse directions on the two halves of the figure— and when they discover that lines in twill fabrics do not chevron, they are convinced that the pattern directions are wrong. As shown in Figure 11-18, the lines should *not* chevron in twill fabrics. It is understandable that the average customer has these misconceptions and that they seem to her to be well-founded complaints. Very probably the pattern companies use the

note "Twill fabrics are not appropriate" to defend themselves against this type of complaint, which is not well founded. If this is so, the experienced reader needs to understand the problems and decide for herself if they can be solved satisfactorily. Then she can use twill fabrics for many patterns which are not recommended for twills.

Lines may slant in either direction Many persons lose confidence when working with twills because they cannot decide whether lines should slant from the right shoulder to the left lower edge or the left shoulder to the right lower edge; confusion grows if they attempt to study ready-to-wear garments, because they find lines slanting either way. The experienced person who has sewn for many years is apt to be more concerned about this issue because she may remember a time when there were definite rules concerning line direction. *The rules no longer exist.* Lines can slant in either direction; the lines in one fabric may slant in one direction while lines on another slant in the opposite direction. In other words, this is one more problem which the customer anticipates but which, in reality, does not exist. There is only one basic rule concerning line direction, as explained in the following section.

To cut twill fabrics

Lines should not chevron but should progress around the body always slanting in the same direction The jacket and sleeve patterns shown in Figure 11-18 have been cut properly, with lines slanting in the same direction; however, they could slant in the opposite direction, depending on how the fabric was woven. The lines should not chevron (reverse direction) on the two halves of the figure. *This is the single basic rule for cutting twills. The worker must understand that lines should slant consistently in one direction and that to a discerning person they look correct that way.* If she is not convinced, she should examine high-quality ready-to-wear; men's departments have many garments made of twills.

The worker with limited experience may assume that the diagonal lines must be matched at corresponding seamlines so

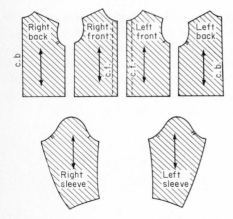

FIGURE 11-18 Lines do not chevron but progress around the body always slanting in the same direction.

that they appear to be long continuous lines. This is another problem which home sewers anticipate but which does not exist. Actually it is impossible to match most seams so that the diagonal lines will appear continuous; the only seam which could be matched is one composed of ruler-straight lines and cut parallel to the grain-lines. Matching is impractical (if not impossible) because the diagonal lines are so close together that they simply are not visible enough to be matched; lines in this series of sketches appear unusually prominent because they are spaced so as to be more conspicuous for illustrative purposes. It is possible that one might wish to match center front and back seamlines (if they are ruler-straight and parallel to the grainline) if the diagonal lines are wide and prominent; a black-and-white twill made with very coarse yards is an example.

When fabric is folded, diagonal lines should fall in opposite directions on the two layers See both layouts in Figure 11-19. Note that the flipped-back corners reveal the proper direction of lines on the two layers; they should fall in opposite directions as shown. After pieces are cut, the diagonal lines will fall in the proper direction (as shown in Figure 11-18).

Twills do not require a with-nap layout The lengthwise layout in Figure 11-19 shows pieces laid with the upper edges consistently placed toward one end of the length of fabric; it is a with-nap layout. The crosswise fold is not a with-nap layout; note the sleeve turned end for end. *Results from these two layouts will be identical.*

Pattern pieces in basic lines create no problems The basic jacket (or coat) and the sleeve shown are typical patterns designed in basic lines. The sketches show jacket pieces, to conserve space; but there are no problems with slim skirts and pants, because they too are designed in basic lines. One can assume that any pattern piece which will fit quite well into a rectangle is a basic pattern piece and can be cut from twill without complications. Note how well the jacket back fills the rectangle; the front, the sleeve, and basic skirts and pants also fill most of the space in a rectangle. See Figure 11-21 for a comparison.

Problems arise if pattern pieces are cut on the bias The under collar in Figure 11-19 is cut on the bias; note that the grainline is placed in such a way that the center-back line falls along a bias line on the fabric. Sketch *a* in Figure 11-20 shows the effect created by the diagonal lines when a pattern piece is cut on the bias; this is the effect even though the under collar was cut from the same layout, which was right for all other pieces. *This unattractive effect will occur on any piece cut on the bias, and obviously it is not visually acceptable.* Many patterns which state that twills are not appropriate do so because this one piece cannot be cut from the layouts shown on the instruction sheet. The under collar will not be visible as the garment is worn; it could be cut in this way, but the effect tends to bother the worker as she tailors the garment and later as she wears it.

The problem of cutting very small pieces (the under collar, band trims, etc.) can be easily solved, as shown in sketch *b*. Cut the two sections on a single thickness, first cutting one, then reversing the pattern (as shown in dashed lines) and placing it down so that the diagonal lines fall in the same direction in both pieces, as shown. Note that it is necessary to place the piece down once with the grainline in the lengthwise direction and the second time with the grainline in the crosswise direction in

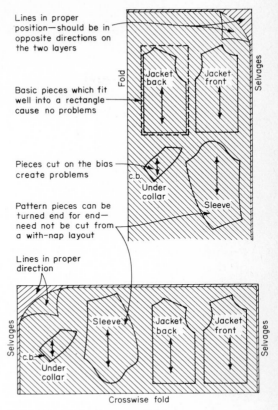

FIGURE 11-19   To cut twill fabrics.

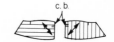

a   The effect when pattern pieces are cut on the bias.

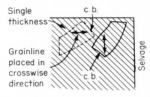

b   To cut the under collar (or other small pieces cut on the bias).

FIGURE 11-20   Problems arise when pattern pieces are cut on the bias.

order to create this more desirable effect. There is little or no disadvantage to cutting a small piece like the under collar on opposing grainlines. However, it would not be wise to do this with large pieces, because grainline direction influences the way fabrics hang on the figure. *Therefore, any pattern with large, structural pieces cut on the bias cannot be cut in twills.*

Problems are comparable if edges of the pattern piece fall along bias lines on the fabric The jacket pieces shown in Figure 11-21 are not basic pieces, because they are combined with sections of the sleeve; note that these pieces do not fill a rectangle. When the jacket sections are cut on the lengthwise grainline, the sleeve sections fall along bias lines of the fabric. Examine the jacket front sections and imagine the sleeve portions in wearing

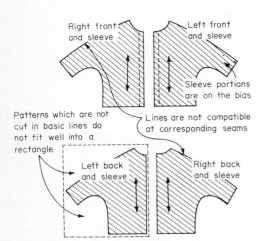

Right front
and sleeve

Left front
and sleeve

Sleeve portions
are on the bias

Patterns which are not
cut in basic lines do
not fit well into a
rectangle

Lines are not compatible
at corresponding seams

Left back
and sleeve

Right back
and sleeve

FIGURE 11-21 Similar problems occur when sections of a pattern are cut on the bias.

position; note that because they fall along bias lines, the diagonal lines on one sleeve will appear in a somewhat horizontal direction on the figure, while those on the other sleeve will appear in a more vertical direction on the figure. This alone is reason enough to rate this pattern as one which cannot be cut in twill. However, there is an additional problem which will be very obvious under wearing conditions. Note that when the corresponding shoulder-and-sleeve seams are stitched, diagonal lines fall in very different directions. Similar problems will occur in flared skirts, pants which flare below the knee, etc. *Therefore, if any edge of any large structural piece of the pattern falls along bias lines on the fabric, the pattern cannot be cut of twill fabrics.*

Pretesting techniques

The very best way to gain much information and understanding is to make quick paper samples, similar to the sketches in Figure 11-19. Roughly sketch diagonal lines on a sheet of notebook paper; lines need not be perfectly spaced or ruler-straight. Then sketch in pattern pieces (a very rough outline will suffice) and cut them out. Separate the two layers and examine the results. If one would like to use twill for a pattern which is not recommended for twill, results can be tested easily and quickly in the store. Examine the chart of pattern pieces. If all of them are in basic lines except the under collar, the pattern can be made of twill by making the simple correction shown in Figure 11-20. If large structural pieces are cut on the bias or if any edge of any large structural piece falls in bias lines, heed the warning and choose another pattern for twill fabric. If in doubt, quickly make the test suggested above, using the pieces pictured on the pattern as a guide.

LEATHER, VINYL, AND SUEDE

Several distinctly different man-made fabrics can be given the look of leather. Those most like leather in stiffness, body, and general character are made of vinyl, and it is this group which requires special handling. Other fabrics can be made to look like leather without having the typical characteristics of leather. Nylon and polyester double knits can be given the look and something of the texture of leather by a heat embossing process; these fabrics may be in suiting weights appropriate for lightweight coats and jackets. They are a welcome addition to the like-leather family for many reasons: They require no special handling during construction, many can be laundered like other polyesters and nylons, they provide some of the body without the characteristic stiffness of the vinyls, and they are softer and warmer to the touch. Because the leather look does not complicate construction in any way, these fabrics can be made into a great variety of designs; simplicity of design is not an issue except that, in general, large expanses of fabric unbroken by seams will allow the unique character of the fabric to be a dominant feature of the costume. These fabrics create no problems with their leather-like facade and are constructed by techniques prompted by their other qualities—fiber content, hand, etc.; they can be tailored in the usual way.

Leather and vinyl are challenging but do not provide good tailoring experience Students working in a classroom situation with an instructor are (and should be) taking the course to gain knowledge and experience (personal, professional, or both) for the future. It is short-sighted to jeopardize long-range goals by choosing a material which does not lend itself to typical tailoring techniques. After glancing through this entire section, review "The Tailored Costume as a Learning Experience" on page 17 to better understand why leather and vinyl are not recommended for classroom projects. This is not to say that there is no value in using these materials; on the contrary, the very experienced person should fortify her basic experiences by undertaking ambitious, unique problems.

These materials do not allow for the best fundamental experience for two reasons: (1) They create many distinctive problems of their own, and these require constant attention, which distracts the worker from the fundamental tailoring techniques she set out to master. (2) If they are used, many basic tailoring techniques must be eliminated. For example, the student will gain little experience in fitting, because these materials should be chosen for loose, free-hanging designs which do not fit close enough to the body to require intricate fitting. Vinyls and most leathers cannot be shaped and molded; this means that the shaping principles, the very foundation of tailoring, cannot be employed. Interfacings are not required; this eliminates the padding stitches which mold and shape the interfacing layer to the fabric in a typical tailored garment. Pressing techniques which further shape the garment cannot be employed. Taping seams is usually not required with these materials, but taping seams is one of the new experiences in a typical tailored garment. And so it goes throughout the entire construction sequence. It follows that it is wise to choose a fabric which adapts well to tailoring techniques when making a project which must also serve as a learning experience. Later, leather and vinyl are an ideal choice for interesting and challenging costumes.

Man-made vinyl and slick-surfaced leather

The vinyls are appropriate for the type of garment that is appropriate in genuine leather—coats and jackets; A-line skirts (simple in line but with some style fullness); accessory items such as hats, clutch bags, and sleeveless vests; and for accent touches (pockets, trims) on wool costumes. The design should have a minimum of seams and darts. Eliminate as many seams as possible; see page 253.

The vinyls and leather will not ease in satisfactorily, so sleeves should be of the raglan or kimono style. Finished edges of hems and facings can best be held flat by top-stitching; it is well to choose a pattern design that is enhanced by top-stitching (casuals, sportswear). They cannot be laundered or dry-cleaned. The surface can be cleaned with a damp sponge, but it is important to choose a lining which can go without attention for the life of the garment; lining fabrics with a smooth surface (which will not attract soil) in dark colors are most appropriate.

Make a muslin copy to test pattern alterations and fit
The vinyls and leather cannot be basted for fitting and machine stitches cannot be removed because needle punctures permanently mar the fabric; therefore, all pattern alteration and fitting problems must be tested by making a muslin copy. After the muslin copy is fitted, corrections are transferred to the pattern before cutting.

Cutting and marking
The fabric may have a design (snakeskin) that must be balanced on the figure (see page 499) and they may require with-nap layouts (see page 496). Heavier fabrics should be cut on a single thickness with an open layout and complete-figure tissue copies of the pattern (see page 493).

Use "Magic"-type transparent tape to tape (rather than pin) pattern pieces in place. If a design must be balanced, pieces must be placed on the right side of the fabric; otherwise tape the pattern pieces to the wrong side of the fabric. Pattern markings are transferred to the backing (wrong side) with pencil or chalk.

Underlinings and interfacings
These are not usually required. The backing acts as an underlining, and the fabric has enough stiffness and body without interfacings.

Machine stitching is a major problem
Use scraps of fabric to test techniques on the particular fabric to be used. Use fine needles (Singer offers a special assortment for vinyls) and one of the elasticized polyester threads. Experiment with the pressure on the presser foot and try using the rolling presser foot; in many of these fabrics a lower pressure will be beneficial, and the rolling presser foot may possibly be helpful. Use a long stitch (eight to ten per inch); short stitches will cut or split the fabric. To replace basting, hold seam edges in place by encasing the edges with short pieces of tape. Pins can be used with supple fabrics if they are confined to the seam allowance or the area between

dartlines. Do not stitch over pins in the usual way because the pressure of the machine foot may permanently mark their imprint on the fabric.

The backing provides a surface that will allow the fabric to flow smoothly through the machine as structural darts and seams are stitched. However, when the shiny side is next to the throat plate or the presser foot (when top-stitching), it adheres to the surface, and if the fabric does not progress at the proper speed, stitches pile up and not only are unattractive but permanently split the fabric. To prevent this serious problem, feed a strip of tissue under the layers as they pass through the machine. To help the machine foot glide more smoothly over the uppermost layer, use another layer of tissue or wipe the area lightly with oil.

Corners must be rounded off as they are stitched because leather-like fabrics will not turn into a point or corner.

Construction techniques Hems and facings can be held in place with some success by an adhesive; experiment with rubber cement and Elmer's glue. With periodic repairs, adhesives may prove adequate. The alternative is to tape the hem allowance or facing in place and top-stitch about ¼ to ½ inch from the finished edge. Front facings must be left full-width (to cover buttonholes), but neck and armhole facings and hem edges can be trimmed down to about ¼ inch from the top-stitched line.

Zippers should be done by the slot-seam method described on page 318. Rather than basting, temporarily hold seam edges to the zipper with tape and then top-stitch in the usual way.

Buttons and buttonholes can be used in vinyl garments. Although it is possible to do a machine-worked buttonhole, it is

not recommended because there is the danger of stitches piling up and splitting the fabric. Test-stitch several samples before deciding on thread buttonholes; the stitches will have to be longer than usual. The better decision is to make bound buttonholes; any method can be used, but the method described in "Novelty Method for Special Uses" on page 393 is strongly recommended. Use tape to substitute for basting. To finish the underside of the buttonhole (made by any method), substitute the following directions: When the facing is permanently in place, top-stitch around the buttonhole from the right side, catching in the facing layer. Then slash down the center of the rectangle of the facing layer and trim the facing close to the stitches, allowing edges to remain raw.

Use strong thread and a minimum number of stitches to sew on buttons. Sew on buttons in the usual way (provide a somewhat longer shank than usual), and always use a reinforcing button.

Linings These are recommended for jackets and coats of high quality. The front edge of the lining must be machine-stitched (in a traditional seam) to the inner edge of the facings. Hems in the lining should be free-hanging and finished separately from the garment.

Pressing Vinyl cannot be pressed with heat or steam. Finger-press seams and darts or flatten them with the clapboard or pounder. Seams can be hand sewn in place by catching stitches through the backing layer only.

Suede

Incorporate all suggestions in the foregoing sections, pretesting all techniques on scraps before beginning work.

The problems of sewing with suede are varied and complex, requiring experience in several areas of clothing construction. The expense of suede, coupled with the difficulty of handling it, rules out experimentation, and only the experienced person should undertake a project as ambitious as this.

Suede is purchased in skin form, therefore it is irregularly shaped. A pattern must be selected that will fit on the irregular skins, and the number of skins required must be estimated for the particular pattern pieces involved. The pattern should be of a simple design because collars, cuffs, encased edges, and complicated construction lines create difficult problems.

Suede has no grain or direction, therefore pattern pieces can be laid on in any direction required by the shape of the skins. However, some attention must be given to shading differences in the suede; select the most uniform and attractive skins for the front and sleeves. Lay the pattern on and cut a single layer at a time; take care to reverse the pattern for the second cutting. Complete-figure patterns are recommended; see page 493.

Pressing suede is a problem and should not be undertaken until tests have been made on scraps. The iron should be moderately warm, the board should be covered with brown wrapping paper, and the suede should be pressed from the wrong side. Avoid great pressure with the iron. For encased edges that are especially heavy, place several layers of paper over the seam and tap lightly with a clapboard; do not attempt to press thick, encased edges.

WASHABLE CONSTRUCTION

If a garment will be laundered at home, all materials (fabrics, findings, etc.) must be washable and must be preshrunk before construction. But washable materials and preshrinking do not ensure a successful washable costume; construction must be handled in such a way that home laundering will not adversely affect the appearance of the finished costume. It is not a simple issue of whether or not the component parts come through the laundering cycle successfully—*the pertinent issue is the appearance of the finished costume after home laundering.* It is important to keep in mind that if a costume is to be washable, it must require little or no pressing and it must be constructed in such a way that seams are accessible for pressing if necessary.

The major problem is that easy-care fabrics taken as a whole have a tendency to pucker at seams; all construction must be aimed at minimizing this problem. It follows that the extra layers of fabric in a traditionally tailored garment (supporting fabrics, lining fabrics) would multiply problems. Because much of tailoring centers on molding several layers together so they act as one, these very techniques (the foundation of tailoring) must be eliminated in washable construction; in short, washable construction and tailoring techniques are not compatible.

Washable construction requires sewing —not tailoring—and it involves very simple construction, especially if the fabric is a double knit. For this reason a washable suit or coat is not recommended as a project in a tailoring class when the major concern is to gain tailoring experience for future professional and personal use. This is not to say that washable construction is inferior in and of itself (quite the contrary); but it is important for the worker to understand that making a suit or coat by washable construction methods does not constitute tailoring and that the washable costume will not give the same elegant, molded appearance she associates with traditionally tailored garments.

There are very obvious advantages of washable construction (economical upkeep, convenience at home and when traveling, etc.); and there is the extra bonus of the sweater-like comfort, which is partly due to the fabric (if it is a knit), and partly a result of having eliminated certain tailoring techniques. Certainly there is much to be said for washable construction.

Ever since the polyesters were introduced, the author has experimented with them in preparation for her professional writing. In general she concentrated on working out the best methods; and to do this she sometimes deliberately set out to break rules in an attempt to test their validity and to determine if and when they might be broken. Some of those costumes will be used to fortify certain points in the following pages.

Selection of fabric and findings

Review "Knitted Fabrics" and "Polyester Double Knits," beginning on page 75. Polyesters, acrylics, and nylon are available in suiting or coating weights; they may be woven or knitted. The wovens have the advantage of performing very much like wool fabrics, but knits are recommended because they will not ravel; seams will have less tendency to pucker if the seams and hem edges can remain raw. The wovens will wash as well, but many are made with

thick yarns (low thread count) and ravel seriously; consequently, seams must be finished in most wovens, and puckering problems will be magnified.

It will be explained later that supporting fabrics (both underlinings and interfacings) should be used sparingly, and so it is important to buy a fabric of an appropriate weight and hand; in other words, buy the fabric in suiting- and coating-weight and do not attempt to work with a lighter-weight fabric which requires the extra body of an underlining to create the desired effect.

These fabrics cannot be straightened if they have been poorly tentered; therefore, if the fabric has the slightest suggestion of a crosswise design, the quality of tentering must be considered before purchase. Read "The Quality of Tentering and Its Implications" on page 63 and "To Prepare Fabric Which Cannot Be Straightened" on page 97.

The polyester knits vary in width; many are 54 to 58 or 60 inches wide, and some are 66 inches wide. This extra width is usually (although not always) an advantage for economical cutting (the 66-inch width offers tremendous savings). Many patterns will state yardage requirements for 60-inch widths; but if the yardage is not stated for a comparable width, it is a wise economy to make a special layout before purchasing fabric. See "To Figure Accurate Yardage Amounts by Making a New Layout" on page 54. The saving cannot be predicted accurately without making a layout. It may be a great deal; for example, a pants suit may require a yard less of 66-inch fabric than the amount listed for a 54-inch fabric.

Linings must be washable Appropriate lining fabrics are evaluated on page 77. Whipped cream or a similar blouse crepe is excellent for dressmaker suits. Cotton-dacron blends combine well with washable cotton suitings. Banlon is an excellent choice for lining knitted garments because it has comparable elasticity.

Findings and trims must be washable Trimming details are available in polyester and acrylics, but cotton trimmings can be used if preshrunk. For example, zippers with cotton tapes are acceptable, although those made with polyester tapes come through laundering in better (flatter) condition. Use the special thread available for polyesters; it will help eliminate the problem of puckering at seams. Some special thought should be given to the choice of buttons, for they must withstand considerable abrasion in the washer and especially as they are tumbled in the dryer.

Preshrinking

Always preshrink the fabric by washing and drying by the same methods that will be used on the finished garment. One of the greatest advantages of making one's wardrobe is this opportunity to ensure against shrinkage. All fabrics that will be used with the garment (underlinings, interfacings, the zipper, tapes, trims, etc.) should be preshrunk along with the fabric.

Most easy-care fabrics do not shrink when washed and line-dried, and they shrink very little if they are dried in the dryer with the proper low temperature setting, *but they do shrink if they are dried*

with a regular setting. The following experiments point out the influence of drying temperature on shrinkage. A dress which had been hand-washed and line-dried for about a year subsequently shrank about one size (2 inches at all levels) when dried at a regular setting on the dryer. A dress length of fabric, dried at the proper setting, shrank only ½ inch in width (60 inches), but the same fabric later dried at a regular setting shrank an additional 1½ inches in width; comparable lengthwise shrinkage also occurred. The fabric does not look or feel different after it is dried at a regular setting, although when dried at the proper setting, the finished garment looks somewhat better (smoother, less need for touch-up pressing).

These experiments are reported to emphasize the importance of drying by the method that will be used for the finished garment. The experiments have resulted in the following suggestions: For maximum shrinkage, use the regular setting on the dryer when preshrinking fabric. This will not harm the fabric and it makes it possible to dry the garment with a load of regular wash (sometimes convenient) and is a precaution against the possibility of forgetting to set the dryer properly. After preshrinking, for best results, use the proper setting when drying the finished garment.

Possibly the center fold of the fabric (as it comes from the bolt) may not press out completely. It is a wise precaution to attempt to press the fold before any cutting is done. If the fold cannot be pressed out, it is well to know it before cutting so pieces can, if possible, be laid on in such a way that the fold can be avoided or be located where it will be least conspicuous. The fold cannot usually be avoided entirely, but in some designs it can be replaced with a seam; for example, in a simple skirt design planned to be cut on a center-front fold, a seam added at the center front would not change the design appreciably.

Pattern sizing and selection

Many designs in the counter catalogues are labeled "suitable for knits" or "for knits only"; these statements cannot be ignored. Patterns planned especially for knits are cut somewhat smaller (have less livability) because the fabric will give or stretch to provide the additional size needed. They may also have less dart-shaping because knitted fabrics will shape to body curves more readily than woven fabrics. However, suit and coat designs will usually be made with the usual amounts of shaping and livability allowances; consequently, they are appropriate for use with a greater variety of suiting and coating fabrics. A pattern planned for multifabric uses is the better choice because it is the safer choice; one can easily remove excess size after the garment is basted for a final fitting test. See the note concerning knits on page 221.

If one chooses a pattern (for example, a pants pattern) made for knits only and uses it with a woven fabric, it is important to make a muslin copy and to suspect that additional size will be required. For example, the author has worked with a pants pattern for several years, perfecting the fit for use with knit fabrics; it has been used for well over a dozen pairs of pants, most of which are made in dress-weight or light-weight suiting knits. But when a heavier knit (similar to wool double knit) is used, the total all-around size must be increased by 1 inch at all levels ($\frac{1}{4}$ inch at each side edge of the front and back) to provide a comparable fit. When the same pattern is used with a woven fabric, the total all-around size must be increased by about

2 inches at all levels ($\frac{1}{2}$ inch at each side edge of the front and back). These statements reveal that the best solution is to make a muslin test copy and see that the pattern fits the figure properly in a woven fabric; then, after the fabric is cut, the garment can be basted together for a final fitting test, at which time the person working with a knit can take in seams to compensate for the stretch of her particular fabric.

Puckering at seams is a chronic problem Seams in easy-care fabrics tend to pucker, and they pucker still more after the completed costume has been laundered. It follows that designs for washable costumes should have a minimum of seams, top-stitching, and intricate applied details; anything that stiffens the seam area increases puckering. For example, top-stitching stiffens the seam and so creates puckering over a wider area. The author recently chose a design with many seams close together, all pressed open and top-stitched $\frac{1}{4}$ inch on each side of the seam-line, and made it up in a light-gray fabric that would reveal the full impact of puckering. With the top-stitching, each seam would pucker along a strip $\frac{1}{2}$-inch wide. In every way, the design promised to exaggerate problems. It was a pants suit, and the four seams of the pants were top-stitched. The long tunic was designed with a mid-riff yoke (both edges of which were top-stitched), and there were seven top-stitched seams in the bodice and seven seams in the skirt. Surprisingly, the costume is quite successful; but its success is a result of beautiful design, excellent fit, becoming color, etc. The seams pucker, of course, but it is wearable—not because it is truly successful when judged by professional standards but because it is attractive in every other way and because viewers have grown to expect puckering in easy-care fabrics and so, in a way, to accept it.

Choose a pattern designed in simple lines, and eliminate as many seams in the pattern as possible. A seam can be eliminated if it is ruler-straight and also parallel to the grainline; in many patterns the seam at the front edge of a jacket or coat and the center-back seam in jackets, coats, and skirts can be eliminated; see more details on page 253.

Supplies

Pins and needles (hand and machine) must be fine and sharp. Use silk dressmaker pins or special ballpoint pins. *Ballpoint needles for machine use are absolutely essential for sewing on single knits and limp woven fabrics.* A rolling presser foot rides more smoothly over thick, soft knits and prevents fabrics from pushing out of line at the machine; it is available on the market for most types of machines.

Interfacings and underlinings

These should be kept to a minimum. Their functional purpose of controlling stretch is of little value because most of these fabrics retain their shape. A supporting fabric used with a knit adversely affects the natural elasticity of the knit by modifying its most dominant and desirable characteristic.

Interfacings may be required in certain small areas (at the neck edge to prevent stretching or underneath bound buttonholes to cushion heavy seams), and if they are lightweight fabrics and are preshrunk, they will not create serious problems. Underlinings which are caught in with seams and darts will create more problems; seams in these fabrics have a natural tendency to pucker, and the additional thickness of even a very lightweight underlining will thicken and stiffen seams, increasing puckering.

In order to preserve elasticity and prevent greater puckering problems, underlinings are not recommended. If they are used (to add body to the jacket of a costume, for example), they should be somewhat limper and lighter in weight than those one would ordinarily use with a fabric of a similar weight; read "Selection of Supporting Fabrics" on page 82.

The author has experimented with several solutions to the problem of interfacing collars and front edges. The most successful costumes (judged after the *completed* costumes were laundered) were those which had no interfacing, provided that the fabric was of suiting or coating weight. An interfacing cut of a lighter-weight polyester (similiar to a dress-weight crepe) or an extra layer of the fabric itself, used as an interfacing, was very effective with dress-weight fabrics. The least successful costumes were those interfaced with traditional interfacing fabrics. Ordinarily, one always interfaces the area under buttonholes; but when working with easy-care fabrics, the interfacing increases puckering. However, these statements need some qualification; see "Buttonholes" on page 517.

Problems of machine stitching on knits

These are not readily revealed in double knits, but they become major problems with limp woven fabrics and supple single knits (Banlon, lingerie fabrics, and other fabrics of comparable character). Because the polyesters are so popular, problems have been given careful thought by many experts in the field; as a result, many innovative construction techniques as well as new findings and equipment have been introduced and these, in turn, are proving useful in solving similar problems in other delicate fabrics of man-made and natural fibers.

The major problem is that machine stitches skip and do not interlock in supple, lightweight fabrics One or two stitches may skip every few inches or several (a length of ½ inch or more) may not interlock; the stitching looks very much as it does when the needle is not inserted in the machine properly. *Here the primary problem is that there is too much play between the pressure foot and the stitching plate,* and the primary solution is to increase the pressure on the presser foot. There is a secondary cause; the plate with a wide slot (necessary for the zigzag setting) allows the needle to carry limp fabrics down into the slot, thereby increasing the play. This can be remedied by using a plate with a single small hole. If the machine does not include this single-hole plate, it will help to set the needle to either the right or left end of the slot for all stitching; this will greatly diminish the play. If the problem persists, feed strips of tissue paper under the seam and stitch through the paper; after the seam is stitched the paper can be easily torn away.

Standard machine needles are not effective with supple fabrics The sharp point of the standard machine needle (even the smallest size) pierces threads in delicate fabrics and tends to snag them or to carry them through the slot, thereby increasing the problem of too much play between the stitching foot and the plate. Ballpoint needles solve the problem. The smooth, rounded point does not pierce threads but rather gently edges its way through the fabric.

Stitched seams have a tendency to pucker This is the reason designs made of polyesters should have few seams. The condition cannot be completely remedied in most fabrics, but it can be minimized. Test-stitch on scraps of fabrics to test the effect of thread tension and stitch length. For most fabrics, looser tensions and stitches slightly longer than are ordinarily used (try ten to twelve stitches per inch) will improve the appearance of seams. Apply slight hand pressure as the fabric passes through the machine by holding the fabric taut both in front of and behind the needle. Top-stitching will multiply puckering problems. If the design requires top-stitching, substitute by hand picking the seam or by using decorative, running hand stitches if test-stitching reveals that top-stitching by machine makes the seam taut and puckered.

Knitted fabrics are elastic and as they stretch, seams tend to pop (stitches break) Seams in knitted garments must respond to the elasticity of the fabric; therefore the thread must have some elasticity. Several companies offer special thread for knits and polyesters which will stretch without breaking. This thread can be used with other fabrics (many professionals are using it for most sewing purposes) and it is a wise choice for any snug-fitting garment that will get stress during wearing; its elasticity at arm-hole and crotch seams is a great advantage. Applying hand pressure as the fabric passes through the machine not only controls puckering but also helps prevent popped seams.

Simple construction for skirts and pants

Stay-stitching is not usually required, because these fabrics are very stable and do not tend to stretch during construction.

One of the characteristics of most easy-care fabrics is their ability to retain crease lines; this is especially true of the wovens. Those who have attempted to alter ready-to-wear garments may have discovered that very often the creases remain after seams are let out or hems let down. To avoid unsightly alteration lines, it is important to baste and fit before stitching and pressing seams. The knits do not create the same problems; in many, hems can be let down and seams let out without any evidence of the former creases.

Linings Skirts and pants can be more easily laundered (and pressed if necessary) if they are not lined. If they are made of knits, skirts, and especially pants, should not be lined, so as to retain the comfortable, elastic qualities of the fabric. However, seams in woven fabrics will have to be finished, or the garment will require a lining. Review "Selection of Lining Fabrics" on page 77.

Linings should be constructed by the couturier (or shell) method, in which the lining sections are joined separately before the completed lining is inserted in the garment. The alternative method, in which the lining is constructed like an under-lining—that is, caught in with seams of the garment—is not satisfactory, because the lining layers stiffen and thicken the seam, increasing puckering problems.

See "Alternative Methods of Finishing the Lower Edge" on page 344; if a lining is used, use the free-hanging method so that seams are more accessible for pressing. In many lining fabrics seams curl and do not retain creases well and so require pressing after laundering. The following suggestion will entirely eliminate the need to press, and it is especially helpful in Banlon, which makes an excellent lining for washable costumes. After the seam is stitched, press it open and hand-pick the seam with rows of stitches ¼ inch on each side of the seamline. Then trim the seam to a width of about ⅜ inch. The seam does not look as neat as it would if it were not hand-picked, but this is no disadvantage in a skirt. Seams in jacket and coat linings can also be hand-picked, although appearance is of course a greater concern in these garments.

Seam and hem finishes Seam and hem edges are left raw in knits because they do not ravel and will be more compatible (more elastic) if they are not held taut by machine stitching. However, woven suitings usually ravel quite seriously and must be finished if the garment is not lined. Even if the garment is lined, seams may require a finish because the lining will be free-hanging. Hems in wovens will require a finish whether or not the garment is lined. The Hong Kong finish (page 287) is recommended; as the final stitching is done—as the raw edge is encased—use hand rather than machine stitches because this will keep the seam from being as taut and stiff and so will reduce puckering.

Construction details for the jacket or coat

The entire sequence is simplified because many tailoring techniques must be eliminated; they result in too much construction —too many layers and too many rows of stitches too close together.

Assemble pieces for a final fitting
See "Shoulder Pads" below and decide if pads will be used. This final fitting is not essential if the fabric is woven, because it will act very much like the muslin used in the test copy. However, if the fabric is knitted, it will be somewhat larger than the muslin copy; this will depend on the weight and hand of the particular knit. Expect to take in structural seams slightly to compensate for the natural (and desirable) stretch of the fabric.

Avoid taping seams when possible
These fabrics, taken as a whole, are very stable, and any stretch under the stress of wearing is temporary. The application of tape stiffens the seam too much and creates puckering. It is possible to tape certain seams (for example, the shoulder seam in certain designs) by the method shown in sketchs *a* and *c* in Figure 8-7 on page 310. The alternative method, in which the tape is caught in with the stitching of the seam (shown in sketch *b*), will cause the seam to pucker seriously.

Seam and hem finishes See the directions under this heading on page 516.

Buttonholes Buttonholes will create no new problems. Actually, they are much easier to make in knits because the fabric is supple and there is no danger of raveling. In woven fabrics, there is the usual problem of raveling.

The one difference has to do with the interfacing usually used at the front edge. The costume will launder much more satisfactorily if this interfacing is eliminated, and experiments made by the author have shown that it can be eliminated in many fabrics. The whole issue is whether or not the bulky underconstruction of the buttonhole will be visible from the outside if the interfacing is eliminated. It will not be if the color is dark, if the fabric has a design (jacquard, plaid, tweed, etc.), or if the fabric has a nubby surface. Make a test buttonhole on a sample without an interfacing, press it lightly, and examine it. The bulky scrap from which the buttonhole lips are made will be visible if the fabric is flat-surfaced and light in color. In that case, use a scrap of interfacing under the buttonhole scrap and trim it about $\frac{1}{4}$ inch larger than the finished scrap. This is better than using the usual interfacing, which is about the size of the front-facing, because when it is caught in with several buttonholes, the front area tends to pucker and appear taut.

Avoid top-stitching when possible
Many times top-stitching can simply be eliminated; but if it is important to the design, it can be done by holding the layers

of fabric taut as they pass under the machine. Alternatively, seams which require top-stitching can be done by hand-picking; this is better, not only because it gives an attractive appearance but also because the hand stitches allow the seam to remain more supple and so reduce puckering.

Shoulder pads These are available in polyester materials that will go through the washing and drying cycle. However, once they are sewn permanently in place, the extra bulk and the extra construction tend to increase puckering. They are very expensive—about three times the cost of a comparable standard pad. An alternative idea is to cover standard pads with matching lining fabric and to sew them in after the garment has been lined; in this way, they can be removed before home laundering. Obviously the garment is not as finished from the lining side, but it is not unattractive.

Linings See "An Evaluation of Lining Methods" on page 450. If the garment will be lined, use the machine method. The hand method, although the more elegant, is not appropriate, because too many layers are held firmly together and this aggravates puckering problems. The novelty Hong Kong method of finishing facing edges (page 470) is not recommended because it involves extra construction that will increase tension and so cause additional puckering. See "Alternative Methods of Finishing the Lower Edge" on page 344; choose the free-hanging method because it will leave seams accessible for pressing if necessary.

If the lining fabric does not retain a

crease well (Banlon does not), press seams open, hand-pick about ¼ inch from the seamline, and trim the seam to a width of about ⅜ inch. This is not as attractive as a plain seam, but it is not unattractive and will very possibly eliminate the need to press the finished garment after it has been laundered.

DOUBLE-CLOTH CONSTRUCTION

Double-weave cloth, popularly referred to as "double cloth," is composed of two separate layers of fabric woven simultaneously on the same loom and held together by threads passing from one layer to the other. It is usually made in coating weight with the layers in two contrasting colors. The appearance of the cloth and the methods of construction it requires make it ideal for reversible costumes, and the effect is enhanced if the two colors are utilized for interesting contrasts.

This cloth, more than any others included in this series of special problems, requires unique construction. None of the tailoring techniques can be used, and even familiar sewing techniques are used in a distinctive way. It is novelty construction and, as such, should be undertaken only after fundamentals have been mastered. It is a worthwhile challenge for experienced readers, but it must be understood that there will be little carryover to the other costumes and that it has no value as a tailoring experience.

Double-cloth construction eliminates the need for facings, underlinings, interfacings, and linings. Collars, cuffs, belts, pocket flaps, etc., are made of a single thickness of the double-layered cloth. Hem allowances should be reduced to the width of a seam allowance. Obviously, this construction is so unusual that the pattern must be modified; many pieces must be eliminated from the layout, and the yardage amount stated in the yardage chart must be revised. Pattern directions will be of little value, and the worker will have to work out details for herself. It is possible to find a pattern planned for double cloth in seasons when the fabric is very fashionable, but the choice will never be great; the author has seen only two of these patterns in her lifetime. Those who wish to do a double-cloth costume, therefore, must select an appropriate pattern and work out the problems that will surely be encountered.

Pattern selection

The design should be simple, with a minimum of seams and intricate details; for example, a cape is an excellent choice. There will be no great problems with standard seams, finished edges, darts, buttonholes, belts, pocket flaps, and other *applied* details. Pockets which can be *applied* (patch pockets) will be successful, but it is very difficult and sometimes impossible to do *set-in* pockets such as those which are set in a seam or pockets of the welt or bound type. It is well to choose a design with a collar, cuffs, or some applied details which can be handled in such a way that color contrasts will provide design interest. It is possible to ease in fullness as a seam is joined; but since this is difficult, it is wise to avoid set-in sleeves. Sleeves of the raglan type or any sleeves cut with the major pattern pieces are better choices.

Fabric selection

Most double cloths are woven in coating weight, and both layers give a matted-together appearance; these are recommended. Suiting-weight double cloth is not recommended, because each individual layer must be too loosely woven in order

that the fabric be lightweight and supple. Glance through the sketches in this series to see that the layers will be ripped apart during the construction processes; loosely woven fabrics are very likely to ravel as the layers are separated. Before purchasing a double cloth, ask the clerk to separate layers at one corner so that individual layers can be examined.

Basic construction techniques

SPECIAL NOTE CONCERNING SKETCHES IN THIS SERIES: **In all other sketches in this text (and in the sketches on the pattern instruction sheet) only the right side of the fabric is shaded, to distinguish between the right and wrong sides. In this series, one layer of the double cloth is shaded on both the right and wrong sides and the other layer is not shaded on either side, to distinguish between the two layers.**

The four techniques described below are basic to all double-cloth construction. The worker will encounter many details, each of which may require special attention and some innovation; but all problems will be solved by using these techniques and making the necessary modifications.

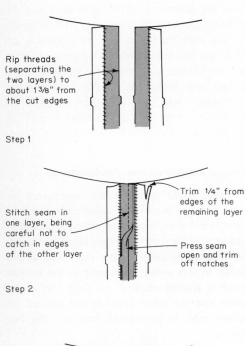

Rip threads
(separating the
two layers) to
about 1 3/8" from
the cut edges

Step 1

Stitch seam in
one layer, being
careful not to
catch in edges
of the other layer

Trim 1/4" from
edges of the
remaining layer

Press seam
open and trim
off notches

Step 2

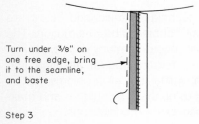

Turn under 3/8" on
one free edge, bring
it to the seamline,
and baste

Step 3

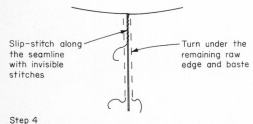

Slip-stitch along
the seamline
with invisible
stitches

Turn under the
remaining raw
edge and baste

Step 4

FIGURE 11-22 To join seams in double cloth.

To join seams See step 1 in Figure 11-22. Just before joining a seam, rip the threads holding the two layers together and separate the layers along the seam edge back to 1⅜ from the cut edges. This will allow for stitching a ⅝-inch seam and pressing it open (a total or 1¼ inches) and for an extra ⅛-inch allowance to keep the seam from looking crowded and taut. Pick out the loose threads.

See step 2. Glance through the sketches to see that the two layers will be seamed independently—one by machine and the other by hand. The machine-stitched seam will be more attractive, and it should be the top layer; decide which layer will be on the outside as the costume is worn or, if the garment is to be reversible, which side will be worn outside most of the time. Join that seam by machine, folding back edges of the other layer and being careful not to catch those edges in with the machine stitching. Trim off notches and press the seam open.

The remaining free edge will be lapped to this line; to reduce bulk and stagger the seam widths, trim ¼ inch from the two remaining edges.

See steps 3 and 4. Turn under ⅜ inch on one remaining raw edge and lap it to the seamline and baste. Then turn under the remaining raw edge, butting the folded edges together and baste. Slip-stitch the two edges along the seamline, slipping the needle in and out of the folds of fabric to keep stitches invisible.

To sew darts See step 1 in Figure 11-23. Just before stitching the dart, slash through the center of the dart almost to its tip. If the dart is wide, trim off the excess, leaving a ⅝-inch seam allowance beyond the dartlines, as shown. Rip the stitches holding the two layers together and separate the two layers back to ¾ inch inside the dartlines. This will allow for stitching the dart and pressing it open and for an extra

⅛-inch allowance to keep the dart from looking crowded and taut. Pick out the loose threads.

See step 2. Stitch the dart along the dartlines in the top layer (the right side as the garment is worn), folding back edges of the other layer and being careful not to catch those edges in with the machine stitching. Press the dart open. To reduce bulk and stagger the width of the seam,

trim some width from the remaining free edges; this amount can be ¼ inch (the same as for seams) if the dart is wide, but it might be just a sliver if the dart is narrow.

See step 3. Turn under the remaining raw edges along the dartlines, butting the fold edges together, and baste. Slip-stitch the two edges together, slipping the needle in and out of the folds of fabric to keep stitches invisible.

Treatment of finished edges   All finished edges are handled the same way. These edges include edges of pockets, flaps, collars, cuffs, belts, and the front and hem edges. See step 1 in Figure 11-24.

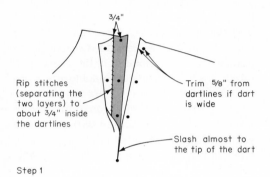

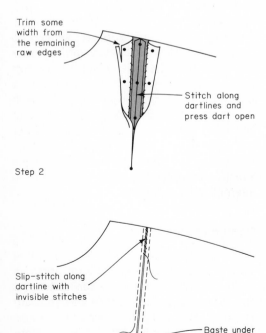

FIGURE 11-23   To sew darts in double cloth.

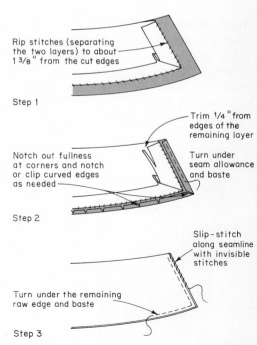

FIGURE 11-24   Treatment of finished edges in double cloth.

Just before finishing the edge, rip the threads holding the two layers together and separate the layers along the seam or hem edges back to 1⅜ inches from the cut edges. Pick out the loose threads.

See step 2. Turn under the seam allowance on one edge and baste. Trim off notches. If the seam is curved in any way, notch out fullness or clip the seam, as needed. If there is a corner involved, notch out the extra fold of fabric to reduce bulk.

To stagger the seam, trim ¼ inch from the remaining free edges, as shown.

See step 3. Turn under the remaining raw edge and baste. Slip-stitch the two layers together, slipping the needle in and out of the folds of fabric to keep stitches invisible.

Buttonholes See Figure 11-25. Buttonholes are done by slitting the fabric, ripping a few stitches surrounding the slit, and turning in edges of the two layers. The edges are held together with slip stitches, as usual, but they must be very secure to withstand the stress of frequent buttoning.

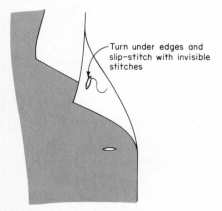

Turn under edges and slip-stitch with invisible stitches

FIGURE 11-25 Slit buttonholes.

MEN'S TAILORING

The early 1970s have seen a revolution in men's fashions. The "uniforms" men formerly wore have been discarded for exciting, newsworthy costumes that have men as committed as women to fashion. Many of the new fashions are casuals in softer lines with a certain unisex character; and the new designs, which look familiar and less forbidding to women who sew, have stimulated women's interest and confidence in sewing for men. And the young men of this decade, no longer so concerned with a need to fit the masculine mold, are themselves embracing the fashion arts. Men whose fathers would have been embarrassed in a costume made at home wear their home-sewn costumes with confidence; many of them are actually boastful if they can claim credit for themselves.

As this text reaches the market, the men's and boys' section in the counter catalogues includes a great variety of costumes, and the offerings can be considered comprehensive when judged by past standards. Each of the four major houses offers a sizable collection, and it is interesting to note that Vogue, a company which formerly specialized in fashions for women, now offers an impressive collection of men's fashions, some of which are designed by world-famous international couturiers.

Design choices

The customer with limited experience is wise to choose a casual design such as a sports shirt, vest, or casual suit for a first project. Although men's wear is constructed very much like women's wear, there are some subtle differences, and there are a few new techniques to be mastered. The techniques are not radically different or necessarily more difficult. However, it is more difficult to get the hard, flat-surface look men expect in a business suit; this is partially a matter of pressing, which is difficult to do with sufficient pressure without the special equipment available to the professional tailor. Pressing problems, coupled with the greater difficulty in sewing with flat-surfaced fabrics (flannel, etc.) that some men favor for business suits, is sufficient reason to delay the ambitious project of a business suit until the worker becomes more confident and proficient.

Suitable fabrics

The choice of fabrics for men's wear is not limited. The old favorites such as corduroy, worsted wools in suiting or coating weights, and denim remain popular. As in women's fashions, the polyester knits have taken over a large percentage of the market. In the decade of the 1970s almost any fabric is appropriate for the man with fashion daring, including such unlikely choices as velvet, brocade, Hawaiian prints, and tie-dyed denim.

Polyester knits have gained great popularity for men's wear because they are comfortable to wear, do not wrinkle, and retain their shape. The fact that they are washable is an asset in only some costumes; although casual slacks are laundered at home, more tailored costumes are dry-cleaned. These knits are offered in many fabric departments in a special collection for men's wear. The reader with limited experience sewing men's wear will be wise to choose a double-knit polyester or wool because they are easily constructed, are somewhat easier to fit, and do not ravel.

First projects must be considered experimental

Regardless of the amount of experience the worker has had in sewing or tailoring women's wear, he or she should approach a first project in men's wear with caution. The experienced person may have a tendency to proceed with what appears to be a familar task without reading the instructions with the pattern; one cannot assume any detail will be done in exactly the same way it would be handled in women's wear. Futhermore, the worker must understand that the pattern companies are also working on familiar but somewhat different problems. The very important matter of choosing the correct size for the figure must certainly be approached with great caution; there are, at this time, additional problems with sizing, as explained below.

The pattern companies are doing an excellent job of writing directions on the instruction sheet. Such details as the fly fastening, waistbands, and pockets are covered well and in detail. It is important for all workers, including those who are experienced, to follow directions carefully.

Sizing

In the past there were relatively few men's patterns sold, and for this reason they are not available in the wide range of figure types offered on the ready-to-wear market. At this time (1974) patterns are offered in only the following sizes: Boy' (sizes 7, 8, 10, 12), Teen-boys' (14, 16, 18, 20), and Men's (in even sizes from 34 to 48). The standard body-measurement charts appear on page 531. Men's patterns are planned for the figure of average build—about 5 feet, 10 inches in height. Because the patterns are available only in even sizes and one figure type, sizing must be considered a major problem at this time. If the market for men's patterns continues to grow, it is entirely possible they may be offered in uneven sizes and additional figure types in the future.

Pattern alterations may be extensive
The worker can expect to make changes in the length of pants and sleeves; it may be necessary to make changes in the length of jackets as well, in order to maintain good proportions. Men who are perfectly fitted in uneven sizes will require pattern alterations because the pattern will be 1 inch too large or too small for their figures.

Pants patterns allow for some adjustment in waist size. Examine the back pattern to see that the seam allowance at the center back is about 1½ inches at the waist and tapers back to the standard ⅝-inch allowance at the crotch; the seam allowance at the center-back edge of the waistband patterns is of a corresponding width. These seamlines should be tailor-tacked, and the pants should be basted for a fitting along the seamline; then the seam can be let out during fitting if necessary.

The pattern will allow about 2 inches for a standard pants hem; the allowance will be about 5 inches for cuffed pants. These widths are somewhat greater than the proper finished hem width because, as in women's designs, the pattern allows some extra hem width for possible small additions in length. The hem allowance for jackets and sleeves will be about 1½ inches.

The principles of altering the pattern are the same as for women's patterns; the fundamental principles, given in great detail in Chapter 5, can be applied with only slight modification.

Before making pattern alterations (and again after the muslin copy is basted), compare measurements with a similar favorite garment in the wardrobe. Compare lengths (outside leg, inside leg, jacket, and sleeve) and placement of pockets. In this way, it will be somewhat easier to establish pleasing proportions on the figure which differs from the average height of 5 feet, 10 inches.

Muslin testing is essential The matter of sizing is a sensitive one; the success of the costume rests on proper sizing and fit. Because patterns are available only in even sizes and one figure type (which leads to more extensive pattern alterations), there is a greater need for testing decisions in muslin. In addition, the muslin copy affords an opportunity to practice new and somewhat different construction details such as the fly fastening, welt and bound pockets, etc. Men are demanding in the matter of fit; they are accustomed to superb fit and comfort and are less willing than women to make do with something less than perfection. For this reason, it is important for the man to test the garment under actual wearing conditions and to wear the test copy long enough to be sure it meets his standards and his demands.

Tailoring the pants

Basic construction details are no different than in women's wear Seams and seam finishes, darts, top-stitching details, etc., are done in the usual way. Pockets are made in essentially the same way a similar pocket would be made in women's costumes. The worker must understand that any detail of construction may differ slightly and so must always refer to the pattern directions to discover any different techniques presented there.

Pockets Pockets are featured on men's wear; they constitute a larger percentage of the design interest of the costume and at the same time serve more functional needs than the same pocket on women's wear. There may be more than one type of pocket on the pants and more than one type on the jacket. For example, one suit may feature patch pockets on the jacket, a bound or welt pocket on the lining at about chest level, inset pockets in the front of the pants, and hip pockets of the welt type. Obviously, the pockets are important; it follows that they must be well constructed. Certainly one cannot decide to eliminate them; without them the costume does not look professional.

Patch pockets are the simplest and most familiar type. They may be lined or unlined. Directions on the instruction sheet will be in detail. For additional help in working for perfection, see "Aids to Accuracy" on pages 296 to 300.

Bound and welt pockets are more difficult to do, partially because there will be weak points which will have a tendency to ravel; they are much simpler to do if the fabric is wool or polyester knit, and it is for this reason among others that double knits are highly recommended for first projects. The pattern companies realize these pockets are difficult and also very important to the successs of the costume, and the instruction sheet will include comprehensive directions. Some portion of the pocket will be cut of a flat, firm cotton fabric (this is not usually done in women's wear); it will be helpful to examine a similar pocket on men's ready-to-wear to see that the visible portions of the bound or welt pocket are cut of the garment fabric, while portions

that will not be visible are cut of a flat, firm cotton fabric, which reduces bulk.

Zipper Women who sew for men must concentrate on the left-over-right lap-over in the trousers and in the jacket. Women are so accustomed to working with a right-over-left lap-over that there is great danger of making a mistake; such a mistake, although understandable, is disastrous.

The standard length of a trouser zipper is 11 inches; this special zipper is somewhat heavier than zippers for women's wear. The trouser zipper is available in many (but not all) notions departments; a 9-inch skirt zipper can be substituted, if necessary.

The fly pattern is used to cut three sections. One layer is used to face the left front-opening edge so that the stitching for the zipper can be done about 1¼ inches in from the finished left front edge. The other two sections are seamed together to form the fly itself; it will lie under the zipper and will be caught in with the stitching when the zipper is stitched to the right front edge.

The directions on the instruction sheet will be given in great detail. For additional help, examine the fly construction in ready-to-wear pants.

Belt carriers If the pants will be worn with a belt, belt carriers will be used; these are placed at more frequent intervals than they are in women's wear. They are simple to do, and instructions will be included with the pattern. Study the directions before making the waistband to see that the carriers are attached to the waist edge before the waistband is applied (this is not always true in women's wear).

Waistband The pattern will include two waistband patterns—a right and a left. The right one differs from the left only in that it is about 1 to 1½ inches longer. The waistband is always seamed at the center back; note that the seam allowance on that edge is more than the usual ⅝ inch to allow for some adjustment in waist size.

Methods of construction The waistband on most men's ready-to-wear is done quite differently from the waistband on women's wear. Examine several pants to see that the typical construction on pants of high quality results in a band that is firm and stiff but not bulky because the band facing is cut of a flat, cotton fabric; the band facing extends about 1 inch below the waist seam. This type of construction is especially good for pants which will be worn without a belt and for men with fuller figures (it will not buckle over as readily). The construction involved is more time-consuming and difficult to execute than other methods; perhaps because of this, this method is seldom pictured on the instruction sheet. The reader who is more experienced may wish to copy this construction from a pair of ready-to-wear pants.

Most of the pattern companies are showing the traditional interfaced band, which is done exactly like a similar waistband in women's wear. In the author's opinion, this is the one detail which is not handled well on the instruction sheet. This band is not ideal for women's wear or men's wear, although it is acceptable for casual pants made of lightweight fabrics such as denim. Read "An Evaluation of Methods" on page 320 to see the disadvantages of this quick, simple construction.

Some patterns, especially those for more tailored suits, show a band which is quite similar to the faced band but which incorporates some of the advantages of the quality men's waistband described above. It is one in which the underside of the band (the band facing) is cut of a firm, flat cotton fabric but which is handled like the interfaced waistband used in women's wear in every other way. This modified band is also used in men's ready-to-wear for casual slacks and for pants in the budget price range. Actually it is somewhat like the stiffened waistband recommended in this text for women's costumes. Read "The Stiffened Waistband" on page 322. This construction, with the underside of the band finished with grosgrain ribbon, can be used effectively on men's wear; it is firm and yet flat, and so it meets the accepted standard for men's wear.

Make decisions based on individual circumstances Decide on an appropriate method by evaluating methods (page 320) and by examining the construction on ready-to-wear. The stiffness of the band is a major decision which can be controlled by the firmness and weight of the stiffening material used. The best choice is a non-woven interfacing (such as pellon) of the desired weight. A nonwoven interfacing with an adhesive surface is a good choice because when it is pressed in place, the two fabrics which are then molded together are stiffer and trimmer than the two would be if combined without an adhesive. The finished band must be stiffer and firmer if it will be worn without a belt or with a very narrow belt. Fuller figures require a stiffer band than slim, lithe figures.

To fasten the waistband Some waistbands feature a buttoned closing as part of the design. The standard waistband should be fastened with one of the large, strong skirt hooks and eyes.

Hems The pattern will include a hem allowance of approximately 2 inches for a standard hem and approximately 5 inches for a hem with a cuff. These allowances are greater than recommended finished widths. Just as in women's patterns, the hem allowance is more than ample to allow for some adjustment in length; the worker is expected to trim the hem to an appropriate width after the finished length has been established.

Standard hems The finished width of the hem should be about 1¼ to 1½ inches, depending on the height of the wearer. If the fabric will not ravel (a double knit), the edge should remain raw so that there will be no extra bulk to make the hem more conspicuous. If heavy, bulky fabric ravels, the raw edge should be finished with a machine zigzag stitch. If flat, summer-weight fabric ravels, allow an extra ½ inch in hem width for a turnunder. Refer to "Hem Finishes" on pages 331 to 336; much of the information included there is applicable to men's wear. The hem should be secured with the tailor's hemming stitch (page 283).

Hem and cuff The finished width of a cuff is about 1½ inches, and it should vary slightly with the height of the wearer to create pleasing proportions. Because it is a visible detail which may be influenced by the design, the width may vary with current fashions. The hem allowance provided on the pattern will be ample and is actually in excess of the required amount to allow for some adjustment in length and cuff width.

After the finished length and the width of the cuff have been established, the hem should be trimmed to an appropriate width. See "Standard Hems" above; the finished width and the method of handling the hem are the same whether or not the pants are cuffed. One suggestion: In order to reduce

bulk and provide for staggered thicknesses, make the finished width of the hem about ¼ inch less than the finished width of the cuff; for example, for a 1½-inch cuff, use a 1¼-inch hem.

Tailoring the jacket or coat

Read the general information on pages 522 to 524. Many of the casual costumes shown in the counter catalogues are quite simple designs, such as vests, sleeveless (and perhaps collarless) jackets, and overblouses. These are sewn, not tailored, and cannot be considered a good choice if the project is to serve as an educational experience in tailoring. These casual costumes can be done by washable construction methods (page 510) and can be laundered at home, provided that they are made of polyester knits or wovens or other easy-care fabrics.

Review "The Tailored Costume as a Learning Experience" on page 17. If the costume will be tailored, it should be a more typical jacket or coat with a collar and sleeves. If it is tailored, the finished garment must be dry-cleaned, even if the fabric is washable.

Basic differences between men's and women's tailoring Women who sew for men must concentrate on the left-over-right lap-over; they must be very cautious when beginning work on buttonholes because there is great danger in putting them on the right front from force of habit. The tailor's buttonhole is the only appropriate buttonhole for men's costumes; see page 395.

Typical men's garments have two-piece sleeves. See "Preparation for Basting" on page 264. Refer to page 418 to see that the functional seams in the sleeve (located so as to be inconspicuous) do not necessarily match seams in the jacket or coat, which are located to create a certain fashion effect.

Men's designs often feature vent openings; there may be a vent at the center back or at seams on either side of the center back. These are more difficult if the back lining will be cut full length; see page 448 before cutting the back lining. The vent may feature a tab and button for better control.

The greatest difference is in the way the back lining will be handled; and the lining method influences many other seemingly unrelated construction details. The entire front is always lined, as are the sleeves, but the back in a jacket is usually lined only down to about shoulder level. Full-length coats may have the same partial back lining, but most winter-weight coats have a full-length lining very similar to the lining in women's wear; the full-length lining may be allowed to hang free or may be attached to the hem, the same as in women's wear. However, any jacket or coat can be fully lined like women's wear, if desired; the worker can decide to do this even if the pattern features a partial back lining. Directions for making lining patterns appear on page 445. A full-length lining is the better choice under the following circumstances: (1) in an overcoat—for greater ease in slipping it on and off; (2) to better utilize the lining as part of the design if a novelty lining fabric in a distinctive color or design will be used; (3) for a more elegant effect in tuxedos, velvet smoking jackets, etc.; and (4) in any garment made of fabric which ravels

seriously, if the worker wishes to avoid binding the raw edges of seams, hems, and vent openings in the areas which would be visible and subject to friction if the shorter lining were used. Because most patterns are for casual costumes, the majority will feature the shoulder-length back lining.

Many construction details are influenced by the method of lining chosen. If a full-length back lining is used, the jacket or coat can be handled very much the same as in similar women's garments; this is because the full-length lining covers all inner construction. If the shorter lining is used, construction must be done so that the garment is visually attractive in the area which will be exposed. Women who wish to gain experience from this project, to benefit them later when sewing women's wear, would do well to decide on the full-length lining. The choice of the lining method must be made very early in the construction sequence because it influences many basic decisions.

Men's garments are not usually underlined This is true partially because the type of fabric designed for men's wear is of a suiting or coating weight and therefore has sufficient body for the purpose for which it will be used. If the typical shoulder-length back lining will be used, the garment *cannot* be underlined in the back, because the underlining would be visible as the garment is worn. There is no reason why men's garments cannot be underlined, however; if the fabric chosen requires extra body, an underlining can be used and handled exactly as it is in women's wear, *if a full-length back lining is used.*

The method of handling the interfacing is influenced by the way the back will be lined Review "Construction Methods for Supporting Fabrics" on page 353, with special attention to the three choices which are appropriate in women's wear. Only the partial interfacing is adaptable to men's wear if the short back shoulder lining is used, because the short lining would not hide inner construction of the two alternative methods.

If the short lining and the partial interfacing method are used, the bias strips of interfacing fabric which are used at hemlines and self-facings cannot be cut ½ inch wider than the hem allowance, as recommended in the directions for women's wear; instead, they must be cut ½ inch narrower than the hem allowance so that they will not be visible beyond the hem and facing edges in the unlined back area.

The pattern directions covering interfacings are very explicit and detailed, and the worker will probably find them much more helpful than the directions in a text—especially if the shorter lining is used. There will be a pattern piece for the front interfacing, and it will cover a larger area on the front than it does in women's wear. There may be an additional pattern piece for a layer of interfacing to be applied to the front shoulder area; in other words, there may be two layers of interfacing in certain portions of the front. The pattern may include a pattern piece for a back shoulder interfacing; if it does not, see directions for making one on page 359. Do understand that if a full-length back lining is used, the worker can decide on any method of construction for the supporting fabric.

NOTE: Interfacings of the press-on type are very effective for the front facing area and the under collar; when pressed in place, they provide a harder, flatter finish than interfacings which are pad-stitched in place. However, the press-on interfacings must be basted because they must be shaped into wearing position before they are pressed permanently in place.

Some seam and hem edges must be bound if a shoulder-length back lining is used Study the instruction sheet to see which seams and edges will be visible and subject to friction. All these edges must be finished to prevent raveling and to give an attractive appearance; the finish should be one of the bound types because a zigzag finish, although functional, is not as attractive. Edges can be bound by the traditional method or by the Hong Kong method (page 287). The binding should match the fabric in color, to be inconspicuous, or match the lining for a coordinated effect. Edges which must be finished are the back edge of the side seam, both edges of any seam in the back, the edges of a vent opening, and the upper edge of the back hem. However, if a full-length back lining is used, these same edges will be covered and protected by the lining and need not be finished.

Shaping principles The technique of shaping the garment in the collar and lapel area is the same as for women's wear; see page 368 for a general discussion and follow specific directions in other sections of the text. Padding stitches are done in the same way, but they may be spaced closer together to give a flatter, firmer effect.

Taping seams The tape which stiffens and strengthens edges is applied and handled the same as in women's wear. Directions on the instruction sheet may show tape along more edges than are shown in this text. The entire armhole (rather than just the upper portion) may be taped. The finished edges of pockets and edges of vent openings may be taped.

Pockets Review "Pockets" on page 525. Pockets are usually dominant features of the design, and their importance cannot be overemphasized. Bound or welt types are more difficult to construct if raveling is a serious problem. If the fabric ravels seriously, it is well to practice making a sample pocket on scraps of the fabric which will be used for the garment.

If there is a pocket on the inside of the jacket or coat (at chest level), it will probably be located partly on the front facing and partly on the front lining; for this reason, the front lining will be seamed to the front facing very early in the construction sequence—before the facing is applied to the jacket and before the collar is attached.

Collar construction The collar construction which appears on most pattern instruction sheets is identical to the one used for women's wear; see more detailed directions in "The Tailored Collar" on page 403.

There is another method of handling collars on men's ready-to-wear. It involves trimming the seam allowances from the under collar, allowing those edges to remain raw, and hand sewing the under collar in place. The under collar may be cut of felt (because it is flat and does not ravel) or it may be cut of the garment fabric if it does not ravel too seriously.

The advantage of this method is that it reduces bulk in the collar, particularily at the collar edges. It is used on ready-to-wear in winter-weight coats or whenever the fabric is thick and bulky, and is also used to create the hard, flat look favored for traditional business suits. Patterns do not usually feature this construction, be-

cause the alternative construction is appropriate for the type of casual jacket or coat most home sewers choose. Strictly tailored business suits or overcoats, which require this special construction, are not good choices for the nonprofessional tailor. However, those who have a great deal of experience and are capable of undertaking these more ambitious projects can choose the special collar construction, using a ready-to-wear jacket or coat as a guide.

Lining the jacket or coat Lining techniques are quite different from those used in women's wear; they are comparable if a full-length lining is used, but there will be slight differences even with that method. The instruction sheet handles these procedures in great detail as an extra customer service because they are different from the methods used in women's wear. The worker should concentrate on the instruction sheet and use the directions in this text only for reference on any similar procedures.

One great difference is that the lining front is usually seamed by machine to the front facing very early in the construction sequence—before the collar is applied to the facing and before the facing is applied to the garment. This must be done if there is a pocket located over both pieces, and it is usually done (even if there is no pocket) because a machine-stitched seam is more serviceable than the hand-sewn seam appropriate in women's wear. Ultimately, the two methods result in the same effect; the only difference is that joining the facing to the jacket and collar is somewhat complicated by having to handle larger pieces.

If a shoulder-length back lining is used, the lower edge of the back lining is finished with a narrow hem. The back lining may be joined to the front lining at the shoulder and side seams by hand or by machine.

If the shoulder-length back lining is used, the side edge of the front lining is turned under and hand-sewn to the pressed open side seam of the jacket or coat; examine sketches on the instruction sheet to see that this reveals the back edge of the side seam; this is the reason the back edge of the side seam must be bound for a serviceable and attractive finish.

Lining procedures are quite similar to those in women's wear if a full-length back lining is used, and yet there will be differences. For example, the front edge of the lining will probably be stitched to the front facing by machine, and this changes the order of construction. Regardless of which lining method is chosen, the worker will benefit by following the very excellent directions on the instruction sheet.

	Boys'				Teen-boys'			
Sizes	7	8	10	12	14	16	18	20
Chest	26	27	28	30	32	33½	35	36½
Waist	23	24	25	26	27	28	29	30
Hip (seat)	27	28	29½	31	32½	34	35½	37
Neckband	11¾	12	12½	13	13½	14	14½	15
Height	48	50	54	58	61	64	66	68

	Men's							
Sizes	34	36	38	40	42	44	46	48
Chest	34	36	38	40	42	44	46	48
Waist	28	30	32	34	36	39	42	44
Hip (seat)	35	37	39	41	43	45	47	49
Neckband	14	14½	15	15½	16	16½	17	17½
Shirt sleeve	32	32	33	33	34	34	35	35

INDEX

INDEX